KENYA CHURCHES HANDBOOK

The Development of Kenyan Christianity, 1498 - 1973

Edited by
**David B. Barrett
George K. Mambo
Janice McLaughlin
Malcolm J. McVeigh**

published by
Evangel Publishing House
P. O. Box 969
Kisumu Kenya

COPYRIGHT - DEPARTMENT OF BIBLICAL STUDY AND RESEARCH,
NATIONAL CHRISTIAN COUNCIL OF KENYA - 1973

BR
1443
.K4
K46

Printed in Kenya
by Evangel Press, P. O. Box 1015, Kisumu,
for
Evangel Publishing House, P.O. Box 969, Kisumu
located at Nyang'ori.

KENYA CHURCHES HANDBOOK

HARVEST   AND

HARVESTERS

**The people of Kenya
have raised up
their own pastors**

Kenya Pastors Conference, 1968

RURAL CHURCHES · 1

80 per cent of all Christians in Kenya live in the countryside

7

HARAMBEE !

Let us build together !

9

11

12

URBAN CHURCHES 14

1

The City of Nairobi has 300 churches

ternational Christians
sit Kenya

17

The evangelist meets the medicine men

I AM THE LIGHT OF THE WORLD

rdained by Archbishop Makarios

*Archbishop of
Canterbury*

20

An archbishop meditates

KENYANS AT WORSHIP

"Let everything that hath breath PRAISE THE LORD"

24

Sing to the Lord a new song

25

*Hear the Word
of the Lord*

26

Right: MINISTRY TO YOUTH

27

**MINISTRY
TO YOUTH**

31

Bible stuay

BROADCASTING + COMMUNICATION + DEVELOPMENT = PROGRESS

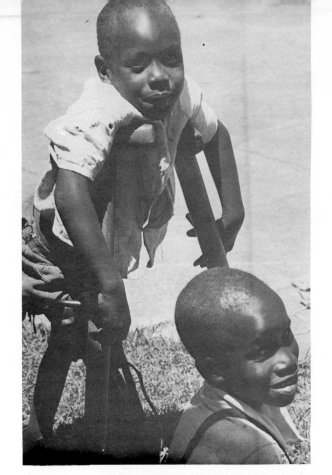

35

SERVING
THE
COMMUNITY

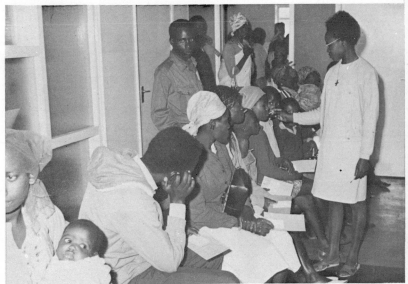

36

Go ye therefore...

...feed my she

3

Part III

Atlas of Christianity and Religion in Kenya

A.   Historical: 1498 – 1962 . . . . Maps 1 –   7
B.   Contemporary: 1963 – 1972 . . . . Maps 8 – 15

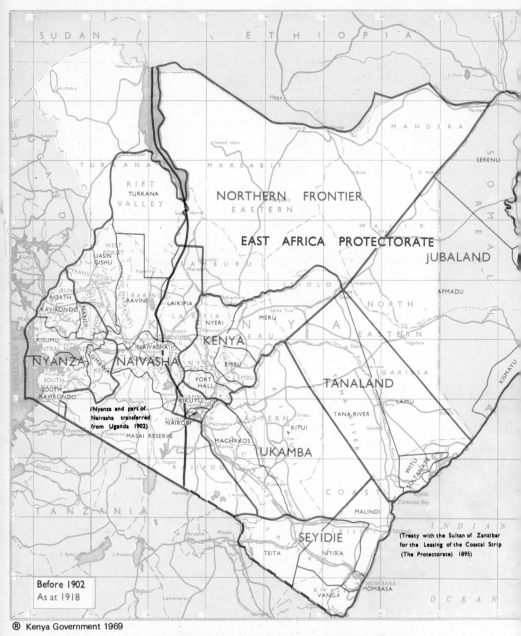

® Kenya Government 1969

1. Political boundaries, 1880-1924

1886, 1890, 1893: Anglo-German agreements. 1895: British East Africa Protectorate declared. 1902: Nyanza transferred from Uganda. 1920: Kenya Colony & Protectorate.

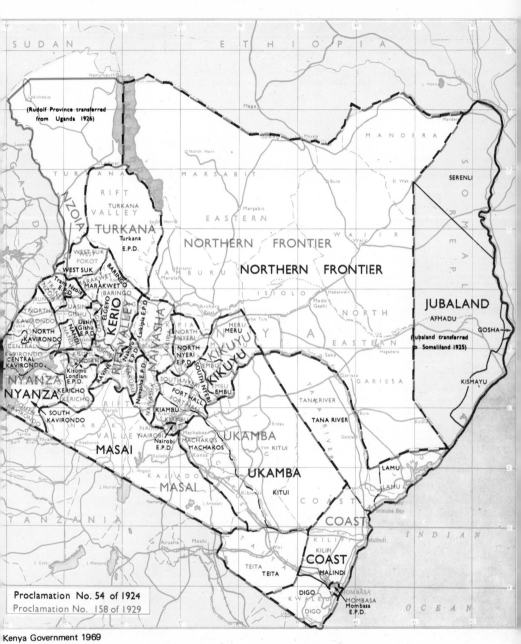

2. Political boundaries, 1924-1933

1924: Treaty of London (Britain & Italy). 1926: Rudolf Province transferred.

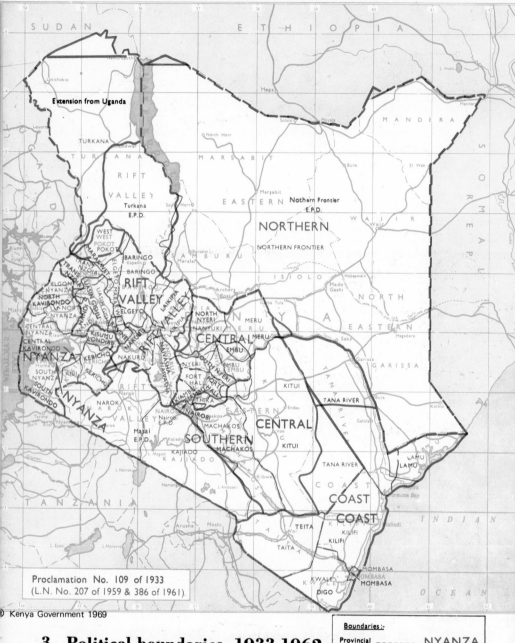

© Kenya Government 1969

3. Political boundaries, 1933-1962

Kenya Colony and Protectorate before Independence.

Proclamation No. 109 of 1933
(L.N. No. 207 of 1959 & 386 of 1961)

Boundaries :-		
Provincial	-------	**NYANZA**
Provincial	-------	COAST

4. Catholic missions, 1498-1952

1498: Vasco da Gama and early missionaries. 1889: beginning of second Catholic missionary entry.

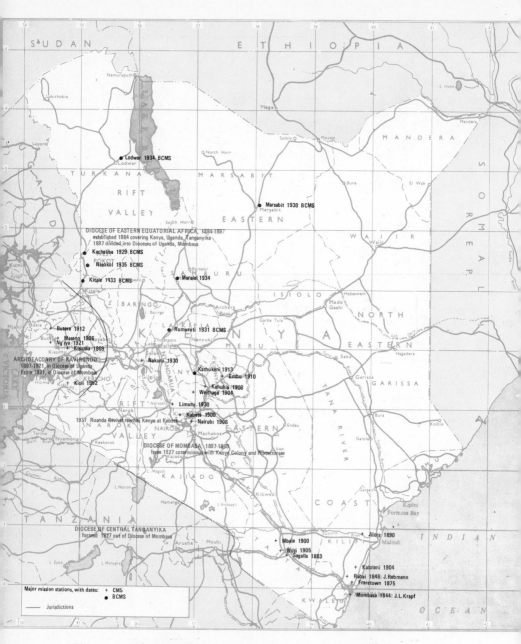

5. Anglican missions, 1844-1959

Creation and evolution of Anglican Diocese of Mombasa and its mission stations.

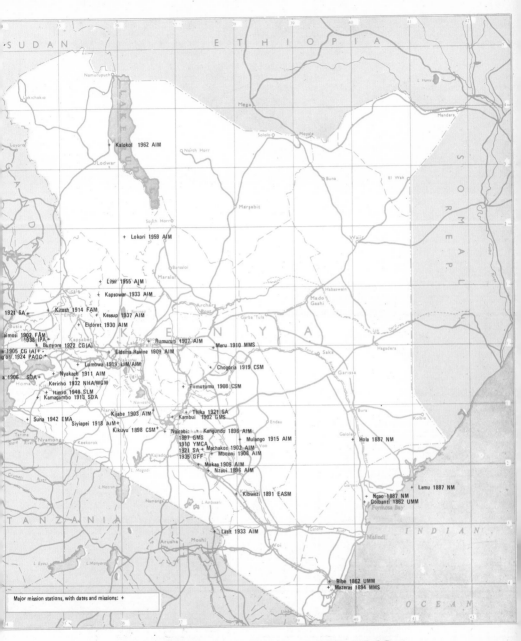

6. Protestant missions, 1862-1962

Location of major Protestant mission stations in the 100 years preceding Kenya's independence in 1963 (for names of missions, see *Index of Abbreviations*).

7. African independent churches, 1914-1962

Headquarters of all indigenous denominations begun by Africans before Independence in 1963 (for names, see *Index of Abbreviations*).

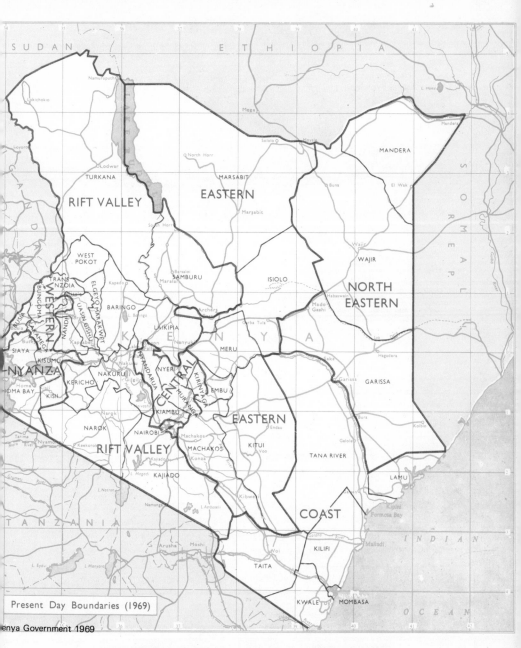

Present Day Boundaries (1969)

enya Government 1969

8. Political boundaries, 1963-1972

Provincial and district boundaries since Kenya's Independence as a Republic in 1963.

KERICHO

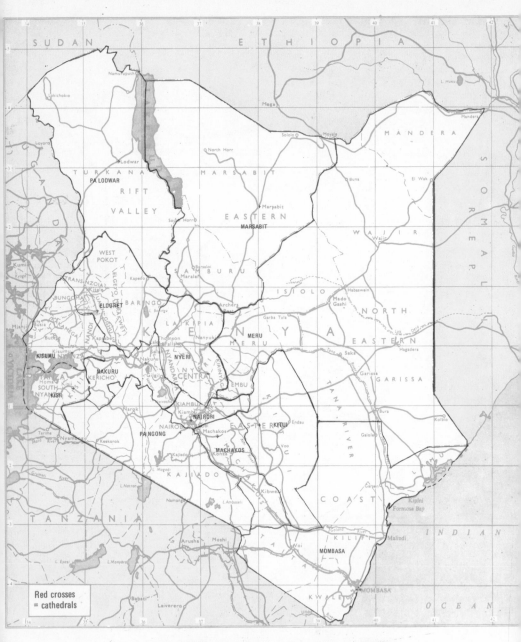

9. Catholic Church, 1953-1972

Development of dioceses since establishment of Ecclesiastical Province of Kenya in 1953.

Red crosses
= cathedrals

10. Anglican Church, 1960-1972

Development of dioceses from creation of Church of the Province of East Africa (1960) to Church of the Province of Kenya (1970).

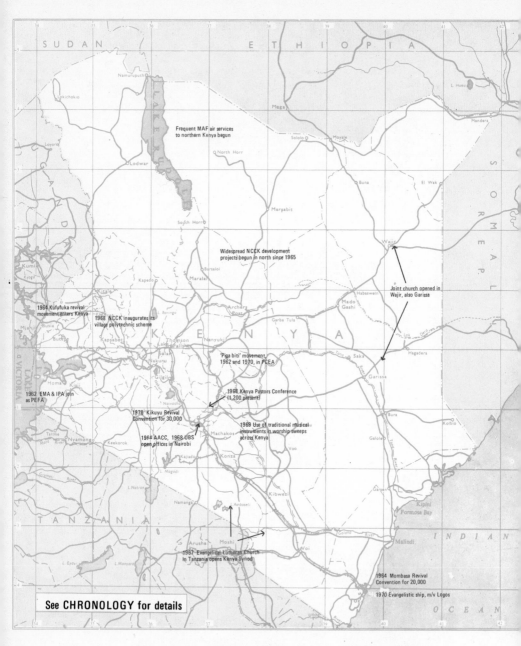

SUDAN

ETHIOPIA

Namuruputh

Lokichokio

Loyoro

Lodwar

Mega

Moyale

Mandera

Sololo

North Horr

L. Huku

Frequent MAF air services
to northern Kenya begun

South Horr

Marsabit

Buna

El Wak

SOMALI

Kumi

Kapedo

Barsaloi

Marala

Wajir

Widespread NCCK development
projects begun in north since 1965

Joint church opened in
Wajir, also Garissa

Kitale

Kapsabet

Boringo

Thomson
Falls

Marala

Habaswein

Mado
Gashi

Archers
Post

Garba Tula

Hagadera

1964 Kufufuka revival
movement enters Kenya

1968 NCCK inaugurates its
village polytechnic scheme

Busia

Butere

K E N Y A

Nyanuki

'Piga biti' movement,
1962 and 1970, in PCEA

Tana

Saka

Garissa

Homa

Kericho

Kisii

Nakuru

Gilgil

Naivasha

1962 EMA & IPA join
as PEFA

1970 Kikuyu Revival
Convention for 30,000

1968 Kenya Pastors Conference
(1,200 present)

1969 Use of traditional musical
instruments in worship sweeps
across Kenya

Bura

Kolbio

Tarime

Mara

Nyamongo

Keekorok

Machakos

1964 AACC, 1968 UBS
open offices in Nairobi

Kajiado

Konza

Voo

Galole

Garsen

L. Natron

Magadi

Kibwezi

Kipini
Formosa Bay

T A N Z A N I A

Namanga

Amboseli

L. Eyasi

L. Manyara

Arusha

Moshi

Voi

Golen

Malindi

INDIAN

1967 Evangelical Lutheran Church
in Tanzania opens Kenya Synod

1964 Mombasa Revival
Convention for 20,000

1970 Evangelistic ship, m/v Logos

See CHRONOLOGY for details

OCEAN

11. Protestant churches, 1963-1972

The map locates a selection of Protestant events in Kenya since 1962.

12. African independent churches, 1963-1972

Headquarters of newly-formed indigenous churches begun by Africans since Independence in 1963 (for names, see *Index of Abbreviations*). Initials with blue dots represent churches with under 10,000 adherents in 1972; with crosses, over 10,000.

Between Islamisation and Islam lines,
residual traditional religion (animism)
still widespread

AKUJ
Turkana 96%

WAH

WAQA
Marsabit

TORORUT
Pokot 90%

Mt. Elgon: Dini ya
Msambwa 1948
ASIS

OIKI

ASIS
Marakwet 57%

WERE

Elgeyo 56%

AKUJ

ASIS ugen 59%

Nandi 41%
CHEPTALIL

Samburu 97%

mugwe
(Meru prophets)

TURURIT
Mt. Kenya, House of God
looked to by Kikuyu,
Embu and Meru

MURUNGU
Meru 54%

Luo **NYASAYE**
Mumbo, in lake

Renowned witchdoctor
Makadudi and large
entourage 1964-72

1964 Witchfinder Kabwere
arrested, sold holy water

Tharaka 61%

ASIS

ERIDBA
Kipsigis 32%

NGAI 28%

Kikuyu 27%

ENYASAYE
Kipsis 41%

NGAI
mukurwe (Kikuyu sacred tree)

Mbere 66%

WAQA

EN-KAI
Maasai 78%

NAIROBI: over 100
medicine men, 1972

HQ, Waganga wa Miti Shamba
(Medicine Men's Society)

MULUNGU
Kamba 39%

MULUNGU

Kilimanjaro, House of God
for Maasai

MULUNGU
Taita 28%

Witchfinder Kajiwe led
movement from 1965;
imprisoned
Giriama 82%

Taita skull caves
of ancestors

Duruma 42%

MULUNGU

Black CAPITALS = tribal names for God
Blue = traditional religion (animism)
Red = Islam line (east of it = 100% Muslim)

13. African traditional religions

Traditional tribal religions are professed and practised by 3 million persons in Kenya.

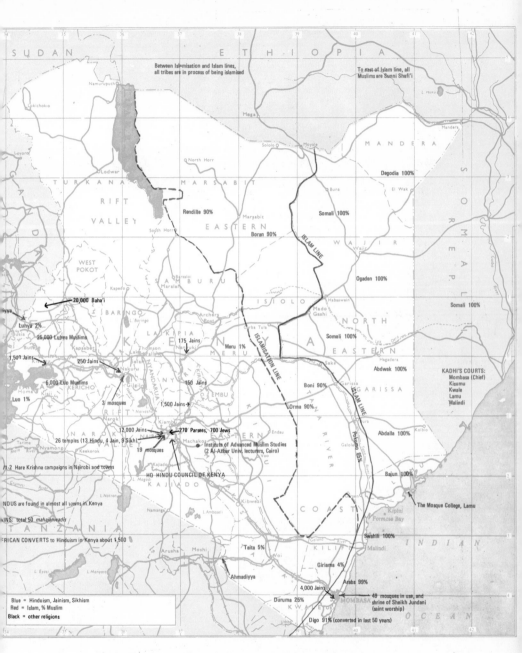

Between Islamisation and Islam lines,
all tribes are in process of being islamised

To east of Islam line, all
Muslims are Sunni Shafi'i

SUDAN

ETHIOPIA

MANDERA

Degodia 100%

Somali 100%

Randille 90%

Boran 90%

ISLAM LINE

Ogaden 100%

Somali 100%

Somali 100%

20,000 Baha'i

Luhya 2%

25,000 Luhya Muslims

Meru 1%

175 Jains

Abdwek 100%

KADHI'S COURTS:
Mombasa (Chief)
Kisumu
Kwale
Lamu
Malindi

1,500 Jains

250 Jains

150 Jains

6,000 Luo Muslims

Boni 90%

Luo 1%

3 mosques

1,500 Jains

Orma 90%

Abdalla 100%

12,000 Jains

270 Parsees, 700 Jews

26 temples (13 Hindu, 4 Jain, 9 Sikh)

Institute of Advanced Muslim Studies
(2 Al-Azhar Univ. lecturers, Cairo)

19 mosques

Pokomo 85%

Bajun 100%

1-2 Hare Krishna campaigns in Nairobi and towns

HQ HINDU COUNCIL OF KENYA

The Mosque College, Lamu

NDUS are found in almost all towns in Kenya

AINS: total 50 mahajanwadis

TANZANIA

Swahili 100%

RICAN CONVERTS to Hinduism in Kenya about 1,500

Taita 5%

Giriama 4%

INDIAN

Ahmadiyya

4,000 Jains

Arabs 99%

49 mosques in use, and
shrine of Sheikh Jundani
(saint worship)

Duruma 25%

MOMBASA

Blue = Hinduism, Jainism, Sikhism
Red = Islam, % Muslim
Black = other religions

Digo 91% (converted in last 50 years)

OCEAN

14. Non-Christian world religions

Of the great world religions, Islam is widely practised in Kenya, together with Hinduism, Jainism and
Sikhism.

15. Tribes and languages of Kenya

African peoples in Kenya are divided into three main linguistic groups, Bantu-, Nilotic- (including Paranilotic-) and Cushitic-speaking. The three areas labelled 'Mixed' above are occupied by settlers from many tribal groups.

4

Part IV

Directory of the Churches in Kenya

Directory of the Churches in Kenya

This Directory is a listing of all denominations and their major dioceses in Kenya. Information is set out as follows:

Official name, in bold type (Initials, if used)   Number
Title and name of senior church leader
Street address or location of office
Postal address, in italics.   *Telephone*

In cases where an official name in Swahili is in use, this is given in italics below the postal address. In actual fact, although all churches and organisations were asked to give their Swahili name, very few have one in use.

Initials are given only when in use by or for the denomination. Exchanges of telephone numbers are the same as town of postal address, unless otherwise shown. 'RN' = Radiocall Nairobi, a special service requested from telephone operator. Note that the vast majority of church headquarters are outside Nairobi and do not have telephone numbers, whereas most Christian organisations (see Part V) are in Nairobi or major towns and have telephones. Most of the places listed in this Directory may be located on the foldout map of Kenya at the end of this Handbook.

Note: The full, correct, postal address is as shown in italics; street address, and words such as 'via', are *not* required on envelopes. Note also that box numbers, offices and telephones are often not exclusive to the user, but belong to some large secular body.

For each church or denomination, brief information of a historical and descriptive nature is then added. For comparative statistics, dates of founding, membership in councils, ethnic (tribal) affiliation of members, and other brief descriptive data on all bodies, the reader should turn to the table *Statistics of the Churches in Kenya* in Part II (page 183).

All denominations and dioceses in existence in January 1972 are included in this Directory, and are given a reference number on the right which is the same as that in the table *Statistics of the Churches in Kenya.* But in addition, the Directory includes a few churches which were in process of coming into existence

in January, 1972, and which subsequently applied for registration; a few churches which have now gone out of existence; as well as a number of alternative titles in use for existing churches; all of these are identified by the *absence* of reference numbers. It should be remembered that the number of denominations is increasing by about one each month; thus, there were 205 in January, 1972, but this total would have increased to about 210 by July, 1972. There is also an increasing number of aspiring denominations; thus from April-June 1972, four each month applied for registration. In addition to those listed in this Directory but not in the table *Statistics,* these included: African Galili Church of East Africa, African Independent Church of the Holy Spirit, Holiness Church of Kenya, Holy Cross Church of God All Over the World in East Africa, Kenya Evangelist Church, Rock Church, Union of Prophet Churches, World Undenominational Apostolic Faith Church.

Changes of names and address
The information supplied here was correct as of, on average, December 1971. Changes in the names of church leaders, and addresses, can be expected at the rate of about 5 per cent each year. Space has been left for the reader to up-date any of these that concern him.

Legal existence
Inclusion of a body in this Directory does not imply it has legal existence or recognition. This is primarily a descriptive directory, listing all bodies known, or thought, to exist in 1972; for their legal status, the reader should consult the table *Statistics of the Churches.* The fact that we include a number of bodies which have no legal existence, or have had their former registration cancelled, is not meant to imply infringement of the law; it takes a long time for the law to be understood, or for the leaders of a dissolved church to disperse their followers or persuade them to join other churches. *(Our survey simply gives their approximate situation and numerical status at the time when information was last available, which in a handful of cases is several years ago.)

Africa Early Church 1
Pastor: Mr. John Luvisha
Mahanga Village, South Maragoli
P.O. Box 109, Maragoli.
    A very small Luhya independent group, whose application
for registration was refused in 1967.

Africa Gospel Church 2
Moderator: The Rev. Jonah A. Cheseng'eny; Executive Secretary:
The Rev. Dean Strong
World Gospel Mission, Kericho
P.O. Box 123, Kericho. *Tel: 123*
    In 1932 a mission was begun in Kericho by the World Gospel
Mission, an international American society in the Holiness
tradition. In 1961 the AGC was formed as an autonomous
church under national leadership. Membership is largely
Kipsigis, with five dioceses: Belgut Area, Kipgelion Area,
Tenwek Area, Longisa Area, Chebolungu Area. In 1964 a
serious dispute resulted in a schism, the Africa Gospel Unity
Church. The AGC runs a ministers' training school, Highlands
Bible College, and Kaboson Bible School; and publishes a news-
paper, *Igondit* (Trumpet).

Africa Gospel Unity Church (AGUC) 3
Founder and Chairman: The Rev. Dishon A. Kesembe
Silibwet
P.O. Box 3033, Bomet.
    An independent church among the Kipsigis begun in 1964
by the first moderator of the Africa Gospel Church, who was
voted out of office in a dispute over missionary personnel, and
seceded with 10 per cent of the membership. Expanding now
from Kericho District to Nandi District.

Africa Inland Church (AIC) 4
Chairman: The Rev. Wellington E. Mulwa
AIC Headquarters: Kinyanjui Road, Ziwani
P.O. Box 13024, Nairobi. *Tel: 25149*
    One of the earliest missions to arrive in Kenya was the Africa
Inland Mission. In 1895 Peter Cameron Scott arrived at Nzani
in Machakos district. The work then spread throughout Kenya,
including to remoter areas like Galole and Woldera (Orma
tribe), and Turkana. The AIC is the national church associated
with the AIM, and became fully autonomous in 1971. Church
work is divided into six church regions: Machakos, Kitui,
Central, Southern, Lake, and Rift Valley. There are seven Bible
schools which have produced over 300 graduates over the years,
at Mumbuni, Mulango, Mukaa, Narok, Ogada, Kapsabet and
Kijabe, with an eighth planned for the Coast. Scott Theological
College, Machakos, trains pastors of secondary education. The
AIM began a large number of secular schools also, and the AIC
is now the sponsor of 667 primary schools; manages over 30
Harambee secondary schools; and has a private school at Kessup
in Elgeyo, with another planned for Kyome, Kitui. A wide range
of other activities includes the Africa Inland Press, mobile units,
and the large complex (Hospital, schools, Rift Valley Academy,
etc.), at Kijabe on the edge of the Rift Valley. Details of these
major institutions are given in Part V, Directory of Christian
Organisations in Kenya.

AIC Stations
    (Correspondence to: Station Manager)
Eldama Ravine, Box 9, Eldama Ravine (T: 14)
Gatab, Box 21010, Nairobi (T: RN 2070)
Kajiado, Box 25, Kajiado (T: 31)
Kalokol, Box 21010, Nairobi (on Ferguson's Gulf) (T: RN 2039)
Kangundo, Box 1054, Kangundo
Kapropita, P.O. Kabarnet (T: RN 2046)
Kapsabet, Box 20, Kapsabet (T: 8)
Kapsowar, Box 130, Eldoret (45 miles north) (T: RN 2004)
Kaptagat, Box 472, Eldoret
Kessup, Box 418, Eldoret (26 miles from Eldoret) (T: RN 2045)
Kijabe, P.O. Kijabe (T: 12Y1 to 12Y9)
Kilgoris, P.O. Kilgoris, Sotik
Kyome, P.O. Migwani, Kitui (40 miles) (T: RN 2068)
Litein, Box 2000, Litein, Kericho (20 miles) (T: Litein 11)
Liter, Box 382, Eldoret (80 miles north) (T: RN 2020)
Loglogo, Box 21010, Nairobi (40 miles south Marsabit) (T: RN
2036)

Lokori, Box 21010, Nairobi (100 miles south of Lodwar) (T:
RN 2005)
Machakos, Box 49, Machakos (Mumbuni, 2 miles) (T: 65)
Mukaa, P.O. Kilome, Machakos
Mulango, Box 49, Kitui (4 miles) (T: RN 2125)
Narok, Box 7, Narok (T: 16)
Njabini Conference Centre, Box 24, South Kinangop
Nyakach, P.O. Sondu, Kisumu (50 miles south) (T: RN 2038)
Ogada, Box 360, Kisumu (7 miles north) (T: RN 2037)
Siyiapei, Box 49, Narok (T: RN 2170)

African Anglican Church, see Church of the Province of
  Kenya

African Brotherhood Church (ABC) 5
Bishop: The Rev. N.K. Ngala
HQ & DS Mitavoni
P.O. Box 32, Machakos.
    One of the earliest large independent churches, formed in
1945 out of members of the Africa Inland Church, Salvation
Army, and other bodies. Mainly Kamba members, but with
congregations in Mombasa, Kwale, Embu, Thika, Magadi,
Kisumu and Kakamega area.

African Christian Church
Lay Reader: Mr. Thomas Ong'idi
Ochuna Branch
P.O. Ahero.
    A Luo independent church that was refused registration in
1954.

African Christian Church & Schools (ACC&S) 6
Chairman: Mr. Stephen Ng'ang'a Wairegi; Gen. Secretary: The
  Rev. S. Mugo Mwangi
HQ: ACC&S Church, Gituru
P.O. Box 291, Thika.
    A large Kikuyu movement out of the Africa Inland Church
in 1947 which drew off almost all 50 Kikuyu mission churches
and schools, due to the desire to expand schooling facilities.
Recently, overseas missionary aid has been invited in, viz. the
Canadian Baptist Overseas Mission Board, who now have 8
missionaries. The ACC&S is a member of the NCCK, and from
about 1966 a member of the East African Church Union Consultation. 29 congregations in 4 parishes (plus one congregation
in Nairobi). Ministers wear black Geneva gowns, with (after
5 years' service) white surplices with a large red cross on. The
church is described in J.W. Kuria's paper (see *Bibliography*),
which is available from the general secretary of the church.

African Christian Church of East Africa 7
Chairman: Mr. Jonah Gaceru
Laikipia District
P.O. Box 258, Meru (P.O. Box 207, Nanyuki).
    An independent group in Laikipia with Kikuyu and Meru
members.

African Church, The (AC) 8
Bishop Isaac Kivai Mbonde
Mutondoni Market
P.O. Box 41, Machakos.
    Founded in 1961 as the Kenya African Church. Largely
Kamba members. Two pastorates: AC Kitui Kyuso, and AC
Nguliya Yatta.

African Church Holy Spirit Independent 9
Chairman: Mr. Johan Nkabu
Upper Chure Church, Ruraja, Abogeta Location
P.O. Nkubu, Meru.
    One of the few independent groups to attempt to register
with a name too close to existing bodies; hence application
refused in 1971.

African Church Mission (ACM) 10
Bishop Erasto Olwande
Gogo School, Sirembe Gem
P.O. Box 33 (or P.O. Box 64), Yala.
    A very early schism (1941) from an existing independent
church, the Nomiya Luo Mission, rejecting that body's practice
of circumcision. This is one of the very few churches in Kenya

to permit post-baptism polygamy. Membership 1,200 Luo, 800 Luhya.

African Church of Holy Spirit (ACHS) 11
High Priest: The Rt. Rev. Kepha Ayub Mavuru; Secretary: Mr. Peter Ihaji
Lugala Headquarters, Isukha, Kakamega-Kapsabet Road
P.O. Box 183, Kakamega.
One of the first independent churches, springing out of the 1927 Kaimosi Holy Spirit revival. Known also as Dini ya Roho, Dini ya Msalaba (Religion of the Cross). Long history of persecution by the mission they left, and by the government. The present High Priest has held office since 1953. Members are distinguished by white robes with red belts and red crosses, beards, turbans, and drums. Sick members do not go to hospitals, but members weaker in faith are permitted to do so. Mainly Luhya members, with Kikuyu and Meru branches. The ACHS was the first independent church in Kenya to send a student to St. Paul's United Theological College, Limuru (1967).

African Church of Jesus Christ in Kenya 12
Bishop: Paul Kibuti
Kiamuthambi Diocese
P.O. Box 47, Kerugoya.
A recent Kikuyu movement among former Anglicans founded by a former Anglican minister associated with the Church of Christ in Africa. Considerable efforts being made to open Bible schools.

African Church of Red Cross, see Lyahuka Church of East Africa

African Coptic Orthodox Church 13
Ecclesiastical General: The Rev. Thomas Munjal
Orthodox Church, Moto Estate, Juja Road, Eastleigh
P.O. Box 28312, Nairobi.   *Tel: 50931*
A recent regrouping of independent bodies in the Orthodox tradition, with three sub-groups of its own, claiming 200,000 adherents in various nations. The leader of this grouping was a Catholic who took part in the founding of Maria Legio in 1962. These realignments are due to dissatisfaction over the small amount of mission aid given over the years by the Greek Orthodox Patriarchate of Alexandria, and an attempt to appeal from the GOC to the Coptic Orthodox Patriarchate of Alexandria. So far neither patriarchate has taken the issue sufficiently seriously. This church (ACOC) exists mainly in Uganda and has a small following in Kenya. It is linked with the Ugandan pioneer independent, Reuban Spartas, and his African Autonomous Orthodox Church, based on Kampala.

African Disciples Church (ADC) 14
Bishop: The Rev. David Musembi
HQ &BS Ngoleni-Kiumoni
P.O. Box 96, Machakos.
Ikanisa ya Amanyiwa ma Yesu. An independent church among the Kamba begun in 1967 and based on the founder's visions. Publishes own journal, *ADC's Gazette* or *The Fulfilment of God's Work in ADC.* Fifteen persons have now graduated from their Bible school.

African Divine Church (ADC) 15
Chairman: Bishop James Lulega Chabuga; Gen. Secretary: David K. Noah
HQ: Boyani
P.O. Box 907, Kisumu.
A schism in 1949 among the Maragoli from the Pentecostal Assemblies of Canada mission, partly over the desire to wear uniforms.

African Eden Roho Society 16
Pastor: Mr. Joel Anyango
Bware School, Kendu Bay
P.O. Kendu Bay.
A Luo independent church with 143 members, formerly known as African Roho Mission.

African Emmanuel Church New Salem 17
Chairman: The Rev. Joshua Otieno
Pap Onditi
P.O. Sondu.

A small Luo independent group in South Nyanza.

African Evangelical Presbyterian Church (AEPC) 18
Moderator: The Rev. David M. Mutava
Waita-Endui Location
P.O. Mwingi, Kitui.
A largely Kamba church, organised by World Presbyterian Missions after this mission was formed in the USA as a split from the Independent Board for Presbyterian Foreign Missions in 1957. Has developed new methods of Sunday-school teaching for children, and to that end has published four books recounting the Bible story from Adam to the Apostles. Four branches: East, Central, West, and Embu.

African Evangelist Fellowship Healing, see Prophecy Evangelist Church of Africa

African God Covenant Brotherhood Church Society, see Holy Spirit Brotherhood Church

African God New Covenant Holy Ghost Church, see Holy Spirit Brotherhood Church

African God Worshippers Fellowship Church Society, see Apostolic Hierarchy Church

African Gospel Church, see Gospel of God

African Greek Orthodox Church, see African Orthodox Church of Kenya

African Holy Ghost Christian Church 19
High Priest: Bishop Daniel Nduti Katuga
Gichagi-ini HQ, Kandara, Murang'a
P.O. Box 644, Thika.
This body emerged as one of the earliest churches out of the original Kikuyu independent Watu wa Mungu (People of God), and has a long history of persecution in colonial times. It was organisationally part of the Kenya Foundation of the Prophets Church until it broke from them in 1968.

African Holy Zionist Church (AHZC) 20
Bishop Shem Ogola; Secretary: Mr. Albert Anono
Kegomori, Maragoli
P.O. Box 76, Maragoli.
Formerly called the Africa Zion Church. Uses drums and instruments; publishes paper *Sauti ya Zion* (Voice of Zion). Registration of 1963 was cancelled in 1972.

African Independent Church of Kenya 21
Archbishop: The Most Rev. Thomas Mutiso Kithele (P.O. Box 9217, Nairobi).
Mutituni Church, Machakos
P.O. Box 73 (and P.O. Box 224), Machakos.
A schism by Kamba members of the Anglican Church in 1943, which subsequently declined over the years from a claimed 8,000 members in 1959, to 1,000 in 1962, and to 670 in 1964. It was registered in 1962, but cancelled in 1969.

African Independent Pentecostal Church of Africa 22
(AIPC)
Bishop: The Rt. Rev. Benjamin Kahihia; Chairman: Mr. L. Kabunga; Secretary-General: Mr. Elijah N. Willy
Central Office
P.O. Box 28133, Nairobi (also P.O. Box 255, Ruiru; P.O. Box 35, Nyeri).
The first independent church among the Kikuyu was founded near Fort Hall in 1921 by Daudi Maina Kiragu, later an AIPC bishop. The AIPC was founded about 1925 as the religious arm of KISA (Kikuyu Independent Schools Association), and in parallel with the rival African Orthodox Church, the AIPC played a notable part in early Kenya nationalism. By 1952, there were 168 KISA schools with over 60,000 pupils in Central and Rift Valley Provinces, each school having its associated AIPC congregation, church and school using the same building (28 in Kiambu District, 38 in Fort Hall, 27 in Nyeri, 16 in Embu, 6 in Meru, 47 in Rift Valley). In 1952 the AIPC was banned along with other Kikuyu organisations, and its members were forced to lapse or to join the PCEA (Presbyterian) and other mission churches. After Independence in 1963, these persons brought about a mass exodus, the PCEA

around Nyeri, for example, losing most of its members. The AIPC was then re-established and given legal recognition in 1964, since when it has experienced phenomenal growth in Kikuyu rural areas, expanding from 18,000 members in 1966 to 496,000 in 14 districts in 1971. Six high priests, 70 priests, 60 deacons and 450 lay preachers minister in 430 churches built since 1963, under four dioceses: Northern Diocese (Nyeri), Central Diocese (Kiambu), Eastern Diocese (Embu), Rift Valley Diocese (Nakuru). Many new church buildings are at present under construction. One of the largest single congregations is that of Muthua-ini, founded in 1928, which has 4,000 followers (see essay by S.G. Kimunge in *Bibliography*). AIPC congregations are also found outside Kikuyu country, from Mombasa, to Isiolo, and in Eldoret and Kitale. Almost the only published account of the AIPC is Welbourn's 'A national church against foreign control' (1961: see *Bibliography*).

African Interior Church   23
Minister-in-Charge: The Rt. Rev. Washington A. Lusuli
HQ: Ebunangwe, Bunyore
P.O. Box 106, Maragoli.
An early schism (1943) of 7 churches and 2,000 members from the Church of God mission from Anderson, Indiana, USA (from 1905 to 1928, the South African Compounds and Interior Mission Interdenominational). The church uses the Anglican Book of Common Prayer, stresses the ordained ministry, and is attempting to finance a theological college.

African Israel Church Association, see East African Israel Church

African Israel Church Nineveh (AICN)   24
Founder and High Priest: Baba M.P. David Zakayo Kivuli; Chief Minister: Jackson Philemon Orwa; Gen. Secretary: Mr. Richard Oloo
HQ: Nineveh (17 miles north of Kisumu)
P.O. Box 701, Kisumu.
An early independent church founded on 1 January 1942 out of the Pentecostal Assemblies of Canada mission at Nyang'ori, earlier called Huru Salvation Nineveh (Free Salvation Nineveh), later AICN, now spread across Kenya, and administered through 23 Ministries under Ministers (21 being in Kenya), which in turn are over 68 Pastorates each with a Pastor, and 274 Churches. A single church can hold 600 persons, and congregations are well-known for their packed seating, energetic worship, and processions moving through the streets with banners, drums and home-made megaphones. In addition, the AICN has 3 Priests devoted to prayer for the sick. The headquarters at the holy city, Nineveh, has a small fish farm. Priests are trained there also by the High Priest himself, though one of his sons recently studied at the United Theological College (St. Paul's, Limuru) of the Protestant churches. The name 'Nineveh' derives from the practice of public repentance (as in Nineveh in the Old Testament) on Thursday evenings before Friday (the AICN holy day).

African Mission of Holy Ghost Church (Kirang'a)   25
Leader: Mr. Daniel Muciri Nganga
HQ: Ngeraria, Muruka Location 4, Murang'a
P.O. Box 511, Nyeri (P.O. Box 111 and 588, Thika).
One of the oldest Kikuyu independent churches, the AMHGC was begun in 1930 from the Watu wa Mungu by Johana Waweru (began preaching 1913, died 1959). Faith healing practiced, opposed to hospitals; white robes; word 'Israel' in red on robes, on drums, on bishop's door, and other places.

African Nabi Roho Maler   26
Chairman: Mr. Peter Odindo Ondu
Reg. Office: Samaria, Sub-Location Dago, Kisumu Location
P.O. Box 55, Maragoli (P.O. Box 347, Kisumu).
A small independent church with Luo and Maragoli members. The name is Luo for 'African Prophet Holy Spirit'.

African Orthodox Church of Kenya (AOC)   27
Metropolitan of East Africa: Archbishop Frumentius Nasios; Vicar-General: Auxiliary Bishop Arthur Gathuna (P.O. Box 21186, Nairobi); Secretary: The Rev. Elaftherios Muiruri Ndwaru (P.O. Box 44, Kikuyu)
HQ: Holy Archbishopric of Irinoupolis: Valley Road, Nairobi,

and Waithaka-Kagira, Wangai Road, Dagoretti
P.O. Box 6119, Nairobi.   *Tel: 28804*
As a result of the Kikuyu female circumcision controversy and the attendant surge of nationalist hopes, from 1928 onwards large members of Kikuyu left the historical mission churches (PCEA, CMS, AIM, *et alia*) forming loose independent groups like the 'Watu wa Mungu' (People of God) and KISA (Kikuyu Independent Schools Association). By 1932 two distinct large independent churches had crystallised out — the AIPC, linked with KISA, and the AOC; in the latter, the first priests were ordained in 1937 by Archbishop Daniel Alexander of South Africa. By 1952, the political-educational society associated with the AOC, Kikuyu Karing'a ('Pure') Educational Association, had 28 independent Kikuyu schools, and the associated AOC congregations had 30,000 active adult subscribing church members, mainly in Kiambu District, in 309 churches (253 in Central and Rift Valley Provinces). With other Kikuyu bodies the AOC was banned in 1952 and its members dispersed, and only emerged after Independence when it was registered as a lawful society in 1965. Since then (as with the AIPC), its former members have flocked back and the church has experienced a phenomenal expansion. Recognised since 1946 as Greek Orthodox under the Patriarchate of Alexandria (Egypt), the church in 1971 was aided by only three Greeks — two priests and the archbishop. A highlight of 1971 was the visit of Archbishop Makarios, President of Cyprus, who baptised 5,000 persons of all ages (almost all hitherto unbaptised Kikuyu who passed through former KKEA schools without being baptised during the years when the AOC was banned) during two open-air services, laid the foundation stone of the new Waithaka seminary, and who is at present aiding its construction from Cyprus. The church expects shortly to change its official name to: the Orthodox Church of Kenya. (For literature on the AOC, see *Bibliography* under F.B. Welbourn, D. Wentinck).

African Revelation Church St. Mission   28
Sondu, Nyanza
P.O. Sondu, Kisumu.
A small Luo independent group in South Nyanza.

African Roho Mission, see African Eden Roho Society

African Sinai Church (ASC)   29
Founder and Bishop: Musa Busolo Anyika
Halahala Mission (3 miles north of Kaimosi)
P.O. Box 10087, Tiriki.
A small independent church among the Tiriki (Luhya), formed in 1965 by schism from the African Divine Church. In 1964 there was a circumcision ceremony in Tiriki Location; those who allowed their sons to participate were excommunicated, and among them was Busolo and other founding members of ASC.

African Spiritual Israel Church, see Roho Church of God of Israel

African United Christian Church, see Kenya African United Christian Churches (in Part V)

Akurinu, see Chosen Church of the Holy Spirit in Kenya

All Africa Nation of Holy Ghost Church Israel, see Israel Holy Ghost Church of Kenya

All Ethiopian Church in East Africa   30
Chairman: Mr. Adam Noor
c/o *P.O. Box 47909, Nairobi.*
One of several independent church groups with few or no members, whose purpose is to serve as rallying-points and foci for attempts to unite all indigenous churches in Kenya by linking them with the Ethiopian and Coptic Orthodox Churches (of Ethiopia, and Egypt).

A-Nabii Church, see Church of the Prophets

Anabii na Atumwo, see African God New Covenant Holy Ghost Church

Anglican Church, see Church of the Province of Kenya

Apostles, see The Gospel of God

Apostles Christian Church of Africa 31
Chairman: Archbishop: The Rev. Paul Njue; Gen. Secretary:
The Rev. Frederick Njeru (P.O. Box 260, Embu).
Diocese of Riandu, Nthawa Location (Siakago), Mbere
P.O. Box 374, Embu.
A recent Embu independent church with four parishes in a
Diocese of Riandu, led by a former Aroti member of the Holy
Spirit Church of Zayun. Turbans not worn.

Apostolic Faith Mission of South Africa
(formerly of *P.O. Box 253, Eldoret*).
A missionary body from the Republic of South Africa,
registered in 1957, later disbanded about 1963 and whose
registration was cancelled in 1967.

Apostolic Faith of Africa 32
General Overseer:.Mr. Willie Nganga Kago
HQ: Thogoto Village
P.O. Box 13, Kikuyu. *Tel: 2174*
A Kikuyu schism in 1959 from the Presbyterian Church of
East Africa, also known as Witikio wa Atumwo (Faith of the
Apostles), and Wa-Mathina (People of Sorrows). Congregations
have spread westwards from Kikuyu country to Baringo, West
Pokot, Kitale, Kericho, and into Uganda.

Apostolic Fellowship Church of God 33
Chairman: Mr. S. Kimaru
Solai Shopping Centre
P.O. Box 5023, Subukia.
A small Kikuyu independent body, registered in 1967.

Apostolic Hierarchy Church 34
Moderator: Mr. Wilfred Kamau Kamanu
Loc. 11/Maragi/1183
P.O. Box 153, Murang'a.
A small break from the Roman Catholic Church tracing its
origins to 1940. Formerly known as African God Worshippers
Fellowship Church Society, then Holy Trinity Church Mission-
ary Society. 580 Kikuyu members, in a strongly Roman
Catholic location.

Arata a Roho Mutheru, see Friends of the Holy Spirit

Aroti, see Holy Ghost Church of Kenya, etc

Assemblies of God, Kenya District Council 35
(KDCAG)
Superintendent: Mr. Charles F. Gallup
P.O. Box 492, Kakamega (and P.O. Box 4927, Nairobi).
A schism in 1968 from International Pentecostal Assemblies,
Kaimosi, led by two lay missionaries from the USA; first known
as Kenya Pentecostal Fellowship. Church-building program is
supported by Christ for the Nations; tracts and equipment from
T.L. Osborn Foundation. Journal *Life Light* (monthly).

Baptist Churches of Kenya, see Baptist Convention of
Kenya

Baptist Convention of Kenya (BCK) 36
Chairman: The Rev. Morris Wanje (Box 442 Malindi); Secretary:
The Rev. John Kariuki
Kariobangi Baptist Church, Outer Ring Road
Secretary, P.O. Box 20312, Nairobi.
The Southern Baptist Convention (USA) began work in
Kenya in 1956, known as the Baptist Mission of East Africa.
There has been a strong emphasis on church-planting based on
sound anthropological and biblical principles; growth has been
very rapid, resulting in 170 churches gathered into 8 Associa-
tions: Nairobi, Mt. Kenya, Maragoli, Western Region, Nyanza,
Kitale, Nakuru, and Coast. The theological college is in
Arusha (Tanzania). There is a monthly journal, *Habari za
Wabatisti* (Baptist News), a large publications programme, and
a communications and radio centre. In 1971, the Baptist Churches of Kenya were formally organised and registered as the Baptist
Convention of Kenya.

Believed Power of Jesus Christ in Kenya, The 37
Archbishop: Pastor Willson Gumba
Rapedhi Lwala Kanyadoto, West Nyokal
P.O. Mirogi.

A small Luo independent movement, whose application
for registration was refused in 1972.

Bible Fellowship Church 38
Founder and Chairman: Miss Stella L. Ross
On road to industrial area, on left before Thika High School
P.O. Box 5, Thika.
A single congregation in Thika begun around 1940 by Miss
Ross, a former missionary of the Gospel Missionary Society
before it merged in 1946 with Church of Scotland Mission to
form the Presbyterian Church of East Africa; Kikuyu and
expatriate members.

Blood of Christ Cleansed Church (BCCC)
Bishop Johanes M. Mutua
Mbiuni Village
P.O. Mbiuni, Machakos.
A small Kamba group of 50 members which was refused
registration in mid-1972.

Canaan Church in Kenya, see New African Canaan Church

Catholic Church in Kenya 39
Archbishop of Nairobi (& Chairman, Kenya Episcopal Con-
ference): H.E. Maurice Cardinal Otunga
Archbishop's Residence, St. Austin's Road
P.O. Box 14231, Nairobi. *Tel: 48932*
As described in the historical section of this *Handbook,* the
first Catholic missionaries arrived on the Kenya coast in 1498.
In the modern era, the first permanent Catholic missions were
planted, again at the Coast, at Kosi (1889) and Mombasa (1890).
The growth of the number of jurisdictions over the years is
shown in Figure 3 (p.179). , and in Maps 4 & 9. With the
establishment of an ecclesiastical province at Kenya in 1953,
the number has grown to (in mid-1972) one archdiocese, ten
dioceses, and two prefectures apostolic.
Full details of the hierarchy, personnel, parishes, etc., are
given in the *Catholic Directory of Eastern Africa, 1971.* In the
present *Handbook,* names and addresses of dioceses, bishops and
parishes are given immediately below; whereas Catholic organisations and institutions (including the Kenya Episcopal Conference, the Kenya Catholic Secretariat, the Apostolic Nunciature in Kenya, AMECEA, St. Thomas Aquinas Seminary,
et alia) will be found listed in alphabetical order in Part V,
Directory of Christian Organisations in Kenya. The rest of the
Handbook has other Catholic information described at the
appropriate points (historical, descriptive, statistical, bibliographical, periodicals, personnel). The location by province and
district of the 1,876 Catholic-sponsored primary schools and 98
harambee secondary schools is shown in Table 3, p. 180.
In the directory that now follows, the addresses of diocesan
officials (vicar-general, education secretary, etc.) are the same
as that of the Ordinary (bishop), unless indicated otherwise.
Every diocese has a large variety of development projects; by
way of illustration, these are detailed only for a few dioceses.
Details for the others may be found in the *Catholic Directory* or
from the dioceses concerned.

—Archdiocese of Nairobi 40
Archbishop of Nairobi: The Most Rev. Maurice Otunga
Archbishop's Residence, St. Austin's Road
P.O. Box 14231, Nairobi. *Tel: 48932*
The first mission in Nairobi was St. Austin's (1899). The
archdiocese was erected in 1953, and subsequently new dioceses
were erected from it: Mombasa (1955), Kitui (1956), Ngong
(1959), Nakuru (1968), Machakos (1969). Statistics as at 31
December 1969: 174,806 Catholics, 25,967 catechumens; mid-
1971, 192,404 Catholics.
Parishes
Eastleigh, Box 2603, Nairobi (T: 50005)
Gatitu, Box 6, Ruiru
Gatundu, Box 692, Thika
Jericho, Box 8069, Nairobi (T: 58529)
Kabochu, Box 23020, Nairobi
Kagwe, Box 265, Kiambu
Kalimoni, Box 25, Ruiru (T: 8Y10)
Karen, Box 24829, Nairobi
Karinga, Box 152, Ruiru

233

Kereita, Box 54, Uplands
Kiambu, Box 177, Kiambu
Kilima Mbogo, Box 8, Thika (T: Donyo Sabuk 4Y1)
Kiriku, Box 49, Thika
Limuru, Box 63, Limuru (T: 424)
Lioki, Box 44, Kiambu (T: Anmer 206)
Makadara, Box 12661, Nairobi (T: 58752)
Mangu, Box 298, Thika (T: Karamaini 216)
Miguta, Box 179, Kiambu
Nairobi: Holy Family Cathedral, Box 891, Nairobi (T: 20971)
Nairobi South, Box 30325, Nairobi (T: 59853)
Ngarariga, Box 220, Limuru
Parklands, Box 14313, Nairobi (T: 55616)
Polish Mission, Box 1889, Nairobi (T: Langata 425)
Riruta, P.O. Kabete, Nairobi (T: 66944)
Ruaraka, Box 8409, Nairobi (T: Ruaraka 2303)
St. Peter Claver, Box 1065, Nairobi (T: 22130)
Thigio, Box 200, Limuru
Thika, Box 33, Thika (T: 2002)
Westlands (Italian Parish), Box 8353, Nairobi (T: 53352)
Westlands, Box 580, Nairobi (T: 60328)

—Diocese of Eldoret 41
Bishop of Eldoret: The Rt. Rev. John Njenga
Bishop's House, Shakespeare Road
P.O. Box 842, Eldoret. *Tel: 2427*
   The prefecture of Eldoret was erected in 1953 out of the diocese of Kisumu, and was raised to a diocese in 1959. Statistics as at 31 December, 1969: 53,660 Catholics, 10,550 catechumens. The diocese is not as clearly delineated by political boundaries as others, since it embraces five districts in Rift Valley Province (Elgeyo-Marakwet, Trans Nzoia, Uasin Gishu, West Pokot and Karapokot), together with parts of Bungoma and Kakamega Districts in Western Province. There are about 114 Catholic-sponsored primary schools in the diocese. A number of development projects exist, with a large programme for initiating new ones in the spheres of agriculture, medical work, home training and home economics, commercial training, water and irrigation schemes, welfare, and a multi-purpose inservice district development centre for government and church rural extension workers.
Parishes
Eldoret, Box 289, Eldoret (T: 130)
Hoey's Bridge, Box 28, Hoey's Bridge
Iten, P.O. Iten, Eldoret
Kaptagat, Box 694, Eldoret
Kiminini, Box 591, Kitale
Kitale, Box 427, Kitale (T: 2648)
Majengo, Box 630, Eldoret
Nerkwo, Box 32, Eldoret
Ortum, Private Bag, Kitale (T: 2432)
Pope John XXIII, Box 774, Eldoret (T: 2432)
Singore, P.O. Iten, Eldoret
Tartar, Box 45, Kitale
Turbo, Box 51, Turbo (T: 8)

—Diocese of Kisii 42
Bishop of Kisii: The Rt. Rev. Tiberius C. Mugendi
Bishop's House
P.O. Box 140, Kisii. *Tel: 95*
   The diocese was erected in 1960, out of the diocese of Kisumu. Statistics as at 31 December 1969: 230,000 Catholics, 6,218 catechumens. There is a variety of development projects, in the following parishes: homecraft centres (Homa Bay, Kisii Town, Asumbi), agricultural project (Homa Bay), agricultural school for the blind (Sikiri), Schuni-Nyansiongo Agricultural Scheme, child care centre (Kisii Town), village polytechnic (Rangenyo), community centre (Nyabururu), marketing co-operatives (Isibania), and a projected hospital (Migori).
Parishes
Asumbi, Box 574, Kisii
Gekano, Box 416, Kisii
Homa Bay, Box 8, Homa Bay
Ichuni, Box 138, Kisii
Isibania, P.O. Isibania, Kisii
Kadern, P.O. Migori
Kisii, Box 484, Kisii
Mawego, P.O. Kendu Bay

Migori, P.O. Migori
Mirogi, P.O. Mirogi
Nyabururu, Box 570, Kisii
Nyamagwa, Box 94, Kisii
Oyugis, P.O. Oyugis, Kisii
Rakwaro, Box 349, Kisii
Rangenyo, Box 129, Kisii
Rapogi, P.O. Sare, Kisii
Rarua, Box 132, Homa Bay
Sengera, Box 433, Kisii
Tabaka, Box 509, Kisii
Tonga, Box 91, Homa Bay
Ulanda, P.O. Sare, Kisii

—Diocese of Kisumu 43
Bishop of Kisumu: The Rt. Rev. John de Reeper: Asst. Bishop: The Rev. Philip Sulumeti
Bishop's House, Catholic Mission
P.O. Box 150, Kakamega. *Tel: 32*
   In 1925, the prefecture apostolic of Kavirondo was erected, raised to vicariate in 1932, and diocese in 1953. Statistics as at 31 December 1969: 454,960 Catholics, 8,260 catechumens; mid-1971, 472,119 Catholics. Most parishes have 4 or 5 religious associations, plus many development projects.
Parishes
Ahero, P.O. Ahero, Kisumu (T: 4)
Aluor, Box 26, Maseno
Amukura, Box 187, Tororo, Uganda
Barkorwa, Box 6, Maseno
Butula, P.O. Butula, Bungoma
Buyangu, Box 7, Maragoli
Chakol, Box 66, Busia Market
Chamakhanga, Box 7, Maragoli
Chelelemuk, P.O. Malakisi, Bungoma
Chepterit, Box 50, Kapsabet
Eregi, Box 436, Kisumu
Erusui, Box 10070, Tiriki
Hambale, Box 7, Maragoli (T: 24)
Kaiboi, Box 374, Eldoret
Kakamega, Box 397, Kakamega
Kibabii, Box 50, Bungoma
Kibuye, Box 50, Kisumu (T: 2627)
Kisoko, P.O. Nambale, Kisumu
Kobujoi, Box 44, Kapsabet
Koru, Box 17, Koru (T:17)
Lutasso, Box 75, Kakamega
Lwak, P.O. Nyilima, Kisumu
Malindi, Box 44, Yala
Mbaga, P.O. Siaya, Kisumu
Milimani, Box 795, Kisumu (T: 2563)
Misikhu, Box 61, Kimilili
Mukumu, Box 123, Kakamega
Mumias, Box 23, Mumias
Mundika, Box 77, Busia Market
Musoli, P.O. Private Bag, Kakamega
Nandi Hills, Box 80, Nandi Hills
Nangina, Box 5070, Funyula
Nyabondo, P.O. Sondu, Kisumu
Nyangoma, P.O. Bondo, Kisumu
Port Victoria, P.O. Port Victoria, Kisumu
Rangala, P.O. Yala
Sega, Box 24, Ukwala
Shibuye, Box 101, Kakamega
Shikoti, Box 75, Kakamega
Tindinyo, P.O. Kaimosi
Yala, Box 32, Yala (T: 7)

—Diocese of Kitui 44
Bishop of Kitui: The Rt. Rev. William Dunne
Bishop's House, near cathedral on main road
P.O. Box 119, Kitui. *Tel: 14*
   In 1956, the prefecture apostolic of Kitui was erected, and raised to a diocese in 1963. Statistics at at 31 December 1969: 16,426 Catholics, 3,467 catechumens; mid-1971, 18,199 Catholics.
Parishes
Ikanga, Box 169, Kitui
Ikutha, Box 155, Kitui

Ithookwe, Box 7, Kitui
Kimangao, P.O. Mwingi, Kitui
Kitui, Box 149, Kitui (T: 14)
Migwani, Box 187, Kitui
Muthale, Box 159, Kitui
Mutito, Box 186, Kitui
Mutomo, Box 155, Kitui
Mutune, Box 119, Kitui
Mwingi, Box 129, Kitui

—Diocese of Machakos 45
Bishop of Machakos
Bishop's House (near hospital)
P.O. Box 344, Machakos. *Tel: 140*
    The diocese was formed in 1969 out of the archdiocese of Nairobi. Statistics as at 31 December 1969: 79,502 Catholics, 23,094 catechumens. The Legion of Mary is found in every parish and in many schools and colleges; so also is the St. Vincent de Paul Society, assisting the poor with food and clothing. Catholic Relief Services have pre-school feeding clinics in 5 dispensaries (300 children monthly). There is also one village polytechnic (Kithayoni).
Parishes
Athi River, Box 14, Athi River
Ekarakara, P.O. Private Bag, Thika
Kabaa, Box 65, Thika
Kanzalu, Box 1012, Kangundo
Katangi, P.O. Private Bag, Thika
Kaumoni, P.O. Private Bag, Machakos
Kibwezi, P.O. Kibwezi
Kilungu, P.O. Kilome, Machakos
Kiteta, Box 65, Machakos
Machakos, Box 56, Machakos (T: 54)
Makueni, P.O. Makueni, Machakos
Matuu, P.O. Kithimani, Thika
Mbitini, P.O. Emali
Mbooni, P.O. Kikima, Machakos
Mwala, P.O. Siathani, Machakos
Tala, Box 1055, Kangundo

—Diocese of Marsabit 46
Bishop of Marsabit: The Rt. Rev. Charles M. Cavallera
Bishop's House, Nanyuki
P.O. Box 281, Nanyuki. *Tel: 2768*
    The diocese was erected in 1964 out of the diocese of Nyeri. Statistics: 2,000 Catholics, 2,500 catechumens, 12 mission stations, 26 priests, 49 sisters, 3 brothers, 64 catechists, 61 lay teachers, one catechists' school, 22 primary schools (1972) with 1,934 pupils, 15 other schools and nurseries, 3 hospitals and 12 dispensaries with 2 doctors; 2 schools for arts and crafts (Maralal, Marsabit), 4 adult literacy schools, 5 homecraft schools (Maendeleo ya Wanawake), one technical school.
Parishes or missions
Archer's Post, Box 74, Isiolo
Baragoi, P.O. Maralal
Laisamis, Box 74, Isiolo
Loiyangalani, P.O. Maralal
Maikona, P.O. Marsabit, Isiolo
Maralal, P.O. Maralal
Marsabit, P.O. Marsabit, Isiolo
Moyale, P.O. Moyale
North Horr, P.O. Marsabit, Isiolo
Sololo, P.O. Marsabit, Isiolo
South Horr, P.O. Maralal
Wamba, Box 74, Isiolo

—Diocese of Meru 47
Bishop of Meru: The Rt. Rev. Laurence V. Bessone
Bishop's House
P.O. Box 16, Meru. *Tel: 49*
    In 1926, the prefecture apostolic of Meru was erected, and was raised to a diocese in 1953. Statistics as at 31 December 1969: 142,300 Catholics, 15,220 catechumens; mid-1971, 160,557 Catholics.
Parishes
Amungenti, Box 238, Meru
Chuka, P.O. Chogoria, Meru
Egandene, P.O. Nkubu, Meru

Egoji, Private Bag, P.O. Meru
Embu Township, Box 99, Embu (T: 18)
Garissa, Private Bag, Garissa
Gatonga, Box 255, Meru
Imenti, Box 16, Meru
Iriamorai, P.O. Siakago, Embu
Ishiara, P.O. Ishiara
Isiolo, Box 25, Isiolo
Kevote, Box 24, Kevote
Kirua, Box 225, Meru
Kyeni, P.O. Runyenjes, Embu
Loire, Box 16, Meru
Materi, Box 16, Meru
Mekinduri, Box 23, Meru
Meru Township, Box 16, Meru
Muthambi, P.O. Chogoria, Meru
Nguvio, Box 109, Embu
Nkabune, Box 97, Meru
Nkubu, P.O. Nkubu, Meru
Rombia, P.O. Siakago, Embu
Tigania, Box 73, Meru
Tuuru, Box 77, Meru

—Diocese of Mombasa 48
Bishop of Mombasa: The Rt. Rev. Eugene Butler
Bishop's House, Nyali (office at Cathedral)
P.O. Box 83131, Mombasa. *Tel: 71320*
    The diocese was erected in 1955 from the archdiocese of Nairobi. In 1965, the islands of Zanzibar and Pemba (Tanzania) were separated from the diocese. Statistics as at 31 December 1969: 62,646 Catholics, 7,420 catechumens. There is a catechetical training school (Bura), 11 convents, a Commission for Non-Christian Religions, 3 private clinics, Kinango Hospital, about 79 Catholic-sponsored primary schools, two private schools (Loreto Sisters), credit unions, a home for handicapped children, an old people's home, the St. Charles Lwanga Home for Boys; also water schemes and irrigation schemes (Tana River).
Parishes
Bura, P.O. Bura, Voi
Changamwe, Box 262, Mombasa (T: 73612)
Chonyi, Box 20, Mariakani
Giriama, Box 20, Mariakani
Kilifi, Box 62, Kilifi
Kinango, P.O. Kinango, Mombasa
Kisauni, Box 9850, Mombasa
Lushangoni, Box 1010, Wundanyi
Makupa, Box 262, Mombasa (T:3749)
Malindi, Box 272, Malindi
Mariakani, Box 43, Mariakani
Mgange Nyika, Box 1009, Wundanyi
Mombasa Cathedral, Box 376, Mombasa (T: 3971)
Ndavaya, P.O. Kinango, Mombasa
Sagalla, Box 21, Voi
Shimba Hills, P.O. Shimba Hills, Mombasa
South Mainland, Box 9850, Mombasa
Taru, Box 43, Mariakani
Taveta, Box 1, Taveta
Timbila, Box 1, Taveta
Voi, Box 21, Voi
Wema, Private Bag, Malindi
Wundanyi, Box 1002, Wundanyi

—Diocese of Nakuru (Catholic) 49
Bishop of Nakuru: The Rt. Rev. Rafael S. Ndingi
Bishop's House, Lanet (10 miles towards Nairobi from Nakuru)
P.O. Box 938, Nakuru. *Tel: Lanet 324*
    The diocese was erected in 1968. Statistics as at 31 December 1969: 72,510 Catholic~, 22,401 catechumens; mid-1971, 76,450 Catholics.
Parishes
Bahati, Box 1660, Nakuru (T: 230)
Bomet, P.O. Bomet, Sotik
Elburgon, Box 29, Elburgon (T: 48)
Eldama Ravine, Box 50, Eldama Ravine (T: 16)
Gilgil, Box 100, Gilgil
Kaplong, Box 90, Sotik

Kericho, Box 178, Kericho (T: 59)
Kipchimjim, Box 162, Kericho
Kituro, P.O. Kabarnet
Molo, Box 105, Molo (T: 73)
Naivasha, Box 9, Naivasha (T: 65)
Nakuru, Box 314, Nakuru (T: 2591)
Njoro, Box 59, Njoro

—Diocese of Nyeri 50
Bishop of Nyeri: The Rt. Rev. Caesar M. Gatimu
Bishop's House, by cathedral
P.O. Box 288, Nyeri.   *Tel: 105*
   Nyeri was established as a Mission in 1905, a vicariate in
1909, and raised to a diocese in 1953. Statistics as at 31
December 1969: 300,000 Catholics, 40,000 catechumens; mid-
1971, 315,000 Catholics.
Parishes
Barico, Box 11, Kerugoya
Bellevue, Box 31, Mweiga
Fort Hall, Box 4, Fort Hall
Gaicanjiru, Box 483, Thika
Gatanga, Box 149, Thika
Gaturi, Box 49, Fort Hall
Gekondi, Box 511, Nyeri
Icagaki, Box 29, Maragua
Kaheti, Box 372, Nyeri
Karatina, Box 30, Karatina
Karema, Box 191, Nyeri
Kerugoya, Box 31, Kerugoya
Kiriaini, Box 393, Nyeri
Kitito, P.O. Makuyu
Kyangonyi, Box 227, Fort Hall
Kianyaga, P.O. Kianyaga, Kerugoya
Mareira, P.O. Maragua
Mathari, Box 25, Nyeri (T: 162)
Mogoiri, Box 44, Fort Hall
Mwea, Box 49, Kerugoya
Mweiga, Box 38, Mweiga
Mwenji, Box 25, Nyeri
Nanyuki, Box 86, Nanyuki
Ngandu, Box 182, Karatina
Njabibe, Box 16, South Kinangop
North Kinangop, Box 1049, North Kinangop, Naivasha
Nyeri, Box 288, Nyeri (T: 105)
Ol Kalou, Box 1049, North Kinangop, Naivasha
Roco, Box 279, Thika
Sagana, P.O. Sagana, Karatina, Nyeri
South Kinangop, Box 12, South Kinangop
Tetu, Box 129, Nyeri
Thego & Kiganjo, Box 60, Kiganjo
Thomson's Falls, Box 173, Thomson's Falls
Tuthu, Box 227, Fort Hall

—Prefecture Apostolic of Lodwar 51
Ordinary: The Rt. Rev. Msgr. John C. Mahon
Catholic Mission, Lodwar
P.O. Lodwar, Kitale.
   The prefecture was erected in 1968. Statistics as at 31
December 1969: 540 Catholics, 550 catechumens; mid-1971,
700 Catholics.
Parishes and missions
Kakuma, Private Bag, Kitale
Kaputir, Private Bag, Kitale
Kataboi, Private Bag, Kitale
Loarengak, P.O. Lokitaung, Kitale
Lodwar, P.O. Lodwar, Kitale
Lorugumu, Private Bag, Kitale

—Prefecture Apostolic of Ngong 52
Ordinary: The Rt. Rev. Msgr. Colin Davies
Bishop's House, Ngong (past police station)
P.O. Box 24801, Nairobi.   *Tel: Karen 2318*
   The prefecture was erected in 1959 from the archdiocese of
Nairobi and the diocese of Kisumu. It covers the Maasai area in
Kenya (15,000 square miles). Statistics as at 31 December
1969: 8,000 Catholics, 490 catechumens; mid-1971, 11,443
Catholics.
Parishes and missions

Ilkerin, Box 50, Narok
Kajiado, Box 27, Kajiado
Kilgoris, Private Bag, Sotik
Kiserian, Box 24876, Nairobi
Loitokitok, P.O. Loitokitok, Nairobi
Lolgorien, Private Bag, Sotik
Nagarie Ngare, P.O. Narok
Narok, Box 50, Narok
Ngong, Box 24801, Nairobi
Rombo, P.O. Loitokitok, Nairobi

Children of God Regeneration Church 53
Archbishop: Killion Orina
Ng'ong'a HQ, Sakwa Location
P.O. Sare, Kisii.
   An early Luo independent movement known in Luo as
'Ayie Remb Yesu' ('I believe in the Blood of Jesus'). Work
divided into 13 areas including Mombasa. The church has 200
rules for administering its members.

Chosen Church of the Holy Spirit in Kenya 54
Chairman: The Rev. Elijah Kinyanjui
Reg. Office: Plot No. 6, Landhes Road, Mithonge Estate, House
No. 51, Nakuru
P.O. Box 672, Nakuru.
   A Kikuyu movement looking to the Watu wa Mungu (Aroti,
Akurinu) of 1930 for its origin, whose earlier title, Church of
the Holy Spirit of God in Africa, was not acceptable for
registration in 1968.

Christadelphian Bible Mission (Kenya) (CBMK) 55
Chairman: Mr. Stephen Sykes; Treasurer: Mr. J. Opiyo
Meetings: Green Acres School, Limuru; Lenana School, Nairobi
(to mid-1972: 3 Vale Close Flats, Westlands)
P.O. Box 14503, Nairobi.
   A group of 50 members scattered in 5 communities (called
Ecclesias) across Kenya, formed 'to preach the Gospel, prepare
for eternal life, obey the laws of Kenya, recognise supremacy
of God's Law, and form communities of believers (called
Ecclesias)'. The Christadelphian community throughout the
world avoids political activity of any kind.

Christ Evangelistic Association 56
Chairman: The Rev. Malachi Odera
P.O. Box 746, Kisumu.
   A Luo movement originating in 1959, experiencing rapid
growth.

Christ Faith Evangelical Church 57
Chairman: Pastor Nashan Olloo
Plot No. 21, Sori via Kisii
c/o R.P. Dixit & Co., P.O. Karungu, Kisii.
   A Luo movement with a considerable following; application
for registration refused in 1972.

Christian Association 58
Chairman: Mr. Isaiah Oguk
Lieng'o Mission, Ringa School, Pap Onditi
P.O. Pap Onditi, Oyugis.
   A Luo movement in South Nyanza.

Christian Brotherhood Church (CBC) 59
Founder and Bishop: The Rt. Rev. Wellington B. Sakwa
HQ & Divinity School, Ibinda
P.O. Khwisero, Yala.
   A Luhya schism from the Anglican Diocese of Mombasa in
1952, which has seen gradual numerical progress under its
founder.

Christian Church in Africa 60
Ministers of Religion: Mr. A.S. Roberts, Mr. P.J.C. van Heerden,
   Mr. Moses Wasike
Hoey's Bridge Scheme No. 2, Plot No. 135
P.O. Box 658, Kitale.
   A small group around Kitale whose name could not be
accepted for registration because too similar to those of
existing churches.

Christian Divine Church, see Divine Christian Church of East
   Africa (Masiza)

Christian Evangelical Church (CEC)   61
Omwassi: His Vigilance O Okello-Olluoko
HQ: Yo-Maler Head Church, Wihembyo (also Victoria Street,
  Kisumu)
P.O. Box 188, Siaya, Kisumu.
  The first Balokole (Revival) schism among the Luo (1948),
from the Anglican Diocese of Mombasa under its founder
Ishmael Noo   Until 1965, it was known as Christian Universal
Evangelistic Union (CUEU) or Fellowship (CUEF), also as
JoMaler (Saints)   Does not practice water baptism nor giving of
Christian names'. Each year in Western Kenya the church holds
three public evangelistic conferences for three days. There is
considerable emphasis on healing of the sick.

Christian Evangelistic Church, see Disciples of Christ in
  Africa

Christian Faith Mission of Kenya   62
Chairman: The Rev. D.R. Thom
Thuthuriki Village, Githunguri Division
P.O. Box 7721, Nairobi.
  A mission from Louisville, Kentucky, USA, which in 1970
was not granted registration.

Christian Holy Ghost Church of East Africa   63
(CHGCEA)
High Priest: Joshua Ng'ang'a Kimani
HQ: Kigumo, Githunguri Division, Kiambu
P.O. Box 76, Ruiru.
  One of the Kikuyu churches which emerged in 1934 from
the original Aroti (Prophets) or Watu wa Mungu (People of God)
Spirit movement. The CHGCEA was until 1958 loosely
affiliated with the HGCK (leader Hezron Tumbo), but then
split with him; the HGCK now represents the liberal wing of the
Aroti, whereas the CHGCEA represents the conservative wing,
strict on ritual uncleanness, and prohibiting medicines, injec-
tions, going to hospital, hand-shaking, photography, and the like.

Christian Science Church of East Africa   64
Chairman: Elisabeth M. Erskine (Lady Erskine)
Kirk Road (Reading Room, University Way)
P.O. Box 30115, Nairobi.   *Tel: 21498*
  'The group began in 1925, became a society in 1930, then in
1943 received status as a branch church of the Mother Church
(First Church of Christ, Scientist, Boston, USA). Daily inter-
national newspaper *Christian Science Monitor*, public reading
room and library. No baptism. Aim: 'to make better disciples
of our Lord Jesus Christ'.

Christian Theocratic Holy Church of God   65
Founder and Archbishop: The Most Rev. Elijah Cephas Muturi
Reg. Office: Plot No. 608, Kawangware Village, Nairobi District
P.O. Box 72355, Nairobi.
  A Kikuyu independent church begun in 1958.

Christian Universal Evangelistic Fellowship, see Christian
  Evangelical Church

Christian Universal Evangelistic Union, see Christian
  Evangelical Church

Church Group of Light   66
Chairman: Mr. Festus Kausi Lumbasi
Lurambi, Matsakha Sub-Location
P.O. Box 82, Broderick Falls.
  A small Luhya group applying for registration in 1972, with
a single temporary church building.

Church of All (CA) and Divinity School   67
Chairman: Mr. Johana Nyaga; Priest: Mr. Livingstone Njeru
Rukuriri Village, Kyeni Location
P.O. Runyenjes, Embu.
  A small Embu group which applied for registration in 1971,
led by two former officers in the Salvation Army (which is
strong in this area) who then joined successively NICA, then
ABC. Registered June 1972 as East Africa Divinity Church.

Church of Christ in Africa (CCA)   68
Presiding Bishop & Bishop of Masogo: The Rt. Rev. A. Matthew
Ajuoga; Gen. Secretary: Asst. Bishop H. Habakuk Ogutu

Dala Hera ('City of Love'), Kibos Road, Kisumu
P.O. Box 782, Kisumu.   *Tel: 2536*
  An Anglican renewal movement begun in 1952 under the
name 'Revival within the Church', or JoHera (People of Love)
which finally separated in 1957 with 16,000 Anglicans from the
CCA. It now has followers across Kenya, and in Tanzania and
Uganda, in 90 Pastorates, 27 Areas, and 6 Area Dioceses in
Kenya (Winam, Homa Bay, Nairobi, Ndere, Kakamega, Kam-
bare) plus Tororo (Uganda) and Musoma (Tanzania). A large
cathedral is being built at Dala Hera, and there are several
institutions: Ogero Youth Centre, Homecraft Training Centre,
Commercial Training College (book-keeping and typing), nursery
schools and a secondary school (the whole being known as
Nyanza Christian College).   There is a monthly newspaper,
Dwond Hera (Voice of Love).

Church of Christ in the Word   69
P.O. Box 246, Lugazi, Uganda.
  An indigenous Pentecostal body from Uganda, strong among
the Baganda, Basoga, Batoro and Bagisu, which has recently
begun work in Mombasa and other parts of Kenya.

Church of East Africa Society
(Former address: P.O. Box 1061, Kangundo).
  A schism from the African Brotherhood Church in 1958 led
by the discredited founder Mulandi Kaasya which in 1969
rejoined the ABC with Kaasya and so was dissolved.

Church of Full Gospel in Africa   70
Chairman: Mr. Peter Mbote
Plot No. 3, Magina Township
P.O. Matathia.
  A Kikuyu group near Limuru at Matathia, one of the more
important originating areas of independent churches. Also
known as Full Gospel Church in Africa (Kenya).

Church of God in East Africa (CGEA)   71
Executive Secretary/Treasurer: The Rev. Byrum A. Makokha
Kima Station (2½ miles northeast of Maseno)
P.O. Box 160, Maseno.
  The Church of God (Anderson) began in the USA in 1880 as
a reformation movement against denominationalism, attempting
to lead to fuller Christian unity by regarding all born-again
Christians everywhere as its members. Work in Kenya began in
1905, and the Missionary Board (known as East Africa Ministries) now works with the national Church of God in East
Africa, which extends across Kenya with congregations in almost
all towns and settlement stations, though still strongest in
Western Province.   The church sponsors about 96 primary
schools, 4 major government-maintained secondary schools, 2
harambee secondary schools, 4 clinics, 4 mobile clinics, a
dispensary and 2 hospitals (Kima and Mwihila), and Kima
Theological College. Social amenities are provided at Kaloleni
and Mariakani Christian Centre, Nairobi. The church press in
Kakamega publishes extensively, including the church newspaper
Mwendo (Progress).

Mission stations
  (each under a board of governors)
Kima Mission Station, P.O. Box 410, Kisumu.
Mwihila Mission Station, Private Bag, Yala.
Shitoli Mission Station
Ingotse Mission Station
Ibeno Mission Station, P.O. Box 23, Kisii.

Church of God (Universal), see Church of the Almighty
  (Kenya)

Church of Holy Communion of God   72
Chairman: Bishop Simon Lunani
Sirende Village, North Kabras, Kakamega
P.O. Box 240, Broderick Falls (P.O. Box 51, Kakamega).
  A recent Luhya independent movement (1969) out of the
East Africa Yearly Meeting of Friends, over tithing, polygamy,
the use of drums, and over-lengthy instruction before member-
ship. Also known as the Friends Balafu (Friends of Light).

Church of Jesus Christ of Latter-day Saints (LDS)   73
  In 1970-2 expatriate American Mormons advertised Sunday

services of the LDS in the newspapers. The addresses and telephone numbers change too rapidly for inclusion here.

Church of Jordan East Africa

Leader: Bishop Samuel Ekamba. (Nairobi) Mr. Samson Macheru
Headquarters: Maragoli
P.O. Maragoli.
Led by a former member of the Pentecostal Assemblies of God, the church was being formed and applying for registration early in 1972. Many members of the two branches of the Divine Christian Church of East Africa (whose registration was cancelled in early 1972) joined the new body. Many congregations in Maragoli, and three in Nairobi. In May 1972 registration was refused.

Church of Messiah 74

Founder and Archbishop: The Rev. Aggrey Peter Kiamba
HQ: Kangundo, Machakos
P.O. Box 1201, Kangundo.
A Kamba schism from the Africa Inland Mission, founded in 1948. 5,000 adult members in Ukambani, Lamu, Mombasa, Nakuru, Uganda, Tanzania and Rwanda.

Church of Quakers in Africa, see Lyahuka Church of East Africa

Church of Saviour, Diocese of Nyakoko 75

Bishop: The Rt. Rev. Isaya Ndisi; Archdeacon: The Rev. Nikolao Odaa
Masogo Market, Plot No. 11
P.O. Box 16, Miwani.
In 1957, a large schism of 16,000 Luo Anglicans (300 congregations) took place in western Kenya from the Diocese of Mombasa, forming the Church of Christ in Africa. In 1960, a majority of the 7 Luo clegy involved seceded from the CCA to form Holy Trinity Church in Africa. Nine years later, several of the same clergy seceded from HTCA to form this new Diocese of Nyakoko, electing one of the original group as bishop.

Church of Spirit in Grace & Truth in Africa 76

Archbishop: Meshak Otieno
Reg. Office: Naya Market, Plot No. 4, Uyoma Naya
P.O. Nyilima, Kisumu.
A small Luo movement in the extreme west of Kenya.

Church of the Almighty (Kenya) 77

Pastor/Chairman: Mr. Joshua Gichuki Silas
Kia-Wabiru Garden, Muyu Sub-Location, Mukurue-ini
P.O. Box 361, Nyeri.
A church emphasising divine physical healing and use of the King James Version of the (English) Bible, which previously attempted to register under the name Church of God (Universal); linked with Church of God (Universal), 626 Salem Avenue, Hagerstown, Maryland, USA.

Church of the Holy Apostles of the Lamb 78

Founder: Kleopa Nyagowa
P.O. Suna, Kisii.
A Luo schism in 1966 from the Seventh-day Adventist Church, after founder had dream instructing him to form a church worshipping not on Saturday but on Sunday. The members, 200 Holy Apostles, wear white surplices with green epaulettes.

Church of the Holy Spirit of God in Africa, see Chosen Church of the Holy Spirit in Kenya

Church of the Kenya Family 79

Founder and Bishop: The Rev. Frederick Njeru (not the same person as in No. 31)
Kanja Village, Embu
P.O. Runyenjes, Embu (or c/o Box 47, Embu).
Beginning in 1948, the founder preached in villages around his home, Kanja Village, in a ministry especially directed towards the sick. By 1965 his following had crystallised into a church, and the founder broke his existing connection with the National Independent Church of Africa. A characteristic of the church is that 'Amen' is regarded as an abusive word, hence it is not used after prayer; instead, members make the sign of the cross with the name of the Trinity, while greeting people.

Yellow turbans (men) and headcloths (women) are worn; pork is not eaten. Strong throughout whole of Embu Division.

Church of the Living God 80

Archbishop: Benjamin Makau Kieti
Plot No. 60, Mavivye, Machakos
P.O. Box 1, Machakos.
A Kamba schism from the Gospel Furthering Fellowship, subsequently reporting a decline in numbers.

Church of the Power of Jesus Christ 81

Archbishop: Kilion Ndisi Obar
Agongo Kuoyo, Katieno, Kanyamkago
P.O. Sare, Kisii.
A Luo movement known in Luo as Ayie kuom Yesu man gi teko' (I believe in Jesus who has Power).

Church of the Prophets (A-Nabii Church) 82

Prophet: Joshua Ali
Ngararia Market
P.O. Box 111, Thika.
A division circa 1960 of African Mission of Holy Ghost Church, in the Roho (Spirit) tradition among the Kikuyu.

Church of the Province of East Africa, see Church of the Province of Kenya

Church of the Province of Kenya (CPK) 83

Archbishop of Kenya: The Most Rev. Festo H. Olang'
Provincial Office: Bishopsbourne, 26 State House Avenue
P.O. Box 40502, Nairobi.   *Tel: 20207*
Kanisa la Jimbo la Kenya. Anglican work in Kenya began in 1844 with the arrival of CMS missionary J.L. Krapf at Mombasa, followed by the Rev. J. Rebmann. In 1884, the Diocese of Eastern Equatorial Africa was created, which again was divided in 1898 into the Dioceses of Uganda and Mombasa, the latter including central Tanganyika. In 1927 this latter was separated leaving the Diocese of Mombasa as the whole of Kenya (including from 1921 Kavirondo, which had become part of Kenya from Uganda in 1902). From 1929 the Kikuyu circumcision and independent schools controversies caused many Anglicans to leave the church, a situation repeated during the 1952-60 Emergency In 1953 the diocese's archdeaconries — hitherto racial — became geographical, and in 1955 the first two African bishops were consecrated — F.H. Olang' for Maseno (Nyanza), and O. Kariuki for Fort Hall (Central Province). In 1960 the church became autonomous from Canterbury with the formation of the Church of the Province of East Africa (CPEA), uniting the Kenya and Tanganyika Anglican churches. By 1970 the churches had grown sufficiently for two separate Anglican provinces to be established, one in each nation, and the Church of the Province of Kenya was created, with Bishop Olang' as the first African archbishop. Property and finance are administered by the Church Commissioners for Kenya on behalf of the 6 dioceses. Candidates for the ordained ministry are trained at St. Paul's United Theological College, Limuru; and supplementary and assistant ministers at diocesan Bible schools. As the pioneer in primary education over the years, the CPK now sponsors 775 primary schools and about 60 *harambee* secondary schools, especially in Mount Kenya diocese; and retains its interests in Maseno and St. Luke's (Kaloleni) Hospitals.
The lists of parishes following the dioceses below set out the differing structures of the six dioceses. In recent years, certain dioceses (Mombasa, Mount Kenya, Nakuru) have abandoned the traditional administrative divisions of rural deaneries (and the post of rural dean) and have opted for the more centralised structures shown.
When writing to Anglican parishes, they are best prefixed with initials thus: 'CPK Butere'.

—Diocese of Maseno North 84

Bishop of Maseno North: The Rt. Rev. James Mundia
Bishop's House, near Anglican Church (up hill from DC's Office)
P.O. Box 416, Kakamega.
Created in 1970 by the sub-division of the former Diocese of Maseno.

DEANERIES & PARISHES
Archdeacon: The Ven. Howell H. Davies (Box 62, Maseno. T:34)

Butere Rural Deanery
Butere, Box 100, Butere
Khwisero, P.O. Khwisero, Yala
Lubinu, Box 11, Mumias
Lunza, P.O. Bukura, Kakamega
Namasoli, Box 38, Yala
Namulungu, Box 109, Mumias
Shiamboko, Box 221, Kakamega
Shinkunga, Box 51, Butere

Maseno Rural Deanery
Ebuhando, Box 94, Maseno
Ebwali, Box 243, Maseno
Esiandumba, Box 124, Maseno
Maragoli, Box 384, Kakamega
Mwichio, Box 14, Maseno

Nambale Rural Deanery
Alupe, Box 1044, Busia
Bukhalalire, P.O. Butula, Bungoma
Khasoko, Box 46, Bungoma
Lugare, Box 5067, Funyula
Nambale, P.O. Nambale, Kisumu
Namboboto, Box 5056, Funyula
Sigalame, Box 5067, Funyula

Bungoma Rural Deanery
Butonge, Box 80, Bungoma
Katakwa, P.O. Malakisi, Bungoma
Kimilili, Box 143, Kimilili

—Diocese of Maseno South 85
Bishop of Maseno South: The Rt. Rev. Evan Agola
Church House, Dhanwant Singh Road
P.O. Box 380 (Bishop: Box 114), Kisumu. *Tel: 2131*
Created in 1970 by the sub-division of the former Diocese
of Maseno. Very largely rural, with three urban areas (Kisumu,
Kericho, Kisii). Served by the Church Missionary Society and
the Church Army.

ARCHDEACONRIES, DEANERIES, & PARISHES

ARCHDEACONRY OF NG'IYA
Archdeacon of Ng'iya: The Ven. H.S. Nyong'o

Ng'iya Rural Deanery
Hono, Box 136, Siaya, Kisumu
Lugare, P.O. Uranga, Kisumu
Mudhiero, Box 13, Butere
Ng'iya, P.O. Ng'iya, Kisumu
Regea, Box 107, Yala
Sawagongo, Box 49, Yala
Yenga, Box 2, Ukwala

Ramba Rural Deanery
Akoko, P.O. Bondo, Kisumu
Chianda, P.O. Nyilima, Kisumu
Ndiru, Box 213, Maseno
Ngere, Box 1710, Kisùmu
Ramba, P.O. Ndori, Kisumu
Ramula, Box 24, Maseno
Usigu, P.O. Ramogi

ARCHDEACONRY OF KISUMU
Archdeacon of Kisumu: The Ven. J. Daniel Omolo

Kisumu-Kericho Deanery
Belgut, Box 434, Kericho
Kericho, Box 181, Kericho
Masogo, Box 459, Kisumu
Ndori, P.O. Ahero, Kisumu
Rae, P.O. Ahero, Kisumu
Kisumu, Box 43, Kisumu
Sinyolo, Box 66, Maseno
Songhor, P.O. Songhor
Sotik, Box 6, Sotik

South Nyanza Rural Deanery
Akoko South, c/o Pe Hill School, P.O. Sare, Kisii
Kisii, Box 121, Kisii
Ogande, Box 16, Homa Bay

—Diocese of Mombasa (Anglican) 86
Bishop of Mombasa: The Rt. Rev. Peter Mwang'ombe
Bishopscourt, Nkruman Road (Fort Jesus Road)
P.O. Box 80072, Mombasa. *Tel: 25984*
The diocese was founded in 1899 on the sub-division of the
former Diocese of Eastern Equatorial Africa. In 1921, Kavir
ondo was added; in 1927, Central Tanganyika was separated off;
in 1960 Maseno, Nakuru and Fort Hall were separated; and in
1964, the Diocese of Nairobi, leaving the Diocese of Mombasa
with Coast Province and the towns of Mombasa, Kilifi, Malindi,
Taveta, Voi. Missions: CMS, CA.

DIOCESAN OFFICERS & PARISHES
Vicar-General: The Ven. S.T. Kiteto (A.C. Rong'e, Box 69, Voi)
Archdeacons: The Ven. J. Kiwinda (Box 1074, Wundanyi), The
Ven. W. Muta (St. Paul's Church, P.O. Rabai)
Provost of Mombasa: The Very Rev. D.G. Givan (Mombasa
Cathedral, Box 81962, Mombasa)

Parishes
Changamwe, Box 85687, Mombasa
Holy Trinity Church, Mahoo, Box 63, Taveta
Immanuel Church, Kisauni, Box 11010, Mombasa
Kaloleni, P.O. Kaloleni, Mombasa
Kigombo, P.O. Voi
Kilifi, Box 48, Kilifi
Kishamba, P.O. Mwatate, Voi
Malindi, Box 263, Malindi
Mariakani, Box 80, Mariakani
Mbale, P.O. Voi
Mombasa Cathedral, Box 81962, Mombasa
Mwakinyungu, P.O. Voi
Rabai, P.O. Rabai, Mombasa
Rong'e, P.O. Voi
Sagalla, P.O. Voi
Shimba Hills, P.O. Shimba Hills, Mombasa
Voi, Box 16, Voi
Weruga, Box 1015, Wundanyi
Wusi, P.O. Mwatate, Voi

—Diocese of Mount Kenya 87
Bishop of Mount Kenya: The Rt. Rev. Obadiah Kariuki;
Asst. Bishop: The Rt. Rev. Ezbon Ngaruiya
Synod Hall, next to St. James & All Martyrs Cathedral
P.O. Box 121, Murang'a. *Tel: 53*
Created in 1961 as the Diocese of Fort Hall on the sub-
division of the Diocese of Mombasa. A very densely-populated
rural diocese with many areas strongly Anglican, which has
opened large numbers of new stone churches in the last decade.
Publishes a quarterly, *Arahuka* (Awake). Missions: CMS, BCMS,
CA.

ARCHDEACONRIES & PARISHES
(Note: for full name, write 'CPK' in front of name of parish,
thus: 'CPK Weithaga')
Vicar-General: The Ven. Sospeter Magua
Cathedral Parish, Box 121, Murang'a

Central Archdeaconry
Archdeacon: The Ven. Eshban Githinji (Weithaga)
Githunguri, Box 550, Thika
Iyego, Box 31, Murang'a
Kahuhia, Box 120, Murang'a
Kahumbu, Box 4, Saba Saba, Thika
Kathukeini, Box 47, Murang'a
Kiru, Box 116, Murang'a
Muguru, P.O. Kangema, Murang'a
Muthiria, Box 44, Maragua
Ndutumi, Box 60, Maragua
Njumbe, Box 63, Murang'a
Weithaga, Box 107, Murang'a

Northern Archdeaconry
Archdeacon: The Ven. Bedan Ireri (Nyeri)
Nanyuki-Doldol, P.O. Doldol, Nanyuki
Nanyuki, Box 279, Nanyuki
NFD-Marsabit, St. Peter's Church; P.O. Marsabit, Isiolo
NFD-Moyale, St. Paul's Church, P.O. Moyale, Isiolo
NFD-Sololo, St. John's Church, P.O. Moyale, Isiolo

Nyeri, Box 229, Nyeri

Eastern Archdeaconry
Archdeacon: The Ven. Dedan Kamau (Kigari)
Embu, Box 133, Embu
Kabare, Box 48, Kerugoya
Kagaari, P.O. Runyenjes, Embu
Kanyuambora, Box 153, Embu
Karaba, P.O. Karaba, Embu
Karungu, P.O. Runyenjes, Embu
Kerugoya, Box 98, Kerugoya
Kiandangae, P.O. Sagana, Karatina, Nyeri
Kianjokoma, Box 76, Embu
Kigari, Box 119, Embu
Mutira, Box 36, Kerugoya
Mwea, Private Bag, P.O. Wanguru, Kerugoya
Ngiriambu, Box 1069, Kianyaga, Kerugoya
Nyangwa, Box 158, Embu

Southern Archdeaconry
Archdeacon: The Ven. John Kago (Thika)
Chania, CPK Kanjuku, Box 679, Thika
Kabete, Box 23031, Nairobi
Kariara, CPK Gatura, Box 192, Thika
Karura, Box 23029, Nairobi
Kiambaa, Box 116, Kiambu
Limuru, Box 271, Limuru
Thika, Box 214, Thika

—Diocese of Nairobi (Anglican) 88
Bishop of Nairobi: The Most Rev. Festo H. Olang', Archbishop of Kenya
Diocesan Office: Bishopsbourne, 26 State House Avenue
P.O. Box 40502, Nairobi. *Tel: 20207*
Created in 1964 by sub-division of the Diocese of Mombasa.

DIOCESAN OFFICERS, DEANERIES & PARISHES
Archdeacon of Nairobi: The Ven. K.E. Stovold (T: 20207)
Provost of Nairobi: The Very Rev. J.H. Okullu (T: 20715)

Nairobi Deanery
All Saints' Cathedral, Box 40539, Nairobi (T: 20715)
Kajiado, Box 21, Kajiado
Lavington Church, Box 25030, Nairobi (T: 48352)
Ofafa Jericho, Box 17174, Nairobi (T: 57580)
St. Francis, Karen, Box 24992, Nairobi (T: Karen 2454)
St. John's, Pumwani, Box 13084, Nairobi (T: 22233)
St. Mark's, Westlands, Box 14407, Nairobi (T: 60471)
St. Paul's Kahawa Garrison Church, Box 48826, Nairobi
St. Stephen's, Jogoo Road, Box 17056, Nairobi (T: 57409)

Ukamba Deanery
All Souls', Box 322, Machakos
Ukia, Private Bag, Machakos
Kithangathini, P.O. Kilome, Machakos
Kitui, St. Martin's Church, Box 100, Kitui
Syongila, Box 100, Kitui

—Diocese of Nakuru (Anglican) 89
Bishop of Nakuru: The Rt. Rev. Neville Langford-Smith; Asst. Bishop: The Rt. Rev. Manasses Kuria (Box 253, Eldoret. T: 2462)
Diocesan Office: Lake Road
P.O. Box 56, Nakuru. *Tel: 2380*
Created in 1961 on the sub-division of the Diocese of Mombasa. A mainly rural diocese covering the Rift Valley, with three large towns, Nakuru, Eldoret, and Kitale. The diocese is served by the Bible Churchmen's Missionary Society, Church Missionary Society, and the Church Army, and has experienced very rapid growth over the last decade.

DIOCESAN OFFICERS & PARISHES
Archdeacon of Nakuru: The Ven. L. Kamau (Box 48, Ol Kalou. T: 7)
Archdeacon of Eldoret: The Ven. Julius Adoyo (Box 391, Eldoret. T: 201)
Provost of Nakuru: The Very Rev. John Mahiaini (Box 244,

Nakuru. T: 2569)

Parishes
Amudat, Private Bag, Kitale
Eldama Ravine, Box 18, Eldama Ravine
Kapcheno, P.O. Kapcheno, Kapsabet
Kapsabet, Box 58, Kapsabet
Mau, Box 171, Molo (T: 53)
Naivasha, Box 159, Naivasha
Nakuru, Box 381, Nakuru (T: 2009)
Nandi Hills, Box 79, Nandi Hills
Nasokol, Private Bag, Kitale
Nginyang', P.O. Marigat
Nyandarua, Box 48, Ol Kalou (T: 7)
St. Peter's, P.O. Marsabit, Isiolo
Soy, Box 24, Soy, Eldoret
The Church of the Good Shepherd, P.O. Maralal
Thomson's Falls, Box 217, Thomson's Falls (T: 115)
Trans Nzoia, Box 245, Kitale (T: 428)
Uashin Gishu, P.O. Eldoret (T: 201)
Wamba, P.O. Maralal

Church of the Truth 90
Chairman: Mr. John Boro
Reg. Office: Ngurionditu Muguga, Plot No. 620
P.O. Box 74, Kikuyu.
A small Kikuyu group affiliated to Apostolic Faith church, Portland, Oregon, USA, which first applied for registration under the name Gospel Proclaimers. Neither application was acceptable.

Communion Church of Africa 91
Chairman: Mr. Christopher Otonglo
Plot No. 3 Nyatao School, Migere Market, North East Kano
P.O. Chemelil.
A Luo church which at first showed Catholic tendencies by appointing cardinals as well as bishops, but which subsequently replaced these by secular titles (chairman, vice-chairman etc.).

Cross Church of East Africa 92
Head: Archbishop Filipo Okatch; Administrative Bishop: Joel Aomo
Ayiengo Village, Kabondo Location
P.O. Kabondo, Kisumu.
Also known as Roho Musalaba (Spirit Cross Church), this is one of several groups claiming the Luo priest-martyr Alfayo Odongo (murdered in 1935) as their founder.

Deliverance Church 93
Evangelist: The Rev. Joseph Kayo; Pastor: The Rev. Albert Likhaya
Penguin House (4th floor), Tom Mboya Street
P.O. Box 28600, Nairobi. *Tel: 20500*
A pentecostal denomination registered in 1971 'to establish indigenous churches', with Deliverance Church (Nairobi) as the Mother Church. Works with YCAF (Young Christian Ambassadors Fellowship).

Dini ya Msambwa, see Religion of the Ancestral Spirits

Disciples of Christ in Africa 94
Chairman: Pastor Francis Njuguna
Karuri Township, Kiambaa, Kiambu
P.O. Box 87. Eldama Ravine (& P.O. Box 47721, Nairobi).
A Kikuyu movement whose leadership broke from Apostolic Faith of Africa; known until 1970 as the Christian Evangelistic Church.

Divine Christian Church of EA (Ludenyo) 95
Chairman: The Rev. Hezekiah Muhindi Ludenyo
Iriva HQ
P.O. Box 526, Kisumu.
In 1967 Ludenyo separated from his former colleague Masiza and won a court ruling to the church's property and name. Registration was approved in 1964 but cancelled in 1972; many members then moved into a new body with the name Church of Jordan East Africa.

Divine Christian Church of EA (Masiza) 96
Founder and Leader: The Rev. Jeremiah Masiza
HQ: Mbale (16 miles from Kisumu and Kakamega)
P.O. Box 505, Maragoli.
A Luhya group founded by Masiza which separated from the African Divine Church in 1964. The name Christian Divine Church was also in use early on. In 1967, Masiza's co-leader Ludenyo separated from him, and Masiza lost the court ruling to the church's property and name. In 1964, registration was approved but eventually cancelled in 1972. Many members then re-formed taking the name Church of Jordan East Africa.

Duond Warruok gi Chang mar Piny ngima, see Voice of
Salvation & Healing Church

Dutch Reformed Church (DRC) 97
In colonial times, a mission of this church from South Africa ministered in the western Kenya 'White Highlands', particularly among settlers. In 1962, it sold 2 of its 3 church buildings in Eldoret to the Dutch missionaries (from the Netherlands) of the Reformed Church of East Africa, with whom it has no connection. There is no minister, but the farmer community organises a monthly service in the Afrikaans language.

East Africa Divinity Church, see Church of All

East Africa Pentecostal Churches (EAPC) 98
Founder and Leader: The Rev. Arnt Walther Olsen
Meru township
P.O. Box 245, Meru.
The EAPC is supported by the Kenya Faith Mission, which began work in Mombasa in 1953 under two Norwegian missionaries formerly linked with the Swedish Free Mission, and then in International Pentecostal Assemblies. They operate two Bible schools, in Meru and in Mombasa. Members are 80% Meru.

East Africa Yearly Meeting of Friends (EAYM) 99
Executive Secretary: The Rev. Thomas G. Lung'aho
HQ: Kaimosi Mission
P.O. Box 10035, Tiriki. *Tel: RN 2047*
One of the oldest missions in Kenya, begun in 1902, was the Friends Africa Mission, staffed by American missionaries, which has now become the largest Friends church outside the Western world. Also known as Quakers, or the Religious Society of Friends, the EAYM is now served by the Friends United Meeting (USA) and the Friends Service Council (UK). There are 103 Monthly Meetings (equivalent to pastorates) and 19 Quarterly Meetings (dioceses or deaneries). In 1971, there were 64,130 Luhya members, 400 Gusii, 400 Ugandans, and 70 Kalenjin. The Quakers do not practice water baptism. Over the years Kaimosi Mission has pioneered in education (the EAYM now sponsors 254 primary schools), teacher training, hospital work (Tiriki Hospital), printing, and industrial mission. Nowadays, the Rural Service Programme of the EAYM is pioneering rural development and teaching the use of artificial fertilizers and hybrid maize seeds, as well as adult literacy, human nutrition, and family planning. A newspaper *Mufrenzi* (Friends) is published three times a year.

East African Church Roho Israel 100
Bishops Daniel Ojwang and Elijah Ajago; Secretary: Mr. Henry Ndege
HQ: Ongeche, West Kano (on Nairobi-Kisumu road)
P.O. Ahero, Kisumu.
An independent group with Luo and Luhya members, formed in 1965 as a schism from the Roho Church of God of Israel in a dispute over leadership. Bishop Ajago lives in Tanzania and visits the headquarters regularly.

East African Israel Church 101
Secretary: Mr. Samuel Ndungu
P.O. Box 252, Thika.
A Kikuyu body originally called African Israel Church Association (Dini ya Roho), until it decided not to affiliate, as proposed, with the African Israel Church Nineveh, but to remain autonomous.

East African Mission (TEAM) 102
Director: Mr. J. Paul Bruton; Secretary: Mr. De Forest Hasch

Nairobi West, LR No. 37/258/15
P.O. Box 30749, Nairobi.
An American mission whose primary objectives are to train pastors and evangelists, to open Bible training schools, to produce Christian literature, to conduct ministerial seminars, and also to open branches.

Ebenezer Gospel Hall 103
Elder/Secretary: Mr. Robert McKinley
Mkomoni (Plot No. 1423, Section 1, Mainland North)
P.O. Box 82252, Mombasa.
An independent congregation founded by Europeans of the Plymouth Brethren tradition, as a sister church of the Nairobi Undenominational Church (Nairobi Chapel).

Eldoret Christian Fellowship Church 104
Representative: Mr. Stanley L. Davies
Nandi Road
P.O. Box 719, Eldoret. *Tel: 2488*
An independent congregation founded by British expatriates in 1948, now affiliated to the UK council, the Fellowship of Independent Evangelical Churches. Formerly a fellowship mainly of expatriates, now almost all attenders are Kenyans. Plans are in hand to make it less a church than a Christian teaching centre serving all churches in the area.

Elim Evangelistic Church, see Pentecostal Evangelistic
Fellowship of Africa

Episcopal Church of Africa 105
Bishop Benson T. O'Otieno; Diocesan General Secretary: Mr. Booker Agogo
HQ: Diocese of Kenya, Ondiek Estate, House No. TP2/60
P.O. Box 1573, Kisumu.
A schism in 1968 from the Church of Christ in Africa, in a dispute over the proper use of church funds, with the name Holy Church of Christ of Africa until this was declared inacceptable for registration. There are 3 parishes (Kisumu West, Kisumu East, Nakuru) in the one Diocese of Kenya, with parishes in Nairobi and Tanzania being organised. Strong emphasis on African churchmanship combined with Anglican worship.

Evangelical Baptist Church in Africa 106
Bishop Johnson M. Chege
P.O. Box 127, Kikuyu.
A Kikuyu body which was first called Baptist Evangelical Church in Africa.

Evangelical Free Mission in Kenya 107
Representative: The Rev. Rhode Struble
Office: Hatheru Road (off Bernard Road)
P.O. Box 47469, Nairobi. *Tel: 66762*
Kanisa la Mungu. In 1960, the Swedish Free Mission (Svenska Fria Missionen), of Pentecostal tradition, began work in Kenya. Its main areas now are Nairobi, Kinangop, Nyeri, Machakos, Loitokitok, Nakuru, Solai, Kakamega and Turkana. The new name EFM was adopted in October, 1971. 'Kanisa la Mungu' (Church of God) is also used, unofficially.

Evangelical Lutheran Church in Tanzania (Kenya Synod) (ELCT) 108
Chairman: The Rev. Nkanileka E. Pazia
P.O. Box 72772, Nairobi.
A large number of Tanzanians migrate to Kenya as labourers on plantations and in the cities and towns, and many belong to the ELCT. These have now been organised into the Kenya Synod. Although quite distinct from the Lutheran Church in Kenya, which is found almost entirely in Western Kenya, merger talks have been urged by the respective leaders.

Evangelistic Church Universal of Africa (ECUA) 109
Spiritual National Chairman: Mr. Ogango Opolo
Rae, Nyakach
P.O. Box 1115, (& P.O. Box 313), Kisumu.
A small Luo group which registered in 1963 but then gradually declined. It original high ideas is revealed in its sub-title 'The First Christ-Church founded in Africa to represent the Christ-Kingdom and to reveal the Truth'

Evangelistic Gospel Church of Holy Morning Star 110
Chairman: The Rev. Joseph Kamau
P.O. Box 47436, Nairobi.
A Kikuyu body, first called Jesus Evangelistic Shepherds Universal Salvation. Linked with Mantle Missions, San Diego, California, USA.

Evangelists Association in Africa 111
Chairman: Mr. Jacob Odegu
East Kano
P.O. Ahero, Kisumu.
A Luo organisation aiming to open branch churches, and composed primarily of itinerant lay evangelists with loose congregational affiliations.

Faith Miracle Church 112
Director: The Rev. Daniel Masaga
Ogada Church
P.O. Suna, Kisii.
A Luo independent movement first called Full Gospel Evangelistic Church (FGEC) until 1971 change of name, despite which registration could not be granted.

Fellowship of Believers 113
Chairman: Mr. Walter Nyasamo (P.O. Box 30,000, Nairobi); Secretary: Mr. J.W. Roberts.
BAT Shauri Moyo, Section H.1, Door No.8
P.O. Box 48808. Nairobi.   *Tel: (Mr. Roberts) 56746*
A small Plymouth-Brethren fellowship group named after the words in Acts 5.14, this is a sister congregation to, but now independent of, Nairobi Undenominational Church, which meets in Ofafa, Nairobi.

Free Church of East Africa 114
Bishop Bigedi; Mission Secretary: Mr. John Mujembi
Nile Road, Nairobi
P.O. Box 72122, Nairobi.   *Tel: 57307*
A largely Luhya independent church, founded in 1968.

Friends of the Holy Spirit (FHS) 115
Founder & Chairman: Mr. Mukaru Muthuria
HQ (Loc. 8) Gaturi
P.O. Box 157, Murang'a.
A Kikuyu secession of Balokole (Saved Ones, Revival) members of the Anglican Church, originally also called Dini ya Ruanda (Religion of Ruanda, i.e. the East African Revival), Ahunjia (Preachers), and Dini ya Kaggia (after Bildad Kaggia, an early pentecostal leader who left to enter political life), and then Arata a Roho Mutheru (Friends of the Holy Spirit). Followers throughout Kenya, loosely organised.

Friends of the Holy Spirit (Kitui) 116
Unorganised groups in Ukambani (Kitui, Mwingi, etc.) Originally a Kikuyu and Kamba movement begun in 1948 through the preaching of Mukaru Muthuria, dissension arose in 1960 when it was discovered that, contrary to earlier rejection of registration with government, the Kikuyu branches had registered, under the Kikuyu title Arata a Roho Mutheru. Henceforth the Ukambani and Nyanza branches broke with the Kikuyu. In Kikamba, the church is called Anyanyae ma Veva Mutheu (Friends of the Holy Spirit). In some areas, members still belong to historical mission churches and form groups within them, with a variety of names: Harambee ya Mungu (God's co-operation) in the Free Gospel Churches of Kenya; Andu ma Kikoka (The Saved People), Ndini ya Kuokoka (Religion of the Saved) in the Africa Inland Church, Salvation Army, and Gospel Furthering Fellowship. Other names are: Andu ma Kavonokya (People of the Saviour), Andu ma Veva (People of the Spirit), Andu Atangue (The Saved Ones). These groups and their doctrines are described in detail, with 59 hymns, in D.N. Kimilu's article (see *Bibliography*).

Full Gospel Church in Africa, see Church of Full Gospel
in Africa

Full Gospel Churches of Kenya (FGCK) 117
Spokesmen: Messrs. Hesekiel Kiptoo (Chairman), Christopher Simon Kariuki; Secretary: Miss Anna-Lusa Arthuri
P.O. Box 5, Koru (Tel: 11), and (Secretary) P.O. Box 285, Kericho (Tel: 84).
Founded in 1949 by the Finnish Free Foreign Mission, a Pentecostal body, the FGCK is a national church under Kenyan leadership, mainly in Nyanza, Rift Valley, Central, Eastern and Western Provinces. Congregations are all under local leadership, with consuetation meetings at a provincial level. The Annual General Meeting of the FGCK is held each February, when three Spokesmen are elected with an Advisory Council of nine Church leaders as members. Five Registered trustees are responsible for all property. Workers are trained at Koru Bible School. Tent meetings, youth camps, and Sunday schools all attract large audiences. There are FGCK medical centres at Chemelil and Kapeddo.

Full Gospel Evangelistic Church, see Faith Miracle Church

Full Gospel Fellowship Mission of Africa 118
Chairman: The Rev. Joaz Onyango
Reg. Office: Sangoro, Kogutu Location, South Nyakach
P.O. Box 862, Kisumu.
A Luo independent group south of Kisumu.

Gethsemane Divinity Church (Kenya)
Chairman: Pastor Jacton Kung'a
Gamuguni Kapseng'ere Sub-Location
P.O. Box 246, Kisumu.
A Luhya group with 210 members, which applied for registration in 1972.

God of Israel Zion Church (Zionists) 119
Bishop: Ephraim Musodzi
Zion (formerly Bware Kanyange), Plot No. 25
P.O. Suna, Kisii.
A Luhya movement referring to themselves as Zionists, who use a flag of green, white and yellow, and set aside Friday as their day for worship and Sunday as their day for preaching to the unconverted.

God of the Universe Church (GUC) 120
Chairman: Mr. Naphtali Ondiany Odewa: Secretary: Mr. Mark T. Anjejo
HQ: Wanganga Village, SE Kano Location
P.O. Box 53, Muhoroni.
A mainly Luo schism in 1962 from the Pentecostal Assemblies of East Africa (now PAG), known at first as Wanganga church. Now six pastorates: Kano, Milambo, Awendo, Koru, Maragoli, Chemelil. The spread of the church is largely due to an unusual method of evangelism through prophecy, or the prophetic naming of contacts. During meetings, evangelists are selected by the Holy Spirit and given, through prophecy, the names and addresses of new and as yet unknown persons who are in dire spiritual need and will receive their message. All the present congregations have been begun in this way, usually accompanied by faith healings.

God's Last Appeal Church (Luong Mogik mar 121
Nyasaye Church)
Pastor: Mr. Harun Owuor; Secretary: The Rev. J.G. Otieno
P.O. Box 5068, Kendu Bay.
A Luo schism in 1966 from the Seventh-day Adventist Church, emphasizing African leadership, faith healing, baptism with the Holy Spirit, and a ministry of praying for the sick. The numbers of sick who attend is placing heavy demands on the church's resources.

God's Word & Holy Ghost Church 122
High Priest: Johana Wangendo
Rusiru Farm
P.O. Box 12, Njoro.
One of the Kikuyu Spirit churches, which originally separated from other Spirit churches over polygamy.

Good News Church of Africa (GNCA) 123

Chairman: The Rev. Simion M. Matonoi
P.O. Box 72708, Nairobi.

A large schism of Kamba members in 1958 from the Gospel Furthering Fellowship mission, with members from other missions then joining also, due to a claimed new revelation concerning the baptism of polygamous wives. Pastors' School at Machakos; also sends pastors to East Africa Bible College, and Scott Theological College, Machakos.

Gospel Furthering Bible Church 124

Chairman: The Rev. Elijah M. Kituku
P.O. Kikima, Machakos.

In 1935, there was a schism from the Africa Inland Mission by missionaries who then formed the Gospel Furthering Fellowship. Their work among the Kamba grew sizeably, but there have been several large schisms to form indigenous groups. The GF Bible Church is under national leadership and is still assisted by GFF missionaries.

Gospel Holy Spirit of East Africa 125

Leaders: Mr. Elfas O. Sagide, Mr. Nathan Keya
Impaka Gospel Holy Spirit Church (Kisumu to Kakamega road, turning right at Mbale Market)
P.O. Box 47, Maragoli.

One of the Luhya groups originating from the 1927 Holy Spirit revival at Kaimosi.

Gospel International Church of Kenya, see International
Pentecost Church of Christian Fellowship

Gospel of God, The 126

Leader: Pastor Arthur Dirorimwe; General Secretary: Mr. Robinson Sichaya Ngube.
HQ: Ngong (formerly Racecourse Road, Nairobi)
P.O. Box 49044 (& 24819), Nairobi.

In Southern Rhodesia in 1932, a Shona prophet named Johane Masowe received a vision on a mountain, as a result of which a large Shona independent church came into being, known as the Vapostori (Apostles), or the Apostolic Church of Johane Masowe (not to be confused with the much larger African Apostolic Church of Johane Maranke, also of Rhodesia), also known as the Apostolic Sabbath Church of God of Johane Masowe, with followers throughout southern Africa. Polygamy is permitted. Nicknamed the Basketmakers (their special trade), they were evicted from South Africa as a community, and are now strong in Zambia and parts of Tanzania. This group of Shona Vapostori in Nairobi began in 1968 and first registered under the name African Gospel Church; it consists of 28 members (11 men, 17 women, children) working at Ngong as fundis and (women) sewing and weaving. They now claim 600 Kikuyu followers, and expect shortly to unite with a Kikuyu church at Ngong, the Holy Church of Evangelistic Apostles Faith; they now share the latter's large mansion on Allen Road, Nairobi.

Gospel Proclaimers, see Church of the Truth

Gospel Tabernacle Church (Mombasa Gospel 127
Tabernacle)

Leader: Pastor J. Ndiwa
HQ: Plot No. 126, Section IX, Tudor Road
P.O. Box 81487, Mombasa. Tel: 20572

A schism of Kamba members led by a missionary (the Rev. George Lyons) from the Gospel Furthering Fellowship mission, circa 1943, which resulted in Mombasa Gospel Tabernacle and a new mission, Africa Faith Mission Inc. Later, the work expanded to 2 congregations in Mombasa (1 English-speaking), 5 in Kitui, and 8 in Kibwezi. The church now has good relations with the GFF, who have supplied a missionary for the Mombasa church.

Greek Orthodox Church, see African Orthodox Church of
Kenya

Greek Patriarchate of Alexandria, see African Orthodox
Church of Kenya

Holy Church of Africa (EA) 128

Bishop: Mrs. Gaudencia Aoko
Awasi, Plot No. 18, NE Kano Location, Ahero
P.O. Box 41, Muhoroni.

In the early days of the Maria Legio breakaway from the Roman Catholic Church in Western Kenya (1963) one of the prominent figures was a 20-year-old Luo girl, Aoko, who claimed to have received a vision after her two infant children had suddenly died, allegedly through sorcery. By 1968 she had claimed to be the original founder, and opened legal proceedings against the other leaders Ondeto, Muga (her brother-in-law) and Atila. Her branch took the name Legio Maria Orthodox Catholic Church, but it failed to attract many followers. In 1969 she attempted to register it under the title Holy Church of Africa (East Africa), with an elaborate constitution including descriptions of the use of yellow flags; but registration was not granted. by 1971 Aoko had retired from public view, and was seeking reconciliation with Ondeto.

Holy Church of Christ of Africa, see Episcopal Church of
Africa

Holy Church of Evangelistic Apostles Faith 129

Leader: Archbishop Joshua W. Kiarie; Bishop Timothy J. Muiruri
HQ: church: stone building at Ngong; Nairobi house: Allen Road
P.O. Box 24885 (& 24819), Nairobi.

An offshoot, affirming polygamy, water baptism and holy communion, which broke from the work of Charles Nielsen, a South African missionary with the Apostolic Faith Mission of South Africa, who was in Kenya 1958-61. (The AFMSA left Kenya about 1963). There are 14 Presbyteries in Kenya from Voi to Kitale, and a Bible school at Ngong is planned for 1972. The church has recently linked up with Shona Rhodesian Christians from the Apostolic Church of Johane Masowe (or, Apostolic Sabbath Church of God of Johane Masowe; or, Vapostori, Apostles) found across southern Africa, and now in Kenya (see The Gospel of God). The church owns a building at Ngong, one in Nairobi, and 10 acres of land at Karen.

Holy Covenant Church Assembly of God, see Holy Spirit
Brotherhood Church

Holy Ghost Church of Kenya (HGCK) 130

Minister: Mr. Hezron Tumbo; Secretary: Mr. Joseph Karugia
Murengeti Village, Uplands Road, Limuru
P.O. Box 184, Limuru.

A church formed from the original 'Watu wa Mungu' (People of God) Kikuyu independent around 1929. It forms the liberal wing of the Aroti (Dreamers, Seers) movement, permitting modern attitudes to society, employment, etc. Opposed to polygamy. In May 1972 the name was being changed to Holy Ghost Church of East Africa.

Holy Ghost Coptic Church of Africa 131

Leader of the Faith and Holy Father: His Holiness John W.S. Juma Pesa; Archbishop: Nehemiah Aineo Owalo (P.O. Ndori)
HQ: St. Stephen's Basilica, Kogore, West Konyango, South Nyanza
HQ (Kisumu): Kakamega Kakamega Road
P.O. Box 1162, Kisumu.

A Luo movement led by a former Catholic, employing Catholic terminology and titles (e.g. mass, basilica).

Holy Mission of Israel Church 132

Chairman: Mr. Peter John Mwariki
Jabini Society, P.O. Box 8, South Kinangop
P.O. Box 48991, Nairobi.

A small Kikuyu group which broke in 1967 from the African Mission of Holy Ghost Church.

Holy Spirit Brotherhood Church 133

Supreme Archbishop: The Most Rev. Benjamin M.P. Mwangi
Kawanguare Village, Plot No. 452. Nairobi District
P.O. Box 72355, Nairobi.

A Kikuyu group with three bishops and an archbishop, with a lengthy theological statement, use of vestments, etc. Polygamists can receive communion but not hold office. Archbishop

Mwangi had made three previous attempts to register, under the titles: (1961) African God Covenant Brotherhood Church Society, then African God New Covenant Holy Ghost Church (also known as Anabu na Atumwo, 'Prophets and Disciples'), then Holy Covenant Church Assembly of God (registered, then cancelled, in 1968). The fourth (HSBC) was also rejected, in 1969.

Holy Spirit Church of East Africa (Dini ya Roho)   134
High Priest: Archbishop Jephatha Zale Ambula
Bukoyari Mission
P.O. Box 78, Maragoli.
One of several Luhya groups originating from the 1927 Holy Spirit revival at Kaimosi. Recently, a few Kikuyu congregations have been formed. The church has sent one ordinand to St. Paul's United Theological College, Limuru.

Holy Spirit Church of Zayun   135
Chairman: Prophet Jathan Muranga
Ngararia
P.O. Box 747, Thika.
A Kikuyu movement known as the 'M' Aroti (Dreamers of the Cross), due to their wearing of a red letter M (for *musolaba*, cross), and red edges, on their robes. Red or blue turbans are worn, but not green, because 'Green is forbidden by the Holy Spirit'. 'Zayun' = Zion.

Holy Trinity Church in Africa (HTCA)   136
Bishop: The Rt. Rev. Joshua Aluoch Gawo
P.O. Box 160, Kisumu.
In 1960, this church was formed as a schism from the Church of Christ in Africa in a dispute over leadership. It now has 16 pastorates and 2 deaneries in a Diocese of Masogo; and congregations across the country to Mombasa, and also in North Mara, Tanzania.

Holy Trinity Church Missionary Society, see Apostolic
Hierarchy Church

Huru Salvation Nineveh, see African Israel Church Nairobi

Independent African Orthodox Church   137
Chairman
Plot No. 39, Klhuti
P.O. Box 85, Karatina.
A Kikuyu independent movement in the Nyeri and Karatina areas, which originated in a dispute over leadership in the African Orthodox Church. In 1967 its chairman was the Rev. Philip Kiande Wamagu, who shortly after was invited to be bishop of the AIPC for a year before his death in 1970.

Independent Assembly of God of Kenya   138
P.O. Box 243, Limuru.
A body registered in 1965 but cancelled in 1969.

Independent Baptist Churches of East Africa   139
(IBCEA)
Chairman: The Rev. Paul Obange
Thika Road Baptist Church (next to Safari Park hotel)
P.O. Box 48227, Nairobi.   *Tel: Ruaraka 2327*
Founded in 1964 by American missionaries of Grace Independent Baptist Mission, now under national leadership. Emphasis is placed on open-air evangelism, Bible School, personal evangelism and instruction in the Word of God.

Independent Churches of God of East Africa   140
Chairman: Mr. Peter Mbote
Magina Town
P.O. Box 204, Limuru.
A split in 1967 from the Local Churches of Kenya.

Independent Lutheran Church (ILC)   141
Patriarch: Bishop (Rabbi) Elam Angali Musinde
Maragoli
P.O. Box 142, Maragoli.
An independent Luhya church founded in 1961 as the African Lutheran Church, and also known as the Loyalists, or Loyalist Religion. Dioceses of Baluyia and Nyanza. No foreign workers, but receives aid from Sweden.

Independent Pentecost Evangelistic Fellowship   142
Bishop: The Most Rev. Samwel Imwendwa (Box 167, Meru).
P.O. Box 34, Rumuruti.
A body whose application for registration was refused in 1969.

Independent Presbyterian Church of East Africa   143
(IPCEA)
Chairman: The Rev. Solomon Muthukya
Migwani Location
P.O. Mwingi, Kitui. (President: P.O. Box 72681, Nairobi, Tel: 20500).

Independent United Churches of Baptist of Christ   144
Chairman: The Rev. Jonah Nzau
Digo Road, Plot No. 80, Eastleigh Sec. 7
P.O. Box 73162, Nairobi.
A body whose application for registration was refused in 1971.

International Bible Students Association, see Jehovah's
Witnesses (also IBSA in Part V)

International Church of God Evangelistic   145
Fellowship
Chairman: The Rev. Joel Njuguna
Kandara Mungaria Village
P.O. Box 517, Thika.
A Kikuyu organisation registered in 1969, but cancelled in 1969.

International Fellowship for Christ (IFFC)   146
Director: The Rev. Chacha M. Omahe
Jericho, House No. AD11-5571
P.O. Box 72654, Nairobi.   *Tel: 59991*
An indigenous Pentecostal organisation founded in 1969 with 8 widely-scattered pastorates across Kenya: Malindi (Coast), Chonyi, Taita, Tana River, Luoro, Nairobi, Kuria, Karungu, Rakwaro. Links with USA and Canadian organisations.

International Jerusalem Church (IJC)   147
Leader
P.O. Meru.
Although the name originally belonged to a movement in Meru around 1960, it was appropriated by a large group who broke off from that church's leaders in 1967, as a result of which the original body changed its name to Pentecostal Church of Christian Fellowship.

International Missionary Society of Seventh-day
Adventist Reform Movement, see Seventh-day Adventist Church, Reform Movement

International Pentecost Church of Christian   148
Fellowship (IPCCF)
Archbishop: The Rev. Joel N. Gitete
Plot No. 15, Lanet Centre
P.O. Box 685, Nakuru.
A Kikuyu body which applied for registration in 1971, then again in 1972 under a new name, Gospel International Church of Kenya (GICK) (P.O. Box 218, Naivasha).

International Pentecostal Assemblies, see Pentecostal
Evangelistic Fellowship of Africa

Israel Anglican Church, see Religion of the Ancestral Spirits

Israel Assemblies of Kenya   149
Chairman: Mr. Joel Muturi Ndogo
Plot No. 34, Tulaga, North Kinangop, Nyandarua District
P.O. Box 219, Naivasha.
An independent Kikuyu group in North Kinangop, which wears turbans. Like many indigenous Spirit groups, water baptism is not practised, being rejected and replaced by Spirit baptism.

Israel Holy Ghost Church of Kenya 150
Founder and Chairman: Stefano Musa Mwangi
Mathare No. 4, Mathare Valley
P.O. Box 28955, Nairobi.
An Aroti ('Prophets') group looking to 1949 for its origin, which finally split in 1972 from African Mission of Holy Ghost Church over the latter's acceptance of polygamy, and sought registration under the name above after earlier name (All African Nation of Holy Ghost Church Israel) had been rejected. Whereas AMHGC does not baptise in water this new group has introduced it.

Jehovah's Witnesses in East Africa, Association of 151
Representatives: Mr. P.S. Palliser, Mr. J.L. Hockett
Kingdom Hall, Woodlands House, Woodlands Road
P.O. Box 47788, Nairobi.   *Tel: 24905*
By 1971 there were in Kenya 18 Kingdom Halls (local congregations) of the worldwide organisation Jehovah's Witnesses (also known as Jehovah's Christian Witnesses, or the International Bible Students Association), which began in the USA in 1884. Witnesses keep detailed statistics of their evangelistic activity, with termenology different from other churches, as can be seen from their Kenya 1970 statistics: average publishers (active adult members), 844; peak publishers (largest number active in year), 947; 225 baptisms during year; 1,242 Bible Studies held; 335,643 hours spent talking about the Bible from house to house; 143,637 back-calls made (return visits); 118,463 magazines distributed; 2803 new subscribers during 1970; and 75,437 other pieces of literature distributed. An annual Christians' convention for four days is held in Nairobi, featuring Bible instruction and the acting of Biblical dramas. Registration as a society was granted in 1962; also licenced to celebrate marriages under the African Christian Marriage and Divorce Act. In 1972 there were 34 foreign missionaries assisting in Kenya. April, 1973: declared banned.

Jerusalem Seventh-day Church of God 152
Chairman: Bishop Samuel M. Wabande; Secretary: Mr. Edward
    Macharia Karuitha
Gitundaga Village
P.O. Box 169, Thomsons Falls.
All Kikuyu members, formerly known as Church of God Seventh-day in Kenya. Began in 1959 when founder contacted Church of God Seventh-day (P.O. Box 568, Jerusalem, Israel). Then in August 1970, 17 ministers were ordained in Kenya by a minister from Jerusalem.

Judah Israel Mission 153
Founder and Bishop: Yohana N. Muhindi; Secretary: Mr
Reming D. Gichuru
Kamusinde Village
P.O. Box 144, Kimilili.
In 1944 a large separatist movement arose east of Mt. Elgon called the Israel Anglican Church and led by a Quaker, Elijah Musinde. By 1948, as Dini ya Msambwa (Religion of the Ancestral Spirits), it had become violent and was declared a prohibited society. As a result of its increasingly political nature, Musinde's assistant Bishop Muhindi broke off in 1961 and formed Judah Israel as a legal body, and (to be an orthodox ecumenical church organisation. Practices include obligatory Friday worship in main temple near Kimilili (which means membership is restricted to those living within 20-mile radius), polygamy, prophecy and dreams, animal sacrifices three times a year, and reverencing of Mt. Elgon as 'Zion'. In 1967 the church sent representatives to the World Conference on Christian Education in Nairobi.

Kendu Roho Church Mission 154
Bishop: Elija Kilion Ogol
HQ: Bware-Nyenjwa, Konyango
P.O. Kendu Bay.
A small Luo sabbatarian independent church begun in 1953 as a split from Musanda Holy Ghost Church, in protest against veneration of founder Odongo, and to stress faith healing and foot-washing. Known in Luo as Chuny Kanisa Mochung' (Spirit Independent Church). Members wear turbans; bishop fasts every Saturday.

Kenya African Church, see African Church, The

Kenya Church of Christ 155
Representative: Mr. Van Tate
Church House, Government Road
P.O. Box 48086, Nairobi.
Kenya Kanisa la Kristo. Begun in 1965 by missionaries of the Churches of Christ (Non-instrumental), USA, with emphasis on church-planting, church growth methods, and Bible school courses. Two areas: Nairobi-Thika, and Kakamega.

Kenya Compassion Church of Christ
Chairman: Mr. James Nyaga
Runyenjes Social Hall
P.O. Runyenjes, Embu.
A small Embu church of 152 members registered in June 1972.

Kenya Evangelical Lutheran Church, see Evangelical
    Lutheran Church in Tanzania

Kenya Faith Mission, see East Africa Pentecostal Churches

Kenya Foundation of the Prophets Church (KFPC) 156
Founder and Minister: Mr. Musa Thuo s/o Chege; Secretary: Mr.
    Samuel Kinyua
HQ: Ithiru, Gatanga Location, Kandera Division
P.O. Box 223 (and Box 89), Thika.
One of the Kikuyu churches originating in 1927 in Location 4, Fort Hall District, from the Watu wa Mungu (People of God) movement, and still led by its 93-year-old founder. They initiated a new form of prayer, for men only, standing on top of Kaguthi Hill with upraised hands, facing Mount Kenya. There are branches among Kikuyu in both Central and Rift Valley Provinces. Other Aroti churches consider that the statistics claimed for this church are too high because they include those of other churches over whom the minister claims jurisdiction.

Kenya Full Gospel Fellowship, see Kenya Revival Centre

Kenya Pentecostal Fellowship, see Assemblies of God,
    Kenya District Council

Kenya Redeemed Church
Chairman: The Rev. Allan Njeru
Plot No. 1112/69, Kubukubu Road
P.O. Box 298, Embu.
A church of 200 Embu members newly registered in 1972.

Kenya Revival Centre 157
Director: The Rev. Richard Kirby; Asst. Director: The Rev.
Geoffrey Kamosche
Kikuyu
P.O. Box 43446, Nairobi.   *Tel: Ruaraka 2438*
Known until 1967 as the Muscoy Community Church Ministerial Fellowship (based on San Bernadino, California, USA), then until 1972 registered as Kenya Full Gospel Fellowship, the Kenya Revival Centre is an association of clergy and Christian workers, with seminars and branches; linked with United Pentecostal Church of Kenya.

Kenya Voice of Gospel Church 158
Chairman: Mr. Joseph Mbogo
MCN
P.O. Box 1092, Nakuru.
Formerly Nakuru Full Gospel Church, this is largely a Kikuyu body which split in 1965 from the Full Gospel Churches of Kenya. Membership declined, the founder left, and the work is almost in abeyance.

Kenya Voice of Liberty Church
Chairman: Mr. Stephen Njeru
Kathangari, Ngandori Location
P.O. Box 298, Embu.
A small Embu group with 50 members, refused registration in mid-1972.

Last Ministry Church 159
Apostle: Simon Manuel Zawadi; Bishop: George Nguru
Wusi, Mtango
P.O. Mwatate, Voi.

A Taita body whose application for registration was refused in 1969. The name is derived from its claim to minister during the last days before Christ returns.

Lavington Church (United Parish) 160
Minister: The Rev. John Bowles
Lavington Road, Lavington Green (Manse: Pytchley Road)
P.O. Box 25030, Nairobi. *Tel: 48352*
In 1960, the Anglican, Presbyterian and Methodist Churches created this as the parish church serving the new Nairobi suburb of Lavington, and to function as the first united church, belonging to and financed by these three bodies. Whilst this experiment in unity has been a marked success, no further such experiments elsewhere have as yet resulted. The church is represented on, and governed by, the synods and assemblies of the three denominations. There are flourishing Sunday schools, Scouts, Guides, Cubs, Brownies, Women's Guild, Urafiki Club (Friendship), Social Service Fund, services in English and Swahili a wide range of other social and evangelistic activities, and a monthly church magazine, *Lavington Messenger.*

Legio Maria Church, see Maria Legio of Africa

Legio Maria Orthodox Catholic Church, see Holy Church of Africa

Legion Catholic African Church 161
Bishop: Vitalis Okelo; Secretary: Mr. Lucas Odhiambo
Suna Location
P.O. Suna, Kisii.
Part of the original Maria Legio schism of 1962 which broke from main body and attempted to register in 1963 claiming 3,500 members, but whose registration was refused in 1964. Subsequently the church declined in influence.

Local Churches of Kenya 162
Chairman: The Rev. Godfrey Kanja; Secretary: The Rev. William Masini
Manyatta Kisumu
P.O. Box 1296, Kisumu.
An indigenous Pentecostal group begun in 1960 as a split from PCEA, uniting independent congregations in Luo, Luhya and Kikuyu areas, with local congregational autonomy and provincial divisions administered by a provincial supervisor.

Lost Israelites of Kenya 163
Prophet of God: Papa Joshua Michael William Wanyonyi
Kimilili Kamalewa, Bondeni, Kitale
P.O. Box 699, Kitale.
In 1960, a group of Christians around Kitale took this name (or, 'Israel with Ten Commandments') with the claim to have been discovered as one of the lost tribes of Israel from Old Testament days. Their followers extend westwards into Uganda. Highly colourful uniforms, flags, pageantry and marching. The Papa wears the number '44,000' embroidered on his uniform, this being the total persons he plans to recruit.

Loyalist Religion, see Independent Lutheran Church

Lumpa Church (Zambia)
This large African independent church, whose name means 'the Church which evangelises abroad', was begun in 1954 in Northern Rhodesia by the prophetess Alice Lenshina Mulenga. A Kenyan, Elmad Ouma Jathim Makadudi, served as her bodyguard and editorial aide. Returning to Kenya in 1964, he attempted to start a Kenya branch, but abandoned the idea and now operates a large business at Manyatta Libya, Kisumu, as a medicine man and herbalist, with other clinics in Nairobi and Homa Bay, and with a large retinue of young herbalists and magicians. The most renowned and feared 'witchdoctor' in modern Kenya, he is a devout Christian who also serves as treasurer of the Independent African Orthodox Church of Kenya. (See article in *Sunday Nation* (Nairobi), 31 October 1971, p. 22).

Luong Mogik mar Nyasaye, see God's Last Appeal Church

Luo Roho Church 164
Archbishop: The Rev. Zablon Ndiege; Secretary: Mr. C. Apolo Bunde

Diocese of Alara, Kandaria Secondary School, Siaya District
P.O. Nyilima, Kisumu. (Secretary: Ralingo Church, P.O. Ndori, Kisumu).
A schism in 1968 from the Nomiya Luo Church over the right to speak in tongues and to pray in the Holy Spirit (Roho). Ministry to the sick, faith healing, circumcision, removal of shoes in church or at open-air services; original Anglican tradition in worship still maintained.

Lurambi Church Group of Light, see Church Group of Light

Lutheran Church in Kenya (LCK) 165
Chairman: The Rev. James O. Nchogu
Itierio Mission
P.O. Box-50, Kisii.
In 1948, the Swedish Lutheran Mission (Bibeltrogna Vanner—Bible True Friends), invited by the Anglican Church, began work in South Nyanza among the Kisii and Luo. Now under national leadership, the church is also assisted by the Evangelical Association of Finland, and the World Mission Prayer League (USA). The LCK sponsors 30 primary schools, and medical centres at Itierio and Matongo. The church paper is *Habari Njema* (Good News), monthly.

Lyahuka Church of East Africa 166
Chairman: Mr. Eliakim Keverenge
Ikivu Church, North Maragoli
P.O. Box 619, Maragoli.
Until 1965 known as the Church of Quakers in Africa, and until 1971 as African Church of Red Cross; claims to be the original Luhya schism from the Friends Africa Mission at Kaimosi in 1927. Lyahuka (or Riahuka) means 'Religious protesters' in the Luhya language.

Magina Pentecostal Church in Africa 167
Leader: The Rev. Albert Oriare
Magina Village, Sub-Location Wawidhi B, SE Kano.
P.O. Ahero, Kisumu.
A Luo schism in 1969 from the Norwegian Pentecostal Mission in Kenya, named after its location. Growing annually.

Maranatha Church 168
Representative: The Rev. Curt Johansson
P.O. Suna, Kisii.
Begun in 1967 by missionaries of the Swedish Maranatha Mission (Maranatha = 'Our Lord, come!' in Aramaic), the church is located in Suna near the border with Tanzania.

Maria Legio of Africa 169
Baba Mtakatifu (Holy Father) & Founder: Simeo Ondeto; Pope: Timotheo Atila; Cardinals: Joanes Muga, Carolus Mumbo, *et alii.* Archbishop, Nairobi Diocese: Herbert Aloo (Room 13, KANU Building, Jeevanjee Street, P.O. Box 73364, Nairobi).
HQ: Kalafari (Calvary), Got Kwer (Mount of Confession), Suna Location
P.O. Box 70, Kisii.
From 1930-60, an unmarried Luo Roman Catholic mystic named Maria (born circa 1876, died 1966) saw visions calling her to initiate an African Catholic church. After several abortive attempts, a mass exodus of Luo and Kisii Catholics took place from the RC Diocese of Kisii in 1960-62, and with her spiritual son Simeo Ondeto, Maria founded the Legion of Mary Church, initially with some 90,000 adherents. After a period of turbulence during which Ondeto was briefly imprisoned, the church was granted registration and organised itself throughout Kenya, Uganda and Tanzania (North Mara district). A survey in 1969 showed that 10% of the members had formerly been Roman Catholics in good standing, 10% former Protestants, about 40% lapsed, nominal or would-be Catholics, and about 40% were pagans before joining. Ondeto is recognised as the spiritual head, Baba Mtakatifu, the special representative of Jesus Christ, with Pope Atila as second-in-command. By 1971 there were 7 cardinals, and the following 10 dioceses led by archbishops (with bishops as assistants in each): the headquarters Diocese of Amoyo (Jerusalem) near Suna, and Nairobi, Nakuru, Mombasa, Kisumu, Ukwala, Kericho, Busia, Kakamega, Siaya. The church combines Luo tradition and culture with conservative Roman Catholicism including retention of Latin in the

246

mass. A detailed description of Maria Legio is given in P.J. Dirven's thesis (see *Bibliography*).

Methodist Church in Kenya (MCK) 170
Presiding Bishop: The Rev. Lawi Imathiu
Conference Office: St. Andrew's Church, St. Andrew's Road
P.O. Box 47633, Nairobi.   *Tel: 24841*

Led by the former CMS missionary Krapf, the first Methodist missionaries came from Britain in 1862 and began work at Ribe near Mombasa. In 1912, the first Meru station was opened, at Kaaga; the work expanded until today the Meru field is far larger than that at the Coast. In 1967, the church became an autonomous Methodist conference, with three Districts (Meru, Coast, Nairobi). The church has long been active in educational and medical work, and today sponsors 166 primary schools, plus 10 *harambee* secondary schools; and also two hospitals (Maua, Ngao) and a medical mobile unit with a doctor based on Garba Tula.

A strong interest in northern Kenya has recently crystallised into the Northern Kenya Mission, begun after the *shifta* (bandit) attacks ceased in 1968. With grants from the Methodist Missionary Society (UK), Oxfam, Bread for the World, *et al.*, substantial help to the Boran people has been provided, and by 1970, 308 Boran had been baptised in the 7 churches in the Mission (including Mandera and Moyale in the extreme north). Social work there includes irrigation schemes, tanneries and children's homes.

Coast District Chairman: The Rev. R.S. Mng'ong'o, P.O. Box 98224, Mombasa.
Meru District Chairman: The Rev. P. Amiraki, Kaaga, P.O. Box 269, Meru.
Nairobi District Chairman: The President
Northern Kenya Mission Minister: The Rev. B. Jinkin, Garba Tula, P.O. Box 3, Isiolo.

Miracle Evangelistic Ministry 171
Chairman: The Rev. Charles O. Yamo
Gendia Village, East Karachuonyo
P.O. Box 5032, Kendu Bay.

A Luo Pentecostal movement, begun in 1970, now found in Kendu Bay, Oyugis, and Uhuru Estate, Nairobi.

Miracle Revival Fellowship Pentecostal Church 172
Director: The Rev. Elisha Chitayi; Deputy Director: The Rev. Morris Mwadime.
Kilifi District
P.O. Box 1, Mariakani.

From 1957, the American Pentecostal evangelist T.L. Osborn held mass rallies in East Africa. After the Mombasa crusade, a number of Taita revivalists in the Anglican Church were excommunicated for 'enthusiasm'. Also known as Weni-Mwanguvu (People of Power), they formed Pentecostal groups in the Taita Hills, from which this denomination is descended. They are said to have 15,000 followers in Uganda also.

Miracles and Wonders Church
Chairman: Mr. Abdulla Davis
Plot No. 296, Sec. 7, Macalisters Street, Eastleigh
P.O. Box 30315, Nairobi.

A small church registered in 1972, with 30 members.

Muolo Roho Israel Church 173
Bishop & Founder: Yona Atiang; Deputy Bishop: 'Nabi' Petro Kariuki
North Nyakach Agoro, P.O. Pap-Onditi, Kisumu
P.O. Box 405, Kisumu.

Muolo' = peacefulness (Luo). A Luo schism from the African Israel Church Nineveh in 1950 over food taboos. The bishop and his deputy inform the congregations concerning prohibited types of meat.

Musanda Holy Ghost Church of East Africa (MHGC) 174
Archbishop: Mr. Jeremiah Aloo; General Secretary: Mr. Michael Owiti Wambogo
HQ: Musanda
Archbishop, P.O. Box 521, Kisumu. Gen. Sec. P.O. Box 19050, Nairobi.

Begun in 1916 by the Rev. Alfayo Odongo-Mango as a Roho Maler (Holy Spirit) revival within the Anglican Church (CMS),

the movement was forced into schism by the murder of Odongo and others in a burning hut in 1934. The church has suffered from several schisms over the years, the largest being that of the Ruwe Holy Ghost Church in 1939, and growth at present is slight. (See biography of Odongo by B.A. Ogot in *Bibliography*).

Nairobi Baptist Church 175
Minister: The Rev. Gottfried Osei-Mensah
Church: Ngong Road, at Green Lane (west of Kenyatta Hospital roundabout)
P.O. Box 44128, Nairobi.   *Tel: 22537*

An independent congregation formally constituted in 1958, affiliated with the Baptist Union of Great Britain and Ireland, the church has been noted for a preaching ministry, and a radio and TV ministry, of the highest quality. Amongst many successful innovations and experiments, the imaginative and informal Youth Church begun in January 1971 doubled the total church attendance within a few weeks. A church newspaper *Outlook*, is published 11 times a year.

Nairobi Chapel, see Nairobi Undenominational Church

Nairobi Undenominational Church (Nairobi Chapel) 176
Secretary: Mr. Bernard Wilson
Protectorate Road, Nairobi
P.O. Box 42312, Nairobi.   *Tel: (Sec.) Langata 386*

Begun 40 years ago as a fellowship of expatriate Christians in the Plymouth Brethren tradition, the church now attracts a large number of Kenyans. It has no ordained ministry but is served by 7 part-time elders. Sister congregations are established at Ofafa Nairobi, and in Mombasa (see Ebenezer Gospel Hall)

National Independent Church of Africa (NICA) 177
Bishop: The Rt. Rev. Willie J.N. Nyaga
Gichiche HQ, P.O. Runyenjes, Embu
P.O. Box 182, Embu.

Part of the Embu and Meru exodus from the PCEA, Methodist and Anglican churches in Central Province circa 1929 during the controversy over female circumcision and independent schools. The church was revived again around 1958 and registered in 1964.

New African Canaan Church 178
Bishop: The Rev. Zakayo Makanga
Essaba Sub-Location, West Bunyore Location
P.O. Box 73, Maseno.

A small independent church among the Luhya with 28 members, first called Canaan Church in Kenya. Their constitution compares the present-day world with that of Canaan in the Bible.

New East African Church 179
Chairman: The Rev. Joshua Muoka Mutua
Kwakivanyu, Mitaboni
P.O. Mitaboni, Machakos.

A recent Kamba independent movement claiming a large following.

New Roho Israel Church (Manyien) 180
Leader: Mr. Paul Omumbo Achola
P.O. Box 105, Kisumu.

In 1962, the leader split from the African Israel Church Nineveh, returned to Roho Church of God of Israel, and eventually in 1970 managed to form his own body under Luo leadership, supported generously from his own resources. 'Manyien' means 'New' in Luo.

Nomiya Ligangala Mabith Sabato Church 181
Bishop Joshua Owino
Dhanji Maji Building, Oginga Odinga Road, Kisumu
(also HQ Kanyakwar Sub-Location)
P.O. Box 766, Kisumu.

A recent Luo schism from the Nomiya Luo Sabbath. The name is Luo for 'He gave me a sharp sword' and 'Sabbatarian'.

Nomiya Luo Church (NLC) 182
Archbishop: The Rt. Rev. Benjamin Oundo; Assistant Archbishop Gideon C. Owalo; Senior Bishop: Mathayo Orwa; Principal Secretary: Mr. Solomon O. Oiro
HQ: Diocese of Oboch, Kisumu

P.O. Box 1283, Kisumu.
Correspondence to: Princ. Sec., *P.O. Box 72917, Nairobi.* Tel: 27401 Ext. 370, 24002.

In 1907, 'the Word of God was given' (in Luo, *Nomiya*) to Johana Owalo, a catechist successively in the Roman Catholic, Seventh-day Adventist, and Anglican missions near Kisumu; after several years of unrest, the prophet broke off in 1914 to form the first African independent church in Kenya, the Nomiya Luo Mission. By 1925, there were 500 adherents, and churches were opened across the country and into Tanganyika. There is now a large cathedral, 'Jerusalem'. at Oboch School, and there are 3 dioceses: Oboch, Kuoyo, and Milambo. Male followers are circumcised, and the church follows strictly the Five Books of Moses (Pentateuch) in the Old Testament. Jesus is accepted as God's Son, above all the prophets, but the church denies that he is God himself. In its rapid expansion, the church has encountered a serious obstacle in that non-Luos do not want to join a body in which prayer books are written only in Luo, services conducted in Luo, and whose title implies a similar restriction. Efforts are now being made at translation and at a universalising of membership.

Nomiya Luo Sabbath (NLS) 183
Archbishop: The Rt. Rev. Jacob Ayoo Paulo (P.O. Box 29, Homa Bay); Principal Secretary: Mr. M.M. Odongo
HQ: Busamia Close, Jericho Estate, Nairobi
P.O. Box 43420, Nairobi. *Tel: 57028*
A schism from the Nomiya Luo Church in 1957, the church emphasises especially certain Muslim influences stressed by the original prophet, Johana Owalo, in 1907: circumcision of males, God is One only, wearing of white robes, prayers 5 times daily. In addition, Saturday is observed as the Sabbath for worship. The church is organised in 5 dioceses in Kenya (South Nyanza Lambwe Valley, Siaya District, Kisumu District, Nairobi, Mombasa) and 3 in Tanzania (North Mara, South Mara, Moshi).

Norwegian Pentecostal Mission in Kenya (NPMK) 184
Chairman: The Rev. Arvid Bustgaard; Secretary: Miss Astrid Tveter
HQ: Nyambare Hill
P.O. Box 15, Ukwala (and Box 10, Muhoroni).
This missionary society from Norway began work in 1955, and has two fields of service, the extreme west of Kenya around Ukwala among the Luo, and Kipsigis and Kisii territory to the east. It operates medical centres at Nyambare Hill and Thessalia, Muhoroni.

Orthodox Church of Kenya, see African Orthodox Church of Kenya

Peace & Mercy Church of East Africa 185
Leader: Mr. Joshua Chuma
P.O. Box 51, Lumbwa.
A schism in 1962 from the Seventh-day Adventist Church among the Kisii and Kipsigis, characterised by polygamy and sabbath-keeping.

Pentecost Africa Church 186
Bishop: Jafeth Odayo
Nyakakana Intermediate School
Private Bag, P.O. Ahero, Kisumu.
A Luo movement beginning in 1967, experiencing very rapid growth. Emphasis on faith healing and miraculous gifts.

Pentecostal Assemblies of East Africa, see Pentecostal Assemblies of God

Pentecostal Assemblies of God (PAG) 187
General Superintendent: The Rev. Charles Gungu
HQ: Nyang'ori
P.O. Box 671, Kisumu. *Tel: Nyang'ori 1Y4*
A large national church begun in 1910 and subsequently supported by the Pentecostal Assemblies of Canada (PAOC). Strongest amongst the Luhya of western Kenya, but now countrywide divided into 5 sub-divisions: Western Region (in Western Province), Luo Region (in Nyanza Province), Gusii Region, Rift Valley Region (in Rift Valley Province), Central-Coast Region (in Central, Eastern and Coast Provinces). The church operates a wide variety of institutions, including Evangel

Press, Evangel Publishing House, Pentecostal Bible College at Nyang'ori with 62 students; and runs a Christian Education Department with organisations for 5-12 years age group (Crusaders) and 13-35 years age group (Christ's Ambassadors).

In Kenya there are 642 churches (active congregations with buildings), 314 assemblies, and 314 pastors; a pastor is a salaried minister (mostly ordained) in charge of from 1-8 congregations forming an assembly (which must be able to pay a pastor). There is a church paper *Mwangazi* ('The Enlightened') published every two months. In recent months a new charismatic movement critical of the organisational aspects of the PAG has arisen among Luo members in Western Kenya.

Pentecostal Christian Universal Church (PCUC) 188
Founder and Chairman: Bishop Peter Willy Masinde
Miendo PCU Church, Kimilili
P.O. Box 287, Broderick Falls.
A Bukusu movement begun in 1968 in Bungoma District with special emphasis on healing of the sick, helping those with personal troubles, and the like.

Pentecostal Church of Christian Fellowship (PCCF) 189
Chairman: The Rev. Reuben Kiugu; Secretary: Jenet Karuru
P.O. Box 167, Meru.
A Kikuyu independent church begun circa 1960 as the international Jerusalem Church, now with five groups, in Meru, Thika, Timau, Thompson's Falls, Nakuru. In 1967 a division occurred concerning the aims of the church and how to instruct the many new converts, as a result of which a large group broke off from the leaders and claimed the name IJC; as a result the remaining officers changed the name to PCCF.

Pentecostal Church, One Faith 190
Chairman: Pastor Simion Sulubu
Matsangoni
P.O. Box 62, Kilifi.
A group of 150 members separated from PEFA (Pentecostal Evangelistic Fellowship of Africa) on the Coast.

Pentecostal Evangelistic Fellowship of Africa (PEFA) 191
Chairman: The Rev. Milburn J. Sickler; Secretary: Miss Clara Rhines
PEFA Central Office, Elim Evangelical Church, Jomo Kenyatta Avenue
P.O. Box 82627, Mombasa. *Tel: 26132*
In 1962 PEFA was formed, uniting the mission work of the International Pentecostal Assemblies (since 1938), and the Elim Missionary Assemblies (since 1942), stimulated and subsequently financially supported by the American Pentecostal evangelist, T.L. Osborn, since his 1957-58 crusades in East Africa. PEFA now has 791 churches in Kenya (Coast 219, Central Region 84, Nyanza 255, Kaimosi 233), plus 135 in Tanzania; the number of churches has increased at the rate of over 200 a year since 1969. The church runs several institutions including the PEFA Bible Institute, PEFA Correspondence Course and Bible School, and Kaimosi Bible School.

Pentecostal Holiness Church of Kenya 192
Pastor: The Rev. Geoffrey Muchoki
Iriaini-Kairia
P.O. Box 394, Nyeri.
A small group in Central Province.

Philadelphia Church of Kenya 193
Chairman: The Rev. Joseph Taiti
Munyange Sub-Location, Nyeri
P.O. Othaya, Nyeri.
A Kikuyu movement emphasising praying for the sick, with 100 members and 2 church plots in 1966 when registration was refused.

Power of Jesus Around the World Church 194
Leader: Pastor Christopher Alando; Chairman: Mr. Edward Tei
P.O. Box 1588, Kisumu (also P.O. Box 10, Muhoroni, and P.O. Box 153, Homa Bay).
A Luo independent church founded in 1955 as a split from the Voice of Salvation and Healing Church, after the founder Filemon Wachara had heard the American evangelist T.L. Osborn preach in Uganda.

Presbyterian Church of East Africa (PCEA) 195
Moderator: The Rt. Rev. J.K. Giatau; General Secretary:
Rev. John G. Gatu
Office: St. Andrews Church, Kirk Road
P.O. Box 48268, Nairobi. Tel: 25095

In 1891 the East African Scottish Mission opened a station at Kibwezi, transferred in 1898 to Kikuyu, after which the number of Christians under the Church of Scotland Mission grew rapidly until the setbacks of 1929-30 due to the female circumcision controversy. In 1943 the church became independent under the name Presbyterian Church of East Africa. In 1946, 2,000 Christians under the Gospel Missionary Society joined the PCEA. From 1962-67 the PCEA was engaged on church union consultations with Anglicans and Methodists, which ended in failure. The history of the PCEA to 1967 is told in detail in R. Macpherson's book (see *Bibliography*). Long a pioneer in educational and medical work, the PCEA today sponsors 275 primary schools, a number of *harambee* secondary schools, and three hospitals (Chogoria, Kikuyu, Tumutumu).

Prophecy Evangelist Church of Africa 196
Missionary: Mr. George Lusuli
Kitulu Village, Mahanga Market Road, Maragoli
P.O. Box 36, Maragoli.

A small Luhya group emphasising music ('The church will adopt using loudspeakers, accordions, guitars and drums-when singing (Psalm 150)' — Constitution). First called African Evangelist Fellowship Healing.

Ramogi Catholicity Church
Founder: Bro. Robert Makodawa
P.O. Box 136, Butere.

A small grouping founded by a former Roman Catholic with the aim of teaching African culture. Related to United Orthodox Independent Churches of East Africa.

Reformed Church of East Africa (RCEA) 197
Chairman of Synod: The Rev. W. Welime
HQ: Kisumu Road, Eldoret
P.O. Box 99, Eldoret. Tel: 2665

From 1909 to 1935 the Rev. Tini Loubser worked as a missionary on settler farms in northwest Kenya. From 1944 other missionaries joined the 'Bwana Loubser Mission' at Plateau (12 miles from Eldoret), many pastors and evangelists were trained, and a presbytery of Eldoret, Trans-Nzoia and Plateau was set up. In 1961, the Reformed Mission League, of the Reformed Church of the Netherlands (Holland), took over this work, and in 1963 created a synod with the name RCEA. The first missionaries from Holland came in 1961, and have since concentrated on ministerial training, schools, hospitals, youth work and literature; a Bible school for 32 students at Plateau, and a conference and lay training centre in Eldoret. Six students have gone to St. Paul's United Theological College, Limuru, and also one staff member. Church work has expanded greatly recently, the number of congregations doubling from 1968-71; and work is now under way in Western Province, and Turkana, Elgeyo and Baringo Districts. The church publishes *Tuzungumze* ('Let us talk together') ten times a year, and *Sauti ya Vijana* ('The Voice of Youth') quarterly. It sponsors 29 primary schools, Plateau Hospital, and various other educational and medical centres.

Religion of the Ancestral Spirits (Dini ya Msambwa) 198
Founder: Elijah Masinde
District: Bungoma, Elgon

The only proscribed (illegal) religious body in Kenya in 1971, the DYM was begun in 1944 among the Bukusu as the Israel Anglican Church under Masinde, a member of the Friends Africa Mission. More a nativistic movement than a Christian church, it regarded Mt. Elgon as Zion, the holy mountain out of which cargo (cars, tractors, etc.) were about to emerge for the faithful. A strongly nationalistic movement, it became violently anti-white, riots occurred, and in 1948 DYM as 50,000 adherents were barred by government. After Independence, DYM was registered as a legal society, but Masinde's continued anti-foreign and anti-government stand resulted in his arrest, and

in 1968 it was declared a proscribed society. After a long series of disturbances, in June 1972 Masinde was again sentenced to jail, for six years.

Roho Church of God of Israel 199
Founder and Bishop: Mr. James Kasibo
HQ: Ibwali Mission, Jemuguni Village, Tiriki Location
P.O. Box 246, Kisumu.

The founder, formerly of the Pentecostal Assemblies of God, later of the African Israel Church Ninevah, had serious illness in 1960 accompanied by a vision, as a result of which in 1963 he led a 'reform Israel' movement out of AICN and formed a church known first as African Spiritual Israel Church, then World Spiritual Israel Church (Roho Mtakatifu Israel Church and Schools), then from 1966 Roho Church of God of Israel.

Roho mar Nyasaye Mission (Spirit of God Mission) 200
Bishop I. Were
Karabondi Village
P.O. Kendu Bay.

A small Luo independent group, registered under the Luo name shown.

Roho Mtakatifu Israel Church & Schools, see Roho Church of God of Israel

Roho Ngima Church of Kendu 201
Chairman: Mr. Joash Muga Okumu
Kendu
P.O. Kendu Bay.

A small Luo movement with 50 members in 1971. The name means Living Spirit Church of Kendu Bay (Luo).

Roman Catholic Church, see Catholic Church in Kenya

Ruwe Holy Ghost Church of East Africa 202
Founder and Archbishop: Yusuf Barnaba Waluoho; Secretary
General: Mr. S. Owuor Opanga
HQ: Ruwe
P.O. Box 159, Butere.

In 1939 the founder was forced out of Musanda Holy Ghost Church of which he was then archbishop, in a dispute over compelling members to wear uniforms glorifying the martyred Founder Alfayo Odongo-Mango. A large number of followers seceded with him. Rival headquarters were then opened at Ruwe. MHGC reported 2,810 in 1956, and 1,440 in 1959; whereas RHGC reported 2,257 in 1959, rising to 2,615 in 1970. Although the dispute aligned leaders wanting white uniforms with red crosses against those wanting red uniforms with white crosses, today both churches wear white with red crosses.

Sabato Maler mar Nyasaye Kanisa 203
Bishop Gerison Akal
Kadongo Market, Kabondo
P.O. Kabondo, Kisumu.

One of the handful of independent churches which has attempted to obtain registration with a vernacular title (in this case, 'Holy Sabbath of God Church', in Luo). Application refused in 1969.

Sabina Church 204
First Prophet: Jakobu Kamau
Worazo Village
P.O. Box 60, Kiganjo.

A Kikuyu group led by three prophets, whose name, (from the Kikuyu word for Noah's Ark) means 'Church of the Ark'.

Salvation & Healing to All Nations, see World-Wide Evangelistic Church

Salvation Army (Jeshi la Wokofu) (SA) 205
Territorial Commander (East Africa Territory): Lt-Commissioner Geoffrey Dalziel
HQ for East Africa: Government Road
P.O. Box 40575, Nairobi. Tel: 20320, 27541/2

A large national body begun in 1921, whose emphasis on music, processions, uniforms and para-military organisation has had wide appeal. In its early days in areas like Embu, many of its converts were disaffected Anglicans or Presbyterians. However the major reason the Army gives for its rapid spread in

249

Kenya is its insistence on the use of Swahili, plus the deliberate and continual posting of officers to places outside their tribal areas. The work is strongest among the Kamba and Luhya (Maragoli and Tiriki). There is an elaborate hierarchy of command, based on Divisional and District headquarters at: Embu, Kangundu, Machakos, Thika, Shigomere, Kisumu, Eldoret, Maragoli (Mbale), Elgon, and Mombasa. The Army does not baptise with water, and most church terminology differs from that of most denominations; adult members are called 'soldiers', ministers are 'officers', children 8-15 years are 'junior soldiers', baptism is replaced by 'swearing-in', places of worship are 'corps'. In Kenya, the Army has long had a wide range of projects in the realm of social service, in addition to sponsoring 96 primary schools. The best known of their 17 social welfare institutions are given in the Directory of Christian Organisations (Part V). Two papers are published: *Sauti ya Vita* ('Voice of Life') monthly, and *Chama cha Wanawake* (Women's League'), quarterly.

Salvation Merciful Church (WHC) 206
Chairman: Mr. Harun Masia Aligula
P.O. Box 131, Molo.
Wokofu Huruma Church. A Luhya independent church with title in Swahili as well as English, and using Swahili initials WHC. Salvation Army origins are revealed in the full title Wokofu Huruma Church, Damu na Moto ('Blood and Fire', the SA motto).

Scriptural Holiness Mission (SHM) 207
Superintendents: Mr. W. Finch, Mr. G. Mulaha
P.O. Box 10, Londiani **Tel: 8Y2**
A British mission (address: 109 Highcross Street, Leicester, UK) which began work in 1948 with the object of promoting the Biblical teaching of personal holiness (in the Methodist tradition). Based on Londiani, the mission has a dozen branches with 6 men and 4 women as lay workers. A paper, *The Highway*, is published three times yearly.

Seventh-day Adventist Church (SDA) 208
Chairman:(East African Union): Pastor D.K. Bazarra; Administrative Secretary: Pastor F.K. Wangai.
HQ: Invergara Grove, off Bernard Road, Nairobi
P.O. Box 42276, Nairobi. **Tel: 66025**
The Adventist mission was one of the first to enter Kenya, starting work in Nyanza in 1906. There are now four conferences known as (in order of size): South Kenya Field (Kisii and Narok Districts), Kenya Lake Field (Central Nyanza, Siaya, Busia part of South Nyanza) Ranen Field (Central, Western, Migori and Kehancha Divisions of South Nyanza District), Central Kenya Field (the rest of Kenya, to the Coast). The Kenya church belongs to the wider East African Union of SDAs (Kenya, Uganda, Seychelles). The mission formerly had 400 primary schools, but now they only count as sponsored the 27 (with 3,540 pupils) which they finance, although they are still linked with 155 altogether. Baptism is administered countrywide on the same days (17 April and 26 September, in 1971) There are Bible schools, active literature evangelists, and a press (Africa Herald Publishing House) and large hospital (Gendia) at Kendu Bay. As throughout the world, the SDAs are sabbatarian (conducting public worship on Saturdays).

Central Kenya Field Chairman: Pastor F.K. Wangai
Chalmer's Square, Shauri Moyo
P.O. Box 1352, Nairobi (T: 58276)

Kenya Lake Field Chairman: Pastor F.E. Wilson
P.O. Kendu Bay

Ranen Field Chairman: Pastor Christopher Odero
P.O. Ranen

South Kenya Field Chairman: Pastor Hezron Kenani
P.O. Box 22, Kisii (T: 22)

Seventh-day Adventist Church, Reform Movement 209
(International Missionary Society of the SDA Reform Movement)
Leader: Mr. James Omwansa
Ntana Mission, North Mugirango
P.O. Box 634, Kisii.

In 1968, a schism from the Seventh-day Adventist Church took place in their strongest area, South Kenya Field, among their Gusii followers. The leader has subsequently got his group linked to an international SDA schism, the SDA Reform Movement (Box 67, Wurzburg, West Germany; and the Religious Liberty Publishing Association, 5420 San Francisco Boulevard, Sacramento 20, California, USA).

Seventh-day Missionary Church (SDMC) 210
Chairman: Mr. Haruni Njuguna
HQ: Ringuti-Thigio Town
P.O. Box 184, Limuru.
One of the earliest Kikuyu independent churches to be registered with government, this church was formed in 1936 as a schism from the Holy Ghost Church of Kenya in order to change the day of worship from Sunday to Saturday.

Sinai Church of East Africa (SCEA) 211
Founder and Bishop: Paulo Masambu
Vitendo, Maragoli
P.O. Box 212, Maragoli (also P.O. Box 20202, Nairobi).
A Luhya schism in 1965 from the African Israel Church Nineveh, endeavouring to stress the need for more educated leadership training. It has only grown slowly over the years, to, by 1971, 300 Luhya and 50 Kikuyu.

Spiritual Church 212
Leader: Bishop Lucas Musasia Nuhu
Munishram Building, Jeevanjee Street
P.O. Box 47909, Nairobi. **Tel: 25217**
One of several independent groups with few or no followers, but whose purpose is to serve as rallying points in the attempt to unite all independent churches in Kenya.

Swedish Free Mission, see Evangelical Free Mission in Kenya

Tana River Independent Church
A schismatic movement among the Pokomo on Tana River which resulted in the secession of 2,000 Methodists in 1965 under Amos Chadhoro; in 1939 the original Neukirchner Mission had been removed because German, and tried to return after the war to claim its work back from the Methodist Church. In 1966, registration for the new church was refused, and in 1967 it joined the Africa Inland Church. By 1971 it was small in numbers and concentrated mainly around Ngao.

Tanganyika Mennonite Church (Kenya) (TMC) 213
Representative: The Rev. J. Clyde Shenk
Macalder
P.O. Suna, Kisii (Repr., P.O. Box 7596, Nairobi, Tel: 28023).
The work of the Eastern Mennonite Board of Missions and Charities (Salunga, Pennsylvania, USA) in North Mara, Tanzania, since 1934 has been among the Luo tribe there. Many Luo have recently re-migrated back to Kenya, and in 1962 the sizeable numbers of Mennonite Luo around Suna in South Nyanza organised themselves into a church, obtained Kenya government registration in 1963, and now constitute a district of the TMC.

Three Holiness Israel Union Church 214
Founder and Chairman: The Rev Stephen John Khaguli
Mbambo HQ, Maragoli
P.O. Box 15, Maragoli.
A schism in 1965 from the African Israel Church Nineveh in dispute over leadership; registered in 1966 as the Three Holiness Church of Kenya. Registration cancelled in 1970.

Truth of the Apostles 215
Archbishop: Mr. Jacob Ongana
Karabok Intermediate School, Kasipul Location
P.O. Oyugis.
A Luo independent movement begun circa 1966.

United International Fellowship for Christ, see International Fellowship for Christ

United Pentecostal Church of Kenya (UPCK) 216
District Superintendent: The Rev. Kenneth Wendell; District Asst. Superintendent: The Rev. John Harris.
Plot 8393, Mountain View Estate, Thika Road
P.O. Box 43446, Nairobi.

A recently-arrived mission sponsored by the United Pentecostal Church International (8855 Dunn Road, Hazelwood, Missouri, USA); linked with Kenya Revival Centre. Campaign in Nairobi in June, 1972, followed by weekly services at central YMCA.

Vapostori, see The Gospel of God

Voice of Prophecy Church 217
Chairman: Prophetess Susanna Nyabulwa
Nyambare, Gem Location
P.O. Homa Bay.
A Luo independent church of Sabbatarian practice, led by a blind charismatic prophetess. Registered in 1963, but registration cancelled in 1970.

Voice of Salvation & Healing Church 218
Missionary Supervisor: The Rev. J.A. Silas Owiti; Secretary: Mr. Eric S. Oloo
P.O. Box 582, Kisumu.
An early Luo schism from the Africa Inland Mission in 1954 after the founder claimed an experience of the Holy Spirit. One of the first independent churches to receive government registration (1956). A Pentecostal movement emphasising healing through the Holy Spirit. Now constructing a large new church in Kisumu.

Water of Life Church (WLC) 219
Modern Seer: Evangelist Dickson Elmad Ouma
Kanyaluo Kobila, Seme, Karachuonyo
P.O. Kendu Bay.
A Luo movement begun in 1964 which regards itself not as a denomination but as a spiritual organisation dedicated to a prayer ministry for the sick and troubled, operating through prayer cards printed in English.

Weni-Mwanguvu (People of Power), see Miracle Revival Fellowship Pentecostal Church

Witikio wa Atumwo, see Apostolic Faith of Africa

Wokofu African Church (WAC) 220
Founder and General: Mr. Matthew Odundo (P.O. Box 82, Turbo); Chairman: Mr. Harrison Keya; Secretary: Mr. Joseph Lusiola
Main HQ: Turbo. Nairobi HQ: St. Aggrey Church, Racecourse Road
P.O. Box 27036, Nairobi.
A largely Luhya schism in 1966 from the Salvation Army over leadership and dissatisfaction with SA's treatment of the problem of healing. In contrast to the SA's white uniforms, WAC members wear yellow uniforms or dresses, with the insignia 'W' ('Wokofu' — Salvation) on their collars; also in contrast to SA obstention from sacraments, WAC now practices

water baptism (for believers over 14 years) and bread-and-wine communion three times a year; and, further, they have abandoned all military terminology except the honorary term 'General' for the founder. There are eight spheres of work, or Divisions: Turbo (HQ), Nairobi, Maragoli, Kinyui (Eastern Region), Mariakani, Molo, Eldoret, Kisumu. There is also a Division in Uganda.

Wokofu Huruma Church, see Salvation Merciful Church

World Christian Soldiers Church 221
Chairman: Mr. Jackton Kissuge
HQ: Ng'ong'a, Marienga School
P.O. Sare, Kisii.
A recent Luo independent movement emphasising music; its Rule 2 reads: 'The member must accept to praise Jehovah with musical instrument necessary'.

World Revival Union Evangelistic Church 222
Founder and Chairman: The Rev. Brother Japhet N. Mwango; Secretary: Mr. Samuel Kombe
HQ: Kaloleni, Giryama
P.O. Box 33. Mariakani.
A Pentecostal movement among the Mijikenda coastal tribes, and one of their first independent churches, with the express aim of uniting all Pentecostal denominations, calling them to 'join together with the Harambee spirit to spread the Gospel of Christ in unity and fellowship "that they all may be one" — John 17.20-1'. Brother Mwango, a former Anglican, started his first church in 1965 at Kaloleni among the Giryama tribe. Revival meetings were held throughout the Coast region from 1969-71. The church is linked with A.A. Allen's organisation Miracle Revival Fellowship, Miracle Valley, Arizona 85645, USA.

World Salvation of Soul Adventist Holy Ghost 223
Church
Chairman: Bishop Astariko Oyieko
Kakelo Ringa, Kamroth Sub-Location, Kasipul Location
P.O. Oyugis.
A small Luo Roho (Spirit) movement begun circa 1964, reporting three bishops, one permanent church building and a declining membership from 150 in 1967 to 70 in 1969.

World Spiritual Israel Church, see Roho Church of God of Israel

World-Wide Evangelistic Church 224
Chairman: Missionary John Adoo
Nyahera Sub-Location, Kisumu
P.O. Box 1492, Kisumu.
A recent Luo independent church, at first known as Salvation & Healing to All Nations.

World Wide Revival, see Voice of Salvation & Healing Church

5

Part V

Directory

of Christian Organisations in Kenya

Directory of Christian Organisations in Kenya

This Directory is a listing of all Christian organisations in Kenya (except churches, denominations and dioceses, given in Part IV) which are of national, or more than local, importance. A handful of the major local churches or congregations are also included here. In addition, a handful of religious organisations of particular interest to Christians are included, although not specifically Christian themselves.

Information is set out as follows:

Official name, in bold type (Initials, if used)
Title and name of main executive officer
Street address or location of office
Postal address, in italics.   *Telephone*

In cases where an official name in Swahili is in use, this is given in italics below the postal address. In actual fact, although all churches and organisations were asked to give their Swahili name, very few have one in use.

Initials are those in use for the organisation, *or* those of the sponsoring or affiliated denomination (see Index of Abbreviations, p. 338). Note that street address, postal address, and telephone are in many cases unrelated, since postal addresses and telephones are widely shared, and are often not exclusively used by the body shown but may belong to some large secular organisation. Exchanges of telephone numbers are the same as town of postal address, unless otherwise shown. 'RN' = Radiocall Nairobi, a special service requested from telephone operator.

Note: The full, correct, postal address is as shown in italics; street address, and words such as 'via', are *not* required on envelopes. Note that most of the places listed in this Directory are shown on the foldout map of Kenya at the end of this Handbook.

In addition to organisations in existence in 1972, a few organisations are listed which are no longer present in Kenya, and brief comments are given on each.

How to use this Directory
All organisations are listed here by their official names in strictly alphabetical order. Since many organisations use several alternative names, or shorter versions of their official names, the reader seeking a particular body should look under all the variations possible; he can also look in the Index under the main subject or keyword in the name he requires.

Changes of address and officers
The names and addresses given here date from, on average, December 1971. Changes can be expected at the rate of 5 per cent each year. Space has been left for the reader to up-date any of these that concern him.

Cut-off point for inclusion
There are also a number of other international organisations who support a small work in Kenya, sometimes with one or two workers. There has to be a cut-off point somewhere for inclusion in this directory, so those which in the editors' judgement are not large enough to be termed Kenya organisations are excluded here.

AAAC Training Centre
Director: The Rev. Canon Yinka Olumide
Sclaters Road (near Church Road)
P.O. Box 14206, Nairobi.   *Tel: 61166*
Opened in 1968 to train Africa's communicators as Christian broadcasters in radio and television. Residential 6-month courses; studio-control rooms, practice rooms; script-writing, programme content, evaluation sessions; library.

Africa Acts Feature Service (AACC)
Director: Mr. Norman Hart
Pioneer House, Government Road
P.O. Box 20390, Nairobi.   *Tel: 33510*
A service begun in 1970 under the AACC to offer monthly packets of feature articles on current topics to periodical editors throughout Africa, and beyond. Non-profit subscription service; articles written by African professional writers, emphasising Christian participation in the new societies of Africa.

Africa Christian Press (ACP)
Regional Editor for East Africa: Miss Joyce Scott
Lantana Road, Westlands
P.O. Box 14721, Nairobi.   *Tel: 60180*
A publishing house (HQ: Accra, Ghana) begun in 1964 for producing Christian books by African writers. Emphasis on writer-training courses and activities. Language: only English, but translation rights into other languages granted. 50 titles to date, sales over 100,000 a year.

Africa Evangelical Office (AEO)
A centre formed in 1962 through which evangelical churches and missions in Africa received information of developments affecting church life and work; published information bulletin; encouraged formation of national Evangelical Fellowship; con-encouraged formation of national Evangelical Fellowships; conferences, radio, literature (see AELO). Since 1971 the AEO has been submerged into the Association of Evangelicals of Africa and Madagascar.

Africa Evangelical Literature Office (AELO)
Director: The Rev. C. Richard Shumaker
Bible House (2nd floor), Jeevanjee Street
P.O. Box 21285, Nairobi.   *Tel: 27070*
A literature service agency to the churches in Africa, begun 1966, associated with AEO; assists with coordination between Christian publishing houses, booksellers, writer trainers; publishes Lit-Helpers; selects trainees in journalism and communications; sponsors workshops. Bulletin *Vocal.*

Africa Faith Mission (AFM)
Director
Tudor Road
P.O. Box 81620, Mombasa.
An American mission which has assisted the Mombasa-based denomination, Gospel Tabernacle Church.

Africa Gospel Light (WGM)
Executive Secretary: Mrs. R.L. Adkins
WGM (on Kisumu road, off to right)
P.O. Box 123, Kericho.   *Tel: 123*
Begun in 1964, operated by AGC, AIC, AIM, WGM, for production and promotion of religious education materials for all age groups.

Africa Herald Publishing House (SDA)
Manager: Mr. D.C. Swan
(between Kendu Bay and Kendu Mission)
P.O. Box 5049, Kendu Bay.   *Tel: RN 2153*

Africa Inland Church Missionary Society
Secretary: Pastor James Mathang'a (AIC Mukaa, P.O. Kilome, Machakos)

AIC Headquarters, Kinyanjui Road, Ziwani
P.O. Box 13024, Nairobi. **Tel: 25149**
   An evangelistic missionary society of Kenyans begun in 1962 to send Kenyans to unevangelised areas in Kenya, Africa or overseas; run by the AIC Missionary Board of the central church council, using offerings from churches on the first Sundays in May and October each year. By 1972 four missionaries have been sent out: to Turkana, to Kitui and Hola (Orma Galla tribe), to Tana River area, and to Garissa area; with another shortly to go to the Mandera-Wajir area, northeastern Kenya.

Africa Inland Church Press
Manager: Mr. R. Wilson
AIC Kijabe Station
P.O. Box 40, Kijabe. **Tel: 12Y7**

Africa Inland Mission (AIM)
Field Secretary: The Rev. Frank C. Frew
AIM Field Office: Kitchener Road (near Adams Arcade)
P.O. Box 21010, Nairobi. **Tel: 67419**
   Founded in the USA by Peter Cameron Scott, the AIM began work in Ukambani in 1895, and today collaborates with the autonomous Africa Inland Church (AIC). In 1972, there are about 250 missionaries engaged in all types of work, including pioneer work among the Turkana, Pokot and Rendille tribes in the north (see under AIC Part IV for full details and addresses of stations).

African Evangelistic Enterprise (Kenya Committee) (AEE)
Convenor for Kenya: The Rev. J.T. Mpaayei
Bible House, Jeevanjee Street
P.O. Box 47596, Nairobi. **Tel:28023**
   The Kenya branch of African Evangelistic Enterprise, headed by the Rev. Festo Kivengere (office: P.O. Box 14381, Kampala, Uganda). Began in 1971; aim, urban evangelism; related to international Africa Enterprise, which in February 1969 held a United Christian Mission to Nairobi, also termed Crossroads Mission (Njia Ipi).

African Independent Communion Churches
Secretary: The Rev. Thomas J. Munjal
Unity Building
P.O. Box 49217, Nairobi.
   Also known as African Independent Community of Churches of East Africa; a federation aiming to speak for the independent churches of Kenya. See: United Orthodox Independent Zion Churches of Kenya, and list of similar federations on p.153.

Afromedia
Secretary: The Rev. E. Alan Roberts
Office: AIC Ziwani Church
P.O. Box 21028, Nairobi. **Tel: 25149**
   Begun 1971 for television film production, under AGC, AIC, Baptist Communications, and Audio Visual Aids Department of Emmaus Bible School.

Ahero Credit and Savings Co-operative Society
Secretary: Mr. Sylfanus Rabari
Ahero Catholic Parish, Multi-Purpose Training Centre
P.O. Ahero, Kisumu. **Tel: Ahero 4**
   Begun in 1969, one of many Catholic-initiated credit unions (Credit and Savings Societies of Kenya); 300 members, assists them save and obtain loans.

Ahero Technical Training Institute
Manager: The Rev. Fr. John Kuntner
(Located on Kisumu-Nairobi road, 23 km before Kisumu)
P.O. Ahero, Kisumu. **Tel: Ahero 4**
   Begun in 1968 by Catholic parish to train school-leavers as masons, carpenters, painters; to find them work and contracts. 40 boys at present. 40 have passed Gr. 3 Test, 30 are members of Ahero Building Construction Co-operative Society.

AIC Literature Department
Chief Executive Officer: Mr. L.M. Weaver
AIC Kijabe Station
P.O. Box 37, Kijabe. **Tel: 12Y7**

AIC Radio Department
Director: Pastor Timothy Kamau
AIC Kijabe Station
P.O. Box 75, Kijabe. **Tel: 12Y4**

AIPC Bible School (Chuo cha Biblia)
Principal
Kiriti
P.O. Box 587, Nyeri.

All Africa Conference of Churches (AACC)
General Secretary: The Rev. Canon Burgess Carr; Associate
   General Secretaries: The Revs. Aaron Su, James Lawson
Pioneer House, Government Road
P.O. Box 20301, Nairobi. **Tel: 33510/1/2/3**
   In French, CETA, Conference des Eglises de Toute l'Afrique . International ecumenical organisation begun in 1963, with 100 member churches and councils in Africa (12% of population of Africa), with the following functions: keeping before churches and councils the demands of the Gospel pertaining to their life and mission, evangelism, witness in society, service and unity; providing common programme of study and research; encouraging mutual sharing of experience between churches; assisting churches in finding, sharing and placing personnel and resources; assisting churches in leadership training, lay and clerical; collaborating with other international Christian agencies. The AACC produces a monthly information bulletin, and a quarterly journal, *Theologia Africana;* and operates a Training Centre (Broadcasting) in Nairobi.

Alliance Girls High School (AGHS)
Headmistress: Mrs. Joan Waithaka
Thogoto, Kikuyu Road
P.O. Box 109, Kikuyu. **Tel: 2102 (HM: 2101**
   Founded as African Girls High School in 1948; in 1972, 480 pupils and 27 staff.

Alliance High School (AHS)
Principal: Mr. A.C.E. Sanders
Thogoto, Kikuyu Road
P.O. Box 7, Kikuyu. **Tel: 2026**
   Begun in 1926 by Alliance of Protestant Missions, with 26 pupils; by 1972, 560 pupils and 30 staff. A well-attended Theological Society (sixth form only) has been in existence since 1964, and a Christian Union run by students.

Alliance of Protestant Missions
Forerunner of the NCCK, from 1918-1935.

All Nations Bible Correspondence Course, see Evangel Outreach

All Nations Gospel Church (PEFA)
Pastor in charge: The Rev. Samuel Mwatha Kangethe
Pumwani Road, near Solidarity Building opposite Quarry Road Post Office
P.O. Box 13004, Nairobi. **Tel: 58995**
   A congregation affiliated to PEFA begun in 1962, with 1,300 church members in Nairobi.

All Saints' Cathedral (Anglican)
Provost: The Very Rev. J. Henry Okullu; Canon
Residentiary: The Rev. W. Richards
Kenyatta Avenue
P.O. Box 40539, Nairobi. **Tel: 20715**
   Construction began in 1917; in 1927, became second cathedral for Diocese of Mombasa, known as the Cathedral of the Highlands. Kindergarten school next to church and hall.

American Bible Society (ABS)
   This New York-based society was originally responsible for the first scriptures in the Luragoli and Lunyore languages (Luhya). It now works through the Bible Society of Kenya.

Anglican Consultative Council (ACC), Research Office
Research Secretary: The Rev. Dr. David B. Barrett
Office: Church House (7th Floor), Government Road
P.O. Box 40230, Nairobi. **Tel: 23649**
   The Anglican Consultative Council is the representative body of the worldwide Anglican Communion, and has now replaced

the decennial Lambeth Conferences of all bishops that met in London. The 50 elected representatives include laity, women and youth. President: The Archbishop of Canterbury. Chairman: Sir Louis Mbanefo. Vice-Chairman: Mrs. H. Kelleran. Secretary General: The Rt. Rev. J.W.A. Howe. Headquarters: 21 Chester Street, London, S.W.1, England. The Nairobi Office deals with surveys and research.

Apostolic Faith Mission of South Africa
A mission from South Africa formerly at work on the farms of the Eldoret Highlands, but which left the country soon after Independence.

Apostolic Nunciature in Kenya
Apostolic Pro-Nuncio: The Most Rev. Pierluigi Sartorelli
Churchill Avenue
P.O. Box 14325, Nairobi.   *Tel: 48468*
The diplomatic representative of the Holy See (Vatican, Rome) to the Republic of Kenya.

Arahuka Book Depot (CPK)
Manager: Capt. Ezra Thiong'o
Kenyatta Avenue, Murang'a
P.O. Box 260, Murang'a.
Diocesan book depot (with reading room) for the Diocese of Mount Kenya (Church of the Province of Kenya). *Arahuka* means *Awake!*

Associated Business Consultants (EA) Ltd.
Director
Koinange Street
P.O. Box 47656, Nairobi.   *Tel: 25176*
A professional firm of market research and survey specialists who can, for a fee, insert questions about religion into their surveys.

Association of Catholic Graduates and Professionals of
Kenya, see Catholic Forum

Association of East African Theological Colleges
(AEATC)
Chairman: The Rev. E.E. Mshana
Lutheran Theological College, Makumira
P.O. Box 55, Usa River, Tanzania.   *Tel: Usa River 35*
Begun in 1959 to co-ordinate work of theological colleges. Members in Kenya: St. Paul's United Theological College, Limuru; Kima Theological College; Trinity College, Nairobi; Department of Philosophy and Religious Studies, University of Nairobi; plus 10 others (including two Roman Catholic seminaries) in Uganda and Tanzania.

Association of Evangelicals of Africa and Madagascar
(AEAM)
Administrative Secretary: Mr. Eric Maillefer
Valley Road (at top, on left)
P.O. Box 49332, Nairobi.   *Tel: 21894*
Begun in 1966, the AEAM provides spiritual fellowship among evangelical Christians, united action, co-operation; promotes evangelism and total outreach. Members: National Associations of Evangelicals in ten African nations. In 1971, the Africa Evangelical Office, begun in 1962 and located in Nairobi, was submerged into the AEAM, which has taken over the AEO's functions.

Association of Sisterhoods of Kenya (AOSK)
Secretary: Sr. Claire M. Callahan
8th Malagasy Crescent, Kenyatta College
P.O. Box 221, Ruiru (also Box 14622, Nairobi). Tel: Templer 254
Comprises 31 religious congregations of women working in Kenya. Its objects are: 'to be of benefit to the individual Sisterhoods in the fuller attainment of their ideals; to foster co-operation between the Sisterhoods; and to promote collaboration on religious affairs of common concern' *(Statutes).*

Association of the Episcopal Conferences in Eastern
Africa (AMECEA)
Secretary General: The Rt. Rev. Vincent McCauley.
Secretaries: The Rev. Frs. Joseph Healey, Joseph Mukwaya.

AMECEA Office, 49 Bernard Road
P.O. Box 21191 and 21053, Nairobi.   *Tel: 66506*
Shirikisho la Mabaraza ya Maaskofu ya Afrika ya Mashariki na ya Kati. Begun in 1961 (initially as ITEBEA, Interterritorial Episcopal Board of Eastern Africa), as the organ of liaison and collaboration between, and service of, the 5 constituent Episcopal Conferences (Kenya, Uganda, Tanzania, Malawi, Zambia); functions through plenary meetings of the 66 bishops, annual executive board, and central office (and Office of Social Communications) in Nairobi. Newsletter: *AMECEA Information.* Operates Pastoral Institute of Eastern Africa, Gaba (P.O. Box 4165, Kampala, Uganda).

Assumption Sisters, see Sisters of the Assumption of Nairobi

Assumption Sisters of Eldoret
Mother General
Convent of Our Lady of Lourdes (on Eldoret-Uganda road)
Private Bag, Turbo.   *Tel: 8*
An indigenous diocesan congregation of 15 sisters, 9 novices, and 3 convents, founded in 1956 for teaching, nursing and social work among people in Eldoret.

Asumbi Brothers, see Congregation of Fraters of Our Lady

Bahati Community Centre (PCEA, MCK)
Warden: Mr. E. Kirimania
Heshima Road, off Jogoo Road
P.O. Box 72582, Nairobi.   *Tel: 58970*
A centre begun in 1954 and run by the Presbyterian and Methodist churches for community work in Bahati, Nairobi, specialising in: youth work, domestic science training, bookkeeping and accountancy, day nursery, and general social and pastoral work.

Bahati Martyrs' Church (PCEA)
Pastor in Charge: The Rev. G. Gikanga
Heshima Road, off Jogoo Road
P.O. Box 72582, Nairobi.   *Tel: 57470*
A church built in 1954 jointly by the PCEA and MCK, now under PCEA. Has associated Bahati Community Centre.

Baptist Communications Centre
Director: Mr. Dale Hooper
Liverpool Road
P.O. Box 50370, Nairobi.   *Tel: 57392, 59076*

Baptist Language School
Principal: Mr. Duncan Marshall
Brackenhurst Baptist Assembly, Tigoni
P.O. Box 137, Limuru.   *Tel: Tigoni 256*
Begun in 1957 to teach BMEA missionaries (and others) Swahili and other languages.

Baptist Mission of East Africa (BMEA)
Mission Chairman: The Rev. Boyd Pearce
Brackenhurst Baptist Assembly, Tigoni
P.O. Box 32, Limuru.   *Tel: Tigoni 256*
A mission of the Southern Baptist Convention (USA), began work in Kenya in 1956. Mission stations: Kisumu, Kitale, Limuru, Meru, Mombasa, Nairobi, Nakuru, Nyeri; 2 high schools (Nyeri, Mombasa) with 296 pupils; medical clinics in Kisumu and Nairobi; and a publishing house and radio-recording studio in Nairobi. For church work, see Baptist Churches of Kenya.

Baptist Publications
Editor: Mr. James Tidenberg; Business Manager: Mr. Jim Hill
Liverpool Road
P.O. Box 30370, Nairobi.   *Tel: 58744*
Begun in 1960 by the BMEA for printing and publishing of books, tracts and Sunday-school materials.

Baptist Reading Room
Director: Mr. A.A. Cummins
Fort Hall Road (below Ngara roundabout)
P.O. Box 14701, Nairobi.   *Tel: 63281*

Berea Farm, see Christian Rural Extension Scheme

Bethany Bookshop (WGM)
Manager: Mr. Gerald W. Fish

Kenyatta Avenue
P.O. Box 583, Kitale.   *Tel: 113*
  Began in 1968 by the World Gospel Mission.

Bethany Bookshop (WGM)
Manager: Mr. David Kellogg
P.O. Box 211, Nakuru.   *Tel: 2695*
  Began in 1966 by the World Gospel Mission.

Bible College of East Africa (IBPFM)
Principal: Dr. William Hawkes
Mirema Estate, on Lumumba Drive, Ruaraka
P.O. Box 41140, Nairobi.   *Tel: Ruaraka 2337*

Bible Churchmen's Missionary Society (BCMS)
Field Representative: The Ven. Howell Davies
Archdeacon's Office: on main road
P.O. Box 62, Maseno.
  In 1922 the BCMS was founded in London in a protest
against alleged modernism in the (Anglican) Church Missionary
Society, and to witness to the Scriptural and reformed character
of the Church's faith. Work in Kenya began in 1931, and the
Society has pioneered missions and linguistic work among the
Pokot, Turkana, Samburu, Boran and other northern tribes.
There are now around 40 missionaries and associates, the
majority working in the Diocese of Nakuru. There is a mobile
medical unit operating from Marsabit.

Bible Society of Kenya
Executive Secretary: The Rev. David M. Gitari; Promotion &
  Information Officer: Mr. Elija Thuu
P.O. Box 72983, Nairobi.   *Tel: 25587, 27338*
  Chama cha Biblia cha Kenya. From the earliest days of
Protestant missions in Kenya, the BFBS (and later ABS) assisted
in translation and publication of the Scriptures in Kenya's
languages. In 1962, the Bible Society in East Africa was formed,
and in 1970 the Bible Society of Kenya. All scriptures are sold
at subsidised prices that people can afford, as a result of
overseas subsidies (and local donations amounting to 2.9% of
total budget in 1971). Local donors (churches and individual
Christians) can become associate members, full members, or life
members, or part of a group membership. Local support and
interest is encouraged by a network of Bible Society Auxiliaries
throughout the country.
  Distribution from Bible House in Kenya for the years 1966-
1971 was as follows:

Year	Portions	Selections	New Testaments	Bibles	Totals
1966	220,323	89,113	39,776	43,615	392,836
1967	509,110	207,902	71,012	52,571	840,595
1968	638,273	278,961	98,579	48,063	1,063,876
1969	493,238	181,124	78,281	54,935	807,578
1970	623,653	245,036	76,866	51,892	997,447
1971	515,591	507,986	72,866	59,724	1,156,167

(Note: There are many factors involved in rising or falling
numbers. A drop in numbers does not necessarily indicate
declining demand, since many versions sell out and cannot be
immediately reprinted). A detailed table giving details of dates
of publication and 1971 sales of Scriptures in Kenya's languages
is given on p. 99.

Boys' Brigade (BB)
Training and Organising Secretary: Mr. John P. Chappell
HQ: off Applecross Road, Lavington
P.O. Box 25190, Nairobi.   *Tel: 48763*
  A British organisation founded in 1883, and begun in Kenya
in the 1940s, and re-organised in 1967; a uniformed Christian
youth movement for 'the advancement of Christ's Kingdom
among boys, and the promotion of habits of obedience,
reverence, discipline, self-respect and all that tends towards a
true Christian manliness'. The BB admits boys from 12 to 19
years (and 8 - 11 years in a Junior Section). Drill, first-aid,
athletics, swimming, physical education, camping, music, drama,
badges and awards. In Kenya, there are 70 Companies with
3,000 members in the major denominations. Branches:

Coast District Chairman: Mr. Johnstone Bwenye, Jibana
  Tsunguni, P.O. Kaloleni, Mombasa
Meru District Chairman: Mr. William Kithara, P.O. Box 67,
  Meru.
Chogoria Chairman: Mr. Ludwin J. Mwirukire, P.O. Chogoria,
  Meru.
Eldoret/Kitale Chairman: Mr. Moses Cherop, P.O. Box 812,
  Eldoret.

Brackenhurst Baptist Assembly
Director: Mr. Dallas L. Bateman
Tigoni
P.O. Box 32, Limuru.   *Tel: Tigoni 529*
  Opened in 1964 as a Christian conference centre owned and
operated by the BMEA, catering to all denominational and
interdenominational groups.

British & Foreign Bible Society (BFBS)
  The first of the modern Bible societies, this body based in
London has been responsible for most of the Scripture transla-
tions to date in Kenya, and now co-operates with the Bible
Society of Kenya.

Broadcasting and Audio Visual Services (BRAVS)
  An organisation of the All Africa Conference of Churches,
formerly with an office in Nairobi, now only in Ilesha and
Ibadan, Nigeria. In 1972 BRAVS has been absorbed into the
new AACC programme cluster on Communication, Interpretation, Training and Information.

Brothers of Christian Schools
Director
P.O. Box 25, Nyeri.
  An institute of Catholic missionary brothers.

Brothers of Our Lady of Mercy, see Congregation of
  Fraters of Our Lady

Brothers of St. Francis Xavier
Provincial Delegate
Xaverian Brothers
P.O. Box 100, Maragoli.
  An institute of Catholic missionary brothers.

Brothers of St. Joseph (Kisumu)
The Rev. Brother Superior
P.O. Box 127, Kakamega.
  An indigenous (Kenyan) society of Catholic brothers.

Brothers of St. Joseph (Nyeri)
Superior: The Rev. Fr. Stephen Wambugu
P.O. Box 25, Nyeri.
  An indigenous (Kenyan) society of Catholic brothers.

Brothers of St. Patrick
Brother Ambrose
St. Patrick's Secondary School
P.O. Iten, Eldoret.
  An institute of Catholic missionary brothers.

Brothers of St. Peter Claver
Superior: The Rev. Fr. F. Egan
Catholic Mission, Kaumoni
Private Bag, Machakos.
  An indigenous society of brothers which began in 1953,
emphasising educational work, technical schools, agriculture,
carpentry, building, mechanics, printing. Now 15 professed
members, 8 novices, 11 postulants.

Campus Crusade for Christ International
Representative: Mr. Gary Fredricks
P.O. Box 21296, Nairobi (& P.O. Box 60, Kijabe).

Canadian Baptist Overseas Mission Board
Missionary representative: The Rev. William J.D. Lewis
ACC&S Church, Gituru (4miles from AIC Githumu)
P.O. Box 291, Thika.
  A mission from Canada (217 St. George Street, Toronto 180,
Ontario, Canada) invited to assist them by the independent
African Christian Church and Schools. The first two couples
arrived in Kenya in December 1970; eight missionaries by 1972.

Carmelite Nuns
Prioress: Mother Ann Petros
Mount Carmel Convent, St. Austins Road
P.O. Box 40958, Nairobi.   *Tel: 48465*

Carpentry School
Director: The Rev. Fr. William Pollard
Lorugumu Catholic Mission
Private Bag, Kitale.

Catechetical Training Centre (Diocese of Mombasa)
Director: The Rev. Brian Carey
Catholic Mission, Bura
P.O. Bura, Voi.

Catechist Training Centre (Diocese of Kisumu)
Director: The Rev. Fr. Ed Karhof
Catholic Mission, Mumias
P.O. Box 75, Mumias.

Catechists' Training Centre (Diocese of Nyeri)
Director: The Rev. Fr. Seraphim Dal Pont
Mugoiri
P.O. Box 44, Murang'a.

Cathedral Parish Co-operative Savings & Credit Society
Chairman: Mr. David Mwangi
Office behind main street
P.O. Box 608, Nyeri.
   Begun in 1967; 1,000 members.

Cathedral Secretarial College (Diocese of Nyeri)
Principal: Sr. Josephine
Consolata Sisters (next to cathedral and bishop's house)
P.O. Box 288, Nyeri.

Catholic Action
Director: The Rev. Fr. A. Gorzegno
Mathari Catholic Mission
P.O. Box 25, Nyeri.   *Tel: 2462*
   A few Catholic dioceses have adopted this movement for
secondary school students, which is based on the principle of
'See, judge and act'; the strongest groups are in the Diocese of
Nyeri, with many members.

Catholic Bookshop
Manager: The Rev. Fr. T. Barron
Cathedral Grounds
P.O. Box 84850, Mombasa.   *Tel: 23953*

Catholic Bookshop
Manager: The Rev. Fr. S.J. Grogan
York Street (behind Holy Family Cathedral)
P.O. Box 30249, Nairobi.   *Tel: 25172*
   Begun around 1940 and moved into its present premises in
1968, this is the largest Catholic bookshop in the world outside
the USA, carrying 15,000 titles (including many Protestant
ones), which is more than bookshops in Catholic countries take
Italy or Ireland. Schools of all kinds in Kenya are supplied.

Catholic Enquiry Centre
Director: The Rev. Fr. Michael O'Donnell
St. Austin's Road
P.O. Box 14600, Nairobi.   *Tel: 60349*
   The only such centre in East Africa, it was begun in 1958.
The Centre sends a free course of 10 booklets in English
covering the chief aspects of Catholicism to enquirers, with 600
envelopes a week posted. Enquirers average 2,300 a year.

Catholic Forum
Chairman: Mr. William Maeke
Meetings: University Chaplaincy Centre, State House Road
P.O. Box 73714, Nairobi.   *Tel: 21613/4*
   A lay organisation to provide a stimulus to modern Catholic
thinking, formerly registered under the title Association of
Catholic Graduates and Professionals of Kenya; discussions,
lectures, films.

Catholic hospitals, see Hospitals

Catholic Lay Council of Kenya
Chairman: Mr. Peter Nyakiamo

Catholic Secretariat, Hughes Building, Kenyatta Avenue
P.O. Box 48062, Nairobi.   *Tel: 21613/4*
   Begun in 1968 as National Lay Council; co-ordinates
activities of Catholic lay organisations, promotes lay/hierarchical
co-operation.

Catholic Printing Press
Director: The Rev. Fr. A. Camillo
Mathari Mission
P.O. Box 25, Nyeri.   *Tel: 2462*

Catholic Prisons Chaplaincy
Senior Catholic Chaplain to Prisons: The Rev. Fr. E. Lawless
Office: Department of Prisons, Bishop's Road
P.O. Box 30175, Nairobi.   *Tel: 29001 Ext. 11*
   For further details, see Kenya Prisons Chaplaincy.

Catholic Relief Services (CRS)
Director: Mr. Matthew C. Heim
Adelaide & Sclaters Road
P.O. Box 49675, Nairobi.   *Tel: 61291*
   The Kenya Program of Catholic Relief Services of USCC
(United States Catholic Conference) was begun in 1964, and
handles direct relief operations, social and economic devel-
opment projects, health, education and welfare work.

Catholic Scouts Society (Scoutists)
General Secretary: The Rev. Fr. J. James
Office 443, Church House, Government Road
P.O. Box 40344, Nairobi.   *Tel: 23323*

Catholic Secretariat, see Kenya Catholic Secretariat

Catholic University Chaplaincy
Chaplain: The Rev. Fr. Patrick Astor
St. Paul's Chapel, Uhuru Highway & University Way
P.O. Box 41512, Nairobi.   *Tel: 60333*
   Begun in 1957, serving the pastoral needs of about 1,000
Catholic staff and students at the University of Nairobi.

CCM Catechist Training Centre
Principal: The Rev. Fr. Michael Musso
Maralal Catholic Church
P.O. Maralal.
   Chuo cha Wakufunzi wa Dini. A centre begun in 1969 for
training catechists in the Diocese of Marsabit. In the first 2-year
course, 16 were trained, another 11 by 1972.

CCM Technical School
Principal: Br. Giuseppe Zenker
Catholic Mission, Marsabit
P.O. Marsabit, Isiolo.
   A Catholic school with 70 trainees learning masonry, carp-
entry, tanning, leatherwork, plumbing. Some catechists have
also learned a trade here.

Center for Religious Research
Secretary: The Rev. Dr. Malcolm J. McVeigh
Church House (7th floor), Government Road
P.O. Box 14728, Nairobi.   *Tel: 23649, 61303*
   Linked with Unit of Research in production of *Kenya
Churches Handbook,* inter alia.

Central Africa Christian Council (CACC)
Chairman: The Rt. Rev. A. Matthew Ajuoga
Dala Hera, Kibos Road
P.O. Box 782, Kisumu.
   An inter-territorial council of Bible-based churches, affiliated
to the International Council of Christian Churches (Amsterdam,
Netherlands).

Changamwe Baptist Centre
Secretary
P.O. Box 82925, Mombasa.   *Tel: 73347*

Charles New Methodist Church
Minister: The Rev. Zabulon Nthamburi
Charles New Road, Ofafa
P.O. Box 47633, Nairobi.
   Opened in 1967 for Meru-speaking Methodists in Nairobi.

Child Evangelism Fellowship

Missionary: The Rev. Herbert Lyon
Sayed Road, Nairobi South 'C'
P.O. Box 47266, Nairobi.   *Tel: 58141*
An international service organisation (Grand Rapids, Michigan, USA) begun in 1936 to assist churches reach children with Gospel, primarily through Bible classes called Good News Clubs, and training classes for potential volunteer teachers.

Children's Church (Christ Church, Westlands)

Lay Reader in charge: Mr. John Ellison
Church Road, Westlands
P.O. Box 43387, Nairobi.   *Tel: 48477*
Anglican and Protestant chaplaincy to Loretto Convent, Msongari, and St. Mary's School, specialising in children's ministry and family worship.

Children's Home (Testimony Faith Homes)

Ramula
P.O. Box 133, Maseno.

Chogoria Hospital (PCEA)

Medical Superintendent: Dr. Andrew Young
Chogoria Mission (50 miles from Meru)
P.O. Chogoria, Meru.
Begun in 1922, this is the largest of the 3 PCEA hospitals, with 200 beds.

Christian Book Centre (AIC)

Manager: Mr. B. Chemoiywa
P.O. Box 545, Eldoret.

Christian Businessmen's Committee, see City Businessmen's Group

Christian Challenge

Chairman: Mr. Charles Muchai
St. Joseph's Secondary School
P.O. Box 202, Kiambu.
A Catholic organisation to spread the love of God among young people, especially those who have left school.

Christian Children's Fund (CCF)

An international body which began aid in Kenya in 1960, assisting a primary school and children.

Christian Churches' Educational Association (CCEA)

Secretary-General: Mr. Richard O. Ondeng
Church House (3rd floor), Government Road
P.O. Box 45009, Nairobi.   *Tel: 22312*
Founded in 1957 to preserve and maintain Christian teaching in schools and colleges, to co-ordinate the churches' work in education, to set up standards, to assist the churches in their dealings with government, to produce RE syllabuses and other materials. Membership: 15 Protestant denominations, 6 teachers' colleges, 59 secondary schools. The CCEA does not sponsor schools itself (except for a handful of jointly-sponsored ones), but it acts on behalf of the denominations, which sponsor 2,613 primary schools and 149 Anglican and Protestant *harambee* secondary schools. Control is by a council meeting four times a year, which has set up an RE Committee and a Curriculum Development Programme. There are District Committees in all districts meeting three times a year.

Christian Council of Kenya, see National Christian Council of Kenya

Christian Education Committee (Diocese of Nairobi)

Chairman: Mr. W. Ochieng'
P.O. Box 40502, Nairobi.   *Tel: 20207*

Christian Education Department (AIC)

Director: The Rev. R. Coon
P.O. Box 49, Machakos.   *Tel: 65*

Christian Education Department (PAG)

Director
Goibei Mission PAG (14 miles from Nyang'ori)
P.O. Box 1828, Kisumu.

A large department catering for all aspects of Christian education in the Pentecostal Assemblies of God, including the 5-12 years age group (Crusaders) and the 13-35 years age group (Christ's Ambassadors).

Christian Fellowship Centre

Manager: Mr. Christopher Munyasia
Anderson Road
P.O. Box 770, Kisumu.   *Tel: 2396*
Operated by the NCCK; accommodation available.

Christian Hostels Fellowship (CHF)

Chairman: The Rev. Peter G. Ward
Pumwani Boys Hostel, St. John's Church, Pumwani
P.O. Box 30035 and 72636, Nairobi.   *Tel: 53634*
Begun in 1969 to provide inexpensive accommodation for secondary school students and young workers. Linked with Lee Abbey Friends (Britain) as a fund-raising body.

Christian Industrial Training Centre (CITC)

Principal: Mr. Tom Fisher (CMS)
Buxton Road
P.O. Box 82012, Mombasa.   *Tel: 20273*

Christian Industrial Training Centre (CITC)

Principal: Mr. Anthony H. Idle
Meru Road, Pumwani
P.O. Box 72935, Nairobi.   *Tel: 24763*
Begun in 1959 by the Rev. Charles Tett (CMS) as the first of three CITCs in Kenya, training primary school-leavers, unable to enter secondary schools, for employment in industry. 1,000 boys have been trained to the end of 1971. There are 2,000 applications a year, but only 144 students can be accommodated (two-year course).

CITC Secretarial College

Principal: Miss. A.P. Wilding
Bonyo Road
P.O. Box 1437, Kisumu.   *Tel: 3046 (Students 2220)*
The third CITC begun by CMS in 1969 (after Nairobi and Mombasa), to train girls (Form 4 leavers) as secretaries, copytypists, stenographers. Intake capacity: 50 day students, one year full-time course June-May.

Christian Literature & Bible Centre

Director
Thika Road
P.O. Box 45887, Nairobi.   *Tel: Ruaraka 2327*

Christian Literature Centre (AGC)

Manager: Mr. J. Tonui
Temple Road
P.O. Box 161, Kericho.   *Tel: 161*

Christian Rural Extension Scheme

Director: Captain David Kinyanjui
Berea Farm and Mission
Private Bag, Nakuru.   *Tel: Bahati 262*
Begun in 1968 by the Anglican Diocese of Nakuru to raise the standard of living of rural workers through groups, 4K clubs, mobile unit (films); supported by World Neighbours.

Christian Rural Fellowship of East Africa

Secretary: The Rev. R.M. Spurin
Khasoko Village Polytechnic
P.O. Box 46, Bungoma.
An interdenominational (Catholic and Protestant) body founded in 1968 to unite all Christians working in rural development. Annual conference for study and fellowship. 200 members in Kenya, Uganda and Tanzania.

Christians at Work

Chairman: Mr. Abednego Ongoma
P.O. Box 72304, Nairobi.   *Tel: 29708/9*
A fellowship of Christians begun in 1966 under the auspices of the Kenya Students Christian Fellowship, which now independently organises conferences, lunch-time meetings, and weekend street meetings in villages. Large membership.

Christian Science Committee on Publication
Chairman: Lady Erskine
Reading Room and Library, University Way
P.O. Box 40132, Nairobi. *Tel: 53331*

Christian Science Monitor
Representative: Mr. F. Hunter
Riverside Paddocks
P.O. Box 43795, Nairobi. *Tel: 53331*

Christian Science Reading Room
Chief Librarian: Mrs. F. Hunter
University Way
P.O. Box 30115, Nairobi. *Tel: 21498*

Christian Social League
Corresponding Secretary: Marta Karwitha (CDO, Meru)
Catholic Mission, Nkubu
P.O. Box 16, Meru.
An association of lay Catholics in the Diocese of Meru for the promotion of social projects, farming schemes, etc.

Christian Student Leadership Centre
Project Chairman: The Rev. Jose Chipenda
University Chaplaincy Centre, State House Road
P.O. Box 48802, Nairobi. *Tel: 26737, 23649*
A project supported by the major churches in Kenya (Catholic, Anglican, Protestant) for the training of students in the University of Nairobi in development, responsibility and leadership in church and state.

Christian Students Council (CSC)
Co-Secretaries: Mr. Gerhard Dilschneider, Miss Christina Odiemo
Limuru Conference Centre
P.O. Box 212, Limuru (& P.O. Box 14783, Nairobi). Tel: Tigoni 347, 443
An interdenominational and inter-organisational body begun in 1968 to link together students (school, college, university, seminary) from differing backgrounds in joint programmes of united prayer, study, service and action. Conferences, work camps, national seminars are held regularly.

Christian Union, University of Nairobi (CU)
Chairman:(student elected annually)
Men's Halls of Residence, State House Road
P.O. Box 30344, Nairobi.
Begun in 1956, the CU has been the major Protestant student-organised Christian body in the University of Nairobi (formerly Royal Technical College), with as objects: strengthening of Spiritual life, witness, service. In 1971-2, 118 registered members. Friday attendance: 200. A Mission to the University was held in 1967, 1970, and every three years.

Christ's Ambassadors, see Pentecostal Assemblies of God (in Part IV)

Church Army Community Centre
Warden: Capt. G. Macharia
Jogoo Road (opposite St. Stephen's Church)
P.O. Box 72584, Nairobi. *Tel: 58253*
About 1,000 students a day attend primary, secondary, typing, book-keeping, and domestic science classes; also a day nursery school for destitute children.

Church Army in Eastern Africa (CA)
General Secretary: The Rev. Crispus Nzano
Jogoo Road (opposite St. Stephen's Church)
P.O. Box 72584, Nairobi. *Tel: 58253*
An Anglican evangelistic organisation begun in England in 1882 and in Nairobi in 1956, which now has 52 captains and 12 sisters, with 9 expatriates, working mainly in the Anglican province of Kenya but also in Uganda and Tanzania.

Church Army Training College
Principal: The Rev. Crispus Nzano; College Officer: Capt. Joseph Kasio
Jogoo Road (opposite St. Stephen's Church)
P.O. Box 72584, Nairobi. *Tel: 58253*
Opened in 1971 to train CA evangelists for Eastern Africa, in a two-year course: 10 men and 5 women.

Churches' Chaplaincy to the University Community (CCUC)
Hon. Secretary: The Rev. D.B. Barrett
Chaplaincy Centre, State House Road
P.O. Box 48802, Nairobi. *Tel: 26737, 23649*
The chaplaincy to the University of the Anglican and Protestant churches in Kenya was begun in 1962, and now has 40 member churches and organisations. Pastoral and evangelistic work is conducted by a Team Ministry of eight part-time workers from various denominations; on average 400 students attend the Sunday University Service, and 300 a week use the Chaplaincy Centre. The CCUC is sponsoring a new ecumenical project, the Christian Student Leadership Centre.

Church Commissioners for Kenya (CPK)
Chairman: The Archbishop of Kenya; Secretary: Mr. Joel K. Buku
Church House (5th floor), Government Road
P.O. Box 48822, Nairobi. *Tel: 25004*
Formed in 1957 as the Church Trust (renamed in 1962) as a company limited by guarantee and not having a share capital, serving the Anglican Church in Kenya. Objects: 'through its proper activities to assist in the spreading of the Gospel and the extension of Christ's Kingdom, and in furtherance of such objects to make a contribution inspired by the Spirit of Jesus Christ to religious, social, economic and cultural life of the people among whom it is established and whom it serves'. Each of the 6 Anglican dioceses in Kenya is represented by its bishop, one clergyman and one layman. These members (Church Commissioners) meet once a year; business is run by a board of governors which meets once a month. The company holds in trust all real properties of each diocese; acts as trustee for a number of schools and colleges of Anglican tradition; handles immigration and financial affairs of all expatriate Anglican workers; and owns and manages investment properties (including Church House, Nairobi) and financial holdings. Income is derived from these properties and other securities, and is applied exclusively for giving assistance to the dioceses, through which the objects of the company are achieved.

Church Guest House, see CPK Guest House

Church, Industry and Commerce Project, NCCK
(Mombasa)
General Secretary: The Rev. Josiah N. Magu
P.O. Box 82275, Mombasa. *Tel: 20172*

Church, Industry and Commerce Project, NCCK
(Nairobi)
Secretary: Mr. Ng'ang'a Njiraini
Church House (5th floor), Government Road
P.O. Box 45009, Nairobi. *Tel: 22264/5*

Church, Industry and Commerce Project, NCCK
(Nakuru)
General Secretary: Mr. Jochen Riess
P.O. Box 1655, Nakuru. *Tel: 2981*

Church Language School, see CPK Language School

Church Missionary Society (CMS)
CMS Representative: The Rev. John Ridout
Office: First Ngong Avenue off Bishop's Road
P.O. Box 40360, Nairobi. *Tel: 20147*
An Anglican society founded in 1799 which began work in Kenya in 1844 as 'a voluntary association of persons united in obedience to the call of God to proclaim the Gospel in all lands and to gather the people of all races into the fellowship of Christ's Church' (CMS Law 1). The Society serves in all six dioceses of the Church of the Province of Kenya, with 102 full missionaries (from UK, Australia and New Zealand), 5 associates, 46 YSAs (Youth Service Abroad), and a total of 227 Members.

Church of God Board of Publications
Director: The Rev. Samuel Wakhu
Kima Mission
P.O. Box 160, Maseno.

Church of God Bookshop
Manager: The Rev. Samuel Wakhu
Kima Mission
P.O. Box 160, Maseno.

Church of God Press
Editor-in-Chief: The Rev. Samuel Wakhu
Kima Mission
P.O. Box 160, Maseno.

Church Training Centre (CPK, Diocese of Nakuru)
Warden
Warden's House
P.O. Box 18, Kapsabet.   *Tel: 33*

Chwele & District Ecumenical Group
Contact: Capt. Dickson Juma (Salvation Army, Kuywa Section)
c/o Chebukaka Catholic Mission, Bokoli Location
P.O. Box 96, Bungoma.
    A local interdenominational grouping which holds united prayer services attended by all local churches (Anglicans, Friends, Catholics, Salvation Army, Baptists, PEFA, PAG, Assemblies of God, Maria Legio, etc.). See photograph on p.152.

Cistercian Order (OCSO)
Superior: The Rev. Father Abbot
Our Lady of Victory Abbey
P.O. Box 40, Lumbwa.   *Tel: 38Y8, 23Y8*
    The abbey was founded in 1956 by monks from Tilburg, Holland, of the Cistercian Order of strict obedience (OCSO), itself founded in 1098 at Citeaux, France, and propagated by St. Bernard of Clairvaux, with the aim of leading a strict contemplative life. Community at present: 32 members (two-thirds Africans).

City Businessmen's Group
Secretary: Mr. John Ellison
P.O. Box 43387, Nairobi.   *Tel: 58525*
    A group that has grown out of the CBMC (Christian Businessmen's Committee) begun in 1963 under the Kenya Christian Graduates Fellowship.

Cloistered Dominican Nuns
Prioress: Sr. Mary
Corpus Christi Monastery, Langata Road
P.O. Box 30589, Nairobi.   *Tel: Langata 598*
    Founded in 1965 as an autonomous monastery under the direct jurisdiction of the Master General of the Order of Preachers, by nuns from Connecticut, USA. Dedicated to the life of prayer. 8 nuns with perpetual vows, 1 nun with temporary vows, 3 novices.

CMS Guest House, see CPK Guest House

Coast Bible Institute (AIC)
Missionary Promoters: The Rev. Frank and Mrs. Frew (AIM)
Malindi Road, Nyali Estate
P.O. Box 81150, Mombasa.

Coast Bible School (CPK, Diocese of Mombasa)
Warden/Caretaker: Mr. Jeremiah Kamunyu
Makupa Road
P.O. Box 98294, Mombasa.
    Although there are no permanent teaching staff, the school is used for a variety of short courses. Accommodation may also be had.

Commission for Non-Christian Religions
Chairman: The Rev. Fr. John Monteiro
Makupa Catholic Parish
P.O. Box 80262, Mombasa.   *Tel: 23749*
    Founded by Catholic Bishop of Mombasa in 1971, to promote dialogue among Muslims, Christians and Hindus.

Committee for Adult Catechesis
Chairman: The Rev. Fr. Bruno Porcu
St. Thomas Aquinas Seminary, Langata
P.O. Box 30517, Nairobi.
    A group formed to produce a handbook for Catholic catechists.

Communications Department (Kenya Catholic Secretariat)
Communications Co-ordinators: Mr. John Irungu, Sr. Janice McLaughlin
(also: Broadcast Committee, Chairman: Mr. John Irungu)
Hughes Building (1st floor), Kenyatta Avenue
P.O. Box 48062, Nairobi.   *Tel: 21613/4*
    Begun in 1967 to co-ordinate the communications activities of the Catholic Church in broadcasting, press, information, and audio-visual activities, and to act as liaison with Voice of Kenya, Kenya News Agency, and the like. The Department has a Broadcast Committee of about 20 members and a National Communications Committee of about 70 members to assist it in these tasks.

Congregation of Fraters of Our Lady, Mother of Mercy
Regional Superior: Frater A.H. Verhoeven
Asumbi Mission
P.O. Box 668, Kisii.
    The Asumbi Brothers (Fraters of Tilburg) began work in Kenya in 1958, at Asumbi and Nyabururu Catholic missions. They run schools, Asumbi TTC, and two specialist centres: East African Braille Press, and the Vocational Training Centre for the Blind, both at Sikri. In 1971 there were 17 fraters at work.

Congregation of Our Lady of the Sacred Heart
Councillor-Director
Sacred Heart Brothers
P.O. Box 25, Nyeri.
    The Scared Heart Brothers are a Catholic institute of missionary brothers.

Congregation of the Holy Ghost (HGM, CSSp)
Superior: The Rev. Fr. N. Delaney
Monagea Road (off Sclater's Road), Westlands
P.O. Box 14621, Nairobi.   *Tel: 61083*
    The first Catholic mission to open permanent stations in Kenya (1889), and one of the three major missions (the other two being CCM and MHM), having been responsible for the areas in the present Dioceses of Mombasa and Machakos and the Archdiocese of Nairobi (in which, in 1971, HGM priests numbered respectively, 45, 38, and 74).

Consolata Catholic Mission (CCM, IMC)
Regional Superior: The Rev. Fr. Peter Baudena
Salisbury Road
P.O. Box 42118, Nairobi.   *Tel: 53597*
    A missionary congregation from Turin, Italy, with the name Istituto Missioni Consolata (named after a famous shrine), which began work in 1901 in Kenya at Tutho Mission, and now works in the Dioceses of Nyeri, Meru, Marsabit and Nairobi. Members of the congregation working in Kenya: 170.

Consolata Sisters (CCM, IMC)
Regional Superior: Mother Germana Tuninetti
Fifth Ngong Avenue
P.O. Box 48301, Nairobi.   *Tel: 26281*
    An Italian missionary congregation (Suore Missionarie della Consolata) from Turin, Italy, which began work in Kenya in 1913, with emphasis on evangelistic and social work in less developed areas. Members in Kenya: 238 in 5 Catholic dioceses (Nyeri 80, Meru 82, Nairobi 49, Marsabit 25, Mombasa 2). Branch addresses: P.O. Box 25, Nyeri; P.O. Box 129, Meru (Tel: 106); P.O. Box 368, Embu; P.O. Box 74, Isiolo.

Co-operative Savings and Credit Society
Field Officer: Sr. Antoinette-Rose Potvin (Catholic Relief Services)
Kenya House, Koinange Street
P.O. Box 49539, Nairobi.   *Tel: 23455 Ext. 2*
    Savings and credit societies at national and local levels have been begun in many countries of the world, with support and initiatives from the Catholic Church in most cases. Objects: to improve financial condition of members, assist saving, supply loans, etc. In Kenya, Catholic Relief Services has assisted many local Societies. The national society (above) works with the government Department of Co-operative Development, the Co-operative College of Kenya, and other bodies. This Directory

includes three examples of local savings and credit societies; see under Ahero, Cathedral Parish (Nyeri), and Shibuyi.

Council of East African Evangelist Societies of God
General Secretary: The Rev. Moses Asewe
Unity Building, Tom Mboya Street
P.O. Box 49217, Nairobi. *Tel: 24831*

An organisation reporting a membership of 10 societies and 1,000 persons, mainly Kikuyu, in 1970, whose objective is to collaborate with all churches in East Africa with regard to 'evangelisation, the World Council of Churches, the International Council of Christian Churches, T.L. Osborn organisation, etc'.

Council on Higher Studies in Religion
Chairman: The Rt. Rev. Professor S.C. Neill
University of Nairobi, College Road
P.O. Box 30197, Nairobi. *Tel: 34244*

A council set up in 1970 to develop all forms of higher studies in religion in Kenya; to serve as a centre for information on work in progress. Representatives of the University Senate, Dept. of Philosophy & Religious Studies, NCCK, KEC, seminaries and other bodies.

CPK Guest House (Church Guest House)
Warden: Miss Edna M. Collins; Asst. Warden: Mr. Joab Odhiambo
Bishop's Road
P.O. Box 48760, Nairobi. *Tel: 23011*

Founded in 1925 and named CMS Guest House until 1971, this is a boarding house for missionaries, church workers and Christian visitors to Kenya, with special terms to Anglican workers in Kenya; owned by the Church of the Province of Kenya. In 1970, 9,020 adult nights were provided (CMS personnel, 3,354; other Anglican personnel, 654; other missions, 3,860; others 1,152).

CPK Language & Orientation School
Principal: Mr. B. Owen Gumba
First Ngong Avenue
P.O. Box 49849, Nairobi. *Tel: 20992*

Begun in 1965 as CMS Language School, offering language and orientation courses to church workers of any denomination, in Swahili, Kikuyu, Luo, Luhya, Kamba, Maasai, English; now operated by CPK (Church of the Province of Kenya). 2,000 students over the last six years. Beginners and advanced courses of 2-15 weeks' duration.

Credit and Savings Societies of Kenya, see Co-operative
Savings and Credit Society

Crusaders
Secretary: Mr. John Ellison
Meeting place: Lenana School
P.O. Box 43387, Nairobi. *Tel: 48477*

Voluntary Sunday Bible classes for boys; part of the interdenominational Crusaders Union (UK), begun in Kenya in 1955, with 3 classes (Lenana School, Nairobi School, Nairobi Primary School; attendances, 75, 75, 100).

Crusaders, see Pentecostal Assemblies of God (in Part IV)

Dagoretti Children's Centre
Supervisor: Miss E.M. Shaw
Kikuyu Road, Karen
P.O. Box 24756, Nairobi. *Tel: Karen 2532*

A rehabilitation centre for physically handicapped disabled children, begun in 1953 by the Kiambu County Council and the Christian Council of Kenya, now run by the Kenya Red Cross Society. Sheltered workshop, nursery school welfare nurses training. Average number of children: 125.

Dala Hera, see Church of Christ in Africa (in Part IV)

Deeper Life Evangelism
Chairman: The Rev. George Washington Ohange
No. 23D, Uhuru Estate, Nairobi
P.O. Box 28118, Nairobi.

A pentecostal evangelistic organisation with mainly Luo members, working for revival and holiness of life; registered in 1972, with 171 members.

Department of Christian Communication (NCCK)
Secretary: Mr. Samuel Munyi
Church House (1st floor), Government Road
P.O. Box 45009, Nairobi. *Tel: 22264/5*

Department of Philosophy and Religious Studies
(University of Nairobi)
Head of Department: The Rt. Rev. Professor S.C. Neill
University of Nairobi, College Road
P.O. Box 30197, Nairobi. *Tel: 34244*

An academic department of the Faculty of Arts, begun in 1969, offering instruction with special reference to the Kenyan background; B.A. and higher degrees. Service courses in Faculties of Law and Education. Six full-time staff, 130 undergraduates.

Diocesan Missionary Associations, *see under* Maseno South, Mount Kenya, Nairobi

Diocese of Mombasa Book Centre (CPK)
Manager: Mr. Julius Riga
Nkrumah Road
P.O. Box 80072, Mombasa. *Tel: 24876*

Begun in 1970; there are also two other book centres and a mobile unit operating in the diocese.

Diocesan Literature Unit (Diocese of Maseno North)
Literature Worker: Capt. Moses Obatsa
P.O. Box 33, Butere.

Formed in 1969 for production of booklets, translation, distribution, training writers, colporteurs, literature workers.

Diocesan Literature Unit (Diocese of Maseno South)
Literature Worker: Mr. Roy Stafford
Church House
P.O. Box 380, Kisumu. *Tel: 2131*

Diocese of Maseno Dental Unit
Dental Surgeon in Charge
Bonyo Road
P.O. Box 380, Kisumu. *Tel: 2425*

An Anglican team begun in 1965 as a service over a large area, with a surgeon, two dental nurses, two technicians and a receptionist, offering all forms of dental treatment out of three surgeries.

Diocese of Mount Kenya Literature Committee
Secretary: Miss Jill Cossar
Kenyatta Avenue
P.O. Box 260, Murang'a.

Distribution of Christian literature through Arahuka Book Depot and mobile book van; literature production; diocesan newsletter *Arahuka* (Awake!).

Diocese of Nairobi Literature Committee
Literature Secretary: Miss Gwen Kerr
Office: Nairobi Diocesan Bookshop, Jogoo Road
P.O. Box 72125, Nairobi.

Diocese of Nakuru Boys' Centre (CPK)
Warden: Capt. G. Karanja
Diocesan Office, Lake Road
P.O. Box 1253, Nakuru.

A rehabilitation centre for homeless boys aged 7-13 years, begun in 1967, with accommodation for 25 boarders and 25 day boys.

Diocese of Nakuru Rural Service Department
Rural Development Worker: Mr. John P. Fowler
Elgon View Gardens, off Elgon View Road
P.O. Box 79, Eldoret. *Tel: 2051*

An Anglican MRI project, the Million Acre Settlement Scheme, supported by the Diocese of Chichester (UK), with work in various parts of Nakuru Diocese (20 projects in Rift Valley Province; see elsewhere in this Directory): Rural Aid Mission, Njabini RTC, village polytechnics, Lugari Extension Programme, Christian Rural Service, Christian Rural Extension Scheme.

Diocese of Nakuru Social Welfare Department (CPK)

Chairman, Social Welfare Committee: Mr. S. Ojuka
Diocesan Office, Lake Road
P.O. Box 1253, Nakuru.

Discalced Carmelite Nuns

Superior (Prioress): The Rev. Mother Anne Petros
Mount Carmel Convent, off Tara Road West (St. Austin's)
P.O. Box 40958, Nairobi.   *Tel: 48465*
    Cloistered, contemplative order of nuns begun in Spain in
1939. The Nairobi Convent has 19 sisters of three different
races.

Discalced Carmelite Nuns

Superior: The Rev. Mother Ann Marie
Tindinyo Carmel
P.O. Kaimosi.
    The second Carmel (Carmelite community) in Kenya, begun
in 1956; 8 African and 4 other sisters. Cloistered con-
templatives, supporting life of prayer by sewing, gardening and
other tasks.

Dominican Nuns (enclosed), see Cloistered Dominican Nuns

Dr. Barnado's Homes, see Thomas Barnado House

Dutch Ursuline Sisters

Sister-in-charge: Sr. Renata
P.O. Box 127, Kakamega.   *Tel: 32*
    An order of nuns from Bergen, Holland, invited in 1928 into
the Vicariate of Kisumu, doing catechetical work, teaching,
needlework, medical work, midwifery training, school for the
deaf. In 1932 they began the Sisterhood of the Sisters of Mary,
formally approved by the Holy See in 1952.

East Africa Christian Alliance (EACA)

General Secretary: The Rev. S. Muthukya
Mercury House (1st floor), Tom Mboya Street
P.O. Box 72681, Nairobi.   *Tel: 28280*
    A council of Protestant, Bible-centred churches in Kenya
begun in 1965; opposed to ecumenical movement, and affiliated
to the International Council of Christian Churches (headquarters: Amsterdam, Holland).

East Africa Ministries (CGEA)

Co-ordinator: The Rev. Douglas E. Welch
Caledonian Road
P.O. Box 47236, Nairobi.   *Tel: 67012*
    Formerly the Missionary Board of the Church of God
(Anderson, USA), which began work in Kenya in 1905, and
which now exists as a service organisation for overseas personnel
sent by the Missionary Board to serve in the Church of God in
East Africa. 20 missionaries, 7 Sunday-school teachers, 2
doctors, 7 nurses, 2 seconded to other bodies. At the beginning
of 1972, mission property and institutions were formally handed
over to the CGEA.

East African Braille Press

Manager: Frater Th. C.M.J. van Rooij
Sikri
P.O. Box 285, Kisii.
    A Catholic enterprise begun at Aluor and moved in 1970 to
a new building at Sikri; specialises in printed materials for the
blind in the Braille language (reading by feeling raised dots on
paper).

East African Consultation on Church Union

Chairman: The Rev. Johana Mbogori
P.O. Box 42726, Nairobi.   *Tel: 26117*
    Formed in 1961 to take further the fifty years of church
union negotiations between Anglican and Protestant churches.
The Consultation foundered after its 1968 Dodoma Conference
largely because it was no longer feasible to discuss uniting
churches in the two separate nations of Kenya and Tanzania. In
1972, the PCEA withdrew in order to seek other ways to unity.
For a description and background, see paper by J. Nyesi in the
Bibliography.

East Africa Religious Education Committee (EAREC)

Chairman: The Rev. Dr. Donald R. Jacobs; Secretary: Miss
    Audrey McKim
CCEA Office, Church House, Government Road
P.O. Box 45009, Nairobi.   *Tel: 22312*
    Formed in 1965 by the Protestant churches of Kenya,
Uganda and Tanzania to co-ordinate religious education, syll-
abuses and teaching materials. Related to JEAREC (Joint, with
Catholics).

East African Religious Films Library

Secretary: The Rev. Clive Boddington
CPK Houses, Bishop's Road
P.O. Box 72361, Nairobi.   *Tel: 25027*
    A small library begun in 1952, now operated jointly with the
NCCK Film Library. Consists of 38 religious films specialising
in Moody science topics.

East African Revival Fellowship (Brethren, Balokole)

(No executives; informal organisation by local, district and
    provincial Teams)
No central office nor address: local fellowships can be contacted
    through pastors and heads of churches.
Fellowship Meeting in Nairobi: second Sunday of the month,
    2.30 p.m., St. Stephen's Church, Jogoo Road, Nairobi.
    Revival broke out in the Kingdom of Ruanda in 1929, within
the CMS mission's work, and the Balokole (Luganda for 'The
Saved Ones') reached Kenya in 1937. Subsequently it has
extended throughout East Africa. The Revival Fellowship is not
an organised body, but consists of Christians living lives of
committed discipleship, and sharing those lives in close fellowship. Most pastors in the Anglican, Presbyterian and Methodist
churches are members, and local fellowship groups meet weekly,
usually in church buildings.
    A major feature of the Revival over the years has been the
mass convention meetings held for several days at a time, on
average every two years. These have always been arranged on an
East Africa-wide basis. Programmes and arrangements are
unstructured, and are usually decided in fellowship by group
decisions of Team Meetings in which laymen have larger
influence than clergy. Each province in Kenya has its Team
Meeting, meeting quarterly or monthly to deal with such
matters, such as the Central Fellowship Meeting which serves
brethren in Central Province and Nairobi.
    In addition to East Africa-wide conventions in Uganda and
Tanzania, the following major nation-wide conventions have
been held in Kenya:

Year	Place	Attendance
1947	Kahuhia	3,000
1948	Kagaari	5,000
1949	Kabete	15,000
1950	Kikuyu	15,000
1951	Maseno	6,000
1955	Chogoria	6,000
1956	Maseno II	12,000
1958	Kahuhia II	6,000
1960	Tumutumu	5,000
1961	Butere	7,000
1964	Mombasa	20,000
1965	Kitui	5,000
1966	Meru	10,000
1967	Kabare	5,000
1969	Wundanyi	10,000
1970	Kikuyu II	30,000
1971	Mumias	6,000

    For further details, see article by G.K. Mambo in Part I of
this *Handbook.*

East African United Churches and Orthodox Coptic Communion

Chairman: Bishop Lucas M. Nuhu
Head Office: General Building Contractors, Jeevanjee Street
P.O. Box 47909, Nairobi.   *Tel: 25217*
    One of the largest and initially most promising of the many
attempts to unify or federate all indigenous independent

264

churches in Kenya. Begun around 1962, it claimed to have 8 million followers in 32 member denominations, and in 1964 claimed as its four sub-groups the Kenya Independent Churches Fellowship, Kikuyu Independent Churches (AIPC), Kenya African United Christian Churches, and African Orthodox Communion. The EAUC announced it was hoping to create 'a state church', and drew up elaborate rules: '3 priests can ordain a priest, 8 priests can consecrate a bishop', and 'The Council of Bishops will not allow any splinter group [to break off]'. Among the members claimed in 1964 were AICN, AOC, ABC, CCA, KFPC, ACHS, HGCK, Ruwe HGC, Nomiya Luo Church, Legio Maria Church, Christian Divine Church, Holy Spirit Church of Zion. Unfortunately, the benefits of membership were not apparent, and member churches began to withdraw their support.

East African Venture Company (EAVC)
Secretary (and Editor, TARGET): Mr. Odhiambo Okite
Mercury House, Tom Mboya Street
P.O. Box 72839, Nairobi.   *Tel: 24437*
    A newspaper publishing company begun in 1964, in association with the CCK (now NCCK) and CCT (Christian Council of Tanzania), which operates as a specialised communications arm of the church in East Africa, to stimulate discussion on matters of public interest such as development. Through its two fortnightly newspapers TARGET (English: circulation, 17,000) and LENGO (Swahili: circulation, 23,000), the church 'speaks for the voiceless and underprivileged and makes this medium the common property of the people'. Staff (editor, sub-editors, reporters, and others): 18. TARGET and LENGO now each contain a separate educational supplement called, respectively, TORCH and NURU.

Eastern Mennonite Board, see Mennonite Board in EA

Eastleigh Community Centre (PCEA)
Director: Mr. K. Njuguna
2nd Avenue, Eastleigh
P.O. Box 72330, Nairobi.   *Tel: 50085*

Ecumenical Programme for Emergency Action in Africa
    A former programme of the All Africa Conference of Churches which in 1970 was merged into the Department of Service of the AACC.

Ecumenical Institute in Africa
    A short-lived overseas extension of the Ecumenical Institute, USA, which operated courses for a time in 1968, based on Limuru Conference Centre and Kenyatta College.

Edelvale Trust, see Sisters of Charity of Edelvale

Education Department (Kenya Catholic Secretariat)
Education Secretary: The Rev. Fr. Joachim Getonga
Hughes Building (1st floor), Kenyatta Avenue
P.O. Box 48062, Nairobi.   *Tel: 21613/4*
    Co-ordinates Catholic-sponsored schools and liases with the Teachers Service Commission, the Ministry of Education and the Christian Churches' Educational Association (CCEA).

Edward Tei Evangelistic Society
Chairman: Evangelist Edward Tei
P.O. Box 95069, Mombasa.
    One of several evangelistic associations formed to sponsor evangelism; 15 Luo members (evangelists). Chairman is also the chairman of a Luo independent denomination, Power of Jesus Around the World Church.

Eldoret Centre (GFF)
Missionary in charge: Mr. Robert Munce
P.O. Box 322, Eldoret.   *Tel: 2531*

Eldoret Churches Unity
Secretary: The Rev. W. Welime (RCEA)
HQ, RCEA: Kisumu Road
P.O. Box 99, Eldoret.   *Tel: 2665*
    An interdenominational committee for ecumenical co-operation.

Eldoret Diocese Communications Team
Secretary: The Rev. Fr. Terry Nash
Plateau Road
P.O. Box 71, Eldoret.   *Tel: 2432*

Eldoret Junior Seminary, see Mater Apostolorum Minor Seminary

Elim Evangelistic Church (PEFA)
Pastor
Jomo Kenyatta Avenue
P.O. Box 82627, Mombasa.   *Tel: 26132*

Elim Missionary Assemblies (EMA)
Field Secretary: The Rev. Milburn J. Sickler
Elim Evangelistic Church, Makupa Roundabout, Jomo Kenyatta Avenue
P.O. Box 82627, Mombasa.   *Tel: 26132, 24316*
    A ministerial fellowship begun in 1924 with headquarters in Lima, New York, USA, which began work in South Nyanza in 1941, and whose work was merged with IPA in 1962 to form the Pentecostal Evangelistic Fellowship of Africa.

Emmaus Bible School
Director: Mr. Bert Banzhaf
Richmond House, Jeevanjee Street
P.O. Box 72725, Nairobi.   *Tel: 25934*
    Founded in Toronto, Canada, in 1941; and in Nairobi in 1952 as (1) a Bible Correspondence School (10,000 active correspondence students in East Africa in 5 languages (pass rate: 85%), 2,000 new courses issued a month; total since 1952, 100,000); (2) Radio Bible School begun in 1968 on Voice of Kenya; (3) Mobile Bible School, showing films, Bible teaching seminars, workshops.

English Ursuline Sisters
The Reverend Mother
Kyeni
P.O. Embu.

Ethiopian Orthodox Holy Spirit & United Churches of EA
Chairman: Bishop Lucas M. Nuhu
Munishram Building, Jeevanjee Street
P.O. Box 47909, Nairobi.   *Tel: 25217*
    An organisation founded in 1970 in the endeavour to unite African independent churches in East Africa.

Evangel Bible Courses, see Evangel Outreach

Evangelical Fellowship of Kenya
    In 1970 the Evangelical Fellowship of East Africa was dissolved in order to permit the formation of separate fellowships in each nation, which would be members of AEAM (Association of Evangelicals of Africa and Madagascar). By 1972 the Kenya body had not yet been organised.

Evangelical Literature Fellowship of East Africa (ELFEA)
Chairman: Mr. Odhiambo Okite; Secretary: Mr. Samwel Magessa
Office: Bible House, Jeevanjee Street
P.O. Box 28567, Nairobi.   *Tel: 27070*
    A fellowship of Christian literature workers (12 publishers, 6 printers, artists, 6 distributors, 4 newspapers) begun in 1960. Seven-day annual conference.

Evangelical Missionary Society of Finland
Representative: Miss Taina Korpivara
Matongo Health Centre
P.O. Sondu.
    A Finnish-speaking mission, with 3 women missionaries working in the Lutheran Church in Kenya.

Evangelische Gemeinde Deutschersprache in Kenya
Pastor: The Rev. Walter Hildebrandt
Riverside Drive (services in Lutheran Church, Uhuru Highway & University Way)
P.O. Box 47094, Nairobi.   *Tel: 53030*
    A pastoral service to German-speaking Lutherans in Kenya and Tanzania.

Evangelistic Sponsors Association

Chairman: Mr. Joseph H. Charo; Pastor: The Rev. Samson Kitsao
Office: Old Buxton School (Block M), Buxton Road, Mombasa
P.O. Box 405, Malindi.

Mfuko wa Injili. A Coast organisation formerly known as Africa Evangelistic Fund Association until 1967, reporting 23 members in 1970, whose aims are 'to propagate the Full Gospel, to support ministers', and allied objectives.

Evangel Outreach

Director: Mr. Shem K. Omolo
Nyang'ori Mission (PAG)
P.O. Box 969, Kisumu.   *Tel: Nyang'ori 1Y5*

A department within Evangel Publishing House begun in 1964, with (1) Evangel Tract Fellowship (distribution of free tracts), (2) Evangel Bible Correspondence Courses, (3) Evangel Book Club, (4) Outreach Evangelism (mobilisation of youth into teams). Mailed-in coupons indicate 500 conversions monthly; 2,300 active enrolled students. The major course is All Nations Bible Correspondence Course, or, Masomo ya Biblia kwa Mataifa Yote (12 lessons, in Swahili or English).

Evangel Publishing House (EPH)

General Manager: The Rev. Cal R. Bombay
Business office: P.O. Box 969, Kisumu (Tel: Nyang'ori 1Y5)
Editorial Office: Bible House (top floor), Jeevanjee Street, Nairobi.
P.O. Box 28567, Nairobi.   *Tel: 27070*

Christian publishing house begun in 1964 by PAG (PAOC), for books, newspapers, Bible correspondence courses, other literature, throughout Africa (English, Swahili, French and other languages). 35 new titles published in 1971, 260 customers (bookshops, churches) in 23 African nations, making this the largest religious publisher in Africa.

Every Home Evangelism

National Director: Mr. Elijah F. Akhahenda
Leslander House, Haile Selassie Avenue
P.O. Box 72933, Nairobi.   *Tel: 25702*

An interdenominational Christian literature organisation begun in 1964 as Every Home Crusade, sponsored by World Literature Crusade (USA). House-to-house tract distribution (8,845 individually placed so far, in homes, schools, prisons, hospitals); 367,429 enquirers to date, of whom 131,000 have completed a correspondence course, and 184,000 are at present enrolled. Monthly periodical *Pray* circulated in English, Swahili and Luo: circulation 30,000. Parallel organisations with nationals as directors in Tanzania, Uganda, Zambia, Rhodesia, and 100 other nations. The former Kenya director, Mr. Barack Odhiambo, is now Continental Director for Africa.

Farmers' Training Centre (SA)

Principal: Captain Paul Latham
Mitubiri Location, Murang'a
P.O. Box 274, Thika.   *Tel: Mitubiri 4Y8*

Since beginning in 1963, this centre has had 4,500 farmers and their wives attending courses on improved farming.

Finnish Free Foreign Mission, see Full Gospel Churches of Kenya (in Part IV)

Flora Hostel (Consolata Sisters)

Sister-in-charge: Sr. Fulvia
Ngong Road at Fifth Ngong Avenue
P.O. Box 48301, Nairobi.   *Tel: 26281*

Foreign Missionary Society of America, see Maryknoll

Franciscan Missionary Sisters for Africa

Regional Superior: Sr. Mary Bernard
Mangu Convent
P.O. Box 283, Thika.   *Tel: Karamaini 257*

A Catholic congregation begun in 1903 who began work in Kenya in 1941, and now have 41 expatriate sisters. Aim: to spread the good news of the Gospel by schools, maternity and child welfare work, disabled children, leprosy care. 8 convents: Mangu (1941: girls' school, dispensary), Kanzalu (1946: health centre, maternity unit) Muthale (1950: 75-bed hospital) Kiminini (1953: girls' school), Nakuru (1955: schools, child welfare group), Nyabondo (1955: St. Joseph's Hospital, 101 beds; home for crippled children), Molo (1957: primary boarding school, private secondary school), Kimangao (1959: health centre, 49 beds, leprosy project).

Franciscan Missionary Sisters of St. Joseph

Regional Superior: Sr. Lelia Kennedy
Franciscan Convent, Kibuye
P.O. Box 408, Kisumu.   *Tel: 2627*

A Catholic congregation dedicated to following Christ in charity in the spirit of the Third Order of St. Francis, in particular through teaching, medical work and nursing, child care and social work. 30 sisters in Kenya in hospitals and schools. 8 convents: Kisumu, Rangala, Kisii, Nyabururu, Kapsabet, Sotik, Asumbi, Victoria Hospital (Kisumu).

Franciscan Sisters of Oudenbouch

Regional Superior: Sr. Mechtilda
Lwak Convent
P.O. Box Nyilima, Kisumu.

A congregation from Holland which began work at Lwak, Diocese of Kisumu, in 1958, specialising in girls' education, and work with the aged and with handicapped children. 26 Dutch sisters, 20 professed African sisters, 6 novices, 7 postulants. 4 convents: Lwak (1958: hospital, schools, noviciate for African sisters), Aluor (1960: blind children's school), Nyangoma (1962: deaf children's school, deaf boys' technical school), Rapogi (1963: hospital, schools).

Franciscan Sisters of St. Joseph

Superior
P.O. Box 574, Kisii.

Fratres of Tilburg, see Congregation of Fraters of Our Lady

Fratres of Utrecht

The Rev. Brother Provincial
P.O. Box 127, Kakamega.

An institute of Catholic missionary brothers from Holland.

Friends Africa Industrial Mission

The original name of the first Friends mission at Kaimosi from 1902 onwards.

Friends Africa Mission (FAM)

The early American Friends mission at Kaimosi, now replaced by EAYM and other Friends' organisations.

Friends Bible Institute (EAYM)

Principal: The Rev. Elisha M. Wakube
Kaimosi Mission (Kisumu-Eldoret road)
P.O. Box 10035, Tiriki.   *Tel: RN 2047*

The sole Quaker Bible institute in East Africa. Trains pastors, Christian education teachers, and secretaries.

Friends Bookshop (EAYM)

Manager: Miss Estella Hollinshed
Kaimosi Mission (Kisumu-Eldoret road)
P.O. Box 10035, Tiriki.   *Tel: RN 2047*

Friends Centre, Ofafa (EAYM)

Wardens: Mr. and Mrs. Titus Mugavana
Rukwa/Kivu Road
P.O. Box 46613, Nairobi.   *Tel: 57920, 58083*

A community centre begun in 1954 for Ofafa Estate; social, educational and recreational activities, including carpentry, secretarial, homecraft centre. Enrolment of all kinds: 1,100.

Friends College

Registrar: Mr. Solomon N. Adagala
Kaimosi Mission (temporary buildings)
P.O. Box 10035, Tiriki.   *Tel: RN 2047*

The first *harambee* (self-help) college of technology to be founded in Kenya (in 1971), also called Kaimosi College of Science and Technology, for young men and women who have completed secondary education. Present courses: secretarial, accounting, business management.

Friends International Centre (EAYM)
Wardens: Mr. & Mrs. Nathan Luvai
Ngong Road (on left from city before Adams Arcade)
P.O. Box 41946, Nairobi.   *Tel: 67601*
     Youth work, discussion groups, Sunday worship centre (average 100).

Friends Service Council (FSC)
Representative: Mrs. Philomena Leech
Kitchener Road
P.O. Box 30260, Nairobi.   *Tel: 67220*

Friends United Meeting (FUM)
Regional Representative
Kaimosi
P.O. Box 10035, Tiriki.   *Tel: RN 2047*
     The FUM is an international body that has replaced earlier Friends groupings for overseas missionary assistance; missionaries largely North Americans.

Garba Tula Rural Training Centre (MCK)
Administrative Secretary: Mr. Robert Burke
c/o D.C. Isiolo
P.O. Box 3, Isiolo.   *Tel: 3*

Garissa Community Church
St. Peter's Community Church
P.O. Box 60, Garissa.
     In this majority Muslim part of Kenya, the church building in Garissa (capital of the Northeastern Province) is a community church used by Christians of all denominations, Protestant and Roman Catholic.

Gideons International
Chairman: Mr. G.W. Kearie
P.O. Box 40061, Nairobi.
     An international organisation for the distribution and placing of copies of the Holy Scriptures in strategic places — hotel rooms, public places, and the like.

Girls Brigade
Worker: Miss Lynda Brett
(Based on Kaago, Meru)
P.O. Box 25190, Nairobi.
     An organisation from Britain, linked with the BB (Boys Brigade); 14 Girls Brigades in Kenya attached to Anglican and Protestant churches.

Githiga Home for Destitute Boys
Warden: The Rev. John Boro
(¼ mile from Githiga shops, 11 miles from Kiambu)
P.O. Box 125, Kiambu.   *Tel: Cianda 224*

Gospel Furthering Fellowship (GFF)
Secretary: Mrs. Woll
Nairobi Centre: Watkins Street
P.O. Box 41141, Nairobi.   *Tel: 50905*

Got Kokech Orphanage
P.O. Box 77, Homa Bay.

Government departments concerned with churches, see Ministry of Education, Ministry of Lands & Settlement

Government of Kenya, legal relations with, see Registrar of Societies

Harvest Fields Bible School
Principal: The Rev. Richard R. Kirby
Thika Road
P.O. Box 43446, Nairobi.   *Tel: Ruaraka 2438*

Health Centre (Reformed Church of East Africa)
Medical officer in charge
Ainabkoi West Settlement Scheme
P.O. Box 724, Eldoret.   *Tel: Ainabkoi 7Y2*

Highlands Bible College, see Kenya Highlands Bible College

Holy Ghost Fathers, see Congregation of the Holy Ghost

Holy Rosary Sisters
Regional Superior
Regional House: Wingate Grove
P.O. Box 42467, Nairobi.   *Tel: 66033*
     A congregation working in 11 countries among women and children in educational, medical and social work. 4 convents in Kenya (Thika, Ortum (West Pokot), Tala (Machakos), Kilima Mbogo); also Turbo and Singore for training African Sisterhood.

Home for the Aged
Sister-in-charge
Mkomani
P.O. Box 84292, Mombasa.
     Begun in 1969 as a home for elderly destitutes, run by the Little Sisters of the Poor. Recently moved from centre of Mombasa to across Nyali Bridge.

Home Industries Programme (St. John's Community Centre)
Director: Mrs. Martha Gikonyo
Digo Road, Pumwani
P.O. Box 72935, Nairobi.   *Tel: 23306*
     Noted for Maridadi Fabrics, a successful cottage industry which produces fine hand screened fabrics; staff of 35 women and 7 supervisors; begun 1966.

Home Industries Centre (NCCK)
Director: Mrs. Elvina Mutua
Sir Ali Street
P.O. Box 82275, Mombasa.   *Tel: 21004*

Hospitals, Catholic and Protestant
     The following list covers all Protestant hospitals (with beds and doctors), Catholic hospitals (with beds but either with or without doctors), and Protestant dispensaries and maternity centres not attached to hospitals (mostly with beds, with trained staff, but without doctors). Bodies with an asterisk * have fuller details listed elsewhere in the Directory, in alphabetical order. The location of all mission hospitals and dispensaries is shown on the map, 'Medical facilities', p.77 in the *National Atlas of Kenya (1970).*

A. Catholic hospitals
     The 63 hospitals and maternity hospitals listed below all have beds and trained staff; 22 have doctors, 41 do not. They are run not by church boards (as with Protestant hospitals) but by congregations of sisters and missionary orders. The dioceses they are under are also shown. In addition (but not shown here) there are about 120 Catholic dispensaries.

Name of Hospital	Diocese	Address
NAIROBI		
Edelvale Maternity Hos.	Nai	Box 17063, Nairobi
Mater Misericordiae Hos.	Nai	Box 30325, Nairobi
CENTRAL PROVINCE		
Baricho Maternity Hos.	Nye	Box 11, Kerugoya
Bellevue Hospital	Nye	Private Bag, Mweiga
Gaicanjiru Hospital	Nye	Box 483, Thika
Gaturi Maternity Hos.	Nye	Box 49, Fort Hall
Gikondi Hospital	Nye	Box 25, Nyeri
Icagaki Hospital	Nye	P.O. Maragua
Kagwe Hospital	Nai	Box 265, Kiambu
Kalimoni Hospital	Nai	Box 25, Ruiru
Kerugoya Hospital	Nye	Box 11, Kerugoya
Kilimambogo Hospital	Nai	Box 448, Thika
Kiriaine Hospital	Nye	Box 393, Nyeri
Kitito Hospital	Nye	Box 25, Makuyu
Miguta Hospital	Nai	Box 172, Kiambu
Mwea Hospital	Nye	Box 49, Kerugoya
Mweiga Hospital	Nye	Box 38, Mweiga
North Kinangop Hos.	Nye	Box 1049, North Kinangop
Nyeri (Mathari) Hos.	Nye	Box 25, Nyeri
Riara Ridge (Nazareth) H.	Nai	Box 9682, Nairobi
Riruta Hospital	Nai	Box 21283, Nairobi
Thego Hospital	Nye	Box 60, Kiganjo
Thika Maternity Hos.	Nai	Box 792, Thika

COAST PROVINCE

EASTERN PROVINCE

Chuka Hospital	Mer	Box 16, Meru
Igoji Hospital	Mer	Private Bag, Igoji, Meru
Ishiara Hospital	Mer	Box 16, Meru
Kanzalu Hospital	Mac	Box 1012, Kangundo
Kiirwa Maternity Hos.	Mer	Box 16, Meru
Kilungu Hospital	Mac	P.O. Kilome, Machakos
Kimangao Hospital	Kit	P.O. Mwingi, Kitui
Kyeni Hospital	Mer	P.O. Runyenjes, Embu
Laisamis Hospital	Mar	Box 74, Isiolo
Muthale Hospital	Kit	Box 159, Kitui
Mutomo Hospital	Kit	Box 155, Kitui
Nkubu Hospital	Mer	Box 205, Meru
Tigania Hospital	Mer	Box 73, Meru

NORTH-EASTERN PROVINCE

NYANZA PROVINCE

Asumbi Hospital	Ksi	Box 574, Kisii
Koru Hospital	Ksu	Box 17, Koru
Lwak Hospital	Ksu	P.O. Nyilima, Kisumu
Mawego Hospital	Ksi	P.O. Kendu Bay
Mbaga Hospital	Ksu	P.O. Siaya, Kisumu
Nyabondo Hospital	Ksu	P.O. Sondu, Kisumu
Nyangoma Hospital	Ksu	P.O. Bondo, Kisumu
Rangala Hospital	Ksu	P.O. Yala
Rapogi Hospital	Ksi	P.O. Sare, Kisii
Sega Hospital	Ksu	Box 24, Ukwala, Kisumu

RIFT VALLEY PROVINCE

Eldama Ravine Hos.	Nak	Box 10, Eldama Ravine
Kabujoi Hospital	Ksu	Box 44, Kapsabet
Kaiboi Hospital	Ksu	Box 374, Eldoret
Kakuma Hospital	Lod	Private Bag, Kitale
Kaplong Hospital	Nak	Box 4, Sotik
Kilgoris Hospital	Ngo	Box 107, Sotik
Lorugumu Hospital	Lod	P.O. Lorugumu, Kitale
Ortum Hospital	Eld	Private Bag, Kitale
Rombo Hospital	Ngo	P.O. Loitokitok
Wamba Hospital	Mar	P.O. Maralal

WESTERN PROVINCE

Amukura Hospital	Ksu	Box 187, Tororo
Butula Hospital	Ksu	P.O. Butula, Bungoma
Eregi Hospital	Ksu	Private Bag, Maragoli
Misikhu Hospital	Ksu	Box 61, Kimilili
Mukumu Hospital	Ksu	Box 127, Kakamega
Mumias Hospital	Ksu	Box 23, Mumias
Nangina Hospital	Ksu	P.O. Funyula, Kisumu

B. Protestant hospitals (Members of PCMA)

The 15 hospitals listed below have beds and doctors, are affiliated to denominations as shown, and are run by boards of governors. A number of them have out-dispensaries, the largest of which is Kima Hospital (CGEA), attached to Mwihila Hospital. For detailed statistics, see under Protestant Churches Medical Association in this Directory.

Name of Hospital	Denom.	Address
Chogoria Hospital*	PCEA	P.O. Chogoria, Meru
Kapsowar Hospital	AIM	Box 130, Eldoret
Kendu Hospital*	SDA	P.O. Kendu Bay
Kijabe Hospital	AIM	P.O. Kijabe
Kikuyu Hospital	PCEA	Box 45, Kikuyu
Lokori Hospital	AIM	c/o Box 21123, Nairobi
Maseno Hospital*	CPK	Box 116, Maseno
Maua Hospital	MCK	P.O. Maua, Meru
Mwihila Hospital*	CGEA	Private Bag, P.O. Yala
Ngao Hospital*	MCK	P.O. Malindi
Plateau Hospital	RCEA	Box 724, Eldoret
St. Luke's Hospital*	CPK	P.O. Kaloleni, Mombasa
Tenwek Hospital	WEM	Box 3039, Bomet
Tiriki Hospital	EAYM	P.O. Tiriki
Tumutumu Hospital*	PCEA	P.O. Karatina

C. Protestant Dispensaries and Maternity Centres not attached to hospitals (Members of PCMA)

Almost all the 19 centres listed below have beds and trained staff, but no doctors. For statistics, see under PCMA in this Directory.

Name of Centre	Denom.	Address
Chemelil	FGCK	P.O. Songhor
Eldama Ravine	AIM	Box 9, Eldama Ravine
Githumu	AIM	Box 41, Thika
Itierio	LCK	Box 50, Kisii
Kabason	WGM	P.O. Sotik
Kapeddo	FGCK	Private Bag, P.O. Nakuru
Litein	AIM	P.O. Litein, Kericho
Lugulu	EAYM	Box 43, Broderick Falls
Marsabit	BCMS	Mobile Medical Unit, Marsabit, Isiolo
Matongo	LCK	P.O. Sondu, Kisumu
Mukaa	AIM	P.O. Kilome, Machakos
Mulango	AIM	Box 49, Kitui
Naikarra	WGM	Box 59, Narok
Nairobi	SDA	Liverpool Road, Box 42276, Nairobi
Nyakach	AIM	P.O. Sondu, Kisumu
Nyanza Baptist Clinics	BCK	Box 598, Kisumu
Nyambare Hill	NPMK	Private Bag, P.O. Ukwala
Siyiapei	AIM	Box 49, Narok
Thessalia	NPMK	Box 10, Muhoroni

Hospitals Chaplaincy of Kenya
Secretary: The Rev. William E. Jacobson
Cedar Road, Westlands
P.O. Box 14424, Nairobi.   *Tel: 60803*

A society registered in 1971 to co-ordinate all Protestant and Anglican hospital chaplaincies, firstly in Nairobi, and then through branches elsewhere in Kenya. Nairobi has about 4,200 beds in 13 hospitals, and chaplains and lay volunteers visit from bed to bed, and conduct ward and private services. There is one small chapel (in Nairobi Hospital).

Ile Relief Camp (NCCK)
Famine Relief Worker: Mr. Jackson Right Matano
P.O. Lodwar, Kitale.

Immaculate Heart of Mary Sisters
Mother General: Mother Mary Celine
Mary Immaculate Convent
P.O. Box 306, Nyeri.   *Tel: 283*

A diocesan religious congregation begun in 1918, a religious order by 1927; 156 professed, 37 novices, 24 postulants; specialising in education and hospitals. 15 medical centres, 10 schools.

Independent Nilotic Mission
An early mission begun in 1906 in Kisumu among the Luo of western Kenya, later amalgamated with the Africa Inland Mission circa 1920.

Independent Board for Presbyterian Foreign Missions (IBPFM)
Secretary: Miss M.W. McNeil
African Mission: Mwingi
P.O. Mwingi, Kitui (or P.O. Box 41140, Nairobi). Tel: RN 2069 (Ruaraka 2337)

The Independent Board for Presbyterian Foreign Missions was founded in the USA in 1933, and began work in Kenya in 1946. Its 18 missionaries co-operate with the Independent Presbyterian Church of East Africa.

Institute for the Blind
Principal
P.O. Box 26, Maseno.

Inter-Christian Churches Denomination
Secretary: Mr. Paul Silas Githenya
Nyeri Parish PCEA, Hospital Road
P.O. Box 182, Nyeri.   *Tel: 251*

A pioneering movement in Christian unity begun in 1963 by Joseph Wahome of the Holy Ghost Church of Kenya, and now linking a large number of churches including PCEA, SA, CPK, PAG, SFM, AICN, FGCK, BCK, and the Roman Catholic Church as well as the HGCK (although RCs withdrew from official participation in 1966). Other names in use for the group are Inter-Churches Denomination Fellowship, and in Kikuyu, *Ngwataniro ya makanitha moothe ma North Tetu Division* (North Tetu Divison Interchurches Evangelism). One-day convention meetings have been held twice yearly in March and September. Numerous other areas of Kenya have requested help from officers in starting similar movements of unity and reconciliation. (See *Bibliography* under D. Waichanguru).

Inter-Church Action Group
Convenor: The Rev. Davis L. Saunders
St. Andrews Road
P.O. Box 48390, Nairobi.   *Tel: Tigoni 224*

International Bible Students Association (IBSA)
Representative: Mr. P.S. Palliser
Kingdom Hall, Woodlands House, Woodlands Road
P.O. Box 47788, Nairobi.   *Tel: 24905*
For fuller details on Kenya activities, see associated body Jehovah's Witnesses.

International Christian Union
Formerly the Indian Christian Union, this body was registered in 1953 and existed until 1962 to unite Christians of Indian origin.

International Missions
Field Secretary: The Rev. Robert D. Brown
Alamgir/Liaquat Ali Khan Road, Nairobi South 'C'
P.O. Box 47531, Nairobi.   *Tel: 58833*
A mission from the USA invited by the AIM which began work among Asians in Kenya in 1957. Now 10 workers in Kisumu, Nairobi and Mombasa, using Sunday schools, libraries, home Bible study groups, annual camping programmes. Around 50 persons have become Christians since 1957. Branches: P.O. Box 83227, Mombasa, and P.O. Box 950, Kisumu.

International Pentecostal Assemblies (IPA)
Field Secretary: Mr. M. LeRoy Davis
Kaimosi Mission Station
P.O. Kaimosi.
An American mission which arrived in 1937 at Kaimosi, and which in 1962 joined EMA to form PEFA, in which it had in 1971 233 churches with 7,377 regular attending members. 3-year Bible training programme at Kaimosi Bible College, with 45 students. Kitale Branch with Good News Reading Room: P.O. Box 933, Kitale.

Interterritorial Episcopal Board of Eastern Africa, see AMECEA

Irish Ursuline Sisters
Mother Superior
P.O. Box 179, Kitui.

Joint East Africa Religious Education Committee
(JEAREC)
Co-Chairmen: The Rev. Fr. K. Flynn, Dr. D.R. Jacobs
Church House (6th floor), Government Road
P.O. Box 47596, Nairobi.   *Tel: 61465*
A joint Catholic/Protestant education advisory committee representing EAREC and AMECEA; formed in 1971.

Joint Refugee Services of Kenya (JRSK)
Executive Officer: Mr. J.N. Bonuke
Diamond Trust Building, Duke Street, Government Road
P.O. Box 45627, Nairobi.   *Tel: 26595*
A joint service with 9 staff assisting 600 refugees (receiving welfare) and 320 refugee students and pupils, operated through 6 donors: Kenya Catholic Secretariat, National Christian Council of Kenya (welfare), United Nations Development Programme (scholarships), UN High Commissioner for Refugees (welfare and scholarships), Swedish Organisation for Individual Relief (scholarships), International University Exchange Fund (scholarships).

Joytown for Cripples, Salvation Army
Principal: Major Leonard Cooper
Kenyatta Avenue
P.O. Box 326, Thika.   *Tel: 2025*

A full primary school begun in 1962 with 204 crippled children in 1971; boarding, physiotherapy department, rehabilitation, crafts training centre for school leavers.

Kaaga Rural Training Centre
Principal: Mr. Gerrard M. Ikunyua
Kaaga
P.O. Box 267, Meru.   *Tel: 3Y3*

Kabete Children's Home, Salvation Army
Superintendent: Major E. Northwood
Churchill Avenue, Kabete
P.O. Box 14454, Nairobi.   *Tel: 48769*
Home for 84 orphaned, homeless or unwanted children, aged 3-17 years.

Kahawa Garrison Church (St. Paul's)
Chaplain
Kahawa (14 miles north of Nairobi)
P.O. Box 48826, Nairobi.

Kaheti Rural Training Centre (CCM)
Chairman: The Bishop of Nyeri
CCM Kaheti
P.O. Box 372, Nyeri.
Since its opening in 1954, the centre has issued nearly 600 Training Certificates to students (Standard VII or higher), in masonry and carpentry. Two-year non-residential (day) courses, to government trade test grade III.

Kaimosi Bible School (EAYM)
Acting Principal: Mr. Elisha Wakube
(on Kisumu-Kapsabet road, 30 miles from Kisumu)
P.O. Box 10035, Tiriki.   *Tel: RN 2047*

Kaimosi Bible School (IPA)
Principal
Kaimosi IPA Mission
P.O. Kaimosi.
A 3-year Bible training programme, run by International Pentecostal Assemblies and PEFA; 45 students.

Kaimosi College of Science & Technology, see Friends College

Kaimosi Junior Seminary (Diocese of Kisumu)
Rector
Private Bag, Kaimosi.

Kakamega Junior Seminary, see St. Peter's Seminary

Kalokol Cottage Hospital (AIM)
Missionary-in-charge: Mr. B.G. Aldridge
AIM Kalokol
P.O. Lodwar, Kitale.

Kalokol Relief Centre (EAYM)
Director: Mr. Easle Kindle
c/o Friends Technical Centre
Private Bag, Kitale.
A Friends centre among the Turkana begun in 1967, linked with the Industrial Department, Kaimosi Mission EAYM, and teaching woodwork and manual skills, assisted by a nurse and a pastor.

Kambui Deaf School (PCEA)
Headmaster: Mr. Philip Kimau
Kambui Road (8 miles from Ruiru on road to Githunguri)
P.O. Box 257, Ruiru.   *Tel: Anmer 203, 226*
Begun in 1965, a school for 50 children born deaf; modern equipment and methods.

Kapsabet School for Deaf Children (AIC)
Headmaster: Mr. Josephat K. Mining
Located east of District Headquarters
P.O. Box 20, Kapsabet.   *Tel: 8*
Begun 1965; 19 boys, 10 girls, 4 teachers.

Kanamai Conference and Holiday Centre (NCCK)
Director: Mr. Robert Munga
On coast 22 km. north of Mombasa
P.O. Kikambala, Mombasa.   *Tel: Kikambala 12Y4*

Begun in 1961, a Christian holiday centre with very inexpensive accommodation in cottages, dormitories or camping, for families, groups and individuals; also training and conference facilities.

Kapsabet Bible School (AIC)
Principal: The Rev. Sam Sennot
P.O. Box 20, Kapsabet.   *Tel: 8*

Kapsowar Hospital (AIC)
Medical Officer: Dr. R.S. Lindsey
P.O. Box 130, Eldoret.   *Tel: RN 2004*

Kaputir Agricultural Scheme
Director: The Rev. Fr. John Callaghan
Private Bag, Kitale.

Kararumo Trades Institute
Principal
P.O. Box 311, Embu.

Kataboi Fishing Village
Director: The Rev. Fr. James Brady
Kataboi Catholic Mission
Private Bag, Kitale.
The project provides rehabilitation of the poor from famine camps.

Kendu Hospital (SDA)
Medical Director: Dr. E.C. Kraft
Kendu Mission (on main road south)
P.O. Box 5053, Kendu Bay.   *Tel: RN 2153*

Kenya African United Christian Churches
Chairman: The Rev. Gideon Omolo Asoyo (Christian Evangelical Church); Pastor: The Rev. Philip Okungu.
P.O. Box 44778, Nairobi, P.O. Box 521, Kisumu.
Known until 1965 as African United Christian Church, this body was formed in January 1961 by its chairman, the Rev. Gideon Omolo, in the attempt to unite all indigenous churches in Kenya. It claimed to be the Kenya version of EAUC, which it held to be too ambitious; whereas the latter condemned its acceptance of polygamous bishops. Like most such attempts, little has come of this effort at unity, although today it claims a membership of 32 African independent churches of all types including CEC, HTCA, Holy Church of Evangelistic Apostles Faith, and the African Independent Pentecostal Church of Africa.

Kenya Anglican Youth Organisation (KAYO)
Provincial co-ordinator: The Rev. Alfred Chipman
CPK Kabare, Kerugoya, Kirinyaga; Chapel (Nairobi), Karura Forest Station
P.O. Box 48, Kerugoya.
Begun around 1963 in Diocese of Mount Kenya as AYO (Anglican Youth Organisation), subsequently extended by 1968 to Kenya-wide organisation, with many groups in all 6 Anglican dioceses. Runs camps, courses, and an annual provincial conference.

Kenya Armed Forces, Chaplains to
Senior Chaplains to the Forces: (Catholic) The Rev. Fr. John Auro. (Anglican) The Rev. William Wanalo
Harambee House
P.O. Box 40668, Nairobi.   *Tel: 27411 Ext. 497, 404*

Kenya Association for Liturgical Music (KALM)
Chairman: The Rev. Fr. J.P. Kealy; Secretary: Sr. M. Edel
St. Thomas Aquinas Seminary
P.O. Box 30517, Nairobi.   *Tel: Langata 405*
Founded in 1970 by Catholics to encourage and co-ordinate work on liturgical music for Kenya. Annual 3-day conference; branches in each Catholic diocese. The secretary edits a newsletter.

Kenya Association of the Church Missionary Society, see
Church Missionary Society

Kenya Beliefs Systems Project
Head: Dr. Okot p'Bitek
Institute of African Studies (near National Museum), University of Nairobi
P.O. Box 30197, Nairobi.   *Tel: 28631/2*
A university research project to promote detailed and comparative studies of distinctive aspects of Kenya's tribal cultures, especially traditional cosmologies, social values and religious beliefs. Publications: annual reports, articles in journal *Mila* (Institute of African Studies), miscellaneous reports and papers.

Kenya Catholic Pastoral & Development Centre
Chairman: The Rt. Rev. Msgr. C. Davies
Hughes Building (1st floor), Kenyatta Avenue
P.O. Box 48062, Nairobi.   *Tel: 21613/4*
A new project to develop a permanent centre for the Catholic Church in Kenya in which pastoral, development and research needs can be catered for.

Kenya Catholic Secretariat (KCS)
General Secretary, & Education Secretary General: The Rev. Fr. Joachim Getonga
Hughes Building (1st floor), Kenyatta Avenue
P.O. Box 48062, Nairobi.   *Tel: 21613/4*
Instituted in 1961, the Secretariat is the centralised working arm of the Kenya Episcopal Conference, which reviews the Secretariat's work at its bi-annual meetings; it is the link between the Catholic Church and government ministries, VOK, NCCK, and other national bodies; and it also co-ordinates the plans and work of the 13 Catholic dioceses.
There are 5 departments, with secretaries as follows (further details are given elsewhere in this Directory, in alphabetical order):
Communications: Mr. John Irungu, Sr. J. McLaughlin
Education: The Rev. Fr. Joachim Getonga
Lay Apostolate and Youth: Mr. Peter Kiarie
Medical Welfare: The Rev. Fr. M. Campbell
Religious Education: Sr. Aloysia O'Sullivan
Also attached is:
Kenya Catholic Pastoral & Development Centre: Mgr. C. Davies

Kenya Christian Graduates' Fellowship (KCGF, or GF)
Secretary: Mr. David Gregory-Smith
Meetings: Chaplaincy Centre, State House Road
P.O. Box 48789, Nairobi.   *Tel: 22829*

Kenya Christian Teachers' Prayer Fellowship (KCTPF)
Secretary: Mr. Albert Taylor
CCEA, Church House (3rd floor), Government Road
P.O. Box 21352, Nairobi.   *Tel: 22312*
A fellowship of Christian teachers begun in 1970, operating as an activity of the CCEA. Termly newsletter, circulation 2,500.

Kenya Church Association
Chairman: The Archbishop of Kenya; Hon. Secretary: Miss Mollie Newton
47 Manor Road, Beckenham, Kent, England.
A society founded in England in 1920 to keep British persons with Kenya interests in touch with the work of the Anglican Church in Kenya, especially by prayer and giving.

Kenya Church History Archives
Principal, Librarian
St. Paul's United Theological College (Library)
Redhill Road
Private Bag, Limuru.   *Tel: Tigoni 338, 421*
A large collection of written interviews (and 100 vernacular tapes) made with surviving early Christians in different parts of Kenya, also documents and papers on Kenya church history.

Kenya Church Language School, see CPK Language School

Kenya Church Music Society (KCMS)
Secretary: Mr. Roy Griffin
P.O. Box 41482, Nairobi.
Formed in 1947 to promote the use of music and singing in worship (Swahili, English). Affiliated to Royal School of

Church Music (UK). About 20 associated church and school choirs. Annual festival service, school service, courses.

Kenya Episcopal Conference (KEC)
Chairman: The Most Rev. Maurice Otunga; Secretary: The Rev. Fr. Joachim Getonga
Office: Hughes Building (1st floor), Kenyatta Avenue
P.O. Box 48062, Nairobi.   *Tel: 21613/4*

Around 1938 a Catholic Bishops' conference was begun, to facilitate conferring on, and co-ordinating of, matters of common interest in church affairs. One of the major tasks then concerned the Church's role in education, and from 1940-1965 the Rev. Fr. J.J. O'Meara served as education secretary. In 1961 the KEC instituted the Kenya Catholic Secretariat in Nairobi as its working arm. Members of the Conference are local ordinaries and auxiliary bishops in Kenya, together with (from 1971) the Bishop of Port Victoria (Seychelles); the Chairman is elected from among the members, for a three-year term.

Kenya Every Home Crusade, see Every Home Evangelism

Kenya Faith Mission
Founder and Leader: The Rev. Arnt Walther Olsen
Meru township
P.O. Box 245, Meru.

Pentecostal mission begun in 1953 by Norwegian missionaries in Mombasa, now working with East Africa Pentecostal Churches. Two Bible schools, Meru and Mombasa.

Kenya Highlands Bible College (AGC)
Chairman: The Rev. Jonah Chesengeny
P.O. Box 123, Kericho.   *Tel: 123*

Kenya High School Chapel
Chaplains: The Revs. P.G. Ward & D.W. Vail
Nairn Road
P.O. Box 30035, Nairobi.   *Tel: 53101*

Kenya Hospitals Christian Fellowship (KHCF)
Travelling Secretary: Miss Mary Sharp
Kanamai Beach Cottage
P.O. Kikambala, Mombasa. (P.O. Box 30024, Nairobi).

An interdenominational fellowship begun in 1964, to unite Christians in hospital, health and medical work. Quarterly newsletter, circulation 500. Many local groups, annual conference in November, monthly Prayer Days (1st Wednesday), annual International HCF Week (1st-2nd Sundays in March).

Kenya Hospitals Church's Ministry (KHCM)
Presd

Kenya Hospitals Church's Ministry (KHCM)
Chairman: The Rev. Jesse A. Andrew Munene
Nakuru Provincial General Hospital
P.O. Box 264, Nakuru.

A ministry to the sick based on Nakuru Hospital.

Kenya Independent Churches Fellowship
Chairman: High Priest M.P.S.D. Zakayo Kivuli
HQ: AICN Nineveh
P.O. Box 701, Kisumu.

One of the first attempts (begun in 1960, registered in 1963) to unite all independent churches in Kenya, which, despite the chairmanship of High Priest Kivuli, only attracted a handful of members including his AICN, DCCEA, African Holy Zionist Church, and African Holy Spirit Church, and African Orthodox Church. Has gradually petered out through lack of resources to offer members.

Kenya Institute of Education, Religious Education Panel
Panel Chairman: The Rev. F. Ronald Dain
KIE (next to Jamhuri High School), Ngara Road
P.O. Box 30231 (Chairman: Box 42493), Nairobi.   *Tel: 28284*

The KIE is a government body, and the Panel is a government advisory panel on syllabuses and the like, parallel to the similar role of the Inspectorate Section (Religious Education), Ministry of Education, which concentrates on primary syllabuses.

Kenya Mental Health Association
General Secretary: Mr. Elijah R. Ikutwa
Health Education Division, Nottingham Road
P.O. Box 30562, Nairobi.   *Tel: 23973, 20651*

Begun in 1971 to educate, promote mental health care facilities, encourage research in mental health and illness. Not a specifically religious organisation, but a number of members were formerly in the NCCK's Sub-committee on Mental Health.

Kenya Keswick Convention
Secretary: Mr. A.T. Hales
Nairobi South 'C'
P.O. Box 45942, Nairobi.

Kenya Prisoners Aid Association
Director: Mr. H.M. Kisia
Department of Prisons, Bishop's Road
P.O. Box 10026, Nairobi.   *Tel: 23933*

A Christian organisation to assist discharged prisoners embark on a new life in society.

Kenya Prisons Chaplaincy
Secretary: Mrs. Jill J. Wambua
Chaplains' Office, Department of Prisons, Bishop's Road
P.O. Box 30175, Nairobi.   *Tel: 29001 Ext.11*

Begun in 1953, and organised into 5 provincial areas with 3 Provincial Chaplains and a Protestant Administrative Chaplain at Prisons Headquarters. Chaplains in 1971: 1 Catholic, 3 Protestant; catechists, 7 Catholic, 9 Protestant; also 20 warder catechists. Quarterly magazine, *Light.*

Kenya Missionary Council
Immediate forerunner of the NCCK, from 1924-1943.

Kenya Revival Centre, see Directory of the Churches in Kenya

Kenya Students Christian Fellowship (KSCF)
Travelling Secretary: Mr. Micah Amukobole
Office: Church House (3rd floor), Government Road
P.O. Box 41718, Nairobi.   *Tel: 29841*

Begun in 1958, aiming to help and co-ordinate the activities of some 400 Christian groups or unions (CUs) in secondary schools (compared with 20 in 1958) and other educational institutions in Kenya; 200 individual associate members, 12-16 annual conferences or camps. Average attendance at school CUs in 1971 was 15% of all school members.

Kenyatta College Chapel
Chaplains: (Protestant) The Revs. F. Ronald Dain & Michael Kagume; (Catholic) The Rev. Fr. M. Drohan
Kenyatta College, Kahawa, Thika Road
P.O. Box 43844, Nairobi.   *Tel: Templer 356*

Kenyatta College, Religious Education Department
Head Tutor: The Rev. F. Ronald Dain
Kahawa (12 miles north of Nairobi on Thika Road)
P.O. Box 43844, Nairobi.   *Tel: Templer 356*

Kerala Christian Congregation in Kenya
Secretary: Mr. Thomas Varughese
P.O. Box 46730, Nairobi.

The Kerala (South India) Association of Kenya (President: Dr. Sunny Samuel) links Hindus and Christians from the heavily populated Kerala State, South India. In Kenya (mostly in Nairobi) there are about 30 Christian families (120 adults, of whom 40 are from the Mar Thoma Church, and the others Orthodox Syrian Church, Church of South India, and others). They do not have separate services but belong mostly to two Anglican parishes, All Saints Cathedral and St. Mark's, Westlands. The Mar Thoma Missionary Bishop, Alexander Mar Theophilus, visited Nairobi in August, 1972.

Kesho Book Centre (AIC)
Manager: Mr. F. Ngilla
Duke Street
P.O. Box 30351, Nairobi.   *Tel: 21031*

Kesho Publications (AIC)
Editor: Mr. John Ndeti
AIC Kijabe Mission
P.O. Box 88, Kijabe.   *Tel: 12Y7*

Keswick Book Society
Manager: Miss M.I. Smyth
Portal House, Portal Street
P.O. Box 10242, Nairobi.   *Tel: 26047*
A Christian bookshop begun in 1959.

Khasoko Village Polytechnic Centre (CPK)
Manager: The Rev. R.M. Spurin
P.O. Box 45, Bungoma.

Kianda College
Principal: Miss Olga Malin
Sclater's Road
P.O. Box 48328, Nairobi.   *Tel: 48388*
Secretarial training school run by the Catholic organisation
Opus Dei.

Kibos School for the Blind
Principal
P.O. Box 477, Kisumu.

Kibuye Welfare Centre (Diocese of Kisumu)
Secretary
P.O. Box 50, Kisumu.

Kijabe Book Shop (AIC)
Manager: Mrs. E. Arenson
AIC Kijabe Station
P.O. Box 85, Kijabe.   *Tel: 12Y7*

Kijabe Guest House (AIM)
Warden: Mrs. Fast
AIC Kijabe Station
P.O. Kijabe.   *Tel: 12Y5*

Kikuyu Hospital (PCEA)
Administrator: Miss. J. Foster
Off Kikuyu Road
P.O. Box 45, Kikuyu.   *Tel: 2057*

Kiltegan Fathers, see Society of St. Patrick for Foreign
Missions

Kima Hospital (Church of God)
Sister-in-charge: Miss Edna Thimes
Kima
P.O. Box 410, Kisumu.

Kima Mission Station (Church of God)
Caretaker: The Rev. Oscar Borden
Kima
P.O. Box 410, Kisumu.

Kima Theological College (Church of God)
Principal: The Rev. Dennis D. Habel
Located two miles from main road to Bunyore Location
P.O. Box 75, Maseno.
Transferred in 1972 from the Missionary Board to the CGEA
under a board of governors. 30 students in training for the
ministry.

Kisii Diocese Communications Team
Co-ordinators: The Rev. Fr. J. Matogo, Sr. Patrick, Sr. Jacoba
St. Paul's Catholic Church
P.O. Homa Bay.

Kisii Junior Seminary, see St. John's Minor Seminary

Kisumu Diocese Communications Team
Co-ordinator: The Rev. Fr. E. Karhof
Mumias Catechetical Centre
P.O. Box 75, Mumias.

Kitui Diocese Communications Team
General Secretary: The Rev. Fr. Harry McCarney
St. Patrick's TTC, Mutune
P.O. Box 189, Kitui.   *Tel: 14*

Kitui Fellowship
Secretary
P.O. Box 126, Kitui.
A fellowship of Christians banded together for service and
witness.

Kitui Junior Seminary, see St. Joseph's Minor Seminary

Kitui School for Deaf Children
Sister-in-charge
(located in the town)
P.O. Box 149, Kitui.   *Tel: 14*
Run by Assumption Sisters.

Kufufuka (Re-Awakened Ones)
(No organisation nor officers, no central office or address).
Monthly Nairobi fellowship meeting in St. Stephen's Church,
Jogoo Road, 2.30 p.m. on first Sunday of month.
A large movement arising since 1967 within the East African
Revival (Fellowship, Brethren, Balokole or Saved Ones) all over
East Africa, claiming to represent a new vision of the resurrected
Christian life, and therefore called Kufufuka (The Re-awakened
Ones, Risen Ones, Resurrection), and holding in many areas rival
meetings separate from the main body of the Balokole. These
groups are particularly strong from Kitui to Mombasa, and also
in Nyanza; the largest section is in Uganda and is known in
Luganda as Okuzukuka (Awakened). In addition to holding the
theology and moral stand of the Balokole, Kufufuka is distinguished by a stricter insistence on the necessity for keeping
accounts, and opposition to ruinous loans and to lavish personal
expenditure.

Kwale Junior Seminary, see St. Mary's Junior Seminary

Laubach Literacy
A Christian literacy programme begun in 1955, whose work
subsequently passed to the Adult Education Division (see
Ministry of Co-operatives and Social Services).

Laws of Kenya, and legal relationships, see Registrar of
Societies

Lay Apostolate, Diocese of Kisii
Director: Mr. Samuel Ntabo
Bishop's House
P.O. Box 140, Kisii.   *Tel: 95*

Lay Apostolate, Diocese of Machakos
Director: The Rev. Fr. U.J. Kioko
Bishop's House, Machakos
P.O. Box 56, Machakos.   *Tel: 54*

Lay Apostolate & Youth Department (Kenya Catholic
Secretariat)
Secretary: Mr. Peter Kiarie
Hughes Building (1st floor), Kenyatta Avenue
P.O. Box 48062, Nairobi.   *Tel: 21613/4*
This department is concerned with animating, co-ordinating
and directing the participation of the laity in the apostolic work
of the church at all levels in Kenya.

Legion of Mary
National Chairman: Mr. John Omolo; Spiritual Director: The
Rev. Fr. J. Kennedy
Meetings: Our Lady of Visitation, Jogoo Road
P.O. Box 40610, Nairobi.   *Tel: 58752*
A Catholic lay organisation from Ireland, founded in Kenya
in 1936 on the visit of an envoy from Dublin, Miss Edel Quinn.
Object: to involve the laity in apostolate by means of house
visiting, weekly meetings, and the like. In some dioceses (e.g.,
Machakos) it is found in every parish and in most primary and
secondary schools, and also in TTCs.

Leipzig Evangelical Lutheran Mission
A German missionary society which in 1893 took over the

two mission stations of the Bavarian Lutheran Mission (begun 1891) in Ukambani; translated St. Luke's Gospel into Kikamba in 1898 (by Hofmann); had four stations in Ukambani by 1907; and whose work was handed over to the AIM on the outbreak of World War I in 1914.

LENGO, see East African Venture Company

Likoni School for the Blind (Salvation Army)
Headmaster: Capt. M. Kiganane
Old Gazi Road
P.O. Box 96089, Mombasa.   *Tel: 76215*

Light of Life Library
c/o Mr. D. Grover
P.O. Box 47531, Nairobi.

Limuru Bookshop (PCEA)
Manager
P.O. Box 186, Limuru.

Limuru Conference & Training Centre
Acting Director: The Rev. Heiner Hofmann
Redhill Road/Tigoni Road corner (16 miles from Nairobi)
P.O. Box 212, Limuru.   *Tel: Tigoni 347, 519*
    Founded in 1959 by the CCK, the Centre now co-ordinates training activities of the NCCK (lay training; church, industry and commerce; youth and social work; national development) through consultations, seminars and conferences. Closely linked with NCCK Kanamai Conference and Holiday Centre. In 1970, 2,943 persons attended conferences in the above areas of concern. There is accommodation for 120 persons in single and double rooms, and a large conference hall seating over 200 with full audio-visual facilities.

Limuru Girls' School
Headmistress: Miss Audrey M. Scott
School Road, Tigoni
P.O. Limuru.   *Tel: Tigoni 355*
    An Anglican foundation, the school was founded in 1922, then assisted by the CMS and later the Colonial (now Commonwealth) and Continental Church Society (UK); 300 pupils, 20 staff.

Litein Bookshop (AIM)
Manager
P.O. Litein, Kericho.

Little Sisters of Jesus
Regional Responsible: Little Sr. Anna Lucia of Jesus
Godawari Road, Nairobi South B (opposite Mariakani)
P.O. Box 49245, Nairobi.   *Tel: 58241*
    Dada wadogo wa Yesu. A contemplative Catholic order supporting themselves by manual labour alongside the populace in factories and farms, with Jesus as their ideal, following their founder Brother Charles de Foucauld (died 1916). There are four communities, called fraternities, in Kenya: Godawari Road (above), Makadara (Box 49245, Nairobi), Mombasa (Box 80262), Kajiado (Box 27).

Little Sisters of St. Joseph
Mother Superior
Kilgoris
P.O. Sotik.

Little Sisters of the Poor
Mother Superior: Sr. Margaret
Kilindini Road
P.O. Box 84292, Mombasa.
    A Catholic order (5,000 throughout the world) dedicated to the care of the elderly poor in 311 Homes for the Aged. Began in Mombasa in 1969.

Loarengak Fishing Village
Director: The Rev. Fr. Fraynot
Catholic Mission
P.O. Lokitaung, Kitale.
    The project provides rehabilitation of the poor from famine camps.

Lodwar Diocese Communications Team
Co-ordinator. The Rev. Fr. Desmond Millar
Catholic Mission
P.O. Lodwar, Kitale.

Lokori Hospital (AIC)
Medical Officer: Dr. R.J.D. Anderson
South Turkana District
P.O. Box 21010, Nairobi.   *Tel: RN 2005*

Loreto Sisters
Provincial: Mother Scholastica
Loreto Convent (Msongari), St. Austin's Road
P.O. Box 30258, Nairobi.   *Tel: 60235*

Lumbwa Industrial Mission
    The Maasai originally called the Kipsigis tribe *Lumbwa* (cultivators). The LIM had connected with both the Friends (FAM) and the AIM, and merged with the latter.

Lutheran World Federation Broadcasting Service
TV Study Director: The Rev. Paul M. Volz
Flowerdale Road (near Lavington Green)
P.O. Box 25061, Nairobi.   *Tel: 48089*
    Radio Sauti ya Injili. A communications arm of the LWF begun in Nairobi in 1970 to study the role and function of the Service in the area of television, with reference to Radio Voice of the Gospel (Addis Ababa).

Maasai Bible School (AIC)
Principal. Mr. J. Bisset
AIC Narok
P.O. Box 7, Narok.   *Tel: 16*

Maasai Rural Development Centre (PCEA)
Director: Mr. Colin P. Crabbie
Olooseos (27 miles from Nairobi on Magadi Road)
P.O. Box 24860, Nairobi.
    An outreach centre begun in 1968, with a demonstration farm, dispensary, children's clinic, water projects, veterinary store, primary school, and church.

Maasai Rural Training Centre (CPK)
Project Manager: Mr. R.P. Slade; Director of Training. Mr. T. Matianyi
Isinya, on main road to Tanzania, halfway from Athi River to Kajiado
P.O. Box 24, Kajiado.
    After the big drought of 1961 when the Maasai lost most of their cattle (300,000 in Kajiado District), this former detention camp was used as a Famine Relief Centre until the RTC was set up in 1963 by NCCK and the Anglican Diocese of Nairobi. Departments: training (land use, adult literacy, Christian Faith), tannery (market for local hides and skins, leathercraft); ranch (2000 acres, 300 cattle, 300 sheep); shamba (crop husbandry), primary school; extension work (Kalema/Olkiramatian, Magadi, Meto; 700 animals vaccinated or attended to per month).

Machakos Diocese Communications Team
Co-ordinator. The Rev. Fr. Hilary Kailu
P.O. Makueni, Machakos.

Maisha Mapya Bookshop (AIC)
Manager: Mr. H. Pollard
P.O. Box 49, Machakos.

Makadara Community Centre (Salvation Army)
Superintendent: Capt. M. Philip Edalia
Off Jogoo Road
P.O. Box 40575, Nairobi.   *Tel: 27541/2*
    Begun in 1953 for the Makadara area of Nairobi. Scouts, Guides, commercial classes, feeding scheme (600 children per month), day nursery school, women's club, youth work (350 members)

Maranatha Mission of Kenya, see Swedish Maranatha Mission

Mariakani Christian Centre ((Church of God)

Mariakani Christian Centre (Church of God)
Warden. Mr. Timothy Litondo
Ghalib Road, Nairobi South 'B'
P.O. Box 18071, Nairobi.   *Tel: 58753*

Marianist Brothers see Society of Mary

Maridadi Fabrics, see Home Industries Programme (Nairobi)

Marsabit Diocese Communications Team
Co-ordinator: Bishop C.M. Cavallera
Bishop's House, Nanyuki
P.O. Box 281, Nanyuki.   *Tel: 2768*

Maryknoll Fathers (Foreign Missionary Society of America)
Regional Superior: The Rev. Fr. J. Morrissey
Regional Centre House: Off Churchill Road (opposite Apostolic Nunciature)
P.O. Box 43058, Nairobi.   *Tel: 48466*
    An American missionary order which began in East Africa in 1946, mostly in pastoral work in Tanzania (100 persons) with a regional centre house in Nairobi (15 persons in Kenya). The initials MM (Maryknoll Missioner) are used after the names of Maryknoll brothers and sisters as well as priests.

Maryknoll Sisters of St. Dominic
Area Chairman. Sr. Carol Schoenecker
Kinango Hospital
Private Bag, Kinango, Mombasa.
    An American missionary order which began working in Kenya in 1969. There are now 16 Maryknoll sisters in Kenya, in 5 dioceses.

Maseno Bible School
Principal. The Rev. John van Emmerick
Sunrise, Maseno
P.O. Box 1, Maseno.   *Tel: 20*

Maseno Depot Village Polytechnic Centre
Project Manager. Mr. Jairo Alela
P.O. Box 1, Maseno.   *Tel. 20*
    An Anglican VP Centre begun in 1968 to train unemployed school leavers in technical skills. 8 instructors, 55 trainees as follows. masonry 26, carpentry 12, accounting 9, tailoring and typing 8 (girls).

Maseno Hospital (CPK)
Superintendent. Mr. Alfred Okuyo
CPK Maseno (past the secondary school)
P.O. Box 116, Maseno.

Maseno South Diocesan Missionary Association (DMA)
Chairman. The Bishop of Maseno South
Church House, Dhanwant Singh Road
P.O. Box 380, Kisumu.   *Tel: 2131*

Mater Apostolorum Minor Seminary, see Mother of
    Apostles Junior Seminary

Maternity 'Safina , Plateau (RCEA)
Sister in charge
Plateau Mission Station
P.O. Box 724, Eldoret.   *Tel: Kaptagat 2Y2*
    Safina' = ship, vessel, Noah's ark.

Matongo Bible School (LCK)
Principal. Mr. J. Otete
LCK Matongo
P.O. Sondu, Kisumu.

Mayfield Guest House (AIM)
Wardens. The Rev. & Mrs. P. Stough
Ngong Road (next to Nairobi Baptist Church)
P.O. Box 21044, Nairobi.   *Tel: 22519*

McGregor Bible School (CPK)
Principal. The Rev. Colin Dundon
CPK Weithaga (15 miles west of Murang'a)
P.O. Box 107, Murang'a.

Mechanic Training School
Director: Mr. John Fox

Lodwar Catholic Mission
P.O. Lodwar, Kitale.

Medical Missionaries of Mary
Regional Superior. Sr. Monica Prendergast
Suam Road
P.O. Box 371, Kitale.   *Tel: 441*
    Catholic order for medical work specialising in mother and child care, operating in Turkana area (Lorugumu, Lodwar, Kakuma, Kataboi).

Medical Services (Reformed Church of East Africa)
Medical Officer in charge: Dr. J.J.J. Goslinga
Maternity Safina, Plateau
P.O. Box 724, Eldoret.
    Begun in 1961, 50 maternity beds in Plateau, 12 in Ainabkoi, dispensaries in Lessos, Ndalat, Sergoit, Lokichar (Turkana).

Medical Mission Sisters
District Superior: Sr. Nichola Lovett
Nangina Hospital
P.O. Box 5057, Funyula, Kisumu.   *Tel: Funyula 5*
    Catholic religious congregation which began in Kenya in 1963; 12 sisters at work in government and mission hospitals.

Medical Welfare Department (Kenya Catholic Secretariat)
Secretary. The Rev. Fr. M. Campbell
Hughes Building (1st floor), Kenyatta Avenue
P.O. Box 48062, Nairobi.   *Tel. 21613/4*
    Begun 1961 for liaison between Ministry of Health and the 63 Catholic hospitals, co-operation with Protestant Churches Medical Association, co-ordination of Catholic medical work, and also refugee work.

Medicine Men's Society, see Waganga wa Miti Shamba (p.312).

Mennonite Board in Eastern Africa
Director: The Rev. Dr. Donald R. Jacobs
Church House (6th floor), Government Road
P.O. Box 47596, Nairobi   *Tel. 28023, 60413*
    Begun in 1965 to co-ordinate and advise on church growth and related development activities in Kenya, Tanzania, Ethiopia and Somalia. 17 missionaries from USA in Kenya, Tanganyika Mennonite Church has small emigrant population in South Nyanza, Kenya.

Mennonite Central Committee (Teachers Abroad Program) (TAP)
East Africa Director. Mr. M. Hershey Leaman
Church House (6th floor), Government Road
P.O. Box 47596, Nairobi.   *Tel: 28023, 60413*
    An American mission program begun in 1962 to second Christian teachers and professionals to existing institutions in Kenya, Tanzania and Somalia, also to assist in famine relief and rural development · activities; in 1971, 20 secondary school teachers in Kenya.

Mennonite Centre Guest House
Hostess. Miss Elizabeth L. Hostetter
71, Church Road, Westlands
P.O. Box 47596, Nairobi.   *Tel: 60264*
    Begun in 1964 for inexpensive hospitality for church workers and missionaries in transit or on leave. Accommodation for 35 guests, occupancy in 1971 averaged 24 nightly.

Menno Travel Service (MTS)
Branch Manager. Mr. Don S. Hedrick; Travel Co-ordinator: Mr. G.G. Kahn
Lullington Street
P.O. Box 40444, Nairobi.   *Tel: 24811, 29487*
    A church-related travel bureau offering service for church travel needs, international tours, and group movements.

Merti Famine Relief & Rehabilitation Camp
Leader. Mr. Daniel Maganjo
c/o D.C. Isiolo
P.O. Box 3, Isiolo.
    Begun in 1968 to care for orphans and destitutes; 450 children and 200 destitutes fed daily; nursery school for 90 children.

Meru Bookshop (Methodist Church in Kenya)
Manager: Mr. Stanley Mwithimbu
Harambee Street
Private Bag, Meru.   *Tel: 99*
　　Christian bookshop begun in 1962 for Meru and northern Kenya; distribution by colporteurs.

Meru Diocese Communications Team
Co-ordinator: Bishop L.V. Bessone
Bishop's House
P.O. Box 16, Meru.   *Tel: 49*

Methodist Book Depot
Superintendent: The Rev. Samuel Ngala
Ribe
P.O. Box 90122, Mombasa.

Methodist Hospital Ngao
Medical Superintendent: Dr. P. Fox
Private Bag, Malindi.   *Tel: RN 2315*

Methodist Isiolo District Medical Unit (Mobile)
Medical Superintendent: Mr. Stanley Bell
Methodist Hospital
P.O. Maua, Meru.   *Tel: RN 3610*

Methodist Rest House
Matron: Miss B. Jones
Dorset Close Road
P.O. Box 25086, Nairobi.   *Tel: 67238*

Mill Hill Mission, see St. Joseph's Society for Foreign Missions

Million Acre Settlement Scheme
Originator: The Rt. Rev. N. Langford-Smith
Lake Road
P.O. Box 56, Nakuru.   *Tel: 2380*
　　A development project under the Anglican Church of the Province of Kenya, providing training and pastoral care for workers on settlement schemes all over Kenya. In some areas (Eldoret) one outcome has been a complex of small non-institutionalised self-help projects.

Ministry of Co-operatives & Social Services
Head, Adult Education Division: Mr. D. Mwandia
Gill House (3rd floor), Government Road
P.O. Box 30276, Nairobi.   *Tel: 23901*
　　The Adult Education Division is responsible for adult literacy work throughout Kenya, with 810 government-aided classes in 1970 and over 450 unaided self-help literacy classes. A fair proportion of these are run by the churches in Kenya. In 1972, 62,000 adults were enrolled. This work continues that begun by the Laubach organisation and the Kenya Literacy Centre.

Ministry of Education, Inspectorate Section
Inspector of Schools i/c Religious Education: The Rev. Fr. Thomas M. Farrelly
Marshall House, Harambee Avenue
P.O. Box 30426, Nairobi.   *Tel: 24344 Ext. 26*
　　The Inspector is appointed by the Minister of Education with responsibility for religious education in all primary and secondary schools, and teachers' colleges, in Kenya, including professional and academic aspects, syllabuses, methodology, books and materials, in-service courses, examinations, school inspections.

Ministry of Lands and Settlement, Kenya Government
Commissioner of Lands
Lands Department, Harambee Avenue
P.O. Box 30089, Nairobi.   *Tel: 27471*
　　This department deals with all questions concerning land, including applications for church plots. A number of church properties have trustees registered here under the Land (Perpetual Succession) Act; in 1972, 69 denominations, dioceses and missions were so registered (see p. 281).

Missionaries of Our Lady of Guadalupe
Centre House: Adams' Arcade, Sonning Road
P.O. Box 21245, Nairobi.   *Tel: 67161*

Missionary Aviation Fellowship (MAF)
Kenya Programme Manager: Mr. L.T. Brown
Hanger 9, Wilson Airport
P.O. Box 21123, Nairobi.   *Tel: 21665, 66414*
　　An interdenominational church and mission air charter service begun in 1945 (Kenya, 1959) especially to help work in underdeveloped areas. Two 6-seat Cessna aircraft, 2 pilots, operating throughout East Africa. Bookings should be made well in advance.

Missionary Board of the Church of God, see East Africa
Ministries

Missionary Home of Jehovah's Witnesses
P.O. Box 84607, Mombasa.

Missionary Sisters of the Precious Blood
Provincial Superior: Mother M. Hemma Krenz
Precious Blood Convent, Riruta, Ngong Road
P.O. Box 21283, Nairobi.   *Tel: 66944*
　　A Catholic order founded in 1885 in Mariannhill, South Africa, specialising in teaching, nursing and social welfare; began at Bura, Voi, in 1908; 1925, Eastleigh; 1927, Kalimoni (approved school, maternity home), 1940, Kilungu (hospital, schools); 1949, Giriama; 1950, Lioki; 1955, Mbitini; 1956, Kiteta; 1959, Kagwe; 1959, Riruta Convent opened as provincial house, noviciate, girls' secondary school, and maternity home. Their associated order for African girls is the Congregation of St. Joseph, autonomous in 1951.

Missionssallskapet B.V. see Swedish Lutheran Mission

cational,

Missions to Seamen (CPK)
Chaplain. The Rev. T. Hearn
Kilindini Road
P.O. Box 80424, Mombasa.   *Tel: 23770*
　　The Kenya Mission was begun in 1921, to cater for the spiritual and physical welfare of all visiting seamen. Services: St. Nicholas Anglican Chapel. Flying Angel Club: open every day. 1970-71 statistics for the year: 38 visits to naval ships, 1,063 to other ships, 1,208 hospital visits, 229 chapel services.

Mji wa Huruma (Village of Mercy) (Salvation Army)
Superintendent: Brigadier Douglas Liyai
Kiambu Road
P.O. Box 27058, Nairobi.   *Tel: 63292*
　　A home for beggars and adult destitutes, aiming to assist them leave the streets of Nairobi.

Moffat Bible Institute (AIC)
Principal: The Rev. E.T. Borman
AIC Kijabe Station
P.O. Box 70, Kijabe.

Mombasa Bible Reading Fellowship
P.O. Box 82476, Mombasa.

Mombasa Council of Christian Congregations
Secretary: The Rev. Elijah Abonyo
St. John's Anglican Church, Buxton
P.O. Box 98316, Mombasa.
　　A combined preaching fellowship which encourages Christians to extend their witness to every part of the area.

Mombasa Diocese Communications Team
Co-ordinator: The Rev. Fr. Noel O'Rourke
Bishop's House, Mombasa Cathedral
P.O. Box 84850, Mombasa.   *Tel: 71320*

Mombasa Gospel Tabernacle
Pastor
Tudor Road
P.O. Box 81487, Mombasa.   *Tel: 20572*

Moral Re-Armament (MRA)
Hon. Secretary/Treasurer: Mr. P.D. Abrams
Gymkhana Road
P.O. Box 20035, Nairobi.   *Tel: 20400*

Mother of Apostles Junior Seminary

Rector
P.O. Box 71, Eldoret.   *Tel: 2432*
Opened in 1960 as a minor seminary (secondary school). 120 students from the Catholic Dioceses of Eldoret, Nakuru and Lodwar. Qualifications: Standard VII, and a possible vocation to the priesthood.

Mothers' Union (Province of Kenya) (MU)

Diocese of Maseno North MU Worker: Mrs. R. Anamini, c/o Bunyore Pastorate, P.O. Box 18, Maseno.
Diocese of Maseno South MU Worker: Mrs. D. Owaga, Church House, P.O. Box 380, Kisumu.
Diocese of Mombasa Chairman: Mrs. P. Mwang'ombe. MU Workers: Mrs. E. Mwaluma, Mrs. E. Mitchell, P.O. Box 72, Mombasa.
Diocese of Mount Kenya Chairman: Mrs. L.W. Kariuki. MU Worker: Mrs. Mbugua, P.O. Box 181, Kiambu.
Diocese of Nairobi Chairman: Mrs. F.H. Olang'. MU Worker: Mrs. R. Mwadime, St. John's Church, P.O. Box 13084, Nairobi.
Diocese of Nakuru Chairman: Mrs. V. Langford-Smith. MU Workers: Mrs. E. Bet, Aldai School, P.O. Kapcheno, via Kapsabet; Mrs. R. Ongolo, P.O. Box 515, Nakuru.
The Mothers' Union is a large Church of England organisation which has now expanded across the world, sending workers to many Anglican dioceses. Members: Britain, 334,000; elsewhere 120,000. Branches: Britain, 9,530; elsewhere, 6,030. Objects: to uphold the sanctity of marriage (the Christian principle of the permanence of the relationship between husband and wife), to train youth, to organise bands of mothers to pray and lead families in purity and holiness of life.

Mount Kenya Bookshop; see Arahuka Book Depot

Mount Kenya Diocesan Missionary Association (DMA)

Chairman: The Ven. Sospeter Magua
Martyrs' Memorial Cathedral
P.O. Box 121, Murang'a.   *Tel: 53*
An indigenous Anglican voluntary association formed in 1962, with 3,000 members including church leaders paying Shs. 5/- a year, to support missionary initiatives within the diocese (northern areas to Ethiopian and Somali borders) and beyond (Sudan), with emphasis on rapid action in case of need. DMA representatives are appointed at congregational level for recruiting, collecting, distributing.

Mucii wa Urata Rural Training Centre

Director: Mr. Elisha Gatuna
P.O. Box 72, Kerugoya.
'Home of Friendship', a community centre.

Mulango Bible School (AIC)

Principal: The Rev. J. Maithiya
P.O. Box 49, Kitui.

Mulango Bookshop (AIC)

Manager: The Rev. J. Maithiya
P.O. Box 80, Kitui.

Mumias School for the Deaf

Headmistress: Sr. Lutgard Streng
(situated one mile from township)
Private Bag, Mumias.
Opened in 1961, a Catholic boarding school with nursery for deaf children aged 4 to 6 years, and full primary school. Oral method used to help children speak and lipread. Sports, outdoor activities. Present enrolment: 140. Leavers go on to Technical School for Deaf Boys; girls to vocational classes (touch-typing, book-keeping, child care, home economics).

Muscoy Community Church Ministerial Fellowship, see Kenya Revival Centre

Mwihila Hospital and School of Nursing (CGEA)

Medical Superintendent: Dr. Roger Bruce
Mwihila, Yala
Private Bag, Yala.   *Tel: RN 2048*

Nairobi Archdiocese Communications Team

Co-ordinators: The Rev. Fr. Nicodemus Kirima, Mr. Patrick Ngare, Sr. Bernadette Munini
St. Thomas Aquinas Seminary
P.O. Box 30517, Nairobi.   *Tel: 89405*

Nairobi Baptist Association (BCK)

Chairman: The Rev. Daniel Mathuku
Shauri Moyo Baptist Church, Ahero Street
P.O. Box 44628, Nairobi.   *Tel: 58880*
Jumuiya Ndogo ya Makanisa ya Nairobi. Begun in 1961, fosters joint work among the 7 Baptist Churches of Kenya congregations in Nairobi area.

Nairobi Baptist Centre & Bookshop (BCK)

Warden: Mr. F. Joe Snyder
Ahero Street
P.O. Box 44628, Nairobi.   *Tel: 58880*
Community centre begun in 1958 under BMEA.

Nairobi Bible Institute (GFF)

Headmistress: Mrs. Ruth H. Munce
Watkins Street (opposite Pumwani Maternity Hospital)
P.O. Box 41141, Nairobi.   *Tel: 50316*
Courses begun in 1954 (Kikamba) and 1967 (English) in Bible knowledge and pastoral and evangelistic ministry. Three-year course: 25 students, 5 faculty, belonging to Gospel Furthering Fellowship.

Nairobi Christian Literature and Bible Centre

Director: The Rev. E. Weaver
Thika Road
P.O. Box 45887, Nairobi.   *Tel: Ruaraka 2327*

Nairobi City Council

Religious Education Officer: The Rev. Fr. J. Hughes; Mayor's Chaplain: The Rev. G. Gikanga (PCEA)
City Hall, Harambee Avenue
P.O. Box 30298, Nairobi.   *Tel: 26561, 24281*

Nairobi Clergy Fellowship

Acting Convenor: The Very Rev. Henry Okullu
Meetings: University Chaplaincy Centre, State House Road
c/o P.O. Box 40539, Nairobi.   *Tel: 20715*

Nairobi Diocesan Missionary Association (DMA)

Treasurer: Mr. S. Mbogo (Box 47512, Nairobi)
Office: 26 State House Avenue
P.O. Box 40502, Nairobi.   *Tel: 20207*
Begun in mid-1972 as a local initiative for evangelism in unevangelised areas of the Anglican diocese of Nairobi.

Nairobi Diocesan Bookshop (CPK)

Manager: Mr. Henry Okola
Church Army Community Centre, Jogoo Road
P.O. Box 72125, Nairobi.   *Tel: 57534*
Vernacular, Swahili and English Christian literature; 2 mobile vans and a bicycle colporteur; wholesaling agent for Central Tanganyika Press and Uzima Press.

Nairobi Evangelistic Team (NET)

Chairman: Mr. Edward Kizza (Department of Mathematics, University of Nairobi)
P.O. Box 30197, Nairobi.   *Tel: 34244*
A part-time team offering their services for short missions to schools and other institutions.

Nairobi Girls Centre (Salvation Army)

Superintendent: Captain M. Pickstone
Quarry Road, Kariokor
P.O. Box 27304, Nairobi.   *Tel: 20936*
Begun in 1964; 32 girls (50 soon); two-year course in domestic training, home nursing, first aid, arts and crafts, singing, dancing, cooking.

Nairobi Gospel Association

Chairman: The Rev. James Ngunyi
Bible House, House 1562 (Flat F/4), Ulu Road, Ofafa Maringo Estate
P.O. Box 72289, Nairobi.   *Tel: 57316*

A branch of All Nations Gospel Tabernacle related to PEFA (Pentecostal Evangelistic Fellowship of Africa) but now independent.

Nairobi Junior Seminary, see Queen of Apostles Seminary

Nairobi Pentecostal Bible College
Principal: The Rev. T.C. Cross
Garden Estate, Thika Road
P.O. Box 30267, Nairobi.   Tel: Ruaraka 2391
Begun in 1971 to provide Bible school training for any undenominational groups, especially those with Full Gospel emphasis. A resident college, and also a Correspondence Course Department (P.O. Box 30207 and 30373, Nairobi).

Nairobi Pentecostal Church (PAG)
Pastor: The Rev. Mervyn Thomas
Valley Road (above Panafric Hotel)
P.O. Box 42254, Nairobi.   Tel: 25366

Nairobi Youth Christian Choirs Association
Secretary: Mr. Dickson O.M. Mpivas
St. Stephen's Church, Jogoo Road
P.O. Box 50005, Nairobi.   Tel: 55168

Nakuru Diocese Communications Team
Co-ordinator: The Rev. Fr. Liam Blayney
P.O. Box 938, Nakuru.   Tel: Lanet 324

Nakuru Literature Centre (CPK)
Secretary: The Rev. John Ball
Uzima Press Building, Normain Estate (on Eldoret Road)
P.O. Box 665, Nakuru.   Tel: 2425
Headquarters for literature work in Anglican Diocese of Nakuru. (See: Uzima Press).

Nakuru Youth for Christ (YFC)
Executive Secretary: Mr. Stan Moss
P.O. Box 430, Nakuru.   Tel: 2895

Nambale Village Polytechnic Centre
Warden: Mr. E.J. Alexander (CMS)
P.O. Nambale, Kisumu.

National Association of Religious Education Teachers
(NARET)
Secretary: Mr. F.G. Welch
Alliance High School
P.O. Box 7, Kikuyu.   Tel: 2026
An association for all who teach RE or have an interest in its place in the educational system. Local branches in Nyeri, Mombasa, Machakos and Nairobi.

National Christian Council of Kenya (NCCK)
General Secretary: Mr. John C. Kamau
Church House (4th floor), Government Road
P.O. Box 45009, Nairobi.   Tel: 22264/5, 27360, 24652
Jumuiya ya Wakristo wa Kenya. An association of churches, missions, and other Christian agencies. The long history of co-operation between the churches in Kenya, described elsewhere in this Handbook, has the following dates as milestones: 1918, forming of Alliance of Protestant Missions; 1924, forming of Kenya Missionary Council; 1943, founding of Christian Council of Kenya; and, 1966, renaming as NCCK. The 25 member denominations and their statistics are listed in Table 5 (pages 183-89) with full details on each in the Directory of the Churches (Part IV). The NCCK has a wide range of activities, operated by 100 salaried staff; for details of these, see Annual Reports in the Bibliography (which also lists the NCCK Constitution, and all NCCK publications).

Administrative staff General Secretary: Mr. John C. Kamau
Deputy General Secretary: Mr. Bethuel A. Kiplagat
Accountant: Mr. Philip W. Scribbins
Secretaries: The Rev. Donald L. Mathews (Christian Outreach & Rural Development Services); Miss Mary Muchai (Project Development and Documentation), Broadcasting Secretary: Mr. Samuel Munyi (for full staff list, see Reports 1971).

NCCK Branches
Eldoret Branch: Secretary, P.O. Box 64, Eldoret.

Coast Branch: Secretary, P.O. Box 82275, Mombasa. T:20172
Kakamega Branch: Secretary, P.O. Box 2066, Khayega, Kakamega.
Nakuru Branch: Chairman, P.O. Box 1600, Nakuru.
Nyanza Branch: Secretary, P.O. Box 770, Kisumu (Christian Fellowship Centre, Anderson Road). T: 2396
Thika Branch: Secretary, P.O. Box 296, Thika.

NCCK Projects
The Council is involved in over 100 Projects, together with over 50 other special projects run by Member Churches (see Annual Reports, 1970, 1971). The following listing gives the major Projects, and their NCCK relationship; addresses and further details of those marked * are given elsewhere in this Directory in alphabetical order.

(a) Operated by NCCK (six departments)
Dept. of Biblical Study & Research (Panel on Evangelism; Panel on Islam)
Dept. of Christian Communication* (Radio-TV; Audio-Visual; Literature; Film Library*)
Dept. of Christian Education & Training (Church & Industry in Nairobi*, Mombasa*, Nakuru*; Overseas Study Committee)
Dept. of Christian Service & Home & Family Life (Social Work projects, Mathare Valley, community centres)

Dept. of Relief, Rehabilitation & Rural Development (Rural training centres; village polytechnics; Home Industries Centre, Mombasa*; Famine Relief Camps (13); Children's Homes (Turkana; Garba Tula); Tractor Contractor Training Scheme, Moyale/Sololo/Dabel Comprehensive Scheme (CPK Mt. Kenya)).
Dept. of Youth (youth leadership training in most provinces)

(b) NCCK legal responsibility, but semi-independent
Limuru Conference & Training Centre*
Kanamai Conference & Holiday Centre (near Mombasa)*
Nakuru Community Centre*
Christian Fellowship Centre (Kisumu)*

(c) Initiated or assisted by NCCK, but now under sponsor shown
Rural Training Centres (run by churches, assisted by NCCK)
Garba Tula (MCK)*
Kaaga RTC (MCK)*
Lugari RTC (EAYM)
Maasai RTC (CPK Nairobi)*
Marimanti RTC (MCK)
Mucii wa Urata (NCCK)*
Njabini RTC (CPK Nakuru)*
Olooseos RTC (PCEA)*
Salvation Army RTC, Thika*
Samburu RTC (CPK Nakuru)

Village Polytechnics (related to or assisted by NCCK, in some cases with government assistance); VP Field Officer: Mr. Edward A. Wanjala.
Akado VP (CPK Maseno South)
Garba Tula VP (MCK)
Ithima VP (MCK Meru)
Kalokol VP (EAYM)
Kaloleni VP (Kilifi County Council)
Karima VP (CPK Nakuru)
Karurumo VP (Salvation Army)
Katakwa VP (CPK Maseno North)
Keveye VP (local chief's council)
Khasoko VP (CPK Maseno North)
Kianjai VP (MCK Meru)
Kisauni VP (NCCK Coast Branch)
Kithoka VP (MCK)
Maseno VP (CPK Maseno North)
Mazeras VP (MCK Coast)
Mbale VP (CPK Mombasa)
Misambi VP (CPK Maseno South)
Mount Kenya VP (CPK Mount Kenya)
Mucii wa Urata VP (NCCK/Govt.)
Muhanda VP (CPK Maseno South)
Nambale VP* (CPK Maseno North)
Narok VP (AIM/RCC)
Ndere VP (CPK Maseno South)
Nyakach Group VP (Nyabondo Catholic Mission):

Katito
Nyalenda
Sang'oro
Nyangoma VP (Ahero Catholic Mission)
Shitoli VP (Church of God in EA)
Sigilai VP (CPK Nakuru)
Soy VP (CPK Nakuru)
Subukia VP (CPK Nakuru)
Weithaga VP (CPK Mount Kenya)
Withur VP (Ahero Catholic Mission)
(18 other VPs are at the enquiry stage of development)

Community Centres in Nairobi
Bahati CC (PCEA/MCK)*
Church Army Centre (CA/CPK Nairobi)*
Eastleigh CC (PCEA)*
Friends' Centre, Ofafa (EAYM)*
St. John's CC, Pumwani (CPK Nairobi) *

Joint NCCK projects with other bodies
Christian Churches' Educational Association*
Protestant Churches Medical Association*

NCCK assistance to other projects
Joint Refugee Services of Kenya*
Turkana Fisheries Co-operative Society*

National Communications Committee (RCC)
Secretary: Sr. Janice McLaughlin
Hughes Building (1st floor), Kenyatta Avenue
P.O. Box 48062, Nairobi.   *Tel: 21613/4*
    Formed in 1970 to co-ordinate communications development in Kenya. Membership: 13 Catholic diocesan communication co-ordinators, 10 Broadcast Committee members, 50 graduates of communications workshops.

National Conference Centre (RCC)
Chairman: The Rt. Rev. Msgr. C. Davies
Kiserian Catholic Mission (17 miles southwest of Nairobi)
P.O. Box 24876, Nairobi.
    Originally built as the Catholic national seminary, now proposed as a conference centre after renovation.

National Council of Catholic Women
Chairman: Mrs. Augusta Karanja
Hughes Building (1st floor), Kenyatta Avenue
P.O. Box 48062, Nairobi.   *Tel: 21613/4*

National Freedom from Hunger Committee of Kenya
(FFH)
General Secretary: Mrs. Jael O. Mbogo
Office: corner of Government Road/Jeevanjee Gardens
P.O. Box 30762, Nairobi.   *Tel: 24023*
    Kushinda Njaa. Begun in 1965 to combat hunger, malnutrition, unemployment and underdevelopment; works closely with church agencies (Bread for the World, Misereor, WCC, SODEPAX, Christian Aid, Fraternal Sharing Campaign, etc.) Supports over 120 development projects in Kenya, including agricultural, educational, nutritional development, and youth mobilisation projects.

National Holiness Association (NHA, WGM)
    A missionary society begun in the USA in 1910, which began at Kericho in 1933, and at Tenwik in 1935, which by 1955 had changed its name to World Gospel Mission.

National Lay Council, see Catholic Lay Council of Kenya

National Liturgical Commission
Chairman: Bishop J. de Reeper; Secretary: The Rev. Fr. J. Leffers
P.O. Box 150, Kakamega.   *Tel: 32*
    Composed of chairmen of Catholic diocesan liturgical commissions.

National Religious Education Commission
Chairman: The Rt. Rev. Msgr. C. Davies
P.O. Box 48062, Nairobi.   *Tel: 21613/4*
    A Catholic commission in process of development.

National United Churches Association of East Africa
Chairman: The Rev. Ayub Njenga

Office: Block V 26, Jericho House
P.O. Box 72782, Nairobi.
    An attempt to federate independent churches in Kenya whose registration application was refused in 1969 because the name was too similar to those of existing bodies.

Navigators, The
Area Representative: Mr. James L. White
19, Harrison Road, Lavington
P.O. Box 47300, Nairobi.   *Tel: 48147*
    Begun in the USA in 1933 to change lives through Christ, emphasising discipleship, personal evangelism, intensive individual training, Bible groups, leading to multiplication of disciples. Nairobi ministry in university through groups, two annual weekend conferences.

Nazareth Sisters
Mistress of Novices
P.O. Box 97, Meru.
    An indigenous congregation of Catholic religious women.

NCCK Film Library
Librarian: Mr. Peter Marangu
Church House (1st floor), Government Road
P.O. Box 45009, Nairobi.   *Tel: 22264*
    A large library of about 700 16mm. sound films (colour, and black-and-white) and 300 35mm. filmstrips, on Bible, OT and NT, church history, church and world, Christian life, and general educational.   See 160-page duplicated *NCCK Film Library Catelogue* for all details of bookings (one month's notice; length of loan, one month).

Neukirchener Mission
    A German interconfessional faith mission of Congregational tradition, with the full title Waisen- und Missionsanstalt e.V. (Orphan- and Mission Institute), founded in 1878 in Neukirchen-Vluyn, Germany, which began work on the Tana River in 1887. During World Wars I and II its missionaries were interned and the work was handed over to the Methodist Church. An attempt after 1945 to recover their lost influence resulted in a schism in 1966 (see Tana River Independent Church).

Newspaper archives
    The two major Kenya newspapers, *Daily Nation* and *East African Standard*, both have extensive archives on religion in Kenya (news cuttings and photographs).

Daily Nation (East African Newspapers (N.S.) Ltd.)
Librarian, Nation House, Tom Mboya Street
P.O. Box 49010, Nairobi.   *Tel: 27691, 21933*
    (Cuttings on 'Religion' under various headings, back to 1966; extensive collection of photographs).

East African Standard (Newspapers) Ltd
Librarian, Liverpool Road
P.O. Box 30080, Nairobi.   *Tel: 57633*
    (3 files of clippings on religion, arranged by subject and denomination; extensive photographs).

Ngong Diocese Communications Team
Co-ordinator: Mr. Stephen Mutuku
Bishop's House, Ngong
P.O. Box 24801, Karen, Nairobi.   *Tel: Karen 2318*

Njabini Rural Training Centre (CPK)
Principal: Mr. S.N. Mbatia
Rural Aid Mission, Kinangop
P.O. Box 15, South Kinangop.   *Tel: 3Y6*
    An Anglican (Diocese of Nakuru) rural service scheme, begun in 1964 and known as Rural Aid Mission, comprising RTC for 1,200 farmers a year (one-week courses), extension work visiting 100 homes, 30 adult literacy classes, and youth work; all done in association with local churches.

Nkubu Junior Seminary (Diocese of Meru)
Rector
Nkubu Catholic Parish
P.O. Box Nkubu, Meru.

Northern Frontier Medical Fellowship
Chairman: The Rt. Rev. N. Langford-Smith; Secretary: Dr. P.S. V. Cox (BCMS, P.O. Marsabit)
P.O. Box 56, Nakuru.   *Tel: 2810*

Begun in 1966 as NFM Mission (name changed in 1971), as an interdenominational fellowship of Christian doctors in government work in Northern Kenya. Active work in Marsabit, Maralal and Kapenguria.

Norwegian Pentecostal Mission
This missionary society is registered as a church (see Part IV).

Notre Dame Sisters, see Sisters of Notre Dame

Nyabondo Home for Crippled Children
Administrator: Sr. Olive Digan
Nyabondo Catholic Parish
P.O. Sondu, Kisumu.
Opened in 1956, now with 85 resident children aged 3-20 years suffering effects of polio, and over 250 outpatients. 7 outpatient clinics on Kano Plains; resident physiotherapists. Two-year course in home economics for crippled girls; orthopaedic workshop, surgery, schools.

Nyanza Christian College
Chairman: Bishop A.M. Ajuoga
Dala Hera ('City of Love'), Kibos Road
P.O. Box 782, Kisumu.   *Tel: 2536*
A complex of institutions operated by the Church of Christ in Africa at their headquarters, including Ogero Youth Centre, Homecraft Training Centre, Commercial Training College.

Nyeri Diocese Communications Team
Co-ordinator: The Rev. Fr. Anthony Mathenge
Mathari Mission
P.O. Box 25, Nyeri.   *Tel: 2462*

Nyeri Interdenominational Evangelism, see Inter-Christian Churches Denomination

Nyeri Junior Seminary, see St. Paul's Minor Seminary

Ofafa Jericho Church & Community Centre (CPK)
Vicar: The Rev. Canon Leonard Mbugua
Lumumba, Rabai Road off Charles New Road
P.O. Box 17174, Nairobi.   *Tel: 57580*
An Anglican centre begun in 1970; typing, book-keeping, primary education, also a parish church.

Office of the Attorney General, see Registrar of Societies

Officers' Christian Fellowship
Secretary: Capt. John Seii, Kenya Army
(Harambee House)
c/o P.O. Box 40668, Nairobi.   *Tel: 27411*
A fellowship of Christians in the 3 services (Army, Navy, Air Force), at present with an informal provisional organisation (Bible Study, prayer meetings), with a monthly associated prayer group.

Ogada Bible School (AIC)
Principal: Mr. J. Ogongo
AIC Station Ogada
P.O. Box 360, Kisumu.

Olooseos Rural Training Centre, see Maasai Rural Development Centre

Operation Mobilization (OM), m/v Logos
Operation Mobilization is an international mission (formerly Send the Light) specialising in book and educational services and unusual missionary methods. m/v *Logos* is an evangelistic training ship which calls at ports for Christian leadership conferences. *Logos* visited Mombasa for such a conference in April, 1971.

Opus Dei
Counsellor: The Rev. Fr. P. Cummings
Strathmore College
P.O. Box 25095, Nairobi.
A Catholic secular society (Sacerdotal Society of the Holy Cross) which supports Strathmore College, Kianda College, and other work in Kenya; in 1971, 5 secular priests served in the Archdiocese of Nairobi.

Organisation for Christian Acts of Mercy
c/o Meru Central Farmers Co-operative Union, Industrial Area
P.O. Box 6, Meru.   *Tel: Nanyuki 2267*

Orthodox Christian Youth Association of Kenya
(OCYAK)
Chairman: Mr. Humphrey G. Ngure (P.O. Box 157, Limuru)
General Secretary: Mr. J. Moses Mugo
Valley Road
P.O. Box 47008, Nairobi.   *Tel: 28804*
Begun in 1966, an AOC (Greek Orthodox) organisation with 1,600 members, to promote understanding of Orthodoxy by festivals (music, sports), leadership seminars. Branches in Elburgon, Kabatini, Maragoli, Matathia, Kikuyu.

Orthodox Seminary and Technical School
Principal
Waithaka
P.O. Box 44, Kikuyu.
Situated at the AOC headquarters a few miles northwest of Nairobi; foundation stone laid officially in a ceremony performed by Archbishop Makarios, President of Cyprus, in March, 1971.

Our Lady of the Mission Sisters
Mother Superior
P.O. Box 304, Machakos.

Pan-African Fellowship of Evangelical Students (PAFES)
Travelling Secretary: Mr. William Adodoadji
Jamhuri Estate
P.O. Box 48789, Nairobi.
A fellowship of university and college evangelical Christian Unions throughout Africa, to encourage Christian students to deeper spiritual life, to witness, and to lead others to Christ. Annual conferences, meetings.

Patrician Brothers, see Brothers of St. Patrick

PCEA Chogoria Bookshop
Manager: The Rev. Elias Kabii
Post office premises near Chogoria Hospital
P.O. Chogoria, Meru.

PCEA Church Union Committee
Secretary: The Rev. David Philpot
St. Paul's United Theological College, P.O. Limuru. Tel: Tigoni 421

PCEA Department of Christian Education
Director: Miss E. Gibbs
Delamere Flats, Kenyatta Avenue
P.O. Box 48268, Nairobi.   *Tel: 25095, 23262*

PCEA Lay Training Centre
Principal: The Rt. Rev. Crispus Kiongo
Thogoto
P.O. Kikuyu.   *Tel: 2135*

PCEA Literature Department
Secretary: The Rev. A.D. Lamont
P.O. Box 439, Nakuru.   *Tel: 2823*

PCEA Stewardship Team
Team: Rev. Stephen M. Cauri, Mr. Alun L. Hughes
704 Church House, Government Road
P.O. Box 48268, Nairobi.   *Tel: 27334*

PEFA Bible School & Correspondence School, see Nairobi Pentecostal Bible College

Pentecostal Assemblies of Canada (PAOC)
Field Secretary: The Rev. W. Cornelius
Mission Office. Jubilee House, Koinange Street
P.O. Box 21176, Nairobi.   *Tel: 28347*
A mission from Canada which began work in western Kenya in 1924, whose national-led church is now the Pentecostal Assemblies of God (PAG). In 1972 there were 42 missionaries in Kenya. For details of institutions, etc., see PAG. The PAOC also operates Lighthouse Christian Travel (Box 73852, Nairobi) from the above office.

Pentecostal Bible College (PAG)
Chairman: The Rev. Shem Irangi
Nyang'ori Mission
P.O. Box 316, Kisumu.   *Tel: Nyang'ori 1Y7*

Pentecostal Revival Church
Pastor: The Rev. Justus A. Odera
Hoblay Road, Mombasa
P.O. Box 98012, Mombasa.
A large congregation affiliated to Pentecostal Evangelistic Fellowship of Africa.

Pioneer Movement
National Chaplain: The Rev. Fr. Patrick O'Toole
Miguta Mission
P.O. Box 179, Kiambu.
A Catholic group founded to help those addicted to drink. Members wear badges and offer prayers.

P.M. Kiti Evangelistic Association
Chairman: Evangelist Peter Mullae Kiti
Ngerenyi Settlement Scheme, Plot No. 893
P.O. Box 68, Kilifi.
A Coast indigenous movement emphasising evangelism, and aiming to spread through opening branches; affiliated to PEFA.

Port Reitz School
Headmistress: Mrs. M. Beetham
Port Reitz (next to Chest Hospital)
P.O. Box 98342, Mombasa.   *Tel: 73567*
A Methodist primary school (begun 1965) for physically handicapped children; boarding and day, physiotherapy, speech therapy; 76 resident children, 24 day pupils, in 8 classes (Standards I to VII, plus remedial class).

Precious Blood Sisters
Mother Provincial
Convent: Riruta, Dagoretti Road
P.O. Box 21283, Nairobi.
Also known as Mariannhill Sisters. Founded in South Africa in 1885; came to Kenya (Mombasa) in 1910; educational and medical work.

Presbyterian Bible School (IBPFM)
Principal: The Rev. Eugene Fawcette
Mwingi
Private Bag, P.O. Kitui.

Priests' Association of Kenya
Chairman. Interim Steering Committee: The Rev. Fr. James Roy
Office: Jericho Parish
P.O. Box 48069, Nairobi.
Catholic priests' council, open to all diocesan and missionary priests working in Kenya; begun 1972. Publishes a *Bulletin* (Editor, Fr. M. Keane, P.O. Box 80262, Mombasa).

Primary School for the Blind
Principal: Captain Lucas
P.O. Box 80, Thika.

Prisoners Pastoral Care Committee
Secretary: Mr. Bramwell Wangusi
P.O. Box 45009, Nairobi.
A committee of the NCCK to co-ordinate the work of prisons chaplaincies and churches.

Project Development and Documentation Office (NCCK)
Staff: Miss Mary Muchai, Miss Irene Herm
Church House (4th floor), Government Road
P.O. Box 45009, Nairobi.   *Tel: 22264/5*

Protestant Churches Medical Association (PCMA)
Secretary: The Rev. Aaron Kerr
PCMA (Flat 3), Lenana Road near Woodlands Road
P.O. Box 30690, Nairobi.   *Tel: 20695*
Formed in 1962 to co-ordinate Protestant medical services, to deal on their behalf with government and local health authorities, and to assist member bodies with staffing, supplies, Christian standards in medicine, and pastoral and evangelistic aspects of medical work. There are 15 Protestant hospitals as members, and

19 dispensaries or maternity centres not attached to hospitals (for names and addresses, see under Hospitals, p. 267-268).

1970 statistics: (a) *hospitals*
Beds: 397 male, 369 female, 241 children, 102 other, 248 maternity
Inpatients: 14,322 male, 15,008 female, 7,866 children, 276 other, 9,574 maternity.
Outpatients: 170,407 new cases, 131,588 return cases.
Operations: 2,046 major, 8,989 minor.
Staff: 24 doctors, 12 managers, 36 clerical, 46 registered nurses, 94 enrolled nurses; total staff 1,205. Students in training (December, 1970) 281.
Outdispensaries: 43, 111 staff, 182,899 new patients, 162,640 return.

(b) *dispensaries, maternity centres not attached to hospitals*
Beds: 82 general, 69 maternity.
Inpatients: 3,833 general, 2,539 maternity.
Outpatients: 531,345 new cases, 98,202 return cases.
Operations: 1,401.
Staff: 27 registered; total, 168.

Provincial Literature Board (CPK)
Co-ordinator: The Rev. John M. Ball
Uzima Press Building, Normain Estate (on main road to Eldoret)
P.O. Box 665, Nakuru.   *Tel: 2425*
Representatives of Anglican dioceses in Kenya; to publish (through Uzima Press) and distribute Christian literature.

Pumwani Boys' Hostel (CHF)
Chairman: Mr. J.W. Leach, Warden: Mr. J. Kisia
Hamilton Street, Pumwani
P.O. Box 72636, Nairobi.   *Tel: 25387*
Opened in 1971 by the Christian Hostels Fellowship to provide inexpensive accommodation for 112 secondary school students and 46 young workers in three buildings. 30 of the students are Sudanese refugees.

Queen of Apostles Minor Seminary (Archdiocese of Nairobi).
Rector
Thika Road, Ruaraka
P.O. Box 48409, Nairobi.   *Tel: Ruaraka 2303*

Radio Emmaus, see Emmaus Bible School

Reformed Mission League
Plateau Road
P.O. Box 617, Eldoret.   *Tel: 2625*

Registrar of Societies, Office of the Attorney-General
State Law Office, Harambee Avenue
P.O. Box 30031, Nairobi.   *Tel: 27461*
This Office handles most aspects of the legal status of churches, denominations and dioceses.
All denominations and other autonomous or independent religious organisations in Kenya with 10 or more members over 18 years old are regarded by government as societies, and have been required to register since 1953. Individual parishes, congregations, local churches, branches, committees, or denominational organisations, are not regarded as separate entities if they recognise the denomination's official name, and so are not required to register if their denomination itself is registered. New dioceses, however, being separate entities, are required to register. The requirements can be seen by obtaining a copy of *The Societies Act 1968*, and *The Societies Rules 1968*, from the Government Printer, Nairobi (5 shillings). The status of all denominations in Kenya in March, 1972, is shown in this Handbook in the table *Statistics of the Churches in Kenya* (p. 183); see also comments at the beginning of the Directory of the Churches in Kenya (Part IV).

Advantages of registration Registration brings certain advantages to churches, including legal status, recognition by local authorities, financial safeguards (often required by banks), crystallisation of what may have been vague situations, safeguarding of members and their money through a constitution and recognised procedures, etc.

The Societies Act 1968   Under the provisions of the Act, any society or association of ten or more persons "shall, in the prescribed manner and within 28 days after the formation thereof, make application to the Registrar for registration or for exemption from registration under this Act" (Section 9). Every society which is not a registered society or an exempted society is an unlawful society, and any person who manages or assists in the management of an unlawful society is guilty of an offence and liable to imprisonment for a term not exceeding 14 years or to a fine not exceeding 50,000 shillings, or to both (Sections 4(1), 5). The Registrar may refuse to register a society where he is satisfied that a society is a branch of, or is affiliated to or connected with, any organisation or association of a political nature established outside Kenya, or if it appears to him that the society has among its objects any unlawful purpose or any purpose prejudicial to or incompatible with peace, welfare or good order in Kenya, or if the name under which the society applies to be registered so nearly resembles the name of any other society as to be likely to deceive the public or the members of either society (Section 11). The registration of a society may be cancelled or suspended if it fails to furnish, when called upon, its constitution, complete list of members, audited accounts, or annual returns to the Registrar (Section 12). Appeal to the Minister is allowed for (Section 15). At the beginning of 1971, there were 3,287 registered societies of all kinds, and 1,376 societies exempted from registration. Details together with full statistics of all aspects of registration, are given in the *Annual Report of the Registrar-General* 1970 (latest edition; Government Printer, 1972).

Application for registration   Application is made on the Registrar's Form A, which requires information about the name of the society, its objects, present number of members (defined as over the age of 18 years), names and titles of officers, and land or premises owned. Form B (location of office, and postal address) must also be returned. A detailed constitution is required; a specimen constitution can be supplied, as a result of which most constitutions tend to follow the same pattern. There is an application fee of Shs 20/-. Once registered, all societies are required to submit an annual return (Form 1) plus annual fee (Shs 5/- where membership does not exceed 25; for 26-100 members, 10/-; for 101-1,000 members, 20/-; and for over 1,000 members, 50/-).

Exemption   Any well-established, well-administered and responsible denomination may apply for exemption from registration (see Act, Section 51), thereby avoiding the necessity for annual returns. In March 1972, 26 denominations and dioceses were exempted (see table *Statistics of the Churches in Kenya*), as well as about 1,400 non-religious societies.

Official notice   Names of all societies newly registered, exempted, refused registration, cancelled, or proscribed, are published weekly in *The Kenya Gazette*. Further, any person may inspect, at the office of the Registrar, the register and documents relating to any society, and obtain copies or extracts on payment of a small fee (Section 48).

Historical review   Registration was first required in Kenya with the promulgation of The Societies Ordinance (1953), from which the present Act has evolved. Many African independent churches applied for registration before or around 1960, the earliest being: ABC (1954), ADC (1955), NLC (1956), AICN (1956), A Interior C (1956), ACHS (1957), HSCEA (1957), CCA (1958), HGCK (1958). Very few applications have been refused; such instances have usually been because the technical requirements of application have not been properly fulfilled. Quite a number of once-registered bodies have subsequently become defunct and ceased to exist, whereupon their registration has been cancelled. There is at present only one proscribed or prohibited society, Dini ya Msambwa. By 1968, about 86 independent churches were registered; by 1972, there had been many new applications (and a number of cancellations), causing the number of independent churches registered to rise to 100. In March 1972, as the table *Statistics of the Churches in Kenya* shows, there was a total of 123 denominations of all types registered, 22 exempted, and a further 12 with their applications under consideration. In addition, a small number of denomina-

tions and dioceses were not registered under The Societies Act but were instead registered as companies or incorporated as charitable bodies under the two acts in the following two paragraphs.

The Companies Act   Another form of registration with government is under The Companies Act, under which churches and other religious bodies wishing to hold land and property as companies may register, through the Office of the Attorney General. There are three kinds of recognised company — private, public, and foreign. In 1972 there were about 30 church or religious companies of all kinds. *Private* companies "must be formed with a view to making profit"; since this is not one of the objectives of churches, there are only three or four church-related private companies (East African Venture Company, Menno Travel Service, Mount Kenya Bookshop). *Public* companies, often limited by guarantee, include several charitable or non-profit bodies, such as: Church Commissioners for Kenya, Church Army, Holy Archbishopric of Irinoupolis, Salvation Army, Seventh-day Adventist Church (EA). *Foreign* companies have to be established abroad; examples include The Navigators, Dr. Barnado's Homes, Southern Baptist Convention, International Pentecostal Assemblies, IBSA, ISKCON, Missions to Seamen, United Bible Societies.

The Land (Perpetual Succession) Act (cap. 286)   Applications under this Act are dealt with through the Commissioner of Lands (see Ministry of Lands and Settlement, p. 275). First promulgated as an ordinance in 1923, the Act states in section 2(1): "Trustees or a trustee may be appointed by any body or association of persons established for any religious, educational, literary, scientific, social or charitable purpose, and such trustees or trustee may apply, in manner hereinafter mentioned, to the Minister for a certificate of incorporation of the trustees or trustee of such body or association of persons as a corporate body" In 1972, 69 church bodies held certificates of incorporation as charitable bodies under this Act, usually being titled as 'Trustees Registered', or 'Registered Trustees'; thereby enabling them to hold land and property. These included: all Catholic dioceses, most foreign missionary societies, most large denominations, six African independent churches, and a few large local congregations.

The African Christian Marriage and Divorce Act   Under this Act, specific ministers or priests of recognised denominations can be licenced to celebrate weddings as registrars of marriages. When first so licensed, the names of the ministers and their churches are published (weekly) in *The Kenya Gazette*. Licensed ministers belong to a wide variety of denominations, from the Catholic Church to the International Bible Students Association (Jehovah's Witnesses) and African independent churches (African Gospel Unity Church, Chosen Church of Holy Spirit in Kenya, International Fellowship for Christ, etc.) At the beginning of 1971, the total of all licensed ministers and priests was 195; during 1970 they celebrated 15,963 marriages under the Act *(Annual Report of the Registrar-General, 1970,* p. 48).

Registration of books and newspapers   Newly published books, and newspapers, have to be registered by the Registrar-General. In 1970, 25 per cent of the 164 books newly registered were on religious subjects, making about 40 new religious books published each year. Of the 60 newspapers published in Kenya, a large number were religious (see 'Index of Kenya Religious Periodicals' at end of *Bibliography* in this Handbook).

Religious Education Department (Kenya Catholic Secretariat)

Secretary: Sr. Aloysia O'Sullivan
Hughes Building (1st floor), Kenyatta Avenue
P.O. Box 48062, Nairobi.   *Tel: 21613/4*
   National office for co-ordinating work of religious education at all levels within the Catholic Church, for co-operating ecumenically with other Christian Churches, and other religions, and with the Kenya Institute of Education, and the Ministry of Education.

Religious Superiors' Association of Kenya (RSAK)

Chairman: The Rev. Fr. J. van Diepen; Sec./Treasurer: The Rev. Fr. J. Gilmartin

P.O. Box 1913, Kisumu.

An organisation, begun in 1967, with as members the superiors of 17 of the 19 Catholic religious communities of men in Kenya. Purposes. to study common problems, to co-ordinate, to facilitate exchange of information and ideas. Seminars, retreats, co-ordination with Association of Sisterhoods.

Rift Valley Academy (AIM)
Principal: Mr. H.C. Downing
AIC Kijabe Station
P.O. Box 80, Kijabe.   *Tel: 12Y1*

Rural Aid Mission, see Njabini Rural Training Centre

Sacred Heart Brothers, see Congregation of Our Lady of the Sacred Heart

St. Andrew's Church, Nairobi (PCEA)
Minister: The Rev. George E. Wanjau   ate Minister. The Rev
Kirk Road
P.O. Box 41282, Nairobi.   *Tel. 22218*

Large Nairobi PCEA church, founded in 1908, 900 members, 200 other active adherents. Weekly University Service run for and by students, regular VOK broadcast services, active support of PCEA projects (hospitals, social work, RTCs, schools for the deaf).

St. Andrew's School, Turi
Headmaster: The Rev. R. Drown
3 miles from Molo, on new road to Nakuru
P.O. Turi, Nakuru.   *Tel: Molo 11*

Begun 1932 as an Anglican foundation; mixed private preparatory school, ages 6-13, 220 boys and girls; 24 staff.

St. Charles Lwanga Home for Boys
Matron
P.O. Box 84392, Mombasa.

In 1963 the Catholic diocese of Mombasa purchased a house to cater for orphan boys; non-denominational; 8 children who attend local schools in Mombasa.

St. John's Community Centre (CPK)
Warden: Mr. Euphantas Mugo
Munyema Street, Pumwani
P.O. Box 72935, Nairobi.   *Tel: 23306*

An Anglican centre with a very diversified programme (Home Industries Programme, etc.).

St. John's Minor Seminary (Diocese of Kisii)
Rector
Rakwaro Catholic Parish
P.O. Box 504, Kisii.

St. Joseph's Minor Seminary (Diocese of Kitui)
Rector: The Rev. Fr. Patrick Donnelly
Mwingi Catholic Parish
P.O. Box 129, Kitui.

St. Joseph's Society for Foreign Missions (MHM)
Regional Representative for Kenya: The Rev. Fr. J. van Diepen
St. Mary's School
P.O. Box 350, Yala.   *Tel: 10*

Catholic society (Mill Hill Mission) founded in Mill Hill, London N.W. 7, in 1866, began in Kenya in 1902. Widespread work in 4 dioceses: Kisumu, 79 priests, 9 brothers; Kisii, 22 priests, 1 brother; Nakuru, 8 priests, 1 brother; Ngong, 12 priests, 4 brothers.

St. Julian's, Limuru
Warden: Miss Barbara Rutherford
Off Redhill Road, Limuru
P.O. Box 48121, Nairobi.   *Tel: Redhill 334*

A Christian lay community (4 women) and quiet guest house for 12 adults, a branch of St. Julian's, Sussex, England (1941; Kenya. 1956).

St. Luke's Hospital, Kaloleni (CPK)
Superintendent: The Rev. Dr. D. Milton-Thompson
A.C. Kaloleni, Giriama
P.O. Kaloleni, Mombasa.

St. Mary's Junior Seminary (Diocese of Mombasa)
Rector
Ndavaya Catholic Parish
P.O. Box 1014, Kwale, Mombasa.

St. Oda School for the Blind
Headmistress: Sr. M.M. Langereld
Aluor Catholic Mission (50 km from Kisumu)
P.O. Box 26, Maseno.

Begun in 1961; 109 children aged 3 years upwards, 8 teachers (6 Kenyans, 2 missionaries); normal primary schooling, plus 3-year home science course for older girls.

St. Patrick's Society, see Society of St. Patrick for Foreign Missions

St. Paul's Minor Seminary (Diocese of Nyeri)
Rector: The Rev. Fr. Anthony Mathenge
Mathari Catholic Parish
P.O. Box 505, Nyeri.   *Tel: 2462*

St. Paul's United Theological College
Principal: The Rev. Dr. Samuel Kibicho
Redhill Road (next to Limuru Conference Centre)
Private Bag, Limuru,   *Tel. Tigoni 338 (staff), 421 (students)*
Begun as CMS Divinity School in 1930, became united Anglican/Presbyterian/Methodist college in 1955 (now also RCEA), training men for the ordained ministry. 1971. 70 students, 10 staff, 3-year course, certificate or diploma in theology (university-related). Extensive field research over the years (see Kenya Church History Archives).

St. Peter's Seminary (Diocese of Kisumu)
Rector
Mukumu Catholic Parish
P.O. Box 2039, Khayega, Kakamega.

St. Stephen's Church (CPK)
Vicar: The Rev. Boaz Oduma
Jogoo Road
P.O. Box 17056, Nairobi.   *Tel: 57409*

In the early years of Nairobi, St. Stephen's was the largest church, built on the site of today's parliament and later transferred to Jogoo Road. In 1916, Sunday attenders numbered 1,500 Africans in two sittings (45% Kikuyu, 35% Kavirondo Luo and Luhya), with 500 at the Friday prayer meeting Similar numbers attend today's services.

St. Thomas Aquinas Regional Seminary
Rector: The Rev. Fr. Silas Njeru
Langata Road (14 miles south of Nairobi city)
P.O. Box 30517, Nairobi.   *Tel: Langata 405*
Founded 1963 as the Catholic national seminary to train future priests, 1972 enrolment, 120 students; 13 staff. Offers a six-year course of studies.

St. Vincent de Paul Society
Chairman of Superior Council. Mr. Peter L.J.O. Nyakiamo
Dagoretti Lane
P.O. Box 30011, Nairobi.   *Tel: 66760*
A Catholic charitable society aiding the poor. Six local conferences in Kenya; branches in many parishes.

Salvation Army Farm
Farm Manager: Major A. Lefeuvre
P.O. Box 274, Thika.   *Tel: Mitubiri 4Y7*

Salvation Army Officer Training College
Principal: Brig. Holmes
Desai Road
P.O. Box 27205, Nairobi.   *Tel: 25586*

Salvation Army Sunset Lodge
Manager: Brigadier E. Evans
Tritton Road
P.O. Box 90531, Mombasa.   *Tel: 23309*
Home for care of elderly people; 12 residents.

Scholasticate for Kenyan Sisters
Chairman: Sr. Claire M. Callahan
Headquarters: Corner of Ngong Road & Garden Road, Adams

Arcade
P.O. Box 14622, Nairobi.
A Catholic resident training centre for Kenyan sisters, with courses in Scripture, theology, etc.

School for the Deaf and Dumb (Diocese of Kisumu)
Sister-in-charge
Mumias Catholic Parish
P.O. Box 23, Mumias.

School for the Deaf and Dumb (Diocese of Kisumu)
Sister-in-charge
Nyangoma Parish
P.O. Bondo, Kisumu.

Scott Theological College (AIC)
Acting Principal: The Rev. David Richardson
Mumbuni
P.O. Box 49, Machakos.   Tel: 65
Founded in 1962 by AIM as a 4-year college training men and women for ministry in the AIC. Training is on 2 levels: (1) those with 2 years' secondary education, (2) secondary school graduates. Enrolment: 30; graduated, 40.

Scripture Union of Kenya (SU)
Organising Secretary: Mr. Harry J. Cotter
Office: Church House (3rd floor), Government Road
P.O. Box 40717, Nairobi.   Tel: 29841
Umoja wa Kujisomea Biblia. International body begun in 1867 to promote Scripture reading and study. Serves the churches in Kenya with daily personal Bible reading materials and in youth evangelism. 1971: about 8,000 users of SU daily

Bible reading notes (English and Swahili), 6,000 users of SU cards (in 5 Kenya languages), 2,000 children taught with SU Sunday school materials.

Secretary School for the Blind (Salvation Army)
Principal: Captain Michael Rich
Workshops Road
P.O. Box 704, Thika.   Tel: 2092

Seelsorgestelle fur die Deutschsprachigen Katholiken
Mother Provincial: Sr. Henna
c/o Missionary Sisters of the Precious Blood, Nakuru Road, Riruta
P.O. Box 21283, Nairobi.   Tel: 66944

Seventh-day Adventist Medical Service
Doctor-incharge:

Seventh-day Adventist Medical Service
Doctor-in-charge: Dr. R.M. Buckley
Medical Surgery, Crauford Road
P.O. Box 48629, Nairobi.   Tel: 26605

Shauri Moyo Baptist Centre
Director: Mr. Joe Snyder
Ahero Street
P.O. Box 44628, Nairobi.   Tel: 58880
Begun 1958 by BMEA; nursery school, 2-year commercial course, adult literacy, library.

Shibuyi Parish Co-operative Savings and Credit Society
Treasurer: Mrs. Rose Amalia Manyonje
Shibuyi Community Centre, Isukha Location
P.O. Box 101, Kakamega.   Tel: 32
One of many self-help groups and credit unions among Catholics; begun 1967, now 171 members. Works: church and convent buildings, harambee schools, social halls, nursery schools, water development project.

Sight by Wings
Secretary: Mr. John Ellison
Wilson Airport
P.O. Box 43387, Nairobi.   Tel: 58525
A flying eye-specialist service under Christian auspices, founded in memory of Philip Morris, operating in the East African territories with one aircraft based on Wilson Airport, Nairobi. Surgeons go out with colporteurs.

Sisters of Charity of Edelvale
Sister-in-charge: Sr. Edel
Edelvale, off Outer Ring Road, Embakasi
P.O. Box 17063, Nairobi.   Tel: Embakasi 258
A Catholic order with 13 sisters in Kenya, at 3 institutions: Edelvale Girls Home (begun 1959 for girls aged 11-16 years referred by social workers), Jamaa Maternity Home (Crescent Road, Uhuru Estate; a work for unmarried mothers begun in 1963), and Waridi Villa (Sports Road, Westlands, P.O. Box 47536, Nairobi; Tel: 61364). The legal entity is the Edelvale Trust.

Sisters of Charity of Eldoret
Superior: Sister Edel Bahati
P.O. Box 17063, Nairobi.   Tel: Embakasi 258

Sisters of Mary of Kakamega
Mother General: Sr. Frances Terese
P.O. Box 127, Kakamega.   Tel: 32
Independent national order of nuns begun 1932 by Dutch Ursuline Sisters, formally approved by Holy See in 1952. 13 by-convents in Kenya, 7 in Uganda. Social work, education, medical work.

Sisters of Mercy (Dublin)
Regional Superior: Sr. Mary Cora
Villa Maria, Sclater's Road
P.O. Box 14188, Nairobi.   Tel: 61012
A Catholic congregation founded in Dublin, Ireland, in 1831, for the service of the poor, the sick and the uneducated. Work in Kenya began in 1956; now 35 sisters, at: Shauri Moyo, Nairobi South B (Mater Misericordiae Hospital, 120 beds), Mbooni, Machakos, Miguta, Makueni. The Sisters of Mercy (Cork) and (Sligo) are different governmental units to the Sisters of Mercy (Dublin) (see below for addresses).

Sisters of Mercy (Cork)
Superior
P.O. Box 10, Eldama Ravine.

Sisters of Mercy (Sligo)
Superior
Karen
P.O. Box 24829, Nairobi.

Sisters of Notre Dame de Namur
Co-ordinator: Sr. Claire M. Callahan
Kenyatta College, Kahawa, Thika Road
P.O. Box 221, Ruiru.   Tel: Tembler 254
A Catholic order (1804, France; 1965, Kenya) specialising in education of the poor; work in dioceses of Meru, Kisumu (Eregi and Hambale), and Nairobi.

Sisters of Our Lady of Africa, see White Sisters

Sisters of St. Joseph
Mother General: Mother Teresa
St. Joseph's Convent, Bura
P.O. Bura, Voi.
Shirika la Masister wa Mt. Joseph. A congregation of African sisters founded in 1939 at Bura by the Precious Blood Sisters from Germany. Vocation: teaching, nursing, catechesis, social work. Work in 8 missions in Catholic Diocese of Mombasa; 44 professed sisters, 25 novices, 19 postulants.

Sisters of the Assumption of Nairobi
Superior General: Sr. Marie T. Gacambi
Assumption Sisters Generalate, St. Austin's Road
P.O. Box 25054, Nairobi.   Tel: 60035
A Catholic congregation founded in 1957 by Archbishop J.J. McCarthy for African girls; 38 professed sisters, 4 novices. Activities: schools, nursing, social work, parish work. Assumption Sisters also work in the Diocese of Kitui (Box 194, Kitui), and of Machakos (Mbooni, P.O. Kikima, Machakos).

Social Training Centre (Diocese of Kisumu)
Director
Kobujoi Parish
P.O. Box 44, Kapsabet.

Social Training Institute (Diocese of Meru)
Sister-in-charge: Sr. Adele Angela
Gitoro
P.O. Box 129, Meru.   *Tel: 106*

Society of Catholic Medical Missions
Reverend Mother
Holy Family Hospital, Nangina
P.O. Ukwala.

Society of Mary (Marianists)
Superior: The Rev. Fr. Robert W. Hertweck
Aquinas High School, Jogoo Road
P.O. Box 72000, Nairobi.   *Tel: 59046*
    A Catholic religious congregation of priests and brothers
founded in 1817 in France, primarily engaged in the education
of youth. In 1961, Marianists from the Cincinnati Province
(USA) began work in Mangu High School (253 students), and in
1963 Aquinas day-school (409 students). These two communities
have a total of 13 Marianists.

Society of St. Patrick for Foreign Missions (SPS)
Regional Superior: The Rev. Fr. J. Gilmartin
St. Austin's Road/Bernard Road
P.O. Box 25084, Nairobi.   *Tel: 48913*
    An Irish order (Kiltegan Fathers) founded 1932, begun in
Kenya 1952, with 119 priests in 5 Catholic dioceses (Eldoret 30,
Kitui 35, Nakuru 31, Lodwar 14, Kisumu 6).

SODEPAX Communications Working Group for Africa
Secretary: Canon Yinka Olumide
AACC Training Centre, Sclaters Road
P.O. Box 14206, Nairobi.   *Tel: 61166*
    Commenced in 1970, a national and ecumenical forum to
co-ordinate the Churches' development and communications
programmes.

SODEPAX Youth Group
Secretary: Mr. John Urunqu
Hughes Building (1st floor), Kenyatta Avenue
P.O. Box 48062, Nairobi.   *Tel: 21614*
    A group of over 50 young Kenyans who follow guidelines
from the SODEPAX Working Group for Africa but who focus
on communication projects. Has 4 working groups: drama,
broadcasting, audio-visuals, and journalism.

South Africa Compounds and Interior Mission (SACIM)
    A mission to Bantu goldminers in South Africa, which in
1914 moved to Kenya and worked with the Church of God
(Anderson) mission at and around Kima for a couple of decades.

Southern Baptist Convention (USA), see Baptist Mission of
East Africa

Span
Secretary for East Africa
P.O. Box 48789, Nairobi.
    A student magazine sponsored by the Pan-African Fellowship
of Evangelical Students.

Spiritans, see Congregation of the Holy Ghost

Strathmore College of Arts and Science
Principal: Mr. David C. Sperling
Strathcona Road (corner of St. Austin's Road)
P.O. Box 25095, Nairobi.   *Tel: 48315*
    Run by the Catholic organisation Opus Dei.

Sunday School by Post
Secretary: Mr. A.W.B. Street
P.O. Box 30223, Nairobi.

Swedish Evangelical Mission Society of Finland
Representative: The Rev. Gustav Norrvack
Atemo Lutheran Parish (LCK)
P.O. Oyugis.
    A Swedish-speaking mission, with 5 missionaries working
with the Lutheran Church in Kenya.

Swedish Free Mission (Svenska Fria Missionen) (SFM)
Secretary: The Rev. Rhode Struble
Office: Hatheru Road (off Bernard Road)
P.O. Box 47469, Nairobi (Box 1420, Nakuru).   *Tel: 66762*
    A pentecostal mission from Sweden now registered as the
Evangelical Free Mission in Kenya (see Part IV).

Swedish Lutheran Mission (SLM)
Mission Secretary: Mr. Erling Hansson
Itierio Mission (5 miles north west of Kisii town)
P.O. Box 165, Kisii.
    The Missionssalskapet Bibeltrogna Vanner (BVM) or Mi-
ssionary Society Friends True to the Bible, is a Swedish
Lutheran mission (Stockholm) founded in 1909, which began
work in Kenya in 1939 among Ethiopian refugees, and in 1948
in South Nyanza. It now works with the autonomous Lutheran
Church in Kenya.

Swedish Maranatha Mission (SMM)
Director: Mr. B. Sundh
P.O. Box 5, Kisii.
    A mission which works with the Maranatha Church (see Part
IV); registered name changed in June 1972 to Maranatha Mission
of Kenya. 'Maranatha' = 'Our Lord, come!' in the Aramaic
language.

Taita Bookshop
P.O. Box 1028, Wundanyi.

Tala Commercial School
Sister-in-charge
(In Tala township)
P.O. Box 1055, Kangundo.
    Run by Holy Rosary Sisters; typing, shorthand, book-
keeping.

TARGET, see East African Venture Company

Teachers' Prayer Fellowship, see Kenya Christian Teachers'
    Prayer Fellowship

T.E. Gikonyo Evangelistic Association
Chief Evangelist: The Rev. Thomas E. Gikonyo
P.O. Box 438, Nyeri.
    Founder was a former politician who on his way to China in
1962, came in touch in Dar es Salaam with American evangelists
in the aftermath of the T.L. Osborn Pentecostal campaigns, and
was physically healed. Beginning in 1963, he evangelised widely
in East Africa, and has congregations in Nyeri and Karatina.

Testimony Faith Homes
P.O. Box 133, Maseno.

Thika Bible Fellowship, see Bible Fellowship Church (in
    Part IV)

Thogoto Home for Aged Destitute (PCEA)
Chairman: Mrs. Elizabeth Kiongo
Kikuyu (near Kikuyu Hospital)
P.O. Box 48268, Nairobi.   *Tel: 25095*
    Founded in 1967, now has 7 aged women, 13 men.

Thomas Barnado House
Manager: Mr. Stanley E. Ablewhite
Langata Road, opposite Wilson Airport
P.O. Box 44261, Nairobi.   *Tel: 23727*
    A branch of Britain's Dr. Barnado's Homes, the House was
opened in 1961 and extended in 1968. There are 70 orphaned,
homeless, abandoned or destitute Kenyan boys and girls aged
from a few days to 16 years old. Girls are trained as nursery
nurses: a 2-year course for the Kenya Roll of Child Care Nurses,
and the National Nursery Examination Board course.

Trappist Fathers, see Cistercian Order

Trinity College (CPK)
                                          (1973) The
Warden: The Rev. Christopher Carey.
Jogoo Road (next to St. Stephen's Church)

P.O. Box 72430, Nairobi.   *Tel: 58655*

284

Founded in 1963 as a post-ordination college for Anglican clergy. Accommodation for 12 students; normal courses 10 weeks.

Trinity Fellowship (TF)
General Secretary: Mr. Godfrey D. Dawkins
c/o Siriba Teachers College
P.O. Box 192, Maseno.　　　　　　　　　　　*Tel: 4*
Founded in 1963, an inter-church non-denominational Christian charismatic youth movement specialising in missions of evangelism in the schools and colleges of Kenya. Illustrated magazine *This is That*, produced in Kenya 3 times a year.

Tumutumu Hospital (PCEA)
Superintendent: Mr. T. Thompson
Tumutumu Road (off Nanyuki Road)
P.O. Karatina.　　　　　　　　　　　　　　*Tel: 341*
Begun in 1912 by CSM; 120 beds.

Tumutumu School for Deaf Children (PCEA)
(4 miles north of Karatina, ½ mile off tarmac)
P.O. Karatina.

Turkana Fisheries Co-operative Society
Chairman: Mr. Ekamate Akeny
Head Office: Kalokol
Private Bag, Kitale.
A fishing co-operative, begun in 1964, now with 2,500 members, for purchase and marketing of fish from Lake Rudolf. One of many projects in which NCCK and the churches have been involved.

Ukamba Bible School (AIC)
Principal: The Rev. W.I. Davis
Mumbuni
P.O. Box 49, Machakos.　　　　　　　　　　*Tel: 65.*
Begun in 1928 by AIM; trains pastors and Christian workers usually of primary school background. 4-year course in English (previously in Kikamba); branch at Mulango, Kitui District, opened in 1962; and 1971, branch at Mukaa.

Union of Catholic Daughters
Sister-in-charge
Sega Convent
P.O. Box 19, Ukwala.
An indigenous organisation begun by a sister in 1971 for training girls in liturgy, Scripture understanding, and renewal in the church. 50 members.

United Bible Societies, Africa Regional Centre (UBS)
Regional Secretary for Africa: Mr. D. Cohen; Consultants: **Mr.** J.H. Girling (production), The Rev. J.M. Mbugori (Distribution), Mr. G.A. Nicholson (Management). Regional Translations Co-ordinator: Dr. H.F. Peacock.
Sunglora House (1st floor), Tom Mboya Street
P.O. Box 42726, Nairobi.　　　　　　　　*Tel: 26117*
A fellowship of all major national Bible societies united for consultation, mutual support and action for the widest possible effective distribution of the Holy Scriptures in the world; in Africa, 24 national Bible houses. Begun 1964; Nairobi office, 1968. During 1970, Scripture distribution in Africa was: Bibles, 1,201,714; New Testaments, 1,021,467; portions, 4,202,555; selections, 3,188,604; total, 9,614,340.

United Christian Mission, see African Evangelistic Enterprise

United Churches of Africa
Chairman: Bishop A.S. Odhiambo
Olympic House (2nd floor), Koinange Street
P.O. Box 16362, Nairobi.
A body with 'membership open to all independent churches', attempting to unite all such churches in Kenya, whose application for registration was refused in 1969. Claimed 3 member churches and 500,000 followers.

United Churches of East Africa
Chairman: The Rev. Joswa Kiarie; General Secretary: Mr. Joseph Lianzika
Ramsingh Photographers House, Tom Mboya Street
P.O. Box 72782, Nairobi.

An attempt to unite independent churches, whose application for registration was refused in 1969.

United Independent Churches of East Africa
Chairman: The Rev. Reuben Mudengani (P.O. Box 11293, Nairobi)
Ramsingh Photographers House, Tom Mboya Street
P.O. Box 72782, Nairobi.
An organisation with 10 member churches aiming 'to unite all independent churches in East Africa', and 'to represent all United Churches at the International Council of Christian Churches, World Council of Churches, T.L. Osborn Evangelistic Association, and to the Government'. Registration refused in 1969.

United Methodist Church Foreign Missions
The first Methodist mission in Kenya, later succeeded by the Methodist Missionary Society.

United Missionary Air Training and Transport, see Wings for Progress

United Orthodox Independent Churches of East Africa
Chairman: The Rev. Evanson Gadhura; Ecclesiastical General: Bro. James Ochwatta; General Secretary: Bro. Robert Makodawa
Penguin House (4th floor), Tom Mboya Street
P.O. Box 28919, Nairobi.　　　　　　　　*Tel: 35376*
Since the visits of Archbishop Daniel Alexander (AOC of South Africa) in the 1930s, many attempts have been made to unite or federate the resulting AOC, AIPC and other large independent churches of Kenya. This organisation was begun in 1971, the latest of a long line of such attempts. Members claimed: AICN, AIPC, AOC, ABC, MHGC, African Coptic Orthodox Church, Holy Ghost Coptic Church of Africa, Holy Spirit Church of East Africa, Holy Spirit Church of Zayun (Zion), and Independent African Orthodox Church. Strenuous attempts have been made to obtain recognition and assistance from, initially, the Greek Orthodox Patriarchate of Alexandria, and, latterly, the Coptic and Ethiopian Orthodox Churches (Egypt and Ethiopia).

United Orthodox Independent Zion Churches of Kenya
Chairman: Nabii Jathan Muranga; General Secretary; The Rev. T.J. Munjal
Juja Road, Eastleigh Section 3
P.O. Box 28159, Nairobi.　　　　　　　　*Tel: 50931*
An attempt to unite independent churches, whose application for registration was refused in 1971.

Unit of Research
Secretary for Research: The Rev. Dr. D.B. Barrett
Church House (7th floor), Government Road
P.O. Box 40230, Nairobi.　　　　　　　　*Tel: 23649*
Begun in 1965 as an Anglican centre for church and mission research in the Church of the Province of East Africa. In 1969, it became an ecumenical team serving all the churches, and assisting persons undertaking religious or theological research. Editors of *Kenya Churches Handbook, World Christian Handbook*, & c.

University Catholic Society
Chairman
St. Paul's Chapel, Uhuru Highway/University Way
P.O. Box 41512, Nairobi.
Society of Catholic students and staff at University of Nairobi; talks, discussions, action groups.

University of Nairobi, see Catholic University Chaplaincy, Christian Student Leadership Centre, Christian Union, Churches' Chaplaincy to the University Community, Council on Higher Studies in Religion, Department of Philosophy and Religious Studies, University Catholic Society

Ursuline Institute (Irish)
Mother Superior
St. Angela's School, Mutune

P.O. Box 179, Kitui.
A Catholic order of sisters from Sligo, Ireland, begun in 1535, specialising in education.

Uzima Press (CPK)
Secretary: The Rev. John Ball
Uzima Building, Normain Estate (on main road to Eldoret)
P.O. Box 665, Nakuru.   *Tel: 2425*
Publishing house of the Anglican Church in Kenya, working with Central Tanganyika Press (Dodoma), and Uganda Church Press (Mukono). Wide range of book titles. 'Uzima' = life, wholeness, soundness, health, maturity.

Vocational Training Centre for the Blind
Principal: Frater A.H. Verhoeven
Sikri, Kisii
P.O. Box 285, Kisii.

Voice of Kenya, Religious Department (VOK)
Religious Programme Producers: Mr. Festus Wanjohi; The Rev. Christopher Gichuhi
Broadcasting House, College Road
P.O. Box 30456, Nairobi.   *Tel: 34567 Ext. 209*
For regular broadcasting schedule, see table on p.

Voice of Prophecy Bible Correspondence School (SDA)
Director: Mr. James Mutero
Karura, off Redhill Road
P.O. Box 43224, Nairobi.   *Tel: 62338*
Courses are offered in Swahili, English, Luo.

Wajir Community Church
P.O. Wajir.
The Northern Province of Kenya is almost entirely Muslim by religion, and Christians of all denominations -- Protestant and Roman Catholic -- use a single community church in Wajir (and also in Garissa, Northeastern Province).

Week of Prayer for Christian Unity
Chairman of Steering Committee (1972): The Very Rev. J. Henry Okullu; Secretary: The Rev. J.L. Paterson (P.O. Box 41282, Nairobi. Tel: 22218).
Annual worldwide interdenominational occasion, in mid-January.

Wesley Lay Training Centre (MCK)
Lay Training Secretary: The Rev. Richard Firth
Wesley House, Mazeras
P.O. Box 98622, Mombasa.
Commenced in 1962 for courses at local church level, youth work, and correspondence courses in English and Swahili, including one on Christian stewardship.

White Sisters
Regional Superior: Sr. Madeleine
Maryhill School, White Sisters Road
P.O. Box 9, Thika.   *Tel: Karamaini 222, 241*

Wings for Progress
Secretary: Mr. J.J. Dames
Safari Air, Wilson Airport
P.O. Box 47331, Nairobi.   *Tel: 29597*
Formerly related to UMATT (United Missionary Air Training and Transport, in Nairobi 1964-67), begun in 1968 as a charitable company to assist all humanitarian agencies in remote or inaccessible areas, by providing air transport.

Wings of Healing Evangelistic Association
Chairman: Mr. Samuel Mwawaka
P.O. Box 72845, Nairobi.
A small organisation directed towards evangelism, reporting 20 members, whose registration was cancelled in 1966.

Women's Guild Home for the Aged
Secretary: Mrs. Grace Kamau
P.O. Box 45, Uplands.   *Tel: Cianda 244*

Women's Social Institute
Chairman: Mr. J. Gituma
Consolata Sisters
P.O. Box 129, Meru.   *Tel: 106*
Begun by Catholics in 1965, offering one- and two-year vocational courses. Graduates since 1966: 32 social workers, 168 nursery teachers, 90 secretaries (commercial courses).

Women's World Day of Prayer
Chairman: Kenya National Committee: Mrs. John Mpaayei
P.O. Box 47180, Nairobi.
An interdenominational worldwide day of prayer held on the first Friday in March each year; prayers prepared each year by women of a different country (1972, Germany; 1973, New Zealand).

Word of Life, Kenya
Director: Mr. Manfred Kettering
Word of Life Youth Centre: Fort Smith Road, Kanyariri, Upper Kabete
P.O. Box 29120, Nairobi.
A camping ministry for young people, begun in 1936 in USA, and in Kenya in 1971; associated with former Kenya visitor Evangelist Jack Wyrtzen. Weekend Bible conferences, youth leaders' courses; in 1972, camping accommodation is open to 200 young people ages 15-30 during vacation months (April, August, December).

World Gospel Mission (WGM)
Executive Secretary: The Rev. Dean W. Strong
WGM Mission (on Kisumu road, off to right)
P.O. Box 123, Kericho.   *Tel: 123*
An American mission begun in 1910 as the National Holiness Association, which began in 1932 in Kenya at Kericho; in the 1950s, the name was changed to WGM. There are now 36 missionaries, mainly working in co-operation with the Africa Gospel Church. The WGM has operated schools for many years and now it and the AGC sponsor 68 primary schools. There are also medical centres: Tenwek Hospital, and centres at Kabason also medical centres: Tenwek Hospital, and centres at Kabason and Naikarra.

World Presbyterian Missions (WPM)
Secretary
Gai Mission
Private Bag, P.O. Mwingi, Kitui.   *Tel: RN 2044*
An American mission which broke in the USA from the Independent Board for Presbyterian Foreign Missions in 1957. Missionaries in Kenya then assisted in the formation of a new body, the African Evangelical Presbyterian Church, in which they now work.

World Student Christian Federation (WSCF)
Secretary, Africa Region: The Rev. Jose Belo Chipenda
Church House (7th floor), Government Road
P.O. Box 14782, Nairobi.   *Tel: 27334*
International student organisation begun in 1895 with headquarters in Geneva, Switzerland; enables national student Christian organisations to function in about 30 African nations. Nairobi office opened in 1969, helping students throughout the continent to meet on national, sub-regional and regional levels.

Xavierian Brothers, see Brothers of St. Francis Xavier

Young Christian Ambassadors Fellowship (YCAF)
National Director: The Rev. Pastor Joseph Kayo; Evangelist: The Rev. Pastor A.M. Likhaya
HQ: Penguin House (4th floor), Tom Mboya Street
P.O. Box 28255, Nairobi.   *Tel: 20500*
An independent Pentecostal group whose denomination is registered as Deliverance Church; oriented towards youth in schools, colleges and institutions, and emphasising charismata, speaking in tongues, divine healing, shouting for victory.

Young Christian Students (YCS)

Chairman: Mr. Michael Toror; Chaplain: The Rev. Fr. M. Drohan
Kenyatta College
P.O. Box 221, Ruiru.   *Tel: Templar 356*
   An international Catholic organisation, begun in Kenya in 1956 and present in all dioceses except Marsabit, working in schools, training colleges and the university among students ages 16-30

Young Men's Christian Association (YMCA)

National General Secretary: Mr. Philip A. Oyango
YMCA, State House Road
P.O. Box 30330, Nairobi.   *Tel: 22217, 23567*
   International interdenominational organisation, begun in Kenya in 1910, to serve all people irrespective of race, religion, class, nationality, or political opinion, meeting their physical, mental and spiritual needs by programmes, hostels, recreational centres, community centres, craft training centre. 1970: 5,000 members, 20,000 participants, 12 staff. *Major branches:* Box 330, Thika; Box 33, Nyeri; Box 1754, Kisumu; Ngewa, Box 200, Ruiru.

Young Women's Christian Association (YWCA)

National Chairman: Mrs. Ann W. Ndegwa, National Secretary:
   Mrs. Margaret Mugo
Kirk Road/Protectorate Road
P.O. Box 40710, Nairobi.   *Tel: 20707*
   Begun in Nairobi in 1912, an interdenominational and international organisation whose purpose is 'to build a fellowship of women and girls devoted to the task of realising in our common life those ideals of personal and social living to which we are committed by our faith as Christians,... as we seek to follow Jesus', and 'to promote community service amongst all people'. In Kenya, membership (1971) is 3,700, with 27 adult women's clubs, 40 youth clubs, 3 hostels for girls (Nairobi, Mombasa, Kisumu), 2 vocational training schools for girls (Nairobi, Mombasa), day nurseries in the three main cities, dressmaking courses, flower arrangement, good grooming, club work, and adult literacy work throughout the country.
Branches Coast Province (General Secretary, Cliff Avenue, P.O. Box 90214, Mombasa. T: 25426), Eastern Province, Nyanza, Nairobi.

Youth for Christ (YFC)

Chairman: Dr. Stephen Talitwala; Director: Mr. C.G.T. Hindley;
   Full-time Workers: Mr. & Mrs. B. Cummins
Meetings: City Hall, Nairobi.
P.O. Box 72435, Nairobi.   *Tel: 23348*
   An international interdenominational organisation, begun in Kenya in 1967, to present the Gospel by means of specialist youth rallies, clubs, film shows, youth activities in co-operation with the churches. Rallies: bi-monthly, normally in City Hall, Nairobi
Branches Mombasa (Secretary: Mr. John Chege); Nakuru.

Youth Service Abroad (YSA)

CMS Representative: The Rev. John Ridout
CMS Office, First Ngong Road, off Bishop's Road
P.O. Box 40360, Nairobi.   *Tel: 20147*
   A scheme to send young persons and graduates abroad from Britain for one year's service under the Church Missionary Society. In Kenya, in 1972 there are 46 YSAs, mostly teachers in Harambee and other schools across the country.

YWCA Vocational Training Centre

Principal: Miss Patricia Tyler
Likoni (near Ferry)
P.O. Box 96009, Mombasa.   *Tel: 76449*
   A residential school begun in 1967 for girls of any religion wanting secretarial and general development training (usually over 18 years, and with School Certificate). One-year course, shorthand, typing, English, office practice.

6

Part VI

Kenya's Other Religions

The Heritage of Traditional Religions

Luo religious specialist in a traditional dance.

John S. Mbiti

Africans are notoriously religious, and each people has its own religious system with its set of beliefs and practices. Religion permeates into all the departments of life so fully that it is not easy or possible always to isolate it. This statement can be applied to Kenya as well as to many other countries of Africa.

It is possible to speak of traditional religions in the plural because there are more than fifty Kenyan peoples (tribes), and each has its own religious system. To ignore traditional beliefs, attitudes and practices can only lead to a lack of understanding of African behaviour and problems. Religion is the strongest element in the traditional background, and exerts probably the greatest influence upon the thinking and living of the people concerned.

Because traditional religions permeate all departments of life, there is no formal distinction between the sacred and the secular, between the religious and non-religious, between the spiritual and material areas of life. Wherever the African is, there is his religion.

Traditional religions are not primarily for the individual, but for his community of which he is part. Chapters of African religious heritage are written everywhere in the life of the community, and in traditional society there are no irreligious people. To be human is to belong to the whole community, and to do so involves participating in the beliefs, ceremonies, rituals and festivals of that community.

These traditional religions in Kenya are not universal; they are tribal. Each traditional religion cannot be propagated in another tribal group. This does not rule out the fact that religious ideas may spread from one people to another. But such ideas spread spontaneously, especially through migrations, intermarriage, conquest, or expert knowledge being sought by individuals of one tribal group from another. Traditional religions have no missionaries to propagate them; and one individual does not preach his religion to another.

Similarly there is no conversion from one traditional religion in Kenya to another. Each society has its own religious system, and the propagation of such a complete system would involve propagating the entire life of the people concerned. Therefore a person has to be born in a particular society in order to assimilate the religious system of the society to which he belongs.

The traditional African world is a unity centred upon man. We can use five categories to describe it:

(i) *God*, as Creator and Sustainer of all things, is acknowledged by each people of Kenya, but some know and say little about Him. To show the variety of these concepts of God, we have appended to this article a table giving a list of African peoples in Kenya, with the traditional names for God that each uses.

(ii) *Spirit beings* are thought to be the occupants of the spirit world which is much like the physical, and not distant from it. They are composed of spirits and off-spring of people who died in the distant past; and the departed of up to four or five generations back, but who are recognised by surviving relatives and friends—and these latter we call the living dead to distinguish them from the other spirits. These are the ones who feature most in African religious practices and ideas.

(iii) *Man*, for whose origin there are different legends from society to society. It is also narrated variously how death came into the world. But after physical death man continues to exist in the spirit world, though it is not generally said or known whether such life comes to an end.

(iv) *Animals and plants*, together with

(v) *Non-living objects*, form the physical environment of man.

This five-fold world is knit together by that invisible and mystical force or 'electricity' of Nature, known by anthropologists as *mana* (using a Polynesian word). Within this totality of existence, man or the other categories cannot be isolated from the rest of the totality without damaging the whole of creation. Balance exists between man and the other modes of existence. Culture and the problems of today are derived aspects of the basic existence of man; they are his creative response (or otherwise) to the other four modes of existence. Morals, ethics, and the like are relative realities arising out of man's interrelationship with men and the rest of ontology.

A great number of beliefs and practices are to be found in African societies in Kenya. These are not, however, formulated into a systematic set of dogmas which a person is expected to accept. People simply assimilate whatever religious ideas and practices are held or observed by their families and communities. These traditions have been handed down from forefathers, and each generation takes them up with modifications suitable to its own historical situation and needs. Individuals hold differences of opinion on various subjects; and the myths, rituals and ceremonies may differ in detail from area to area. There are no creeds to be recited; instead, the creeds are written in the heart of the individual, and each one is himself a living creed of his own religion. Where the individual is, there is his religion, for he is a religious being. It is this that makes Africans so religious; religion is in their whole system of being.

TABLE 1
NAMES FOR GOD OF KENYAN PEOPLES

A majority of these names refer to attributes of the Deity ('Creator', 'Omnipotent'). Translations are given in *Concepts of God in Africa*, p. 327 - 336.

Bajun	*Allah*
Boran	*Waqa*
Digo	*Mulungu*
Dorobo	*Asis, Tururit*
Duruma	*Mulungu*
Elgeyo	*Asis*
Embu	*Ngai*
Galla	*Waqa*
Giriama	*Mulungu*
Gusii	*Erioba*
Kamba	*Mulungu, Ngai, Mumbi, Mwatuangi, Asa*
Kikuyu	*Ngai, Murungu, Mwenenyaga*
Kipsigis	*Asis, Chebtalel, Chebongolo*
Kuria	*Enyasaye*
Luhya	*Wele, Were, Nyasaye, Nabongo, Khakaba, Isaywa*
Luo	*Nyasaye, Wang', Chieng', Nyakalaga, Tham*
Maasai	*En-kai, N'gai, Ai, Parsai, Emayian*
Marakwet	*Asis*
Mbere	*Ngai, Murungu*
Meru	*Murungu, Ngai, Mwene inya*
Nandi	*Asis, Cheptalil, Chepkeliensokol, Chepopkoiyo, Chebonamuni*
Pokomo	*Muungu*
Pokot	*Tororut, Ilat*
Rabai	*Mulungu*
Rendille	*Wah*
Swahili	*Mungu*
Taita	*Mlungu*
Turkana	*Akuj*

LITERATURE

There is a vast literature on African religions and traditional concepts. The heritage of traditional religions in Africa as a whole is described in two works by J.S. Mbiti, *African religions and philosophy* (New York: Praeger, 1969, and in Kenya: Heinemann) from the opening chapter of which parts of the present article have been adapted, and *Concepts of God in Africa* (London: SPCK, 1970), from which the preceding table has been adapted. In Kenya, there have been a number of studies of traditional religion in particular tribes; these will be found in the Bibliography to this Handbook.

Witchcraft eradication leaders:
Two practitioners reviving traditional religious practices in recent years: left: Kajiwe (or, Tsume Washe); bottom left: Kajiwe in action as a witchfinder; bottom right: Kabwere (or, John Bosco Bakari, Ali Bin Kabwere).

Friday prayers at Jamia Mosque, Nairobi.

Islam in Kenya and Relations with the Churches

James D. Holway

Islam in Kenya

There are in mid-1972 some 770,000 Muslims in Kenya. Most of them live along the Coast and in North-Eastern Province. Between Tanga and Mombasa there is the Digo tribe, about 130,000 of whom live in Kenya, and form the only wholly Muslim Bantu tribe in the country. There are 30,800 Arabs, all Muslims, living in Mombasa and along the Coast northwards. Other smaller Muslim groups whose home is at the Coast include the Swahili-Shirazi (8,000), the Bajun (24,000) and the Pokomo, of whom some 33,000 are Muslim. In North-Eastern Province the Somali form the largest ethnic group of Muslims, numbering 273,000. Muslims of Asian origin are concentrated in Mombasa and Nairobi; in the whole of Kenya they number about 50,000, of whom 13,000 are Ismailis (or Khojas), 3,000 are Ithnasher-is, and perhaps 2,000 are Bohoras (or, to use the spelling in Asia, Bohras), the rest being Sunnis.

Besides these major groups there are minor communities scattered throughout the country in village-type communities, made up for the most part of people of diverse ethnic origin. The chief populations of this nature at the district level are the 25,000 mainly Luhya Muslims in North Nyanza and about 5,000 in Central Nyanza. In addition to these may be mentioned tribes such as the Boran, Gabbra, Sakuye and Orma, totalling about 80,000, who are pagans with some small Islamic influence.

Recent Events

The most important Muslim event in recent years in Kenya was the long-awaited publication in 1969 of Sheikh Abdullah Saleh al-Farsy's translation of the Qur'an into Swahili. This translation is a breach of the traditional view that the Qur'an is untranslatable; but Sheikh Abdullah felt it was necessary because of the Ahmadiyya translation of the Qur'an, which is stated by Sunnis to contain deliberate mistranslations favouring Ahmadiyya doctrine. His commentary on the text is mild towards Christianity but severely hostile towards the Ahmadiyyas. The translation was published in Nairobi by the Islamic Foundation and made possible by a donation from the ruler of Qatar.

In regard to other religious observations, 467 people made the pilgrimage to Mecca in 1971. Ramadhan, the month of fasting, is widely observed in 1972 lasted approximately from 9 October to 8 November; all Muslim festivals advance by about twelve days each year). The festival of Id al Fitr which marks the end of Ramadhan, and Id al-Hajj held when the pilgrims are at Mecca (27 January in 1972), are gazetted by the government as public holidays for Muslims. Attempts over a number of years by Muslim members of Parliament to make them general holidays have not so far been very successful. However, in 1971 President Kenyatta decreed that Id al-Fitr should be a general public holiday. Milad al-Nabii, Muhammad's birthday, is celebrated in May.

International leaders of the various Muslim sects visit Kenya from time to time. Thus Dr. Syedna Mohammed Burhanuddin Saheb, head of the world Bohora community, came in August, 1968. Maulana Hafiz al-Haj Muhamed Ibrahim Khustar visited Kenya from Mauritius in July 1970 to give lectures on Islam. The Aga Khan comes from time to time, the last occasion being in February, 1972.

Muslims in Kenya are conscious of their international links. Thus they close their shops as a mark of respect for the death of a foreign Muslim national or religious leader, such as President Nasser in September, 1970, and the Ithnasheri scholar and religious leader al-Haj Syed Mohsin al-Hakim in July 1970. Or they may hold special celebrations as the Ismailis did at the birth of Princess Salima, daughter of the Aga Khan, on 25 July, 1970. Islam in Kenya receives a good press, helped by the controlling interest of the Aga Khan in the *Nation* series of newspapers, and all events of interest to Muslims are reported. Both the Nairobi daily newspapers, the *East African Standard* and the *Daily Nation*, devoted a great deal of space throughout much of 1970, both in news and correspondence columns, to the 'forced brides' issue in Zanzibar. Despite the mobilisation of public opinion on this humanitarian issue, Kenya Muslims were unable to bring any pressure to bear.

Divisions within Islam in Kenya

The principal sects of Islam are all represented in this country. The chief division is into Sunnis and Shias, and there is also a small Ahmadiyya community.

1. Sunnis

Most African and Arab Muslims in Kenya are Sunnis. For them the basis of the community is the *sharia*, the infallible law, which derives primarily from the Qur'an and the Hadith, which are the traditions handed down about what Muhammad said and did in different circumstances. Together these form the basis of a legal system which governs every aspect of life for a devout Muslim to the minutest degree; for example, it specifies with which foot one should cross the threshold on entering or leaving a house. The system has been extended by analogy to cover situations and environments beyond those in which Muhammad lived. Sunnis guard against complete innovations, and the application of the principle of analogy becomes forced at times.

A Sunni may belong to any one of the four Muslim law schools: Hanafite, Malikite, Shafiite or Hanbalite. Called *madhhab* in Arabic and *madhehebu* in Swahili, the law schools are not analogous to Christian denominations. In Kenya most Sunnis are Shafiites, although about 10,000 Asian Sunnis are Hanafites.

Within the Sunni community there are two customs which may be encountered at the Coast. First is the practice of saint-worship. Processions are made with chanting and dancing to the grave of Shaha Mshaham bin Hisham (died 1592) on a cliff on Mombasa Island facing Kisauni. In the centre of Mombasa there is the Sheikh Jundani mosque containing the sheikh's grave, which is visited by Muslims to deposit offerings and to make requests; his intercession is considered to be very powerful. There are buildings in the ruined towns on Manda and Pate islands containing the graves of saints, to which visits are made.

Secondly, some Sunnis are members of Sufi or Dervish orders. A select number of men form a group which celebrates the *dhikr* (Arabic for 're-membrance of God'), a form of worship which involves chanting the name of God to the accompaniment of swaying and jumping in unison. Sunnis also hold *maulidi*, evening gatherings at which poems in praise of Muhammad are chanted.

2. Shias

The Shias in Kenya are almost exclusively Muslims of Asian origin. For them the basis of the community is the Imam, the infallible leader, a descendant of Muhammad through his cousin and son-in-law Ali. Veneration of Ali is an important part of Shia worship. ('Shia' derives from *shi'at 'Ali*, Arabic for 'the party of Ali'). The different sects among the Shias arose over disputes in the succession, although once separated, they became further differentiated as time went on by other variations in belief and practice.

(a) Ithnasheris

Ali was regarded as the first Imam in a line of succession of descendants of Muhammad. After the death of the sixth Imam, Jafar, in AD 765, one of two rival groups recognised his younger son Musa al-Kazim as the seventh Imam. This line continued as far as the twelfth Imam, who disappeared in AD 878, hence this group is known as the 'Twelvers' or Ithnasheris (Arabic *Ithna'ashariyya*). They expect the twelfth Imam to reappear one day. This sect is the official religion of the nations of Iraq and Iran. Ithnasheris go on pilgrimage to Najaf, Karbala and the tombs of the Imams in Iraq, in addition to the pilgrimage to Mecca. Karbala was where Ali's son, Husain, was killed in battle by Sunni opponents in AD 680. His death occurred on the tenth day of Muharram, and each year the anniversary is an occasion for Ithnasheris to mourn his death. It has been called the Muslim Good Friday.

Insofar as there is a world leader of the Ithnasheri community it would be His Exalted Eminence Ayatullah al-'Uzma, Aqai Syed Mohsin al-Hakim Tabatabai, Grand Mujtahid, who resided at the principal centre of Ithnasheri religious learning at Najaf until his death in July 1970. His successor has not yet been appointed.

In Kenya, Ithnasheris are found chiefly in Mombasa and Nairobi. At Mombasa they maintain a small Bilal Mission. The town is also the seat of the Supreme Council of the Federation of Khoja Shia Ithna-Asheri Jamaats of Africa, representing about 17,000 people.

(b) Ismailis

We have mentioned above the two rival groups of AD 765. The second maintained that the succession should pass through Imam Jafar's eldest son, Ismail. Ismail was in fact already dead, and they therefore recognised his son Muhammad as the seventh Imam. Within this group, there was yet another disputed succession in AD 1094. After the death of the Fatimid caliph al-Mustansir, the army leader in Egypt recognised the late caliph's younger son al-Musta'li as Imam, whilst the easterners recognised his eldest son Nizar. The followers of Nizar have continued to the present time with yet another disputed succession in 1310 producing a small sect in Syria; and the 49th Imam in this line is Karim, His Highness the Aga Khan. His followers are known as Ismailis, or Khojas. The full title which they give their community is the Shia Imami Ismailia.

Ismailis in Kenya are organised under three Provincial Councils at Nairobi, Mombasa and Kisumu. In addition there is the Council for Kenya, and the Executive and Supreme Councils for Africa, all with offices in Nairobi. The community has large modern hospitals in Nairobi and Mombasa, open to all communities, and a maternity home at Kisumu. Education is organised under the provincial councils with a number of nursery, primary, and secondary schools in each of these three cities.

The principal Ismaili building in a town is called the jamatkhana by Ismailis, and frequently the Khoja Mosque by non-Ismailis. It contains a mosque, but is more than just a place of worship. The jamatkhana is a community centre in every sense of the term, with a library, offices, and facilities for communal meals, recreation and social functions.

(c) Bohoras

After the disputed succession of AD 1094, the supporters of Musta'li followed his succession down to the 21st Imam al-Taiyib, who as an infant

Ahmadiyya translator of the Koran into Swahili presents a copy to Mzee Kenyatta in 1958.

299

was 'taken into concealment'. The Bohoras believe that the Imams, successors of al-Taiyib, are living in total secrecy somewhere, and will reveal themselves on some future occasion. In the meantime the community is ruled by a line of deputies called the *dai al-mutlaq*. The present deputy is the 52nd, His Holiness Dr. Syedna Mohammed Burhanuddin Saheb, who resides in Bombay and occasionally visits Kenya. Disputes in the succession of *dais* have caused schisms. One of these in 1588 divided the community into the Dawoodis (in India) and the Sulaimanis (in Yemen); so that from the point of view of religious succession, the community in Kenya should be called the Dawoodi Musta'li Ismaili Shias. In practice they call themselves the Dawoodi Bohoras, the word *bohora'* being supposed to mean 'traders', though its origin is in doubt. The representative of the reigning Dai in East Africa is Amil Janab Taherbhai Saheb Ezuddin Saheb.

3. Ahmadiyyas

There is also the Ahmadiyya or Qadiani sect, begun near Lahore (now Pakistan) in 1890, which is regarded as heretical by other Muslims. They have missionary stations at Nairobi, Mombasa and Taveta, and numerous followers in North Nyanza; their following, figures for which they do not divulge, probably does not exceed 2,000. They publish a monthly paper in English, *East African Times*, and one in Swahili, *Mapenzi ya Mungu*, and a range of booklets in English and Swahili, all strongly anti-Christian. The first printing of their translation of the Qur'an into Swahili, with commentary, was of 10,000 copies in 1953, and this is still on sale.

Relations with the Churches

Relations between Muslims and Christians in Kenya are distant but not hostile, each community accepting the existence of the other. Many Christians in non-Muslim areas think of Islam as yet one more in the plethora of Christian denominations existing in the country, and this point of view suits Muslims very well. Muslims are a minority and resist any attempts at conversion to Christianity. The number of Muslims who do become Christians is in any case small and very few Christians have any taste for the unrewarding work of evangelising Muslims, so that both sides are content with the status quo. Such conversions as do occur from Islam to Christianity are mainly as a result of the need for formal education. Conversion of Christians to Islam is chiefly due to marriage, every pressure being put upon the Christian partner in a mixed marriage to become Muslim and to raise the children as Muslims.

The National Christian Council of Kenya in 1964 appointed an adviser on Islam, the Rev. James Ritchie, who worked for two years at Mombasa in connection with the Islam in Africa Project (an ecumenical Christian organisation). The IAP aims at creating in Christians a greater desire to present the Gospel to Muslims. Where there is hostility it tries to generate a spirit of love towards Muslims in Christian hearts. The IAP is active in

West Africa, where there is a study centre, at Ibadan, and a number of local advisers in each country. The IAP has not met with much response in Kenya, but the NCCK's Department of Biblical Study and Research has a small Panel on Islam which organises occasional meetings.

LITERATURE

J.S. Trimingham's *Islam in East Africa* (Oxford: Clarendon Press, 1964) is the best book on Islam in Kenya, although since it covers the three East African countries it is not always clear how much the subject-matter applies to Kenya. A.Guillaume's *Islam* (London: Penguin Books, 1954) is an inexpensive book covering the religion of Islam as a whole. *Qurani Takatifu* (Nairobi: The Islamic Foundation, 1969) is the Qur'an in Arabic with a Swahili translation and commentary by an orthodox Muslim, A.S. al-Farsy. In modern English, there is a translation of the Qur'an by N.J. Dawood: *The Koran* (London: Penguin Books, 1956), which is relatively inexpensive. Lastly, on relations between Islam and Christianity, there is an excellent book by J.H.S. Crossley, *Explaining the Gospel to Muslims* (London: Lutterworth Press, 1960), also available in Swahili as *Kuwaeleza Waislamu Injili,* and in Arabic as *Kaifa Ya'malu al-Injilu.*

Three Africans, who have become Hindus, in the Arya Samaj temple, Nairobi.

Hinduism, Jainism and Sikhism in Kenya

Terence P. Day

I. HINDUISM

The Kenya census of population over the years have recorded the growth of the Asian community from 11,787 in 1911, to 43,623 in 1931, 97,687 in 1948, 176,613 in 1962 (of which 55 per cent were Hindus and 12 per cent Sikhs), falling to 139,037 in 1969, and rising again to an estimated 155,000 in 1972. In the 1969 census, 60,994 Asians were recorded as Kenya citizens, the rest being Indian citizens and British passport holders with a few thousands whose status was still to be determined. These figures compare with 105,000 for the total Asian population of Tanzania, and 80,000 for Asians in Uganda in 1970 dropping to almost zero by 1973.

According to the rough estimates of the present survey, the proportion of Kenya Asians in 1972 who are Hindus, Jains or Sikhs is still about 66 per cent, with the remainder being mostly Muslims. Jains form at least 30 per cent of the non-Muslim Asians of Kenya and of East Africa, and Sikhs comprise around 12 per cent. This means that in Kenya today, out of an Asian population of 155,000, approximately 60,000 are Hindus, 30,000 are Jains, and the Sikhs (who numbered 21,169 in 1962) have fallen to 13,000. 50,000 are Muslims, a gradual increase from their total of 40,057 in 1962.

Concerning the Hindus of Kenya, these do not belong to one single community, nor to one religious system. According to the recently founded Hindu Council of Kenya, there are well over fifty different Hindu organisations, most of which are religious foundations or have religious social functions. The distinction between them is rarely on doctrinal grounds, but mostly on geographical ones, with linguistic and historical factors coming second. In Duke Street, Nairobi, is located a Punjabi temple and a Gujarati temple. Bengali-speaking Kenya Asians are more at home in the Mahakali Sevashrama, though Goddess Kali or Durga has a strong following also in Gujarat in India. Some of the associations are devoted to a particular spiritual function such as the Gita Pracharak Society, others to a particular interpretation of Hinduism such as the Arya Samaj, which claims as members as many as 15 per cent of all Kenya Hindus. The Shri Satsang Mandal is the expression of one particular sect, the followers of Swami Narayan whose monastic order and following is very large in Gujarat. All of these and many others reflect the wide variations to be found within Hinduism itself in the Indian subcontinent, though what is new is their unity and the spirit of cooperation within one major representative organisation, the Hindu Council of Kenya.

In the religious sphere, there is little outward difference between the Hinduism which their forbears followed in India, and that of present-day Asians in Kenya. One reason for this is that since Hinduism is, for most Hindus, the observance of certain day-to-day customs on the basis of several unquestioned traditional beliefs and attitudes, there has not been an intellectual stimulus or critical impulse at work to change the definition of Hinduism in East Africa. Close family ties, and the influence of the womenfolk in the home, have tended toward the preservation of the old traditions, while the involvement of the menfolk in commercial professions has provided little room for critical reflection and religious reforms. Nevertheless, there are differences between the Hinduism of India and that of Kenya. Indians in Kenya have not felt the cultural, social, religious and political forces which have swept over India since her independence in 1947. Moreover, there have been significant changes in East Africa which Hindus themselves have hardly noticed. First of all, there is among them a noticeable openness in their response to enquiries about their faith, a readiness to communicate which makes the study of Hinduism easier for an outsider in

Kenya than is the case in India. Secondly, the detachment of Hinduism from its motherland, from the geographical centres which scriptural legend has sanctified by centuries of devotion, has tended to make East African Hinduism less and less a religion of holy places and holy festivals and more and more the religion of a Book. The reading and study of scriptures as the main source of spiritual inspiration and sustenance, and the exposition of religious ideas rather than pilgrimages and dependence upon holy places, is much more in evidence in Kenya than in India. Thirdly, the reduction of religion to a series of ideas, beliefs, and doctrines, which are presented to others as being true, profound, and relevant to their spiritual lives, has made Hinduism in East Africa more plainly the vehicle of a universal faith which commends itself to all men and which others may accept and submit to as their own personal religion.

The Arya Samaj, which perhaps is in the forefront of this intellectualising of Hinduism, has long been able to receive converts into the Hindu fold. As the Samaj understands it, a Hindu is not one who belongs to a certain place in India and is born of a certain caste or subcaste into a particular Hindu community; but he is one who believes and accepts the central doctrines of Hinduism, such as the eternity of the soul, transmigration and Karma, Dharma, and the like, as being true for mankind and relevant to his personal life. Since anyone may accept such belief, anyone may become a Hindu

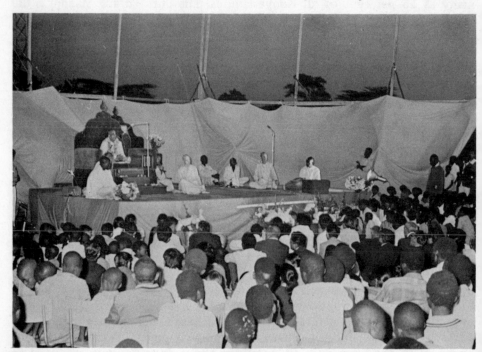

World Hare Krisna Movement Festival led by Swami Prabhupada; a 1972 Nairobi meeting.

either inwardly or outwardly through the Samaj's rite of initiation, and at least 1,000 Africans are estimated to have already done so.

Another Hindu sect actively engaged in proselytism in Kenya is the International Society for Krishna Consciousness, commonly called the Hare Krishna movement. Founded by Swami Prabhupada, ISKÇON entered Kenya during 1971, and recorded its first African convert in December. A five-day World Hare Krishna Movement festival was held in Nairobi in January, 1972.

Other Hindu communities and sects of Kenya also accept, in principle, the idea and the possibility of conversions to their beliefs among peoples who are not Asians; though in no case, other than the Arya Samaj and ISKCON, did the author of this article find evidence in Kenya of an active desire to make converts or even to spread their beliefs through the publication of English and vernacular literature for general readership. On the contrary, the requirement that proselytes must learn Hindi, Gujarati or Punjabi, as a first condition even of attending worship and lecture meetings, has ruled out the likelihood of any sizeable flow of African and European converts to Hindu beliefs and practices. Despite this deficiency, however, there is open recognition of the idea and the possibility of conversions to the various Hindu sects and communities of Kenya; and it is this 'open recognition' which constitutes a spirit which is barely evident in India outside of the handful of Hindu renaissance missions such as the Arya Samaj and the Ramakrishna Mission.

The most recent and most significant social development among Hindus of Kenya has been, as already referred to, the founding of the Hindu Council of Kenya in January, 1971, as a registered society with a constitution approved by the Government of Kenya. The Council is an impressive effort to bring together all Hindus, Jains and Sikhs of Kenya through their diverse associations into a common fellowship and partnership for action based upon their common beliefs, ideals and needs, as well as their social and national objectives. The constitutional aims and objectives of the HCK include the following: to provide a common platform of discussion and joint action for all Kenya Hindu associations on social, religious and cultural problems; to promote and diffuse knowledge of the ethical and spiritual principles and practices of Hinduism as 'suited to modern times in all parts of Kenya as a whole'; to publish literature and to open centres for this purpose; to organise public celebrations of Hindu social and religious festivals in a manner expressive of the spirit and beliefs of Hinduism and meaningful to the general public; and in general to define and express the rights and responsibilities which all Kenya Hindus share with other social and religious communities of Kenya toward the nation and society in which they live.

This constitutional statement is an impressive document containing an ambitious programme for unified Hindu expression. Such a programme needs sizeable resources both in money and in personnel for its successful implementation. Such resources have not been provided so far, but a start has been made. With the wholehearted support of the member associations, the HCK may go far to implement its far-reaching proposals.

Almost all of the fifty or so Hindu religious and social organisations in Kenya have become member organisations of the HCK, and have representative membership on its committee of management. A nominal annual subscription from each of these organisations has already enabled the Council to conduct some impressive public meetings during the course of 1971. It is still too early to expect to see structural evidences of the HCK in terms of libraries, offices, cultural centres, clubs, and so on, built and run by Kenya Hindus as a whole. But already, the public celebrations of Diwali, the formation of joint welcoming committees for the reception of Hindu religious leaders, and other public gatherings, have borne sufficient testimony to the seriousness of its purpose, the breadth of its possibilities, and the promise of a dynamic growth for this new expression of religious and social identity among Kenya Hindus.

Hindu Festival — Vijay Dashmi, celebrated in Nairobi each year.

306

II. JAINISM

Jains have been in Kenya for nearly one hundred years. The first migrations of Jains to East Africa took place from western India between 1886 and 1896. The early migrants probably came as business employees of Muslim traders who were Memons and Ismailis; but the need for independence and economic self-sufficiency led them into small retail businesses which gradually expanded into wholesale businesses and 'middleman' enterprises serving both Europeans and Africans. The outcome of this desire for self-sufficiency is that most Jains in East Africa are engaged in private business enterprises, so that their communities as a whole are self-supporting and independent of government aid or patronage. The Jains are by far the most successful of the Asian business communities of East Africa.

In East Africa, Jains number about 40,000 members, of whom some 30,000 are in Kenya. It is estimated that 25 per cent of these are Kenya citizens and about 5 per cent are Indian citizens. The largest proportion are British subjects without United Kingdom citizenship.

The Jains of East Africa do not comprise a single religious community. They are broadly divided into two groups, Digambaras and Svetambaras; and since the Svetambaras are dominant in Gujarat, India, most East African Jains, some 80 per cent, are Svetambaras. Within these two broad groups are several Jain communities and castes. The Visa Oshwals are the largest group and comprise as many as 70 per cent of all East African Jains. An additional 25 per cent of Jains are Dasa Oshwals, and a small number are Pancha Oshwals. There are also small communities of Nauvnathvanik and Sthanakvasi Jains. All have originated from the Indian state of Gujarat, though their earliest origins may have been in north-eastern India before migrating via Rajasthan into Gujarat during the 12th century A.D.

In Gujarat the Visa and Dasa Oshwals were farmers and landowners and the Nauvnathvanik Jains were traders. Even so, the Oshwals were the wealthiest and most influential of the Cutchi-Gujarati dialect-speaking groups and remained so even after establishing themselves in East Africa as traders.

Not all the Visa Oshwals are Jains. In East Africa Jains comprise 90 per cent of the Visa Oshwal caste, and Hindus 10 per cent. Nevertheless, both groups recognise their social parity and so some intermarriage takes place between them, with the understanding that the bride in each case acquires, without social discrimination, the faith of her husband.

Some common surnames among the Jains of Kenya are Shah, Seth, Sangrajka, Haria, Dodhia and Gudka. These however are not always sufficient to indicate the particular Jain sect and subcaste to which their owners belong. The cognomen 'Shah' is common to all sects of Jains, though the Harias, Dodhias, and Gudkas are all Svetambara Visa Oshwals. The Sangrajkas are either Sthanakvasis or Nauvnathvaniks.

An inclusive general estimate of Jains of all communities in Kenya according to their geographical locations is as follows: Nairobi 18,000 (where Visa Oshwal Jains own 95 per cent of the Asian retail shops in Bazaar Street); Mombasa 6,000, Thika 2,500, Fort Hall 300, Nyeri 250, Nanyuki 300, Nakuru 350, and Kisumu 2,000. In proportion also is the number of their *mahajanwadis*, community centres (of which there are about fifty throughout Kenya) and of their temples *(dahrashars* or *mandirs)*. Nairobi has four Jain temples, two being Svetambara, one Sthanakvasi and one Digambara. The Visa Oshwal community has plans to build a new temple at the cost of K£50,000 on the site of the Visa Oshwal Mahajanwadi in the Limuru Road which commences building in 1972. This is a significant indication of the size and resources of the Visa Oshwal Jain community in Kenya. In Mombasa there is a large worship centre belonging to the Svetambara Visa Oshwals, and a mandir for Digambaras also.

An impressive feature of Jain communal and social activity in Kenya is the highly sophisticated educational and social-relief work financed and maintained by the Visa Oshwal Jains through the Visa Oshwal Education and Relief Board, begun in 1941. In particular, their educational institutions are nearly of the size and calibre of the Ismailia institutions of the Aga Khan. Like them, Jain schools provide the same kind and quality of education for boys and girls irrespective of their racial origins or religious affiliations. In the Visa Oshwal Secondary School in Westlands, for example, a small prayer-room houses both Jain, Hindu, Christian and Muslim images and symbols, so that all inmates equally may feel it to be their place of private worship and meditation. Such a room, of course, reflects the wide spirit of tolerance which is characteristic of Jainism and is propounded in the Jain philosophical doctrine of *anekantavada.*

Nevertheless, despite the openness of Jain educational institutions and their undiscriminatory social relief work, there is little cultural or spiritual interaction between Jainism, Islam, Christianity and other religions in East Africa. The Jain communities of Kenya are self-contained spiritual and cultural units; mere contact with other communities and peoples, rather than integration and identification with them, has been the most that their favourable circumstances in East Africa have warranted. What difference there is between Jainism in India and that in Kenya is primarily a greater degree of open acceptance of other communities; but it is principally a question of recognition without integration. The older generation of Jains in Kenya still observe strict vegetarianism as required by the Jain doctrine of *ahimsa.* However, Kenya Jains, owing to the exigencies of their business and social life, eat both vegetarian and non-vegetarian food and no longer apply the Jain rule of taking the last meal of the day before sunset. None of them could have migrated to East Africa in the first instance if they had observed the conservative Jain rule of travelling nowhere by wheeled or mechanical transportation but only so far in one day as one can travel on foot.

For this reason it may be asked to what extent traditional Jain beliefs and values are maintaining their hold upon young members of Jain families who have been born and educated entirely outside India. To some extent strong family ties, social traditions, good community organisation, and practical community considerations are all playing a part in maintaining Jainism as a living force among them in every place in the world to which they have migrated. In Jain educational institutions, religious instruction classes are intended to meet the challenge of materialism and indifference to religious values, both ubiquitous influences in this secular age. Unfortunately, the Jainist taboo against travel overseas by mechanical transportation has prevented the establishment of schools of *acharyas* (religious teachers) in East Africa who could have taken up, as efficiently as Jain educational and relief work, the task of religious education also. The result is that such religious instruction as exists is quite inadequate to inculcate strong religious ideals and to produce young men and women who are committed to those values. On the other hand, the general appeal of Jain ethical principles to Asians of every religious community is extremely strong, especially when these are presented as universal principles of life and religion by such able exponents as Munishree Chandraprabhasagarji (Chitrabhanu) who visited Kenya for two months' teaching mission in July, 1971. His daily discourses on the universal essence and spirit of Jainism drew regular audiences in the Nairobi Visa Oshwal Mahajanwadi of up to 10,000 persons including Hindus, Jains, Muslims, and some Europeans. Later he proceeded to similar marathon preaching and teaching tours in the U.S.A. and in Britain. This demonstrates that, despite contrary influences, Jainism contains the qualities of spiritual validity, efficacy and vitality which in relation to the common needs and aspirations of humanity are demonstrating the growing claim that Jainism is a universal religion for all mankind.

III. SIKHISM

In their homeland in the Punjab, India, Sikhs today number about 8 million. By comparison, Sikhs in Kenya are a small community, numbering about 13,000 having nine *gurdwaras* (hostels and worship-places) in Nairobi, two each in Mombasa, Nakuru, Kisumu, Eldoret, Kitale, and one in Makindu, making a total of about 21 places. The number of 13,000 may be compared with the approximate figures of 7,500 Sikhs in Tanzania and 5,700 in Uganda, in each case comprising approximately 12 per cent of the non-Muslim Asian populations. These figures also contrast with those of U.K. (100,000), Singapore (20,000), Malaya (10,000), Canada (7,000), U.S.A. (5,000), Burma (5,000), South Africa (4,000), Iran (2,000), Australia (1,800), and China (500).

The Sikhs of Kenya are mainly from Eastern or Indian Punjab, especially the districts of Jullunder, Ludhiana, Ambala, and of course from Amritsar the holy city of the Sikhs. Some also hail from Delhi Province into which large numbers came as refugees from Pakistan and have achieved a dominant position in the social and commercial life of India's capital city. Others come from the part of Punjab which is now the state of Hariyanna.

Sikhs are normally Punjabi-speaking, with Hindi and English as second and third languages. Their public worship and conferences are conducted in Punjabi which is written in the script of the Punjabi dialect of Gurmukhi which Nanak himself spoke.

In Kenya the Sikhs have largely abandoned the agricultural and military roles of their forebears in favour of trade, crafts, and the full range of commercial enterprise, in all of which they have proved their efficiency and enterprise.

In India, various distinct groups of Sikhs can be recognised. Not all Sikhs are Singhs, the latter being a title and surname adopted by those who, after a period of instruction in the tenets of Sikhism, submit themselves to the initiatory rite of Khandaydi-Puhul by which they enter the Khalsa or Sikh Brotherhood. Other distinctions are between Nanakpanthis, Namdharis, Akalis, Nirmalas and Udasis, although all worship the Granth. In Kenya no visible evidences of such group distinctions are to be found. Only two

Five Sikh swordsmen, guarding the Granth Sahib (the Holy Scriptures), process through Nairobi.

broad distinctions are made — between Khalsas (members of the Sikh Brotherhood) and Sahajdharis (novices who have not been initiated). The Khalsas or Elect Ones have received formal initiation under vows to honour the memory of Nanak and his successors, to make their watchword 'Hail Guru', to revere no object save the Holy Granth, to wear the five K's which testify to their distinctive identity as Elect Ones, and to visit and bathe in the Pool of the Sacred Temple of Amritsar. (The 'five K's' are the five characteristics of the Sikhs, which begin (in Punjabi) with the letter K: uncut hair, steel comb, steel wrist bangles, white undergarments, and a knife held in the sock). Every April near the Christian Easter, at the festival of Vaisakhi, a public ceremony in all the gurdwaras includes 'receiving the *amrit*' at a common meal, the *guru ka langar.* It is an annual 'holy communion' which serves also as the occasion for the renewal of the baptismal vows and the sense of joyous solidarity with the Sikh Brotherhood. As in India, Kenya Sikhs attend their gurdwaras on Sundays and special days such as the feastdays of the ten Gurus. Sunday has no special religious significance for Sikhs, being only that day which has become free for worship since British colonial days. Morning worship on Sundays is between 5 a.m. and 8 a.m., and in the evening for one hour. Anyone who is not a Sikh and is not restricted by the Punjabi medium of worship, may attend Sikh worship-services; the gurdwaras are open to all. None are excluded, provided they observe the rules and requirements — washing of feet and covering of the head when in the temple precincts.

There is an openness among the Sikhs in Kenya, as well as in India, including a readiness to explain Sikhism and to communicate the teachings of Guru Nanak. Sikhism is a missionary faith, and pious Sikhs genuinely look forward to the time when all men will recognise the universal spiritual principles which Nanak expounded and will accept them as their personal faith and discipline. This means that, in principle, Kenya Africans and Europeans as well as Asians may become Sikhs. It is said that in Nairobi itself 'quite a number' of Africans are *sahajdharis* employed in the gurdwaras and receiving instruction in Sikhism. But many Sikhs are doubtful concerning whether these novices will ever receive the initiatory rite of Khandaydi-Puhul, together with the 5 K's, and thus find full acceptance into the Khalsa.

LITERATURE ON ASIANS IN KENYA

Delf, George, *Asians in East Africa.* London:Oxford, 1963.
Ghai, Dharam P. *Portrait of a minority.* Nairobi:Oxford, 1965.
Hollingsworth, W. *The Asians of East Africa.* London:Macmillan, 1960.
Mangat, J.S. *A history of the Asians in East Africa.* Oxford:Clarendon, 1969.
Pandit, Shanti, *Asians in East and Central Africa.* Nairobi:Panco Publications, 1963.

The author of this article wishes to express his gratitude to Messrs. V.S. Sikand, C.P. Gupta, J. Shah, P.J. Dedhia and M. Singh for their help in providing information for this article.

311

Directory of Islam, Hinduism and Other Religions

The major religions and bodies listed here are described in detail in the preceding articles by James Holway and Terence Day. Traditional religion, described by John Mbiti, is almost entirely unorganised and uninstitutionalised, except for the first organisation in this listing. Notes are added for a handful of other bodies not dealt with in the preceding texts.

TRADITIONAL RELIGION

Waganga wa Miti Shamba Society
Chairman: Mr Samuel Katiku; Treasurer: Mr Kadhiya Mbeneka
Office: Plot No. 909/123, Machakos Township
P.O. Box 334, Machakos.
'Medicine Men's Society', 'Witchdoctors' Society': the major organisation of traditional healers in Kenya and the closest to an institutionalised form of traditional religion and medicine in Kenya; over 110 medicine men from various tribes, particularly Kamba; registered in 1971. Objects: 'to promote the art of curing diseases using medicinal herbs', and 'to ensure that unqualified persons do not practice'. In the city of Nairobi, there are at least 100 medicine men, most of whom work as individuals but located mainly in seven areas as shown on the fold-out map in this Handbook, *Churches and Temples in Nairobi*. See also the article here by J.S. Mbiti (p. 291) with the photographs of two of Kenya's most famous medicine men, Kabwere and Kajiwe.

ISLAM

SUNNI

High Court of Kenya
Chief Kadhi of Kenya: Sheikh Abdulla Saleh el-Farsy
P.O. Box 90140, Mombasa.   *Tel: 26471*

Kadhi's Courts:
P.O. Box 90140, Mombasa. Tel: 26471
P.O. Box 16000, Kwale. Tel: 8
P.O. Box 41, Lamu. Tel: 35
P.O. Box 2, Malindi. Tel: 17
Sheikh Ahmed Omar, P.O. Box 126, Kisumu. Tel: 2771

Anjuman Himayat-e-Islam (EA) Muslim Religious Body
Secretary: Mr. Rashid Chaudry
Jamia Mosque, Kirparam Road
P.O. Box 40065, Nairobi.   *Tel: 23900*

Anjuman Islam Mombasa, Muslim Religious Body
Kaderbhoy Building, Nkrumah Road
P.O. Box 633, Mombasa.   *Tel: 4486*

Central Muslim Association
P.O. Box 40278, Nairobi.

Department of Philosophy and Religious Studies,
University of Nairobi
Reader in Islam: Mr. Said Hamdun
University of Nairobi
P.O. Box 30197, Nairobi.   *Tel: 34244*

East African Muslim Welfare Society
Provincial Council
P.O. Box 10434, Nairobi.

Islamic Foundation
P.O. Box 30611, Nairobi.

Kenya Muslim Welfare Association
Chairman: Dr. Yusuf Ali Eraj
Corner House, Kimathi Street
P.O. Box 43789, Nairobi.   *Tel: 24592*

Nairobi Muslim Housing Corporation Society Ltd.
P.O. Box 11900, Nairobi.

University of Nairobi Islamic Society
Chairman: Mr. Abdulla Mohamed Ahmed
P.O. Box 47510, Nairobi.

Wakf Commissioners for Kenya
White Fathers Road
P.O. Box 80272, Mombasa.   *Tel: 4581*

ISMAILI

H.H. the Aga Khan Ismailia Supreme Council for Africa
Chairman: Sir Eboo Pirbhai (Box 30098, Nairobi. Tel: 65049)
Jamatkhana Building, Government Road
P.O. Box 40555, Nairobi.   *Tel: 25114*

H.H. the Aga Khan Imami Ismailia Council for Kenya
Chairman: Alija Abdul Ismail Sanji
Jamatkhana Building, Government Road
P.O. Box 44500, Nairobi.   *Tel: 25329*
In 1972 there are about 13,000 Ismailis in Kenya (roughly 6,500 in Nairobi, 2,500 in Kisumu and Nyanza, 3,000 at the Coast, 100 in Thika, 100 in Nakuru). There are about 120 African Ismailis, some of 12 years' standing.

H.H. the Aga Khan Ismailia Provincial Councils
P.O. Box 40190, Nairobi. Tel: 20928
P.O. Box 1, Kisumu. Tel: 2547
P.O. Box 80115, Mombasa. Tel: 5719

H.H. the Aga Khan Education Department
Administrator: Mr. Ismail Dawood
IPS Building, Kimathi Street
P.O. Box 48430, Nairobi.   *Tel: 23217*

BOHRA (BOHORA)

Dawoodi Bohora Jamaat Corporation
Head Priest: Dawoodi Bohora Amil Saheeb (P.O. Box 81943, Mombasa. Tel: 4687)
Bohora Mosque, near Old Port
P.O. Box 81766, Mombasa.   *Tel: 5850*

Dawoodi Bohora Jamaat Corporation
Bohora Mosque
P.O. Box 10936, Nairobi.   *Tel: 23053*

ITHNASHERI

Khoja Shia Ithnasheri Jamaats of Africa, Supreme Council of the Federation of
Nehru Road
P.O. Box 81085, Mombasa.   *Tel: 5856*

Bilal Muslim Mission
P.O. Box 82508, Mombasa.

AHMADIYYA

Ahmadiyya Muslim Mission (or, Association)
Missionary-in-charge
Fort Hall Road
P.O. Box 40554, Nairobi.   *Tel: 25091*

OTHER MINOR COMMUNITIES

Cutchi Sunni Muslim Jamaat Corporation (Memons)
P.O. Box 85153, Mombasa.

Kokni Muslim Jamat
P.O. Box 82086, Mombasa.

Luhar Wadha Jamat
P.O. Box 85325, Mombasa.

Mombasa Lohana Community
P.O. Box 82031, Mombasa.

Muslim Bhadala Jamat
P.O. Box 82578, Mombasa.

MISCELLANEOUS ORGANISATIONS

Islamic Foundation
Secretary: Mr. A.R. Bazmi
Jamia Mosque, Kirparam Road
P.O. Box 30611, Nairobi.   *Tel: 24251*

National Union of Kenya Muslims
Chairman: Mr. Issa Kuria
P.O. Box 40896, Nairobi.

Supreme Council for Islamic Affairs
P.O. Box 13174, Nairobi.

Young Muslim Association
Kirparam Road
P.O. Box 40629, Nairobi.   *Tel: 29896*

Young Muslim Women's Association
P.O. Box 83561, Mombasa.

HINDUISM

Hindu Council of Kenya (HCK)
Chairman: Mr. Virendra Singh Sikand; Secretary: Mr. B.R. Aggarwal
P.O. Box 49012, Nairobi.   *Tel: 27054*
   A body co-ordinating the affairs of almost all Hindu, Jain and Sikh communities in Kenya. The earliest such body was founded around 1910 (Cutchhi Gujarati Hindu Union), and the HCK, dating from 1969, links all such unions.

Arya Samaj (Vedic Churches of East Africa)
Chairman:
Vedic House, Queensway
P.O. Box 4023
P.O. Box 40243, Nairobi.   *Tel: 21573*

Bhagini Samaj
Chairman:
P.O. Box 27245, Nairobi.

Bhartiya Swayam Sevak Sangh
Chairman:
P.O. Box 10720, Nairobi.

East Africa Satsang Mandal
Chairman:
P.O. Box 41371, Nairobi.   *Tel: 24860*

International Society for Krishna Consciousness
(ISKCON) (also known as Hare Krishna)
Acharya: His Divine Grace A.C. Bhaktivedanta Swami Prabhupad; Secretary: Jagannivas Das Brahmachary (Steven Donnelly)
Services: Shri Sanatan Dharam Sabha, Kamukunji Park (4 times a week)
Office: c/o G.N. Shah Ltd., National House, Koinange Street
P.O. Box 28946, Nairobi.

Kenya Brahma Sabha
Chairman:
P.O. Box 46314, Nairobi.

Maharashtra Mandal
Chairman:
P.O. Box 45452, Nairobi.

Nairobi Surti Mochi Gnati Mandal
Chairman:
P.O. Box 49259, Nairobi.

Sanatan Dharma Sabha
Chairman:
P.O. Box 40032, Nairobi.

Shree Cutchi Gujarati Hindu Union
Chairman:
Duke Street
P.O. Box 40204, Nairobi.   *Tel: 24189*

Shree Lohana Mahajan Mandal
Chairman:
Desai Road
P.O. Box 40335, Nairobi.   *Tel: 28648*

JAINISM

Shree Sthanakvasi Jain Mandal
Chairman:
Imtiazali Road
P.O. Box 46469, Nairobi.   *Tel: 25831*

Visa Oshwal Community
Chairman:
P.O. Box 40638, Nairobi.   *Tel: 20340, 34779*

SIKHISM

East African Namdhari Sangat
Chairman:
Ngara Road
P.O. Box 11308, Nairobi.   *Tel: 27936*

East African Ramgarhia Board
Chairman:
Ramgarhia Road
P.O. Box 40845, Nairobi.   *Tel: 22128*

Sikh Missionary Society
Chairman:
Ramgarhia Road
P.O. Box 10339, Nairobi.   *Tel: 22128*

Siri Guru Singh Sabha
Chairman:
Byramjee Street
P.O. Box 40496, Nairobi.   *Tel: 25340*

BAHA'I

National Spiritual Assembly of the Baha'is of Kenya
Secretary: Mr. Bonaventure Wafula
Baha'i Centre, Sykes Road
P.O. Box 47562, Nairobi.   *Tel: 24175*

The international Baha'i religion is neither Muslim nor Hindu, but claims to be a synthesis of all religions. Its mission to Kenya began in 1951, and the movement now claims 700 'local spiritual assemblies (each of 9 or more members) in Kenya, with over 30,000 followers, almost entirely Africans (especially Luhya, also Coast, Kikuyu, Luo), with about 50 Asian and 15 European followers. These are all grouped in 2,000 localities' (areas in which Baha is reside) across Kenya. There are 400 Baha'is in Nairobi. There are no priests or ministers In July 1972, 16 Persian young men and women Baha'is arrived in East Africa for a year's volunteer preaching at Baha'i centres.

PARSEEISM (ZOROASTRIANISM)

Nairobi Parsee Zoroastrian Anjuman
Chairman: Mr. Kersey Moddie, Priest. Mr. Sohrab Rabady (Box 40894, Nairobi, Tel. 22671)
Parsee Club, Dalgairns Road, Westlands
P.O. Box 30075, Nairobi.   *Tel. 67058*
Followers of the ancient dualistic religion of Persia (Zoroastrianism). Parsees in Kenya numbered 97 in the 1911 census, and numbered 270 in 1972. A feature of their religion is the fire temple (as in Bombay, India), but there are none in Kenya.

OTHER RELIGIOUS GROUPS

Divine Life Society of East Africa
c/o Karamshi & Co. Bazaar Street
P.O. Box 41022, Nairobi.   *Tel: 23524*

Freemasons, District Grand Lodge of East Africa
Grand Master: Colonel S.G. Ghersie
Masonic Temple. Freemasons Hall, Kirk Road
P.O. Box 41148, Nairobi.   *Tel: 23666*
Not a religion but an international brotherhood affirming belief in the Supreme Being and revering the Bible as the Volume of the Sacred Law. First Freemasons came to Nairobi 1905; 1926, District Grand Lodge formed, now 36 lodges in Kenya (14 in Nairobi), with 3,400 subscribing members of all races, not

restricted to Christians (Ismailis, Hindus and others are members in Kenya). Rites steeped in the religious symbolism of masonry, traced back to King Solomon's temple in Israel, are held in the Masonic Temple, Nairobi, on many days each month. Over the outside entrance to the Freemasons' Hall is inscribed in large gold letters. God said of King Solomon, He shall build Me an house and I will establish his throne for ever'.

Nairobi Hebrew Congregation
Rabbi: (Kirk Road)
Nairobi Synagogue, University Way & Uhuru Highway
P.O. Box 40990, Nairobi.   *Tel: 22770*
In 1912 the foundation stone of the first synagogue in East Africa was laid in Nairobi. The number of Jews in Nairobi has varied from 100-200 over the years since, reaching 300 practising members by 1972 with about 250 non-practising; a synagogue was built in Nakuru in 1956, and there have been Jewish communities in the major towns of Kenya, although no services are held now outside Nairobi. No Africans belong to the Jewish community.

Rosicrucian Order AMORC
A movement based in the USA, which was registered in Nairobi in 1960 but cancelled in 1963.

Temple of Knowledge
Principal: Mr. M.P. Dhall
2nd Avenue, Eastleigh Section 1
P.O. Box 8705, Nairobi.   *Tel. 50285*

Theosophical Society of East Africa
Chairman: Mr. B.P. Yadav, Hon. Secretary. Miss B.L. Vadgama
Nairobi Lodge. No. 55A, Third Avenue, Parklands
P.O. Box 45928, Nairobi.   *Tel: 55174*
The Theosophical Society was begun in India in 1873 as a cultural religious organisation, to study comparative religion, and to form a nucleus of the Universal Brotherhood of humanity without distinction of persons. The TSEA is a registered society in Kenya, with 17 registered branches and 280 members. Weekly lectures in English and Gujarati; annual conventions during public holidays.

7

Part VII

Bibliography of Christianity and Religion in Kenya

Bibliography of Christianity and Religion in Kenya

This bibliography lists the great majority of all published and unpublished material written on the subject of religion in Kenya, and in particular on the history and contemporary situation of Christian missions and churches, including a small number of items on other subjects but which contain significant sections on religion. Each entry gives first the name of the author (men: surname and initials; women: surname and first name) and the title of the work, followed by the place of publication, name of publisher or distributor, and date of publication. In cases where the title of an entry does not adequately describe its contents, a brief descriptive annotation has then been added.

Published books (almost always printed) are shown here by titles in italics; published articles by titles in single quotation marks followed by the title of the journal in italics. Entries with no italics in them are usually unprinted and unpublished duplicated reports, or typed or handwritten manuscripts; 'Dissertations' here refer to manuscripts presented for doctoral degrees, and 'theses' refer to manuscripts presented for master's degrees; both are usually unpublished, and are deposited in the libraries of the universities or colleges shown.

Entries are listed here in alphabetical order by name of author or editor. In the case of corporately written material with no authors stated, entries are alphabetised on the words of the title itself.

This bibliography contains several Kenya-produced English writings of the non-Christian religions. It should be noted, however, that although not included here there is also a large literature in other languages (Swahili, Hindi, Punjabi, Gujarati) describing Islam, Hinduism, Sikhism, and the various Asian sects.

Published material listed here can usually be consulted in libraries, or, if still in print, can be purchased from the publisher shown. Unpublished material can usually be consulted by contacting the author or the sponsoring body; in the case of recent duplicated or mimeographed papers, copies are usually available for sale.

It is interesting to note that, of the 600 entries listed here, 200 were written or edited entirely by Africans from Kenya; in addition, of course, Africans have contributed information, data, opinions, translations, paragraphs, even articles, to virtually all the rest.

The following standard abbreviations should be noted:

ms. = single handwritten manuscript
typescript = single typed document
mimeo = mimeographed (duplicated)
n.d. = no date specified (editors' estimate in brackets)
4, 3 or IV, 3 for a journal or periodical means Volume 4, Issue, number 3.

Abbott, Sally. 'The education policy of the Kenya government, 1904-1935'. Dissertation, University of London, 1969.
    Interaction between government and mission agencies in the early years of Western education in Kenya.
Abonyo, Agnes A. 'Johera: independent church in Kasagam'. Paper, Kenyatta College, 1970 (ms).
    An account of the Johera (People of Love, or Church of Christ in Africa).
Adelphoi (pseudonym). *His Kingdom in Kenya.* London: Hodder and Stoughton, 1953.
    An anonymous inter-racial group discusses working together between Christians of different races.
African education in Kenya. Report of a committee appointed to inquire into the scope, context, and methods of African education, its administration and finance, and to make recommendations. Nairobi: Government Printer, 1949.
    The 'Beecher Report', named after its chairman.
African socialism and its application to planning in Kenya. Nairobi: Government Printer, 1965.
    This sessional paper of the Kenya Government, the blueprint for Kenya's 'policy of positive non-alignment', contains this statement on p. 4: 'Another fundamental force in African traditional life was religion which provided a strict moral code for the community. This will be a prominent feature of African Socialism'.
After school what? A report by the Youth Department of NCCK and the Christian Churches' Educational Association. Nairobi: Ministry of Health, 1966.
    A report dealing with further education, training and employment of primary school leavers.
Amisi, A. 'How Luo people thought of God and their way of life'. Paper, Kenyatta College, 1970 (mimeo).
An audience survey report in Kenya. Ministry of Information and Broadcasting. Nairobi: Associated Business Consultants (EA), 1969 (computer tables, about 400 pages).

Anderson, Dick. *Team for Turkana.* London: Africa Inland Mission, 1969.
    The work of the AIM in Turkana by its first medical missionary in the district.
Anderson, J.D. *The struggle for the school: the interaction of missionary, colonial government and nationalistic enterprise in the development of formal education in Kenya.* London: Longmans, 1970.
——. 'Selection and adaptation outside the government/missionary framework: the independent schools', in Anderson, *The struggle for the school,* p. 112-131.
    The rise of KISA and KKEA, with their associated AIPC and AOC.
Anderson, W.B. 'The experience and meaning of conversion for early Christian converts in Kenya', in D.B. Barrett (ed.), *Theory and practice* (1968), p. 157-167.
——. 'History of the Holy Spirit Church of East Africa'. Typescript (19 pages) in library of St. Paul's United Theological College, Limuru, n.d. (circa 1970).
——. 'Development of leadership in Protestant churches in Central Kenya'. Paper, St. Paul's United Theological College, Limuru, 1970 (mimeo).
——. 'Feeling after God: the African Brotherhood Church'. Typescript (20 pages), St. Paul's United Theological College, Limuru, n.d. (circa 1971).
——. 'Children of Jakobo: a history of the Holy Spirit Church of East Africa', *Risk* (Geneva), vol. 7, no. 3 (1971), p. 14-19.
——. 'The man facing out: the story of Mwangi Nyarari'. Manuscript, 1971.
    A full-length biography of the best-known pioneer faith-missionary of the Kikuyu, who had been brought up in the Gospel Missionary Society area.
....and some fell on good ground': issue on the African independent churches. *Risk* (Geneva), vol. 7, no. 3 (1971).
    Includes articles and photographs on Kenyan independent

churches.

Aoko, D. 'High Priest David Zakayo Kivuli: biography of an African independent church founder', *Risk* (Geneva), vol. 7, no. 3 (1971), p. 20-22.

——. 'Language use within the independent African churches of Nairobi', chapter 10 in W.H. Whiteley, *Language in Kenya* (Nairobi: Oxford, 1972).

A report on Islam in Kenya. Nairobi: Department of Biblical Study and Research, CCK, 1960 (mimeo, 36 pages).

Arisi, D. 'The SDA Church in Kisii'. Paper, Kenyatta College, 1969 (ms).

Ashimala, E. 'Aspects of ministry emphasised by a selection of Christian denominations in Kenya'. Typescript (84 pages) for diploma in theology, University of East Africa, n.d. (circa 1965).

Ashton-Gwatkin, F. 'Dini ya Msambwa (Cult of the Ancestors)', *Spectator* (London), 11 August 1950, p. 173-174.

Astor P 'Evolution of a multi-religious student community: University College, Nairobi, 1964-69', in D.B. Barrett (ed.), *Theory and practice* (1968), p. 401-408.

- Atieno-Odhiambo, E.S. 'Some aspects of religious activity among the Uyoma fishermen: the rites connected with the launching of a fishing vessel', *Mila* (Nairobi), 1, 2 (1970), p. 14-21.

A United Liturgy for East Africa (3rd draft). Nairobi: East African Church Union Consultation, 1966.
A liturgical service for use with or without communion, prepared for the Anglican, Lutheran, Methodist, Moravian and Presbyterian churches in East Africa. A Swahili version is also available.

Ayoo, J.W.O. 'Life and work of the Rt. Rev. Bishop A.M. Ajuoga'. History Research Paper B/3/1, Dept. of History, University of Nairobi, n.d.
On the founder of the Church of Christ in Africa.

Azals, F. 'Etude sur la religion du peuple Galla', *Revue d'ethnographie et des traditions populaires* (Paris), vol. 7 (1926), p. 113-120.

Bahati, Sr. Edel. 'Moral dilemmas in the life of modern girls in Kenya'. Paper, Pastoral Institute of Eastern Africa, Gaba, 1970.
From the standpoint of religious sociology.

Baker, Mabel. *[A history of the Church of God in East Africa]* (in Lunyore). 50th anniversary publication. Kima: Church of God, 1955 (mimeo).

Barker, R. St. Barbe. 'Beliefs of some East African tribes', in *Religions in the Empire* (London, 1926), p. 341-357.
Papers of a conference on some living religions within the former British Empire. The article includes material on Bantu religious ideas.

Barnett, Anne. 'Christian home and family life in Kenya today', *International Review of Missions*, vol. 49 (1960), p. 420-426.

Barrett, D.B. 'Urban pressures on religion and church'. S.T.M. thesis, Union Theological Seminary, New York, 1963.
A study of the Luo, their former religions, their present religious situation, and the future of religion in the towns.

——. *Schism and renewal in Africa: an analysis of six thousand contemporary religious movements.* Nairobi: Oxford, 1968.
Gives data on independent churches in all Kenyan tribes.

——, (ed.). *Theory and practice in church life and growth: 56 studies in Eastern, Central and Southern Africa over the last hundred years.* Nairobi: Workshop in Religious Research, 1968.

——, (ed.). *African initiatives in religion.* Nairobi: East African Publishing House, 1971.
Five of the 21 papers deal with Kenyan initiatives.

——. 'Who's Who of African independent church leaders', *Risk* (Geneva), vol. 7, no. 3 (1971), p. 23-34.
Contains brief biographies with photos of 56 AIC leaders, including five from Kenya.

Barton, G.A. 'Sacrifice among the Wakamba', *Journal of American Folklore*, 12 (1899), p. 144-5.

Baxter, P.T.W. 'Acceptance and rejection of Islam among the Boran of the Northern Frontier District of Kenya', in I.M. Lewis (ed.), *Islam in Tropical Africa* (New York: Oxford, 1964), p. 233-252.

——. 'Repetition in certain Boran ceremonies', in M. Fortes and G. Dieterlen, *African systems of thought* (London: Oxford, 1965), p. 64-78.

Bayley, M. 'Attitudes to the Church in Kenya today: a report of an enquiry undertaken in August-September, 1961'. Nairobi: Christian Council of Kenya, 1961 (mimeo).

Bedford, F.J. *The Bible in East Africa.* London: British & Foreign Bible Society, 1954.
A historical and descriptive account, with maps and chronology.

Beech, M.W.H. *The Suk: their language and folklore.* Oxford: Clarendon, 1911.
Section on religious beliefs, p. 19-25.

——. 'The sacred fig-tree of the A-Kikuyu of East Africa', *Man*, vol. 13, article 3 (1913), p. 4-6.

——. 'A ceremony at a Mugumu or sacred fig-tree of the A-Kikuyu of East Africa', *Man*, vol. 13, article 5 (1913), p. 86-89.

Beecher, L.J. 'The African explains witchcraft: three Kikuyu', *Africa*, vol. 8, no. 4 (1935), p. 516-519.

——. 'Missionary education in Kenya', *East and West Review*, V, no. 4 (October, 1939).

——. *The Kikuyu.* Nairobi: CMS, 1944.

——. 'The Revival Movement in Kenya', *World Dominion*, XXIX, no. 1 (Jan. - Feb., 1951).

——. 'Au Kenya: nationalisme et eglises separatistes africaines', *Monde non-chretien* (Paris), p. 324-336.

——. 'African separatist churches in Kenya', *World Dominion*, XXXI, no. 1 (1953), p. 5-12.

——. 'Polygamy, female initiation rites, etc., in Kenya: a reply to Dr. L.S.B. Leakey by the Bishop of Mombasa'. London: CMS, 1954 (4 pages).

——. 'Rehabilitation in Kenya: the Churches' part in establishing a new way of life', *Times British Colonies Review*, vol. 14 (1954).

——. 'The Gospel in Kenya'. Unpublished typescript, 1957.
A history of the Anglican Diocese of Mombasa.

——. *Vocabulary of Hebrew words in Swahili.* Unpublished typescript, 1967.
A study of the derivation of a number of Swahili theological terms (*damu*, etc.) from the Hebrew.

——. *An archbishop remembers.* Unpublished typescript (forthcoming).
Autobiography of the first Anglican Archbishop of East Africa.

Beetham, T.A. *Christianity and the new Africa.* London: Pall Mall, 1967.
An overall survey, with several references to Kenya.

Bellagamba, A. 'La Chiesa Kikuyu e fondata (The Kikuyu Church is established)', *Missioni Consolata* (Turin), 63, 15 (1961), p. 15-20.

Bennett, N.R. 'Some letters of J.L. Krapf', *Boston University Graduate Journal*, IX, 2 (December, 1960), 45-58.

——. 'The Holy Ghost Mission in East Africa, 1858-1890', in *Studies in East African history* (Boston University Research Studies No. 4, 1963), p. 54-75.
History of the period immediately preceding the start of HGM work in Kenya.

——. 'The Church Missionary Society at Mombasa, 1873-1894', in J. Butler (ed.), *Boston University Papers in African History*, Vol. I (Boston, 1964).

Beresford-Stooke, G. 'An Akamba fortune-telling ceremony, divination by throwing seeds', *Man*, 137 (1928), p. 189.

Berg, F.J. & B.J. Walter. 'Mosques, population and urban development in Mombasa', in B.A. Ogot (ed.), *Hadith 1* (Nairobi: EAPH, 1968), p. 47 - 100.
Describes 49 mosques in use in Mombasa (7 for all Muslims, the rest for communities), and 8 other disused ones.

Bernard, G.M. 'The "Weni-Mwanguvu" Igange Congregation'. Paper, Kenyatta College, 1969 (mimeo).
Description of a Taita Pentecostal church formed from the Anglican Church after the 1957-58 Osborn crusades. The name means 'People of Power'.

Bernardi, B. *The Mugwe, a failing prophet: a study of a religious and public dignitary of the Meru of Kenya.* New York: Oxford, 1959.

Bertolino, G. 'La nuova setta auche nel Meru (The new sect among the Meru)', *Missioni Consolata* (Turin), 36, 6 (1934), p. 86.

Bessem, J. 'Scripture translations in East Africa', *African Ecclesiastical Review*, IV, 3 (July, 1962), p. 201-211.
 Lists and describes Catholic as well as Protestant translations.

Bewes, T.F.C. *Kikuyu conflict: Mau Mau and the Christian witness*. London: Highway Press, 1953.
——. 'The work of the Christian church among the Kikuyu', *International Affairs* (London), vol. 29 (1953), p. 316-325.
——. 'Kikuyu religion, old and new', *African Affairs* (London), vol. 52, no. 208 (1953), p. 202-210.
——. 'The Christian revival in Kenya', *World Dominion* (London), 34, 2 (1956), p. 110-114.

Biermans, J. *A short history of the Vicariate of the Upper Nile, Uganda*. Kampala, 1920.
 By one of the first bishops.

Blakeslee, Helen V. *Beyond the Kikuyu curtain*. Chicago: Moody Press, 1956.
 Autobiographical account by a former AIM missionary.

Bonaya, T.W. 'The Young Buu Association, 1944-1956', in B.G. McIntosh (ed.), *Ngano* (Nairobi: East African Publishing House, 1969).
 The work of the Neukirchner Mission and the United Methodist Mission among the Buu clan of the Pokomo, Tana River, leading to the Young Buu self-help enterprise

Bostock, P.G. *The Taita*. London: Macmillan, 1950.
 By a CMS missionary. Brief mention of ancestor worship, religion and missions.

Boxer, C.R. & C. de Azevedo. *Fort Jesus and the Portuguese in Mombasa, 1593-1729*. London: Hollis & Carter, 1960.

Bridges, R.C. 'Krapf and the strategy of the mission to East Africa, 1844-1855', *Makerere Journal*, no. 5 (1961), p. 37-50.

Britton, J. 'Mission task in Kenya', *International Review of Missions*, vol. 12 (1923), p. 412-420.

Brown, Evelyn M. *Edel Quinn: beneath the Southern Cross*. London: Burns & Oates, 1967.
 Biography of the founder of the Catholic Legion of Mary in Kenya, who lived from 1907-1944, and arrived in Kenya in 1936.

Brutzer, E. *Begnungen mit Wakamba*. Leipzig: Evangelical Lutheran Mission, 1903.
——. *Der Geisterglaube beiden Kamba*. Leipzig: Evangelical Lutheran Mission, circa 1904.

Bryson, S.M. *Light in darkness: the story of the Nandi Bible*. London: Perry Jackman, 1959.
 By the first AIM translator of the Nandi Bible; deals also with early missionary work in Nandi country.

Bujra, Janet M. 'Language loyalties within a religious community in Nairobi'. Project, Institute of African Studies, University of Nairobi, 1971.

Bunger, R.L. 'An historical study of the process of Islamization among the Pokomo and other peoples of Coastal Kenya'. Project, Institute of African Studies, University of Nairobi, 1970.

Buxton, C.R. 'Missionaries in East Africa', *Contemporary Review*, April, 1933.
 A British M.P. answers critics of missionary work after a personal visit to East Africa, including Kenya.

Byrne, F. 'The role of the primary teacher in the local church in Kenya'. Paper, Pastoral Institute of Eastern Africa, Gaba, 1969.
 The teacher's role within the wider Christian community, and the multi-functional character of the school in Africa.

Cagnolo, C. *The Agikuyu: their customs, traditions and folklore*. Nyeri: Mission Printing School, 1933.
 Contains material on Kikuyu religion and an account of the early years of the Consolata Mission.
——. 'Uno schisma nella chiesa Protestante del Kikuyu (A schism in the Kikuyu Protestant church)', *Missioni Consolata* (Turin), 46, 7 (1944), p. 55-7; 46, 8, p. 69-72.
 An account of the African Orthodox Church.

Capon, Martin. *A history of Christian co-operation in Kenya*. Nairobi, 1947.

——. *Towards Christian unity in Kenya*. Nairobi: CCK, 1962.

Carey, W.J. *Crisis in Kenya: Christian commonsense on Mau Mau and the color bar*. London: Mowbray, 1953.

Carlebach, J. *The Jews of Nairobi, 1903-1962*. Nairobi: Nairobi Hebrew Congregation, n.d. (1962).
 By a former rabbi of Nairobi.

Carothers, J.C. *The African mind in health and disease*. Geneva: World Health Organisation, 1953.
——. *The psychology of Mau Mau*. Nairobi: Government Printer, 1954.

Catholic Directory of East Africa, 1950. Mombasa: Apostolic Delegation, 1950.

Catholic Directory of Eastern Africa. Tabora: T.M.P. Book Department, 1971.
 Names and addresses for 70 dioceses in Kenya, Uganda, Tanzania, Sudan, Zambia, Malawi. Previous editions: 1965, 1968.

Catholic Directory of East and West Africa, 1958. Mombasa: Apostolic Delegation, 1958.

Catholic Handbook of East Africa. Mombasa, 1932.

Cayzac, P. 'La religion des Kikuyu (Afrique orientale)', *Anthropos*, vol. 35 (1910), p. 309-319.
——. 'Witchcraft in Kikuyu', *Man*, vol. 12, article 67 (1912), p. 127-128.

'Centenary Pamphlets. The Methodist Church in Kenya'. No. 1 'March 24, 1862'; No. 2 'One hundred years: the earlier days'; No. 3 'Tharaka'; No. 4 'Translation of the Scriptures into Kimeru'; No. 5 'Autonomy, Jan. 7, 1967'. Nairobi: Methodist Church in Kenya.
 In English and Swahili.

Cherotich, Sarah. 'The Nandi female initiation and the Christian impact upon it', *Dini na Mila* (Kampala), vol. 2, nos. 2-3 (1967).

Chilson, Edna. *Ambassador of the King*. Wichita, Kansas, 1943.
 By the wife of Arthur Chilson, FAM missionary under whom the 1927 Holy Spirit revival began, who served in Kenya in 1902 and from 1907-1927.

'Christian living and Christian giving'. Report of a conference at Limuru Conference Centre, 1961. Nairobi: Church Information Board, 1961 (mimeo).

'Church and state in education: Kenya', in *World Book of Education*. London: Evans, 1966.

Church, J.E. 'Quest for the highest: an autobiographical account of the East African Revival Movement'. Typescript (265 pages), Kampala, 1971.

Church Missionary Intelligencer (London), 1849-1919.
 Monthly CMS missionary journal containing much information on Kenya.

Coats, Victoria T. *David Charters: engineer, doctor and missionary, 1864-94*. London: A. & C. Black, 1925.
 Graphic biography, compiled from his letters, of a pioneer of the East African Scottish Mission who disappeared at Kibwezi in 1894.

Cole, E.K. *Mau Mau mission*. Sydney: Testimony Press, 1954.
——. *A history of church co-operation in Kenya*. Limuru: St. Paul's College Press, 1957.
——. *After Mau Mau: the Church in Kenya today*. Sydney: Testimony Press, 1957.
——. *Kenya: hanging in the middle way*. London: Highway Press, 1959.
——. 'The Anglican Church in Kenya'. Dissertation, Australian College of Divinity, 1964.
——. *The Cross over Mount Kenya*. Nairobi: Church Missionary Historical Publications, 1970.
 History of the Anglican Church in the Diocese of Mount Kenya, 1900-70.

Collister, P. & E. Vere-Hodge, *Pioneers of East Africa*. Nairobi: Eagle Press, 1956.
 Includes frequent references to pioneer missionaries.

Colpi, E. *Credenze religiose e moralita Kikuyu*. Turin: Ed. Filosofia, 1953.

Conquest for Christ in Africa, 1902-52. A history of the Consolata Fathers in Kenya. Nyeri: Catholic Printing School, 1952.

Consolata journals (Edizioni Missioni Consolata, Turin): *La Consolata, Missioni Consolata* (the official journal), *Da Casa*

Madre (internal house bulletin of Consolata Fathers), *Eco* (journal of Consolata Sisters).

Constitution of the National Christian Council of Kenya, (1966) (Katiba ya Jumuiya ya Wakristo wa Kenya). Nairobi: NCCK, 1971.

Corfield, F.D. *Historical survey of the origins and growth of Mau Mau.* Nairobi: Government Printer, 1960.
An official report: p. 41, 45, the African Orthodox Church; p. 171-90, Kikuyu Independent Schools.

Cox, P. *Amudat story.* London: Patmos Press, circa 1965.
The work of a BCMS station in Karapokot (Kenya/Uganda), by a medical missionary.

Crawford, E. May. *By the equator's snowy peak.* London: Church Missionary Society, 1913.
Accounts of the founding of the CMS missions at Kahuhia (Fort Hall) and Kigari (Embu).

Crawford, J.W.W. 'The Kikuyu medicine-man', *Man* (London), vol. 9 (1909), p. 53-56.

Dain, F.R. 'Religious education in Kenya', *Association for Religious Education Bulletin*, 9 (1972).

Davidson, R.T. *Kikuyu.* London: Macmillan, 1915.
The 74-page statement on the Kikuyu conference by the Archbishop of Canterbury.

Davies, L. 'The growth of the Africa Inland Church'. Thesis, School of World Mission, Fuller Theological Seminary (California), 1970.

Dawson, E.C. *James Hannington, first Bishop of Eastern Equatorial Africa.* London: Seeley and Co., 1886.
——. *The East African journals of Bishop Hannington.* London, 1888.

Dena, L.C.T. 'A comparative study of the impact of the differing traditions of Christianity on some of the Coastal tribes of Kenya'. Limuru: St. Paul's United Theological College, n.d. (typescript).

Development Plan 1970-1974. Republic of Kenya. Nairobi: Government Printer, 1969.
This 571-page volume details the government's development policies in the whole range of fields, in many of which the churches co-operate.

Dini ya Sikh (Sikh religion). Nairobi: Sikh Students Federation, 1968. (Also available in English and Gujarati).

Dirven, P.J. 'The Maria Legio: the dynamics of a breakaway church among the Luo in East Africa'. Dissertation, Pontificia Universitas Gregoriana, Rome, 1970.

Dodoma Conference report. Kikuyu: East African Church Union Consultation, 1965 (mimeo, 24 pages).

Dougall, J.W.C. *'Missionary education in Kenya and Uganda:* a study of co-operation'. London: International Missionary Council, 1936.
——. *Building Kenya's future.* Edinburgh: Church of Scotland Foreign Missions Committee, 1955.

Du Plessis, J. *The evangelisation of pagan Africa.* Cape Town: Juta, 1929.
Massive history of Protestant missions across Black Africa, west to east.

Dutto, C.A. 'Nyeri townsmen: a case study of social participation'. Paper, Institute of African Studies, University of Nairobi, 1972; and dissertation, Catholic University, Washington DC, USA (forthcoming).
9,400 out of the population of 20,000 in Nyeri town are school pupils. Every Sunday, 50 per cent of the population attend church.

Eglin, Lorna. *Child of two worlds.* Cape Town: Africa Inland Mission, 1971.
The story of a Maasai girl at an AIM boarding school.

Emerson, Elizabeth. *Emory Rees, language pioneer.* Gowanda, NY: Niagara Frontier Publishing Co., 1958.
The life and work of a pioneer FAM worker, largely responsible for the translation of the Bible into Luragoli.

Evans-Pritchard, E.E. 'Ghostly vengeance among the Luo of Kenya', *Man* (London), 50, 133 (1950), p. 86-87.
A study of the Luo belief in *jacien* (a troublesome ghost) as the primary cause of sickness and other misfortunes, and thus an important factor in maintaining social mores.

Extracts from Voice of Kenya audience survey: quick-reference buyers' guide for 1970. Nairobi: Ministry of Information

and Broadcasting, 1969.

Falda, B. *Ricordi personali* (Personal remembrances). 3 vols. Turin: Edizioni Missioni Consolata, 1969.
Manuscripts in Italian covering the work of a pioneer Consolata brother who worked in Kenya from 1904 for fifty years.

Farson, N. *Last chance in Africa.* London: Victor Gollancz, 1949.
Contains material on Dini ya Msambwa, the Watu wa Mungu, and Dini ya Jesu Kristo.

Fokken, H. 'Gottesanschauungen und religiöse Uberlieferungen der Masai', *Archives fur Anthropologie*, vol. 15, no. 4 (1917), p. 237-252.

Forbes-Watson, R. *Charles New.* London: Nelson, 1950.
Life of the pioneer Methodist missionary in Kenya.

Forde, C.D. (ed.). *The ethnographic survey of Africa.* London: International African Institute, 1950-60.
All the monographs in this series on African peoples, including those on Kenya tribes, have a section on religion.

Freeman-Grenville, G. 'The martyrs of Mombasa, 1631', *African Ecclesiastical Review*, IX, 4 (October, 1967), p. 353-364.

Frere, Sir Bartle. *East Africa as a field for missionary labour.* 1874.

Fueter, P.D. 'A Christian council in action: the Christian Council of Kenya', *International Review of Missions*, vol. 49 (1960), p. 291-300.

Furley, O.W. 'The historiography of Mau Mau'. Paper, Historical Association of Kenya annual conference, 1971 (mimeo).

Gale, H.P. *Uganda and the Mill Hill Fathers.* London: Macmillan, 1959.
History of the first Roman Catholic mission in Kavirondo, Western Kenya, over the period 1895-1914.

Gallea, G. *Istituto Missioni Consolata: nascita e primi sviluppi.* Vol. 1 (1880-1909), Vol. 2 (1910-1922), vol. 3 (1923-1928). Turin: Edizioni Missioni Consolata, 1970-1.
This work in Italian will eventually be the official Consolata history.

Gatu, J.G. 'Revival in East Africa: a critical review'. Unpublished manuscript, Nairobi, 1971.
Deals with the problem of the Kufufuka movement across East Africa.

Gertzel, Cherry (ed.). 'Religion', in *Government and politics in Kenya: a nation building text* (Nairobi: East African Publishing House, 1969), p. 53-69.
A handful of newspaper items and quotations from two church constitutions.

Ghai, D.P. (ed.). *Portrait of a minority: Asians in East Africa.* Nairobi: Oxford, 1965.

Ghilardi, P. 'Religion and beliefs of the Agekoyo', *Annale Lateranensi* (Vatican), vol. 19 (1955), p. 333-348.

Githae, M. 'The place of religion in African traditional education'. Department of Education, University College, Nairobi, 1968 (ms).

Githii, Hannah. 'Church discipline: a contemporary problem of the Church in Kikuyu'. Hancock Memorial Prize Essay, Makerere University College, Kampala, 1967.

Glazier, J. 'A study of the role of religion and church in socio-economic development among the Mbere people of Kenya'. Project, Institute of African Studies, University of Nairobi, 1970.

Glen, R.M. *Historia ya Ukristo: ramani na nyakati zake.* Dodoma: Central Tanganyika Press, 1971.
The last 11 pages of maps deal with Christianity in East Africa.

Goldthorpe, J.E. *Outlines of East African society.* Kampala: Department of Sociology, Makerere University College, 1958.
Chapter VIII, 'Religious groups' (p. 190-231), has thorough coverage of the entire religious situation in the mid-1950s.
——. 'Asians', chapter IX in *Outlines of East African society* (Kampala, 1958), p. 108-128.
Includes detailed religious information on the various Asian groups.

Good News is for telling: one hundred years of Bible Society work in East Africa. Centenary booklet. Nairobi: Bible Society, 1969.

Gray, Sir John. *Early Portuguese missionaries in East Africa*. London: Macmillan, 1958.

Gray, R. 'Roman Catholic missions and the response in tropical Africa from the 15th to the 18th centuries'. London: School of Oriental and African Studies, n.d., circa 1968 (mimeo, 23 pages).

Greaves, L.B. *Carey Francis of Kenya*. London: Rex Collings, 1969.
　Biography of the CMS missionary who was successively headmaster of Maseno School and Alliance High School.

Grimshaw, E. 'A short history of the Vicariate of the Upper Nile'. Manuscript (2 parts), circa 1945.
　Lengthy and detailed account of the period 1894-1944.

Groves, C.P. *The planting of Christianity in Africa*. Vol. 4, 1914-1945. London: Lutterworth, 1958.
　The definitive history of Christianity and Christian missions in Africa, with sections on Kenya in the last two volumes.

Grubb, N.P. *Alfred Buxton of Abyssinia and Congo*. London: Lutterworth Press, 1942.
　Deals briefly with the establishment of BCMS work in Kenya.

Gulliver, P.H. 'A preliminary survey of the Turkana'. A report compiled for the Government of Kenya. School of African Studies, University of Cape Town, 1951.
　Part 4 deals with the magico-religious aspects of Turkana life (p. 229-51).

Hake, A.A.G. 'An urban-industrial ministry in Kenya', in D.B. Barrett (ed.), *African initiatives in religion* (Nairobi, 1971), p. 242-252.
　History and description of the Christian Council of Kenya's industrial mission in Nairobi, 1959-67.

—— & G.K. Mambo. *Seventy young workers*. Nairobi: Christian Council of Kenya, 1962 (mimeo, 55 pages).
　A study of 70 youths previously trained in the Christian Industrial Training Centre, Pumwani, Nairobi.

Hakes, J.E. *A study guide for Kenya*. Boston: African Studies Centre, Boston University, 1969.

Hamilton, G. *In the wake of Da Gama: the story of Portuguese pioneers in East Africa, 1497-1729*. London: Skeffington, 1951.

Harambee na makanisa. Uhuru Souvenir. Nairobi: NCCK, 1963.
　A description of the churches' involvement in development before Uhuru (Independence) in 1963.

Harries, L.P. *Islam in East Africa*. London: Longmans, 1952.

Harris, Grace. 'Possession hysteria in a Kenya tribe', *American Anthropologist*, LIX, 6 (1957), p. 1046-1066.
　A study among the Taita.

Heavenly melodies. Machakos: Scott Theological College, 1971 (mimeo).
　A collection of 25 traditional or original hymns composed by Kenyan theological students, with words in Nandi, Kamba, Kikuyu, Pokot, Swahili, as well as English.

Hemelrijk, H.M. *The church in education in Kenya*. Kisumu, 1968 (mimeo).

Hewitt, G. 'Kenya', in *The problems of success: a history of the Church Missionary Society, 1910-1942*, vol. 1 (London: SCM, 1971), p. 121-173.
　A detailed history of missions, churches, education, church union and related subjects up to 1942.

Hinde, Hildegarde. *Some problems of East Africa*. London: Williams & Norgate, 1926.
　The wife of an administrative officer on topical and religious problems.

Hinsley, Cardinal A. 'The martyrs of Mombasa', *East African Annual*, 1932.

Historia ya Kanisa. Mombasa: Coast Bible School (Anglican), 1965 (mimeo, 28 pages).

'Historical notes concerning the educational work of the United Methodist Church Mission, Meru', in 'The Report of the Missions', 1908.

Hobley, C.W. *Ethnology of A-kamba and other East African tribes*. London, 1910 (Cass, 1971).
　Chapters 18-22 refer to religion, beliefs, magic, medicine men, prohibitions, omens, etc.

——. 'Further researches into Kikuyu and Kamba religious beliefs and customs', *Journal of the Royal Anthropological Institute*, vol. 41 (1911), p. 406-457.

——. 'Kamba protective magic', *Man*, vol. 12, no. 1 (1912), p. 4-6.

——. *Bantu beliefs and magic*. London, 1922 (Cass, 1967).
　An early study with particular reference to the Kikuyu and Kamba tribes.

Hofmann, J. *Geburt, Heirat und Tod bei Wakamba*. Leipzig: Evangelical Lutheran Mission, 1901.

Hollingsworth, L.W. *The Asians of East Africa*. London: Macmillan, 1960.
　Although the book is outdated and the situation of Asians has changed markedly since 1960, chapter XI on religions, 'Hindu and Muslim in East Africa' (p. 127-150), has still valid descriptions of the various communities — Hindus, Muslims, Ismailis, Ismaili Khojas, Ithna'ashri, Bohras, and Ahmadiyya.

Hollis, A.C. *The Masai: their language and folklore*. Oxford: Clarendon, 1905.
　Pages 264-356 deal in both general and specific terms with religious beliefs, magic, superstition, etc.

——: 'The religion of the Nandi', *Transactions of the Third International Congress for the History of Religions*, Vol. 1 (1908), p. 87-91.

——. *The Nandi: their language and folklore*. Oxford: Clarendon, 1909.
　Pages 6-100 deal with religious beliefs, magic, superstition, etc.

——. 'Some Dorobo beliefs', *Man*, vol. 9, no. 101 (1909), p. 177.

Holway, J.D. 'The religious composition of the population of the Coast Province of Kenya', *Journal of Religion in Africa*, III, 3 (1970), p. 228-239.

——. 'The extent of interconversion between Islam and Christianity in East Africa'. Dissertation, University of East Africa, 1970.
　A study of the extent and the causes of conversion to and from Islam, and to and from Christianity, with particular emphasis on Kenya peoples.

——. 'The Qur'an in Swahili: three translations', *The Muslim World*, LXI, 2 (1971), p. 102-110.

——. 'Islam and Christianity in East Africa', in D.B. Barrett (ed.), *African initiatives in religion* (Nairobi, 1971), p. 262-273.

——. 'Contact with Islam in Kenya by the Church Missionary Society before 1914', *Journal of Religion in Africa* (1972).

——. *Islam and Christianity in East Africa: a study of interconversion*. Forthcoming.

Hooper, C. *Down our street (Kenya)*. London: Church Missionary Society, 1959.

Hooper, H.D. 'Kikuyu churches in united action', *Church Missionary Review*, no. 825 (March, 1919), p. 15-23.
　On the Kikuyu Missions Volunteer Carrier Corps.

——. *Leading strings: native development and missionary education in Kenya colony*. London: CMS, 1922.
　Author was a CMS missionary in Kenya, 1916-1926, and later Africa Secretary of CMS.

——. 'Expression of Christian life in primitive African society', *International Review of Missions*, XIII (January, 1924), p. 67-73.

——. *Africa in the making*. London, 1924.

——. 'Gold in Kenya', *Church Overseas*, vol. 6, no. 22 (1933), p. 99-112.

Hooper, M. Cicely. *Beyond the night*. London: Highway Press, 1929.
　A fictionalized account by a missionary of the founding of a girls' dormitory in Kikuyu country, with background of missions in the 1920s.

Hooton, W.S. & J. Stafford Wright. *The first twenty-five years of the Bible Churchmen's Missionary Society (1922-47)*. London: BCMS, 1947.
　Deals with inauguration of BCMS work in Kenya.

Hopkins, A.J. *Trail blazers and roadmakers.*
By an ordained UMM (Methodist) missionary in Kenya.
Hoskins, Irene. *Friends in Africa.* Richmond, Indiana: American Friends Board of Foreign Missions, 1944.
Hotchkiss, W.R. *Sketches from the dark continent.* London, 1903.
By a pioneer AIM missionary who later founded the Lumbwa Industrial Mission.
——. *Then and now in Kenya Colony: forty adventurous years in East Africa.* London: Oliphants, 1937.
Hughes, H.R. 'Church buildings in Kenya', *Church Buildings Today* (January, 1962), p. 5-13.
——. 'The churches of Kenya', *East African Annual* (July, 1964).
An architectural description.
——. 'The designing of a cathedral', *Kenya Weekly News* (January, 1965).
Huntingford, G.W.B. 'Ghosts and devils in East Africa', *Man*, vol. 28, no. 55 (1928), p. 76-78.
On the Nandi and Luhya.
——. 'Note on some names for God', *Man*, vol. 28, no. 138 (1928), p. 189-190.
On the Nandi.
——. 'Further notes on some names for God', *Man*, vol. 30, no. 79 (1930), p. 102-103.
——. 'Genealogy of the Orkoiik (religious leaders) of Nandi' *Man*, vol. 35, no. 24 (1935), p. 22-3.
——. *The Nandi of Kenya.* London: Routledge and Kegan Paul, 1953.
Chapter 7 (p. 122-58) deals with religion.
Hurd, A.E.S. *Serving the church in Kenya.* London: Bible Churchmen's Missionary Society, 1963.
Huxley, Elspeth. 'The rise of the African zealot', *Corona* (London), 2, 5 (1950), p. 163-166.
The Watu wa Mungu of the Kikuyu, the Dini ya Msambwa of the Bukusu, and the roots of such movements in secret societies.
——. *A thing to love.* London: circa 1960.
Fiction. Describes a mission station and Christian refugees during the Emergency period.
Huxley, Julian. 'Missions and the life of Africa', in *Africa view* (New York: Harper, 1931).
Critical discussion by agnostic scientist and humanitarian.
In African accents. A report of a conference on communications in development: AMECEA, Lusaka, December 1971. Lusaka: Multimedia Zambia, 1972.
Indaru, P. *The man with the iron heart.* Nakuru: Uzima Press (forthcoming).
Biography of Canon Ezekiel Apindi, Anglican pioneer in South Nyanza.
Irvine, Cecilia. 'Report on a survey of African independent church (separatist) congregations in Nairobi city, July, 1967' Nairobi: NCCK, 1967 (mimeo, 47 pages).
Jacobs, D.R. 'The culture themes and puberty rites of the Akamba'. Dissertation, New York University, 1961.
Jones, T.J. *Education in East Africa.* New York: Phelps — Stokes Fund, circa 1926.
Jumbale, A. 'Traditional religion of the Chonyi tribe'. Limuru: St. Paul's United Theological College, 1969 (mimeo, 13 pages).
Kabugi, J. 'The history of Wahundura Church'. Paper, Kenyatta College, 1969 (ms).
History of an Anglican church in Murang'a District.
Kaggia, Bildad. *Roots of Freedom.* Nairobi: East African Publishing House, 1972.
Chapter on his relations with the CMS and beginnings of the 'Dini ya Kaggia'.
Kajuki, D. 'The growth of the Methodist Church in Meru'. Typescript (15 pages) in library of St. Paul's United Theological College, Limuru, n.d. (circa 1962).
Kamau, P. 'The coming of Christianity to Kabete'. Paper, Kenyatta College, 1969 (ms).
Kamenyi, J. *Prophets (Aroti): Turban people Andu a Iremba.* Nairobi: Christian Council of Kenya, circa 1960 (mimeo).
Kikuyu independents, by a theological student.
Kanyua, J.N. 'The traditional religion of the Embu people'.

Limuru: St. Paul's United Theological College, n.d., circa 1970 (mimeo. 38 pages).
Karhof, E. 'The catechist in East Africa after the Council'. Paper, Pastoral Institute of Eastern Africa, Gaba, 1968.
Karioki, P. 'Unemployment and its challenge to the church: a special study in Kiambu District'. Typescript (22 pages) in library of St. Paul's United Theological College, Limuru, 1970.
Karp, I. 'A socio-structural study of African Christian churches in Baluhyia (Khayo), Western Province, Kenya'. Project, Institute of African Studies, University of Nairobi, 1971.
Kaufmann, H. 'Zwischen Zauberei und Christentum (Between magic and Christianity)', *Frankfurter Allgemeine Zeitung*, 134 (12 June 1965).
An account of Maria Legio.
Keller, Marian. *Twenty years in Africa.* Toronto: Full Gospel Publishing Co., n.d.
By a pioneer missionary of the Pentecostal Assemblies of Canada in Kenya.
Kenya, 1898-1948: the Jubilee Book of the Church of Scotland Mission, Kenya Colony. Kikuyu: Church of Scotland Foreign Mission Committee, 1948.
Kenya Church Review and Year Book. A yearly report on the work of the Anglican Church in Kenya. Nairobi: Church Information Board, annually from 1955-64.
Contain a large number of short articles on Anglican work in different parts of Kenya.
Kenya present and future: a statement of Christian principles. Nairobi: CCK, n.d. (1961).
Kenyatta, Jomo. 'Kikuyu religion, ancestor-worship and practices', *Africa*, vol. 10, no. 3 (1937), p. 308-328.
——. 'The new religion in East Africa', in *Facing Mount Kenya* (London: Secker and Warburg, 1937), p. 269-279.
Attributes new sects to the blindness of missionaries, especially in opposing polygamy, and describes in detail one Kikuyu group, the Watu wa Mungu (People of God).
Keymer, R.C. 'Lighting the torches: the story of the East African Scottish Mission'. Tumutumu, 1967 (mimeo).
Kibicho, S.G. 'The interaction of the traditional Kikuyu concept of God with the Biblical concept', in D.B. Barrett (ed.), *Theory and practice* (1968), p. 381-390.
Kieran, J.A. 'The Holy Ghost Fathers in East Africa, 1863 to 1914'. Dissertation, University of London, 1966.
——. 'The Christian Church in East Africa in modern times', *Neue Zeitschrift fur Missionswissenschaft*, 25, 4 (1969), p. 273-287.
Kihara, N. 'A history of the Church at Ng'enda'. Paper, Kenyatta College, 1969 (ms).
History of an AIM Kikuyu congregation near Kambui begun in 1905, then handed over to the Gospel Missionary Society, which later became part of the PCEA.
Kikuyu: 1898-1923. Semi-jubilee book of the Church of Scotland Mission. London: Blackwood, 1923.
Published for the 25th anniversary of the Church of Scotland Mission.
Kikuyu, 1918. Report of the United Conference of Missionary Societies in British East Africa. London: CMS Bookshop, 1918.
Kimilu, D.N. 'The Separatist Churches', *Dini na Mila* (Makerere University), vol. 2, 2-3 (1967). p. 11-61.
A detailed examination of the history, beliefs and practices of the Kamba branches of the Friends of the Holy Spirit, including the words of 59 hymns.
Kimunge, S.G. 'The Muthua-ini Independent Pentecostal Church of Kenya'. Paper, Kenyatta College, 1969 (mimeo).
History of one local church in the AIPC (African Independent Pentecostal Church). Founded in 1928, this congregation was taken over by the PCEA in 1952-3, but after Independence in 1963 was reopened as AIPC. It has 4,000 followers and is growing rapidly.
——. 'Karima Mission of the Italian Consolata Fathers'. Paper, Kenyatta College, 1969 (mimeo).
King, K.J. 'The American Negro as missionary to East Africa: a critical aspect of African evangelism'. Conference paper. Kampala: University of East Africa Social Sciences Council, 1968.

———. 'The Kenya Maasai and the protest phenomenon, 1900-1960', *Journal of African History*, XII, 1 (1971), p. 117-137.
Refers to early AIM mission work among the Maasai, and the first Maasai converts.

———. *Pan-Africanism and education; a study of race, philanthropy and education in the Southern States of America and East Africa*. Nairobi: Oxford, 1971.
Discusses church and mission roles in education in Kenya.

———. 'A biography of Molonket Olokorinya ole Sempele', in K.J. King & A. Salim (eds.), *Kenya historical biographies* (Nairobi: East African Publishing House, 1971), p. 1-28.

King, N.Q. 'The East African revival movement and evangelism', *Ecumenical Review*, 20, 2 (1968), p. 159-162.

Kinyua, P. 'The foundation and growth of Tumutumu Presbyterian Parish, Kenya', *Dini na Mila* (Makerere University College), vol. 4, 1 (October, 1969), p. 12-27.

Kipkorir, B.E. 'Christianity comes to Marakwet'. Arts Research Prize Essay, Makerere University College, 1961.
The coming of the AIM and other missions to a Kalenjin people.

———. 'The Alliance High School and the making of the Kenya African elite, 1926-1962'. Dissertation, Cambridge University, 1969.

———. 'The sectarian factor and Kenya's first African secondary school'. University College, Nairobi. 1967 (typescript).

———, with F.B. Welbourn. *The Marakwet of Kenya*. Nairobi: East African Literature Bureau, 1972.
Refers to Marakwet religion as an integral part of Marakwet society.

Kirima, N. & J. Mugambi. *African religious heritage, with special reference to East Africa*. Nairobi: Oxford, 1973.
Textbook for 'O' level, EACE.

Kiriro, A.K. 'Church growth among the Embu of Mount Kenya, 1900-66', in D.B. Barrett (ed.), *Theory and practice* (1968), p. 397-400 (mimeo).

Kirkman, J.S. *Men and monuments on the East African Coast*. London: Lutterworth, 1964.
Covers the Arab and Portuguese centuries.

Kitabu cha kusifu. Nairobi: Majestic Printing Works, n.d.; also Nakuru: Uzima Press, 1972.
A printed hymnbook with 8 hymns of the East African Revival Fellowship, including the hymn *Tukutendereza* translated into 20 languages.

Kiute, Christine W. 'The development of the church in Kasigau-Taita'. Paper, Kenyatta College, 1969 (mimeo).
A case study of CMS and the Anglican church in the Taita Hills when faced with the challenge of both Pentecostal and Balokole revivalists after 1959.

Kiwaria, J.C. 'Missionary work in Taita District'. Typescript (12 pages) in library of St. Paul's United Theological College, Limury, n.d. (circa 1961).

Koren, H.J. *The Spiritans: a history of the Congregation of the Holy Ghost*. Pittsburgh: Duquesne University, 1958.
Numerous references to Kenya, with maps of early Catholic jurisdictions.

Krapf, Johannes Ludwig. *Travels, researches and missionary labours during an eighteen years' residence in Eastern Africa*. London: Trubner, 1860.
Journals of the pioneer Anglican missionary to Kenya who arrived in 1844.

Kulbeck, Gloria. *What God hath wrought*. Toronto: Full Gospel Publishing House, 1958.
A history of the Pentecostal Assemblies of Canada, including their mission in Kenya.

Kupalo, Sr. Ancilla. 'Religious education in Kenya'. Paper, Pastoral Institute of Eastern Africa, Gaba, 1971.

Kurani Tukufu (The Holy Qur'an, in Swahili). Nairobi: E.A. Ahmadiyya Muslim Mission, 1953.

Kuria, J.W. 'The separated brethren'. Paper, Kenyatta College, 1969 (mimeo).
A history and description of the African Christian Church and Schools (ACC&S).

La Fontaine, S.H. 'Taveta customs and beliefs in connection with religion, burial and disease', *Journal of the African Society*, vol. 13, no. 52 (1914), p 385-394.

Langford-Smith, N. 'Revival in East Africa', *International Review of Missions* (January, 1954), p. 77-81.

Langley, Myrtle. 'Deviation in three rites of passage: initiation, marriage and divorce over the past fifty years in Nandi (with special attention to the influence of missions)'. Dissertation, Bristol University (forthcoming).

——— & T. Kiggins. *A serving people: the church in East Africa*. Nairobi: Oxford, 1973.
Textbook for 'O' level, EACE.

Latourette, K.S. *Christianity in a revolutionary age*. Vol. 5. New York: Zondervan, 1958.
Latourette's definitive history of the expansion of Christianity throughout the world in the 19th and 20th centuries. P. 474-77 deal with the 'Complex Pattern in Kenya' with regard to the development of Christian religious bodies and beliefs.

La vita nell'Istituto. Vols. 1-3 (1908-1921); Vol. 4 (all issues of internal house journal *Da Casa Madre*, 1918-1919). Turin: Missioni Consolata (typescript).
Diaries on life in Consolata.

Leakey, L.S.B. 'Some notes on the Masai of Kenya Colony', *Journal of the Royal Anthropological Institute*, LX (1930).
Includes a section on Maasai religion.

———. 'The Kikuyu problem of the initiation of girls', *Journal of the Royal Anthropological Institute*, LXI (1931), p. 277-285.
Written by an anthropologist at the time of the controversy within the Kikuyu Protestant churches.

———. 'Mau Mau as a religion', *Manchester Guardian*, June 24-5, 1954.

———. 'The religious element in Mau Mau', *African Music* Roodepoort, Transvaal), 1, 1 (1954), p. 77.
A note on Mau Mau hymnbooks setting new words to Christian tunes.

Lemi, J. 'Work done by Catholic Church missionaries in Mikinduri Location, 1920-69'. Paper, Kenyatta College, 1969 (ms).

LeVine, R.A. 'Witchcraft and co-wife proximity in southwestern Kenya', *Ethnology*, 1, 1 (1962), p. 39-45.
The relationship between the two phenomena in three Kenyan tribes, the Gusii, Kipsigis and Luo.

Lewis, I.M. *Peoples of the Horn of Africa*. London: Ethnographic Survey of Africa, 1955.

Leys, N. *Kenya*. London: Hogarth Press, 1926.
Discusses work of missions in Kenya.

Lindblom, K.G. *The Akamba in British East Africa*. Uppsala: Appelberg, 1920.

———. *Kamba tales of supernatural beings and adventures*. Uppsala: Appelberg, 1935.

Liturgia ya Umoja kwa Afrika ya Mashariki. Limuru: St. Paul's United Theological College, 1967.
Swahili edition of United Liturgy for East Africa.

Livingstone, David. *On Tana River; a story of Kenya's Tana Church*. London: Cargate Press, n.d. (c 1965).
A description of the Methodist mission and church in the Tana River area over the last hundred years.

Lloyd, T.E. *African harvest*. London: Lutterworth, 1953.
The work of the Africa Inland Mission, with chapters on Kenya.

Lonsdale, J.M. 'Politics and society in Kavirondo, 1894-1945'. Dissertation, Cambridge University, 1963.
The development of political expression in Nyanza, CMS encouragement, and the search for a paramount chief.

———. 'Archdeacon Owen and the Kavirondo Taxpayers Welfare Association', in *Proceedings of the Conference of the East African Institute of Social Research*, 1963 (mimeo).

———. 'European attitudes and African pressures: missions and government in Kenya between the wars', in B.A. Ogot (ed.), *Hadithi 2* (Nairobi: East African Publishing House, 1970).

Macharia, A. 'Rural Aid Mission'. Paper, Kenyatta College, 1969 (ms).
Description of an Anglican agricultural mission on the Kinangop begun in 1963.

Macnaria, E.G. 'The establishment of the Anglican Church, Kahuhia'. Paper, Kenyatta College, 1969 (mimeo).

———. 'The establishment of the Catholic Church at Mugoiri'. Paper, Kenyatta College, 1969 (mimeo).

Macpherson, R. *The Presbyterian Church in Kenya: an account of the origins and growth of the PCEA.* Nairobi: PCEA, 1970.

Madoka, A. *Taita na Kanisa la Kristo katika miaka hamsini, 1900-1950.* Taita Rural Deanery, 1950.
Swahili: book on the Taita & CMS work over fifty years.

Magut, P.K. arap. 'The rise and fall of the Nandi Orkoiyot, c1850-1957', in B.G. McIntosh (ed.), *Ngano: studies in traditional and modern East African history* (Nairobi: East African Publishing House, 1969), p. 95-108.

Maina, A. 'The coming of Christianity to Kabete' - Paper, Kenyatta College, 1969 (mimeo).

Maina, Daudi wa Kiragu, *Kiria giatumira Independent igie* (What caused the Independent Church). Nairobi, n.d. (Kikuyu).
By one of the founding leaders of the African Independent Pentecostal Church, who began his first three churches near Fort Hall in 1921.

Makokha, C.C. 'The rise of African sects among the Baluyia'. Arts Research Prize, Makerere University College, 1951 (typescript).

Maloney, I.J. 'Acculturation among the Nandi of Kenya: Islam — its impact and potential'. Dissertation, Washington, St. Louis, USA, 1960.

Mambo, G.K. 'The shape of the urban church: the problem of Africanization', in *The Church meets life in the town* (Dar-es-Salaam: CCT and AACC, 1964), p. 111-116.

——. 'Million acre settlement scheme: survey of progress to date, December 1968'. Nairobi: NCCK, 1968.
An Anglican rural development and pastoral scheme in the whole of Kenya, especially Rift Valley (Diocese of Nakuru), Diocese of Maseno, and Diocese of Mount Kenya.

——. 'Use of African traditional medicine in Pumwani, Nairobi'. Typescript (33 pages), Department of Philosophy and Religious Studies, University of Nairobi, 1972.
A study of eleven medicine men practising in the city of Nairobi.

Mangaya, S. 'Worship in the African Brotherhood Church'. Paper, St. Paul's United Theological College, Limuru, n.d., circa 1970 (mimeo, 31 pages).

Manyara J. 'The African Independent Pentecostal Church of Kenya, Meru Branch'. Paper, Kenyatta College, c1970 (manuscript, 39 pages).
Detailed history and description of one of a group of 9 AIPC congregations west of Meru town.

Maps of the dioceses: Church of the Province of East Africa. Nairobi: Church Information Board, n.d. (1966) (mimeo, 14 maps).

Masembe, J. & D.N. Okunga. 'Paganism old and new'. Unpublished paper, 1956.
Includes an account of Elijah Masinde and Dini ya Msambwa.

Massam, J.A. *The cliff-dwellers of Kenya.* London, 1927 (Frank Cass, 1968).
Chapters 12-14 are on magic, religion and superstition, among a Kalenjin people in the Rift Valley, the Elgeyo (Keyu).

Mathu, G. 'C.M.S. enterprise in Gikuyu country to 1923'. Project, Institute of African Studies, University of Nairobi, 1971.

Matson, A.T. 'The Holy Ghost mission at Kosi on the Tana River', *Bulletin of the Society for African Church History*, II, 2 (1966), p. 174-179.
The first Roman Catholic mission to be begun in Kenya, in 1889, although it lasted less than a year.

——. 'Reflections on the growth of political consciousness in Nandi'. *Hadith 4* (forthcoming).
Contains comments on Nandi opposition to a multiplicity of Christian denominations, and their attitude towards African independent churches.

Mau Mau and the Church. Edinburgh: Church of Scotland Foreign Mission Committee, 1953.

Mbaire, Sr. Redempta. 'Kikuyu sacrifice'. Paper, Pastoral Institute of Eastern Africa, Gaba, 1971.

Mbiti, J.S. 'The African concept of time', *African Theological Journal, 1* (1968).

The concepts of *sasa* (present time) and *zamani* (ancient time), expounded from the standpoint of Kamba understanding.

——. *African religions and philosophy.* New York: Praeger, 1969.
An overview of Black Africa with numerous references to Kenya tribes.

——. *Concepts of God in Africa.* London: SPCK, 1970.
A study ranging across 300 African tribes, including many in Kenya. P. 327-336 contains a 'List of African peoples, their countries and names for God'.

——. *New Testament eschatology in an African background: a study of the encounter between New Testament theology and African traditional concepts.* London: Oxford, 1971.
A case study of the Akamba of eastern Kenya.

Mboya, P. *Luo kitgi gi timbegi* (The Luo people and their customs). Kisumu, 1950.
Survey of Luo customs by a senior chief from south Nyanza.

McIntosh, B.G. 'Archival resources of the University College, Nairobi, relative to missionary work and independent churches in Kenya', *Bulletin of the Society for African Church History* (Aberdeen), 2,4 (1968), p. 350-351.

——. 'Kenya 1923: the political crisis and the missionary dilemma'. Social Sciences Council Conference, University of East Africa. Kampala: Makerere University College, 1969 (mimeo, 24 pages).

——. 'The Scottish Mission in Kenya, 1891-1923'. Dissertation, Edinburgh University, 1969.
Early history of the PCEA.

'Memorandum prepared by the Kikuyu Mission Council on female circumcision'. Kikuyu: Church of Scotland Mission, 1931 (mimeo).

Merker, M. 'Religion und Tradition der Masai', *Zeitschrift fur Ethnologie* (Berlin), vol. 35 (1903), p. 733-744.

——. *Die Masai.* Berlin: Dietrich Reimer, 1910.
Chapter 21 (p. 203-211) deals with the religion of the Masai.

Methodist Church in Kenya: Minutes of 5th Conference, Limuru, 14-18 December, 1970. Nairobi (mimeo, 90 pages).
Report published annually since 1966.

Middleton, J. & E.H. Winter. *Witchcraft and sorcery in East Africa.* London: Routledge and Kegan Paul, 1963.

—— & G. Kershaw. *The Kikuyu and Kamba of Kenya.* London: International African Institute, 1953 (rev. ed. 1965).
P. 87-96 deal with religious beliefs and rituals, magic, sorcery and spirit possession.

Milikau, D.S. 'A brief history of Musoli Catholic Church'. Paper, Kenyatta College, 1969 (ms).

Millar, Catherine S. *The life of Peter Cameron Scott: the unlocked door.* London: Parry Jackman, 1955.

Miller, P.M. *Equipping for ministry in East Africa.* Dodoma: Central Tanganyika Press, 1969.
A study of congregations and the East African Revival in Kenya, and the relevance of dispersed theological education and the tent-making ministry.

Millikin, A.S. 'Burial customs of the Wa-Kavirondo of the Kisumu province', *Man,* vol. 6, no. 35 (1906), p. 54-55.

Minney, R.P. 'Divine compulsion: a study of vocation, leadership and Christian action in Kenya', in D.B. Barrett (ed.), *Theory and practice* (1968), p. 168-176.

Mockerie, P. *An African speaks for his people.* London: Hogarth, 1934.

Moriondo, B. 'Come conobbi l'Archivescovo ortodosso (How I met the Orthodox Archbishop)', *Missioni Consolata* (Turin), 46, 8-9 (1944), p. 92-94.
On the African Orthodox Church.

Morris, H.S. 'The divine kingship of the Aga Khan: a study of theocracy in East Africa', *Southwestern Journal of Anthropology* (New Mexico), 14 (1958), p. 454-472.

Mosii, T.M.K. 'Sabaot traditional religion'. Paper, Kenyatta College, 1970 (ms).

——. 'The Salvation Army: church history'. Paper, Kenyatta College, 1970 (ms).

Mpoke, Mary. 'Traditional religion among the Masai — past

forms and present relevance'. Paper, Kenyatta College, 1970 (mimeo).

Mruka, J. 'Religious specialists among the Luo'. Paper, Department of Philosophy and Religious Studies, University of Nairobi, 1972.(manuscript).

Muhoho, G.K. 'Gikuyu polygamy and Christian monogamy'. Thesis, National Seminary, Morogoro (Tanzania), 1962.
——. 'The Church's role in the development of the educational policy in the pluralistic society in Kenya'. Dissertation, Pontifical Urban University, Rome, 1970.

Muindi, B. 'Survey of the PCEA Church in Meru country'. Typescript (7 pages), St. Paul's United Theological College, Limuru, 1961.

Mulwa, W. (ed.) *Sura mpya ya Kanisa: historia ya Africa Inland Church.* Kijabe: Africa Inland Press, 1971.
'A new chapter for the Church: the history of the Africa Inland Church'; a Swahili history of the AIC and AIM, compiled by the 1971 president of the AIC.

Murdock, G.P. 'African cultural summaries'. New Haven: Human Relations Area Files, 1958 (photocopied).
Summaries of anthropological data on all African tribes, including Kenya's peoples.

Muriu, N. & W. Njaga. 'Revival in Kikuyuland', in *Religion and social change in modern East Africa* (Kampala: Makerere College, 1956), p. 9-19 (mimeo).

Murray, F. 'The diaconate in East Africa', *African Ecclesiastical Review,* VII, 4 (October, 1965), p. 346-350.

Murray, Jocelyn. 'Life of Jason Kilee Nguta'. Unpublished typescript, Nairobi, 1967 (100 pages).
Biography of rising young church leader of the Africa Inland Church who was killed in 1963.
——. 'A survey of Christian and educational work among the Kenya Maasai, undertaken to establish the feasibility of a church-connected literacy project'. Nairobi: NCCK, 1967 (typescript, 16 pages).
——. 'The present status of "female circumcision" among Kikuyu and Embu secondary schoolgirls, with reference to the historical background'. Report (mimeo), Nairobi, July 1972.
——. 'The Kikuyu female circumcision controversy of 1928-31: background, comparisons and perspectives'. Dissertation, University of California, Los Angeles (forthcoming).

Mwambanga, R. 'A short history of the Christian Churches' Educational Association (CCEA)'. Typescript (38 pages) for diploma in theology, University of East Africa, n.d. (circa 1965).

Mwangi, J.H. 'Beggars in Nairobi: an analysis and suggestions for action to the churches'. Typescript (22 pages), St. Paul's United Theological College, Limuru, 1970.
——. 'Development of Christian leadership in African Independent Pentecostal Church, Gituamba'. Typescript (9 pages), St. Paul's United Theological College, Limuru, 1971.

Nagle, J. 'The Legion comes to East Africa', *African Ecclesiastical Review,* I, 2 (April, 1959), p. 130-135.
The Legion of Mary, begun in Kenya in 1936.

NCCK Annual Reports for 1970. Nairobi: NCCK, 1971 (mimeo, 146 pages).

NCCK Reports 1971. Annual General Meeting, July 4-6, 1972. Nairobi: NCCK, 1972 (mimeo, 138 pages).

NCCK Souvenir Report, 25th Anniversary, 1969. Nairobi: NCCK, 1969 (mimeo, 118 pages).

Ndegwa, R. *Religion and Politics.* 1969.
A former Seventh-day Adventist theologian and minister on slowness of africanisation.

Ndirangu, J., Ondiek, G., & J.B. Ouma. 'Students and religion at the University of Nairobi: a survey' Report, Department of Philosophy and Religious Studies, University of Nairobi, 1972.

Ndungu, J.B. 'Gituamba and Kikuyu independency in church and school', in B.G. McIntosh (ed.), *Ngano* (Nairobi: East African Publishing House, 1969).
The founding of KISA and the AIPC at Gituamba, Fort Hall.

New, Charles. *Life, wanderings and labours in eastern Africa.* London: Hodder & Stoughton, 1873.

Newing, E.G. 'Concepts of mediation among the Kenya Highland Bantu compared with those of pre-Exilic Israel: a study in methodology', in D.B. Barrett (ed.), *Theory and practice* (1968), p. 149-156.
——. 'Baptism of polygamist families in the Church of the Province of East Africa: a contrast between theory and practice'. Paper, Theological Workshop in African Religions Today, St. Paul's United Theological College, Limuru, 1970.
——. 'Recruitment for the ministry of the church in Central Province, Kenya: a look at two denominations'. Paper, Theological Workshop in African Religions Today, St. Paul's United Theological College, Limuru, 1970.

Ngaira, Jemima. 'Independent churches in Idakho, Isukha and Tiriki districts (Luhya)'. Typescript, St. Paul's United Theological College, Limuru, 1966.

Ngari, Sam. 'Towards an African liturgy'. Paper, Pastoral Institute of Eastern Africa, Gaba, 1969.

Ngugi, James. *The river between.* London: Heinemann, 1965.
Fiction: the conflict between the Kikuyu people and missions over female circumcision forms a central theme.

Nida, E.A. 'Akamba initiation rites and culture themes', *Practical Anthropology,* vol. 9, no. 4 (1962), p. 145-155.

Njabani, N. 'The establishment of Chuka Catholic Church'. Paper, Kenyatta College, 1969 (ms).

Njagi, J. 'Church development in Embu AC'. Typescript (17 pages), library of St. Paul's United Theological College, Limuru, circa 1962.

Njai, Cicely. 'The Gikuyu traditional religion'. Paper, Kenyatta College, 1969 (mimeo).

Njehiah, G. 'Gikuyu second birth according to both guilds'. Typescript, St. Paul's United Theological College, Limuru, n.d.

Njoroge, J.A.C. 'The history of St. Immanuel's Church (CPEA) Weithaga'. Paper, Kenyatta College, 1969 (ms).

Njuguna, G.M. 'Tradition, church laws and civil laws in conflict over marriage and family relations'. Typescript (28 pages), St. Paul's United Theological College, Limuru, n.d.

Noble, D.S. 'Demoniacal possession among the Giryama', *Man,* 61 (1961).

Nottingham, J.C. 'Sorcery among the Akamba in Kenya', *Journal of African Administration,* vol. 11, no. 1 (1959), p. 2-14.

Ntarangwe, R. 'The work of the Methodist Mission in Meru'. Typescript (12 pages) in library of St. Paul's United Theological College, Limuru, n.d. (circa 1962).

Nyangweso. 'The cult of Mumbo in central and south Kavirondo', *Journal of the East Africa and Uganda Natural History Society,* 38-9, (1930), p. 13-17.
A study of the origins, followers and beliefs of a nativistic cult which began in 1913.

Nyesi, J. 'A historical survey of church union negotiations in East Africa'. Typescript (32 pages) for diploma in theology, University of East Africa, n.d. (circa 1967).
A detailed survey over the years 1908-1967.

O'Conor, Sr. Margaret. *Report on Pastoral & Research Centre study.* Nairobi: Kenya Episcopal Conference, 1971 (mimeo).
Results of a questionnaire survey to 1,700 Kenya Catholics, with 500 interviews.

Oded, A. 'A congregation of African Jews in the heart of Uganda', *Dini na Mila* (Kampala), 3, 1 (1968) p. 7-11.
Describes the Bayudaya just across the Kenya border at Mbale.

Odhiambo, J.E. 'The independent schools movement in Nyanza'. Department of History, University College, Nairobi, 1967 (typescript).

Odinga, Oginga. *Not yet Uhuru: the autobiography of Oginga Odinga.* London: Heinemann, 1967.
By a foremost Luo nationalist and former CMS teacher at Maseno School; numerous references to missions.

Ogot, B.A. 'Reverend Alfayo Odongo Mango, 1870-1934', in K. King & A. Salim (eds.), *Kenya historical biographies* (Nairobi: East African Publishing House, 1971), p. 90-111.
A biographical study of the founder of the Luo Roho churches in the context of land and political and religious problems in western Kenya.

325

——. 'Revolt of the elders: an anatomy of the loyalist crowd in the Mau Mau uprising'. Presidential address, Historical Association of Kenya annual conference, 1971 (mimeo).
Refers to the role of Kikuyu Christians among the loyalists during 1952-1956.

Ojiambo, H.H. 'The psychology of witchcraft', *East African Journal*, vol. 2, no. 4 (1965), p. 23-25.

Okite, O.W. 'Christianity and political development in Kenya'. Thesis, Wheaton College, Illinois, USA, 1968.

Okola, Z. *Weche moko mag Luo* (Luo traditions). Nairobi: Ndia Kuu (Highway) Press, 1936, 1947.

Okullu, J.H. *The Christian in African society today.* Nakuru: Uzima Press (forthcoming).

Okumu, D.S. 'Some social aspects of Warruok, a revival movement in Central Nyanza'. History Research Paper C/4/1, Dept. of History, University of Nairobi, n.d.
Warruok (the Luo for 'salvation') is the East African Revival (Brethren) among the Luo.

Okwemba, Florida. 'A comparative analysis of the causes of religious independency in the Western Region of Kenya (Luhya)'. Paper (31 pages) in library of St. Paul's United Theological College, Limuru, n.d. (1968).

Oldham, J.H. *White and black in Africa.* London: Longmans, Green, 1930.
Former Secretary of the International Missionary Council on the racial situation in Africa, including Kenya.

——. & B.D. Gibson. *The remaking of man in Africa.* London: Oxford, 1931.
By a former Secretary and Assistant Secretary of the IMC: deals with Kenya in places.

Oliver, R. *The missionary factor in East Africa.* London: Longmans, 1952.
The definitive history of the planting of the Gospel in East Africa.

Ongolo, D.W. 'The Maria Legio of Africa movement'. History Research Paper C/3/6, Dept. of History, University of Nairobi, n.d.

Orchardson, I.Q. 'Supernatural beliefs of the Lumbwa', *Journal of the East Africa and Uganda Natural History Society*, vol. 14 (1919), p. 417-420.

——. 'Some traits of the Kipsigis in relation to their contact with Europeans', *Africa*, vol. 4 (1931).
P. 469-70 deals with beliefs and customs.

——. 'Religious beliefs and practices of the Kipsigis', *Journal of the East Africa and Uganda Natural History Society*, vol. 47-48 (1932-33), p. 154-162.

——. 'The African explains witchcraft: Kipsigis', *Africa*, vol. 8, no. 4 (1935), p. 509-515.

——. 'Religious beliefs', in *The Kipsigis*, 1st ed. 1961 (Nairobi: East African Literature Bureau, 1970), p. 20-33.

Osogo, J. 'Educational developments in Kenya, 1911- 1924'. Paper, Historical Association of Kenya annual conference, 1969 (mimeo).

Owaka, B. 'The establishment of African Israel Church Nineveh in Central Nyanza'. History Research Paper 6/5/2, Dept. of History, University of Nairobi, n.d.

Owen, W.E. 'The missionary in politics', *Church Missionary Review* (June, 1921), p. 135 ff.

——. 'Empire and Church in Uganda and Kenya', *Edinburgh Review*, vol. 245 (1927), p. 43-57.

——. 'The relationship of missionary and African in East Africa', *Church Missionary Review*, LXXVIII, 857 (1927).

——. 'Some thoughts on native development in East Africa', *Journal of the African Society*, XXX, 120 (1931), p. 225-237.

——. & A. Stanway. 'The CMS in Kenya'. Book III, 'Nyanza Province'. Typescript.

Owuor, H.A. 'Spirit possession among the Luo of Central Nyanza'. Kampala: Makerere College, n.d. (typescript).

Oyigo, D. 'Who was Obondo Mumbo?', *Kisii School Magazine*, 1961.
Origins of the Mumbo cult in south Nyanza.

Painter, L.K. *The hill of vision: the story of the Quaker movement in East Africa, 1902-1965.* Nairobi: East Africa Yearly Meeting of Friends, 1966.

Parkin, D.J. 'Medicines and men of influence', *Man*, N.S. 3, 3 (1968), p. 424-439.
Includes analysis of Kajiwe's witchcraft eradication movement among the Mijikenda, 1966.

——. 'Politics of ritual syncretism among the Kenya Mijikenda'. Unpublished paper.
The significance of Islamic magic as a vehicle of Muslim expansion behind the Kenya coast.

Parsons, R. *Towards one people.* Nairobi: Department of Biblical Study and Research, NCCK, 1970.
A study of the ethnic relations in eleven African churches in Nairobi and the implications for Christian nurture.

Pastoral perspectives in Eastern Africa after Vatican II. AMECEA Study conference record, September 1967. Nairobi: AMECEA, 1968.

p'Bitek, Okot. *African religions in Western scholarship.* Nairobi: East African Literature Bureau, n.d. (1971).

Peel, W.G. & J.J. Willis. *Steps towards reunion: a statement for the Consultative Committee.* London: Longmans, Green, 1914.
By the Anglican bishops of Mombasa and Uganda.

Penley, E.W. 'Superstition among the Turkana: a southern Turkana heaven', *Man*, vol. 30, article 113 (1930), p. 139-140.

Pentreath, R. 'Superstitions in North Kavirondo', *Uganda Journal*, vol. 3 (1936), p. 318-321.

Peristiany, J.G *The social institutions of the Kipsigis.* London: Routledge and Kegan Paul, 1939.
Chapter XI deals with religion and magic.

Perlo, F. *Karoli, il Constantino Magno del Kenya.* Torino: Institute missioni conzolata, circa 1925.
In 1902, the Kikuyu chief Karuri of Fort Hall, the 'Constantine of Kenya', invited in both the Consolata mission and the CMS without informing the other.

Perrin Jassy, M.F. *La communaute de base dans les eglises africaines.* Bandundu (Zaire): Centre d'etudes ethnologiques, 1970.

Petro, D.N. *Jubilee: A.C. Kigari and A.C. Kabare (1910-1960).* Embu Rural Deanery, circa 1960.
Written in Kikuyu (although with an English title), describing two of the first CMS stations.

Phillips, K.N. *From Mau Mau to Christ.* London: Stirling Tract Enterprise, 1958.
Stories of persons who found faith in detention camps.

——. *Tom Collins of Kenya: son of valour.* London: Africa Inland Mission, n.d. (1965).
Biography of an AIM missionary, pioneer of Christian work among the Pokot.

Philp, H.R.A. *God and the African in Kenya.* London: Marshall, Morgan and Scott, n.d. (1933).
Short biographical sketches of Kikuyu converts.

——. *A new day in Kenya.* London: World Dominion Press, 1936.
A detailed survey of missions in the various tribes and peoples of Kenya.

Pich, V.M. 'I falsi profeti al Kenya (False prophets in Kenya)', *Missioni Consolata* (Turin), 36, 6 (1934), p. 84-86.

——. 'Les aspects religieux du mouvement Mau-Mau', in *Devant les sectes non-chretiennes* (Louvain: Semaine de Missiologie, 1961), p. 125-139.

Picking up the pieces. Report of a SODEPAX Conference on the churches in development planning and action, Limuru, January 1971. Geneva: SODEPAX, 1971.

Pirouet, M. Louise. 'A comparison of the response of three societies to Christianity (Toro, Teso, Kikuyu)'. Conference paper. Kampala: University of East Africa Social Sciences Council, 1968.

Plowman, C.H. 'Notes on the Gedamoch ceremonies among the Boran', *Journal of the Royal African Society*, vol. 18 (1919), p. 114-121.

Porcu, B. 'New approach and rural catechumenate'. Paper, Pastoral Institute of Eastern Africa, Gaba, 1971.
Rural catechetics based on an extensive appreciation of values, applied to the Kikuyu situation.

Potts, Margaret I. *St. Julian's: an experiment in two continents.* London: SCM Press, 1968.

Poulton, J. *Christian literature in Kenya and Tanzania: a survey and recommendations to the Christian Councils of Kenya and Tanzania.* London, 1966 (mimeo, 160 pages).

Price, P. *God in the valley.* London: Patmos Press, 1970.
The bringing of the Gospel to the Mwino Valley, Pokot, 1953-1964, by a BCMS missionary.

Priestly formation in Africa after Vatican II. Study and recommendations, Katigondo, Uganda, 1966/7. Nairobi: AMECEA, 1967.

Prins, A.H.J. *The Coastal tribes of the northeastern Bantu.* London: International African Institute, 1952.
A study of the Pokomo, Nyika and Teita, including sections on religion.

Proceedings of the Sixth General Assembly (10-14 March, 1970). Nairobi: Presbyterian Church of East Africa, 1970 (mimeo, circa 180 pages).
Detailed reports of all aspects of PCEA work.

Proposed basis of union. Pamphlet issued by Conference on Church Union, 1932.

Proposed scheme of federation of missionary societies working in British East Africa. Nairobi, 1913.

Purcell, W. *Fisher of Lambeth.* London: Hodder & Stoughton, 1969.
Chapter XI, 'The Archbishop abroad', deals with the visits to East Africa and Kenya of the former Archbishop of Canterbury.

Radio listenership: a survey with particular reference to religious programmes. Nairobi: Marco Surveys, 1965 (for Christian Council of Kenya).

Raux, M. 'Penetration musulmane de l'Est africain', *Grands Lacs* (Namur), 3 (1947), p. 5-8, 149-152.

Ready for change: development in Northern Kenya. Nairobi: NCCK, 1972 (duplicated).

Rees, Emory, J. *Setting the language milestones.*
By a pioneer FAM worker, translator of the Luragoli NT.

'Religion', in *Kenya Population Census, 1962,* vol. III 'African population' (Nairobi: Ministry of Economic Planning & Development, 1966), p. 45-50.
The only official census report of the religion of Africans in Kenya (none before, nor subsequently).

Report, Conference on Christian Co-operation, Nairobi, 1934.

Report and constitution, 1938. Kikuyu Independent Schools Association. Nyeri: Executive Committee of KISA, 1938.

'Report of the National Young People's Congress, Limuru, Kenya', Limuru Conference Centre, 1971.

Report of the United Conference of Mission Societies in British East Africa. Kikuyu, July 23-26, 1918.

Report of the United Missionary Conference. Nairobi, 1909.

Richards, C.G. *Archdeacon Owen of Kavirondo: a memoir.* Nairobi: Highway Press, n.d. (1947).

———. *Krapf: missionary and explorer.* London: Nelson, 1950.
Biography of the first CMS missionary to Kenya, 1844.

———. 'History of the CMS in the Highlands'. Typescript, Makerere University Library, Kampala.

Richards, Elizabeth. *Fifty years in Nyanza, 1906-1956: the history of the CMS and the Anglican Church in Nyanza Province, Kenya.* Maseno: Nyanza Jubilee Committee, 1956.

Richardson, K. *Garden of miracles.* London: Africa Inland Mission, 1964.

Rickman, Mary. *Seven whole days: a week of life on a country mission station in Kenya, East Africa.* London: Highway Press, 1950.

Roland, H. 'Strange sects of Kenya', *Times Survey of the British Colonies.* London, 1950.

'Roman Catholic/Protestant dialogue'. Report on a conference at Limuru Conference Centre, 1965 (mimeo, 19 pages).

Rosberg, C.G. & J. Nottingham. *The myth of Mau Mau.* New York: Praeger, 1966.
Refers to the early work of missions in Kenya and the rise of independent churches.

Routledge, W.S. *With a prehistoric people: the Akikuyu of East Africa.* London: E. Arnold, 1910.
The method of life and mode of thought of a nation in its first contact with European civilisation. P. 225-282 deal with the religion of the Akikuyu (the Deity, sacrifice, the soul, snake worship, morals and medicine men).

Ruel, M.J. 'Religion and society among the Kuria of East Africa', *Africa,* vol. 35, 3 (1965), p. 295-306.

Rules of the Kikuyu Independent Schools Association. Executive Committee of KISA, South Nyeri, November 1935.

Sales, L. *Il servo di Dio Canonico Guiseppe Allamano.* Turin: Edizioni Missioni Consolata, 1944 (3rd ed.).
Life of the founder of Consolata society, with many references to the Kenya missions.

Salim, A. *The Swahili-speaking communities of the Kenya coast, 1895-1965.* Nairobi: East African Publishing House, 1972.

Sandgren, D.P. 'The early church among the Kikuyu: the Africa Inland Mission, 1901-1930'. Dissertation, University of Wisconsin (forthcoming).

Sangree, W.H. 'Contemporary religion in Tiriki'. Conference Papers 64, Makerere Institute of Social Research, Kampala, 1956 (mimeo).

———. *Age, prayer and politics in Tiriki, Kenya.* London: Oxford, 1966.
Analysis of the traditional social structure and the impact of British bureaucracy and missions.

Saunders, D.L. 'A study of lay leadership in selected emerging Baptist congregations in East Africa', in D.B. Barrett (ed.), *Theory and practice* (1968), p. 446-454.

Schmidt, W. 'Die Religion der Galla', *Pontificio museo Missionario etnologico del Laterano* (Citta del Vaticano), 1937, p. 83-152.

Schneider, H.K. 'Pakot resistance to change', in W.R. Bascom & M.J. Herskovits (eds.), *Continuity and change in African cultures* (Chicago: University of Chicago Press, 1959), p. 144-167.

Scott, Mrs. H.E. *A saint in Kenya.* London: Hodder & Stoughton, 1933.
Biography of Marion Stevenson, pioneer Church of Scotland missionary in Kenya.

Seminar on ecumenism. Nairobi, March/April 1970. Nairobi: AMECEA, 1970.

Shorter, A. 'The catechist in Eastern Africa', *African Ecclesiastical Review* (January, 1970).

——— & E. Kataza (eds.). *Missionaries to yourselves: African catechists today.* London: Geoffrey Chapman, 1972.
A detailed survey and analysis of Catholic catechists in East Africa, including Kenya.

Shumaker, C.R. 'Preparing Africans for Christian literature careers'. The Lit-Helper Series, No. 2. Nairobi: Africa Evangelical Literature Office, 1971.

Silvano, Prisca L. 'The impact of the missionaries on Bunyore society'. Part I (1905-1930), Part II. Typescript (89 pages), St. Paul's United Theological College, Limuru, n.d.

Sluiter, Greet. 'Confidential report on migrant labour & connected matters in four villages in the Kiambu Reserve of Kenya'. Nairobi: CCK Dept. of Social Service Training and Research, n.d. (1957) (mimeo).

Smith, Cynthia B. 'History of the Giriama in the nineteenth and twentieth centuries'. Dissertation, University of California at Los Angeles (forthcoming).
Ritual and symbolic leadership; witchcraft eradication; the Giriama reaction to Islam and Christianity and the reasons they have remained impervious to both.

Smoker, Dorothy E.W. 'Decision-making in East African revival movement groups', in D.B. Barrett (ed.), *African initiatives in religion* (Nairobi, 1971), p. 96-108.
Describes the group-decision approach of revival Team Meetings in Kenya and Tanzania in 1967.

'Some notes on the attitude of the Methodist Missionary Society in connection with the initiation ceremony known as the circumcision of girls'. Nairobi: Methodist Church in Kenya, n.d., circa 1921 (typescript in archives).

Spashnikov, G.A. *Religii stran Afriki* (Religions of Africa). Moscow: Nauka, 1967.
Extensive surveys and maps of religions in Africa have been produced by the Institute for Ethnic Statistics and Cartography, Moscow, USSR. This study (in Russian, with an English summary), which has 4 pages on Kenya, is by the author of the large-scale multi-coloured map, 'Religions in Africa'.

Spencer, P. 'The dynamics of Samburu religion'. Conference paper, East African Institute for Social Research, Makerere University College, 1959 (mimeo).

Stam, N. 'The religious conceptions of the Kavirondo', *Anthropos*, vol. 5 (1910), p. 359-362.
    A study of some religious beliefs of the Luo, with the suggestion that the rites are directed to the sun and moon rather than to God, implying origins in Egyptian religion.

——. 'The Bahanga', *Catholic Anthropological Conference* (Washington), vol. I (1929), p. 143-179.

——. 'A short history of the Vicariate of Kisumu, 1904-44', 1944 (typescript).
    By a former Catholic vicar apostolic of Kisumu.

Status missionum, anni 1945-46. Mombasa: Delegatio Apostolica Africae Orientalis et Occidentalis Britannicae, n.d. (1946).
    Statistics of all Roman Catholic dioceses in East and West Africa; part of a regular series.

Steggell, A. *The Taveta Chronicle*, circa 1896.
    The first booklet to be printed in East Africa.

Stock, E. *The history of the Church Missionary Society*. 4 vols. London: Church Missionary Society, 1899 (vols 1-3) and 1916 (vol. 4).
    The standard history of the early years of the Society has numerous references to Kenya.

——. 'Bishop Peel and the Diocese of Mombasa', *Church Missionary Review*, vol. 67 (1916), p. 443-454.

Stovold, K.E. *The CMS in Kenya. Book 1: The Coast, 1844-1944*. Nairobi: CMS Bookshop, n.d. (1946).

Strandes, J. *The Portuguese period in East Africa*. 1st ed. 1899. Nairobi: East Africa Literature Bureau, 1961.

Strayer, R. 'CMS educational policy in Kenya'. Dissertation, University of Wisconsin, 1971.

Suenens, L.—J. *Edel Quinn: envoy of the Legion of Mary to Africa*. Dublin: C.J. Fallon, 1953.
    Biography of founder in Kenya of the Legion of Mary (from Ireland), by Mgr. Suenens, now Cardinal Primate of the Catholic Church in Belgium.

Sulumeti, P. 'Church missionary in Kenya in the light of Vatican II'. Dissertation, Pontifical Urban University, Rome, 1970.
    By the Catholic auxiliary bishop of Kisumu.

Tate, F.V. 'Patterns of church growth in Nairobi'. Thesis, Fuller Theological Seminary, California, 1970.
    A study of membership growth in ten Nairobi city congregations.

Taylor, R.J. 'The success and failure of the MRI projects of the Church of the Province of East Africa'. Thesis, Anglican Board of Theological Studies, Christchurch, New Zealand, 1972.
    A study of the pan-Anglican scheme Mutual Responsibility and Interdependence, as it has operated in Kenya and Tanzania from 1963-1970.

Temu, A.J. 'Missionary attitudes and actions towards forced labour, native paramountcy and African politics in colonial Kenya (1919-1923)'. Paper, Historical Association of Kenya annual conference, 1971 (mimeo).

——. 'The role of the Bombay Africans on the Mombasa coast, 1874-1904', in B.A. Ogot (ed.), *Hadithi 3* (Nairobi: East African Publishing House, 1971).
    CMS work at the Coast at the end of the 19th century.

——. 'The British Protestant missions on the Kenya coast and highlands, 1873-1929'. Dissertation, University of Alberta, 1967 (published version forthcoming, Nairobi, Longmans, 1973).

The Archbishop of Canterbury's tour of Kenya. Department of Information, Government of Kenya. London: Pitkin Pictorials, n.d. (1956).

'The Cathedral of the Highlands, 1917-1950'. Nairobi: East African Standard, 1950.

The Church and development. AMECEA-Misereor Seminar, Limuru, December 1970. Nairobi: AMECEA, 1971.

'The Church and public affairs in Kenya: Christians challenged to improve inter-racial co-operation', *East Africa and Rhodesia* (London), vol. 30 (1954), p. 574-575.

'The Church and the Churches: Kikuyu', *Candid Quarterly*, vol. 1 (1914), p. 513-526.

'The Churches' role in Kenya'. A report of the Conference on the role of the Churches in Independent Kenya, January, 1964. Nairobi: Christian Council of Kenya, 1964.

The Church meets life in the town. Report of a consultation. Dar-es-Salaam: East Africa Committee, Urban Africa Programme (CCT and AACC), 1964.
    A number of papers and reports on the shape of the urban church in society.

The Church Missionary Juvenile Instructor for the year 1848. Vol. VII. London: Church Missionary Society, 1848.
    Contains the first printed account of J.L. Krapf's missionary work in Kenya.

The Constitution of Kenya. Kenya Gazette Supplement No. 27 (Acts No. 3). Nairobi: Government Printer, 1969.
    Freedom of conscience and religion, freedom to change religion or belief, freedom to propagate religion in worship, teaching, practice and observance, are described in Section 78 (pages 41-2) of Chapter V, 'Protection of fundamental rights and freedoms of the individual'.

'The crisis in the Christian ministry in Kenya'. Report of a consultation on recruitment for the Christian ministry. Limuru Conference Centre, Sept. 29th-Oct. 1, 1964.

The Eastern Equatorial Africa Mission of the Church Missionary Society. London: CMS, 1891.
    A 106-page history of the first Anglican diocese in East Africa.

'The place of education in the mission of the church'. Report of a consultation held at Limuru Conference Centre. CCEA and CCK, 1961 (mimeo).

The priest in Africa today. AMECEA Study Conference record, Lusaka, Zambia, August 1970. Lusaka: AMECEA, 1970.

'The Societies Act 1968'. Nairobi: Government Printer, 1968.
    This 26-page booklet sets forth how every society of 10 or more persons must register with government within 28 days after its formation.

'The Societies Rules 1968'. Nairobi: Government Printer, 1968.
    This 11-page booklet describes the procedures by which societies register with government.

'The village polytechnic: report of a consultation, February, 1969'. Limuru Conference & Training Centre, 1969.
    'A village polytechnic is a very simple low-cost training centre for school leavers, training for self-employment and rural development'.

Therese, Sr. Paul. 'Renewal in catechetics for primary schools'. Paper, Pastoral Institute of Eastern Africa, Gaba, 1971.
    Contains an appendix of original songs.

Thomson, C.R. *Revival in Africa*. Calcutta: Evangelical Literature Depot, 1952.
    Description of the East African Revival, including the great conventions.

Thuku, Harry: an autobiography with assistance from K.J. King. Nairobi: Oxford, 1970.
    Refers to the work in Kiambu of the Gospel Missionary Society, in which Thuku was an early convert.

Totty, L.H. *et al. The people and district of West Suk*. Nairobi: Highway Press, 1944.
    By a BCMS missionary.

Trimingham, J.S. *Islam in East Africa*. IMC Research Pamphlet no. 9. London: Edinburgh House, 1962.
    A 47-page forerunner of his later book of the same title.

——. *Islam in East Africa*. New York: Oxford, 1964.
    A study of the history, organisation, beliefs and practice of Islam in East Africa and the effects of recent change.

Tucker, A.R. *Eighteen years in Uganda and East Africa*. 2 vols. London: E. Arnold, 1908.
    By the first Anglican bishop of Uganda.

Twenty Africans write on communications in action. Kampala: Gaba Publications (Pastoral Institute of Eastern Africa), 1972.

Twenty-five years in East Africa. Richmond, Indiana: American Friends Board of Foreign Missions, 1927.

Ueda, H. 'A study of the process of social change among the Kitui Kamba with particular reference to changes in folk beliefs and religion'. Project, Institute of African Studies, University of Nairobi, 1971.

'Unto a perfect man'. Report of a conference on Christian education in home and school. Nairobi: Christian Churches' Educational Association, n.d. (1964).

Usher-Wilson, L.C. 'Bishop's study of "Dini ya Msambwa": first published account of a dangerous African movement', *East Africa and Rhodesia*, 1414 & 1416 (1951), p. 282-3, 345-346.

van den Dries, J. 'Credit unions in developing countries', *Millhilliana* (Mill Hill, London), 4 (1966), p. 142-155.
A Catholic missionary initiative; detailed descriptive sections on numerous countries, including Kenya.

van Diepen, J. & F.R. Dain. *Good News for all: Luke's story about Jesus Christ the Universal Saviour.* Nairobi: Oxford, 1973.
Textbook for 'O' level, EACE, on St Luke's Gospel and its relevance for Africa today.

Village polytechnic handbook. Nairobi: NCCK, 1970.
Describes a new development programme in Kenya and the 21 polytechnics already begun.

Voice of Kenya Omnibus Survey. Nairobi: Associated Business Consultants (EA), 1971.

Wagner, G. 'Die Religion der Bantu von Kavirondo', *Zeitschrift fur Ethnologie*, vol. 71, nos. 4,6 (1939).
——. *The Bantu of North Kavirondo.* London: Oxford, 1949 (vol. I) and 1956 (vol. II).
Section on religious beliefs and practices.
——. 'Der logi- und vila-Zauber bei den Logoni (Kavirondo-Bantu)', in A.E. Jensen, *Mythe, Mensch und Umwelt: Beitrage zur Religion, Mythologie und Kulturgeschichte* (Hamburg, 1950), p. 265-277.
——. 'The Abaluyia of Kavirondo (Kenya)', in D. Forde (ed.), *African worlds* (London: Oxford, 1954), p. 27-54.

Waichanguru, Deborah. 'The Nyeri Interdenominational Evangelism . Paper, Kenyatta College, 1969 (ms).
A pioneering movement in Christian unity between the historical Protestant and Catholic churches, and some indigenous churches, in Nyeri District.

Wakin, E. 'A unique sort of church', *Maryknoll*, 66, 1 (January, 1972), p. 38-40.
Brief description and photographs of the Nomiya Luo Church.

Wamatu, C. & J. Kago. 'East Africa awakens: revival in Kenya'. Unpublished paper, 1961.

Wambugu, Ada. 'Ecumenical youth service'. Paper, Kenyatta College, 1969 (ms).

Wandabusi, M. 'A history of a Roman Catholic church, Kibabii, 1930-69'. Paper, Kenyatta College, 1969 (ms).
Description of one of the largest Catholic parishes in Kenya (near Bungoma).

Wangai, J.M.P. 'The development of Kagwathi Seventh-day Adventist Church (Murang'a)'. Paper, Kenyatta College, 1970 (ms).

Wanjohi, Mary. 'The history of Emmanuel Church, Othaya'. Paper, Kenyatta College, 1969 (ms).

Ward, C.E. 'Notes on sun-worship amongst the Kipsikis or Lumbwa', *Journal of the East Africa and Uganda . Natural History Society*, vol. 24 (1926).

Warren, M.A.C. 'The "Revival" in East Africa: an essay in understanding'. London, 1952 (mimeo).
Earlier version of book on the subject.
——. *Revival: an enquiry.* London: SCM Press, 1954.
An examination of the Balokole (Saved Ones) of the East African Revival.

Waruiru, C. 'The female initiation controversy at CSM Tumutumu, 1912-37'. History Research Paper c/5/3, Dept of History, University of Nairobi, n.d.

Watt, Mrs. Stuart. *In the heart of savagedom.* London: Pickering & Inglis, 1912.
Autobiographical account of a Christian settler family in Ukambani.

Watts, E.R. (ed.) *New hope for rural Africa.* Nairobi: East African Publishing House, 1969.
Deals with the Churches' participation in rural development.

Weatherby, J.M. 'The Sebei prophets', *Man*, vol. 63, article 223 (1963), p. 178-179.

19th-century prophets among the Sebei-speaking peoples of Mount Elgon.

Webster, J.B. *A bibliography on Kenya.* New York: Syracuse University, 1967.
A comprehensive listing on all subjects (including religion and missions), with 461 pages and 7,210 titles published up to October, 1966.

Welbourn, F.B. 'Independency in East Africa', *Ecumenical Review*, XI, no. 4 (1959), p. 430-436.
——. *East African rebels: a study of some independent churches.* London: SCM, 1961.
P. 113-161 deal with the Kikuyu independent churches, the AIPC and the AOC, and the female circumcision controversy of 1929-32.
——. 'A national church against foreign control: the Kikuyu Independents', in Welbourn, *East African rebels* (London: SCM, 1961), p. 144-161.
A detailed analysis of the history of KISA, the AIPC and the AOC.
——. *East African Christian.* London: Oxford, 1965.
A concise overall summary of the historical, cultural and missionary background, with numerous references to Kenya.

Welbourne, F.B. & B.A. Ogot. *A place to feel at home.* London: Oxford, 1966.
A detailed study of the origin, history and present structure and theology of the Church of Christ in Africa among the Luo, and the African Israel Church Nineveh, among both Luo and Luhya.

Welch, D.E. 'From the first day until now: a history of the Church of God in East Africa'. Unpublished manuscript (1972).

Welch, F.G. *Towards an African church.* Nairobi: Christian Council of Kenya, 1962.
——. *Training for the ministry in East Africa.* Limuru: Association of EA Theological Colleges, 1963.

Wentink, D.E. 'The reaction of the once independent African Orthodox Church to the foreign Greek Orthodox mission it invited in', in D.B. Barrett (ed.), *Theory and practice* (1968), p. 135 - 142.
——. 'The Orthodox Church in East Africa'. *Ecumenical Review* (Geneva), XX, 1 (January, 1968), p. 33 - 43.

Were, G.S. 'Politics, religion and nationalism in Western Kenya, 1942 - 1962: Dini ya Msambwa revisited'. Conference paper, Historical Association of Kenya, 1971 (mimeo).

Werner, Alice. 'A Galla ritual prayer', *Man*, vol. 14 (1914), p. 129 - 131.
——. *Myths and legends of the Bantu.* 2nd ed. London: Frank Cass, 1968.

Westervelt, Josephine H. *On safari for God: an account of the life and labors of John Stauffacher, a pioneer missionary of the Africa Inland Mission.* New York, n.d.
Pioneer missionary in Maasai country.

Weston, F. *The case against Kikuyu.* 1915.
The bishop of Zanzibar's defence of his accusation of heresy and schism against CMS Anglicans at the 1913 Kikuyu Conference.

Whisson, M.G. The will of God and the wiles of men: an examination of the beliefs concerning the supernatural held by the Luo with particular reference to their functions in the field of social control'. *East African Institute of Social Research Conference Proceedings.* Kampala, 1962 (mimeo).

——. 'Economic and social change among Kenya Luo'. Report to CCK Dept. of Biblical Study and Research, n.d. (mimeo).

——. *Change and challenge: a study of the social and economic changes among the Kenya Luo.* Nairobi: Christian Council of Kenya, 1964.
This study describes traditional life, analyses the impact of colonization on the economic and social spheres of Luo life, and emphasizes the role Christians and Christianity can play in helping the Luo solve these problems.

——. 'Some aspects of functional disorders among Kenya Luo', in A. Kiev (ed.), *Magic, faith and healing: studies in primitive psychiatry today* (New York: Free Press, 1964).

Luo beliefs concerning the causation of disease, including God, witchcraft, magic, sorcery, angry ancestors and 'juogi' (free-roaming spirits).

White, G. 'East African Province: a guide'. *Episcopal Overseas Mission Review*, 10, 3 (1965), p. 18 - 23.
On the Anglican province of East Africa.

——. 'The Kikuyu Conference of 1913'. Dissertation, School of Oriental and African Studies, University of London (forthcoming).

Whiteley, W.H. (ed.) *Language in Kenya*. Nairobi:Oxford, 1972.
Chapter 10 deals with language use in the African independent churches in Nairobi. Chapter 12 contains survey material on the language usages of Catholic and Protestant churches and missions (p. 324 - 332).

Who controls industry in Kenya? Report of a working party. Nairobi: East African Publishing House, 1968.
An NCCK survey.

Whyte, Susan R. 'Marakwet religion'. Dissertation, University of Washington, 1971.

Willis, J.J. (Bishop of Uganda). *Kikuyu Conference: a study in Christian unity*. London, 1913.

——. 'Presentation of Christianity to primitive peoples: a statement by Christian converts in Kavirondo addressed to their heathen friends'. *International Review of Missions*, IV (July, 1915), p. 382 - 395.

Willis, J.J. *et al. Towards a united church, 1913 - 47*. London: Edinburgh House Press, 1947.

Wipper, Audrey. 'The cult of Mumbo'. Conference paper, East African Institute of Social Research, Makerere University College, Kampala, 1966 (mimeo).
Historical study of an anti-European movement with a new god, Mumbo, among the Luo and Gusii of southwest Kenya from 1914 until today.

——. 'Elijah Masinde — a folk hero', in B.A. Ogot (ed.), *Hadith 3* (Nairobi: East African Publishing House, 1971).
Study of the founder of Dini ya Msambwa.

——. 'African Christian movements in Kenya: Maria Legio and Nomiya Luo'. Manuscript, 1972.

——. *Priests, prophets and protest*. (Forthcoming).
A study of two social movements in Kenya.

Wiseman, Edith M. *Kenya — then and now*. London: CMS, 1950.

——. *Kikuyu martyrs*. London: Highway Press, 1958.
Biographical accounts of Kikuyu Christians killed during the Mau Mau conflict, 1952 - 54.

——. *The story of the Church Missionary Society in Kenya*. London: Church Missionary Society, 1954.

Wouters, A. *Mission and development in Kisumu*. A survey of opinions on missionary development activities in the Diocese of Kisumu, Kenya. Tilburg (Netherlands): Stichting Band Kisumu—Tilburg, 1968.

Wray, J.A. *Kenya — our newest colony, 1882 — 1912*. London: Marshall, 1928.
A personal and historical account of 30 years in Kenya by an early CMS missionary in Sagalla (Taita).

Wrong, Margaret. *Across Africa*. London: International Commission on Christian Literature for Africa, 1940.
Ch. II deals with Christian literature in Kenya.

Yannoulatos, A. 'Brief diary of a tour among the Orthodox of West Kenya', *Porefthendes* (Athens), VII, 2 (1965), p. 24 - 8, and VII, 3 - 4 (1965), p. 48 - 52.
Impressions of editor of journal of Inter-Orthodox Missionary Centre, Athens, Greece.

Yokoo, S. 'Death among the Abaluyia'. Dissertation, Makerere University College, Kampala, 1966.

Youth leaders' handbook. Nairobi: NCCK, 1969.
Describes experience of youth leaders in Kenya, and gives practical advice on all aspects of youth work in the churches.

Index of Kenya Religious Periodicals

In this index are listed most of the periodicals (newspapers, journals, magazines, newsletters), published in Kenya for widespread Kenya consumption, together with a handful published in Kenya for international consumption (*AACC Bulletin, Theologia Africana, Presence, Vocal, etc.*). There are some surprising gaps; for example, no Muslim periodicals are published in Kenya in English, Swahili, or African languages, by any of the major communities (Sunni, Ismaili, etc.); the only Muslim papers are the two Ahmadiyya ones shown below. The 38 periodicals whose titles are given in italics below are printed; the other 44 are not printed but are only duplicated or mimeographed. Sample copies of most of these periodicals are on file for inspection at the Office of Social Communications, AMECEA, P.O. Box 21053, Nairobi (Tel: 66506). In addition to the 80 periodicals listed below, a considerable number of church-related secondary schools publish elaborate printed or duplicated school magazines or annuals (examples: *Limuru Girls School Magazine*, written by girls in English, Swahili and French; *The Sun* (St. Mary's, Yala), *St. Mary's* (Nairobi), *Aquinas High School Magazine* (Nairobi), and those of Alliance High School, Alliance Girls' High School, etc. etc.).

The layout followed below is:—
Title (if not in English, a translation into English is added in brackets), *Sponsor, Frequency* (number of issues per year: 12 = monthly, 6 = bimonthly, 4 = quarterly; c = occasional), *Language* (English, French, Swahili, Kikuyu, Luo, Kamba, Kipsigis, Meru, English/Swahili/Kikuyu combined, English & Swahili, Swahili and English, Luhya and English, Kikuyu and English). If the sponsor is described elsewhere in the Handbook, the address is not given here; the reader can find it by looking up the sponsor's initials in the *Index of Abbreviations* (page 338) then looking the sponsor up in Part IV or Part V. The abbreviations 'Dio' and 'Archdio' refer to Catholic dioceses and the archdiocese; Nbi = Nairobi.

Title (italics = printed periodicals)	Sponsor	Frequency each year	Language
AACC Bulletin	AACC	12	English
ADC's Gazette	ADisC	c	English
Africa Communicator	BMEA	c	English
Afrika ya Kesho (Tomorrow's Africa)	AIC/AIM	12	Swahili
Afromedia Presents	Afromedia	c	English
Afroscope	AEAM	4	English
AMECEA Information	AMECEA	4	English
Analecta (Record)	Dio. Kisumu	6	English
Arahuka (Awake!)	CPK Mt. Kenya	4	Kikuyu/Eng
Association of Sisterhoods News and Information	AOSK	c	English
Assumption Sisters Newsletter	Assump Sisters	12	English
Bible Society of Kenya Newsletter	Bible Society	c	English
Boys' Brigade Bulletin	BB	12	English
Catholic Mirror	Archdio. Nbi	12	English/Swa
Catholic Secretariat Newsletter	KCS	12	English
CETA Bulletin	AACC	12	French
Challenge: youth in action	Box 47954, Nbi	4	English
Chama cha Wanawake (Women's League)	SA	4	Swahili
Communication	KCS	4	English
Contact	Dio. Meru	c	English

Title	Organisation	No.	Language
Cord	CSC	c	English
CPA Bulletin	Priests Association	c	English
CSSp Newsletter	CSSp	12	English
Dwond Hera (*Voice of Love*)	CCA	12	Luo
Daraja (*Bridge*)	Cath. Dio. Nakuru	c	Swahili
East African Times	Ahmadiyya Muslim	12	English
Encounter	YCS	4	English
Fikira (*Reflection*)	Aquinas Seminary	2	English
Habari kwa Mwalimu (*Teacher News*)	Prefecture Ngong	4	Swahili
Habari Njema (*Good News*)	LCK	12	Swahili
Habari za Wabatisti (*Baptist News*)	BMEA	12	Swahili
Igondit (*Trumpet*)	AGC	c	Kipsigis
Jitegemea (*Self-reliance*)	PCEA	4	Eng/Swa/Kik
Journal of All Saints Cathedral	CPK Cathedral Nbi	6	English
Kanisa Leo (*The Church Today*)	AIC/AIM	12	Swahili
Kesho, see Afrika ya Kesho			
KHCF Newsletter	KHCF	4	English
Kimuri (*Torch*)	PCEA	4	Kikuyu
KSCF Newsletter	KSCF	c	English
Kwetu (*Ours*)	Dio. Nyeri	12	English/Swa
Lavington Messenger	Lavington Church	12	English
Lengo (*Target*)	EAVC	24	Swahili
Life Light	KDCAG	12	English
Light	K Prisons Chaplaincy	4	English
Mapenzi ya Mungu (*The Will of God*)	Ahmadiyya Muslim	12	Swahili
Mbeu Yetu (*Our Seed*)	Dio. Meru	2	Meru
Mnara wa Mlinzi (*Watchtower*)	Jehovah's Witnesses	25	Swahili
Morning Star (*Nyota ya Asubuhi*)	EACA	25	English/Swa
Mufrenzi (*Friends*)	EAYM	4	Luhya/Eng
Mugambo wa Youth (*Voice of Youth*)	PCEA Youth	c	Kikuyu
Mwangazi (*Informer*)	PAG	6	Swahili/Eng
Mwendo (*Advance*)	CGEA	6	Swahili
NCCK Newsletter	NCCK	c	English
Nuru (*Light*)	EAVC	24	Swahili
Nyota ya Asubuhi, see *Morning Star*			
Omba (*Pray*)	Every Home Evang	12	Swahili
Outlook	Nbi Bapt Church	11	English
Pastorale	Dio. Kitui	c	English
Pray	Every Home Evang	12	English
Presence	WSCF	2	English
Presence	WSCF	2	French
Rafiki Yetu (*Our Friend*)	Cath. Dio. Mombasa	12	Swahili
Sauti Nyikani (*Herald of His Coming*)	PAG	6	Swahili
Sauti ya Vijana (*Voice of Youth*)	RCEA	4	Swahili
Sauti ya Vita (*Voice of Life*)	SA	12	Swahili/Eng
Sauti ya Zion (*Voice of Zion*)	AHZC	c	Swahili
Sikiliza (*Listen*)	SDA EA Union	2	Swahili
Sisters of Mary Newsletter	S of M Kakamega	c	English
Target	EAVC	24	English
Teachers' Prayer Fellowship Newsletter	KCTPF	3	English
The Highway	SHM	3	English
The Light	YCS, Kitui	2	English
The Link	Dio. Machakos	c	English
The Scroll	Strathmore College	3	English
The Voice	Catholic Action	4	English
Theologia Africana (*African Theology*)	AACC	4	English
This is That	Trinity Fellowship	3	English
Thome (*Courtyard*)	Dio. Kitui	6	Kamba
Today in Africa	AIC/AIM	12	English
Torch	EAVC	24	English
Tuzungumze (*Let us converse*)	RCEA	10	Swahili
Urban Africa	AACC	3	English
Vocal	AELO	4	English
Voice of St. Patrick	SPS	c	English
Wathiome Mukinyu (*True Friend*)	Dio. Nyeri	12	Kikuyu
Watu Wote (*All People*)	Dio. Eldoret	4	Swahili/Eng

8

Part VIII

Appendixes
and
Indexes

Polyglot Glossary of Religious Terminology

There are about 70 African vernacular languages indigenous to Kenya, in addition to immigrant African, European and Asian languages. The official language is English; Swahili is also used in official correspondence, and is to become the national language after 1975. The following table lists the major religious words in use in the churches, giving their equivalent in the eight major languages spoken today, alphabetised on the English words only (heavy type). We omit words which are used in most languages in their English or closely anglicised form, such as 'diocese'; however, to see the great variety possible when an English word is transliterated, the reader should glance along the line for 'Christianity' or for 'sacrament'. Note that, as with all translated words, the equivalents seldom have exactly the same meaning. To read this table correctly, one should start with the English column, then find the word in the column required, which is the nearest equivalent in that language. In practice, one English word may have several near equivalents in another language, in the same way as one word in Swahili (or other language) will have several English near equivalents. Note also that the single equivalent we give here is not necessarily in universal use; often there is a Catholic equivalent and one or more Protestant equivalents (for the various churches). In such cases we select one of the more 'original' or 'vernacular' words, which may be either Catholic or Protestant.

Comprehension. The first line of the table gives the percentage of the inhabitants of Kenya who speak or understand each language, and the second line the estimated number of speakers (the whole community, including children and infants) in mid-1972; the Swahili and English figures are based on recent sample surveys across Kenya and refer not to persons fluent or literate in these languages but to persons with a reasonable comprehension in speaking. The third and fourth lines then give the estimated numbers of professing Protestants (including Anglicans and Independents) and professing Catholics, respectively, who speak each language (including their children and infants.) These numbers are computed from Table 4 in Part II (p.178) with Swahili speakers assumed to have somewhat lower Protestant/Catholic proportions that the whole nation, and English speakers somewhat higher proportions.

Literacy and education. In 1944, about 22% of the population over 15 years was literate (in any language, including vernaculars); in 1972, about 40% were literate; with a national target of 100% by the year 1990. In 1972, some 62,000 adults were enrolled in 810 government-aided and 450 unaided literacy classes, a fair number of the latter were being run by the churches. In 1968, 61% of all children of primary school age were enrolled in school, with a national target of 75% by 1974. In the 1969 census, 27.1% of the whole population including children (or, 59.1% of those aged 15-19 years) had, or were having, school education; 72.9% had had none.

335

Line 1 = speakers as % of nation
Line 2 = number of speakers
Line 3 = Protestant speakers
Line 4 = Catholic speakers

	Swahili	English	Kikuyu	Luo	Luhya	Kamba	Kalenjin	Gusii
1.	70%	25%	21.2%	13.9%	13.3%	11.0%	9.6%	6.4%
2.	8,500,000	3,000,000	2,562,900	1,681,200	1,605,800	1,323,400	1,164,800	775,300
3.	3,000,000	1,500,000	1,187,600	840,600	883,200	622,000	431,400	333,400
4.	2,200,000	1,200,000	682,000	655,700	626,300	185,300	309,600	302,400

Swahili	English	Kikuyu	Luo	Luhya	Kamba	Kalenjin	Gusii
kilembwekezi	ancestor	agu	kwaro	vakulu	umae	kugo	chisokoro
mtume	apostle	mutumwo	jaote	muveka	mutume	kiyogindet	omotomwa
kubatiza	baptize, to	kubatithia	tiso	okhubatisa	kuvatisa	kibatisan	okobatisa
ubatizo	baptism	kibatithio	batiso	shibatiso	uvatiso	abatisanet	ebatiso
Biblia	Bible	Ibuku ria Ngai	Muma	Likhusa lya Nyasaye	Mbivilia	Bukuit ne Tilil	Bibiria
askofu	bishop	mubicobu	askof	mupiskopi	askof	askofu	omosikobi
baraka	blessing	kirathimo	gwedh	khuitsomia	uathimo	kaberunet	ogogesenia
Kristo	Christ	Kristo	Kristo	Kristo	Klisto	Kristo	Keresito
mkristo	Christian	mukirithitiano	jakristo	omukristo	muklisto	chitap Kristo	omokeresito
Ukristo	Christianity	Ukirithitiano	Dini mar Kristo	Obukristayo	Uklisto	Kristoinatet	Obokeresito
kanisa	church	kanitha	kanisa	igeresia	kanisa	kaniset	ekerisia
amri	commandment	riathani	chik	lilako	mwiao	ng'atutiet	richiko
meza ya Bwana	communion	ngwataniro	sawo	livukana	ngwatanio	kibagenge	emesa
jamaa	community	muingi	gweng'	eshina	nguthu ya andu	bik che menye uwak	egasaku
maungamo	confession	uumburi	hulo richo	bwikanili	umbuli	ng'andaet	okoangama
kundi	congregation	gikundi	chokruok	livukana	wumbano	tuiyet	omasangererekano
wongofu	conversion	kugaruruka	lokruok	khuhonyinywa	kualyuka	walet	ogonchora
jumuiya	council	kiama	bura	ibarasa	nzama	kapkirwok	ekeombe
msalaba	cross	mutharaba	musalaba	omusalaba	ngelanio	kimurtoiyot	omosalaba
dhehebu	denomination	dini	dini	evisomero	muvia	tinit	edini
shetani	devil	ngoma	jachien	shetani	satani	oindet	ekerecha
mwinjilisti	evangelist	muhunjia	jaland wach	mwirwatsi	mutavania	amdoindet	omorandia
imani	faith	witikio	yie	busuviri	inee	kayanet	okwegena
kufunga	fasting	kwiima irio	riyo kech	khufunga	kutiia kuya	rugutet	okwerina
ushirika	fellowship	ngwataniro	lalruok	livukana	ngwatanio	yamdaet	obomo
Mungu	God	Ngai	Nyasaye	Nyasaye	Ngai	Kamuktoindet	Nyasae
Injili	Gospel	Uhoro Mwega	Injili	Injili	Uvoo Musea	Logoiywek che miach	Ebanjili
neema	grace	kirathimo	ng'wono	litsanzalia	muuo	mieindo	obuya
mbingu	heaven	matu-ini	polo	omwikulu	ituni	kipsengwet	igoro
jahanam	hell	kwa-ngoma	mach	ewashetani	mwakini	emet ap mat	riera riomorero
Roho Mtakatifu	Holy Spirit	Roho Mutheru	Roho Maler	Omwoyo Mutakatifu	Veva Mutheu	Tamirmiriet ne Tilil	Omoika Omochenu
wimbo	hymn	ruimbo	wer	olwimbo	wathi	tiendo	ogotera
huru	independent	kwibungia	mochung'	muvoholole	kwiyatha	ne bou ge	ogwetenenera
Jesu	Jesus	Jesu	Yesu	Yesu	Yesu	Jesu	Yeso
Bwana	Lord	Mwathani	Ruoth	Omwami	Mwiai	Kiptaiyat	Omonene
upendo	love	wendo	hera	vuyanzi	wendo	chomiet	ogwancha
uganga	magic	kiama	uriri	ovolochi	kyama	indorenik	oborogi
mtu (watu)	man (men)	mundu (andu)	ng'ato (ji)	omundu	mundu (andu)	chito (bik)	omonto
mganga	medicine man	mundu mugo	jathieth	mufumu	mundu mue	chepkerichot	omorwaria
mchungaji	minister, a	mutungatiri	jakwath	omulindi	mutavania	potiriot	omobasta
mtawa	missionary	mumiceni	jaote	omukambi	mumiseni	kiyogindet	omomiseni
Agano Jipya	New Testament	Kirikaniro Kieru	Muma Manyien	Lilako Lihya	Utianio Mweu	Arorutiet ne Lel	Emuma Enyia
sadaka	offering	igongona	chiwo	shihanwa	nthembo	konunet	ekerugwa
Agano la Kale	Old Testament	Kirikaniro gia tene	Muma Machon	Lilako Liakhale	Utianio Mukuu	Arorutiet ne bo keny	Emuma Enkoro
nguvu	power	hinya	teko	tsingufu	vinya	kimnatet	chinguru
sala	prayer	mahoya	lamo	lisayo	mboya	saet	ogosaba
muhubiri	preacher	muhunjia	jayalo	muirwatsi	mutavania	amdoindet	omorandia
mahubiri	preaching	mahunjio	yalo	khuirwatsa	utavania	amdaet	okorandia
kasisi	priest	mugathithi	jadolo	musalisi	muvea	potiriot	okorandia
nabii	prophet	munabii	janabi	muprofeti	mwathani	maotiot	omosasiroti
dini	religion	dini	dini	itini	uthaithi	tinit	edini
tubu, toba	repentance	kwirira	lokruok	bwikaniri	kwilila	sigunet	okoangama
ufufuo	resurrection	kuriuka	chier	khusimukha	kusyuka	ng'etiet	okoboka
sakramenti	sacrament	thakaramendi	sakramenti	lisakaramento	sakalamendi	sakramenti	esakaramento
dhabihu	sacrifice	igongona	musango	musango	nthembo	tiseiywek	ekengwanso
mtakatifu	saint	mutheru	jamaler	mtakatifu	mutheu	ne tilil	omochenu
wokofu	salvation	uhonokio	warruok	okhuhonywa	utangiio	sorunet	ogotoreka
mahubiri	sermon	mahunjio	loso	mirwatso	utavany'a	amdaet	okorandia
ibada	service (worship)	muhoere	lemo	lisala	mboya	amdaet	ogosaba
dhambi	sin	mehia	richo	ubwoni	nai	ng'ogisto	ebibe
mlozi	sorcerer	murogi	janawi	omulosi	muoi	bonindet	omorogi
moyo	soul	muoyo	chuny	mwoyo	ngoo	sobondo	omoyo
roho	spirit	roho	tipo	mwoyo	thayu	tamirmiriet	omoika
mwiko	taboo	thahu	kwer	omuchiro	nai	indorenik	ekebe
ushuhuda	testimony	uira	neno	khuirwatsa	ukusi	baornatet	okoangama

Swahili	English	Kikuyu	Luo	Luhya	Kamba	Kalenjin	Gusii
mila	traditions	mitugo	timbe	ebiima	kithio	kasibutik	chingencho
Utatu	Trinity	Utatu	Nyadidek	Vubaka	Utatu	Kipsomok	Batato
mchawi	witch	murogi	jajuok	mulosi	muoi	bonindet	omorogi
uchawi	witchcraft	urogi	juok	vulochi	uoi	bondit	oborogi
mganga	witchdoctor	mundu mugo	ajuoga	omukanga	mundu mue	chepsogeiyot	omorwaria
mshahidi	witness, a	muira	janend.	musaiti	ngusi	baoriat	kerori
ibada	worship	kuhoya	lemo	lisala	mboya	saet	ogosaba

Notes

1. This glossary was produced *de novo* independently of any other listings. It should be noted, however, that there is a similar section in T.P.Gorman (ed.), *A Glossary of English, Kiswahili, Kikuyu and Dholuo* (London: Cassell, 1972), which is valuable in that it places religious words in the context of over 100 pages of secular words (for the four languages only).
2. The Kikuyu language is spoken by the Kikuyu and Embu tribes.
3. The Kalenjin language is spoken by the Kipsigis, Nandi, Tugen, Elgeyo and Marakwet tribes.
4. The whole subject of language use is exhaustively surveyed and analysed in W.H.Whiteley (ed.), *Language in Kenya* (Nairobi: Oxford, 1972). Whiteley's surveys of Swahili usage in rural Kenya, for example, showed that 75 per cent of rural Bantu claimed some minimal competence in Swahili, 60 per cent of whom claimed to know 'quite a lot'. Competence for non-Bantu was considerably lower (Kipsigis 61%, Luo 33%). In urban Kenya competence in Swahili approaches 100 per cent in most areas. Those who claimed some competence in English varied from 95 per cent in Kikuyu and Embu areas, to 57 per cent in Kamba, 56 per cent in Taita, 51 per cent in Meru, 36 per cent in Luo, 34 per cent in Gusii, 18 per cent in Kipsigis, and 10 per cent in one Pokomo area.

Index of Abbreviations

This index gives all abbreviations and initials in use among the Kenya churches and on the religious scene, including a handful of organisations from outside the country. Also included are a very few organisations no longer active in Kenya, and older names no longer in use.

AAA	A. A. Allen (Miracle Revival Fellowship)
AAC	African Anglican Church
AACC	All Africa Conference of Churches
ABC	African Brotherhood Church
ABS	American Bible Society
AC	African Church (Kenya African Church)
AC	Anglican Church
ACC	Anglican Consultative Council
ACC&S	African Christian Church & Schools
ACHS	African Church of Holy Spirit
ACM	African Church Mission
ACP	Africa Christian Press
AD	archdiocese
ADC	African Divine Church
ADisC	African Disciples Church
AEAM	Association of Evangelicals of Africa and Madagascar
AEATC	Association of East African Theological Colleges
AEE	African Evangelistic Enterprise
AELO	Africa Evangelical Literature Office
AEO	Africa Evangelical Office
AEPC	African Evangelical Presbyterian Church
AFM	Africa Faith Mission
AGC	Africa Gospel Church
AGHS	Alliance Girls High School
AGOC	African Greek Orthodox Church
AGUC	Africa Gospel Unity Church
AHS	Alliance High School
AHZC	African Holy Zionist Church
AIC	Africa Inland Church
AIC	African independent church
AICM	African independent churches movement
AICN	African Israel Church Nineveh
AICs	African independent churches
AIM	Africa Inland Mission
AIntC	African Interior Church
AIPC	African Independent Pentecostal Church of Africa
AMECEA	Association of Episcopal Conferences in Eastern Africa
AMHGC	African Mission of Holy Ghost Church
AOC	African Orthodox Church of Kenya
AOSK	Association of Sisterhoods of Kenya
ASC	African Sinai Church
BB	Boys' Brigade
BCK	Baptist Churches of Kenya
BCMS	Bible Churchmen's Missionary Society
BFBS	British and Foreign Bible Society
BMEA	Baptist Mission of East Africa
BRAVS	Broadcasting and Audio Visual Services
BVM	Bibeltrogna Vanner
Bw.	Bwana (Mr.)
CA	Church Army
CA	Church of All
CACC	Central Africa Christian Council
CBC	Christian Brotherhood Church
CBMK	Christadelphian Bible Mission (Kenya)
CCA	Church of Christ in Africa
CCEA	Christian Churches' Educational Association
CCK	Christian Council of Kenya
CCM	Consolata Catholic Mission
CCUC	Churches' Chaplaincy to University Community
CEC	Christian Evangelical Church
CGEA	Church of God in East Africa
CGSD	Church of God Seventh-day

CHF	Christian Hostels Fellowship
CHGCEA	Christian Holy Ghost Church of East Africa
CITC	Christian Industrial Training Centre
CMS	Church Missionary Society
CPEA	Church of the Province of East Africa
CPK	Church of the Province of Kenya
CRS	Catholic Relief Services
CSC	Christian Students Council
CSM	Church of Scotland Mission
CSSp	Holy Ghost Mission (Congregation of Holy Ghost)
CU	Christian Union (colleges, schools)
CUEF	Christian Universal Evangelistic Fellowship
CUEU	Christian Universal Evangelistic Union
D	diocese
DCCEA	Divine Christian Church of East Africa
DMA	Diocesan Missionary Association
DRC	Dutch Reformed Church
DYM	Dini ya Msambwa
EACA	East Africa Christian Alliance
EAPC	East Africa Pentecostal Churches
EAREC	East Africa Religious Education Committee
EAVC	East African Venture Company
EAYM	East Africa Yearly Meeting of Friends
ECUA	Evangelistic Church Universal of Africa
ELCT	Evangelical Lutheran Church in Tanzania
ELFEA	Evangelical Literature Fellowship of East Africa
EMA	Elim Missionary Assemblies
EMBMC	Eastern Mennonite Board of Missions and Charities
EPH	Evangel Publishing House
FAM	Friends Africa Mission
FFFM	Finnish Free Foreign Mission
FFH	Freedom from Hunger
FGCK	Full Gospel Churches of Kenya
FHS	Friends of the Holy Spirit
Fr.	Father
FSC	Friends' Service Council
FUM	Friends United Meeting
GF	Kenya Christian Graduates Fellowship
GFF	Gospel Furthering Fellowship
GIBM	Grace Independent Baptist Mission
GICK	Gospel International Church of Kenya
GMS	Gospel Missionary Society
GNCA	Good News Church of Africa
GUC	God of the Universe Church
HCK	Hindu Council of Kenya
HGCK	Holy Ghost Church of Kenya
HGM	Holy Ghost Mission (CSSp)
HSCEA	Holy Spirit Church of East Africa
HTCA	Holy Trinity Church in Africa
IBCEA	Independent Baptist Churches of East Africa
IBPFM	Independent Board for Presbyterian Foreign Missions
IBSA	International Bible Students Association
ICCC	International Council of Christian Churches
IFFC	International Fellowship for Christ
IJC	International Jerusalem Church
ILC	Independent Lutheran Church
IMC	Istituto Missioni Consolata (Consolata Fathers)
IPA	International Pentecostal Assemblies
IPCCF	International Pentecost Church of Christian Fellowship
IPCEA	Independent Presbyterian Church of East Africa

JEAREC	Joint East Africa Religious Education Committee
JMU	Jumuiya ya Makanisa Ulimwenguni (WCC)
JW	Jehovah's Witnesses
KALM	Kenya Association for Liturgical Music
KAYO	Kenya Anglican Youth Organisation
KCGF	Kenya Christian Graduates Fellowship
KCMS	Kenya Church Music Society
KCS	Kenya Catholic Secretariat
KCTPF	Kenya Christian Teachers Prayer Fellowship
KDCAG	Assemblies of God, Kenya District Council
KEC	Kenya Episcopal Conference
KFPC	Kenya Foundation of the Prophets Church
KHCF	Kenya Hospitals Christian Fellowship
KHCM	Kenya Hospitals Church's Ministry
KISA	Kikuyu Independent Schools Association
KKEA	Kikuyu Karing'a Educational Association
KSCF	Kenya Students Christian Fellowship
LCK	Lutheran Church in Kenya
LDS	Church of Jesus Christ of Latter-day Saints
LWF	Lutheran World Federation
MAF	Missionary Aviation Fellowship
Mch.	Mchungaji (Pastor)
MCK	Methodist Church in Kenya
Mgr.	Monsignor (bishop, prefect)
Mgsr.	Monsignor
Mhe.	Mheshimiwa (Honourable)
MHGC	Musanda Holy Ghost Church of East Africa
MHM	Mill Hill Mission (St. Joseph's Society)
MM	Maryknoll Missioner (fathers, sisters and brothers)
MMS	Methodist Missionary Society
MRA	Moral Re-Armament
MRI	Mutual Responsibility and Interdependence
MTS	Menno Travel Service
MU	Mothers' Union
m/v	motor vessel
NARET	National Association of Religious Education Teachers
NBI	Nairobi Bible Institute
NCCK	National Christian Council of Kenya
NET	Nairobi Evangelistic Team
NHA	National Holiness Association
NICA	National Independent Church of Africa
NLC	Nomiya Luo Church
NLM	Nomiya Luo Mission
NLS	Nomiya Luo Sabbath
NPMK	Norwegian Pentecostal Mission in Kenya
OCSO	Cistercians (Trappists)
OCYAK	Orthodox Christian Youth Association in Kenya
OFM	Friars Minor
OFMCap	Capuchin Friars Minor
OM	Operation Mobilization
OP	Dominican Fathers (Order of Preachers)
PA	prefecture apostolic
PAEA	Pentecostal Assemblies of East Africa
PAFES	Pan-African Fellowship of Evangelical Students
PAG	Pentecostal Assemblies of God
PAOC	Pentecostal Assemblies of Canada
PCCF	Pentecostal Church of Christian Fellowship
PCEA	Presbyterian Church of East Africa
PCMA	Protestant Churches' Medical Association
PCUC	Pentecostal Christian Universal Church

PEFA	Pentecostal Evangelistic Fellowship of Africa
PWC	Pentecostal World Conference
RCC	Roman Catholic Church
RCEA	Reformed Church of East Africa
Rev.	Reverend
RML	Reformed Mission League
RN	radiocall Nairobi (telephone number)
ROTA	VOK rota of broadcasting denominations
RSAK	Religious Superiors' Association of Kenya
RTC	rural training centre
Rt. Rev.	Right Reverend (Bishop)
SA	Salvation Army
SACIM	South Africa Compounds and Interior Mission
SBC	Southern Baptist Convention, USA
SCEA	Sinai Church of East Africa
SDA	Seventh-day Adventist Church
SDARM	Seventh-day Adventist Church, Reform Movement
SDMC	Seventh-day Missionary Church
SECAM	Symposium of Episcopal Conferences of Africa and Madagascar
SFM	Swedish Free Mission
SHM	Scriptural Holiness Mission
SJ	Jesuits (Society of Jesus)
SLM	Swedish Lutheran Mission
SM	Society of Mary (Marianists)
SMM	Swedish Maranatha Mission
SODEPAX	Committee on Society, Development and Peace
SPS	Kiltegan Fathers (Society of St. Patrick for Foreign Missions)
Sr.	Sister
SU	Scripture Union
T	telephone number
TAP	Teachers Abroad Program
TEAM	East African Mission, The
TF	Trinity Fellowship
TMC	Tanganyika Mennonite Church
TPM	Thessalia Pentecostal Mission
TTC	teacher training college
UBS	United Bible Societies
UMMS	United Methodist Missionary Society
UPCK	United Pentecostal Church of Kenya
VA.	vicariate apostolic
Ven.	Venerable (Archdeacon)
VOK	Voice of Kenya
VP	village polytechnic
W	Wokofu (salvation)
WAC	Wokofu African Church
WARC	World Alliance of Reformed Churches
WCC	World Council of Churches
WF (orPA)	White Fathers (Peres d'Afrique)
WGM	World Gospel Mission
WHC	Wokofu Huruma Church
WLC	Water of Life Church
WPM	World Presbyterian Missions
WSCF	World Student Christian Federation
YCAF	Young Christian Ambassadors Fellowship
YCS	Young Christian Students
YCW	Young Christian Workers
YFC	Youth for Christ
YMCA	Young Men's Christian Association
YSA	Youth Service Abroad
YWCA	Young Women's Christian Association

339

Index of Church Officials & Religious Personnel

This index lists, in alphabetical order by surname, all present heads of denominations, all executive officers of Christian organizations, executive officers of a few secular organizations of assistance to the churches, religious superiors and mission executives, and sundry other church leaders. The reader can locate the work, whereabouts, address and telephone number of any leader or official he needs to find by turning to the page indicated after his name. All titles (Rev., Dr., Fr., Bro., Miss, Mr., etc.) are omitted here except Bp. (Bishop), Abp. (Archbishop), Mo. (Mother), Mrs. and Sr. (Sister).

Ablewhite,S.E., 284
Abonyo,E., 275
Abrams,P.D., 275
Achola, P.O., 247
Adagala, S., 266
Adele Angela, Sr., 284
Adkins, Mrs. R.L., 255
Adodoadji, W., 279
Adoo, J., 251
Adoyo, J., 240
Agogo, B., 241
Agola, Bp. E., 239
Ajago, Bp. E., 241
Ajuoga, Bp. A.M., 237, 259, 279
Akal, Bp. G., 249
Akeny, E., 285
Akhahenda, E.F., 266
Alando, C., 248
Aldridge, B.G., 269
Aleta, J., 274
Alexander, E.J., 277
Ali, J., 238
Aligula, H.M., 250
Aloo, Abp.H., 246
Aloo, Abp. J., 247
Ambrose, 258
Ambula, Abp. J.Z., 244
Amiraki, P., 247
Amukobole, M., 271
Anamini, Mrs. R., 276
Anderson, R.J.D., 273
Anjejo, M.T., 242
Anna Lucia, Sr., 273
Ann Marie, Mo., 264
Anono, A., 231
Anyango, J., 231
Anyika, Bp. M.B., 232
Aoko, Bp. G., 243
Aomo, J., 240
Arenson, E., 272
Arthuri, A.-L., 242
Asewe, M., 263
Asoyo, G.O., 270
Astor, P., 259
Atiang, Bp. Y., 247
Atila, Bp. T., 246
Auro, J., 270

Bahati, Sr. E., 283
Ball, J.M., 277, 280, 286
Banzhaf, B., 265
Barrett, D.B., 256, 261, 285
Barron, T., 259
Bateman, D.L., 258
Baudena, P., 262
Bazarra, D.K., 250
Beetham, Mrs. M., 280
Bell, S., 275

Bessone, Bp. L.V., 235, 275
Bet, Mrs. E., 276
Bett, E.A., 230
Bigedi, Bp., 242
Bisset, J., 273
Blayney, L., 277
Bombay, C.R., 266
Bonuke, J.N., 269
Borden, O., 272
Borman, E.T., 275
Boro, J., 240, 267
Bowles, J., 246
Brady, J., 270
Brett, L., 267
Brown, L.T., 275
Brown, R.D., 269
Bruce, R., 276
Bruton, J.P., 241
Buckley, R.M., 283
Buku, J. K., 261
Bunde, C.A., 246
Burke, R., 267
Bustgaard, A., 248
Butler, Bp. E., 235
Bwenye, J., 258

Callaghan, J., 270
Callahan, Sr. C.M., 257, 282, 283
Camillo, A., 259
Campbell, M., 270, 274
Carey, B., 259
Carey, C., 284
Carr, B., 256
Cauri, S.M., 279
Cavallera, Bp. C.M., 235, 274
Chabuga, Bp. J.L., 231
Chappell, J.P., 258
Charo, J.H., 266
Chege, J., 287
Chege, Bp. J.M., 241
Chemoiywa, B., 260
Cherop, M., 258
Cheseng'eny, J.A., 230, 271
Chipenda, J.B., 261, 286
Chipman, A., 270
Chitayi, E., 247
Chuma, J., 248
Cohen, D., 285
Collins, E.M., 263
Coon, R., 260
Cooper, L., 269
Cornelius, W., 279
Cossar, J., 263
Cotter, H.J., 283
Cox, P.S.V., 278
Crabbie, C.P., 273
Cross, T.C., 277
Cummings, P., 279

Cummins, A.A., 257
Cummins, B., 287

Dain, F.R., 271
Dalziel, G., 249
Dames, J.J., 286
Davies, Bp. C., 236, 270, 278
Davies, H.H., 238, 258
Davies, S.L., 241
Davis, A., 247
Davis, M.L., 269
Davis, W.I., 285
Dawkins, G.D., 285
Delaney, N., 262
Digan, Sr. O., 279
Dilschneider, G., 261
Dirorimwe, A., 243
Donnelly, P., 282
Downing, H.C., 282
Drohan, M., 271, 287
Drown, R., 282
Dundon, C., 274
Dunne, Bp. W., 234

Edalia, M.P., 273
Edel, Sr. B., 270, 283
Egan, F., 258
Ekamba, Bp. S., 238
Ellison, J., 260, 262, 263, 283
Erskine, E.M., 237, 261
Evans, E., 282
Farrelly, T.M., 275
Fast, Mrs., 272
Fawcette, E., 280
Finch, W., 250
Firth, R., 286
Fish, G.W., 257
Fisher, T., 260
Foster, J., 272
Fowler, J.P., 263
Fox, J., 274
Fox, P., 275
Frances Terese, Sr., 283
Fraynot, Fr., 273
Frew, Mrs. F. 262
Frew, F., 256, 262
Fulvia, Sr., 266

Gacambi, Sr. M.T., 283
Gaceru, J., 230
Gadhura, E., 285
Gallup, C.F., 233
Gathuna, Bp. A., 232
Gatimu, Bp. C.M., 236
Gatu, J.G., 249
Gatuna, E., 276
Gawo, Bp. J.A., 244
Getonga, J., 265, 270, 271
Gibbs, E., 279

Gichuhi, C., 286
Gichuru, R.D., 245
Gikanga, G., 257, 276
Gikonyo, T.E., 284
Gikonyo, Mrs. M., 267
Gilmartin, J., 281, 284
Girling, J.H., 285
Gitari, D.M., 258
Gitete, Abp. J.N., 244
Githenya, P.S., 268
Githinji, E., 239
Gituma, J., 286
Givan, D.G., 239
Gorzegno, A., 259
Goslinga, J.J.J., 274
Gregory-Smith, D., 270
Griffin, R., 270
Grogan, S.J., 259
Grover, D., 273
Gumba, B.O., 263
Gumba, Abp. W., 233
Gungu, C., 248

Habel, D.D., 272
Hales, A.T., 271
Hansson, E., 284
Harris, J., 250
Hart, N., 255
Hasch, F., 241
Hawkes, W., 258
Healey, J., 257
Hearn, T., 275
Hedrick, D.S., 274
Heim, M.C., 259
Henna, Sr., 283
Herm, I., 280
Hertweck, R.W., 284
Hildebrandt, W., 265
Hill, J., 257
Hindley, C.G.T., 287
Hockett, J.L., 245
Hofmann, H., 273
Hollinshed, E., 266
Hooper, D., 257
Hostetter, E.L., 274
Hughes, A.L., 279
Hughes, J., 276
Hunter, F., 261
Hunter, Mrs. F., 261

Idle, A.H., 260
Ihaji, P., 231
Ikunyua, G.M., 269
Ikutwa, E.R., 271
Imathiu, L., 247
Imwendwa, Bp. S., 244
Irangi, S., 280
Ireri, B., 239
Irungu, J., 262, 270

Jacobs, D.R., 264, 269, 274
Jacobson, W.E., 268
Jacoba, Sr., 272
James, J., 259
Jinkin, B., 247
Johansson, C., 246
Jones, B., 275

Josephine, Sr., 259
Juma, D., 262

Kabii, E., 279
Kabunga, L., 231
Kago, W.N., 233
Kagume, M., 271
Kahihia, Bp. B., 231
Kahn, G.G., 274
Kailu, H., 273
Kamanu, W.K., 233
Kamau, D., 240
Kamau, Mrs. G., 286
Kamau, Jakobu, 249
Kamau, Joseph, 242
Kamau, John C., 277
Kamau, L., 240
Kamau, T., 256
Kamosche, G., 245
Kamunyu, J., 262
Kangethe, S.M., 256
Kanja, G., 246
Karanja, Mrs. A., 278
Karanja, G., 263
Karhof, E., 259, 272
Kariuki, J., 233
Kariuki, Mrs. L.W., 276
Kariuki, Bp. O., 239
Kariuki, Bp. P., 247
Kariuki, C.S., 242
Karuga, Bp. D.N., 231
Karugia, J., 243
Karuitha, E.M., 245
Karuru, J., 248
Karwitha, M., 261
Kasibo, Bp. J., 249
Kasio, J., 261
Kayo. J., 240, 286
Kealy, J.P., 270
Keane, M., 280
Kearie, G.W., 267
Kellogg, D., 258
Kenani, H., 250
Kennedy, J., 272
Kennedy, Sr. L., 266
Kerr, A., 280
Kerr, G., 263
Kesembe, D.A., 230
Kettering, M., 286
Keverenge, E., 246
Keya, H., 251
Keya, N., 243
Khaguli, S.J., 250
Kiamba, Abp. A.P., 238
Kiarie, J., 285
Kiarie, Abp. J.W., 243
Kiarie, P., 270, 272
Kibicho, S., 282
Kibuti, Bp. P., 231
Kieti, Abp., B.M., 238
Kiganane, M., 273
Kimani, J.N., 237
Kimaru, S., 233
Kimau, P., 269
Kindle, E., 269
Kinyanjui, D., 260
Kinyanjui, E., 283

Kinyua, S., 245
Kioko, U.J., 272
Kiongo, J., 249
Kiongo, Mrs. E., 284
Kiplagat, B.A., 277
Kiptoo, H., 242
Kirby, R.R., 245, 267
Kirima, N., 276
Kirimania, E., 257
Kisia, H.M., 271
Kisia, J., 280
Kissuge, J., 251
Kiteto, S.T., 239
Kithara, W., 258
Kithele, Abp. T.M., 231
Kiti, P.M., 280
Kitsao, S., 266
Kituku, E.M., 243
Kiugu, R., 248
Kivuli, M.P.S.D.Z., 232, 271
Kiwinda, J., 239
Kizza, E., 276
Kombe, S., 251
Korpivara, T., 265
Kraft, E.C., 270
Krenz, Mo. M.H., 275
Kung'a, J., 242
Kuntner, J., 256
Kuria, Bp. M., 240

Lamont, A.D., 279
Langereld, Sr. M.M., 282
Langford-Smith, Bp. N., 240, 275, 278
Langford-Smith, Mrs. V., 276
Latham, P., 266
Lawless, E., 259
Leach, J.W., 280
Leaman, M.H., 274
Leech, Mrs. P., 267
Lefeuvre, A., 282
Leffers, J., 278
Lewis, W.J.D., 258
Lianzika, J., 285
Likhaya, A.M., 240, 286
Lindsey, R.S., 270
Litondo, T., 274
Liyai, D., 275
Lovett, Sr. N., 274
Ludenyo, H.M., 240
Lumbasi, F.K., 237
Lunani, Bp. S., 237
Lung'aho, T.G., 241
Lusiola, J., 251
Lusuli, G., 249
Lusuli, Bp. W.A., 232
Luvai, N., 267
Luvisha, J., 230
Lyon, H., 260

McCauley, Bp. V., 257
Macharia, G., 261
Macheru, S., 238
Madeleine, Sr., 286
Maeke, W., 259
Maganjo, D., 274
Magessa, S., 265
Magu, J.N., 261

341

Magua, S., 239, 276
Mahiaini, J., 240
Mahon, J.C., 236
Maillefer, E., 257
Maithiya, J., 276
Makanga, Bp. Z., 247
Makodawa, R., 249, 285
Makokha, B.A., 237
Malin, O., 272
Manyonje, Mrs. R.A., 283
Marangu, P., 278
Margaret, Sr., 273
Marshall, D., 257
Mary, Sr., 262
Mary Bernard, Sr., 266
Mary Celine, Mo., 268
Mary Cora, Sr., 283
Masaga, D., 242
Masambu, Bp. P., 250
Masinde, E., 249
Masinde, Bp., P.W., 248
Masini, W., 246
Masiza, J., 241
Matano, J.R., 268
Mathang'a, J., 255
Mathenge, A., 279, 282
Mathews, D.L., 277
Mathuku, D., 276
Matianyi, T., 273
Matogo, J., 272
Matonoi, S.M., 243
Mavuru, Bp. K.A., 231
Mbatia, S.N., 278
Mbogo, J., 245
Mbogo, Mrs. J.O., 278
Mbogo, S., 276
Mbogori, J.M., 264, 285
Mbonde, I.K., Bp., 230
Mbote, P., 237, 244
Mbugua, L., 279
Mbugua, Mrs., 276
McCarney, H., 272
McKim, A., 264
McKinley, R., 241
McLaughlin, Sr. J., 262, 270, 278
McNeil, M.W., 268
McVeigh, M.J., 259
Mechtilda, Sr., 266
Millar, D., 273
Milton-Thompson, D., 282
Mining, J.K., 269
Mitchell, Mrs. E., 276
Mng'ong'o, R.S., 247
Monteiro, J., 262
Morrissey, J., 274
Moss, S., 277
Mpaayei, J.T., 256
Mpaayei, Mrs. J., 286
Mpivas; D.O.M., 277
Muchai, M., 260, 277, 280
Muchoki, G., 248
Mudergani, R., 285
Muga, Bp. J., 246
Mugavana, T., 266
Mugendi, Bp. T.C., 234
Mugo, E., 282
Mugo, J.M., 279

Mugo, Mrs. M., 287
Muhindi, Bp. Y.N., 245
Muiruri, Bp. T.J., 243
Mujembi, J., 242
Mukwaya, J., 257
Mulaha, G., 250
Mulwa, W.E., 230
Mumbo, Bp. C., 246
Munce, R., 265
Munce, Mrs. R.H., 276
Mundia, Bp. J., 238
Munene, J.A.A., 271
Munga, R., 269
Munini, Sr., B., 276
Munjal, T.J., 231, 256, 285
Munyasia, C., 260
Munyi, S., 263, 277
Muranga, J., 244, 285
Musembi, Bp. D., 231
Musinde, Bp. E.A., 244
Musodzi, E., 242
Musso, M., 259
Muta, W., 239
Mutava, D.M., 231
Mutero, J., 286
Muthukya, S., 244, 264
Muthuria, M., 242
Mutua, Mrs. E., 267
Mutua, J.M., 233, 247
Mutuku, S., 278
Muturi, Abp. E.C., 237
Mwadime, M., 247
Mwadime, Mrs. R., 276
Mwaluma, Mrs. E., 276
Mwandia, D., 275
Mwangi, Abp. B.M.P., 243
Mwangi, D., 259
Mwangi, S.M., 230, 245
Mwango, J.N., 251
Mwang'ombe, Bp. P., 239
Mwang'ombe, Mrs. P., 276
Mwahiki, P.J., 243
Mwawaka, S., 286
Mwirukire, L.J., 258
Mwithimbu, S., 275

Nash, T., 265
Nasios, Abp. F., 232
Nchogu, J.O., 246
Ndege, H., 241
Ndegwa, Mrs. A.W., 287
Ndeti, J., 272
Ndiege, Abp. Z., 246
Ndingi, Bp. R.S., 235
Ndisi, Bp. I., 238
Ndiwa, J., 243
Ndogo, J.M., 244
Ndungu, S., 241
Ndwaru, E.M., 232
Neill, Bp. S.C., 263
Newton, M., 270
Ngala, N.K., 230
Ngala, S., 275
Nganga, D.M., 232
Ngare, P., 276
Ngaruiya, Bp. E., 239
Ngilla, F., 271

Ngube, R.S., 243
Ngunyi, J., 276
Ngure, H.G., 279
Nguru, Bp. G., 245
Nicholson, G.A., 285
Njenga, A., 278
Njenga, Bp. J., 234
Njeru, A., 245
Njeru, F., 233
Njeru, Bp. F., 238
Njeru, L., 237
Njeru, S., 245, 282
Njiraini, N., 261
Njue, Abp., P., 233
Njuguna, F., 240
Njuguna, H., 250
Njuguna, J., 244
Njuguna, K., 265
Nkabu, J., 230
Noah, D.K., 231
Noor; A., 232
Norrvack, G., 284
Northwood, E., 269
Ntabo, S., 272
Nthamburi, Z., 259
Nuhu, Bp. L.M., 250, 264, 265
Nyabulwa. S., 251
Nyaga, James, 245
Nyaga, Johana, 237
Nyaga, Bp. W.J.N., 247
Nyagowa, K., 238
Nyakiamo, P.L.J.O., 259, 282
Nyasamo, W., 242
Nyong'o, H.S., 239
Nzano, C., 261
Nzau, J., 244

Obange, P., 244
Obar, Abp. K.N., 238
Obatsa, M., 263
Ochieng', W., 260
Ochwatta, J., 285
Odaa, N., 238
Odayo, Bp. J., 248
Odegu, J., 242
Odera, J.A., 280
Odera, M., 236
Odero, C., 250
Odewa, N.O., 242
Odhiambo, Bp. A.S., 285
Odhiambo, J., 263
Odhiambo, L., 246
Odiemo, C., 261
Odongo, M.M., 248
O'Donnell, M., 259
Oduma, B., 282
Odundo, M., 251
Ogol, Bp. E.K., 245
Ogola, Bp. S., 231
Ogongo, J., 279
Oguk, I., 236
Ogutu, Bp. H.H., 237
Ohange, G.W., 263
Oiro, S.O., 247
Ojuka, S., 264
Ojwang, Bp. D., 241
Okatch, Abp. F., **240**

ACKNOWLEDGEMENTS

The editors wish to acknowledge with gratitude the assistance of a number of persons and groups, in addition to those named elsewhere, who have contributed to the material in this *Handbook* and to its interpretation.

Firstly, since so much of the data covering the various churches and Christian organisations has come directly from the bishops, priests, pastors and lay officers of those bodies, this survey is very much their own achievement. Material was painstakingly collected by them, in many cases by commissioning special enquiries, and transmitted to us in such a spirit of collaboration that it augurs well for the future co-operation between the churches in Kenya.

Next, credit is due to the group of volunteers who attempted to compile this mass of material and to get it into some sort of manageable shape. Although it is not possible here to name all the persons involved, we wish to thank David Aoko and John and Carmen Ward, who started off the process, and Jocelyn Murray who made substantial contributions to the chronology, the atlas and the bibliography. Valuable assistance on the indexes was provided by Mary Linda Hronek.

We are indebted to a number of organisations who assisted in the compilation of the book in one way or another: in particular, to the Department of Biblical Study and Research, National Christian Council of Kenya, for its encouragement in initiating the project and for providing grants to cover the field work and part of the research; and to the Kenya Episcopal Conference and to its working arm, the Kenya Catholic Secretariat, for placing its resources at our disposal. We wish also to thank the Survey of Kenya for their assistance in reproducing their several maps of Kenya and Nairobi, and the Attorney General's office for permission to quote from the Constitution of Kenya and the various governmental education acts.

We are grateful to several publishers and authors for allowing us to reproduce the following material: to Heineman Educational Books Ltd., Nairobi, for extracts from *African Religions and Philosophy* by John S. Mbiti; to *Risk* for the article on independent churches by Odhiambo Okite and Marylou Rose's imaginative art work; and to *African Ecclesiastical Review* for portions of the article on African traditional music by Stephen Mbunga.

We also wish to acknowledge with gratitude the co-operation of a number of photographers and holders of photographic libraries in the assembling of a collection of photographs which would do justice to the rapid development of Kenya and its churches. Half the photographs in this *Handbook* are the editors' own; the other half were supplied from the following organisations and persons, to whom special appreciation is extended:

Kenya Information Services; *Daily Nation; East African Standard;* East African Venture Co. *(Target); New York Times; Risk* (Geneva); Weld Dixon International Ltd.; National Christian Council of Kenya; Kenya Catholic Secretariat; Limuru Conference Centre; Christian Institute of Southern Africa; Canadian Baptist Mission, Pentecostal Assemblies of Canada; Salvation Army; Ahmadiyya Mission; Arya Samaj Mission; Dr. J.E. Church; the Rev. Victor Lamont; Mr. Otieno Makonyango; Mr. Leo Odera Omolo; Mr. E. Arenson; Mr. H. Richard Hughes, FRIBA.

THE NATIONAL ANTHEM OF KENYA (1963)

O God of all creation
Bless this our land and nation
Justice be our shield and defender;
May we dwell in unity
Peace and liberty
Plenty be found within our borders.

CONTENTS - A SUMMARY

	Editorial Foreword	XV
	Preface	XVII
Part I:	Aspects of Kenyan Christianity	19
Part II:	The Expansion of Christianity in Kenya, AD 1900 - 2000	155
	Photographic Essay	193
Part III:	Atlas of Christianity and Religion in Kenya	211
Part IV:	Directory of the Churches	227
Part V:	Directory of Christian Organisations	253
Part VI:	Kenya's Other Religions	289
Part VII:	Bibliography of Religion in Kenya	315
	Kenya Religious Periodicals	331
Part VIII:	Appendixes and Indexes	323
	Polyglot Glossary of Religious Terminology	335
	Abbreviations	338
	Church Officials	340
	Towns and Cities	344
	Subjects	346
	Foldout Maps: Nairobi, and Kenya	

TABLE OF CONTENTS

Acknowledgements VII
List of Tables XII
List of Figures XII
List of Maps XIII
List of Photographs and Illustrations XIII
EDITORIAL FOREWORD XV
PREFACE: The Rev Professor John S. Mbiti XVII

PART I: ASPECTS OF KENYAN CHRISTIANITY 19

1. Chronology of Christianity in Kenya, 1498 - 1972 21
2. A History of the Kenya Churches 29
   The Rev W.B. Anderson, PCEA, the Rev Fr S. Clements, CSSp and others
3. Kenya's Cultural Heritage and Tradition 40
   The Rev Dr Donald R. Jacobs, Mennonite Church in East Africa
4. Church and State in Kenya 43
   The Rt Rev Rafael Ndingi, Catholic Bishop of Nakuru
5. Religious Education in the Schools 49
   The Rev Fr Thomas Farrelly, CSSp, Ministry of Education, Nairobi
6. Religious Architecture and Planning 59
   H. Richard Hughes, FRIBA, Chartered Architect, Nairobi
7. The New Surge in Indigenous Christian Music in Kenya 65
   The Rev Fr Stephen Mbunga, Diocese of Songea, Tanzania;
   The Rev Fr John P. Kealy, CSSp, Kenya Association for Liturgical Music;
   Mrs Eva Christian, Scott Theological College, Machakos
8. Religious Broadcasting in Kenya 85
   Moses Wesonga, NCCK, & Prof John W. Ward, Boston University
9. Production of Christian Literature 93
   Jocelyn Murray, Church Missionary Society
10. Communications: Key to Development 100
    Sr Janice McLaughlin, Catholic Secretariat & Prof. J. W. Ward
11. African Society and the Foreign Legacy in the Churches 106
    The Rev Fr Joachim Getonga, General Secretary, Kenya Catholic
    Secretariat
12. The Revival Fellowship (Brethren) in Kenya 110
    George K. Mambo, All Africa Conference of Churches
13. Politics of Africa's Independent Churches 118
    Odhiambo W. Okite, Editor TARGET & LENGO, Nairobi
14. The Rise and Persecution of the Aroti Prophets, 1927 - 1948 124
    Prophet Elijah Kinyanjui, Chosen Church of the Holy Spirit
15. Varieties of Kikuyu Independent Churches 128
    Jocelyn Murray, Church Missionary Society
16. Theological Issues Related to Kenyan Religious Independency 135
    The Rev Dr Malcolm J. McVeigh, University of Nairobi
17. Diversity, Divisions and Denominationalism 144
    The Rev Professor John S. Mbiti, Makerere University
18. Co-operation Between the Churches 149
    The Rev Thomas A. Beetham, St. Paul's United Theological College,
    Limuru

PART II: THE EXPANSION OF CHRISTIANITY IN KENYA
AD 1900 - 2000 155
   The Rev Dr D.B. Barrett, Anglican Consultative Council

PHOTOGRAPHIC ESSAY: 'Fields white unto harvest' 193

PART III: ATLAS OF CHRISTIANITY AND RELIGION
              IN KENYA   211

PART IV: DIRECTORY OF CHURCHES IN KENYA   227

PART V: DIRECTORY OF CHRISTIAN ORGANISATIONS
              IN KENYA   253

PART VI: KENYA'S OTHER RELIGIONS   289
              The Heritage of Traditional Religions   291
                The Rev Professor J.S. Mbiti, Makerere University
              Islam in Kenya and Relations with the Churches   295
                James D. Holway, Islam in Africa Project
              Hinduism, Jainism and Sikhism in Kenya   302
                The Rev Dr Terence Day, University of Nairobi
              Directory of Other Religions in Kenya   312

PART VII: BIBLIOGRAPHY OF CHRISTIANITY AND RELIGION
              IN KENYA   315
              Index of Kenya Religious Periodicals   331

PART VII: APPENDIXES AND INDEXES   333
              Polyglot Glossary of Religious Terminology   335
              Index of Abbreviations   338
              Index of Church Officials and Religious Personnel   340
              Index of Kenya Towns and Cities   344
              Subject Index   346

FOLDOUT MAPS:
        1. Churches and Temples in Nairobi
        2. The Republic of Kenya

LIST OF TABLES

Development in education in Kenya, 1961 - 1971   55
Religious sponsorship of primary schools in Kenya, 1971   56
Distribution of church-sponsored schools by administrative areas, 1970 - 1971   57
Results in Bible knowledge in Kenya secondary schools, 1969 - 1971   58
Church buildings in a rapidly-growing Kenya denomination   64
Numbers of known traditional musical instruments of the major Kenyan peoples   72
Kenya traditional musical instruments and church usage, 1972   73
Christian radio broadcasting schedule on the Voice of Kenya   91
Translation and distribution of Scriptures in Kenya   99
Major Kenya conventions of the East African Revival Fellowship, 1947 - 1971   113
Councils of African independent churches in Kenya   153
Christianity in Kenya, AD 1900 - 2000   160
Professing Christians in Kenya, 1948 - 1962   163
Annual church weddings in 19 Anglican and Catholic dioceses in Kenya   180
Race, tribe and religious profession in Kenya, 1962 - 1972   181
Statistics of the Churches in Kenya   183
Names for God of Kenyan peoples   293
Index of Kenya religious periodicals   331
Polyglot glossary of religious terminology   335
Index of abbreviations   338

LIST OF FIGURES

Expansion of Christianity in Kenya, 1890 - 2000   158
Instantaneous response to Christianity among five Kenyan peoples   169
Development of Anglican and Catholic churches in Kenya, 1844 - 1972   178

LIST OF MAPS

ATLAS OF CHRISTIANITY AND RELIGION IN KENYA   211

   A.   HISTORICAL: 1498 - 1962

       1. Political boundaries, 1880 - 1924   212
       2. Political boundaries, 1924 - 1933   213
       3. Political boundaries, 1933 - 1962   214
       4. Catholic missions, 1498 - 1952   215
       5. Anglican missions, 1844 - 1959   216
       6. Protestant missions, 1862 - 1962   217
       7. African independent churches, 1914 - 1962   218

   B.   CONTEMPORARY: 1963 - 1972

       8. Political boundaries, 1963 - 1972   219
       9. Catholic Church, 1953 - 1972   220
    10. Anglican Church, 1960 - 1972   221
    11. Protestant churches, 1963 - 1972   222
    12. African independent churches, 1963 - 1972   223
    13. African traditional religions   224
    14. Non-Christian world religions   225
    15. Tribes and languages of Kenya   226

CHURCHES AND TEMPLES IN NAIROBI, 1972   Inside back cover

THE REPUBLIC OF KENYA   Inside back cover

LIST OF PHOTOGRAPHS AND ILLUSTRATIONS

President Kenyatta opens Parliament, 1972   43
Prayer service over Kenya army colours, 1970   45
Independence celebrations, 1963: religious leaders   47
2.0 million pupils study in Kenya's schools   49
Krapf-Rebmann Memorial Church, Kilifi   59
Alliance Girls High School, Kikuyu, extended (interior)   60
Traditional village meeting place called *bwalo*   61
Trinity College chapel, Nairobi   62
YMCA Prayer House, Nairobi   63
Scott Theological College students with instruments   65
'Praise Him upon the stringed instruments'   69
Scott students combine traditional and Western instruments   71
Survey of 177 Kenyan traditional musical instruments   74 - 83
Broadcasting technician at work in radio studio   85
Roman Catholic sister & AICN member at broadcasting workshop   86
Workshop members learn to use radio equipment   87
One million scriptures were bought and read in Kenya in 1971   95
Anglican minister explains making a beehive to youths   100
Communications conference displays   102
Communications are the key to reaching youths   104
Revival fellowship gathering   110
Interpretation in four languages (East African Revival)   114
Butere Convention, 1961. Bishop Olang' speaking   116
Holy Father of HGCCA conducting mass in Nairobi   119
Uniforms prominent in Lost Israelites of Kenya   120
The Prophet of God of the Lost Israelites of Kenya   121
Prophet Elijah Kinyanjui, Chosen Church of the Holy Spirit   124
Members of a Kikuyu Spirit church visit President Kenyatta   128
Bishop Benjamin Kahihia inaugurates new AIPC church   130
ACC&S baptism in 1971   131
A pentecostal congregation: the Local Churches of Kenya   132
Aroti women at worship: the Holy Ghost Church of Kenya   134

Speaking in tongues in African Israel Church Nineveh 135
Holy Father Ondeto blesses Maria Legio faithful 137
Outdoor communal service in Nairobi held by AICN 139
Faith healing and exorcism in Maria Legio 142
One of the more than 210 denominations in Kenya 144
Grass-roots Christian unity: a dozen denominations meet 152
In Kenya, 500,000 a year are joining the Christian faith 157
Boys and girls arriving in church for instruction 161
Children and infants must be counted in statistics of attendance 165
Palm Sunday, 1972: a million Catholics process in witness 167
Simultaneous audible prayer in Western Kenya (PAG) 170
AICN congregations assembling for march through countryside 171
Kenyan clergy of the African Orthodox Church at dedication service 172
New churches in the African idiom: Church Army Training College, Nairobi 173
Mass open-air baptism of 250 adults, PAG Tsimbalo 174
Archbishop Makarios baptises 5,000 Orthodox, March 1971 174
Independent church (Vapostori) conducting infant baptism 174
About 90,000 rural baptisms a week take place in Africa 177
Sunset baptism in a local river 182
Photographic essay: 'Fields white unto harvest' 193 - 210
1. The average age of Kenyans is 14½ years.
2 - 4. Contemporary Kenyans (3 photos).
5. Bible society translator, and country pastor.
6. 1,200 Kenyan ministers at the 1968 Kenya Pastors' Conference.
7. A rural denomination with 15,000 white-clad sisters.
8. Catholic bishop addressing laity in rural Machakos diocese.
9. Constructing a rural church building through *harambee* self-help.
10. AICN high priest with disciples at holy village of Nineveh.
11. Representation of AICN on the move, on door of high priest's residence.
12. Cardinal Otunga with Bishops Njenga and Ndingi at the latter's enthronement.
13. President Kenyatta inaugurates a new AIPC church in Central Province.
14. Salvation Army cadets march at officer training college, Nairobi.
15. The first Kenyan to become a Catholic bishop is now Kenya's first cardinal.
16. The city of Nairobi: 300 churches, 450,000 Christians.
17. American evangelist Billy Graham meets medicine men in Kisumu.
18. Billy Graham preaching, interpreted by Bishop Olang' and Bishop Kivengere.
19. Archbishop Makarios ordains a Kikuyu priest in the Orthodox Church.
20. Archbishop of Canterbury.
21. Private meditation: Maurice Cardinal Otunga in his Chapel.
22. A theological student blows a traditional Bajun horn in worship.
23. Theological students accompanying hymns with traditional instruments.
24. Pastor keeping time with handclapping in Western Kenya (PAG).
25. Handclapping assists congregational worship (Assemblies of God).
26. A bishop preaching with an interpreter in Nyanza (Maria Legio).
27. Students outside science lecture theatres, University of Nairobi.
28. Bishop of Mount Kenya greets students after university service.
29. Christian couple being married in an Anglican church.
30. Christian student leaders listening to Archbishop of Canterbury.
31. Novice sister entering on the religious life.
32. Widespread Bible study groups spread knowledge of the Scriptures.
33. Broadcasting, communication and development spell progress.
34. MAF air services assist the churches reach the northern deserts.
35. Handicapped child ready for football at Port Reitz School.
36. Medical clinic.
37. Young worker belonging to African Israel Church Nineveh.
38. Service to the poor and needy, the hungry and the destitute.

Luo religious specialist in a traditional dance 291
Practitioners of traditional religion: Kabwere and Kajiwe 294
Friday prayers at Jamia Mosque, Nairobi 295
Ahmadiyya translator presenting Swahili Koran to Mzee Kenyatta 299
African converts to Hinduism in Arya Samaj temple 302
World Hare Krishna Movement Festival, Nairobi 304
Hindu Festival: Vijay Dashmi, in Nairobi 306
Sikh swordsmen guarding Granth Sahib in Nairobi 310

EDITORIAL FOREWORD

This *Handbook* describes the churches of Kenya and their contribution to development, nation-building, the bettering of the human condition, the renaissance of African culture, and the new trends that African initiatives in religion are taking in this nation. It describes the growth and development of a form of Christianity in the modern world that has sometimes been termed (after the Kenya national motto, *Harambee* — 'Let us pull together!') *harambee* or 'community self-help' Christianity.

We recognize that there are negative elements in the historic expression of Christianity in Kenya, but we believe the overall picture presented here is both an encouraging and positive one. We are aware that from certain points of view the data we present are capable of adverse interpretation. The vast proliferation of denominations in Kenya revealed in these pages is sure to cause unfavourable comment. But we would remind the reader familiar with the 'chaos of cults' on some other continent — the USA with its 700 denominations, Britain with its 300, or Japan with its 130 Christian denominations and 200 Buddhist ones — that such criteria of judgement must not be imported onto the Kenya scene, because the circumstances are entirely different. The USA, UK and Japan are all highly industrialized countries, each speaking a single national language, and with a network of communications so vast and rapid that all sects exist aware of the existence of the others. In Kenya, the large number of mutually unintelligible languages spoken — seventy indigenous to the country, plus a multitude from outside — and the relatively undeveloped communications and transport networks, result in most of the denominations and organisations not knowing of the existence of most of the others.

From this point of view then, what we find in Kenya is an attribute that characterised the early church in New Testament days — diversity. In each place, or area, or language group, there has been a response to the calling of Christ; but because we human beings are so different, these responses have been very diverse. In a nation where, during its nine years since Independence the keywords have been *Harambee* and *Umoja* (Unity), this grass-roots diversity is bound to be modified as communications expand and as Christians get to know of each other's existence. We can therefore expect and eagerly anticipate a new era of co-operation and collaboration in Kenya among the churches themselves, and also between Christians and other organisations.

What this future pattern of unity in Kenya might be is exciting to speculate on. The initiatives demonstrated here make it certain that this pattern will be bold, imaginative, unusual, realistic, and genuinely related to the servant role of the church in the modern world. Visits to independent churches during interviews for the *Handbook* have revealed that, while desiring to maintain their own distinctive structures, many churches are anxious to co-operate with other Christian groups by joining, as full members, national and international organisations. A prominent member of one of the largest independent churches in Kenya emphatically remarked: 'We can no longer afford operating in isolation from other Christian groups in such a free country.' It is not impossible that the churches may come to new expressions of conciliar unity or may even find themselves able to move further on the road toward unity in diversity through joint witness.

All the churches, too, seem to be increasingly aware of the need for cultural adaptation. African songs and instruments as well as vernacular languages are being used in church services. These external changes are being accompanied by a serious study of traditional African religions and philosophy. Already a special paper on the African religious heritage has been completed by the Joint Churches Panel for the East African School Certificate. This africanisation of the very mentality of the church stems from a deepening awareness that Christianity comes to fulfill rather than to destroy. As this trend develops, the church will become less foreign and more deeply rooted in the lives of the people.

There is also a new emphasis on the importance of the laity. This is evident not only in the independent churches but also in churches which have traditionally been dominated by clerics. In fact, the Catholic Bishops of Kenya have declared 1972 the 'Year of the Laity', and have requested that every parish form a council of lay people who will participate in decision-making and planning, and that every diocese have a similar council composed of priests, sisters and lay people.

The publication of this *Handbook* at this stage of Kenya's evolution is designed to assist in this whole process of development. The material in it clearly reveals the extent to which freedom of worship is enjoyed by Kenya's people. Moreover, it shows the rapid rate at which Christianity is growing and the diverse modes of its expression. We believe that Christianity is now making a profound contribution to social life and will continue to play a positive role in nation-building. While making this study, we have sensed the movement of the Holy Spirit in the churches; we are convinced, therefore, that the future is bright with possibilities for the Faith.

Nairobi
August, 1973

David B. Barrett
George K. Mambo
Janice McLaughlin
Malcolm J. McVeigh

Preface

The Rev. Professor John S. Mbiti

This *Handbook* is a disturbing revelation. Nobody could have guessed the statistical surprises contained in this book, and, worse still, nobody has even begun to come to terms with the religious situation in Kenya. Somehow, both religious leaders (Christian, Muslim, Hindu and others) and government officials in the nation have simply assumed that there were various religious groups in the country; but exactly what they were, how many they were, what they really did, when they came into existence, what were their teachings and distribution of their membership, could only be guessed, and that very wrongly. Now for the first time we have these and many other facts in a single source of information. This is the first handbook of its nature in the whole of Africa, and one of the very few in the world. It will be greatly welcomed in Kenya and beyond.

The information contained herein shatters many preconceived notions about Christianity in Kenya, and its data leave no doubt that Kenya has become very much a Christian country. Christianity has taken on a volcanic dimension in Kenya, not only in the explosive increase of adherents, nor in its sectarian growth at the current rate of one new denomination every month, but also organisationally and in its outreach, as is witnessed by the information contained in Parts IV and V. In the first half of this century, Christianity was confined almost exclusively to education, medical work, evangelisation and to a lesser extent agricultural enterprises. The picture is now different, and the churches are involved in a vast variety of concerns ranging from internal questions like Christian music to the wider issues of society, communication and development.

This ever-expanding range of interests is clearly a sign of maturity, for the message of Christianity is the total wholeness of the individual and of society at large. The Christian faith does not only concern and cater for those who embrace it; by its very nature it is public property, hence it stretches its tendrils in every direction of human existence. This is precisely what is happening in Christian activities going on currently in Kenya.

Yet the information in this Handbook makes one wonder whether the churches have begun to realise their full potentialities and opportunities in Kenya. It calls for their joint consultation to discover themselves, to plan together and to act together, to witness together, to pool resources, and above all to thank God together for what He has accomplished through the churches within such a relatively short period in the history of Christianity in Kenya. For example, it is remarkable that the word 'church' occurs in almost every one of the denominations listed in the Handbook; and that the words 'Africa(n)', 'Spirit' and 'Fellowship' are used in about eighty of the denominational names. Do these churches really know the meaning of those four terms which seem so central in Kenyan Christianity today?

It is also very remarkable that the running of the churches in Kenya is in the hands of African Christians, with the few exceptions of the Roman Catholic Church, Anglican Church, Africa Inland Church and the Baptist Churches of Kenya whose proportion of foreign ministers to indigenous ones is still very high if not rather unhealthy for our day. Organisationally, Christianity has become an indigenous undertaking in Kenya, and nearly all the churches are sufficiently equipped in human and financial resources to run and exist on their own, as is evidenced by the 156 independent churches only two of which have staff from overseas. While lamenting the luxury of denominational divisions, it is to their credit that independent churches run their programmes and ministries without financial and personnel assistance from overseas. Surely this is something that mission-founded churches can copy and grow into.

One of the tantalising questions about Christianity in Kenya is what the causes are which have brought about this sudden increase in numerical affiliation, together with the creation of such a vast number of small church groups. The Handbook does not address itself to this question, which it will no doubt be interesting to answer in another context. But it is interesting to note that, over one hundred years after the arrival of the first Protestant missionary to Kenya, J.L. Krapf, there can still be Christian bodies in recent years which have taken titles like African God Worshippers and Religion of the Ancestral Spirits. It is tempting to think that the deep religious heritage of African peoples has prepared the ground for the ready acceptance of Christianity by African peoples. Yet this is not the place to make out a case for this hypothesis; but one feels that Christianity in Kenya (and Africa for that matter) has to come to at least dialogue terms with African traditional religion, on whose legacy it has unofficially depended so largely for its rapid expansion.

Kenya, clearly, is not ashamed of being religious, and this Handbook shows that people are not only keenly interested in religious life but are actively engaged in it.

1

Part I

Aspects of Kenyan

Christianity

Chronology of Christianity

in Kenya 1498-1972

EARLY MISSIONARY CONTACTS

1498   Arrival of Portuguese explorer Vasco da Gama at Malindi, with Roman Catholic missionaries in his company.

1542   Francis Xavier, pioneer missionary on his way to India, talks with Muslim leaders in Malindi.

1564   Portuguese viceroy of India orders Gospel to be preached around Mombasa; 1567, Augustinian monastery established there.

1592   Fort Jesus on Mombasa island begun by Portuguese; not completed till 1639.

1597   Augustinian friars at Mombasa claim 600 African converts (slaves, Swahili, and Bantu from the interior), including exiled King of Pemba.

1598   Three Augustinian priests stationed at Lamu, Pate and Faza. Muslim governor of Faza helps build church; flourishing Christian community results.

1607   Brethren of Mercy arrive in Mombasa to care for converts from Islam.

1626   Swahili sultan of Mombasa, Yusuf bin Hassan, returns from Goa as Catholic (Dom Jeronimo Chingulia), but later apostatises.

1631   'Martyrs of Mombasa': prior of Mombasa, two priests, and about 280 lay persons, massacred by Chingulia after refusing to renounce Christian faith.

1688   Mission on Faza abandoned on invasion by Arabs from Muscat.

1698   Capture of Fort Jesus by Arabs from Muscat after two-year siege.

1728   Portuguese re-occupy Fort Jesus, but soon evicted.

1740   Final extinguishing of Portuguese influence along East African coast.

1824   Temporary British protectorate in Mombasa (for two years).

1841   Representative of Bombay Government (British) established in Zanzibar.

THE MODERN ERA OF MISSIONS

1844   Arrival of Johann Ludwig Krapf, pioneer CMS missionary, at Mombasa; death of wife and child.

1846   Johann Rebmann joins Krapf, CMS station established at Rabai.

1847   Krapf translates Genesis 1-3 into Mombasa Swahili.
        Evangelistic exploration: Rebmann to Taita, Krapf to Ukambani.

1848   St. Luke's Gospel translated into Nyika (Rabai) by Krapf.

1850   Krapf translates first Kamba scriptures: St. Mark's Gospel.

1851   Baptism of first Anglican convert, a dying cripple named Mringe, by Rebmann.

21

1853	Strategy differences in CMS: inland mission rejected by Rebmann, Krapf resigns.
1860	Prefecture of Zanzibar, including Kenya, established by Holy See.
	Krapf publishes *Travels, Researches and Missionary Labours in East Africa.*
1862	Krapf returns with four missionaries of United Methodist Mission (Britain) to establish mission aimed at inland Africa. By end of year only survivor, Wakefield, settles at Ribe, near Mombasa.
1863	Zanzibar Prefecture entrusted to Holy Ghost Mission; 1883, Vicariate.
	Charles New joins Wakefield at Ribe; first baptisms, 1870.
1869	Opening of Suez Canal speeds up communications between Kenya and Europe,
1873	Death of Charles New while attempting to establish inland station.
	Treaty abolishing slave trade signed by Sir Bartle Frere and Sultan of Zanzibar.
1875	Freetown, near Mombasa, established by CMS as colony for freed slaves; 1879, first slaves baptised.
	Baptism of first Giriama converts (CMS).
1878	First translation of a gospel into Mombasa Swahili.
1883	David Koi, teacher-evangelist at Fulodoyo (refuge for runaway slaves) assassinated — Kenya's first Christian martyr.
	CMS establishes first inland extension from Coast at Sagalla.
1884	Anglican diocese of Eastern Equatorial Africa formed, including Uganda, Kenya and Tanganyika, with James Hannington as first bishop.
1885	Berlin Conference for the partition of Africa; British and German spheres of influence defined.
	British East African Association founded for development of trade.
	First ordinations of Africans to Anglican ministry: Ishmael Semler and William Jones, ex-slaves.
	First unmarried woman missionary, Miss Harvey, arrives, and begins in Freretown; twenty-three other CMS single women follow, 1888-1894.
	UMM missionaries, John and Annie Houghton, killed during Maasai raid on Golbanti, among Galla of Tana River.
	Bishop Hannington murdered in October at Mumias on his way to Buganda.
1887	Neukirchener Mission begins at Lamu, later moves to Ngao, Tana river.
1889	First modern Roman Catholic mission in Kenya begun at Kosi on Tana River, by Holy Ghost fathers; but lasts less than a year.
	Divinity training started at CMS Freetown for evangelists, later clergy.
1890	Holy Ghost fathers establish mission at Mombasa, and (1891) Bura.
1891	East African Scottish Mission station opened at Kibwezi.
	Bavaria Evangelical Lutheran Mission (Germany) opens stations at Ukambani; 1893, taken over by Leipzig Mission; 1914, turned over to AIM.
1892	Scriptures in inland languages first published: gospels in Giriama and Taita.
1893	Independent missionary Stuart Watt, with wife and family, walks from coast to central Kenya, settles at Ngelani in Ukambani.
1894	Vicariate of Upper Nile (including Western Kenya) created (Mill Hill Mission).
	Pokomo first scriptures: St. Mark's Gospel (Neukirchener Mission).
1895	Coastal Strip leased from Sultan of Zanzibar as Protectorate.
	IBEA Company sells rights to British government; protectorate of British East Africa proclaimed, covering area from Mombasa to Naivasha.
	Africa Inland Mission begins in Ukambani; founder Peter Cameron Scott dies soon after.
1896	CMS catechist Johana Gona translates St. Matthew's Gospel into Giriama.
	Beginning of railway from Mombasa into interior, built with 32,000 coolies from India.
1897	Influx of missions into Nairobi area begins: GMS (1897), CSM (1898), HGM (1899), CMS (1901), AIM (1901).
1898	East African Scottish Mission transferred to Kikuyu.
	Samuel Isenberg, Digo teacher-evangelist, killed at initiation ceremony.
1899	Railway reaches Nairobi (Mile 326), and opened to public.
1901	Railhead reaches Port Florence (Kisumu), on Lake Victoria, at Mile 582.
	Giriama Old Testament published (before New Testament completed).

Pokomo New Testament translated by Neukirchener Mission.

1902 Nyanza and Rift Valley transferred from Uganda Protectorate to Kenya.
Friends Africa Industrial Mission begins at Kaimosi.
Italian Consolata missionaries arrive in Nairobi.

1903 Mill Hill fathers from Uganda establish missions at Kisumu and Kakamega.
First Kikuyu scriptures: St. John's Gospel (CMS and BFBS).
AIM headquarters station at Kijabe opened.

1904 First influx of white settlers, from South Africa.

1905 James Mbotela of Freretown visits Britain for technical training; returns to
missionary work in central Kenya.
Missionary Board of the Church of God (Anderson, USA) begins at Kima.
First Maasai translation of a gospel.
Vicariate of Zanzibar divided; Kikuyuland becomes Mission under Consolata.

1906 Establishment of Maseno school by CMS archdeacon J.J. Willis.
South African Compounds and Interior Mission begins at Kima with Church of
God.
Seventh-day Adventists begin work at Kendu Bay, South Nyanza.
First GMS converts baptised: Wanyoike Kamawe and four others.

1907 Philip Karanja baptised as first Presbyterian convert.
Winston Churchill visits Nairobi: 'Every white man in Nairobi is a politician; and
most of them are leaders of parties'.
First baptisms by Consolata missionaries in Kikuyuland.
Independent Nilotic Mission begins work at Nyakach.
Catholic catechist Johana Owalo claims visions of africanisation of Christianity:
'Nomiya' ('The Word of God has been given to me').

1908 Further influx of white settlers to Plateau, west of Rift Valley.
Giriama Bible completed with separate publication of New Testament.
A nativistic movement, the Mumbo cult, sweeps South Nyanza.

1909 Beginning of inter-mission co-operation: United Missionary Conference held at
Nairobi. Comity areas of mission influence agreed on.
First 'Native Conference' of Kikuyu Protestant Christians at CSM Thogoto.
New Testament completed in Mombasa Swahili (CMS and BFBS).
Molonket ole Sempele, one of first Maasai Christians, sells cows, travels to
America, studies three years at Bible college.
Yohana Mbila, South African pioneer missionary at Kima, killed.
Nyeri Vicariate formed with Filippo Perlo as first vicar apostolic.

1910 First Anglican and Protestant baptisms in western Kenya at Maseno and Kima.
YMCA begun in Nairobi; building opened following year.

1911 Luo first scriptures: St. Mark's Gospel.

1912 First Methodist minister in Kenya, the Rev. Joseph Jara (a Pokomo), walks from
Mombasa to begin pioneer Meru mission.
Apostolic Faith Mission of Iowa (USA) begins work at Nyang'ori (later PAOC).
Kipsigis first scriptures, translated by Lumbwa Industrial Mission.

1913 CMS Divinity School opened in Freretown.
First Meru UMM students at Kaaga locked in burning hut; five killed.
Mathayo Onduso of Gem becomes first Christian chief in Kenya.
June 17-22: United Missionary Conference (Kikuyu I) at CSM Thogoto. Five
missions decide to federate to build one united African church.

1914 World War I begins. Kenya drawn into fighting in German East Africa.
Bible completed in Mombasa Swahili (CMS and BFBS).
Johana Owalo forms first African independent church in Kenya, Nomiya Luo
Mission.

1915 Chief Karuri of Fort Hall baptised into Catholic Church.
Federation of missions (proposed 1913) rejected by Archbishop of Canterbury
after heresy charge by Bishop Weston of Zanzibar.
Somali first scriptures: St. Mark's Gospel in Ogaden-Harti (BFBS).
Yohana Owenga of Kima dies in Congo as pioneer missionary.

1916 Mass movement into churches, Protestant and Catholic, begins in Nyanza and Central Kenya.

Roho (Holy Spirit) revival within Anglican church led by Alfayo Odongo.

1917 Mission Volunteer Carrier Corps formed in Kenya, recruiting Christians from various missions to assist military campaign in German East Africa.

1918 Kenya swept by famine, influenza and bubonic plague.

Alliance of Protestant Missions formed: AIM, CMS, CSM, UMM. Purpose: to found a united church in Kenya. Lasted until 1935.

1919 Alliance protests forced recruitment of African labour for settler farms.

1920 Kenya Colony and Protectorate proclaimed, the latter composed of Mombasa and a ten-mile strip on the Coast.

Kamba New Testament completed (AIM and BFBS).

1921 Meru first scriptures: St. Mark's Gospel (UMM).

Salvation Army begins in Nairobi, Thika, Malakisi, Embu.

First Kikuyu independent church founded near Fort Hall by Daudi Maina, later of AIPC.

1922 New Testament translated into Maasai by Tagi Oloiposioki and AIM.

Troubles in CMS over modernism; formation in Britain of Bible Churchmen's Missionary Society.

1923 British government publishes Devonshire White Paper, *Indians in Kenya*: 'Primarily Kenya is an African territory... interests of the African native must be paramount'.

Lunyore first scriptures: St. John's Gospel (SACIM and ABS).

Kavirondo Taxpayers' Welfare Association founded by CMS archdeacon W. E. Owen.

1924 Phelps—Stokes Commission visits Kenya, urges expansion of out-schools.

AIM resigns from Alliance on grounds of modernism; then returns.

Kenya Missionary Council formed for all Protestant missions, leaving Alliance freer to pursue the ideal of a united church.

1925 Jubaland (west of Juba river) transferred from Kenya to Somaliland.

First Catholic Scripture translations: OT extracts and Sunday Gospels, in Kikuyu.

1926 Rudolf Province transferred from Uganda to Kenya.

Meru made a prefecture under leadership of Mgr. A. Balbo.

First Presbyterian ordinations to ministry: Musa Gitau and seven others.

Nandi first scriptures translated.

Kikuyu and Luo New Testaments completed (Kikuyu: CMS, CSM, GMS, AIM, BFBS, main translator A.R. Barlow; Luo: CMS, BFBS).

Alliance High School inaugurated at Kikuyu by Alliance of Protestant Missions, with 26 pupils. First principal: G.A. Grieve (CSM).

1927 Holy Spirit revival in FAM, western Kenya, led by the Rev. Arthur Chilson.

Aroti (Dreamers) or Watu wa Mungu (People of God) begin to emerge in Kikuyu country and Rift Valley.

First African Catholic priests ordained: James Camisassa, Thomas Kemango.

1928 Survey of Catholic missions in Kenya by Mgr. (later Cardinal) Arthur Hinsley.

Holy Spirit revival in FAM, western Kenya, led by the Rev. Arthur Chilson.

Broadcasting begins under British East African Broadcasting Company.

1929 Kikuyu Independent Schools Association formed.

Gusii first scriptures: St. Matthew's Gospel (SDA).

Controversy over female circumcision, and membership of KCA, cause widespread secession from Anglican and Protestant missions in Kikuyu, Embu and Meru. *Muthirigu*, dance-song mocking missionaries and Christians opposing circumcision, spreads widely.

1930 Establishment in Mombasa of Apostolic Delegation of Africa for the Missions, under Archbishop Hinsley.

Muthirigu dance banned by government.

CMS Divinity School transferred from Freetown to Limuru.

1931 Bible Churchmen's Missionary Society begins work among West Suk (Pokot).

1932	Gold rush in North Nyanza for a year; over 1,000 European and other prospectors.
	Conference on Church Union held at Nairobi (CMS, CSM, MMS, AIM), resulting in pamphlet *Proposed basis of union.*
	Vicariate of Kisumu established under Mgr. G. Brandsma.
	National Holiness Association (later World Gospel Mission) begins at Kericho (1935, Tenwik).
1933	Violent controversies in western Kenya between mission adherents and Roho Christians.
	New Testament translated into Nandi by AIM.
	KISA requests Anglican bishop for ministerial training at Limuru; rejected.
1934	Conference on Christian Co-operation, Nairobi.
	First scriptures in Union Swahili.
	Boran first scriptures: St. Luke's Gospel (BCMS and BFBS).
	Murder of Anglican pastor Odongo in burning hut; followers secede as MHGC.
	'Ndaragu Forest affray': three Kikuyu Aroti prophets killed by police.
1935	Archbishop Daniel Alexander (South Africa) arrives to help Kikuyu and Meru secessionists set up an independent church.
	Christian Council for Race Relations formed by Kenya Missionary Council.
	Administration persecution of Watu wa Mungu (Aroti) increases until late 1940s.
	Schism among AIM missionaries to form Gospel Furthering Fellowship.
1936	Gospels in Kikuyu first published by Catholics.
	Visit of Edel Quinn, envoy from Ireland; local Legion of Mary begun.
	Pokot (Suk) first scriptures: St. Mark's Gospel (BCMS and BFBS).
1937	Catholic Bishops' Conference begun; 1960, becomes Kenya Episcopal Conference.
	Archbishop Alexander ordains Kikuyu priests for AOC and AIPC.
	Visit of first team from Ruanda Revival (Balokole); meetings in Nairobi, Weithaga, Kabete, and elsewhere.
1938	African members of the Christian Council for Race Relations withdraw.
	Kenya African Keswick convention at Kikuyu; Ruanda Revival speakers William Nagenda *et al.*
	International Pentecostal Assemblies (USA) begin in Kaimosi.
1939	First complete Bible in a single volume in an East African language: Nandi.
	Ruwe Holy Ghost Church formed, taking large number of MHGC members.
	St. Paul's Minor Seminary opened by Consolata fathers at Nyeri.
1940	Kenya involved in World War II, against Italians on Ethiopian and Somali borders. Later, Kenya troops serve in North Africa, India and Burma.
	Carey Francis (CMS) appointed second headmaster, Alliance High School, Kikuyu (till 1962).
1942	African Israel Church Nineveh secedes from PAOC, Nyang'ori Mission.
	Entry of Elim Missionary Assemblies (from UK) into South Nyanza.

EMERGENCE OF AFRICAN CHRISTIANITY

1943	Philip M'Inoti, first Meru Methodist minister, opens Njuri Nceke (Meru ruling elders) to Christians by entering eldership with *njuri ya mauku* (initiation swearing on a Bible).
	Formation of autonomous Presbyterian Church of East Africa.
	African Independent Church of Kenya, Kamba schism from Anglican Church.
	Kenya Missionary Council votes to become the Christian Council of Kenya (CCK).
1944	Nativistic movement Dini ya Msambwa erupts near Mt. Elgon under Elijah Musinde.
1945	African Brotherhood Church begun; largest Kamba independent movement.
1946	Jomo Kenyatta returns to Kenya from England.
	African Orthodox Church accepted into communion by Greek Orthodox Patriarchate of Alexandria (Egypt).
	Gospel Missionary Society, with 2,000 Christians, joins PCEA.
1947	Kahuhia Convention, first of many vast African-organised East African Revival conventions; movement sweeps across central Kenya.

	Establishment of Apostolic Delegation to British East and West Africa. African Christian Church & Schools, a Kikuyu secession from AIM.
1948	Kagaari Convention spreads East African Revival to Embu and Meru. New Testament in Gusii published (PAOC). Catholics first publish Gospels in Swahili. Dini ya Msambwa proscribed.
	First Balokole schisms: FHS among the Kikuyu, and CUEU among the Luo. Swedish Lutheran Mission enters South Nyanza on Anglican invitation.
1949	Large Revival convention at Kabete: 8,000 present. *African education in Kenya* published ('The Beecher Report'). Finnish Free Foreign Mission begins work, in Nyanza. African Divine Church, a secession in Maragoli from PAOC
1950	Vast Revival convention at Kikuyu (Thogoto) with 15,000 present, following East Africa-wide Kaako Convention (Uganda): theme, 'Jesus Satisfies'. Union Swahili New Testament published.
1951	Kikuyu Old Testament published (separate from NT). Luragoli Bible published (by ABS).
1952	Union Swahili Bible completed and published. Eruption of violence in Kikuyu areas: many Christians killed. October 7: assassination of Chief Waruhiu; State of Emergency declared. Society of St. Patrick for Foreign Missions begins in Eldoret, Lodwar and Kitui. Revival Within the Church founded within Anglican Church in western Kenya in opposition to Balokole. Kuhama (Migration) a spiritual movement out of the allegedly worldly Anglican Church, begins across Kenya. First signs of disaffection within Roman Catholic Church: Luo mystic Mariam Ragot attempts to found Dini ya Mariam.
1953	Catholic ecclesiastical province of Kenya formed, with one archdiocese (Nairobi) and 3 dioceses (Kisumu, Meru, Nyeri). Kikuyu independent churches (AOC, AIPC) suppressed due to closing of independent schools. *The Societies Ordinance;* registration of all churches ordered. Opening of Church House, Nairobi (CMS); first multi-storey office building.
1954	Luo Bible published (CMS, SDA and BFBS). Anglicans, Presbyterians, Methodists create St. Paul's United Theological College, Limuru. Initial book of Union Luhya Bible published (Genesis).
1955	First African bishops of Anglican Church in Kenya consecrated in Uganda by Archbishop of Canterbury: Festo Olang' and Obadiah Kariuki. Catholic diocese of Mombasa and Zanzibar erected out of archdiocese of Nairobi. First church radio studio: AIM Kijabe.
1956	Catholic Kikuyu New Testament first published. Maseno Convention, first East African Revival convention after 5 years of State of Emergency; 12,000 present. Catholic Swahili New Testament first published. Kamba Bible published (AIM and BFBS). Church Army (Anglican) begins work in East Africa. Southern Baptist Convention (USA) begins mission, known as BMEA.
1957	Maurice Otunga consecrated as first Kenyan to become a Catholic auxiliary bishop (Kisumu). Christian Churches' Educational Association formed. Large secession from Anglican Church in Nyanza: Church of Christ in Africa. T. L. Osborn crusade at Mombasa results in widespread pentecostal movement. Christian newspaper *Rock* begun by CCK (1964: *Target/Lengo*). CCK industrial mission begun in Nairobi. Church Trust (1962, Church Commissioners for Kenya) formed to handle finance and property for Anglican Church.
1958	Bible House, Nairobi, built. Second East African Revival convention at Kahuhia; 6,000 present.

Large schism from GFF, later named Good News Church of Africa.

1959   Catholic diocese of Eldoret, and Prefecture of Ngong, erected.

Missionary Aviation Fellowship commences operations.

1960   State of Emergency in Kenya declared ended.

Anglican Province of East Africa formed (Kenya and Tanganyika); L. J. Beecher first archbishop. In 1961, four dioceses were then formed in Kenya.

Establishment of Apostolic Delegation to Eastern Africa (in Nairobi).

Catholic diocese of Kisii erected.

American evangelist Billy Graham visits Kenya: crowds of 15,000 in Kisumu, and Nairobi.

Kenya Independent Churches Fellowship: first attempt to unite such bodies.

Anglicans, Presbyterians, Methodists create united parish in Lavington, Nairobi.

1961   Release of Mzee Jomo Kenyatta from detention: he exhorts Kenyans to 'forget the past' and 'love your neighbour as yourself'.

Kenya Catholic Secretariat instituted in Nairobi.

Catholic conference AMECEA constituted; 1964, office opened in Nairobi.

Butere Convention (East African Revival); 7,000 present.

1962   Television launched in Kenya, under Kenya Broadcasting Corporation; religious programmes follow.

Gospels in Luo first published by Catholics.

Bible Society in East Africa formed.

Scott Theological College (AIM) founded in Machakos.

Piga biti ('striking the beat'), spontaneous dancing movement in PCEA, begins.

Large schism from Roman Catholic Church: Legio Maria, mainly in Luo country.

Pentecostal Evangelistic Fellowship of Africa formed by union of IPA and EMA.

1963   Founding of St. Thomas Aquinas Seminary (Catholic) outside Nairobi.

John Kamau appointed as first African general secretary of CCK.

Catholic diocese of Marsabit erected.

Voice of Kenya broadcasting service begun, with regular religious programmes.

December 12: Kenya's Uhuru, Independence.

KENYA SINCE INDEPENDENCE

1964   John Mpaayei first Kenyan appointed executive secretary of the Bible Society in East Africa.

Vast East African Revival convention: the Mombasa Convention at Buxton School, with 20,000 present. Theme: 'Jesus the Way'.

Kufufuka (Awakening) revival movement begins from Kampala and Mombasa, spreads throughout Kenya.

Catholic diocese of Marsabit erected.

Increase in use of African traditional medicine: John Bosco Bakari, alias Ali bin Kabwere, travels through Central and Rift Valley Provinces selling 'holy water'; 1965 arrested at Nakuru.

All Africa Conference of Churches moves headquarters to Nairobi.

Meru Bible published (MMS and BFBS), with a Catholic edition for Diocese of Meru.

1965   Establishment of Apostolic Nunciature in Kenya.

East African Church Union Conference, Dodoma, Tanzania (CPEA, PCEA, MCK, Lutherans, Moravians, also some Independents: ACC&S, CCA).

First Mijikenda independent church, World Revival Union Evangelistic Church.

Pokomo schism from Methodist Church; registration as Tana River Independent Church refused by government.

Witchcraft eradication (witchfinding) movement on the Coast for several years, led by Kajiwe (later imprisoned).

1966   Death of Mwangi wa Nyarari, Kenya's greatest volunteer evangelist, apostle to Kithangari, Meru.

AACC Churches Training Centre (broadcasting) opened in Westlands, Nairobi.

Kikuyu Bible published in a single volume.

United Liturgy for East Africa produced (Anglican, Presbyterian, Methodist).
Wokofu African Church, a schism from the Salvation Army.

1967 AMECEA Plenary Meeting, 'Pastoral perspectives in Eastern Africa after Vatican II'.
Methodist Church in Kenya created; Ronald Mng'ong'o first president.
Church union consultations over several years finally end in failure.
Catholic edition of 1952 BFBS Union Swahili Bible published.
World Methodist Congress meets in Nairobi.
World Council of Christian Education meets in Nairobi.
PCEA General Assembly issues challenge for churches to unite by Easter Day, 1972; 1970, call for covenant on final date of union; 1972, because no response, PCEA withdraws from East African Consultation on Church Union.
Trinitarian Bible Society (UK) publishes Pokot New Testament after BFBS rejects orthography.

1968 United Bible Societies open Africa Regional Office in Nairobi.
Catholic diocese of Nakuru, and Prefecture of Lodwar, erected.
The Societies' Act (1968) becomes law, requiring annual church returns.
Vapostori (Apostles, Shona Christians from Rhodesia) begin near Nairobi.
Launching of village polytechnics scheme by NCCK.
1,200 African pastors (Kenyans) attend 4-day Kenya Pastors' Conference at Kenyatta College; totals: CPEA 186, PAG 160, PEFA 144, AIC 129, CGEA 100, PCEA 88, SA 50; and 131 Independents.
Pentecostal evangelist Oral Roberts conducts healing rallies in Nairobi; 10,000 present daily.
Management of 4,000 mission-founded primary schools transferred to Kenya government; churches appointed sponsors responsible for religious instruction.
Dini ya Msambwa again declared a prohibited society.

1969 Catholic diocese of Machakos erected, with first Kamba priest Rafael Ndingi as first bishop, consecrated in Uganda by Pope Paul VI.
Crossroads Mission held in Nairobi by Africa Enterprise.
Kuria first scriptures translated: St. Mark's Gospel.
Regional church leaders' conferences on nation-building begun by NCCK: 1969 Mombasa (30 participants), 1969 Eldoret (200), 1970 Kakamega (160), 1970 Embu (55), 1971 Embu (40).
Use of indigenous musical instruments in churches gathers momentum across Kenya.
Department of Philosophy and Religious Studies begun at University College, Nairobi; by 1971, 135 undergraduates.

1970 Bishop Festo Olang' elected first Kenyan Archbishop in newly-formed Church of the Province of Kenya (Anglican).
World Alliance of Reformed Churches meets in Nairobi.
Bible Society of Kenya inaugurated.
Largest East African Revival Convention ever, held at Kikuyu: 30,000 present.
Visit to Mombasa of evangelistic ship m/v Logos (Operation Mobilization).

1971 Anglican Consultative Council, representing world Anglicanism, holds its inaugural meeting in Limuru.
Christian Communications Congress (Africa) held at Limuru.
Archbishop Makarios, President of Cyprus, baptises 5,000 into African Orthodox Church, lays foundation stone of seminary.
Bishop Maurice Otunga appointed first African Catholic Archbishop of Nairobi.

1972 Dr. Samuel Kibicho appointed first African principal of St. Paul's United Theological College, Limuru.
Laity Year proclaimed by Catholic Church.
Catholic catechetical congresses: National (April), AMECEA (December).

A History
of the Kenya
Churches

The history of the planting of Christianity in Kenya and its subsequent expansion is similar to that in Black Africa as a whole—an unsuccessful attempt in the 16th century, virtual obliteration, a second attempt in the 19th century, and finally massive expansion in the 20th.

Early Catholic missions, 1498-1889

In 1498, the Portuguese explorer Vasco da Gama reached the Kenya coast at Malindi, and in his company were several Roman Catholic missionaries. Although they did not remain to take up sustained evangelistic work, sporadic contacts were made with the local population. The pioneer missionary, Francis Xavier, stopped on the coast in 1542 on his way to India by sea and had conversations with Muslim leaders in Malindi. Some time later, in 1598, three missionary priests moved to Lamu, although their work only endured for a few years. Next we hear of Augustinian friars who built a church on Mombasa island at the site of the present Old Customs House, and soon were claiming 600 converts from among the local populace. Other churches were built in Mombasa by the Portuguese, including one superintended by the Brothers of the Misericordia (Mercy), which also cared for orphans and widows; the Chapel of Our Lady of Good Hope, the ruins of which may be seen on the island's golf course; chapels at Shimanzi and Makupa; and the so-called Portuguese Cathedral which by 1846, according to a French traveller, had deteriorated into use as a cattle shed.

29

No records remain of any further Catholic activity after the Arabs regained control of Mombasa in 1729. Virtually nothing is known of Christian work during this period, and indeed there probably was none.

Although there remained a handful of Christians, mostly traders from India, organised missionary work in Mombasa had thus collapsed long before the arrival of the first Protestants. Even fifty years later in 1890, when the first Catholic missionaries of the modern era began work in Mombasa, we read that the only Catholics they found were fifty Goans in the town itself.

Protestant pioneers, 1844-1890

In 1844, a German Lutheran preacher employed by the Church Missionary Society of London, Johann Ludwig Krapf, landed at Mombasa, and thus the modern era of Christianity in East Africa began. Except for Fort Jesus and some remnant church buildings erected by the Portuguese, there were no traces of the earlier Christian period. Krapf preached the Gospel to all who would hear; but only one person, a dying cripple named Mringe, was baptised as a result of his stay. Along with his co-worker the Reverend John Rebmann, who arrived in 1846, Krapf pioneered in languages, being the first to produce a Swahili dictionary and to translate the Scriptures. He wanted to move inland where it was healthier and the people were more receptive; but his comrades, particularly Rebmann, opposed this plan as impractical, whereupon Krapf left the CMS and sailed from Kenya. Remaining behind also were the graves of his wife and child who had died of fever two months after their arrival.

Back in Europe, Krapf wrote his famous book, *Travels, Researches and Missionary Labours*, as a result of which the British United Methodists commissioned him to pioneer a new mission, whose object would be to reach the Galla empire which was believed to stretch from Kenya to Ethiopia. This Methodist mission, launched in 1862, suffered a series of disasters over a period of fifty years. Frustrated in the attempt to move inland, the mission settled at Ribe, barely eight miles from the CMS post at Rabai. At the end of the first year, only one missionary, Wakefield, had survived. More recruits then came, and the Methodists gathered together a small community at Ribe. When they finally reached the Galla people at the Tana river, John and Annie Houghton were speared to death by raiding Maasai. Fever and disease took a fearful toll, and in this the Methodists were only slightly less unfortunate than the CMS.

A new vision of missionary work was brought soon after by Sir Bartle Frere, governor of Bombay in India and a convinced evangelical Christian. While in East Africa to sign a treaty ending the slave-trade, he took the trouble to examine the state of the missions. The CMS and the Methodists, he reported, lacked direction; they were preaching the Gospel and were pioneering in linguistics, but were not meeting other pressing needs of the day. They were too 'bookish' and not sufficiently practical. Frere recommended that they should take an active part in opposing slavery and the slave-trade. Heeding Frere's advice somewhat reluctantly, the CMS in 1875 founded Freretown, which was to serve as a colony for freed slaves across from Mombasa island. In a short time, new settlements were established to accommodate the streams of such persons brought to Freretown. Added to those brought by British warships were slaves who had escaped from local slave-owners. Missionaries were concerned about possible violence from Arab masters, and were worried concerning the legality of harbouring runaways; but African Christians were far less inhibited, hiding runaways by the hundreds. One Giriama Christian, David Koi, was invited to become teacher of a large settlement of these runaways at Fulodoyo. An Arab gang swept through the huts in 1883 and beheaded Koi, who thus became Kenya's first Christian martyr. Out of Freretown and other communities of ex-slaves came Kenya's first schools, the first African teachers and evangelists, and in 1885 the first ordained ministers. By 1890, there were about 2,000 baptised Anglicans and a few Methodists, Kenya's first form of organised and enduring Christianity.

Three Catholic societies, 1889-1940

To understand the evangelistic initiatives of the Roman Catholic Church in Kenya, which date from 1889, it is necessary to go back thirty years to 1858, when Bishop Armand Maupoint of Reunion sent his vicar-general Fava to explore the possibilities of opening a mission at Zanzibar. After he had begun a base of operations there in 1860, a mission from France, the Holy Ghost Fathers, was asked to assume responsibility for the work. Three years later two priests, Anthony Horner and Edward Baur, together with two brothers, settled on the island.

In 1883 Zanzibar (called Zanguebar until 1906) was raised from the rank of prefecture to vicariate and John de Courmont was named vicar apostolic. He was a man of energetic disposition and was anxious that the work should be expanded. A Holy Ghost priest, A. Le Roy, made the first visit to Mombasa in 1885, and during the next five years a series of expeditions to the Kenya coast was made by Courmont, Le Roy and Charles Gomneginger. But it was not until 1889 that the first mission was begun, at Kosi on the Tana river; it lasted less than a year, and in 1890 a permanent mission was established at Mombasa.

In 1891 the Holy Ghost Mission opened a station at Bura, near Voi, and by 1899 they had reached Limuru, west of Nairobi.

Ukamba country was explored in 1907, and the construction of the Kabaa station and school in Machakos district was initiated in 1913. By the beginning of World War I in 1914, there were Holy Ghost missions among the Kikuyu, in Ukambani, at Bura and Mwanda in Taita, and at several points along the coast.

From 1896-1913, Bishop Emile Allgeyer served as vicar apostolic, then was succeeded by Bishops John Neville (1913-1930) and John Heffernan

(1932-1945).

In 1902 Bishop Allgeyer welcomed Fathers Tommaso Gays and Filippo Perlo of the Missionary Institute of the Consolata, a new society from Turin in Italy, and they began work in Kikuyuland. Before long there was disagreement between the Consolata mission and the Holy Ghost mission as to the boundaries of their respective work. The conflict was not finally resolved until 1931.

In 1906, Propaganda in Rome divided the Vicariate of Zanzibar, entrusting Kikuyuland to the Consolata Mission. Three years later the Nyeri Vicariate was formed with Filippo Perlo as its first vicar apostolic. In 1907 the first baptisms were recorded, and the year 1911 saw the initial entry of four Consolata priests into Meru district. During 1922, Father Maraviglia opened the first out-stations at Baricho and Kianyaga, in Embu district, and before the end of 1926 Meru had become a prefecture under the leadership of Mgr. G. Balbo.

The work was greatly aided by several orders of sisters, the first to arrive being the Daughters of St. Vincent in 1903. By 1918 there was formed a sodality of African sisters called Immaculate Heart of Mary Sisters, which became a religious congregation in 1927. The first African mother superior was Sister Giulia Wamboi, elected in 1946.

The training of an African clergy was also given priority. An initial attempt to open a seminary was made at Tuso in 1914. The year 1927 saw the ordination of James Camisassa and Thomas Kemango, the first African Catholic priests in Kenya. In 1939 a much more adequate training facility, St. Paul's Minor Seminary, was opened at Nyeri.

In the meantime western Kenya, then known as Kavirondo, was being evangelised by St. Joseph's Society for Foreign Missions of Mill Hill, England. The White Fathers in Uganda, finding themselves at a disadvantage as a predominantly French society in a British territory, had requested the help of the Mill Hill Mission to show that Catholic religion was not synonymous with French nationalism.

The Vicariate of the Upper Nile was created in 1894 and placed under the leadership of Bishop Henry Hanlon of the Mill Hill Mission. The southern boundary of the new vicariate included a line through Lake Victoria from Kampala along the Anglo-German border to Kikuyu; the eastern border ran from Kikuyu through Mt. Kenya to Kafa, north of Lake Rudolf; and the northern and western boundaries went from Kafa through Favira to Kampala.

·In addition to Bishop Hanlon, the pioneer party consisted of four priests: Thomas Matthews, James Prendergast, Gregorius Kestons and Luke Plunkett. Leaving Mill Hill in May 1895, they travelled to Zanzibar and Mombasa and thence trekked on foot through the heart of Kenya, arriving at Kampala in September.

Their early activity was concentrated in eastern Uganda, and it was not until the turn of the century that they were able to begin work in Kavirondo. A conflict with the Holy Ghost Mission regarding the eastern boundary of the vicariate was settled in 1902. The same year saw the arrival of the first Franciscan Sisters of St. Mary's Abbey, Mill Hill, and the initial visits of Fathers Matthews and van den Bergh to Nakuru and Biermans and Kallen to Nandi country. By 1903 a mission had been established at Kisumu, and the following year van den Bergh was posted there. From then on the work progressed rapidly. The first station at Kakamega was opened in 1906, and within three years there were four mission centres operating in Kavirondo. In 1908 Plunkett moved to Nakuru to build a church to meet the needs of a community of 30 Catholics, who until then had been attending a monthly mass in the railway station.

During 1910 Father G. Brandsma entered Kisii country, and the following year a new mission was started at Nyabururu. After the retirement of Bishop Hanlon in 1911, John Biermans was named vicar apostolic. He served with distinction until 1924 when he was succeeded by Mgr. J.W. Campling.

Kisumu was elevated to the rank of vicariate in 1932, and thereafter considerable advance was made under the leadership of Mgr. Brandsma as vicar apostolic.

The proliferation of Protestant missions, 1890-1940

The missionary movement in Kenya changed radically after the beginning of the colonial era, particularly when the new rail line had extended inland to Lake Victoria. Many new missions came in, not all waiting for the railway. The CMS moved to Taita in 1883, and a German and Scottish mission started work in Ukambani. Stuart Watt, an independent missionary, walked from the coast to Kikuyuland with his family in 1893 and then settled in Ukambani. When the railway reached Nairobi in 1899 and Kisumu in 1901, Protestant missions sprang up in every direction.

Once established and settled in, missionaries began asking themselves the question: how could the Gospel be spread most effectively? The freed-slave colony phase was over. New ways had to be tried. In 1895, a pioneer missionary of the Africa Inland Mission, Willis Hotchkiss, arrived. The AIM's policy at first was solely evangelism, as had been that of Krapf and Rebmann. Six years later, Hotchkiss returned to Kaimosi with the Friends Africa Industrial Mission, for he had come to believe that evangelism alone was not enough. He wanted to introduce practical training, teaching men to be carpenters and brick-makers and farmers. A CMS missionary, J. J. Willis, had another method: at Maseno he introduced elite education. He invited Luo chiefs to send their sons to the new school, but only the dispossessed and unwanted were sent. Fifteen years later the chiefs discovered that Willis' disciples were displacing the traditional chiefs. Western education turned out to be the most popular missionary method, especially when combined with medicine and evangelism.

As different missions flooded in, the need for co-operation became apparent. The early meetings were pre-occupied with dividing the field, to avoid overlapping in their work. Willis foresaw a more distant danger, namely that each mission would eventually establish its own denominational African church. Could not the missions, he asked, build together in such a way that one African Church would be the result? On two occasions, in 1913 and 1918, missionaries hammered out plans to make real such a dream. Strangely enough, Willis' dream became a reality in India, where missionaries were struck by Kenya's initiative and launched what eventually became the Church of South India. But in Kenya the plans came to naught.

The missionaries themselves were a varied group. Most were ordinary people, without great gifts. Some displayed fundamental human weaknesses. One early missionary at Kima was accused of immorality. A CMS missionary at Sagalla shot a local inhabitant, putting the mission in jeopardy. Some missionaries were harsh, others cruel; but most are remembered for their love and self-sacrifice.

Interestingly enough, not all of the early missionaries were whites. One of the first Church of God missionaries at Kima was Yohana Mbila, a Shangaan from South Africa. Mbila introduced the modern hoe, and was the outstanding Kima evangelist in the early days. As a result of his example, Mbila's first convert, Yohana Owenga, journeyed into Congo with a missionary party in 1914. Owenga and a number of white missionaries perished on a further journey in 1915, when Kima itself was only nine years old. Another African, Shadrack Mliwa from Taveta, accompanied the first CMS missionaries into central Kenya, settled at Kerugoya, lived out his years there, and died in the early 1960s surrounded by a large and flourishing Kikuyu church. Many of the first African Christians were spiritual giants; others embodied the tensions of the old and new ways of life. Nairobi's first African minister, the Reverend Simeon Kalume, is said to have regularly worn *hirizi* (charms) around his waist to protect himself while preaching the Word of God. Yet it was through such pioneers as these, ordinary and extraordinary, black and white, that Kenya was evangelised, and a foundation was laid for modern schooling and medicine.

Around the year 1915, massive numbers began to pour into the Protestant churches and schools. Before World War I, attendances of pupils in outschools had fluctuated considerably—one hundred pupils one month, and twelve pupils the next. After 1920 the demand for schools became acute and attendances rose and became more regular. The 1920s and 1930s were years of great growth for all the missions and churches in central and western Kenya.

The response differed from place to place. The Maasai and Mijikenda of the coast did not readily accept the Gospel, although evangelists and missionaries had visited them from earliest times. Some places received a greater concentration of missionaries and Christian witness than others. The Tugen,

Elgeyo and Marakwet tribes were entered relatively early on after World War I, and the drier northern area of Samburu and Pokot in the 1930s; but the Turkana, Boran and Somali have only recently had regular contact with Protestant missions.

In these early years Christianity was preached as the way both to heaven and to a better life on earth. For African Christians, the Christian life brought sweeping changes to their traditional systems. Christians initiated many new customs: burial of the dead, preaching in villages, washing with soap, attending and founding schools, wearing clothes, riding bicycles, praying with eyes closed, visiting clinics. Christians looked different, used different music, played different games, and even smelt different from their neighbours. Christians in inter-tribal schools like Maseno, Alliance High School, and Buxton School, Mombasa, learned to understand and appreciate persons of other tribes.

Like their Catholic counterparts, Protestant missions over the years achieved enormous numerical success, but there were many problems. The early vision of working towards a single United African Church was soon shattered. The Alliance of Protestant Missions was badly shaken when the CMS, which had suffered a split in Britain in 1922 during the controversy over modernism, split in Kenya too with the appearance of a new Anglican body, the Bible Churchmen's Missionary Society. Again, the AIM withdrew from the Alliance in 1924, once more over alleged modernism, and the Alliance was badly paralysed until the AIM reconsidered its position and rejoined.

At this period, Kenya appeared to be rapidly moving towards political control by the white settler community. As a result, missions made strong representations in London, and some of the more repressive measures were withdrawn or modified.

Several missionaries of that period are still remembered for their espousal of African interests. Archdeacon Owen of Kavirondo insisted on the rights of the African majority, openly opposing a fellow missionary, Arthur, in London in 1923. Owen also began the Kavirondo Taxpayers Welfare Association, a highly successful organisation aimed at teaching civics and aiding economic development. For a time, Owen became very popular with Africans, but by 1930 most missions were being considered anti-african. After 1935, even Owen had become suspect in the eyes of many Africans.

The Protestant missions, then, founded church organisations and gave a certain measure of responsibility to Africans, but there was increasing discontent which occasionally erupted in one way or another. In 1927, a sudden surge of revivalism swept the Friends Africa Mission in Kaimosi, later known as the Holy Spirit revival. Prophets emerged denouncing sin and leading people to mass public confession. African elders in the Friends church confronted the prophets and demanded an end to this embarrassing practice. Large numbers refused, and seceded to begin the Roho (Holy Spirit) churches of western Kenya, which gradually became a powerful spiritual force. An important leader in this movement was Alfayo Odongo Mango, an Anglican minister burned to death in 1934 in a clash with other Anglicans over land. By 1940 at least a dozen separatist churches had broken off from the Protestant missions in the west.

Meanwhile, Kikuyu and Meru Christians in central Kenya were also protesting, and with greater vehemence. In 1929, African politicians turned their attention to a new challenge: Protestant missions, they declared, had no right to forbid the tribal custom of female circumcision. A number of missions then demanded that African Christians fall into line and affirm their loyalty. As a direct result, in a vast number of areas Protestants left the churches in large numbers, and formed the nationalist independent churches, AIPC and AOC, together with their independent schools organisations. Profound bitterness divided the so-called 'political' Christians from the 'loyal' Christians. The political Christians attempted to negotiate with the Anglican church, but the negotiations collapsed when the Anglican bishop refused to ordain priests who would not be under his direct supervison. In 1935, Archbishop Alexander of the African Orthodox Church (South Africa) visited Kenya, and two years later ordained Kikuyu priests who then set up independent churches which asserted that Christianity and traditional ways were not necessarily diametrically opposed at every point.

At the close of this period in 1940, therefore, Protestantism had become seriously divided, and substantial separatist bodies existed in both western and central Kenya.

Development and africanisation of the churches

It would be wrong to imagine that the africanisation of the churches in Kenya is only a late development. There were African Catholics as far back as 1590, and African Protestants dating from Mringe's baptism in 1851. There were African martyrs like David Koi, African clergy like William Jones and Ishmael Semler (Anglicans ordained in 1885), and the vast majority of evangelists and catechists since those days have always been Africans. There have been many outstanding and internationally-known African pioneers, too. Yohana Owenga preached in the Congo, before he died on safari in 1915. Many Africans took seriously the evangelistic challenge from the beginning: the Kikuyu pioneer evangelist Mwangi wa Nyarari walked 150 miles into Meru country to pioneer the Gospel there in 1928. A vast team of Kamba lay evangelists visited areas far and wide to preach the Gospel and plant churches in Ukambani and Tharaka. These are but a few examples among many. The expansion of Christianity in Kenya has been largely an African achievement due to African initiatives, aided at this point and that by expatriate missionaries.

But in recent decades, missionary leadership in the churches has been more seriously challenged. Sometimes this has occurred violently. A flood of independent churches during and after World War II has followed the example of the independents of the 1920s and 1930s. Some have resulted from personal rivalry and struggles for leadership. Some have reflected the racial tension then existing in Kenya. Others have come from revivals and the explosion of new Spirit movements in the mission churches.

Even the larger and more established mission churches did not remain unaffected. Nominal Christianity in the Anglican, Presbyterian and Methodist churches was abruptly called in question by the East African Revival, an African lay movement of renewal which had begun in Ruanda in 1927 and spread to central Kenya by 1937. Although the Revival had little effect on other denominations, it had a profound overall effect in western and central Kenya from 1947 to 1950, and subsequently throughout the country, and widespread and undisputed African leadership broke through for the first time. Since these conventions were entirely organised by Africans from mission churches, they gained invaluable experience in administration and planning. The Revival re-interpreted the faith and produced its own unique theology, hymnody, evangelism and organisation. Salvation was no longer only an event at the beginning of the convert's life; instead, it became interpreted as the continual transforming work of Jesus, saving the Christian day by day through repentance and faith. Repentance, the keynote of the Revival, involved public confession of sin and restitution, as it had in the earlier Holy Spirit revival of 1927.

Christianity's most persistent problems in Kenya have been its relation to the nationalist movement. At first Roho churches and mission churches alike tended to remain aloof or even hostile. The vast majority of other independent churches, on the other hand, were staunch exponents of nationalism right up to the time of Independence in 1963. During the Emergency in the 1950s, these differences produced acute hostility. Revival Christians were persecuted by freedom fighters and oath administrators for being traitors. Some Revivalists had indeed backed the colonial government, although the majority were pacifists and refused to join either side. In 1952 the colonial government banned the nationalist schools and churches, forcing their Christians either to lapse or to join one or other of the mission churches; but after Independence, the tables were turned and the independents flooded back. Many Christians today either avoid political affairs altogether, or are uncritical supporters of whatever authorities are in power. A number of Christian leaders have not been afraid to speak their mind. The Rev. Gideon Nzoka of the Africa Inland Church, and Canon Awori of the Anglican Church, stood with a foot in both camps, as Owen had done thirty years before. And throughout this whole period and up to the present day, a good number of Kenya's leaders have been devout and practising Christians.

The crisis of the Emergency propelled the churches into new and more relevant forms of service. As a result of the social disruption of those days, Christians began to be seriously concerned with social, economic and political problems in the country. The Christian Council of Kenya began industrial ministries in Kenya's mushrooming cities and urban areas. And in the city of Nairobi itself, community centres were opened by the churches to serve the social and educational needs of the masses migrating from the countryside.

In terms of organisation, rapid progress has characterised both the Protestant and Roman Catholic churches since 1950. The Society of St. Patrick for Foreign Missions, from Ireland, arrived in 1952, providing missionaries for Kenya's growing Catholic parishes in Eldoret, Lodwar and Kitui. The following year, 1953, the Vicariate of Zanzibar became the Archdiocese of Nairobi under Archbishop John J. McCarthy, formerly Vicar Apostolic of Zanzibar, and two years later the Diocese of Mombasa-Zanzibar was separated from Nairobi.

Even before Independence in 1963, there had been a proliferation of new posts of leadership and their gradual assumption by Kenyans. In 1957 Maurice Otunga was consecrated auxiliary bishop in the Diocese of Kisumu, the first African Catholic bishop in Kenya; and in 1971 he succeeded to the post of Archbishop of Nairobi. At the present time Kenyan bishops serve in the Dioceses of Nyeri, Kisii, Machakos, Eldoret, Nakuru and Nairobi.

A similar development has been evident among Anglicans and Protestants. The Presbyterian Church of East Africa was formed in 1943 and its first African moderator, Charles M. Kareri, was elected in 1964. In 1955 the Anglican Church appointed Festo Olang' and Obadiah Kariuki as assistant bishops in the Diocese of Mombasa, with both becoming diocesan bishops in 1961 in the newly autonomous Church of the Province of East Africa. All six Anglican bishops in Kenya in 1972 are Kenyans, and five of them are Africans. Bishop Olang' was elected Archbishop of Kenya in 1970. The first Kenyan appointed general secretary of the Christian Council of Kenya was John Kamau, who has served in that capacity since 1963. The autonomous Methodist Church in Kenya was created in 1967, with a Kenyan, Ronald Mng'ong'o, as its first president. The year 1971 witnessed the autonomy of the Africa Inland Church, under the leadership of the Rev. Wellington Mulwa, served by the Africa Inland Mission. Similar steps have been taken by virtually all the other major Protestant missions and churches over the past decade.

In sum, then, Christianity has been remarkably successful in Kenya, and has clearly been adopted as their own religion by the majority of Kenya's citizens. Twenty thousand stone, thatch or other types of church building or site dot the countryside. The Christian faith is taught in the country's schools. The cities of Nairobi and Mombasa abound with religious activities in the streets, in the markets, in the bus stations, and in the churches themselves. The Spirit of God who led the early pioneers and who guided the subsequent thousands of prophets and evangelists is thus still guiding the churches today.

FOOTNOTE

This history of the churches in Kenya was compiled from two drafts, one on the Protestant churches by the Rev. William B. Anderson, the other on the Catholic Church by the Rev. Fr. S. Clements. A number of persons then read the combined document, and substantial additions were made.

There is at present no single published history of the churches, Protestant or Catholic, in Kenya. There are however a large number of detailed accounts of individual missions and local churches, including a fair number of unpublished papers by Kenyan students and churchmen. All of these are listed in the Bibliography in Part VII of this Handbook.

The best introduction to the subject is still Roland Oliver's classic, *The Missionary Factor in East Africa*, which sets the Kenya story in the whole East African context. It deals with events up to 1949.

Kenya's Cultural Heritage and Tradition

Donald R. Jacobs

As far as cultural heritage and tradition are concerned, Kenya must be one of the most varied and colourful places in the world. The nation is a mosaic of many cultural traditions, or better yet, a kaleidoscope in which there is constant movement and activity. One phrase can summarise the cultural scene in this lovely land: 'infinite variety.'

Four thousand years ago, hunters lived on the plains reaping a harvest from what must have appeared to be unlimited wild game. They were click speakers who are now represented in East Africa by a few remnants like the Sandawe and Hadza in central Tanzania. About three millennia ago, the southern Cushites, who farmed and tended cattle, moved in from the north. They were probably the first 'settled' people. They had a highly sophisticated religious system, which no doubt had a profound effect on those who were to arrive later. These Cushites now appear as peoples in remnants such as the Wambulu, Mbugu, and Iraqw. Then followed the great Bantu migrations, probably from the south moving up along the coast. In the early part of the Christian era, they were carving out their farms on the rich Kenya land and were developing institutions which persist into our time. At about the same time, Nilotic and Paranilotic peoples moved into the area from the north and occupied the expansive land areas which they required for their great herds of cattle. They brought Sudanic cultural traditions with them, which added yet another interesting factor to the already varied scene. While they were consolidating their interests in the plains areas of central and western Kenya, another group known as the eastern Cushites came into the plains region to the northeast. The most significant group of these people in Kenya are the Galla, who continue to participate in the life of the nation.

These represent the large migrations. Each wave of people contributed yet another cultural and religious tradition. They lived shoulder to shoulder in this land of promise. While each was unique, they influenced one another through wars, trade, and sometimes intermarriage. For at least four thousand years, Kenya has been at the very centre of the movement of peoples on the eastern seaboard of Africa. It is a land where the major cultural groups from the north, south, and east meet. In order to understand the infinite sociological and religious variety, it is necessary to keep this phenomenon of multiple migrations constantly in mind.

Arab traders were next to arrive, coming from Arabia and lands to the north. Wherever they settled for purposes of trade, they established centres of Islamic culture. These traders influenced the coast and inland populations to an astonishing degree. In fact, the Arab settlements became the nuclei of a new culture, the Swahili people, whose language was basically Bantu but whose vocabulary included many Arabic words and concepts. It is interesting that the word used by the Swahili for 'civilization' was, and still is, *ustaarabu* (Arabness).

Before long European ships bearing the Portuguese flag began to bring their cultural cargoes to the shores of Kenya. Then followed the British and the Germans. The British at first thought of Kenya as a barren tract of land that one had to go through to get to Uganda. And go through they did, but the Kenyan peoples very smartly taxed these safaris and at times engaged in armed struggle with them. When the British built the railway from 1896-1901, they introduced yet another cultural tradition into Kenya, the Asian culture. They transported into Kenya many thousands of Asians, mostly Indians and Goans, to assist in the construction of the railway. Many of these were Hindus, a new feature on the Kenyan religious map.

Then from 1904-1930 came the European settlers, whose influence upon all of the peoples was completely out of proportion to their numbers. They were not content simply to settle but organised and administered the entire nation. This they did with great diligence under the British flag, and made thereby a significant imprint upon the life of the nation.

At about the same time, wave after wave of European, American, and Canadian missionaries moved in, built churches, schools, and hospitals with great devotion, and succeeded in making an unprecedented impression upon almost every ethnic group in Kenya.

As though the picture were not yet complete, modern technicians and technocrats are bringing yet another factor onto the scene. These are the American businessmen, Israeli builders, the United Nations' communications experts, Scandinavian agricultural specialists, and all who bring yet another new process or product into the nation.

And lastly, just to sprinkle the cultural meal with some pepper, almost a half million tourists come to Kenya each year to add their bit to an already highly seasoned Kenya.

Each of these communities makes a contribution to national life and each in turn is being influenced by the Kenya ethos, which is becoming yet another part of the picture.

Given this very diverse scene, it is little wonder that the religious picture portrayed in this Handbook should be so varied. Every group makes its own contribution to the total, ever-changing picture.

Until very recently, all of the peoples nurtured by this land were extremely religious people. They lived their lives in the acknowledged presence of God and of the spirits. They did not treat their faith as a matter of convenience, but their religious concepts formed the core around which they organised their lives. The Kenyans of the 1970s likewise demonstrate an extraordinary interest in religious matters. In the nation's schools, colleges, and the university, religious subjects are popular; and community life is very definitely based upon religious considerations.

Yet it will never be possible to pour all Kenyans into the same religious mould. And it would be a great loss to Kenya and the world at large if this should be attempted.

The Christian faith today is not the novelty it was fifty years ago, an innovation for a few which could be tried and then thrown away if not useful. It is now being authenticated by people in practically every ethnic group in the Republic.

The religious scene in Kenya is therefore of great interest, not only for Kenyans but for the church international which can witness in this land the undeniable presence of Jesus Christ at work in a most amazing fashion.

LITERATURE

There are a number of published studies on Kenyan peoples, some of which deal with individual tribes, others with a wider survey. Most of these are listed in the Bibliography (Part VII); for these, we give below only author and date. For a general survey of the peoples of Kenya, there is G.W.B. Huntingford, 'The peopling of the interior of East Africa by its modern inhabitants', *History of East Africa*. Vol. I, ed. R. Oliver & G. Mathew (Oxford: Clarendon, 1963), p. 58-93. Several works deal with both the *Kikuyu* and *Kamba:* Hobley (1922 and 1967) and Middleton & Kershaw (1965). Goldthorpe (1958) provides notes on the *Kikuyu, Nandi* and *Kipsigis.* The *Pokomo, Nyika* and *Taita* are treated in Prins (1952), while studies of Kenyan Paranilotic peoples are presented in two works: G.W.B. Huntingford, *The Southern Nilo-Hamites* (London: Ethnographic Survey of Africa, 1953), and Pamela Gulliver & P.H. Gulliver, *The Central Nilo-Hamites* (London: Ethnographic Survey of Africa, 1953). The following studies of individual peoples are useful: *Dorobo:* G.W.B. Huntingford, 'The social institutions of the Dorobo', *Anthropos,* 46, i/ii (1951), p. 1-48; *Elgeyo:* Massam (1927); *Gusii:* R.A. Levine, *Nyansongo, a Gusii community in Kenya* (New York: Wiley, 1966); *Kamba:* Lindblom (1920), and D.R. Jacobs (1961); *Kikuyu:* Kenyatta (1938), and H.E. Lambert, *Kikuyu social and political institutions* (London: Oxford, 1956); *Kipsigis:* Peristiany (1939); *Kuria:* Ruel (1965); *Luhya:* Wagner (1949 and 1956), and J. Osogo, *A history of the Baluyia* (New York: Oxford, 1966); *Luo:* B.A. Ogot, *History of the Southern Luo* (Nairobi: East African Publishing House, 1967); *Marakwet:* Whyte (1971); *Meru:* Bernardi (1959); *Maasai:* A.H. Jacobs, 'The traditional political organisation of the pastoral Maasai' (Dissertation: Oxford University, 1965), and O. Sankan, *Maasai* (Nairobi: East African Literature Bureau, 1971); *Nandi:* Huntingford (1953); *Samburu:* Spencer (1959); *Somali:* Lewis (1955); *Swahili-Shirazi:* Salim (1972); *Turkana:* P. Gulliver, *The family herds: a study of two pastoral tribes in East Africa, the Jie and Turkana* (London: Routledge and Kegan Paul, 1955).

President Kenyatta opens Parliament March 1972 in presence of religious leaders.
(right): Catholic Archbishop, Anglican Archbishop, Muslim Chief Kadhi; (in front of them) Maasai
traditional priest, PCEA Moderator.

Church and State in Kenya

Bishop Rafael Ndingi

Church and state are each a society, and independent societies at that. For the purpose of this article, we define society as 'an organised group of persons or communities, with the same common end, using the same means to attain that end, governed by the same rules for the public (common) good of its members both in person as well as in property, not only here and now but also in the future, as far as it can be foreseen, provided and guaranteed by a clearly defined goal of the group'.

It is clear from the foregoing that the common goal of the society is the key point; and since the group, whether ecclesiastical or civil, is composed of men, man and his welfare are the central issue. It is on him that society focuses attention. In the Book of Genesis we are told that 'God created man in the image of Himself... male and female He created them... God blessed

43

them saying, "Be fruitful, multiply, fill the earth and conquer it". 'For man to fulfil the mission given by his Creator, he needs the help of other men in an organised form, that is society. Any society to be true must include the necessary elements: persons, a community of aim, a stability of bond, a co-operation of effort, and authority. These elements go to safeguard man's rights and to make him capable of executing those duties which flow directly and simultaneously from his very nature; they are, therefore, universal and inalienable,, namely the right to be fruitful, to multiply and to conquer the earth. The church is primarily concerned with the spiritual welfare of man as entrusted and commissioned to her by Christ. The state by the will and agreement of its people, expressed in an agreed form, is charged with the material welfare of man. Each of these two societies pursues its objectives according to circumstances of time, place, means and ability, but the fundamentals are the same—the common good: the one the spiritual common good, and the other the material common good.

Here in Kenya we stand in a very good position as far as church-state relationships and co-operation are concerned. This co-operation is in accordance with the African traditional motto, *Harambee* (Let us pull together). It is in fields such as education, medicine and social work in its various forms, and in other related fields, that church and state in Kenya are noticeably co-operative. This working together did not only begin after Kenya gained its political independence, but was also present during the colonial period. There is however no doubt that church-state relationships and co-operation were highlighted and received a new impetus from Kenya's first president, Mzee Jomo Kenyatta, when in 1964 he called upon the people of Kenya and other residents, irrespective of race, religion or origin, to join hands to build our country. The church took this call as a challenge. More than ever before the church became involved in harambee projects. Many harambee schools, both primary and secondary schools, and nursery centres, were started by the church under the general direction and advice of the Kenya Ministry of Education. Many such schools continued to function for a long time before they received government aid.

The church has used and still uses its personnel and other resources to teach the *wananchi* (citizens), particularly in remote areas, and thus helps them to eradicate ignorance, poverty and disease. Here the church's role is not only the spiritual welfare of man, but the welfare of the whole man. It is true to say that the first secondary schools in the country—Kabaa/Mangu and Alliance High Schools—were pioneered and completely run by the churches. Within these three, to name only a few, have been educated many high-ranking personalities both in the church and state. Such leaders have had great influence in creating the good climate prevalent in Kenya today.

At the present time all institutions for higher education are fully government-aided, and church and state personnel work together in the true spirit of Harambee. The church still provides high- and middle-level manpower whenever possible to fill any gaps for which the state does not have personnel. The co-operation that exists between church and state in Kenya is outstandingly demonstrated also in the medical field. Not only does the state encourage the use of church doctors, but it also pays them a decent wage. The state in recent years has introduced free medicine; but, cognisant of the importance of medicine reaching every *mwananchi* no matter in what remote area he might live, the state has permitted and encouraged church personnel to continue their efforts to eradicate disease. In this connection special tribute is due to Catholic sisters and their helpers, and to Protestant missionaries in rural areas, who labour in difficult circumstances to help us build 'the Kenya we want'.

The African is fundamentally a believer in God. The Kenya government is aware of this fact, and has guaranteed freedom of worship and religion in our constitution.[1] The state has always called upon religious leaders to offer prayers and supplications at every official opening of Parliament and at many other public functions. A further proof of this good church-state relationship is the fact that today in our freely and democratically elected Parliament there sits one Member who is also a church minister, something which is rare indeed, even in developed countries.[2]

It seems to me that the Kenya government policy of *Turudi Mashambani* (Let us return to the fields) had already been anticipated by the National

Prayer service over Kenya Army Colours 1970. Left to right Commander Kenya Army, acolyte. Catholic Archbishop Otunga, Anglican Archbishop Olang', Senior Chaplain to the Forces, Muslim Chief Kadhi el-Farsy.

Christian Council of Kenya in its village polytechnic programme of rural development. Here the NCCK provides special opportunities for youths who have little or no chance of obtaining higher education, or employment at the completion of primary education. Village polytechnic schools give practical training in such fields as carpentry, masonry, building, domestic science, tailoring, and in many other areas. A candidate who has satisfactorily completed the course usually becomes self-employed in rural areas. Such opportunities reduce the influx of youths into the cities and towns, thus saving public authorities many headaches. Government co-operation and help in church-sponsored schemes such as village polytechnics is granted in various ways.

We are all aware of the great efforts the government is making to uplift the socio-economic condition of the *mwananchi*. It is satisfying to note that, in spite of the underlying emphasis on communal development in all the harambee projects, the government has encouraged, supported, assisted and requested private undertakings. This is in keeping with the church's teaching on social development and the ownership of private property, particularly as formulated by Pope John XXIII in his encyclical letter on 'The social question in the light of Christian teaching' (*Mater et Magistra*). The late Pope, speaking on the right ordering of values between private initiative and the intervention of public authorities in the field of economics, wrote: 'It should be affirmed that the economic order is the creation of the personal initiative of private citizens themselves working either individually or in association with each other in various ways for the prosecution of common interests'. In other words, in all efforts to encourage and promote socio-economic development, the 'principle of subsidiarity' should be maintained. The higher should not do what the lower can and should do. Church and state relationships in our country, based on the principle of subsidiarity, have to date steered on the right course. This is a remarkable achievement, and one which other states might well look on with envy.

In recent years the church, both in Kenya and in the world at large, has shifted her perspective from purely religious matters to the secular domain. This is in keeping with the Second Vatican Council's emphasis on the unity of man. It is also in keeping with Christ's work of redemption, for He came to redeem man. The church continues the work of Christ, of bringing man to Christ and Christ to man. The same God creates both the soul and the body. As in the Old Testament, God hates and resents our worship—our cultic performances—when and if they are separated from our secular obligations. Hence it seems that good relationships between church and state for the service of man flow from the nature of these two societies and the design God had in creating man. The Bible tells us that 'God created man in His own image and likeness'. God endowed man with capacities of knowing and loving Him. Furthermore, He gave man a clear mandate to master nature by subduing it, thus using it not only for his own development, but also for that of the whole human community.

In conclusion, let me say that while we are all appreciative of and alive to our present good church-state relationships, the church should never be so identified with the state that she cannot speak to it, nor be so remote from the state that again she cannot speak to it, particularly in matters of conscience of the faithful.

I take this opportunity to express my deep regret that no real or official national ecumenical movement exists as yet in Kenya.[3] I am aware of real but private ecumenical efforts which have borne much fruit to date. But what prevents us from establishing an official church channel for working together at the grass roots? Is it shame or fear? Is it lack of faith, or of charity or of courage? Do we not believe Christ when He says: 'I shall be with you all the time until the end of the world'? Whatever the cause may be, let us ignore it and begin now, and we shall never regret it.

Independence celebration, 12 December 1963. Left to right Mgr. Njenga now Catholic bishop of Eldoret, Bishop Otunga, two Muslim Sheikhs, Chaplain Page, Anglican Bishop Kariuki, Governor of Kenya Malcolm MacDonald, H.R.H. Prince Philip, Mzee Kenyatta.

[1] The relevant section in *The Constitution of Kenya* is reproduced below.
[2] The Rev. Thomas Kalume, MP, is an ordained Anglican clergyman.
[3] The only organisations in this category by March 1972 are: Joint East Africa Religious Education Committee (and Joint Panels of CCEA/KCS for primary and secondary syllabuses), Joint Refugee Committee, SODEPAX Communications Working Group for Africa. For details, see Directory of Christian Organisations in Kenya.

FREEDOM OF WORSHIP IN THE CONSTITUTION

Extract from The Constitution of Kenya (1969), *chapter V* 'Protection of fundamental rights and freedoms of the individual', *78 'Protection of freedom of conscience'*

78. (1) Except with his own consent, no person shall be hindered in the enjoyment of his freedom of conscience, and for the purposes of this section the said freedom includes freedom of thought and of religion, freedom to change his religion or belief, and freedom, either alone or in community with others, and both in public and in private, to manifest and propagate his religion or belief in worship, teaching, practice and observance.

(2) Every religious community shall be entitled, at its own expense, to establish and maintain places of education and to manage any place of education which it wholly maintains; and no such community shall be prevented from providing religious instruction for persons of that community in the course of any education provided at any place of education which it wholly maintains or in the course of any education which it otherwise provides.

(3) Except with his own consent (or, if he is a minor, the consent of his guardian), no person attending any place of education shall be required to receive religious instruction or to take part in or attend any religious ceremony or observance if that instruction, ceremony or observance relates to a religion other than his own.

(4) No person shall be compelled to take any oath which is contrary to his religion or belief.

(5) Nothing contained in or done under the authority of any law shall be held to be inconsistent with or in contravention of this section to the extent that the law in question makes provision which is reasonably required—

(a) in the interests of defence, public safety, public order, public morality or public health; or

(b) for the purpose of protecting the rights and freedoms of other persons, including the right to observe and practise any religion without the unsolicited intervention of members of any other religion,

and except so far as that provision or, as the case may be, the thing done under the authority thereof is shown not to be reasonably justifiable in a democratic society.

(6) References in this section to a religion shall be construed as including references to a religious denomination, and cognate expressions shall be construed accordingly.

2.0 million pupils study in Kenya's schools.

Religious Education
in the Schools

Thomas Farrelly

Historically the Christian missions have played a leading part in the development of education in Kenya. In fact, it would be no exaggeration to say that the educational system was a creation of the Christian missions. This is not to ignore the existence of informal education in traditional African society or of Islamic learning at the Coast. However, formal education in the modern sense, and the schools in which it is given, owe their origin in Kenya to the Christian missions.

Government involvement in education was slow to develop during the colonial period. Even as late as 1949 when the Beecher Report (*African Education in Kenya*) was written, the churches still bore the burden of supporting and staffing most of the schools in Kenya. By 1964, the writers of the Ominde Report (*Kenya Education Commission Report*), the first national report on education since Independence, felt that 'the time had come to relieve the churches of their remaining responsibilities for the management of maintained schools' (Paragraph 30). The report, however, recommended 'arrangements to secure the continuing participation of the church in the religious life of the school' (Paragraph 30). This was in fact the policy which inspired the framing of the clauses in The Education Act 1968 concerning religious education. We may refer to this policy as one of 'participation'.

The policy of participation rejects on the one hand a purely secular school system, such as that followed in some other countries. 'We do not see fit to recommend for Kenya', says the Ominde Report, 'the extreme secular solution adopted in some other countries' (Paragraph 72). On the other hand, it also rejects the opposite solution found in countries with an established state religion: 'We wish to dissociate religious teaching in schools from the particular objectives of any church' (Paragraph 72). The policy of participation is embodied in The Education Act 1968 by the institution of sponsorship for primary schools and by granting representation to the former managers on the boards of governors of secondary schools and teachers' colleges.

The Act gave the former managers of primary schools the role of sponsorship, while management was transferred to the local authorities and later to the central government. The aim of sponsorship was to ensure 'that the religious traditions of the schools should be respected' (Section 8). The Act also stipulated that the granting of sponsorship should depend on the wishes of the community served by the school.

Thus participation of the churches in education at the primary level is exercised mainly through sponsorship. This involves responsibility for maintaining the religious traditions of the school. The meaning of sponsorship is further clarified by a ministerial circular which recognises that some approved syllabuses will include 'teaching closely connected with the pastoral aspects of religion' (Circ. 68/19). At the same time, the clause concerning the wishes of the community indicates that the Act sees the school as serving the whole community and not the adherents of one particular church.

It is noteworthy that religious education is the only teaching subject specifically mentioned in The Education Act 1968. This is an indication of the importance which the Government of Kenya attaches to the subject. In general the Act did not change the position of religious education in the schools; it merely gave its statutory benediction to the already existing situation. It did not make religious education obligatory, as did the 1944 Education Act in Britain. However, Section 26 assumes that religious instruction and worship will be provided by schools. Secondary schools and teachers colleges, as well as primary schools, come under the provision of this section, which refers to all 'public' schools, i.e. schools maintained from public funds.

Thus the Act and regulations assure the place of religion in the schools, under the control of the Minister, while safeguarding the rights of parents, of the local community, and of the churches. Unlike some other countries which exclude all church influence from the educational system, Kenya offers the churches the opportunity of participation in the education of the country's youth. Thus the churches are free to contribute their experience, expertise and personnel to the immense task of religious education in the country's 6,000 primary schools and 800 secondary schools.

Although relieved of responsibility for the management of maintained schools, the churches have retained their educational structures to promote religious education and to deal with the many unaided secondary schools—*Harambee* schools—with which they are still involved. There are two main church structures concerned with education. On the Protestant side there is the Christian Churches' Educational Association, and on the Catholic side there is the Kenya Catholic Secretariat. Each of these has its national office in Nairobi headed by an educational secretary general. The secretaries general provide liaison with the Ministry of Education at national level. Before the passing of The Education Act 1968, church managements were represented at district level by education secretaries. Now their functions are greatly reduced and they work in an honorary capacity, since the government grant-in-aid for their support has been withdrawn.

Of growing importance, however, is the team of religious education advisers in both organisations. They are called directors in Catholic dioceses, and a national director of religious education in the Catholic Secretariat co-ordinates their activities. They are the counterparts of the government inspectors of schools. The advisers perform a very useful service, particularly for primary schools, by working closely with their counterparts in government service. Their activities include the organisation of in-service courses and the provision of advice and information for teachers.

The churches are also making a contribution to religious education by means of research and curriculum development projects. The CCEA Curriculum Development Project assists in the production of syllabuses and materials for schools. The Catholic Secretariat provides a similar service. In addition, the Kenya Episcopal Conference is actively planning a national pastoral and research centre which will include a religious education section. On the East African level, the Pastoral Institute of Eastern Africa at Gaba, Kampala, has a religious education department which offers a one-year course for teachers and conducts research and curriculum development projects. This is a Roman Catholic institution which works closely with other churches and with ministries of education.

In Kenya, co-operation between the Christian churches is an outstanding feature of religious education work in recent years. It has grown, particularly in the last four years, through the work of the Joint Secondary Panel for Religious Education. The greatest achievement of this panel has been the development of common syllabuses acceptable to both the Protestant and Catholic churches. A joint panel for primary schools has recently been established. A similar structure for East Africa is known as the Joint East Africa Religious Education Committee. Another result of co-operation has been the setting up of the National Association of Religious Education Teachers, (NARET), which aims to stimulate interest in religious education and to assist teachers by means of talks, discussions and courses.

Participation of the churches in education has been greatly facilitated by the Kenya Institute of Education. It has proved to be the bridge joining the educational structures of the churches and of the government. The KIE Religious Education Panel works closely with the church panels already referred to. In this way religious education syllabuses have been produced which are more relevant to the needs of students in East Africa.

The major problem for which a solution must now be found is the provision of textbooks and materials for the new syllabuses. Since the syllabuses have been prepared specifically for East Africa, special textbooks will also be needed. The Joint Secondary Panel have decided to meet this need by sponsoring the preparation and publication of textbooks for the new EACE (East African Certificate of Education) syllabus. Each book will be written jointly by a Protestant and a Catholic author. The Joint Panel itself will not publish the books, but is acting as an intermediary to bring the authors and publishers together and as an advisory body to assist the authors.

It is noteworthy that all the work outlined above is being done with a minimum of finance and a minimum of permanent staff. Thus the panels are made up almost entirely of practising teachers and tutors who serve on the panels in an honorary capacity. On the government side, there was no inspector of schools in charge of religious education until the present writer was appointed in January, 1971.

Teachers of religious education in secondary schools are educated either in the Department of Philosophy and Religious Studies at the University of Nairobi, or in the Religious Education Department of Kenyatta College. It is encouraging for the future of religious education to note that enrolment in both departments is high. Primary school teachers are prepared for the teaching of religious education in primary teachers' colleges.

The same interest in religious education is to be noted in the numbers taking it in public examinations where it is an optional subject. During 1971, a total of 20,464 candidates entered for the subject in the examination for the East African Certificate of Education. Close on 10,000 candidates take it in the Kenya Junior Secondary Examination. At Higher School Certificate level, a total of 179 school candidates and 349 private candidates sat for the subject in 1970.

To conclude, a word should be said about the contribution of religious education to the curriculum in Kenya. The obvious contribution of religious education to the education of good citizens need not be stressed. The value of religion in character-building and in the fostering of high moral standards has always been recognised. However, the value of religious education in preparing the pupil to take his place in society in Kenya today has other aspects also. Three of the most important may be noted here, namely, education for unity, education for change, and education in the African cultural heritage.

Religious education contributes to unity by the fact that it accustoms pupils to think of brotherhood under God, irrespective of race or tribe. It contributes to education for change by equipping the pupil with a view of the world which provides stability in the midst of change, when things seem 'to fall apart'. Finally, it provides continuity in culture by stressing what is most fundamental in African culture, namely religion. This basic sympathy for African culture is shown by the inclusion of a paper on African Traditional Religion in the EACE syllabus for religious education.

DOCUMENTATION

We reproduce below extracts concerning religious education from four documents: *The Education Act 1968, The Education (Education Standards) Regulations 1968, Kenya Education Commission Report* (1964), and *A statement by the Christian Church in Kenya* (1963).

THE EDUCATION ACT 1968

Part III — Management of Schools
8. (1) Where a transferred school was managed by a church, or an organisation of churches, and it is the wish of the community served by the school that the religious traditions of the school should be respected, the former manager shall be appointed by the local authority to serve as the sponsor to the school.
    (3) Where the former manager of a transferred school has been appointed by the local authority to serve as the sponsor to the school—
    (a) the Teachers Service Commission, or any agent of the Teachers Service Commission responsible for the assignment of teachers to schools on behalf of the Teachers Service Commission, shall assign teachers so far as may be compatible with the maintenance of proper educational standards at the school and the economical use of public funds, with the agreement of the sponsor.
    (b) the sponsor shall have the right to use the school buildings free of charge, when the buildings are not in use for school purposes, after giving reasonable notice of his intention to do so to the Headmaster of the school:
        Provided that any additional expenses and the cost of making good any damage incurred during or in consequence of the sponsor using the building shall be defrayed by the sponsor; and
    (c) religious instruction shall be given at the school in conformity with a syllabus prepared or approved under regulations made under Section 19 of this Act after consultation with the sponsor.

Part V — Inspection and Control of Schools
    (19) The Minister may make regulations with respect to the conduct and management of schools and such regulations may—
    (b) provide for the preparation or approval of curricula, syllabuses, books and other educational materials.

Part VIII — Miscellaneous
26. (1) If the parent of a pupil at a public school requests that the pupil be wholly or partly excused from attending religious worship, or religious worship and religious instruction, in the school, the pupil shall be excused such attendance until the request is withdrawn.
    (2) Where the parent of a pupil at a public school wishes the pupil to attend religious worship or religious instruction of a kind which is not provided in the school, the school shall provide such facilities as may be practicable for the pupil to receive religious instruction and attend religious worship of the kind desired by the parent.

THE EDUCATION (EDUCATION STANDARDS) REGULATIONS 1968

5. The curriculum of a school, the syllabuses used in any school and the books or other teaching aids used in connexion with such syllabuses shall be such as the Minister is willing to approve; but in a sponsored school, syllabuses, books and other teaching aids used for religious education shall be those prepared or recommended by the sponsor and approved by the Minister.

KENYA EDUCATION COMMISSION REPORT, Part I (1964)

The Constitution

Our approach must be the approach of the secular state, pledged to respect the convictions of persons of all religions, and of none. To the secular state, the use of any public service to entrench the claims of any religion is repugnant. Consequently, we have had to reconsider the whole question of the relationship of Church and State in education. (Para.8)

Religion and national unity

One possible misunderstanding must be disposed of at the outset. In Kenya, there is no question of the worship of the state taking the place of the worship of God, or of nationalism supplanting religion. The Constitution of Kenya very clearly establishes freedom of conscience and worship as being among the fundamental rights of Kenya citizenship. As we see it, therefore, the problem we have to consider is one that accepts the existence of different religions and denominations in Kenya as a given fact in the life of the nation.

There is, unfortunately, ample historical evidence of the divisive influence of religion in many countries in the world, Kenya not excepted. One of the main arguments advanced to us by witnesses against Church participation in education was the inter-confessional rivalry, and indeed enmity, which has been the experience in many parts of Kenya. Fortunately, we were satisfied that these hostilities are now a matter of history and we have been impressed not only by the extent of interdenominational co-operation in the Protestant sections of the community that has arisen under the auspices of the Christian Churches' Educational Association, but also by the clear evidence of a spirit of partnership between Catholics and Protestants.

Religious instruction in schools

The content and nature of religious instruction must be treated as an academic subject on educational lines. To make this clear, we feel that we must draw a distinction between the educational mission of church or mosque and the purpose of a school. A church (using this term to include all religious organisations) is primarily entrusted with the pastoral care of its members, the extension of membership to others and the instruction of those seeking membership. Accordingly, its educational mission is linked with conversion, an increase of faith and the exposition of doctrine. A school, on the other hand, is dedicated to growth—growth of mind, body and spirit. Salvation, in the specific religious sense, is not its purpose or concern.

It will be seen, therefore, that we do not see fit to recommend for Kenya the extreme secular solutions adopted in some countries and that we wish to dissociate religious teaching in schools from the particular objectives of any church, and to apply to it the best that can be found in the way of modern educational principles and practice. (Paras. 69-72).

A STATEMENT BY THE CHRISTIAN CHURCH IN KENYA (1963)

(The statement, of which we reproduce here about a quarter, was signed by the Bishop of Mount Kenya, chairman CCEA, and the Archbishop of Nairobi, chairman Kenya Episcopal Conference).

The Church

The Church has a divine mandate to teach all men and has inalienable rights in the education of her children. She is concerned not only with faith and morals but also with the whole of man's life since all human actions have an inevitable bearing on God's purpose for man. By its nature and mission the Church is committed to education as the search for truth and the process by which man comes to maturity and responsible participation in society.

54

The State

The Church recognises the State under God has responsibility to ensure that adequate facilities are provided for the education of all its children and its young people and, indeed, all its citizens.

Continuing service of the Church

Now that the task of building a nation is being undertaken by a government of the people themselves, the Churches as voluntary associations of citizens wish to make their maximum contribution. We would work for mutual understanding and unity within a national system of public schools, respecting the rights of non-Christian parents. As the State takes over more and more responsibility for the administration of schools the position of the Church in educational matters must be safe-guarded to ensure that she can carry out her divine commission and give service of the highest quality. When the people so wish the resources of the Churches should be used for school management.

Conclusion

In Kenya today an educational system closely adapted to the changed circumstances and needs of the country must be worked out; such a system would take into account the best traditions of the people. With all this the Church is in complete sympathy and pledges the fullest co-operation. Her concern is that the full religious development of her children be assured. The Church is convinced that an educational system without religion can bring only disaster whereas a system with religious foundations will be the greatest assurance of the well-being of the country.

TABLE 1

DEVELOPMENT IN EDUCATION IN KENYA, 1961 - 1971

	1961	1962	1963	1964	1965	1966	1967	1968	1969	1970	1971	1972	Growth %
PRIMARY EDUCATION													
Schools			6,058	5,150	5,078	5,699	5,959	6,135	6,132	6,123	6,372	6,500	4.1
Pupils	870,448	935,766	891,553	1,014,719	1,042,146	1,043,416	1,133,179	1,209,680	1,282,297	1,427,589	1,525,498	1,630,000	6.9
Teachers				27,828	30,592	33,522	35,672	37,923	38,305	41,278	49,396	55,000	20.0
SECONDARY EDUCATION													
Schools			151	222	326	400	542	601	708	783	809	830	3.3
Pupils	22,167	26,586	30,120	35,921	47,976	63,193	88,779	101,361	115,246	126,855	140,722	150,000	11.0
Teachers			1,530	2,000	2,494	3,004	4,053	4,645	5,260	5,881	6,371	6,900	8.3
TEACHER TRAINING													
Colleges			37	35	33	33	28	28	27	27	27	27	0
Pupils			4,119	4,849	5,355	5,474	5,904	6,634	7,145	8,017	8,628	9,200	7.6
Teachers			354	316	366	400	424	468	515	575	605	630	5.2
TRADE & VOCATIONAL													
Schools			7	8	8	8	7	11	10	10	10	10	0
Pupils			1,022	1,043	1,247	1,349	1,479	2,036	2,344	2,359	3,051	3,500	
Teachers			267		133		94	130	145	141	182	200	
HIGHER EDUCATION													
Pupils:													
Kenya Polytechnic					1,146	1,540	1,811	1,889	2,006	2,858	2,811	2,800	
Mombasa Technical Institute							472	490	623	883	953	1,000	8.0
University of Nairobi			471	536	662	826	1,021	1,297	1,478	1,906	2,553	3,400	34
Overseas education	1,576	1,576					4,413	3,643	2,852	1,993	4,331		

Notes

1. The final column shows the annual growth rate, per cent, from 1970 – 1971.
2. The figures for 1972 are rough projected estimates only, based on the rates in the final column.
3. Sources: *Ministry of Education Annual Report 1970* (Nairobi: Government Printer, 1972), p.95, past *Reports.*

TABLE 2
RELIGIOUS SPONSORSHIP OF PRIMARY SCHOOLS IN KENYA, 1971

1. **CHURCH SPONSORSHIP** — **4706**
   - a. Catholic Church in Kenya — 1876
   - b. CCEA (Christian Churches' Educational Association) — 2613
     - Church of the Province of Kenya (Anglican) (CPK) — 775
     - Africa Inland Church (AIC, AIM) — 642
     - Presbyterian Church of East Africa (PCEA) — 275
     - East Africa Yearly Meeting of Friends (EAYM) — 254
     - Methodist Church in Kenya (MCK) — 166
     - Pentecostal Assemblies of God (PAG) — 124
     - Church of God in East Africa (CGEA) — 96
     - Salvation Army (SA) — 96
     - Africa Gospel Church (AGC, WGM) — 68
     - Lutheran Church in Kenya (LCK) — 30
     - Reformed Church of East Africa — 29
     - CCEA jointly-sponsored schools — 21
     - African Christian Church & Schools (ACC&S) — 20
     - Pentecostal Evangelistic Fellowship of Africa (PEFA) — 6
     - Bible Fellowship Church — 6
     - African Brotherhood Church (ABC) — 3
     - Seventh-day Adventist (one school only) — 1
     - Independent Presbyterian Church — 1
   - c. Independent (non-members of CCEA) — 217
     - Seventh-day Adventist Church (SDA) — 155
     - Elim Missionary Assemblies (PEFA) — 40
     - African Brotherhood Church (ABC) — 19
     - Baptist Churches of Kenya (BCK) — 2
     - Church of Christ in Africa (CCA) — 1
2. **NON-CHRISTIAN RELIGIOUS SPONSORSHIP** (Muslim, Hindu) — **10**
3. **NO RELIGIOUS SPONSORSHIP**
   - Government, local government, municipal, county, DEB — 1407

TOTAL PRIMARY SCHOOLS IN KENYA — **6123**

Notes
1. Except in the case of the handful of jointly-sponsored schools, the CCEA does not sponsor schools on its own accord, but acts on behalf of the denominations themselves.
2. A large number of schools without formal religious sponsorship (category 3 above) were originally begun as independent schools by the major African independent churches (AIPC, AOC), and are still closely linked with them.
3. No Muslim or other religious groups sponsor schools in the legal sense, though they have a few private schools
4. In addition, there are a few other private schools not included in this table.
5. In addition to the AIC/AIM schools shown, there were 25 others in Baringo not listed on government records in 1970.

TABLE 3

DISTRIBUTION OF CHURCH-SPONSORED SCHOOLS BY ADMINISTRATIVE AREAS, 1970-71

	PRIMARY EDUCATION (Standards I-VII, ages 7-14)					SECONDARY EDUCATION (Forms I-VI, ages 15-20)								
	Primary schools:					Secondary schools:			Church-linked schools				Enrolment	Teachers
Children Under 16	Total	Church-sponsored		Enrolment	Teachers	Total Maint'd & Ass'd	Unaided (Harambee)		Maintained		Unaided			
		RCC	CCEA						RCC	CCEA	RCC	CCEA		
1	2	3	4	5	6	7	8	9	10	11	12	13	14	15
Nairobi 183,900	103	28	17	61,238	1,844	65	28	37	6	0	4	0	23,695	1,118
Central Province 887,700	1,008	418	466	349,378	10,129	191	70	121	24	27	34	50	28,953	1,306
Kiambu 247,700	287	150	133	102,776	2,909	66	27	39	9	9	14	10	12,140	534
Kirinyaga 112,300	122	34	55	31,429	1,051	18	7	11	3	2	5	7	2,569	121
Murang'a 236,500	277	92	153	94,613	2,578	50	17	33	7	11	7	23	5,456	250
Nyandarua 96,700	108	46	49	34,713	1,089	8	4	4	1	0	0	0	1,376	56
Nyeri 194,500	214	96	76	85,847	2,502	49	15	34	4	5	8	10	7,412	345
Coast Province 423,100	442	50	147	83,983	2,699	49	23	26	4	4	0	3	11,815	490
Kilifi 142,300	146	37	70	20,895	699	9	4	5	1	2	0	0	1,301	49
Kwale 97,100	105	10	20	13,854	548	6	2	4	0	0	0	0	854	34
Lamu 9,700	11	0	0	962	35	1	1	0	0	0	0	0	41	2
Mombasa 91,900	47	1	5	26,164	742	22	9	13	2	0	0	3	8,257	345
Taita 56,200	83	2	52	18,218	538	9	5	4	1	2	0	0	1,207	52
Tana River 25,900	50	0	0	3,890	137	2	2	0	0	0	0	0	155	8
Eastern Province 976,900	1,313	341	477	289,867	8,361	136	45	91	11	18	20	30	17,343	750
Embu 94,800	120	54	57	29,295	816	20	9	11	0	0	5	6	2,517	114
Isiolo 13,800	9	0	0	2,530	79	1	0	1	0	0	0	0	83	4
Kitui 170,400	227	67	55	42,615	1,269	15	7	8	3	3	0	0	2,052	88
Masaku (Machakos) 374,800	548	133	180	130,337	3,612	53	14	39	4	7	6	9	7,754	314
Marsabit 22,900	14	11	3	2,148	74	1	1	0	0	0	0	0	154	6
Meru 300,200	395	76	182	82,942	2,511	46	14	32	4	8	9	15	4,783	224
North-Eastern Prov. 121,900	20	0	0	3,432	116	1	1	0	0	0	0	0	154	7
Garissa 33,300	9	0	0	1,628	54	0	0	0	0	0	0	0	0	0
Mandera 46,800	6	0	0	874	32	0	0	0	0	0	0	0	0	0
Wajir 41,800	5	0	0	930	30	1	1	0	0	0	0	0	154	7
Nyanza Province 1,104,800	1,315	495	389	234,912	7,263	133	46	87	12	21	17	18	16,656	773
Kisii 388,100	502	185	105	84,867	2,902	47	15	32	6	7	5	4	5,133	205
Kisumu 190,600	195	42	133	41,481	1,175	26	10	16	1	5	3	5	3,979	195
Siaya 190,500	224	95	104	48,213	1,338	23	9	14	2	6	6	4	2,849	137
South Nyanza 335,600	394	173	47	60,351	1,848	37	12	25	3	3	3	5	4,695	.236
Rift Valley Prov. 1,101,400	1,085	292	575	202,992	6,289	104	42	62	4	9	21	19	15,412	702
Baringo 81,000	92	13	79	12,244	385	6	4	2	0	2	2	0	822	44
Elgeyo Marakwet 77,500	77	19	43	11,673	354	10	4	6	2	0	4	2	1,091	43
Kajiado 41,200	40	11	17	7,627	229	3	1	2	0	0	0	0	604	25
Kericho 255,500	274	41	139	53,344	1,745	25	9	16	1	3	1	12	2,833	123
Laikipia 33,500	41	27	11	7,981	296	3	2	1	0	0	4	0	4,957	211
Nakuru 144,400	133	53	64	37,885	993	26	8	18	0	0	0	0	867	37
Nandi 102,000	133	46	67	23,272	735	10	5	5	0	3	1	4	1,071	63
Narok 60,800	45	18	22	5,965	235	3	2	1	0	0	0	0	427	18
Samburu 33,800	22	14	8	2,079	90	1	1	0	0	0	0	0	75	3
Trans Nzoia 65,100	67	16	20	15,286	429	6	3	3	1	0	0	1	926	35
Turkana 69,600	13	0	8	1,409	67	1	0	1	0	0	0	0	89	4
Uasin Gishu 96,300	119	23	80	21,191	629	8	2	6	0	0	8	0	1,417	86
West Pokot 40,700	29	11	17	3,036	104	2	1	1	0	0	1	0	233	10
Western Province 727,000	837	252	542	201,787	4,778	104	45	59	12	23	6	29	12,827	735
Bungoma 191,000	241	83	126	58,398	1,519	26	12	14	2	7	5	9	3,311	153
Busia 103,800	136	84	37	27,813	772	14	9	5	6	3	1	1	2,010	85
Kakamega 432,200	460	85	379	115,576	2,487	64	24	40	4	13	0	19	7,506	497
Totals for Kenya 5,526,500	6,123	1,876	2,613	1,427,589	41,479	783	300	483	73	102	98	149	126,855	5,881

Notes

1. The statistics above apply to the year 1970. Annual increases as follows are taking place (as shown in Table 1, final column); primary schools 4%, enrolments 7%, secondary schools 3%, enrolments 11%. This means on average for the whole country, a couple of hundred new primary schools a year, and 20 or so new secondary schools a year. In most districts therefore, the number of schools in 1972 is not likely to have changed from the figures shown.
2. Column 1 gives the total number of children under 16 in each district, based on the 1969 Kenya population census.
3. Data in columns 2, 5, 6, 7, 8, 9, 10, 15, are taken from the *Ministry of Education Annual Report 1970*, Tables 5, 7, 18. The figures for enrolment (columns 5, 14) and teachers (columns 6, 15) refer to all schools, both church-sponsored and other.
4. The management of all primary schools was taken over by government in 1968. In all schools begun by churches, (column 3, Roman Catholic Church; column 4, Protestant and Anglican Churches through the CCEA), the churches retain legal responsibility as sponsors, entailing control of the religious part of the syllabus. (See preceding article and extracts from *The Education Act 1968*).
5. Secondary schools are now divided into two categories. (1) *Maintained* and *assisted* schools (column 8) are managed through boards of governors on which the former managers are usually represented. Where these former managers were churches, there usually remains considerable church influence, though not control or sponsorship (such schools are shown in columns 10 and 11). (2) *Unaided* or *harambee* schools (column 9) receive no government support and are run privately by local communities or churches. Columns 12 and 13 show the number of Catholic and Protestant *harambee* schools (totals, 98 and 149 respectively, in 1970).

TABLE 4

RESULTS IN BIBLE KNOWLEDGE IN KENYA SECONDARY SCHOOLS, 1969 - 1971

Year	*CANDIDATES*		*RESULTS* (Percentage passes)		
	EACE Candidates	*Candidates in Bible Knowledge*	*Passes with Very Good (Grades 1-2)*	*Passes with Credit (Grades 1-6)*	*Passes (Grades 1-8)*
1969	20,224	13,952	4.0	40.2	72.9
1970	22,931	16,407	4.9	45.2	75.3
1971	27,533	20,170	5.0	41.5	72.0

Notes

1. Candidates are those who sat for the joint examination for the East African Certificate of Education and School Certificate, Kenya, in secondary schools at the end of Form IV. This certificate correspondes to General Certificate of Education 'O' (Ordinary) level in England and Wales.'
2. The above figures include private candidates numbering around 25 per cent.
3. 'Passes' include Passes with Credit, and 'Passes with Credit' include Passes with Very Good.
4. The figures for 1969 and 1970 are taken from the *Annual Report of the Local Examinations Syndicate* (Cambridge, England); those for 1971 are supplied by the Ministry of Education, Kenya.

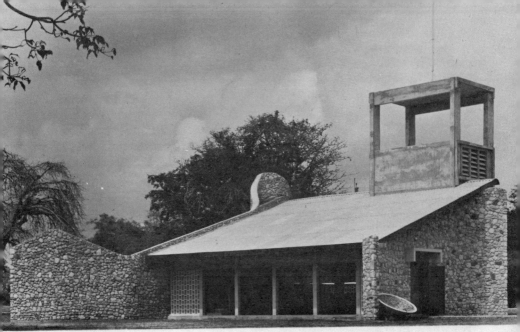

Krapf-Rebmann Memorial Church, Kilifi. Built 1961. Cost £2,500. Seating 150 - 200.

Religious Architecture and Planning

H. Richard Hughes

It is perhaps true to say that few countries of the world offer a greater variety of church architecture than Kenya; from stone cathedrals reminiscent of 19th-century England reflecting early settler and missionary ideas of what a church should be, to grass-roofed mud sheds epitomising the lack of affluence of their congregations. Today a small but growing number of new churches, built of simple materials and exhibiting a different understanding of worship, are beginning to make their appearance.[1]

Theological factors are vitally important in any analysis of religious architecture; for in a real sense the church proclaims its message not only in words and deeds but also in its buildings. Unless the theological dimension is brought to bear on architectural planning, the various denominations are likely to find that they have spent hard-earned money on buildings which, although superficially attractive, may serve only to emphasise the irrelevance of the Christian message for the contemporary world.[2]

The fundamental questions which must pervade all discussion relating to church architecture are these: What is Christian worship? How do church buildings contribute to worship?

On the whole most churches constructed in the past have tended to be rectangular, usually long and narrow. Roman Catholics and Anglicans, while emphasising the importance of the altar, have commonly separated it as far as possible from the congregation, placing it in the deepest recesses of the chancel. Priests perform their liturgical functions largely with their backs

Alliance Girls High School, Kikuyu, extended (interior). Built 1959, extended 1971, £2,000. Seating 500 - 600.

to the congregation, stressing the mysteries of sacramental worship life. Protestants on the other hand have often so de-emphasised the sacraments as to exclude from their buildings any sign of altar or communion table, concentrating their attention on the pulpit from which the Word is preached. Once again the pulpit is not set among the people but over against them, giving physical emphasis to a common belief that the Word of God is largely a word of judgment.

But if these are past realities whose influence is still prevalent, it is also true to say that different emphases are becoming evident. These reflect a fresh theological search for the meaning of worship and its influence on the relationship between church architecture and the message which the church proclaims. It is important to note that uneasiness with existing structures cuts across denominational boundaries and is not confined to any single segment of the church.

Many Christians have increasingly come to feel that valid Christian worship must hold a proper balance of Word and Sacrament and that the building must be so constructed as to emphasise the corporate nature of worship. They believe that both clergy and laymen contribute jointly, each according to their own proper function, toward a sense of participation and mutual sharing in worship.

To achieve this goal, emphasis is now being placed on square, hexagonal or circular buildings rather than long, narrow rectangular ones. The altar is taken away from the wall so that the priest or minister may perform his liturgical task facing the congregation. The Word in turn is proclaimed by the minister as he stands in the midst of his people. The people gather round the altar on three sides with the bishop or president and his clergy completing the circle. This makes possible a sense of corporate worship, even for large congregations, and contributes to the creation of a new relationship between clergy and laity in which both celebrant and people have a role to play.

Thirty years ago, the missionary writer Edwin W. Smith called upon the churches of Africa to take into consideration the African *bwalo*,[3] the circular village meeting place (pictured below), in planning their church architecture.

Traditional village meeting place called bwalo among the Ila of Zambia.

One wonders what such an emphasis, if taken seriously at the time, might have contributed not only to the churches of Africa but to the idea of Christian worship everywhere.

The attempt to create church buildings which reflect the African character serves to show the relevance of the Christian faith for contemporary Africa and to counteract any tendency which continues to regard Christianity as a foreign import.

All this has relevance for cathedrals (or urban headquarters churches) as well as for chapels and village churches.[4] Cathedrals present an unusual challenge in that they not only meet the needs of a local congregation but also serve as centres where large groups can gather from throughout the diocese and beyond. The essential problem of the architect is to make allowances for vast diocesan or nation-wide gatherings without losing the sense of intimacy necessary to the worship life of the local community.

If such a cathedral is properly planned, large numbers can be accommodated for special events without creating a sense of inadequacy on the part of the regular congregation, by the use of spacious aisles outside the columns, and by wide doors opening on to a courtyard. The doors can be so constructed as to make possible a view of the altar by a majority of the overflow crowd outside.

Trinity College Chapel, Nairobi. Built 1963. Cost £2,000, seating 50.

Y.M.C.A. **Prayer House**, Nairobi. Built 1964. Cost £1,750, seating **50.**

Such a cathedral would be unconventional by European standards in the rigid economy and simplicity of its materials and finishes. The structure is designed to speak for itself without added ornament — movement, colour and excitement coming from the people themselves as they gather for worship. Designs should be appropriate for an African church whose worshippers are not affluent, and should attempt to express a new sense of worship in the context of the African ethos.

The new mood in Kenya church architecture lays emphasis on the construction of buildings which are representative of the community in which they are set. They are built of simple local materials, reflecting the economic level of their parishioners, without looking cheap. They fit into the local surroundings but are not lost in that setting. Passers-by know that it is a church, but the architecture suggests that it is a Kenyan church, not an English or an Italian one, and that it is a church with a centuries-old message having a special relevance for the present day. On the outside such churches are attractive but not pretentious. The inside is theologically functional, emphasising a balance of Word and Sacrament, all contributing to an intimate sense of community in corporate worship.

REFERENCES

[1] H. Richard Hughes, 'The churches of Kenya', *East African Annual* (July 1964).
[2] Raymond Nichols, 'Is there a "theology" of church architecture?' (unpublished manuscript).
[3] Edwin W. Smith, *et al.*, 'The indigenous African church', in *The Church Conference on African Affairs* (Westerville, Ohio: Otterbein College, 1942), p. 13.
[4] H. Richard Hughes, 'The designing of a cathedral', *Kenya Weekly News* (January, 1965).
[5] H. Richard Hughes, 'Church buildings in Kenya', *Church buildings today* (January, 1962), p. 5-13.

Editors' note
The buildings illustrated in this article were designed by the author himself specifically to meet the theological considerations he describes, and also to utilise inexpensive local materials. Since the 20,000 congregations in Kenya in 1972 are increasing by 700 a year, it is urgent that such questions be properly discussed by the churches. Even rapidly-growing rural denominations build a large number of new permanent buildings each year; to illustrate this we append below a table showing the relative proportions of permanent and temporary church buildings, and open-air worship sites, in one of the fastest-growing denominations in Kenya, the Pentecostal Evangelistic Fellowship of Africa.

CHURCH BUILDINGS IN A RAPIDLY-GROWING KENYA DENOMINATION

Of the 20,000 Christian congregations in Kenya in mid-1972, about 900 belong to PEFA (Pentecostal Evangelistic Fellowship of Africa). The following survey of types of buildings refers to 1970 statistics, and illustrates how in a rapidly-growing denomination almost 83 per cent of all congregations have either temporary buildings, or none at all.

		Region in Kenya		
	Coast	Central	Nyanza	Totals
Number of congregations	219	84	488	791
Adult member Sunday attenders	15,023	3,177	19,300	37,500
Attenders per congregation	69	38	40	47
Percentage of congregations with:	%	%	%	%
Metal roof (permanent) church	17	21	17	17
Thatched roof (temporary) church	62	37	71	65
No building	21	41	12	18

The New Surge in Indigenous Christian Music in Kenya

I. THE VINDICATION OF AFRICAN TRADITIONAL MUSIC
Stephen Mbunga

We must acknowledge with sincere joy and gratitude that foreign missionaries have worked well sowing the seed of the Kingdom of God, and we recognise that the soil of East Africa has been especially favourable to its
growth and fruitfulness. Nevertheless, faced in the early stages with the difficulties of a strange land, people, language, culture, customs and music, most
early missionaries did not have the time, capacity or patience to go into
these matters sufficiently. Instead, they thought that by abandoning any
attempt to unearth what was good in the African way of life they would cut
off all pagan associations; and thus they were able to introduce their own
familiar music as the church music of East Africa. This substitute for African

65

music sprang out of the national treasures of the various missionaries. Consequently, we find across Africa today a patchwork of European church music in the different missions, as varied as are the nationalities of the Europeans who brought the faith. Thus East Africa started by inheriting from outside more than any single European nation had ever done.

Except for a very small group of missionaries seriously interested in African music, this has not until recently been seen as a problem. We do not question the good faith of pioneer missionaries who invited their flocks to join in singing God's praises in the ways they themselves were accustomed to, although in fact they rendered a disservice to music and, music being the most spiritual of the arts, to the work of civilisation. Moreover, missionaries have commonly assumed that Western civilisation and Christianity are two aspects of the same gift which God has commissioned them to offer to the rest of mankind. This then has given rise to the unfortunate assumption that African music is by nature inferior, primitive, crude, and useless in the church. African converts and their children after them have accepted this misconception without question.

Since the Second Vatican Council of 1962-1965 a new note has been sounded. The new theme is that of baptising the culture of a country rather than only individual converts, training a clergy and laity out of the people and for them. As a result of this note, the spirit of indigenous church music has now begun to revive noticeably. The church has responded by encouraging and harnessing it, making use of whatever can be carefully collected, tested and found suitable out of the wealth of material now available, not only for special occasions, but also in the regular worship of the church. A new freedom of expression of the faith has already begun to manifest itself in hymns and lyrics composed and sung in indigenous idiom and music, with such indigenous musical instruments as drums and songs augmented by handclapping. Naturally, such hymns spread easily and widely and become sources of encouragement and inspiration; they make Africans feel at home in worship, deeply stirred, attracted and touched at emotional depths which foreign liturgies cannot reach.

The constant and universal foundation of African tradition is the spiritual view of life—a deep, broad and universal concept which considers all living beings and the visible universe itself as linked with the world of the invisible and the spirit. This concept, perceived rather than analysed, lived rather than reflected on, was expressed in the past in very different ways, art and music being the prominent ones, which served to cement the African community. In talking about African art and music, one talked of a common language that expressed faith in God. African art and music were part and parcel of the daily life of the community from the cradle to the grave, in joy and sorrow, in love and battle, in work and prayer. Music was simple in style, yet had great influence within the culture because of its functional role; the purpose of religious dancing, for instance, was to induce a devotional frame of mind and ecstasy of spirit. There were beautiful songs with profound wisdom hidden therein, such as those of the rainmaking ceremonies, harvesting dances, circumcision celebrations, marriage rites, dances for success in battle or thanksgiving after victory, and so forth.

All of this takes on considerable significance when one examines the new surge in indigenous Christian music in Kenya that will now be described in detail.

II. CATHOLIC PROGRESS WITH TRADITIONAL MUSIC
John P. Kealy

The Second Vatican Council signalled a new spring for liturgy and for liturgical music in particular. New songs, new sounds, new instruments are now everywhere to be heard. Previously, plainsong, the organ and the Latin language were predominant in Catholic church services, and little encouragement was given to local genius or culture. Choirs, too, tended to dominate the singing during regular services. The Council therefore stressed: 'In certain parts of the world, especially mission lands, there are peoples who have their own musical traditions, and these play a great part in their religious and social life. For this reason due importance is to be attached to their music and a suitable place is to be given to it... adapting worship to their genius... Therefore when missionaries are being given training in music every effort should be made to see that they become competent in promoting the traditional music of these peoples both in schools and in sacred services'. A recent instruction has developed this further: 'All means must be used to promote singing by the people. New forms of music suited to different mentalities and to modern tastes should also be approved by the episcopal conference'.

It is good to note that these recommendations are being taken seriously in most parts of Kenya. In 1970 in the Cistercian Monastery at Lumbwa, a meeting was held to share and co-ordinate efforts being made throughout the country and to encourage new ventures. Enthusiasts both lay and clerical were present from all over Kenya, and the Kenya Association for Liturgical Music was formed. The results can be heard today in many Catholic churches in Kenya. New compositions have been produced and are judged at annual meetings. A short list of the main compositions shows their variety in the different languages. The Rev. Fr. Boniface J. Ndegwa was one of the first to produce an original mass in both the Swahili and Meru languages. Fr. J. Matogo has written one for the Gusii language group. Fr. C. O'Brollchain has several masses in both English and Kikuyu, and Fr. E. Corcoran has one in Swahili. The most successful so far has been the beautiful mass composed by Fr. J. O'Connell to a Taita air, from which we reproduce here the *Gloria* in Swahili. It is already sung all over Kenya, and its popularity is remarkable.

UTUKUFU KWA MUNGU JUU

(Glory be to God on High)

Lively Beat — Leader — People

Fr. J. O'Connell

Allow an empty bar between each verse. In the following verses, syllables followed by a hyphen are held for two quavers.

2. Sifa! Sisi tu - na - ku - sifu
   Heshima! Sisi tu - na - kuheshimu
   Tunakuabu - du Sisi tunakuabu - du   (repeated)
   He - shi - ma!

3. 'Tukufu! Sisi tu - na - kutukuza
   Shukrani! Sisi tu -na - kushukuru
   Kwa 'jili ya utukufu Utukufu wa - ko - mkuu   (repeated)
   Shu - kra - ni !

4. Ee Mungu! E - e - Bwa - na - Mungu
   Ee Baba ! Mfal - me - wa - Mbin - guni
   Ee Mungu Ba - ba - Mungu Baba Mwen - ye - zi   (repeated)
   Ee - Ba - ba!

5. Ee Bwana! Ee - Bwana Ye -su - Kristu
   Ee Mwana! Kris - tu - Mwana wa Pekee
   Mwa - na wa Ba - ba - Mwana Kondoo wa Mun - gu   (repeated)
   Ee - Mwa - na!

6. Mwokozi! Mwenye Kuondo - a - Dhambi
   Huruma! Dham - bi - za - du - nia
   Utuhurumi - e - Po - kea ombi le - tu   (repeated)
   Hu - ru - ma!

7. Ee Yesu! Kwa - ni - ndiwe Mtakatifu
   Ee Kristu! Kwa - ni - ndi - we - Bwana
   Ee - Yesu Kris - tu - Ndiwe Peke Ya -ko - Mkuu   (repeated)
   Ee - Kris - tu!

8. Umoja! pamoja na Roho Mtakatifu
   Milele! Katika - U - tu - kufu
   'Tukufu wa Mungu Baba Kris - tu - anai - shi   (repeated)
   Mi - le - le!

Accompaniment - drum, kayamba.
From Mass based on a Taita song
Oct. 1970

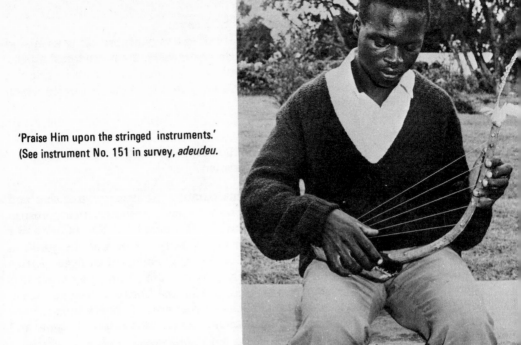

'Praise Him upon the stringed instruments.'
(See instrument No. 151 in survey, *adeudeu.*

KALM organised its third annual conference in January, 1972, at Loreto Convent, Msongari. About forty people attended from all parts of Kenya, some for the first time. The conference was opened by Bishop Rafael Ndingi, who stressed the importance of music and singing as an aid to the spiritual life and deeper understanding of the mass and urged people to write their own songs and tunes to bring Christ nearer to all. Reports were then given of the work that had been done in setting songs and the canon of the mass to Kenyan tunes. At the monastery of Our Lady of Victory, Lumbwa, much had been done with Luo music, and drums were the regular accompaniment to the services. In districts as far apart as Taita and Kitale, work had been going on, especially in schools. A discussion on the use of traditional instruments in worship was led by Mr. Peter Kibukosya, with illustrations on drums, kayamba, and other instruments. Fr. O'Brollchain gave a demonstration of how to start setting words to local tunes, stressing that the words must come first and the music take its inspiration from them. The highlight of the day was the celebration of mass in the evening. The Taita mass by Fr. O'Connell was particularly popular. Settings from Kwale and Mukumu were also heard.

The KALM conference gave to all a greater awareness of the widespread eagerness that has sprung up for using traditional tunes in worship in order that the laity can participate more fully. This impetus has been felt particularly in country areas over the last five years; and it is expected that it will spread rapidly into the towns and cities of Kenya.

Thus progress has been made, a variety of instruments are being used, and there is great hope for the future. Encouraging too is the ecumenical aspect, since music knows no bounds. If Catholics and Protestants learn to sing the same songs to the same melodies, it will be a step towards that unity which Christ so ardently desired.

III. PROTESTANT CHOIRS OF TRADITIONAL INSTRUMENTS
Eva Christian

Music and the Kenyan? They are inseparable! Kenyans would sing and play musical instruments all day if it were possible. 'Since African musical instruments give such a delightful picture of the people of Kenya, why not see if they can be used in churches for God's glory?' This was the question which came to a group of students at Scott Theological College (Africa Inland Church), Machakos, in the early part of 1969. Dare they enter this unknown venture? The answer was 'Yes!' Asking the Lord for clear guidance, they began to investigate the possibilities in this area of church music. Very few indigenous instruments had been seen in churches up to that time, and few indigenous hymns were to be found in hymnbooks.

After making several instruments, the students together with the Rev. and Mrs. Cecil Christian decided to take these to certain AIC congregations to see what the response would be. Some instruments were associated with traditional medicine men, some were used at beer parties, some during circumcision ceremonies, and some for casual entertainment, but few if any had been seen in the churches. Throughout 1970, Gospel-Choir teams utilised a number of these instruments together with European ones to accompany their singing. Each time they went to a new church, they explained carefully that any instrument could be used either for Satan or for God just as our own bodies can serve either purpose. The instrument within itself had no quality of good or evil, but how it was used determined its value. Since God was the One who had created these materials, why not utilise them for His glory? The response from Christians was warm. In December of 1970, a television programme was prepared for the Voice of Kenya, in which several indigenous instruments were demonstrated together with indigenous hymns.

In the meantime, students were collecting traditional folk-song melodies from their tribes, and writing Bible truths in poetry form to fit the tunes. A few of these were used by the Scott Choir in the churches. Again Christians applauded their efforts.

In addition, instruments were taken into market-places and used when the Word was proclaimed, to see how non-Christians would react. People crowded around to see and hear, and many came to the Lord. In the Nyakach area during a week-long evangelistic campaign, instruments were taken into homes during home Bible studies; and before long, other Christians were picking them up and playing them in rhythm to the hymns being sung.

Some students began soon to compose both their own words and music. This resulted in a small mimeographed hymnbook, *Heavenly Melodies*. Then came the exciting discovery that rural churches were using hundreds of indigenous hymns which had never been recorded on paper. These hymns were strongly rhythmic, as indeed most African music is. Realising that the combination of indigenous hymns and instruments would have great appeal to Kenya Christians with their natural rhythm of movement, the students began to collect and record these hymns on tapes and paper. These were mimeographed, used by choir members in churches and enthusiastically received. 'May I have a copy of that hymn?' was a question asked again and again.

The work begun at Machakos has had a profound effect on the Africa Inland Church, and a Christian Music School is being planned to improve music in local churches. The need to indigenise church music is increasingly seen by other denominations also. Imagination and creativity of a high order are needed in this effort to fashion a Christian music which is truly African.

Scott Theological students combine traditional and Western instruments.

KENYAN TRADITIONAL MUSICAL INSTRUMENTS AND THE CHURCHES:
A SURVEY

A large number of traditional musical instruments have been collected during the years 1969-1972 by students of Scott Theological College, Machakos. The possible varieties of percussion, string and wind instruments are almost limitless, and 177 examples for 39 different Kenyan peoples are surveyed below. Scott students have added many of these to the college band, and are

TABLE 1

NUMBERS OF KNOWN TRADITIONAL MUSICAL INSTRUMENTS OF THE MAJOR KENYAN PEOPLES

The number of different known musical instruments belonging to each people, and illustrated in the survey that follows, is given after each people's name. For the Luhya, in addition to 10 general instruments, details are given for 7 Luhya sub-tribes; 5 Meru sub-tribes, and two under Taita.

Bajun	8	Kipsigis	5	Luo	16	Nandi	10
Boran	4	Kuria	8	Maasai	3	Pokomo	1
Digo	2	Luhya	10	Marakwet	1	Pokot	10
Duruma	3	- Isukha	3	Mbere	2	Rabai	1
Elgeyo	7	- Kakelwa	1	Meru		Rendille	2
Embu	3	- Maragoli	9	- Chuka	2	Somali	1
Giriama	5	- Nyore	2	- Igembe	4	Taita	2
Gusii	3	- Samia	3	- Imenti	1	- Kasigao	1
Kamba	20	- Teriki	3	- Tharaka	1	- Taveta	1
Kikuyu	12	- Tsoto	1	- Tigania	1	Turkana	5

TOTAL   177

using them for church services in the Machakos area. Their work received national attention through a 1971 concert given over Voice of Kenya television.

In addition to these 177 instruments, this survey discovered a small number of others not listed here. This means that the grand total of distinct different traditional instruments in use in Kenya today numbers at least 200, and may even exceed this figure.

In this survey, we give first a list of the major peoples of Kenya, and the number of known instruments used by them. Next follows a table in which we classify them into 26 major categories, describe the main traditional uses of each category, and state the present extent of their known usage in Catholic, Anglican, Protestant and African independent churches in Kenya.

Then follows the detailed descriptive survey of instruments, arranged alphabetically by tribal group, and then within each group in the order set forth in Table 2 (alphabetically in three categories). For each instrument, we give a diagram, also the vernacular name for it, the English equivalent, and brief notes describing its construction, traditional use, and church usage if any. Note that in this particular survey, 'AIC' stands for the Africa Inland Church, and not the African independent churches.

Research indicates that there has been a considerable amount of borrowing across tribal lines, so that an instrument which was traditional among one tribe may now be found commonly used by other peoples. No attempt has been made to investigate the tribal origin or to show the degree of sharing involved; the list simply identifies the people using it today.

Whatever the original purposes of these time-honoured instruments, Scott theological students explain that their use in churches today is 'to glorify the Lord'. Not all of them originally served as musical instruments. Some are cattle or goat bells. Others are still employed to frighten away wild animals, to call people together, or simply for entertainment. However, all may now be considered of potential value in church music. It is primarily a question of studying their properties to see how they may best be utilised by church choirs. This study is under way at Scott Theological College. Lastly, as noted earlier, in concerts and church services the Scott band frequently combines the use of traditional instruments with Western instruments.

TABLE 2
KENYA TRADITIONAL MUSICAL INSTRUMENTS AND CHURCH USAGE, 1972

This table summarises the following illustrated survey of indigenous instruments in the 39 major tribes and sub-tribes in Kenya, and lists the various types in use today, the number of each type, and their known usage in worship by the churches as a result of the instrumental revival beginning in 1969.

Type	Instrument	Number	Main traditional uses	Church usage in worship			
				Catholic	Anglican	Protestant	Independent
Percussion		111		Widespread	Frequent	Frequent	Frequent
	Bells:	57		Widespread	–	Frequent	Frequent
	Chain bells	30	Dances, ceremonies	Widespread	Spreading	AIC	–
	Single bell	27	Cattle, ceremonials	Widespread	–	AIC(TV)	–
	Block	1	Dances	–	–	–	–
	Board	2	Dances, rites, frighten animals	–	–	–	–
	Drums	24	Announcements, games, dances	Widespread	Widespread	SA, AIC etc.	Universal
	Gourd	1	Ceremonies	–	–	AIC	–
	Horn & stick	2	Wedding processions, ceremonies	–	–	–	–
	Marimba	1	Entertainment	Widespread	–	AIC(TV)	Occasional
	Rattles	16	Rites, divination, social	Widespread	Spreading	AIC	Frequent
	Sticks	4	Beer parties, rites	–	–	AIC, SA	–
	Tambourine	1	Entertainment	Widespread	–	AIC	AICN
	Triangles	1	Weddings	Occasional	–	AIC	–
	Xylophone	1	Circumcision, parties	–	–	AIC(TV)	–
Strings		25	Solos, private songs	None	Rare	Rare	None
	Banjo	2	Entertainment	–	–	–	–
	Bowl Lyre	10	Entertainment, ceremonies	–	–	–	–
	Fiddle	3	Entertainment	–	–	–	–
	Guitar	2	Entertainment	–	–	–	–
	Harp	1	Entertainment	–	–	–	–
	Musical bow	5	Divination, entertainment	–	Beginning	AIC(TV)	–
	Zither	2	Entertainment	–	–	–	–
Wind		41		None	Occasional	Occasional	Rare
	Bugle	1	Announcing death, meetings	–	–	AIC	–
	Flute	10	Entertainment	–	–	–	–
	Horn	4	Frightening beasts, enemies	–	Occasional	AIC	–
	Oboe	2	Wedding processions	–	–	–	–
	Trumpet	22	Initiation ceremonies, alarms	–	–	AIC	Luo Roho
	Whistle	2	Entertainment	–	–	–	–

TOTAL INSTRUMENTS   177

Key
–   no known church usage
AIC   used in Africa Inland Church
AICN   used in African Israel Church Nineveh
SA   used in Salvation Army
TV   used on Voice of Kenya Television

BAJUN

1. *goma kuu*   drum

Beaten by men during special ceremonies; log is hollowed, one end covered with skin and fastened by wooden pegs.

2. *kitwari*   drum

Played by women at social gatherings; hollow tree trunk, covered on ends with skin.

3. *pembe*   horn

A cow horn, beaten with stick by women marching through village in wedding procession, the evening before wedding, utilised on radio and in AIC (Africa Inland Church) churches by Scott choir.

4. *msondo*   tambourine

Used by women or girls for entertainment and in processions before weddings; brought by early missionaries but adopted as African instrument; 8 inches in diameter; played extensively in rural AIC churches.

5. *pembe*   rattle

Buffalo horn filled with small stones.

6. *kayamba*   reed rattle

Shaken by women at social gatherings, and in processions preceding weddings; women clap hands as they march and sway to rhythm; two layers of reeds from swampy area woven together with grass, inside filled with smooth stones or tiny pieces of metal, frame of carved wood 6 to 15 inches; used by Scott choir in AIC churches, on radio and TV; occasionally used in Catholic diocese of Mombasa.

7. *zomari*   oboe

Played at front of procession through village the evening before wedding; the only wind instrument in Kenya using a reed mouthpiece (double reed); cow horn with metal tube, reed from date palm, sealed with beeswax.

8. *siwa*   filigree blow trumpet

The most important Arab instrument; can be made of brass; original at D.C.'s office in Lamu, carved from elephant tusk; played by men; cow horn on end with mouthpiece, hollow bamboo in middle with solid wood on other end; some AIC usage.

BORAN

9. *bilbil*   bells

8 bells attached to leather strip around waist hang to mid-thigh; worn by wives of young men undergoing 8 years of initiation rites; worn at waist and on cowrie-beaded straps over shoulder by mother of baby and uncircumcised father, while initiation period incomplete; made from top of gourd, wooden or metal clapper; 8 inches long.

10. *koke*   wooden bell

Worn around neck of camel; movement of animal causes bell to ring keeping herdsman informed of whereabouts; made of soft wood; wooden clappers 10 inches long; sisal string handles.

11. *bilbil*   bell

Made from tops of gourds fastened to cowrie; decorated strap worn by man giving feast at occasion of son's naming ceremony.

DIGO

12. *hagalo*   bell

8-inch bell used by boys at circumcision.

13. *ndonga*   rattle

Used by medicine man as he performs his ceremonies; formed from gourd, beads wound around and carved head at top; filled with various types of seeds; 12 inches long.

14. *nzumari*   oboe

Instrument has Arab background and is similar to *zomari* of Bajun and other Coastal peoples; carving on bell notably beautiful; reeds of mouthpiece made of borassus palm leaves.

DURUMA

15. *dzuga*   bells

Small silver ankle bells containing tiny piece of steel (e.g. nail); worn for dances; AIC Scott choir usage.

16. *nzuga*   bells

Black iron ankle bells with small pieces of iron inside; 4 inches long with leather string; used in churches, on radio and TV by Scott choir.

17. *ngunda*   trumpet

Played by men; formerly worn by slave-catchers who also wore wooden masks and carried Grant's gazelle horn; one man dressed as woman so he could catch women, the other caught men.

ELGEYO

18. *kipkurgurik*   bells

1-inch bells worn by men while walking on long journeys to prevent loneliness; small silver-coloured bells with piece of steel inside.

19. *kipgurgurik*   bells

5-inch black iron bells, worn around men's thighs for dances, one belt containing 3 bells on each thigh; women also wear them when girls finish month of circumcision initiation.

20. *chebombumbu*   singing board

2½-foot board with leather or sisal string; men, who have already undergone circumcision rite, play this secret instrument at night outside the house where young initiates are lodging, purpose is to test courage and see if ready to undergo ceremony following day; they are informed noise is due to wild animals.

21. *chepkombis*   drum

Clay pot with leather cover, tightened with sticks.

22. *likembe, merimba*   marimba

Found only in Africa; used by youth for entertainment; hollow wooden or metal box, prongs made from umbrella stays; played by plucking end of stay with thumbnail.

23. *kurerut*   flute

3-foot bark flute, used by young shepherds for entertainment; blown gently like whistle; has 4 notes.

24. *ikondit*   trumpet

Made from hollow tree limb covered with skin for decoration; blown by men at dances or by girls calling each other for special ceremony to take place following day.

EMBU

25. *mbugi*   bell

Worn by woman circumciser on strand slung across shoulder when ready to perform rite; 3-inch black metal; heard at AIM missionary conference in 1971.

26. *njangiri*   bell

Worn by youth *(ndio)* six months before initiation as part of special costume, indicating wish to be circumcised; 6-inch black iron filled with small stones or small pieces of steel.

27. *coro*   horn

Large 15-inch cow horn sounded to call men to war; Scott choir usage.

GIRIAMA

28. *kivumanzi*   bell

2-inch brass bell fastened on neck strap made of thin strips of skin wound around until 2-inch strap is formed; worn by medicine men.

29. *ngoto*   horn

Buffalo horn beaten by rainmaker during rainmaking ceremony; sacrifices chicken or goat while beating horn and praying for rain standing by small shrine.

30. *kayamba*   reed rattle

The most common instrument providing rhythm for Giriama songs; 2 layers of dried reeds with seeds between which rattle; thumb hits wooden bar in middle marking rhythm, and seeds rattle as *kayamba* shaken from side to side. Used frequently in Catholic churches, occasionally in Anglican churches.

31. *chivoti*   flute

Small instrument, very pleasing sound.

32. *gunda*   trumpet

Oryx horn blown by rainmaker while seven assistants beat buffalo horns *(ngoto)* before shrine where sacrifices to rain divinities are offered.

GUSII

33. *chinchigiri*   bells

Worn around ankles as man plays bowl lyre; moves or stamps feet up and down.

34. *chinchigiri*   bells

Warrior wears two rows of these 3-inch black iron bells around ankles in ceremonial dances.

35. *obokano*   bowl lyre

Very large man's instrument; bowl held under left arm, both hands used to pluck sinew strings; strings tuned by turning banana fibres around which strings are wound.

KAMBA

36. *syamba*   bells

Worn by men for entertainment and dances; fashioned of small pieces of tin with stones inside, wire or skin passed through centre to tie them together, or ½-inch silver bells filled with steel pieces; tied to back of leg below knee, sound produced by stamping leg.

37. *nzili* bells

Worn for pleasant sound on long journeys, on ankle or placed on right hand of left-handed child to encourage use of right hand; small steel 1-inch bells filled with stones or iron pieces. Employed by Scott students.

38. *kithembe* drum

Beaten with stick to produce warning signal; ends of hollow wooden tree trunk covered with skin from skull of old ox or buffalo; top can be removed and drum used for storing honey; skin handle.

39. *kithembe* drum

Heard in many rural AIC churches making choir rhythm; 2 feet high; fashioned of hollowed sisal trunk covered with skin.

40. *mukanda* drum

Beaten for entertainment and dances; tree trunk hollowed at both ends, covered with goat skin on one end, other end covered with monitor skin (dotted), hit by hand to produce tune; players usually men; 4 feet long.

41. *mwase* drum

Constructed of wood; covered on top with skin, bottom remaining open; played for woman at ceremony in which she becomes fully recognised *kumwa*, medicine practitioner.

42. *ithembe* drums

Drum 10 inches high attached to 7-inch drum, fastened with rubber strips to 3½-foot wooden stand; drums hollowed wood covered with skin; played regularly in African Brotherhood Church, and for wedding ceremonies.

43. *nzele* percussion gourd

Utilised by medicine men; wires cut from bicycle wheels or umbrella stays; bottom is part of gourd.

44. *ileve* rattle

Shaken by men at circumcision ceremony; debi made of tin (previously, gourds) with stones inside; tied on back of leg and foot stamped in rhythm to music.

45. *kikulu* rattle

Operated in AIC and Catholic rural churches to mark rhythm of choir; made of sisal filled with small bits of iron; about 6 inches long.

46. *kiamba* rattle

10-inch forked tree branch with soda bottle caps or pieces of tin which slide on piece of wire; used in some rural AIC churches in Kyome area marking rhythm for choirs.

47. *kititi* rattle

Utilised by diviners to tell future; curved gourd with small mouth, filled with seeds of different colours; gourd (10 inches) is shaken, seeds spilled out and future told, after diviner has sung song calling on divinities while rhythmically shaking gourd; Scott choir usage, radio/TV.

48. *miti* sticks

Struck in many AIC rural churches to mark rhythm for choir; can be bamboo, but usually two sticks from any tree; 8 inches long.

49. *kanini kabuinga* musical bow

Utilised for entertainment when boy is born; expresses hope that he will become warrior and bring stolen cattle from neighbouring tribe; used also by not-fully-qualified medicine man to attract followers; money given; sisal string on small wooden bow, and wire string on second wooden bow with split gourd in middle.

50. *uta wa kwausya* musical bow

Used by diviner; wooden bow and wire string with half gourd between, amplifying sound; sound made by striking string with any thin stick; Scott choir usage, radio/TV.

51. *mukuta* flute

Played by men for entertainment and dances; made from tree branch, soft centre removed, hole at one end blocked; other end left for blowing, holes made near mouth for controlling sound; 2 small 4-inch reeds; end sealed with beeswax, bound with yarn.

52. *ndumali* flute

Boys entertain themselves with it while chasing birds; fashioned from stalk of sorghum plants; played mostly during harvest; 10-12 inches long.

53. *nzongoi* trumpet

Blown by men for sounding alarm; made from horn of eland; tapering end not hollowed, but blowing hole drilled just beyond solid part.

54. *nguli* trumpet

Antelope horn, used by herdsmen for moving cattle; when blown, cattle rise and move on.

55. *ithua* trumpet

Blown to frighten away elephants, also by dancers to bewitch opponents in competitive games and to show boldness marching onto playing field; bamboo handle, gourd bell; sealed with beeswax; 4 feet long; Scott choir usage.

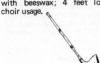

KIKUYU

56. *njingiri* bells

1-inch silver bells with small pieces of iron inside; bound to legs and arms to help mark rhythm; relieves tedium during long marches. Scott choir usage, radio/TV.

57. *ngengere* bell

Goat bell of grey-black iron, beautiful tonal quality; 4 inches; handle made of banana tree fibre.

58. *kihembe* drum

Hollow tree trunk, goat skin stretched over ends with string; beaten after marriage ceremony when woman has arrived at home of husband, or for entertainment after defeat of enemies.

59. *gichandi* rattle

11-inch bottle-gourd painted with Kikuyu hieroglyphics, with long thorns inserted and hard seeds enclosed, stopped with beeswax, decorated with seashells on long string; player travels as itinerant story-teller. Scott choir usage, radio/TV.

60. *githoguo* rattle

7-inch tins flattened at top, filled with pieces of bottles and small stones; tied to men's right leg, controls rhythm of *mucung'wa* dance of circumcised warriors for entertainment, especially during harvest.

61. *kigamba* rattle

Shaped from small tin as with *githoguo* above; shaken by boys and girls during night preceding circumcision.

62. *tuthanju* sticks

Bundle of 5 or 6 sticks which boys carry on days following their circumcision; alternating song with rattling of sticks; tied together with sisal string, grass or leather strips.

63. *wandende* fiddle

2-stringed (wire or cow tendon) instrument, hollow wooden sound box, strummed by boys to entertain selves at night; sounds like pipe organ.

64. *biringi* flute

Shaped from hollow reeds 4 inches long, holes sealed with beeswax, covered with paper, bound together with fine wire; length determines tone. Blown at upper end. Seen at dances.

65. *muturiru* flute

Bark from green twig removed and 4 holes made, producing 4 deep sounds (or octave higher if force employed to blow it); used as children's toy or by shepherds watching sheep or goats.

66. *coro* horn

5-inch horn of bull or other animal; no mouthpiece except slit ½ inch long; sounded for alarm against enemies, to call people to special meetings and propitiatory sacrifices; used during *mucung'wa* dance and other ceremonies; Scott choir usage.

67. *thongori* trumpet

Bamboo cane fastened to neck of gourd bell, sealed with beeswax; cut made at end of cane for blowing; blown to call people to special meetings or to announce propitiatory sacrifices to be offered by whole population; sounds like bugle; Scott choir usage.

KIPSIGIS

68. *sugutit* drum

Beaten during competitions and when crops are harvested; people make circle around player; fashioned from hollow wood, ends covered with skin; beaten with two sticks; tied around neck.

69. *chepkongo* bowl lyre

Played during ceremonies, when crops are harvested or when boys or girls are circumcised; one of the three most important instruments. Wooden box covered with skin, hole made, 7 wires attached.

70. *chepkesem* harp

Played by old men when resting; rarely found today; made of two-branched stick, three wires used for strings; attractive in sound and shape.

71. *chepogogo* musical bow

Played by boys looking after cows, sheep or goats or when resting; two ends of gourd cut off and covered with goat or sheep skin; on opposite side, hole is made, stick put through it and tied with single wire.

72. *igondit* trumpet

Blown to call people to war or when returning from war; only for important occasions; made from horn of cow or wild animal; used during elections. Scott choir usage. Used as title of Africa Gospel Church's magazine.

KURIA

73. ikibirii bells

1-inch small silver bells, worn by warriors around ankles.

74. ituriani bell

Worn hanging over right shoulder reaching mid-chest; sometimes carried loosely over arm; used by medicine men or women; 8-inch black iron on beaded leather strap.

75. entongori bell

Carried by dancer; 5-inch iron bell carried by young men in right hand as they jump around with wooden blocks (*omotambo*) attached to ankles.

76. omotambo wooden block

12-inch wooden blocks strapped to male dancer's feet, giving solid, rhythmic beat to music.

77. embegete drum

Hollow wood, open at one end, covered with skin on other end; played with hands; carried by strap over left shoulder; 5 feet long; played by boys or men at dances.

78. egetomo drum

Beaten by boys or men at dances; hollow wood, sometimes covered with zebra hide; 2 feet long.

79. iritungu bowl lyre

3-foot hollow wooden bowl covered with painted or tarred cowhide; used in divination; vibrations of strings give required answers as medicine, man pulls them in sequence.

80. urutira trumpet

Cow horn, 15-24 inches; blown by musician at dances.

LUHYA

81. bichenje bells

Rung by person performing circumcision to test boy's bravery; also tied to legs of children who survive when many others have died; 1-inch silver metal bells with small pieces of steel inside; AIC and Scott choir usage.

82. chinyimba bells

Round bells with handles attached to ring of steel on wrist of boy to be circumcised; used every other year. Scott choir usage, radio/TV.

83. sikhutu bell

Worn at back of waist of widow until she remarries; for mourning and lamentation. Steel.

84. eng'oma drum

Beaten by chief to call meetings of great importance, and to announce birth of twins and entertain the parents.

85. sukuti drum

Previously played to entertain people after defeating an enemy; now used to entertain football players and men at beer parties. Anglican usage (see No. 109)

86. ebisala sticks

Used by older people at beer parties together with *litungu*; sticks beat piece of wood; Scott choir usage

87. litungu bowl lyre

Played by elders at competition dances and home beer parties; often heard together with a piece of wood beaten by sticks. 7 strings between two wooden brackets, hollow wood, skin cover, one hole for producing sound.

88. shiriri or zeze fiddle

Strummed by young people for dances, accompanied by bells; two wire strings played with bow made of sisal string and wood.

89. kumulele reed flute

Played by newly circumcised young men to deaden pain when treating selves with special ash and herb.

90. ekhombi trumpet

Cow horn blown to warn people of approaching enemies, also to summon soldiers to war, or after war to celebrate victory.

—ISUKHA (Luhya)

91. likhuli, ing'imba bells

3- or 4-inch black metal bell; many worn around neck by women rainmakers; circumciser wears bells just above both knees during ceremony.

92. ing'oma, indindi drum

Beaten at circumcision ceremony to see if boy can be frightened; if he shows fear, must pay a goat; hollowed sisal trunk covered with cow hide; played with stick.

93. litungu   bowl lyre

Played by man; 7 strings of sinew, sounding bowl hollowed wood covered on top with cowhide; held over left shoulder with cowhide strap when played; strings wound around banana tree fibres which are twisted to tune strings to desired pitch; for entertainment.

—KAKELWA (Luhya)

94. vikuli   bells

Worn by young married women who have not yet borne a child; leather strap decorated with cowrie shells (symbol of fertility) from which metal rings are attached, and on which hang small bells.

—MARAGOLI (Luhya)

95. omughango   bells

Waistbelt worn by women while planting grain; iron rings hold 1-inch bells as charms against pain and snakebite, on leather belt.

96. isungandi   drum

Used in worship as well as for dancing; player stands but makes a dancing movement while people dance in a circle; beaten like a drum. Hollowed wood covered with skin, carried by wooden handle.

97. kimunga   rattle

Employed by practitioners in their ceremonies; shaken, stones inside rolled onto ground; 12-inch gourd usually has corn cob stopper; found in AIC churches. A similar gourd rattle, *eshimuka*, is used by the Anglican Diocese of Maseno North.

98. amangemo   banjo

Used for entertainment by boys and girls sleeping away from parents;' young people hum, no words used; played with thumb and first fingers.

Wooden box and arm with 4 sinew strings; 2 feet long.

99. ulukungi   banjo

For boy's entertainment; skin over wood, sounding box a gourd (bottom half) with wooden arm and one string fastened to nail or peg at end of arm.

100. inangali   guitar

Strummed by adults of both sexes during dancing or at a death; hollow wooden bowl covered with cowhide, 6 tendon strings fastened to wooden pegs. Player stands, uses upward movement of fingers; not used in traditional worship.

101. indienyi   guitar

Heard at beer parties; entertainer sits to play, uses downward movement of fingers.

102. uvuta   musical bow

Used by medicine men in ceremonies; consists of 4½-foot bow with thin wire beaten with wooden stick. Often called *lukuji*; when played resonated by mouth and chest, mouth holding bow at one end. Scott choir usage.

103.. olwika   trumpet

Impala horn blown by men to call people together or at time of war; 24 inches long. Scott choir usage. Also used at communion by Anglican Bishop and Diocese of Maseno North.

—NYORE (Luhya)

104. chindeke   horn

Cowhorn, used for funerals and to announce victory. Anglican usage (see No. 103).

105. esiliba   horn

Small goat horn, sometimes used with *olwika*, sometimes played alone to signal victory or funerals.

—SAMIA (Luhya)

106. chindeke   bells

Worn by female medicine specialist around ankles, above knee, and one row below knee. Black metal bells 2½ inches in size.

107. enyimba   bell

Metal bell hung on necklace of cowrie shells.

108. libobo   bell

Worn on strap of beads over shoulder and under arm of warrior, hanging to mid-chest; 6-inch iron bell with leather strap.

—TERIKI (Luhya)

109. sukuti   drum

Teriki funeral drum; hollow tree trunk 2 feet in diameter, covered with skin. Used in worship by Nyore Anglicans (Diocese of Maseno North).

110. litungu   bowl lyre

Hollow wooden .bowl covered with cowhide, 4½ feet long; tendon strings, string strap; strummed by specialist for entertainment.

111. makhana   raft zither

Made of millet stalks 2½ inches long, fastened together with thin strips of bark or grass. On each stalk, skin slit and wood slipped under end; strips are then plucked with thumb and forefinger. For entertainment.

—TSOTO (Luhya)

112. *engoma* — trumpet

Blown by men to announce war or death; gourds fastened together by rubber or wire, with antelope or animal horn at top end; tip of horn cut off, player blows into open end.

LUO

113. *gara* — bells

Small 1-inch bells with piece of steel inside, on leather or sisal string, rung by players of bowl lyres to beat time; mothers tie bells on babies to encourage them to walk; worn also by worriors; Scott choir usage; also used in Anglican Diocese of Maseno North and South.

114. *mbororo* — bells

Steel bells filled with small stones worn by female medicine specialist around upper part of body, also hung above doorway of her hut. Two strands worn around ankles of Luo warriors; Held in hand to accompany hymns during Scott choir usage.

115. *okot* — bell

5-inch iron cow bell with unusual leather strap.

116. *bul* — drum

Beaten with 2 sticks by men at funerals and as signal for meetings; leather and 4-foot long hollow tree trunk. Widelu used, e.g. by Anglican chur ches.

117. *bul mar jolemo* — drum

Used by many African independent churches (AICN, HGCK, etc.) and by Salvation Army; wood covered with skin, 3 feet long.

118. *kalapapla* — drum

Used by women and girls after a burial is over; beaten by sister of dead woman who thus informs husband he should take her as new wife; sisal trunk inside, covered with cow skin.

119. *ajawa* — rattles

Shaken to propitiate evil spirits; also by medicine man who pours seeds onto ground for fortune telling, studying position to give information sought; gourd filled with small stones, 10 inches high, Scott choir usage.

120. *ongeng'o, nyangile* — triangles

Struck by girls on wedding day of girl friend; two pieces of steel and drum. Heard in rural AIC churches to accompany choirs.

121. *nyatiti* — bowl lyre

Used by older people for entertainment and at funerals; eight strings tuned to a musical scale, sounding like piano; small hinged door on back of bowl padlocked to store money, bells, personal effects; door opened for greater sound. Hollow wooden bowl covered with leather; tendon string, decorated with paint; 2 feet long. Used by medicine men also.

122. *orutu* — musical bow

Utilised by young men for entertainment at night; one stringed instrument sounding like European violin; wire string on instrument, sisal string on bow; bowl of hollowed wood or tin can, wooden handle; hollow wood sounding box covered on one end with skin; 15 inches long. Youths playing similar bow, *ahinioi,* are being increasingly heard in Anglican churches.

123. *nyabond tiang* — raft zither

Used by children at play and women; made of millet stalks, played by gently plucking thin strips of outer peeling slit from stalks like strings.

124. *abu* — bugle

Blown at funerals or sports; largest Luo wind instrument, made of gourd and bamboo stems, bamboo handle with gourd bowl; 4 to 6 feet long; Scott choir usage.

125. *asili* — flute

Played by boys when herding; made of reed or bamboo; sometimes white web of large house spider glued to open end to seal it.

126. *oporo* — trumpet

Blown to drive elephants away, or to announce war or invasion of locusts; gourd bell with bamboo handle, fastened with inner tube rubber; 4 feet long. Widely used; Scott choir usage also.

127. *tung* — trumpet

Sounded to announce war or a death, also as ceremonial horn on special occasions, when political prisoners released; Scott choir usage.

128. *tung* — trumpet

Modern version of trumpet, made of tin 3 feet long. Used in Luo Roho churches for singing, also as megaphone for preaching and announcements.

MAASAI

129. *oltuala* — bells

1-inch black iron ankle bells on leather strap, worn by warriors or by young men at dances.

130. *oltuala*   bell

Small 3-inch metal bell. Now being used in Catholic churches during worship (at Sanctus)

131. *emouuo*   trumpet

Only warriors and the uncircumcised use this; at circumcision rites, played in different tone from that used by warriors; also blown when warriors go on lion hunt. Some AIC usage.

MARAKWET

132. *kipgururoik*   bells

Two rows of 3-inch black iron bells filled with small pieces of iron, tied below knees of warriors; AIC usage, radio/TV.

MBERE

133. *kibeere*   bells

6-inch black iron bells worn below knees by warriors.

134. *muriempe*   drum

Used at dances, hung over right shoulder and held between legs; players beat while dancing. Hollow 4-foot wooden tree trunk covered at one end with skin.

MERU

--CHUKA (Meru)

135. *ruogo*   rattle

Played by boys; held in hand and shaken at dances; 5 feet long, carved and wood-burned board with steel rings hanging down to make rattling

sound; rope handle carried in hand by boy undergoing circumcision rites.

136. *choro*   trumpet

Cow horn covered with hide; blown by one or two boys during circumcision initiations; always kept inside player's hut; other would-be players must pay a chicken.

--IGEMBE (Meru)

137. *ntuara*   bells

3-inch metal bells worn by diviner on strap around chest as he performs.

138. *ntuara*   bell

5-inch iron bells; boys undergoing circumcision rites wear 3 of these over shoulder and under arm.

139. *kirimiiria*   bell

7-inch iron bell with leather strap, carried over a *simbi*; worn by boys at circumcision time.

140. *mbugu ya muga*   rattle

Diviner's gourd filled with seeds of various colours, top adorned with end of cow's tail; after shaking rhythmically and calling on spirits, seeds poured on to ground and prophecy expounded.

--IMENTI (Meru)

141. *ncingiri*   rattle

Worn over boy's shoulder and shaken to scare birds from shamba; soft wooden bars, millet or bamboo, with both sides identical.

--THARAKA (Meru)

142. *kibeere*   bell

Made of black iron, filled with small pieces of iron; worn by circumcised Tharaka youth as part of unusual costume to frighten new circumcision candidates; 6 inches long.

--TIGANIA (Meru)

143. *kirimiiria*   bell

Bravest warrior of clan who leads people into battle, wears three leather strips down his back; each is decorated with cowrie shells and 4 to 6-inch black iron bells; believed to frighten and confuse the enemy, so must never be captured.

NANDI

144. *muyawek*   bells

Worn by men below knees at dances; 3½-inch black iron with 2 or 3 steel pieces inside for tinkling sound.

145. *kipkurguriet*   bells

Worn by girls at their circumcision above knee; black iron, 4 inches long.

146. *twoliot*   bell

Rung by girls during circumcision ceremony; worn at back of waist.

147. *kipkurkuryet*   bell

7-inch rattle-like black iron bell on beaded leather strap, worn at dances by young men.

148. *sugutit*   drum

Used during times of happiness to entertain guests, also during traditional dancing; hollowed sisal covered with cowhide.

149. *amadinda* — xylophone

Played at beer parties, by medicine men, and in circumcision rites; boy lies between sticks, fires lighted at ends to test courage and manhood; constructed of pieces of wood of varying lengths, laid across banana stems, with 1-inch twigs separating boards; 5-12 feet long, 2 or more players. Popular in churches; AIC usage, radio/TV.

150. *kipugantet* — fiddle

Hollow wood bowl covered with skin, wire string; bow with plain string; used by men for entertainment.

151. *adeudeu* — bowl lyre

Played by young man for entertainment; girl may propose marriage if he plays well; 15 inches long, hollowed wooden bowl covered with skin, tendon strings.

152. *kibucondet* — bowl lyre

Operated when young men dancing; bowl of hollowed wood covered with cowhide, strings made from cow tendons.

153. *igondii* — trumpet

Oryx horn blown in play, also as warning when danger has become apparent.

POKOMO

154. *ngaji* — drum

Hollow wood trunk, covered with skin at one end, solid wood at other end; stick pushed through hole in skin into can of water on inside of drum; when twirled, stick vibrates in water, making terrifying sound, supposed to be the voice of a monster; operated to frighten away enemies, robbers or wild animals.

POKOT

155. *kurkur* (pl. *kurkuris*) — bells

Small 1-inch silver bells worn around ankles for entertainment on journey. Name also applies to 5-inch black bells on thighs during dances; and on women's thighs when girls emerge from month of circumcision rites.

156. *adeng'o* or *twoliot* — bell

Soft iron 4-inch bell worn on specially cut leather strap around warrior's neck.

157. *tolion* — bell

Worn by goats to notify herdsman of their location; 5-inch black iron.

158. *kadong'ot* — bell

Iron bell placed on cows to prevent straying.

159. *neur* — singing board

Flat board whirled around men's heads to frighten away wild animals; sound is said to resemble cry of leopard. Only men who have undergone circumcision ceremony are allowed to use it.

160. *ketitum* or *kirokon* — musical sticks

Sticks 10 inches long beaten together rhythmically by men at dances.

161. *pugan* — bowl lyre

6-stringed harp, 3 feet long; formerly strings were of tendon, modern ones use wire; hollowed wooden bowl covered with skin; played by experts, for entertainment.

162. *kuroru* — flute

Bark flute slipped off small branch; employed by young shepherds to entertain themselves; 3 feet long.

163. *kondu* — trumpet

Shaped from branch of tree with partly hollow stems, covered with skin except for end and blowing hole; blown by men at dances and by girls in evening to call other girls to special ceremony next day.

164. *sirinni* — whistle

Modern 3-inch metal whistle blown at dances by men and boys.

RABAI

165. *ngoli* — whistle

7-inch musical whistle made from end of antelope horn; used by men at dances.

RENDILLE

166. *koke* — bell

Largest and flattest bell carved by any tribe; made from soft desert wood, shaped when wet, decorated with reddish-brown mud; 9-10 inches; Scott choir usage.

167. *araab* — trumpet

Blown about 6 pm on special occasions, signal to parents of sons that it is time to offer sacrifice; blood put over the doors, families remain awake all night; in morning, blood put on every one, milk offering poured out to God; all gather for prayer-song; sons then receive blessing from married priest who has a son; 5 feet long. Also sounded to call important meetings.

SOMALI

168. korr   bell

7-inch wooden bell with rope handle, wooden clapper inside, carving on outside.

TAITA

169. njuga   bells

Black iron bells of Maasai design on leather strip, small pieces of steel inside; four strands worn below right knee; seen at dances.

170. mgamda   drum

Hollow 3-foot diameter wooden drum covered with cowhide fastened with wooden pegs; used at dances.

—KASIGAO (Taita)

171. njugha   bells

Two strands of small silver bells worn below knee of medicine man.

—TAVETA (Taita)

172. njugha   bells

7 strands of black bells worn around legs of girl during 4 days of seclusion while she receives adult instruction; a small piece of steel, often a ¼-inch piece of nail, placed inside; leather string.

TURKANA

173. ecorot (pl. ngicoroi)   bells

Black iron 3-inch bells worn by members of Leopard group; leather strap fastened below knees and bells placed on top of the leather and tied.

174. ekadong'ot   bell

5-inch cowbell to notify herdsmen of cow s location.

175. akwuma, ekagologolot   bell

6-inch wooden cowbell with wooden clappers tied in with leather; leather on rope strap around cow's neck.

176. ebune or apili   bark flute

Used by youths to entertain selves when herding cattle; inside pulled out of bark; 16 inches long.

177. atom or atoroth   trumpet

3-foot trumpet of leather-covered wood, made from tapered branch partially hollowed.

ACKNOWLEDGEMENTS

The editors are grateful to several collaborators who helped them compile this article, especially the authors indicated. Fr. Mbunga's article was adapted with his permission from his 'African Church Music' in *African Ecclesiastical Review*, October 1968. The rest of the material has not been published previously in any form.

The diagrams and basic information for the survey of traditional instruments were provided by Mrs. Eva Christian from materials gathered by Scott Theological College students in Machakos. Photographs were taken by the Rev. Ed Arensen, AIM. Catholic usage of percussion instruments was supplied by Mr. Peter Kibukosya, Ministry of Education, Nairobi. Additional vernacular names were traced by Mr. George K. Mambo, and Mr. Henry Anyumba, Institute of African Studies, University of Nairobi. The survey was compiled and edited by Mrs. Marion McVeigh.

Religious Broadcasting in Kenya

Moses Wesonga & John Ward

The broadcasting situation

In Kenya, as much time is given to religious broadcasting over a national network—the Voice of Kenya—as can be found in almost any place in the world: 13.5 hours a week without charge on radio, plus TV epilogues and religious music programmes. This broadcasting service is in the interest of the welfare of the people, since surveys show how often they dial in religious programmes of Sunday services (in several languages), religious news, and religious music over secular programmes. One survey reported that 61 per cent of radio listeners tune in regularly to religious programmes, with Sunday service broadcasts surprisingly popular.[1]

With 797,000 radio sets in Kenya, over 4.5 million adults or 77 per cent of the adult population are usual radio listeners.[2] This means that religious broadcasting in Kenya by radio is reaching over 2.7 million adults and perhaps an even greater number of children under 16, namely a total of around 5.8 million persons. To serve these people, it is no wonder that the government-owned and -operated station VOK employs a full-time staff in its Religious Department to manage a very demanding schedule.

Radio listenership in East Africa as a whole is interesting, as shown by the following quotations from another survey:

Four out of every five adults (aged 16 and over) among the African urban and peri-urban peoples of East Africa claim to listen to radio, albeit with differing regularities.

The only significant stations listened to are, in order: Voice of Kenya, Tanganyika Broadcasting Corporation, Radio Uganda, Radio Voice of the Gospel, British Broadcasting Corporation.

The proportion of listeners among pagans and agnostics is considerably less than among Christians and Muslims.

Roman Catholic sister interviews a member of the African Israel Church Nineveh at joint broadcasting workshop, April 1971.

Almost as high as the proportion of listeners who claim 'ever' to listen to radio news bulletins, is the proportion who claim to 'ever' listen to music request programmes (8 out of 10 Africans). Of these there are more women than men, and the preponderance of respondents claiming this programme type as being 'most listened to' is among the youth population.

Generally speaking, religious programmes appear to be favoured (in terms of frequency of listening) in greater proportions among the following sub-groups: females, elderly people, people aged 35 years and over, people who are not literate in English, people who have not advanced beyond elementary education, the middle socioeconomic group, and people living in Kenya.[3]

By comparison, television broadcasting for 5½ hours daily in the evening reaches a more limited audience, since there are only 31,500 sets in Kenya.[4] An estimate of viewers at best would be 297,790 based on the average number of viewers per set.[5] Television coverage clearly is only a fraction of the radio audience. This is understandable since TV service was only begun in 1962. Surveys seem to indicate that TV tends to reach proportionately more Asians and Europeans than Africans and the more affluent people concentrated in Nairobi and Mombasa.

The Voice of Kenya handles the language problem by broadcasting in Swahili (the National Service, with 4.2 million adult listeners), and in English (the General Service, with about 300,000 adult listeners), at the same time carrying on broadcasts in vernacular languages (Kikuyu, Maasai, Meru, Kamba, Luo, Luhya, Gusii, Kalenjin, Turkana, Hindustani). With surveys indicating that up to 70 per cent of the people understand Swahili, there is understandably an emphasis on strengthening national identity through broadcasting in this language.

Muslim as well as Christian programmes are broadcast. There is every interest on the part of VOK to broaden religious offerings in order to serve all the people.

Centres for Christian broadcasting

Much of the recording of Christian programmes to be broadcast later is done in VOK studios: Kisumu for the Western Area, Nairobi for the Central Area, and Mombasa for the Coastal Area. In all these cases, the staff of VOK assist church leaders to record their programmes.

Working with the Religious Department of VOK are a number of church centres and council groups. The Communication Department of the Kenya Catholic Secretariat, for instance, is responsible for a minimum of 31 programmes each month in Swahili, Meru, Kikuyu, and English. In a rotation system with other churches, the department is responsible every month for programmes like the four-minute *Epilogues* (a devotional at the close of the broadcasting day), Sunday programmes of discussion and music, as well as specials for Christmas and Easter. Interviews on programmes like *Mambo Leo* and *Contact* are also arranged by the communications secretary.

Apart from VOK studios, church centres for recording and other studio activities are used to meet a demanding schedule of religious broadcasting. These centres make tape recordings for later transmissions of programmes on VOK. At the present time, there are five centres for radio use being utilised, as shown below; and much of the Protestant broadcasting is carried on in these studios. (Addresses and names of executive officers will be found in the Directory, Part V).

1. The *Africa Gospel Church Studio* (about 200 miles west of Nairobi at Kericho), begun in 1961, is especially helpful in producing vernacular programmes, particularly in Kalenjin.

2. The *Africa Inland Church Studio* at Kijabe (about 35 miles northwest of Nairobi) produces over 100 programmes per month for VOK and is the largest single producer of religious programmes. Perhaps this is due to the fact that it was the first Christian studio to be established in Kenya, in 1955. Using a variety of formats, the studio has worked on as many as a dozen different titles using half a dozen languages.

3. The *All Africa Conference of Churches Training Centre*, located on Sclaters Road in Westlands, Nairobi, was opened in 1968 to train African leaders from all over the continent in broadcasting for their respective churches.

4. The *Baptist Communications Centre*, a studio completed in 1969, is situated in the industrial area of Nairobi on Liverpool Road.

5. *Trinity College Studio*, located on Jogoo/Liverpool Road in Nairobi, is a small Anglican-sponsored studio equipped for introductory work in broadcasting.

While the Religious Department of VOK often records or broadcasts programmes from churches directly, it seeks the assistance of the National Christian Council of Kenya through its Department of Christian Communication to co-ordinate the efforts of churches in the planning and scheduling of programmes. A broadcasting secretary working with a staff and the Broadcasting Committee of the NCCK plan 'ROTAs' (a systematic rotation system of churches taking their turn in broadcasting) so that Protestant and Catholic churches alike may be represented effectively. It is expected that in 1972 additional African independent churches will participate in the ROTA.

Television

The good-will created over the years between the VOK and the Kenya churches through radio broadcasting is also evident in the relatively recent introduction of TV into the country. Once again, free time is made available for the production and transmission of Christian programmes. Epilogues of 3-4 minutes' duration are broadcast as the last programme of the day from Sundays to Thursdays. Each Sunday evening 30 minutes are given over to religious singing in which Christians are involved although not exclusively.

The NCCK has plans to produce twelve new programmes in 1972 dealing with such human needs as work among the handicapped, relief aid to drought-striken areas, and the like. These will be produced under the direction of NCCK and Africa Inland Church staff using technical equipment loaned by the AIC.

Plans are also being made by a new organisation Afromedia to build a TV-radio studio in Nairobi, to serve as a production centre for not only Kenya but other African countries also. The project, sponsored by AGC, AIC, Baptist Communications, and the Audio Visual Aids Department of Emmaus Bible School, is expected to cost shs. 6,000,000, and it is hoped that it will be launched by 1974.

The realisation of Christian vision

In establishing the Department of Christian Communication in 1964, the Christian Council of Kenya listed its function as follows: 'to encourage religious broadcasting and television to bring the Gospel to all people in Kenya'.[6] Another way of expressing this intent has been reported in this manner: 'to work for understanding, development and use of the mass media in effective and faithful communication of the Gospel in witness to and in service of people'.[7]

Church leaders in their broadcasting endeavours have worked to respond to this high resolve. The record of broadcasting service to the people of Kenya is now a well-established fact.

The temptation is to continue designing programmes that fulfilled the needs of yesterday without meeting the demands of tomorrow's Kenya. The devotional approach may be better for church gatherings, for instance, than for broadcasts. Already church leaders are working on new formats for effective Christian communication in our day. Perhaps a few examples illustrative of new imperatives may help.

Churches and councils must continue to increase their ways of working together. Fragmentation of broadcasting activities presents a blurred image of the church. Mutual co-operation among Christian groups not only has the encouragement of VOK but also has the endorsement of all those who realise the need of combined resources to accomplish this complex job of broadcasting.

Fortunately, there is already evidence that church groups are carrying on many projects in this manner. For instance, when in 1971 the NCCK and the Kenya Catholic Secretariat worked with the AACC Training Centre to provide a two-week broadcasting workshop open to all religious groups, the event made news headlines. The *East African Standard* (May 7, 1971) reported the event in this way:

> A Roman Catholic sister interviews a member of the African Israel Church Nineveh. A Lutheran pastor, a Seventh-day Adventist and a Church Army Captain hold a panel discussion on polygamy. A Catholic priest prepares a religious music programme featuring the Beatles. These were familiar scenes at a two-week radio workshop which ended recently. The workshop was the first ecumenical broadcasting venture to be held in Kenya. The fifty participants, coming from various churches in all parts of Kenya, learned by doing.

It was clearly a historic occasion.

Yet another example of the co-operation of the churches with each other and with the government is the programme of religious education broadcasts to the schools. Each Thursday at 2.40 p.m. the VOK National Service broadcasts in English a 20-minute Form I religious education programme which is available to those secondary schools which wish to make use of it. Most schools take advantage of the opportunity by tuning in as it is broadcast. Some schools receive tapes of the broadcast for use at other times. There are also two religious education programmes designed to help school teachers: Mondays, 4.30-4.45 p.m. for Form I teachers, and Tuesdays, 3.40-4.00 p.m. for upper primary teachers. The religious education broadcasts are co-ordinated by the Schools Broadcast Division of the Ministry of Education.

Conclusion

The churches are very much involved in Christian broadcasting in Kenya. Radio has long dominated the field, but the challenge of TV is increasingly recognised as one which cannot be ignored. Perhaps the greatest need of all remains that of leadership development, the training of Christian broadcasters whose skill may be used to the full for the advancement of the work of the Church and the development of the country.

REFERENCES

[1] Kenya Government Survey reported by the Rev. H. Olsen in *International Christian Broadcasters Bulletin*, March, 1966.

[2] The pamphlet *Extracts from Voice of Kenya Audience Survey for 1970* (Nairobi: Ministry of Information, 1969) listed 774,400 home radio sets with 6,000 in public places.

Out of an adult population 16 years of age and over of 4,534,000, 77 per cent or 3,500,000 adults were considered to be 'usual listeners'. Using the same figure of 77 per cent, usual adult radio listeners in 1972 are estimated to be 4,500,000. According to the *Voice of Kenya Omnibus Survey* of May 1971 (Nairobi: Associa.ed Business Consultants, 1971), 1,759,000 adults either own a radio personally or live in households where a radio is owned. The same survey estimates that there are now 797,000 radios in use throughout the country. Since 1969 there has been no distinction in licensing procedures between home and public sets, so it is no longer possible to determine how many sets there may be in public places.

3 *A survey and recommendations to the Christian Councils of Kenya and Tanzania* by John Poulton, chapter 11: 'The position of radio/TV in Kenya and Tanzania; and links between these and the literature activities of the church', September, 1966.

4 In 1969 there were 22,000 TV sets in homes and 850 in public places. By 1972 the total number of TV sets in the country had risen to 31,500 of which an estimated 1,100 may be located in public places.

5 The 1969 *VOK Audience Survey* lists 7.1 viewers per home set, and 74.5 viewers per set in public places.

6 *Annual Reports from Committees for the Annual General Meeting of the Christian Council of Kenya,* May 4-5, 1965, p 27.

7 Report of Paul M. Volz, 'Television in Africa Study Project' to the LWFBS Board Meeting, Addis Ababa, Ethiopia, Jan. 19-21, 1971, p. 6.

TABLE 1
CHRISTIAN RADIO BROADCASTING SCHEDULE ON THE VOICE OF KENYA

(as at 1 January, 1972)

Station	Name of programme	Days	Time	Duration in minutes	Programmes per year	Hours per year	Producers	Listeners (over 16)
Nairobi	Wazo la Usiku	Daily	11.00 pm	4.5	365	27.3	ROTA	401,200
National	Wazo la Siku	Mon-Sat	6.00 am	4.5	313	23.5	ROTA	1,200,500
Service	Nyimbo za Sifa	Sunday	6.30 am	13.5	52	11.7	AIC	1,383,400
(Swahili)	Ibada ya Asubuhi	Sunday	8.30 am	27.5	52	23.8	Variable	810,900
	Wimbo Niupendao	Sunday	2.30 pm	45	52	39	AIC	477,000
	Ibada ya Injili	Sunday	10.00 pm	27.5	52	23.8	ROTA	858,600
	Salamu na Nyimbo	Monday	2.15 pm	45	52	39	AIC	190,700
	Mazungumzo ya Kikristo	Tuesday	4.45 pm	13.5	52	11.7	ROTA	381,500
	Mid-week Service	Wednesday	4.45 pm	13.5	52	11.7	ROTA	381,500
	Chochote Chaweza Kutokea	Wednesday	2.15 pm	45	52	39	AIC	333,900
	Mafundisho ya Biblia	Thursday	8.30 am	30	52	26	ROTA	572,400
	Robo Saa ya Watoto	Thursday	4.45 pm	13.5	52	11.7	ROTA	477,000
	Salamu na Nyimbo	Friday	2.15 pm	45	52	39	AIC	477,000
	Makanisa Wiki Hii	Sunday	9.15 am	8	52	7	NCCK	524,700
Nairobi	Epilogues	Daily	11.00 pm	4.5	365	27.3	ROTA	95,300
General	Lift Up Your Hearts	Mon-Sat	6.50 am	4.5	313	23.5	ROTA	191,000
Service	Daily Service	Mon-Sat	9.15 am	4.5	313	23.5	ROTA	53,300
(English)	Singing I Go	Saturday	3.00 pm	27.5	52	23.8	AIC	–
	Our Man on the Mike	Sunday	7.45 am	13.5	52	11.7	BCK	47,600
	Morning Services	Sunday	8.00 am	43.5	52	37.3	Variable	47,600
	Sunday Music	Sunday	2.00 pm	27.5	52	23	AIC	47,600
	Evening Service	Sunday	6.30 pm	53	52	46	Variable	47,600
	The Torch (Church News)	Sunday	7.25 pm	6	52	5.2	NCCK	143,100
Nairobi	Kikuyu Epilogue	Mon-Sat	8.00 pm	5	313	26	ROTA, RCC	286,200
Central	Kikuyu Service	Wednesday	12.00 noon	27.5	52	23.8	ROTA	–
Service	Kikuyu Catholic Talk	Thursday	7.15 pm	13.5	52	11.7	RCC	–
(Vernacular)	Kikuyu Hymn Time	Friday	7.15 pm	13.5	52	11.7	ROTA	286,200
	Kimeru Catholic Talk	Wednesday	5.00 pm	13.5	52	11.7	RCC	48,100
	Kimeru Service	Friday	5.00 pm	13.5	52	11.7	MCK	–
	Maasai Service	Thursday	7.00 pm	13.5	52	11.7	AIC	48,100
	Kikamba Service	Friday	5.45 pm	13.5	52	11.7	SA, ABC, AIC	95,400
Western	Kisii Service	Monday	4.45 pm	13.5	52	11.7	AIC, LCK	95,400
Kenya	Kalenjin	Tuesday	5.45 pm	13.5	52	11.7	AIC, AGC	143,100
(Vernacular)	Luo	Wednesday	8.00 pm	13.5	52	11.7	LCK, CPK, AIC	238,500
	Luhya	Thursday	7.15 pm	13.5	52	11.7	BCK	95,400

NOTES on above table:

1 The table gives in the last column 'usual radio listeners'; the number is based on the 1969 *Voice of Kenya Audience Survey,* plus a 5 per cent increase across the board as indicated in a further VOK sampling completed in May 1971.

2 For daily programmes, average figures have been used since the audience varies considerably with the different days of the week.

3 The principal criterion affecting the number of listeners is not the quality of the pro-

gramme but the time when it is broadcast. The chart demonstrates the significant variation in listeners, depending upon broadcast time.

[4] There are three ROTAs composed of the following producers:

Kiswahili ROTA = ABC, AGC, AIC, BCK, CPK, MCK, PCEA, RCC, SA, SDA.

English ROTA = AGC, AIC, BCK, CPK, KCTPF (Kenya Christian Teachers Prayer Fellowship), MCK, PCEA, RCC, SA.

Kikuyu ROTA = AIC, BCK, CPK, PCEA, SDA.

[5] The 1969 *VOK Audience Survey* did not record the number of listeners to the Nairobi Central Station for Wednesday, 12.00 noon nor Thursday, 7.15 p.m. For Saturday, 3.00 p.m. (General Service) and Friday, 5.00 p.m. (Nairobi Central Station) the audience was listed as less than 500. However, the numbers are substantially larger at the present time.

[6] The term 'variable' (under Producers) refers to broadcasts, either live or from tapes, of regular church services, and includes Catholic, Protestant, Anglican and Independent worship services.

Production of Christian Literature

Jocelyn Murray

Introduction

In Kenya, as in many other African countries, Christian missionaries were early involved in the writing, printing, publishing and selling of books. They translated the gospel portions which were in many cases the first written materials in a language; and simple catechisms, school readers, collections of folk stories and proverbs all came from the missionary presses. As missionary involvement in education increased, there was a corresponding increase in the production and distribution of educational materials, meeting needs not yet catered for by government or commercial agencies. Although Christian literature and Bible translation needs were not neglected, the situation was not altogether satisfactory. In 1957, the biggest mission bookshop organisation in Kenya, the CMS Bookshops, were sold to a commercial firm, signalling the intention of the church most heavily involved to withdraw from what had become largely an educational service and not a means of evangelistic outreach.

Thus in the last two decades distribution and also publishing agencies have had to devolve themselves from functions adequately catered for in other ways, and have faced the necessity of redefining their aims and purposes in terms of *Christian* literature. This has occurred at the same time that demands for the training of Kenya nationals to carry on such work have been increasing. Neither task has yet been completed.

Writing

At a time when an increasing number of books by African authors are coming from the commercial presses, Christian publishing houses in Kenya have not yet been able to show a similar advance. Translations, adaptations and books by expatriates are still in the majority. A number of promising writers have studied at Africa Literature Centre, Kitwe, Zambia, but most are now in commercial journalism. This is no more than can be expected, for in no country is it easy for free-lance writers to make a living. The Africa Christian Press, based in Ghana, has published books by several East African including Kenyan authors. This has been made possible largely due to the painstaking and dedicated one-to-one help given to young writers by the ACP representative in East Africa. Other ACP books have been prepared by group writing teams, usually consisting of nationals and expatriates. This method has been used by other organisations with success; and the church manuals in Kikuyu, published over the last five years by the Presbyterian Church of East Africa, have been prepared in this way by a local/expatriate team. The Christian Writers Club, organised by the AELO office in Nairobi, is a creative effort to train young Christians in writing.

The editor of the Africa Inland Church's Kesho Publications programme is one of several Kenyans in full-time church literature work; in addition to his journalistic activities he has had full-length books published by both commercial and Christian publishers. The AACC-related Christian news feature service based in Nairobi, Africa Acts, reports that a number of young Africans are now coming forward with articles. A beginning has been made, but clearly we are still a long way from seeing the Christian message presented adequately in print by Africans to Africans.

Publishing

All the larger denominations in Kenya, and many of the smaller ones, publish for their own needs, chiefly instructional and devotional material, but some aim at a wider public. A few have their own printing presses which normally allow books to be sold at a price lower than would be possible if a commercial press was used. The advantage gained in the short term needs to be weighed against the greater difficulties of africanisation because of the need for technically competent staff, and the 'hidden subsidies' in the form of missionary personnel, not always allowed for in costing. It may be questioned whether the present lower prices could be maintained in an exclusively African-staffed Christian press.

Africa Inland Press and Evangel Publishing House are the two largest

Christian publishing houses in Kenya today, and EPH is the largest religious publisher in Africa. The AIM has its own press. Their lists of publications in English, Swahili and Kenyan languages (also French and West African languages for EPH) are growing, and both organisations have a wide vision of evangelism through literature. The editor of Kesho Publications (AIC) has already been mentioned as one of the leading Africans in literature work in Kenya; again, the Church of God Press is managed by another talented Kenya Christian. Another type of organisation, without its own press and with a minimum of superstructure, is Uzima Press, recently set up by the Anglican Province of Kenya to replace a former organisation. It publishes material offered to or commissioned by any of the six Anglican dioceses of the

One million scriptures were bought and read in Kenya in 1971.

Province, or in certain cases channels material to other publishers.

Publications coming from other African countries are widely distributed in Kenya. Much Swahili material comes from Tanzanian organisations such as the Central Tanganyika Press, and Inland Publishers. English material, aimed mainly at young people, comes from the Africa Christian Press of Ghana and the Daystar Press of Nigeria. In Roman Catholic dioceses, the most useful locally-produced material, some of it written by African Christians, is coming from the Pastoral Institute of Eastern Africa, Gaba, in Uganda.

Distribution

There was a time when every mission station in Kenya had its little book-stall, often run by a missionary wife or a pastoral worker. The present utilisation of missionary personnel limits this type of distribution, and the disposal of the CMS Bookshops to a commercial agency has been another important reason why new avenues for distribution have been needed. A number of new bookshops have been opened and others extended in the last few years, and many of these have African managers. These include Kesho Book Centre (AIC) in Nairobi, with branches in Eldoret and Machakos, Nairobi Diocesan (formerly Church Army) Bookshop, the Christian Literature Centre in Kericho and Bethany Bookshop in Nakuru (Africa Gospel Church), Arahuka Book Depot (Diocese of Mt. Kenya) in Fort Hall, the Methodist Bookshop in Meru and the Friends Bookshop at Kaimosi. Almost all these bookshops include out-reach selling through mobile units, three-wheeled vehicles or bicycle colportage. For the setting up and maintenance of such work generous grants have been received from Christian literature organisations overseas, such as the United Society for Christian Literature, Lit-Lit of New York, and JACLO (Joint Action Christian Literature Overseas). The Catholic Bookshop in Nairobi, with a branch in Mombasa, is the largest Catholic bookshop in the world outside the United States, although it sells large quantities of general and educational as well as specifically religious books and supplies. There are other Roman Catholic bookshops at Kitale, Kisumu, Nyeri and Meru. In Nairobi itself the Keswick Book Society has continued to expand and provides a most valuable service.

Despite this network of fairly large bookshops through the main centres of the country, it is still true to say that many Christians in Kenya find it difficult to obtain the books they want, let alone enjoy the chance to see new books. Nor can it be said that evangelism through sale and free distribution of Christian literature is seen as a priority. In the long run, one answer may be a greater use of the facilities offered by commercial bookshops and village stores, rather than setting up more Christian bookshops with their heavy drain on capital resources. For this to be done, and indeed for the simplification of management in existing bookshops, wholesale supplies need to be easily obtained at commercial rates, preferably from one wholesale outlet. At the moment, this is not possible in Kenya, and unfortunately more than one plan for a wholesale warehouse has fallen through in the last few years. A co-operative approach to wholesaling is vital if distribution is to be efficient and if locally-trained personnel, who will inevitably be less experienced as they commence, are to effectively take over full management of Christian bookshops.

Periodicals

A number of churches publish small denominational papers, but only a few are designed for a wider audience and are sold through bookshops and newsstands. The *Catholic Mirror*, in English and Swahili, with a circulation of about 10,000, appears monthly. *Kesho* in Swahili and *Today* in English are published by the Africa Inland Church, with circulations of about 14,000 and 8,000 respectively. These are designed as general evangelistic papers rather than denominational ones, but they do carry news of the sponsoring church. *Target* (English) and *Lengo* (Swahili) are published monthly by the East African Venture Company, and first appeared in 1964 in place of *Rock*, a monthly paper published from 1957 by the Christian Council of Kenya. At present these papers, which are sold in both Kenya and Tanzania, have circulations of approximately 17,000 and 21,000 respectively. A point to bear in mind with all these papers is the high number of readers per paper. Many subscriptions are to colleges and schools, and recently adult literacy classes have used the special supplements in *Lengo*. Since late 1971, *Target* has had a regular educational development supplement each month named *Torch*, with *Nuru* as the counterpart for *Lengo*.

The publication of Christian periodicals presents many difficulties, not least of which are the financial ones. All these periodicals have to be heavily subsidised by profits from bookshops or by subsidies and grants from the sponsoring church or from overseas donations. The East African Venture Company estimates that 85 per cent of the cost of producing *Target/Lengo* has to come from outside sources, despite rising circulations and increased income from advertising.

Target and *Lengo* have had from 1968 a Kenyan national as editor—first Henry Okullu, succeeded recently by Odhiambo Okite. These men have developed further the experiments of their expatriate predecessors in using the papers to give a Christian viewpoint on political and social matters in East Africa. Not all church leaders have approved of this, and some have in fact boycotted the papers in the past. This type of opposition seems to be lessening as respect for the uncompromising stand on matters of Christian and national interest has grown. Readers are of all denominations, including Roman Catholic, as news items and letters to the editor show, and the papers have often been quoted in the commercial press.

The Bible Society

The Bible Society of Kenya as a separate organisation dates from 1970, but it continues the functions of the Bible Society of East Africa. In its various departments—retail and wholesale sales, publication, promotion, mobile distribution and at the executive level, the Bible Society has given an outstanding example of the utilisation of local personnel without lowering of standards. The Executive Secretary since 1964, John Mpaayei, handed over that task in 1971 to David Gitari in order to concentrate on the translation of the Maasai Bible. Other translations are under way in the Boran, Gusii and Turkana languages, and the full Luo and Union Luyia Bibles are close to completion and publication. Other new ventures are a translation of the New Testament into popular Swahili, being undertaken by Thomas Kalume, and the publication of Swahili gospels in Arabic script. The Swahili New Testament has also been published with the line illustrations made famous in *Today's English Version*, and illustrated gospels and portions in Kenya languages have been produced. A chronology of Scripture translations published in Kenya, with annual distribution figures for 1971, is given here in Table 1. Almost all of the work has been due to the Bible Society and its sister societies in Britain (BFBS) and the USA (ABS); but a Pokot New Testament has been published by the Trinitarian Bible Society (UK), and a handful of Catholic versions has been published (e.g. Kikuyu New Testament in 1955; see *Chronology of Christianity in Kenya*) though few remain in print today.

Most Bible Society publications are still sold at subsidised prices, and as yet only a small proportion of the gifts needed for this work come from local sources. But Bible Society Auxiliaries in Kenya are reported to be showing an encouraging interest in the support of translation work for those peoples of Kenya who are as yet largely unevangelised, such as the Boran, Turkana and Galla.

Conclusion

In surveying the extent of Christian literature work in Kenya at the beginning of the 1970s, one is left with the feeling that much is carried on by individual enthusiasts, whether expatriate or national, and that there is no great depth of concern on the part of church leaders and members. Christian literature tends to be seen as one department, and a not very vital one, in a church's organisation, rather than as an invaluable adjunct to every department — youth work, Christian education, women's work, stewardship, evangelism and the rest. A mark of this is seen in the fact that the Literature Committee of the National Christian Council of Kenya has not met, at the date of writing, for twenty months, and that inter-church co-operation in literature is in some areas less advanced than it was a few years ago.

This is not to overlook valuable co-operative efforts inspired by two other bodies, neither of which are, however, confined to Kenya. The Evangelical Literature Fellowship of East Africa (ELFEA) has done much to inspire and help literature workers in all spheres at its annual conferences. The Africa Evangelical Literature Office also is in Nairobi, and provides information, assistance and expert advice to organisations throughout Africa; because of its location it has been of special benefit to Kenya.

Nevertheless, greater interest from church leaders, and renewed efforts in inter-church co-operation, are certainly needed. Special weaknesses in Kenya seem to be the lack of an overall wholesaling policy, and the lack of trained and dedicated African Christians now being prepared for future leadership. Some there are, without doubt, and a number of those already in positions of leadership have been referred to above. But if all missionaries in Kenya were suddenly to leave, Christian literature work would suffer much more severely than many other departments of Christian work. In the matter of the actual message which the books produced in Kenya aim to spread, we are still not seeing enough Kenya Christians writing for their own people. These challenges need to be met vigorously if the future church in Kenya is to be a reading, thinking, growing church.

TABLE 1
TRANSLATION AND DISTRIBUTION OF SCRIPTURES IN KENYA

| Language | Year of first publication | | | Scripture sales from Bible House, Kenya, 1971 | | | | | | | | | |
| | Gospel or Portion | NT | Bible | Gospel or Portions | | | | | | NTs | Bibles | Selections | TOTALS |
				Matthew	Mark	Luke	John	Acts	Portions (total)				
Boran	1934	1973										188	118
Digo	—												0
Duruma	—												0
Elgeyo: use Kalenjin													
Embu: use Kikuyu													
Galla (Orma)	1878			Discontinued										0
Giriama	1892	1908	1908	Discontinued										0
Gusii	1929	1948		2,417	1,828	14,026	3,275	—	21,546	3,426		16,688	41,660
Kalenjin (Union)	1958	1968		4,508	2,501	3,962	3,109	—	14,080	1,996	5,925	24,590	46,591
Kamba	1850	1920	1956	4,127	4,361	5,054	5,522	5,160	24,224	632	5,083	17,756	47,695
Kikuyu	1903	1926	1951	13,542	18,130	11,233	10,718	9,664	63,287	2,854	4,676	22,252	103,069
Kipsigis	1912	1953		Discontinued: Kalenjin used									0
Kony: use Sebei													
Kuria	1969				4,367				4,367				4,367
Luhya:													
Hanga	1914	1939		Discontinued: use Union Luhya									0
Nyore	1923	1936		Discontinued: use Union Luhya									0
Ragoli	1911	1925		375	327	872	889	—	2,463	1,395	1,260	8,816	13,934
Union	1911	1968	1974	2,266	1,925	8,076	5,865	1,303	19,435	2,750		8,464	30,649
Luo	1911	1926	1953	6,860	4,748	10,696	6,428	4,430	33,162	4,773	7,528	27,181	72,644
Maasai	1905	1922								396			396
Marakwet: use Kalenjin													
Meru	1921	1952	1964	9,103			8,016		17,119	1,420			18,539
Nandi	1926	1933	1939	Discontinued: use Kalenjin									0
Nyika:													
Rabai	1848			Discontinued									0
Ribe	1878			Discontinued									0
Pokomo	1894	1901		Discontinued									0
Pokot (Ng'ala)	1936	1967										109	109
Samburu (Maasai)	1961				796				796				796
Somali	1915	1973				604							604
Swahili:													
Mombasa	1878	1909	1914	Discontinued									0
Union	1934	1950	1952	16,851	18,049	16,602	52,251	7,159	110,912	10,921	8,192	319,445	449,470
Taita:													
Dabida	1904	1922		Discontinued									0
Sagalla	1892			Discontinued									0
Taveta	1892	1906		Discontinued									0
Tharaka	1934			Discontinued									0
Tugen: use Kalenjin													
Turkana	1972									558			558
English	1972											1,679	1,679
Other non-Kenyan languages				35,847	43,485	50,696	45,392	28,194	203,614	33,083	25,584	61,115	323,396
									252	82	56		390
TOTALS				95,626	100,517	121,821	141,465	55,910	515,591	72,866	59,724	507,986	1,156,167

Anglican minister Shadrak Opoti explains how to make a beehive to village polytechnic youths.

Communications: Key to Development

Janice McLaughlin & John Ward

A pre-school nutrition clinic closes because mothers fail to attend; voters fail to register for party elections; the exodus to the cities continues despite 'back to the land' pleas; farmers refuse to use a new cattle dip in their area. Apathy or ill-will? or are these simply examples of a failure to communicate?

Success or failure in any development effort can often be traced to communication. Communication can mean the difference between change or resistance, interest or indifference, acceptance or rejection.

100

Money cannot buy development

The churches have traditionally communicated their concern for development through schools and hospitals. Today the churches are striving to communicate a new vision of development which goes beyond educational, medical or economic growth: a vision which recognises the freedom, dignity and equality of all men, which does not assume a superiority of developed nations over the developing world, and which takes into account the whole man. A theology of development is emerging. Already the church in East Africa has contributed to this growing awareness. Thus, the AMECEA MISEREOR Seminar in 1970 on 'The Church and Development' defined development as:

the growth of the whole man and of all men in solidarity with the whole human race. It is therefore the progressive humanisation of life embracing liberation from famine, disease and ignorance as well as emancipation from all servitude and *dominatio*. It goes further to embrace that integral human development which includes the higher values of love and friendship, prayer and contemplation and in Christ, the perfector of men, finds ultimate fulfillment in communion with God himself.[1]

Similar insights emerged from the Limuru Consultation on Development organised in 1971 by SODEPAX, the international committee for the promotion of society, development and peace. The thirty-three participants agreed as follows:

The redeeming love of God which sets us free is a challenge to share our freedom by liberating those who are oppressed by injustice, by despair, by the forces of evil associated with poverty, disease, ignorance or resignation. This liberation from oppression is the process of encouraging men as individuals and as members of a community to realise their fullest potential as the created Sons of God. It is this that we mean by development.[2]

The National Christian Council of Kenya also held a special consultation at Limuru in 1971, discussing what development meant in Christian terms. Here are a few of its summary statements:

Development (is) more than just economic growth... It embodies such intangible aspects as seeking to bring about social equality and justice... Development involves growing; not doing things for people, but helping them to be conscious of their needs and problems and removing the obstacles; helping people to acquire the means to do this; giving all the same chance; involving the participation of all, both weak and strong, in interdependent effort.
Development is a comprehensive process aiming at the whole person and the wholeness of human beings. We cannot allow the distinction between man's spiritual needs and his physical need.[3]

The consensus of many participants was that development is the outcome and expression of evangelism--a way of reconciling and restoring a deprived social order to wholeness.

Still another way of understanding what development means comes from Marie F. Perrin Jassy from Musoma, Tanzania:

In sociological terms, development is the growing ability of people to use and increase their own resources. To promote development is to educate the people to this end. It is therefore mainly a problem of communication, of the transmission of ideas and techniques from one group to another. We all know that one of the main problems met in any development program is to get the understanding, participation, and responsibility of the people involved... The family, the clan, or any other traditional form of grouping, may not have the proper structures and channels of communication to receive and use new concepts and techniques... Christianity offers an exceptionally good basis to build a new social structure adapted to development. It replaces the idea of blood kinship with the idea of spiritual kinship, leading to a universal society. It offers a world view based upon the development of mankind towards salvation, thus providing a mythological explanation for progress in the material world, for social and economic development.[4]

As these concepts are communicated, the theoretical framework will continue to evolve. The next task is to transform these ideals into action. A leading spokesman on the urgency of this effort is President Julius Nyerere of Tanzania, who warns:

> The Church should accept that the development of peoples means rebellion. At a given and decisive point in history men decide to act against those conditions which restrict their freedom as men. I am suggesting that, unless we participate actively in the rebellion against those social structures and economic organisations which condemn men to poverty, humiliation and degradation, then the Church will become irrelevant to man and the Christian religion will degenerate into a set of superstitions accepted by the fearful. Unless the Church, its members and its organisations express God's love for man by involvement and leadership in constructive protest against the present conditions of man, then it will become identified with injustice and persecution.[5]

Communicating development in Kenya

A full-time task of communication in the church would be simply to inform members concerning the projects and engagements in development that are already under way. There are several ways that this can be done. At the AACC Training Centre in February, 1971, young people were introduced to the challenges of a week-end conference on 'Communications and Development' inspired by SODEPAX and sponsored jointly by the Youth

Department of the National Christian Council and the Catholic Secretariat. Another example is the part Kenyans played in joining forty countries in the Hunger Walk, May 9, 1971, many going the full twenty-five miles in order to raise funds for nutritional, agricultural and water development projects in Kenya. These intentional communications events have done much to bring to the attention of the public the pressing needs of less fortunate people.

But other reminders are needed to show what is left to be done, and what in fact the church is at present doing in development. For instance, how many people know that there are 79 Catholic sponsored primary schools in the Mombasa Diocese, including 14,000 students and 8 secondary schools with 1,500 students? Or that this same diocese has a mobile unit that visits 25 neighbouring villages, treating an average of 200 patients monthly? Or that the healing ministry of the Protestant Churches' Medical Association includes at least 14 hospitals with resident doctors and 16 dispensaries and maternity centres? The church responds to human need wherever it is found, as shown by a statement made by the Rev. Fr. Joachim Getonga, General Secretary of the Catholic Secretariat, after a visit to Northern Kenya:

> The whole development in this area depends on water. People at times have to make journeys over 15 miles to fetch water. The Church has faced this challenge valiantly and from its little resources has provided over 20 bore holes for water and built five dams for collecting water.[6]

Development incarnate

The NCCK carries on extensive work in many areas of development: agricultural training through seven rural training centres; training primary school leavers in numerous village polytechnics[7]; social development through nine community centres, and others. Concerning the number of people helped, one report lists the following statistics: 15,000 people receiving assistance from caseworkers, 20 per cent of their work being with church members and 80 per cent with non-church members.[8]

Perhaps more significant for the development of the entire social order is the involvement and assistance of government in many of these projects, such as the village polytechnics program. Many schools now are being turned over to government under the sponsorship of the churches. The merits of the Kenya government working with the churches in development areas may well serve as a precedent for other developing nations.

Communications in Development Conference, December 1971

Those engaged in the work of communications for the Kenyan churches are increasingly aware of their role in development. In December 1971, forty delegates from Zambia, Malawi, Tanzania and Kenya, including representatives from the Kenya Catholic Secretariat and the NCCK, participated in a conference held in Lusaka, Zambia, whose theme was 'Communications in Development'.

Considerable consensus was achieved at the meeting, some underlying principles of which may well be cited here:

> We believe that development will take place where Christian service and the Christian message are effectively communicated. We see development as the building up of the whole nation.
> In development, governments and churches often share the same goals. Communicators can help in defining these common goals and in reaching them. At the same time, we recognise that, in its proper desire to work with governments in serving the people, the Church must preserve its integrity as the Church. Christian communicators can be especially effective in the fields of the life of the society and the community, education, nutrition and medicine.
> Churches and their communicators should make a thorough study of their government's plans to see where their contribution can be effective. We recognise that many of those implementing government plans will be Christians, and that the Church's contribution may effectively be made through them as well as through official church representation in development programmes. We believe that our churches will readily offer personnel to development projects in our countries, as well as any other help they can give.
> We see the advantage of using the African respect for leaders, of Church and of community, in adding weight to the ideas of development which are communicated. We see the need for the voice of the people to be heard through the Church's com-

munications media.[9]

. To achieve these goals, the conference recommended that serious consideration be given to the establishment of a National Ecumenical Communications Projects Board in each of the five countries, composed of Catholic, Protestant and Independent churchmen in addition to representatives from government, United Nations, and voluntary agencies. The purpose of such a board would be to co-ordinate all communications and development projects in order to achieve maximum co-operation in service to their respective countries.

In Africa, by Africans

The conference also stressed the need for a more local approach. 'We can increase the effectiveness of our communication,' the participants agreed, 'by making sure that our material is produced in Africa by Africans and bearing in mind the specific needs of Africa.' Already, attempts are being made in Kenya to use traditional African approaches to communication. Improvised dramas are being performed by the SODEPAX Youth Group to illustrate the

growing gap between rich and poor. Mothers in Western Kenya are being taught nutrition in mission clinics through Swahili songs and jingles. Riddles, proverbs and folktales are being heard on the Voice of Kenya's religious broadcasts.

Africa offers a wealth of images and symbols. By utilising this rich natural resource, communicators preserve it for future generations. Perhaps in this way communicators will succeed in bridging the gap between old and new, and will thus help to prevent the sacrifice of traditional human values to /the new idols of technology. Up to the present time little has been done in this direction. Indeed, a critic evaluating existing communication systems has observed:

> Neither the local programmes nor those from abroad go far to help Christians or general listeners meet problems related to the breakdown of local cultures or the inroads of Western secular culture.[10]

Undoubtedly, this state of affairs can only be corrected by an increase in trained Kenyan communicators. The churches can make a great contribution to Kenya's development by training such professionals. These communicators can be the spokesmen for African aspirations. They can give the Third World a voice in international forums and a hearing through worldwide news media. They can rescue Kenya from the scramble for its airwaves and from the foreign monopoly of its information and communication systems. Then and only then will Kenya be both the agent and the beneficiary of its own development.

FOOTNOTES

1 AMECEA-MISEREOR Seminar on the Church and Development, Limuru, Kenya, December 1-4, 1970, p. 13. For AMECEA see Part V (Directory). MISEREOR is a German Roman Catholic funding organisation.

2 *Picking up the pieces.* A report of a SODEPAX Conference on the Churches in Development Planning and Action, Limuru, January 1971, p. 5.

3 A report of discussions on the theme of development by the staff of the National Christian Council of Kenya at Limuru Conference Centre, February 1-10, 1971.

4 Marie F. Perrin Jassy, a paper, 'Education for development at the rural parish level,' delivered at the AMECEA-MISEREOR Seminar, Limuru, December 1970, p. 55.

5 President Julius Nyerere's Address to the General Assembly of the Maryknoll Sisters, October 16, 1970, p. 11.

6 Kenya Catholic Secretariat Press Release, February, 1971.

7 See Part V (Directory) under NCCK for a listing of these village polytechnics.

8 NCCK *Annual Reports for 1969*, May 5-7, 1970, p. 58. The statistics in the foregoing sentence have been updated to early 1972.

9 Minutes of the Communications in Development Conference, Lusaka, Zambia, December 13-20, 1971.

10 James E. McEldowney, 'Christian communications in developing nations', *Target* (March, 1971), p. 10.

African Society and the Foreign Legacy in the Churches

Joachim Getonga

Society, according to St. Thomas Aquinas, is a moral and stable union of many people aspiring with their actions to one common end.

Any given society has its own morals and culture which strengthen that moral and stable union and guide the people bound together towards the common good or end. There is no society without culture, and culture as defined by Lowie is 'the sum total of what an individual acquires from his society, those beliefs, customs, artistic norms, food-habits and crafts which come to him not by his own creative activity but as a legacy from the past, conveyed by formal or informal education'.

When the church came to Kenya a century or so ago, she found the people of Kenya with both a society and a culture. They had a moral code, not written, but engraved in their hearts, and customs which bound them together, guided, protected and made the stability of society to be respected by the people themselves. With stability, people were able to aspire and to work together for the common good. People fought against enemies together, such as invading tribes, wild animals and thieves. They prayed and offered sacrifices to their Creator for the common good, including for rain, good harvests, the elimination of epidemics by God, and other calamities which from time to time befell their society.

All these peoples, then, had their own culture, composed of language, beliefs, customs, songs, artistic norms, food-habits and way of clothing, which they had acquired not by imposition from outside but as a legacy from the past. The relations between church and society in this country should therefore be examined within the context of people's culture.

Jesus Christ said that He did not come to destroy the law but to build upon it. With this intention He was born into Jewish society. He followed the moral code of that people, and adapted Himself to Jewish culture. Even today Christianity still enjoys much of Jewish culture. The Apostles followed the footsteps of their Master, and wherever they went, they preached Christ. They respected and adopted the culture and good customs of the people to whom they preached the Word of God. Christianity became integrated with the cultures of peoples. In fact almost all church liturgy today is based on Jewish or Roman culture. Church robes or vestments, songs, ways of worship, materials for sacraments, and ways of administering sacraments, are all based either on the Roman style or on Western culture of the Middle Ages.

When the first missionaries came to Africa to preach Christ, despite their goodwill they imagined that they were coming to a particularly primitive, disorganised and uncultured people. With that unfortunate approach Christianity was brought to Africa, Kenya included. From the very first, also, the church was brought to Kenya by different people of differing faiths, nationalities, cultures and customs. Although they preached one Christ, yet they disagreed on fundamental theological beliefs. Nor did they only disagree; they even fought and hated one another. This destroyed the common spiritual good the people had, and even the common material good which they possessed. African society was confronted with differing beliefs by different missionaries. Families were divided into different faiths. They came to the point of hating one another and sometimes they even came to blows, especially when a member of a family decided to change from one faith to another.

Society itself was divided into zones of different faith. One zone belittled the other as inferior or backward simply because that zone adhered to a faith which the other one did not like. Missionaries willingly or unwittingly brought with them the biases they had in their respective countries. All this destroyed the spiritual and moral unity which was essential for a stable society.

To be regarded as a true Christian in those days, a person had to abandon almost all the culture which he had acquired from his own African society. He had to detach himself from virtually all the beliefs of his parents, throw away his native clothes and put on Western dress or ornaments, in order to be accepted into the Christian faith. Tribal dances in particular were considered diabolical.

With regard to worship, almost nothing native was considered genuine. No matter how good traditional prayers and songs might be, they could not be integrated into the Christian way of worship. Association with people who adhered to their ancient customs was completely prohibited. Christianity took it as its duty through the missionaries to change the most fundamental cultural values of society. This drastic change, this refusal to adapt Christianity to cultural values, has not helped the spread of Christianity. From the very beginning, people came to resent Christianity. At the beginning only innocent children came forward for baptism. Adults considered the new faith as alien, European, and dangerous to their cultural heritage. Any member of society joining Christianity was considered to have become an outcast, a traitor to African culture. On the other hand, any new Christian who still associated himself with his cultural heritage was excommunicated. Even today after centuries of evangelisation this attitude still persists in some areas of Africa and also of Kenya. It is not surprising, then, that in many regions conversion to Christianity has been very slow. In Kenya, in fact, there are today more non-Christians than there were a century ago, notwithstanding the last hundred years of evangelisation.

Why has it taken so long to convert people to Christianity here in Kenya? Is it because missionaries were few? I do not think so, because even around the largest mission stations you can still find many old people who have not yet been convinced. Is it because Christianity is difficult to practice? I do not think so. Traditional religions were often far more difficult to follow, with all their superstitions and the prohibitions contained in them.

The reasons why conversion has been so slow in many areas is because Christianity forced itself on society as a strong, rough wind of change rather than as a calm breeze bringing in fresh air and removing stale air without people being any the wiser.

It is, therefore, the duty of all Christian preachers to rethink the place of their cultural heritage and to reconstruct what was destroyed during those pioneering days of evangelisation. It is also unfortunate that our African society had the bad luck to be the recipient of a divided Christianity. That is an accident of history, so far as we are concerned. But people are responsible for history, and it is now the responsibility of the churches to make new history. Now the churches have a challenge in front of them towards society. At first they created a society which had to be ruled and told everything; but now there has emerged a new society conscious of its own existence and which attaches great importance to its cultural heritage, although regrettably this has almost been swallowed up and submerged by foreign culture.

Fortunately, today most of our churches have realised the mistakes of the past in disregarding African cultural values, and in fragmenting society through the importation of foreign religious divisions and differences. This realisation has brought the churches at last to the conference table to open a dialogue between them and society, and even between the churches themselves.

In the churches, moreover, we are now beginning to see and hear African music and singing being introduced. Research is even going on concerning African traditional religions to see what can profitably be introduced into school syllabuses.

Ecumenism is another dynamic factor which is little by little bridging the gaps created by former Catholic/Protestant antagonism. Church leaders, led by the love of Christ, are coming together to sort out their differences. Even if at present they cannot fully agree on certain doctrinal matters, yet they can and do agree concerning many things they have in common.

It is thus most encouraging to see that today the churches are working together on a common syllabus of religious education for all Christian-sponsored schools in Kenya—something which would have been unthinkable ten years ago. At present, they have agreed to use a single version of the Bible, whereas before they had insisted on either Catholic or Protestant Bibles. The feelings and prejudices which existed among Christians against one another are diminishing.

The Revival Fellowship (Brethren) in Kenya

George K. Mambo

The widespread movement of spiritual life in Kenya, commonly called the Revival Fellowship, or Brethren, is a part of what is widely known as the East African Revival Fellowship, or Balokole (Luganda for 'Saved Ones'), whose origins go back forty years or so to the Ruanda Revival. A person becomes a member of this Fellowship by accepting Jesus Christ as personal Saviour leading to daily salvation. Assurance of salvation comes through a deep religious experience, which results in spontaneous open confession of sin. Emphasis is placed on the Blood of Jesus shed on the Cross making possible the certainty of God's forgiveness. Members of the Revival refer to each other in the Swahili language as *ndugu* (brother) or *dada* (sister) in Christ, and are called collectively *Wandugu* (Brethren).

Origins of the Revival Fellowship in Kenya

By the year 1916, a great mass movement into the churches of Kenya had begun. Over the next decade, the New Testament was published in the major languages of this mass influx, namely in Kamba (1920), Luhya/Ragoli (1925), Kikuyu (1926), and in Luo (1926). This had a significant effect on the direction Christianity was to take in Kenya. Many Christians who then read the New Testament in their mother tongue for the first time came to a different understanding of New Testament teaching from the way it had been presented by missionaries. One result was the emergence of separatist or independent churches especially during the decade 1920-1930. Other Christians, although equally moved by the New Testament message in their own language, remained devoted and faithful members within the historical or mission churches. The Holy Spirit was at work to a unique degree in the lives of such Christians, many of whom were unknown to each other, and of most of whom no record remains today. The soil was being prepared for a new and genuine type of African Christianity.

Meanwhile far to the west in the kingdom of Ruanda, a quiet and markedly African lay revival movement (possibly influenced by the Oxford Movement and the Keswick Convention, both of England) had broken out from 1927 onwards, sweeping through Uganda and its large Anglican Church in the mid-1930s. In 1937 the first envoys of the Revival visited Kenya. This team, as they had come to be called, remained for several days, preaching to Christians around Kabete. Before their departure, a small group of Christians including a prominent Anglican clergyman experienced a deep sense of salvation. Within the same year another group of Christians had been similarly converted in Nyanza through contact with members of the Revival from Uganda.

Towards the end of 1938 a second Revival team visited Kenya from Ruanda, holding even more successful preaching services at the Pumwani CMS station in Nairobi. A number of Christians were 'saved', to use the new language of the Revival. These persons came from different tribes across Kenya, and included several more Anglican clergy and a number of prominent laymen educated at Alliance High School, Kikuyu. Through this brief preaching tour in the capital city, the team had sown the seeds of revival in the religiously fertile soil of Kenya.

Between the years 1937 and 1945 this new Revival Fellowship faced severe opposition from the established churches. Members were not permitted to participate in normal church activities. Church leaders particularly resented the Brethren's open confession of sin and their constant claim to have been born again. There were also the inevitable misunderstandings that arise when Christianity penetrates non-Christian cultures and languages. Luo Brethren seeking for a Luo word for 'fellowship' — to describe their central experience of the close, intimate fellowship meeting of a handful of Brethren sharing their thoughts — eventually chose *lalruok*, a word which meant in

Luo the huddling together of thieves conspiring together to commit a robbery; inevitably, then, the Brethren were referred to as 'that gang'. Similarly, Kikuyu members were accused of reintroducing the primitive Kikuyu traditional rite of *guciaruo ringi* (second birth), although in fact they were referring to the Christian experience of rebirth in Christ. Throughout Kenya at that period the Fellowship was contemptuously referred to as 'Dini ya Ruanda', and by some missionaries as the 'Ruanda Heresy'. In many places Brethren were not allowed to hold meetings in church buildings, and at times their meetings were violently disrupted by opponents. Nevertheless, the Brethren continued to come together in homes, in the bush and at times under trees near churches.

After World War II the Revival Fellowship developed rapidly in Kenya and increased greatly in membership, particularly in the Anglican, Presbyterian and Methodist churches. Gradually also it gained the confidence of those churches as a result of its dynamic evangelistic influence in many parts of the country.

During this period of rapid growth from the mid-1940s, however, a controversy arose when numbers of leading members received the pentecostal gift of tongues, and this led to an incipient crisis. In the end 'tongues' were rejected by the Fellowship as a whole; but a number of Brethren separated from the Fellowship as a result. Some present-day pentecostal churches trace their origin to this period.

The rise of the great Revival conventions

A major development in the last twenty-five years has been the rise of vast conventions of several days' duration each, entirely organised by African Brethren themselves. Indeed, many people see the conventions as a major factor in the emergence of nation-wide African Christian leadership. Even more important, the conventions have been a source of great spiritual inspiration for many thousands of ordinary Christians. They have brought about the spiritual awakening of large numbers, and have challenged the churches to intensify their evangelistic and missionary concern. During the state of Emergency in the 1950s, no large conventions could be organised, but their small local conventions were prophetic occasions, praying for the reconciliation of man to man and of man to God and stressing forgiveness and mercy towards all.

The attached table lists the major Revival conventions of the past twenty-five years, including the approximate numbers attending, and the Biblical themes that evolved in each. About half were national in scope, the rest catering for only a single province or region.

The organisation of the Fellowship

In organisation, the Revival is quite different to normal ecclesiastical ad-

112

TABLE 1

MAJOR KENYA CONVENTIONS OF THE EAST AFRICAN REVIVAL FELLOWSHIP, 1947 - 1971

The second column gives the place where a convention was held, though sometimes local people used a different name for the convention itself (thus Butere 1961 is often referred to as the Sigalame Convention, from the village where it actually met).

In the third column is shown the scope of each convention; some (shown as R) were organized on a regional or East-Africa-wide basis, for the entire region of Uganda, Kenya and Tanzania; some (N) on a Kenya-wide basis; while others (P) were intended primarily to be provincial, catering for the needs of a single province in Kenya.

In the fourth column are given estimated figures for total aggregate attendance. Not that this does not imply that the whole number were present at every meeting; many could only get to a few meetings, and there has been a large fringe of 'interested' or 'casual' attenders, partial attenders, relatives of attenders, etc.

In the last column, the theme of the convention is given, followed in parentheses by the related Biblical text.

Year	Place	Scope	Attendance	Theme and Text
1947	Kahuhia	P	3,000	'God wants all men to be saved' (1 Timothy 2.3-4)
1948	Kagaari	P	5,000	'Christ is the Head of the Church' (Ephesians 5.23)
1949	Kabete	N	15,000	'Come let us reason together' (Isaiah 1.18)
1950	Kikuyu	N	15,000	'Jesus satisfies' (based on John 7.37)
1951	Maseno	N	6,000	'Make haste and come down' (Luke 19.5)
(During the period 1952-55, the State of Emergecy was at its height, and conventions could only be organised at the district or local level.)				
1955	Chogoria	P	6,000	'Understandest thou what thou readest?' (Acts 8.30-1)
1956	Maseno 2	R	12,000	'Jesus our Peace' (Ephesians 2.14)
1958	Kahuhia 2	R	6,000	'Jesus the Head' (Ephesians 1.22)
1960	Tumutumu	P	5,000	'Behold I stand at the door and knock' (Revelation 3.20)
1961	Butere	R	7,000	'Christ in you the hope of glory' (Colossians 1.27)
1964	Mombasa	R	20,000	'Jesus the Way' (John 14.6)
1965	Kitui	P	5,000	'Come and dine' (John 21.12)
1966	Meru	P	10,000	'No peace for the wicked' (Isaiah 48.22)
1967	Kabare	P	5,000	'There is salvation in no one else' (Acts 4.12)
1969	Wundanyi	P	10,000	'Live, and grow like a plant' (Ezekiel 16.6-7)
1970	Kikuyu 2	R	30,000	'One in Christ' (John 17.21)
1971	Mumias	P	6,000	'Sir, we would see Jesus' (John 12.21)

ministrative structures. There are no officials, no executives, no salaried workers; no headquarters, no offices; no bureaucracy, no paperwork, no minutes; no budgets, no membership lists, and no annual subscription fees. Unlike the churches to which virtually all its followers belong, the Fellowship is informal, unstructured, spontaneous, and group-led. What little organisation exists is designed merely to facilitate meetings, conventions and itineraries. At the local village level, the Brethren continue to hold small group meetings in private homes, under trees, and now also in church buildings. These meetings are primarily devotional, providing opportunity for testimony and mutual encouragement, prayer and Bible reading, and including frequent singing of the Revival chorus, *Tukutendereza* (We praise Thee, Jesus). This general pattern is also followed at higher levels of the Fellowship, up to the provincial and national.

Such organising as is required centres around a loose framework of planning occasions at various levels, known as team meetings. 'Team meeting' is the name given to a representative group of Brethren who regularly meet to discuss matters of mutual spiritual interest and to co-ordinate the activities of the Fellowship in the different parts of Kenya. We shall briefly describe these meetings at four levels, beginning with the one with the widest responsibility.

At the national level there is the Kenya Team Meeting. This is composed of some twenty Brethren as representatives of most of the seven provinces of Kenya. The Kenya Team Meeting meets periodically, its main function being to organise Kenya-wide conventions and to invite Brethren from outside the country to participate. It also receives reports from the provinces, and co-ordinates their activities on the national level. The Team Meeting discusses strategy for provincial conventions and suggests the names of preachers for consideration by Provincial Teams. The Team sends preachers throughout Kenya as well as making available small teams for work outside the country. In July 1971, two Brethren were sent to preach in the Kasai Province of Zaire Republic, and a month later three others were delegated to preach in north-eastern Zaire; both teams were assisted by Brethren from Uganda.

At the provincial level there is a Provincial Team Meeting consisting of around twenty Brethren, representing the various districts of the province. Similarly, in each province there are District Team Meetings, composed of about twenty representatives from within the district. Lastly, within each district there are Divisional Team Meetings with usually around 25 members. All these Team Meetings perform functions similar to the Kenya Team except on a smaller scale. At the district and divisional levels the teams provide

Interpretation into four languages is usually essential.

for monthly or fortnightly Fellowship gatherings or open-air evangelistic meetings, while conventions are organised at the provincial and national levels. It is worth noting that all decisions made in Team Meetings have to be unanimous; majority voting is never practised in the Revival Fellowship.

Finance: Mfuko ya Bwana

There are no explicit rules regarding financial arrangements for the Revival Fellowship. There is, however, what is commonly known in Swahili as *Mfuko ya Bwana* ('The Lord's Bag'), namely a fund into which individual Brethren are free to contribute according to their financial ability. It is not obligatory to contribute to the *Mfuko;* it is generally assumed that the amount of money one gives is a matter between only oneself and God.

The Team Meetings at the different levels are responsible for the Lord's Bag in their respective areas. The Fellowship does not have a monthly or annual budget as such. Rather, Brethren are requested to contribute to the Lord's Bag when an urgent need arises such as the organising of conventions, transportation of preaching teams both within and outside Kenya, and building houses or providing aid for poor, aged or disabled Brethren. At times help may be sent to Brethren faced with such problems as death, flood or drought. All such financial help is processed through the Lord's Bag.

The rapid influx of new members, the spread of a money economy throughout the countryside, the rising level of wages, and the growth of 'tithing' among members (the donating of 10 per cent of all income to the Mfuko), have created a serious problem for the Revival in view of its distaste for bureaucracy and its determination to remain a fellowship and not an organisation. The question of how to administer and account for these large sums of money has become increasingly acute. In Tanzania, the solution adopted by the Brethren has been to form an organisation, New Life Crusade, specifically to act as the bank account of the Revival and to handle all financial transactions as a public body to the satisfaction of all parties concerned. In Uganda and Kenya, however, a majority of the Brethren including church leaders have seen the value of introducing normal budgeting, accounting and auditing procedures, but have also been aware of the danger of creating a financial organisation distinct from that of the churches. Numbers of other Brethren, however, have held to a more conservative line opposing the deadening effect of organisation on spiritual renewal. Since 1964 some of these Brethren have formed themselves into a new movement within Revival called in Uganda, Okuzukuka (Awakening) and in Kenya, Ufufuo or Kufufuka (Resurrection) or Kuamka (Awakening, the Re-Awakened Ones), the names coming from the Epistle to the Ephesians 5:14-15. In many areas these Brethren, whose testimony is that they have been awakened by God to see the evils caused by money—lavish personal expenditures, ruinous loans, and lust for wealth—have formed rival weekly meetings separate from the rest of the Brethren. In other areas, however, the Brethren participate in the regular Fellowship meetings but claim to have a fresh testimony of *kuamka* or *kufufuka*.

The theology of the Fellowship

The Brethren hold that they have no theology distinct from that found in the major historical churches, Anglican, Presbyterian and Methodist. In fact, the whole history of Revival has been closely bound up with those churches, and it has continued as a movement of renewal within them up to the present day.

Nevertheless, it is possible to identify certain distinctive emphases of the Revival. The Brethren claim that they have received a deeper insight into the meaning of several New Testament passages because of their experience of Jesus as personal Lord and Saviour. They emphasise the necessity of being born again spiritually. Stress is also placed on the hope of new life after death, and the forgiveness of sins. They particularly emphasise daily spiritual deliverance, cleansing and power for Christian living, through the Blood of Jesus which was shed on the Cross. All this, they believe, takes place through a deep religious experience similar to St. Paul's conversion on the road to Damascus. The Crucifixion of Jesus and the shed Blood stand out as the central symbols in the thinking of the Brethren.

Butere Convention 1961, Bishop Olang' addresses over 7000.

The Revival Fellowship and the churches

From its origins the Revival Fellowship has always been non-denominational in outlook. The rapidly increasing membership of Revival today includes Christians from all Kenya's major churches including the Roman Catholic Church. Many churches have found that the zeal of the Brethren has a major role to play in their evangelistic endeavours, and are reaping the benefits in their own increasing memberships. It is today a common practice for Brethren to give their testimony during and after Sunday services. Moreover, the Revival hymn *Tukutendereza* in thirty languages is sung during Sunday worship in many denominations.

It is estimated that over 90 per cent of all clergy in the Anglican, Presbyterian and Methodist churches, including the whole of their national leadership, belong to the Revival Fellowship, together with prominent laymen in various churches. Weekly meetings are now normally held in church buildings, in which Brethren sit in a circle facing each other to facilitate free participation for all. Church pulpits are rarely used in such meetings.

The Revival in Kenya has performed an important service in helping to create a new sense of fellowship within the historical churches. It has made possible the full participation of men, women and youth in worship and has opened up avenues for the use of charismatic gifts in preaching by the laity, including women, who had tended to become mere observers in the churches. Thus the Revival remains a continual source of renewal and rededication to the meaning of the church's existence.

LITERATURE

Considering the importance of the Revival Fellowship, the literature describing it is startlingly small. What little there is will be found in the Bibliography in this Handbook, under the following authors. The clearest book describing the movement in East Africa is still Max Warren's *Revival: an enquiry*, even though it is now nearly twenty years old. The fullest account is the autobiographical history of Revival by Dr. Joe E. Church, *Quest for the highest* (1971), although it deals mainly with Ruanda and Uganda. Lesser accounts include C.R. Thomson (1952), and P.M. Miller (1969). There are also brief published articles by Bishops Beecher (1951) and Langford-Smith (1954), and Dorothy Smoker (1971). In Kenya, there are short accounts by N. Muriu and W. Njaga (1956), and T.F.C. Bewes (1956).

The hymns of Revival, particularly the chorus *Tukutendereza* in 20 languages, are printed in the Uzima Press hymnbook, *Kitabu cha kusifu* (Book of Praise), 1972.

Politics of Africa's Independent Churches

Odhiambo W. Okite

African independent churches—once known as schismatic movements, then as break-away churches, and nowadays referred to in some circles as renewal movements—are certainly and rapidly gaining acceptance and respectability. This increasing status, and rapid growth in both numbers and members, make these churches of some importance to the future of the Christian faith in Africa.

Not all of these churches can, by any means, be described as Christian. Neither do they all have a chance of surviving the test of time. But quite a number of them seem to have a good grasp of the Christian belief and practice; and some are developing such an originally African type of Christianity that they seem well assured of a future in Africa.

In this ecumenical age it is unfortunate that African Christianity should experience the pains of schism; but the African Christian soil is still fertile for division. Predictions that political independence in Africa would arrest church independency have not come true; instead the trend has picked up pace. In fact, politics itself is still a major factor in church independency.

Politics becomes a factor in church independency when the 'mother' churches become so submerged in a certain political situation that they fail to see the elements of evil in it. These churches lose their prophetic role in the situation. They cannot see it in the full perspective of human experience, and they lack the vision of the vast possibilities of the future should the circumstances change.

Holy Father John Juma Pesa of the Holy Ghost Coptic Church of Africa preaching at a congregational mass in Nairobi.

This was the failure of the majority of·missionary-led churches in Africa in the colonial days. The missionaries—not all of them, of course, but quite a number—could not envision a politically free Africa in which everyone enjoyed equal political and economic opportunity. They defended the 'lawfully constituted authorities', and were passionate in favour of peace and order, and condemned those African Christians who got involved in 'subversive political activities'.

The issue was really very simple: it was whether or not the churches supported the exterior peace and order of the state over and above the interior peace and order of the human soul. Those African Christians who felt that there could be no compromise on human rights and on justice, but who knew their faith well enough to know that Christ was on their side, had no choice but to leave the missionary-led churches, and form their own churches. These were not necessarily the educated African people, who in fact had many privileges in the new societies and the new religious communities. But these rebel religious leaders had a clear, if emotional, vision of something better in a new future.

Political independence could not in any way put a stop to this kind of prophetic involvement in politics. In the newly independent states of Africa, political leaders have seemed to some church leaders to have more authority in human affairs than the Lord Jesus Christ himself. A situation like this is ripe for schism.

But there are many other situations in the African Church which continue to create the old conflicts which led, and are still leading, to divisions. The new African-led churches have inherited the economic imbalance of the colonial churches, with leaders paid from abroad, and living in luxury while asking their subordinates to sacrifice to the maximum. Until the church leaders can really control the sources of their upkeep, until they actually begin to suffer the full range of headaches which go with their high offices, until they begin to sacrifice, their positions will continue to be surrounded by that unrealistic and almost irresponsible splendour, which will remain a real bone of contention.

Uniforms play a prominent part in the Lost Israelites of Kenya.

The Prophet of God of the Lost Israelites of Kenya on parade.

Those churches with a local financial base, either in investments or in well-trained laity, seem to have developed leaders with a keen sense of financial responsibility, and seem to have got rid of the complaints of economic imbalance.

Cultural tensions continue to be as strong in the Christian churches in politically independent Africa as they were in colonial Africa. Political independence brought with it self-awareness, self-confidence and the hope for the revival of traditional African values and culture. The basic orientation of Christian life in Africa remains perhaps as the strongest expression of Western influence in Africa today. This still invites rebellion.

Should these churches decide to unite to form a united front, they would become a formidable force for good for African Christianity. But there is one equally formidable problem on the way. There is the human factor, the arrogance, the sweet taste of power and prestige, the lack of patience and tolerance, the personality conflicts, the misuse of power. Without these there would be few theological problems.

121

The independent churches in Africa have not generally been founded by theologians, or even clerics. They are creations of concerned laymen, all of whom, having left their mother churches, found themselves at the mercy of the historical and cultural circumstances surrounding them. The new churches naturally adopted a traditionally African world-view, in which human events are seen to be primarily controlled by spiritual forces. Birth, death, health, harvest, road-accidents, thunderstorms, political elections, are not merely physico-natural phenomena, but purposive acts of spiritual powers, evil or benevolent. This accounts for the very central place given to prayer in the life of the churches, for praying means confronting an all-powerful God with the lower, evil powers.

This also accounts for the belief in and practice of spiritual healing and of prophecy, and for the great importance attached to dreams and visions.

Another common characteristic of these churches is the very vigorous community life which they enjoy. The churches have become the new kinship group controlling all economic life as well as social relations. Sense of identification can get so strong that uniforms become necessary in certain cases. In the face of the general break-down of the extended family system everywhere, the new church communities have provided the new social units, where hospitality is extended without the slightest reluctance, where marriage contracts are arranged, where business advice is freely given, where the individual in every way finds his roots once again.

The new churches are also giving women an interesting and challenging new role to play. In some of the independent African churches, women are the top executives, and in nearly all of them, women are in key leadership positions. This is a factor requiring a whole study in itself, for certainly there is something significant in this. There is something of the feminine religious genius which the old churches are not taking advantage of.

The worship services of these new churches also present a challenge to the older churches. While some churches have the regular weekly hour of service on Sunday in a building, all of them are ready for a service any time, any place where a congregation can be gathered up. The services are lively, theologically sound verses are put to traditional African tunes, and the full participation of the congregation is encouraged.

Another interesting characteristic of these churches is their deep devotion to Bible reading and Bible study. Some of them had earlier in their history rejected the Bible, but some of these are now bordering on bibliolatry. Bible translations into local languages and dialects have also helped to give the Bible its immense prestige as the Word of God applicable to anyone, anywhere.

Moreover, they see in the Bible a world-view that is very close to their own, and in the Biblical characters they see faith in its most simplified form, uncomplicated by theology.

The very valuable contributions that these churches can make to the life of the Church in Africa can be made possible only if the mother churches and the Christian councils develop an openminded approach to them, taking practical steps to establish bridges of understanding and reconciliation. The councils should also help them in their training programmes, as this would help stabilise their theologies, standardise their structures, and rub out some extreme practices and beliefs from their leaders.

All this is possible only in an atmosphere of mutual respect, with each group recognising their weaknesses and strengths.

The Rise and Persecution of the Aroti Prophets, 1927-1948

Elijah Kinyanjui

(The following article, a condensation of a 50-page manuscript, has been written in Kikuyu by one of the last surviving members of the early Aroti Prophets, which he joined in 1930. The Prophet (pictured above) is now president of the Chosen Church of the Holy Spirit, one of the dozen or so Kikuyu Spirit Churches (analysed in the article following this one, and described elsewhere in this Handbook). He compiled his manuscript from 1969 onwards with the aid of his amanuensis, Samuel Mungai, and the text was translated into English by Gereshom Mahiaini. The translation preserves the style, rhythm and repetitions of the original).

The origins of the church of the Akurinu

Before the year 1900, the ways of life and traditional customs in this land of Kenya had not been upset by the foreign mission religion. At that time there were only our own tribal customs in the land of Kenya.

But the foreign mission teaching amongst us, the Kikuyu, started at Kijabe in 1903,[1] and that is when the foreign missions in Kenya started teaching people from the Word of God, the Bible, in the land of Kenya, but with this Bible and their own culture and customs all mixed up together. Some time later in 1918 and 1919, therefore, the Lord God chose people who had gone to mission schools; from the very beginning He had chosen them and had set them aside by His own will. Firstly, he chose some to demand Independence for the land of Kenya; and secondly, he chose others by the Spirit of Jesus in God to preach and to teach the news from the Word of God.

And again, several years later in 1927, God chose men from among those He had selected as politicians, who then began to work for Independence in the Dominion of this mountain of Kirinyaga, working together to serve God in this land of Kenya.[2]

The people of Kenya before those days had always called upon God and prayed to God together. But from 1927 God began a new work and raised up some to be *Aroti*[3] (Dreamers), people of the Holy Spirit, or prophets; and everybody called them *Akurinu*,[4] since they were prophets and interpreters of the Word of God, preaching and praying in this land of Kenya.

God also chose a third group of people, men who called themselves 'independent', who relied not on foreigners but upon their own efforts, waiting for the Spirit of Pentecost while standing on their own feet in the Independent churches.[5] This matter arose throughout the land of the Kikuyu, from Nairobi north to Meru and west to Ngong.

These three groups whom God had raised up, the politicians, the Akurinu, and the Independents, each began to establish themselves independently from 1927 onwards, in this land of Kenya. The members of these three groups were very strong in faith, praying to God with one heart that He would remove the Europeans and send them back to their own country, leaving this country to its rightful owners. It was clearly revealed to some of these prophets by the Holy Spirit that the Europeans must in the end go and leave Kenya. This is a matter about which they prayed to God, that in the end the Europeans would go away from Kenya. I, Elijah Kinyanjui, am sure of this matter, and I have heard it—this account is the truth—both from Akurinu and from Independents, the two groups of churches of the Kikuyu in this land of Kenya. These things were revealed to Africans by God in Kenya. He showed them new and holy prayers, and also new interpretations of the Word of God, and a spiritual way to read it and to grasp it in the heart just as the Holy Spirit reveals it to a man. For, a certain part of the Word of God must be read in the light of the prophecy that has reached us at the end of these times. (*Read:* Acts 2:16-22, and Hebrews 8:8; Acts 2:38-42; and Luke 24:47-50).

Some foreigners in this country, white farmers and traders and members of the British Administration in Kenya during the years 1919 to 1934, believed that the Europeans would never leave Kenya, until in fact it finally happened in 1963. Similarly, many mission followers in the European churches did not believe that the new churches of the Akurinu and the Independents belonged to God; they did not even believe that the politicians who were saying that the Europeans would go were in fact speaking the truth. Therefore the company of all the mission churches greatly disturbed the Akurinu with blasphemies and heaped abuse on the Independent churches into the bargain.

These things have not been thus written before by any other person. This is the first time that we have ventured to speak openly on this subject, I, Elijah Kinyanjui, together with this young man Samuel my amanuensis, who is the only person who has offered to write on my behalf, before whom nobody assisted me. Samuel has asked me to let him do this so as to preserve, and to protect and to establish, the correct proceedings in all these matters.

What happened in Kenya after the murders of 1934

In February, 1934, three of our Akurinu were killed at Ndaragu Forest in a clash with the British Administration; they were Samuel Muinami, Joseph Ng'ang'a, and John Mung'ara. After their deaths, there arose many difficulties, and severe ones, from the Administration. The district commissioners gave orders to the chiefs and to the tribunal court elders, and also to the tribal police who guarded the villages, to be on the alert concerning the aims and objectives of the Church of the Holy Spirit, because the Akurinu used to travel with bows and arrows in those days.[6]

At that time in 1934, in the third month, a group of Akurinu were arrested, those who were looked upon as leaders in the village of Magina. This group of people kept bows and arrows, and carried their quivers with them while travelling, and two-bladed swords as well, because at that time there was a widespread prophecy that a great war would soon be coming.

In those days, then, the church of the Akurinu, the people of God and the prophets, experienced great tribulations and were often beaten up badly. We were thrown into prison and some of us were locked up in dungeons. (Read: Luke 21:12-20; Revelation 3:10-13; Matthew 10:22). The members of the church of the Akurinu rejoiced in these tribulations and trials, and, as Jesus and his disciples did, they preached the Word and prayed to God with one heart.

For fifteen years after these three Akurinu were killed by the British Administration in Kenya, there came about even worse trials and temptations, but the Akurinu overcame them by faith and prayer. God helped them to take courage and have patience; He gave them the Holy Spirit; they increased in numbers; and those who repented of their sins and believed were baptised in the name of the Father, the Son and the Holy Spirit.

The subsequent years[7]

During the last forty years the names Aroti and Akurinu have become widely known in Central Kenya. These Christians suffered trials in the early days because they believed in their God. They were beaten up and persecuted because they would not have fellowship with people who did not know God. For many years, it was considered most unseemly for young men and women to join this new religion, because it was thought that those who did would never marry. Many people also believed that the Akurinu had gone mad when they came to know God. This was because they did not do many of the things done by people who do not believe in God; they refused to shake hands, to eat meat they had not themselves slaughtered, to go to hospital or take medicines, and so on. They did not visit witchdoctors, nor take herbal medicines. They believed that if they prayed to their God when they were sick, then they would recover without recourse to medicines, either European or African.

This then is the story of how God sent the Holy Spirit in the early days to our people in this our land of Kenya.

NOTES

[1] Kijabe, located on the edge of the Rift Valley, is the headquarters of the Africa Inland Mission and reputedly the largest mission station in the world.

[2] In 1927, the Kikuyu Central Association (founded 1922) moved its offices from Kahuhia to Nairobi and invited Jomo Kenyatta to become secretary; he began work early in 1928. By 1927 also considerable agitation was under way, over land, and also for the release of Harry Thuku (detained 1922-1930).

[3] *Aroti* is the plural form; the singular is *Muroti.*

[4] The meaning of the name *Akurinu* is obscure and still disputed. Some Aroti claim that it means 'Who is the Redeemer?'; more probable is the interpretation 'roaring prophets' based on the OT references to the prophets roaring like lions (Isaiah 5:29-30, etc.), i.e. 'enthusiasts'.

[5] The reference is to the great nationalist churches, the African Independent Pentecostal Church, and the African Orthodox Church.

[6] The Administration at that time used to send police informants to Aroti services and meetings, and had forbidden the carrying of arms even for self-defence.

[7] The final section of this manuscript is identified as an addition composed by the amanuensis.

Members of a Kikuyu Spirit Church visit President Jomo Kenyatta.

Varieties of Kikuyu Independent Churches

Jocelyn Murray

To write of 'independent' churches presents an initial problem of definition, for the Kikuyu churches planted through the work of Western missionary societies are now independent also, although most continue to receive financial aid and personnel from overseas. Some of the churches originally founded by Kikuyu Christians to be independent of mission control have now established links with wider Christian communities and stand in relationships precisely similar to the mission-seeded churches. Nevertheless, a group

128

loosely labelled independent can be distinguished from the mission-seeded churches, although within it are churches of very different types. Up to the present, very little has been recorded of these churches, of whose existence many Kenya Christians are scarcely aware. In this preliminary survey I offer a tentative division of these churches, on historical and theological grounds, into four categories. It will be seen that any single independent church may have far more in common with a mission-seeded church than with another independent church, and the time is very near when any discussion in terms of independent and mission-seeded will be completely invalid. But detailed studies of most of these churches are still awaited, and in the meantime this survey may be useful as a basis for further investigation.

1. Nationalist churches

These churches emerged out of the political, educational and cultural struggles of the 1920s and 1930s, when, as a result of dissatisfaction over the type of education offered by mission and government agencies, anxiety over land, and resentment of attempts at forced cultural change (proscription of female circumcision and polygamy), Africans who had been members of mission churches left and formed churches independent of mission control. Parallel with the churches—and historically preceding them—were associations for the management of schools.

The first and still the largest church of this type, the African Independent Pentecostal Church, was associated with the Kikuyu Independent Schools Association, which was founded in 1929. Polygamy and acceptance of female circumcision are not bars to membership of the AIPC, but there are not great theological differences between it and the churches (Anglican and Presbyterian in the main) from which its founders separated. However, out of the same general movement a second church emerged which introduced a new tradition into Kikuyu Christianity. This is the church which, beginning in 1932 as the African Orthodox Church, is now also known as the African Greek Orthodox Church, or the Orthodox Church of Kenya, part of the Greek Patriarchate of Alexandria and in communion with the world-wide Eastern Orthodox Churches.

There are other, smaller, churches which have separated themselves from both of these churches, chiefly on leadership grounds rather than for theological reasons. Two such are the National Independent Church of Africa and the Independent African Orthodox Church. Although the AIPC and other national churches, and the AOC and other Orthodox churches, have now diverged widely, they share a common early history, and also have in common a 'church' rather than a 'sect' orientation. They aim not to be the refuge of a chosen few, but the religious home of a total community.

2. Secessionist churches

In many parts of Africa independent churches are found which have originated in a clearcut schism or split from a mission-founded church over some question of policy or leadership. The resulting church usually covers a geographical area formerly occupied by the mission church, encompassing total congregations. In Kikuyu country I know of only one large church which comes strictly into this category: the African Christian Church and Schools, formed in 1947 by members and adherents of the Africa Inland Mission in southern Fort Hall District. The cause was a dispute with missionaries, chiefly over educational policy; but in matters of faith, church order and rules of conduct, the ACC&S has maintained the traditions of its parent mission. Since 1954 the ACC&S has been a member church of the Christian Council of Kenya; it has sponsored students at St. Paul's United Theological College, and has recently invited in the help of four missionaries from the Canadian Baptist Overseas Mission Board. Here we see a church originally formed to be independent of missionary control now welcoming foreign missionary co-workers, in a relationship similar to that which now exists between the Africa Inland Church and the Africa Inland Mission.

3. Revival-Pentecostal churches

A third category consists of a number of churches which have arisen at different times and in different circumstances but which have a number of features in common which enable them to be considered together. They practice believer's baptism by immersion and hold that the Christian must

Bishop Benjamin Kahihia inaugurates new AIPC church, a nationalist-type church.

receive the baptism of the Holy Spirit, marked by charismatic gifts. Probably the first Kikuyu church of this type arose in Fort Hall in the 1940s among Anglican Christians who had been influenced by the Ruanda Revival message but did not, like the main body of Revival Christians, reject charismatic gifts. It has been known as 'Dini ya Kaggia', after Bildad Kaggia who was for a few years one of its most prominent leaders, but its official name, Arata a Roho Mutheru (Friends of the Holy Spirit) better indicates its emphasis. Independent churches in Western Kenya and Ukambani, now organisationally separate, have developed out of the preaching of Arata leaders.

In the late 1950s a member of the Presbyterian Church at Kikuyu, after his conversion and subsequent association with the local Revival Fellowship, asked his minister for re-baptism as a believer. This was refused, and he was baptised by a white South African missionary of the Apostolic Faith Mission. Later he experienced the baptism of the Holy Spirit, and finding that this was not acceptable within the Revival Fellowship, he commenced the church called Apostolic Faith of Africa, which was registered in 1963. The missionary had left Kenya in 1961; another church arising out of his ministry still continues, but no longer connected with the founding church, namely the Holy Church of Evangelistic Apostles Faith.

ACC&S baptism in 1971 (a secessionist-type church).

No early missions in Kikuyu country were of the pentecostal type, but in recent years the Pentecostal Assemblies of God, and the Finnish and Norwegian Pentecostal missions, have established work. A pentecostal movement has gained strength among Christian students of all denominations. Thus it seems likely that many more churches of this type will be formed in the future, as pentecostal teaching spreads. One or two recently-established churches have links with the Apostolic Faith of Africa; one of these is the Disciples of Christ in Africa.

4. Spirit churches

This final category consists of churches whose members are known to outsiders as Akurinu, Aroti (Dreamers), Anabii (Prophets), or Andu a Iremba (Turban People). To the Colonial Administration in the 1930s they were the

'Watu wa Mungu' (People of God or Men of God). They have many features in common with the Roho churches of Western Kenya; some Kikuyu Spirit churches are now linked to Roho Churches, but most remain completely separate.

All the Spirit churches trace their origin to the late 1920s, that disturbed period in the Kikuyu colonial experience out of which the AIPC and the AOC also emerged. But where these two latter churches sought self-determination in their religious practices, and extension of education within the model received from the West, the early Watu wa Mungu rejected Western education, clothing, amenities, medicine, and even their own Kikuyu traditions, and sought guidance only from the Scriptures and the Holy Spirit. They were imprisoned for holding illegal meetings, having gained an undeserved reputation for violence after an incident in 1934 when a small group encountered a police patrol who killed them (the 'Ndaragu Forest affray') and because of the activities of an extreme fringe, the 'Dini ya Jesu Kristo', in 1947-48. Despite persecution, small groups continued throughout Kikuyu country and among the Kikuyu of the diaspora in the Rift Valley, where indeed they have always been particularly strong.

A revival-pentecostal church: prayer for the sick in the Local Churches of Kenya, at Kamarithu, Limuru. Raising hands to the sky is defended as both traditional Kikuyu praying (see J. Kenyatta, *Facing Mount Kenya*, p.18, 246), and also biblical (see Psalm 68.31, 1 Timothy 2:8).

In the last years of the State of Emergency (which ended in 1960) registration of Kikuyu societies was again permitted, and divisions between different leaders and groups became crystallised as registrations were made under official names. One cause of division has been rejection or acceptance of polygamy; more recently the use or rejection of Western medicines has caused further separations. Some groups have become increasingly liberal in attitudes to education and Western amenities; others have remained conservative. There are also differences over the rigidity with which the Levitical laws of the Old Testament concerning food and ritual uncleanness should be followed. Baptism is by the Spirit only, without the use of water, and the celebration of Holy Communion is not observed.

Probably the largest of these churches today is the Holy Ghost Church of Kenya, with its headquarters at Murengeti, Limuru; others are the Christian Holy Ghost Church of East Africa, the Kenya Foundation of the Prophets Church, the Holy Spirit Church of Zayun, the African Mission of Holy Ghost Church, and God's Word and Holy Ghost Church.

Conclusion

What do these four types of churches, considered together as independent, have in common? In the beginnings of all four there was undoubtedly the desire for self-determination—the right to establish policy, to exercise initiative, to become a genuinely African church, and not just a pale copy of a Western church. The use of words like 'African', 'national', and 'Kenya', in the names of churches in all four groups expresses this desire.

The churches in the first two categories I have defined—Nationalist, and Secessionist—have not in theological terms been particularly innovative. They have continued in the traditions of the churches that they have separated from—or separated towards, in the case of the African Orthodox Church. The churches of the last two categories—Revival/Pentecostal, and Spirit churches—though very different in many ways, all emphasise the person and work of the Holy Spirit, as their names indicate. All stress also personal holiness of life, and in this have very much in common with the East African (Ruanda) Revival Fellowship, which draws its adherents from many churches in Kikuyu country, Anglican, Presbyterian, ACC&S, and the Africa Inland Church. Although in liturgy, styles of singing, robes, vestments and the like, there are many visible differences between these types of churches, it is fair to say that very often one cannot know from the sermon preached whether one is listening to an Anglican clergyman or to a Muroti prophet.

As the mission-founded churches continue to grow more confident in their independence, and as independent churches develop more links both overseas and among themselves, the already fluid situation in Kikuyu country is likely to become even more so. Leaders and members of churches, both mission-seeded and independent, need to know more of their fellow-Christians in other churches, their beliefs and practices, so that suspicions and

Aroti women at worship: the Holy Ghost Church of Kenya, a spirit-type church.

jealousies arising out of past history may not continue, hindering the growth of what should not, in the last analysis, be considered as anything else but Christ's own church.

NOTE ON SOURCES

Full citations for books and articles mentioned below will be found in the Bibliography in this Handbook. The origins of the two largest Nationalist churches, the AIPC and the AOC, are well documented in F.B. Welbourn's *East African rebels*, section III, 'Kikuyu' (chapters 6-8). Some of the same ground is covered in C. Rosberg and J. Nottingham's study of nationalism in Kenya, *The myth of Mau Mau*, chapter 4, 'Cultural nationalism'. An article by L.J. Beecher published in 1953 surveys the situation at that time: 'African Separatist Churches in Kenya', in *World Dominion*, vol. XXX, no. 1. The book by Daudi Maina wa Kiragu, *Kiria giatumira Independent igie*, gives the point of view of a leader in the AIPC.

Virtually nothing seems to have been written up to the present concerning the ACC&S and the Revival/Pentecostalist churches. The forthcoming book by Bildad Kaggia, *Roots of freedom* (to be published by EAPH) gives his account of the founding of the 'Dini ya Kaggia' after the Second World War.

On the 'Spirit' churches, Mzee Jomo Kenyatta's chapter on the 'Watu wa Mungu' in *Facing Mount Kenya* is often quoted. A journalist's report on Kenya in 1947-48, Negley Farson's *Last chance in Africa*, deals with the Watu wa Mungu and the 'Dini ya Jesu Kristo', including a copy of a document by H. Lambert, DC of Kiambu in 1942, on various sects in Kiambu. Unfortunately Farson's account, which covers the Gatundu murders of December 1947, has served to perpetuate the belief in the violent nature of the Spirit churches. Most other accounts I have read are based on these, but there is original material in a duplicated article around 1960 by John Kamenyi, at that time a student of St. Paul's United Theological College, entitled 'Prophets (Aroti): turban people'.

My survey is based on the above materials, on files in the Kenya National Archives, and on personal interviews with leaders of various churches and attendance at their services.

Speaking in tongues in African Israel Church Nineveh.

Theological Issues Related to Kenyan Religious Independency

Malcolm J. McVeigh

The independent churches are increasingly recognised as an important element in African Christianity. To date little notice has been given to the theological foundation on which they are built. Yet their theology is of great interest and significance. This study is an attempt to deal in a preliminary fashion with theological questions and to show their importance in any assessment of Kenyan independency.

Christology

An analysis of African independency in general and Kenya in particular makes it abundantly clear that the traditional theological controversies of

Europe have had little effect on the African scene. Disputes about Christology, which have rocked the Western church from the earliest days to the modern period, have few African parallels.

Nevertheless, Kenya is not entirely free from Christological conflict as seen for example in the official statement of belief of the Nomiya Luo Church. This is the oldest of Kenya's independent churches, having split from Anglicanism in 1914. As Archbishop Benjamin Oundo admits today, his denomination is unusual in that it does not recognise Jesus as God. Displaying a strong Old Testament orientation, Jesus' role is seen as that of a prophet who reminds men of the covenant given to the Jews:

> Our Church is a unique sort of church in that we do not accept that Jesus is God, but we recognise him as one of the God-sent Prophets. We hold him high above the other Prophets because we believe God vested him with that grand name of being His Son who came to earth to accomplish what other Prophets had preached before, especially the Laws of Moses and God's covenant to our Grandfather Ibrahim (Abraham). Our Church therefore strictly follows the teachings contained in the Old Testament, especially the first Five Books of Moses.

Being one of the few churches manifesting genuine doctrinal conflict in its split from Anglicanism, it is perhaps not surprising that doctrinal questions should have proved to be a continuing source of controversy in the church. Archbishop Zabulon Ndiege of the Luo Roho Church justifies the schism which resulted in the creation of his church from the Nomiya Luo Church in 1968 on the basis that the Nomiya leaders were neglecting both the Holy Spirit and Jesus. He insists that the Nomiya Luo Church does not want Jesus' name mentioned, since he is to them merely one of the apostles, not the Son of God. This is strictly speaking not true according to the testimony of Archbishop Oundo, quoted above, but obviously the emphasis placed on Jesus as prophet rather than God has confused and upset many of the members.

With rare exceptions, Kenyan independent churches characteristically accept the orthodox Christological position of their parent bodies. Africans seem to manifest little difficulty in accepting Jesus as either Son of God or God. Nevertheless, these churches not uncommonly display more interest in the Holy Spirit than in Jesus. Jesus remains for them an important historical figure who is now at the right hand of the Father, but their attention is centred on God's living presence in their midst. Great emphasis is placed on the signs of the Spirit, such as shaking and speaking with tongues, and often their very existence is explained on the basis of the failure of the historical churches to take the Spirit seriously.

Messianism

Messianic tendencies, as seen in Shembe's Nazirite Baptist Church in South Africa and Kimbanguism in Zaire Republic, are not widespread in Kenya. Out of some 150 independent churches, only a few examples can be noted.

Perhaps the most significant is that of Maria Legio of Africa, a 1962 split from Roman Catholicism. The founders of the church were Holy Mother Maria, who died in 1966, and Holy Father Simeo Lodivicus Malkio Messias Ondeto, the present leader. The hierarchy below him includes Pope Timotheo Atila, seven cardinals and numerous archbishops and bishops. The church headquarters is Amoyo, also called Jerusalem, in South Nyanza. Holy Father Ondeto's own self-understanding of his position is not fully clear. At times he states merely that he is one sent by God as teacher of the world, but he has also been heard to say: 'My followers call me the Son of God ... they know best'. Evidently, the deeds of supernatural power attributed to him by Maria Legio members suggest to the faithful that he is more than a prophet. Although he avoids identifying himself with the promised Christ, his disciples have no such reservations. He is for them the true Messiah, Jesus Christ to the present generation.

Another messianic tendency, although of minor importance as compared with Maria Legio, is that displayed by Paul Omumbo Achola of the New Roho Israel Church (Manyien) in Kisumu. Unlike Simeo Ondeto, who seems to make less claims for himself than those attributed to him by his followers, Paul Achola's major pre-occupation is to persuade others of his position as

Holy Father Ondeto blesses Maria Legio faithful.

137

God's special representative, the one whom God consults before He does anything on earth. Some of the leaders of the other Roho Churches in the Kisumu area insist that he claims to be God himself. Thus far he has had little success; for, although he has been trying to establish an independent church since 1962, his group remains small and controversial.

Yet a third example is that evident in the Musanda Holy Ghost Church, which looks to Apostle Alfayo Odongo Mango as Spiritual Father. Odongo was burnt alive by enemies within the Anglican church in 1934, as a result of which his followers seceded. Following his martyrdom, the faithful insist that he went straight to Heaven where he now guides their destinies before God. He is no longer their apostle but their Spiritual Father, the one who sends messages to them through his chosen representatives. Along with other duties a true church member is required to accept Alfayo Odongo as the Spiritual Father and Teacher and have faith in his holy teachings and sayings.

In spite of these examples, however, Kenyan independency taken as a whole is remarkably free of messianism. The majority of Kenya's independent churches resist the tendency to divinize their leaders. Indeed, reaction against messianic tendencies has occasionally produced schism. Bishop Elijah Ogol states that the excessive veneration of Alfayo Odongo Mango in the Musanda Holy Ghost Church was an important causative factor in his establishment of the Kendu Roho Church Mission in 1953.

It is true that the leaders of independent churches are men of recognised ability and charismatic personality. One cannot fail to notice the influence that they exert over their followers. They sometimes give the impression of being modern counterparts of the traditional chiefs who have now largely lost their function in a modern African state. They are regarded generally as having had special visions and being men of the Spirit, but one sees little inclination to elevate them beyond the sphere of prophets or servants of God.

Community

Independent church leaders are identified by numerous lofty titles (archbishop, bishop, high priest, prophet, etc.) and clearly play an important role in the life of their denominations. Yet it would be a mistake to overemphasise their authority or to suggest that these churches are dominated by their leaders. On the whole they are more community-centred than leader-centred. There are several evidences of this.

Generally the leaders work closely with their church committees and are careful to avoid arbitrary personal decisions. Undoubtedly they are aware of the ease with which dissatisfied factions are able to create schism in a church. When asked to fill out the questionnaire for the *Kenya Churches Handbook*, Bishop Benjamin Kahihia of the African Independent Pentecostal Church replied that he was only a bishop and could not assume such a responsibility on his own. A decision of the church council was required before the form could be completed.

The centrality of the community is also evident in worship. Most worship services are not monopolised by any single individual. In fact, one often gets the impression that the services are leader-less, with a succession of persons rising to speak followed by the active participation of all in dancing and drumming. A visitor sometimes has great difficulty in identifying the pastor.

Although major denominations such as the African Independent Pentecostal Church and the Church of Christ in Africa have numerous large congregations, in others many congregations do not number more than 50 members. Meeting in small buildings, the participants are afforded an extraordinary sense of intimacy and mutual sharing. Following a lengthy Saturday afternoon worship service of the Cross Church of East Africa outside Kisumu, visited unannounced by *Handbook* editors, the people joined in a communal meal of cooked corn served from a common pot. The sense of togetherness evident in both the service and the meal was striking. Given the pressures on traditional society in modern Africa, this attempt to create a new sense of community in the independent churches is of great significance.

Sacraments

Yet another aspect of independent church theology is an often novel approach to the sacraments. The lack of interest in the sacraments on the part of African independent churches has been recognised by many observers and scholars, and this is also evident in the Kenyan situation. There seems to be a general view on the part of many that, since the Holy Spirit is a reality, they need no material approaches to effect any special presence. Hence there is no need of sacraments. Even where baptism forms part of the regular church ritual, it is not uncommonly a baptism of the Holy Spirit without water. When inquiries are made as to why water is not used, reference is made to the fact that John used water whereas Jesus baptised with the Holy Spirit.

Even in those churches which practice Spirit baptism, there are often recognised vehicles of its expression. So for example in the thought of the African Mission of Holy Ghost Church the shaking of the hands of the bishop is the effective instrument of baptism. In the Muolo Roho Israel Church, baptism is effected by the sign of the cross without the use of water, and an anointing with oil is added to the ceremony.

Although there are notable exceptions, it is not incorrect to state that independent churches tend to place less emphasis on the Holy Communion than baptism. Yet even here, a deeper probing into the question often produces novel theological explanations. The Muolo Roho Israel Church celebrates the Holy Communion by a Scripture reading, no food being regarded as necessary since Jesus already gave his body on the cross for the faithful.

In the Kendu Roho Church Mission, which celebrates the Lord's Supper with conventional elements five times yearly, a general foot-washing with all members participating precedes the distribution of the sacrament.

It should not be assumed that the position of any given church is rigidly fixed in regard to its view of the sacraments. There is in fact evidence of a tendency on the part of a number of churches, which previously have shown little sacramental interest, to consider them more seriously.

Even the statement that independent churches show less interest in the sacraments than their parent bodies needs qualification. The Wokofu African Church, which split in 1966 from the Salvation Army (a Western church practising neither water baptism nor communion), now practises both baptism and the Holy Communion. When asked why they use a water baptism, General Matthew Odundo replies by quoting John 3:5: 'Unless one is born of water and the Spirit, he cannot enter the kingdom of God.'

Healing

The interest of Africa's independent churches in healing has often been noted. However, to date little attention has been directed to the theological thought which lies behind this pre-occupation and how it manifests a concern to provide Christian answers for traditional problems.

As with African traditional religion, the independent churches show great interest in the problem of misfortune. Yet when asked the origin of sickness, for example, they do not give traditional answers. They insist that the departed ancestors are not a cause of illness. The 'living dead' have gone on. Those who had faith are with God, awaiting the arrival of the living, whereas those lacking faith are in Hell.

Once again witchcraft is not the cause. They do not deny the reality of witchcraft, but they insist that it is no longer a problem for them. Witches have no power over those who are faithful to Christ. The power of the Holy

Spirit is greater than the power of witches; so there is protection in the church. One of the great attractions of the independent churches is the freedom it gives: they need fear witches no longer.

But if neither witches nor the departed ancestors are the cause of sickness and misfortune, what is? The independent churches are pre-occupied with this question. There is no unified answer; yet all relate it to biblical perspectives in one way or another. Although the possible solutions are not mutually exclusive and tend to overlap several different emphases may be discovered.

One answer is to picture sickness as a testing of faith in which both the Devil and God play a part. In the thought of the African Holy Ghost Christian Church, according to Ayub Nduti, the brother of Bishop Daniel Nduti Karuga, Satan may ask God for permission to test a person. One sees immediately the influence of the Book of Job in the Old Testament. The cause of illness being spiritual, faith healing alone is allowed. This church broke from the Kenya Foundation of the Prophets Church in 1968 because the latter group now allows its people to go to hospital for treatment. Sickness as a testing of faith is one explanation for illness, but it is by no means universally accepted by the independent churches. Nabi Petro Kariuki of the Muolo Roho Israel Church insists that Jesus tempts no-one.

Another response attributes sickness to God as a punishment for sin. Illness is a manifestation of sin, the result of a broken relationship between man and God. Only prayer and confession can resolve the problem. When asked regarding illness, informants of the Cross Church of East Africa relate the problem immediately to God rather than Satan. Although upon further questioning the Devil may be pictured as playing a role in the process, the first reply is that illness is a manifestation of God's anger at man's sin. Prayer and confession are agents of healing in that they make possible God's forgiveness.

Still a third solution identifies sickness entirely with the work of the Adversary. As in the previous case, the way is opened for the Devil's activity by human sin. In the thought of the Friends of the Holy Spirit, all sickness is of the Devil due to sin. Since illness is caused by Satan, medicine, whether of the traditional or modern variety, is evil. There is no need of or value in going to hospital since only faith can heal.

Nabi Kariuki states that God neither tempts nor punishes. Sickness is of the Devil who is God's opponent. Sin opens the way to Satan's activity, but prayer and confession based on faith give God the opportunity to defeat the Adversary. Similar views are expressed by the Voice of Salvation and Healing Church, and the Power of Jesus Around the World Church. God is not involved as a cause of sickness. Satan is the sole author whose activity is made possible by human sin. Through prayer and confession, the sin is obliterated, making possible the casting out of Satan's influence. Healing is

Faith healing and exorcism in Maria Legio.

the visible material result that proves the efficacy of the spiritual transformation.

It is evident from the above discussion that the independent churches are extremely interested in theological questions. Very few have worked them out in terms of doctrinal treatises or catechetical statements. But clearly they are discussed by the leaders and members of these churches. In other words they seek an intellectual formulation of the Christian position regarding the vital spiritual questions of interest to Africans in traditional society. Yet perhaps even more significant than their intellectual formulations is the emotional satisfaction that these groups are able to provide for their people. The members feel that their real problems are dealt with in the Christian context.

The amount of genuine theological reflection and discussion now taking place in the independent churches, informal and unwritten though it may be, suggests that these churches have an important contribution to make in the quest by Christians of all denominations for a theology uniquely relevant to Africa. Indeed, it may be anticipated that the efforts of this search will reach beyond the continent, benefitting world Christianity as well.

FURTHER READING

The material for this article was largely compiled from questionnaires and field interviews. As noted above, there are few published sources on the theology of Kenyan independent churches. However, for further study, the following works may be consulted; for full bibliographical details, see Bibliography in this Handbook.

P.J. Dirven's 'The Maria Legio: the dynamics of a breakaway church among the Luo in East Africa' (1970) is an extensive study of the background and causes of the Maria Legio schism, with brief mention of some of its theological implications. A popular account of the place of Simeo Ondeto in the Maria Legio, written after a visit by *Drum* correspondents, is 'The Man they call Jesus Christ', *Drum* (June, 1971). B.A. Ogot's 'Reverend Alfayo Odongo Mango, 1870-1934' presents a brief biography of the founder of the Musanda Holy Ghost Church of East Africa, with brief mention of the veneration accorded him by contemporary followers. E. Wakin's article 'A unique sort of church' (1972) is a short description of the worship life of the Nomiya Luo Church which reproduces also the church's official statement of belief. Lastly, F.B. Welbourn and B.A. Ogot, *A place to feel at home* (1966) provides studies of two independent churches, the Church of Christ in Africa and the African Israel Church Nineveh, including theological reflections.

One of the more than 210 denominations in Kenya.

Diversity, Divisions and Denominationalism

John S. Mbiti

Statistically Kenya is one of the most Christian countries in Africa. Already in 1962 over 53 per cent of its population was Christian, and by 1972 the figure had risen to 66 per cent. The statistics in this Handbook reveal many startling facts, one of which is the large number of denominational groups and organisations in the country. Since there are 49 mission (or historical) denominations served by 70 Western Protestant missionary societies and 50 Catholic missionary societies and orders, 156 independent churches, 15 national church councils and conferences, as well as 10 inter-

144

national church councils based in Kenya, this points clearly to the fact that Christianity in Kenya is by no means homogeneous.

Every major tradition of Christendom is represented in Kenya: Roman Catholicism, Anglicanism, Orthodoxy, Presbyterianism or the Reformed tradition, Lutheranism, Methodism, Independent churchmanship, Baptists, Quakerism, Seventh-day Adventism, and so on. Similarly, a number of theological positions are represented in the country, such as liberalism, fundamentalism, evangelicalism, reformationism, conservatism, radicalism, ecumenism, etc. And all this in such a small country as Kenya, all in the name of Christianity.

Christianity in Kenya has mushroomed denominationally, and the mushroom has now been turned into a messy soup. This excessive denominationalism is absolutely scandalous. It could well generate confusion and strife among Christians, and in the long run it will not be in the national interests of our country to tolerate and maintain this type of division precisely when we are attempting to create national unity. The denominational mushroom soup is boiling over and this invites someone to call a halt; and if that someone is not the churches themselves, then it may well be the government. Christianity must not be allowed to become a cloak and cover for divisiveness in the country, and religious freedom must not be abused through this denominational proliferation which courts national disunity and throws shame upon an otherwise breathtaking expansion of the Christian faith in Kenya.

That church divisions are sinful there is no doubt; that many of them are created and sustained by the self-interests of church leaders cannot be denied; that the majority of African Christians do not know and do not care about the theological and historical grounds for these divisions is also undeniable; and that denominational division in mission churches is sustained through financial assistance from Europe, from Britain and America, is another fact that can be substantiated. We have been hypnotised into living with divisions in the church; we are made to fight harder to defend denominational Christianity than to spread the cause of the Gospel. We duplicate Christian service and our meagre financial and human resources of the church under the umbrella of trying to give an Anglican, or a Roman Catholic, or a Methodist witness. One group teaches this while another teaches something different, if not contradictory at times; one denomination allows smoking and drinking of alcohol while another body forbids them both; one sect admits into membership individuals from polygamous families while another excommunicates them or keeps them on the periphery of church membership; one group stands up to pray and sits down to sing while next door another group sits or kneels to pray and stands up to sing; one church uses incense, candles and Latin in church services while another condemns them all as idolatrous. What a cacophony of traditions and practices, as each denomination tries to proclaim its own glory that it and it alone holds the final truth of Christianity and is the emblem of the true church! Each group has a false image of itself and of the others.

Some people will argue quite rightly that each of the 210 or so denominations and sects in Kenya brings into the common church a particular tradition and ecclesiastical insights. This is fair enough. But must we pay the heavy price (I would say penalty) of denominationalism for the sake of these traditions and insights? Surely the same insights could be generated under one and the same church if given the freedom to exercise a diversity of taste, culture, situations and theological views. We do not have to disfigure the Body of Christ first, in order to claim that we have enriched it with different traditions.

Attempts have been going on since the early decades of this century to remedy this denominational mass proliferation. But the pace of these ecumenical discussions is so carefully guarded that one wonders whether we are not receding from rather than proceeding towards church unity in Kenya. In any case, when a new denomination or sect is formed every month, surely much more serious work has yet to be done in the ecumenical direction to keep pace with, let alone overtake and reverse, this high rate of divisions. Even the National Christian Council of Kenya, founded as the CCK in 1943, is hardly anything more than an administrative organisation embracing only 21 of the 203 denominations in the country (this is 10.3 per cent of all denominations); the Evangelical Fellowship of Kenya is made up of the more fundamentalist groups of churches; the Kenya Independent Churches Fellowship, the United Churches of Africa, and other similar councils concern themselves with only a few of the independent churches in the country. Indeed this proliferation of councils only means that in addition to denominational divisions there are also groupings of churches along lines of theological taste and church government, to add to the confusion of the layman and to distort the already damaged image of Christianity that these many churches have given.

It seems to belong to the nature of the Christian faith that, in spite of these obvious divisions and their implications, the churches are making a living contribution to national life and to the life of the individuals who find spiritual refuge and hope under even their rugged umbrellas. Churches are not Christianity, even if they each proclaim something of Christianity. Christianity is not the churches. The Christian faith is not grounded on either the churches or even the religious system called Christianity itself. Because the nucleus of the faith is grounded and centred upon Jesus Christ, we can afford to have divisions in the church with all their shame and embarrassment, without necessarily missing the essence of the Christian faith. Christ is not divided even if His Church is divided and maimed a thousand times and more. We must admit that, in one form or another, each of these many denominations and churches is mediating Christ to the individual and to society at large. It is striking that the word 'church' is used in the names of almost all of

146

these 210 denominations and sects, and even where it is left out it is implied in the use of other words. Thus each group shows a genuine wish and concern to depict the church of Christ, to witness to the fact of Christ as proclaimed in the universal church, and to be *the* or *a* church whatever else outsiders may think or whatever other image of itself it may give. The intention is there, and this intention to be the church is certainly a unifying factor even if organisationally the number of churches continues to mushroom.

Denominationalism and its proliferation, then, are the product of human selfishness and weakness. Our church leaders in Kenya, present and past, African and expatriate, have made a mess of the church through inheriting and agreeing to accept divisions, through multiplying divisions, and through perpetuating divisions. But the spirit of Christ is one of unity, reconciliation and harmony. This is the spirit which gives us the courage and confidence to owe allegiance to Him in spite of, and beyond, the denominational walls. The essentials of the Christian faith have remained intact, so that the causes and the fact of denominational division are fundamentally peripheral to, and not an essential of, the Christian faith which otherwise is grounded on Jesus Christ who Himself is unchangeable and indivisible. Perhaps Kenya is learning to live above denominationalism and to reap the benefits of the Christian faith in spite of the divided churches on its soil; yet the nettle's sting of denominationalism remains, and as long as it is there no Christian can rest comfortably.

Finally, the information in this Handbook makes one wish to appeal to the Government of Kenya to set up a ministry of religious affairs. It is not enough for the government simply to register the over two hundred church sects and denominations in the country, it is not enough to allow religious freedom in the country, it is not enough for the government and the churches to co-operate in matters like education and religious broadcasting. A greater formal involvement is called for between the churches and the government, if the religious energy in the country is to be fully harnessed and utilised for the good of the country. In advocating that a governmental ministry of religious affairs be set up, I am aware that a lot of people, especially non-Africans, will start shouting that this would bring about government interference in church affairs; but surely the Kenya Government is powerful enough to need no ministry for the sake of interfering in religious matters were that to be the case. If we can have ministries dealing with items like natural resources and tourism, is it not high time that we had a ministry to cater for the religious life of our peoples all of whom owe allegiance to a religious tradition? Can the government afford to ignore the presence of hundreds of church denominations in the country, over 66% of the population claiming to be Christian, scores of Western missionary societies, and dozens of international church councils based in Kenya, to say nothing of the many church projects in industry, urban life, mass media, women's organisations, relief work, refugees' concern, etc., without taking formal interest in the life and work of the churches and other religions in Kenya? It would be a grave loss to both the country and the churches as to other religious bodies, to continue much longer without the beneficial services that could be rendered through an effective, efficient and well-organised ministry of religious affairs. This Handbook shows that people in Kenya are not only keenly interested in religious life but are actively engaged in it. This religious picture calls, therefore, for a formal governmental recognition whatever outsiders may say about it. I hope that the Handbook will stir up serious thinking in this direction, and that the Government of Kenya will be bold enough to take this courageous step forward in the interests of its people and in appreciation of the value that African peoples attach to religion.

Co-operation Between the Churches

Thomas A. Beetham

In the directory of auxiliary Christian movements and organisations which this *Kenya Churches Handbook* contains, there are many instances of working together by Christians who have widely different experiences and interpretations of the Christian faith. This article seeks to bring together these significant trends, with some reference to action elsewhere in Africa.

The list of these points of co-operation is impressive: it includes education, medicine, social and development programmes, Bible translation, training of ministers, university chaplaincy work, student Christian fellowships, religious broadcasting. It has to be seen against a history of separation, at times exclusiveness, brought from ecclesiastical and theological differences in the church overseas, and at times intensified by the very enthusiasm and zeal for the new-found faith of men and women in Kenyan towns and villages. And if to many young people today the remaining differences are felt to be unnecessary stumbling-blocks to their faith in God through Jesus Christ, let them, without abating their impatience, read the history of the great revival movements from which existing denominations have sprung—let them see there not only littleness of vision and a legalism not found in the

149

teaching of Jesus, but also the courage to stand for Christ at the cost of worldly position and possessions, and even of life itself.

In Kenya, as in many African countries, the earliest development in co-operation was in education. It is true that in the days when almost all schools were maintained by missions and churches, it was necessary to act together in relation to government. So, while far-sighted Christians saw educational co-operation as a point where differences could be overcome and a foundation laid for further unity, others only saw it as a means of Christian self-defence. The more positive aspect lives on today in the Alliance High School, and in the Christian Churches' Educational Association. Today, in the era of state-managed schools, the CCEA reflects the concern of many in the community that a religious interpretation of life shall underlie the school curriculum. This is seen in the drawing up of agreed religious education syllabuses by the CCEA jointly with the Roman Catholic education authorities; that for secondary schools is now complete and was examinable for Forms I and II for the first time in 1971. Work on the primary syllabus is still in progress. This is at the Christian level. The great differences between the major religions of Kenya, particularly Islam, Hinduism and Christianity, do not make it possible for a common religious syllabus for schools on a wider basis. It could be that for one term towards the end of the primary, and again of the secondary course, there might be a series of lessons on 'human conduct' which brings contributions from all these religions to illustrate certain basic ethical standards; such a course, with passages from the Bible and the Qu'ran, has been attempted in West Africa in Cameroon.

The second major area of Christian co-operation has been in the field of that other great institutional activity of Kenya churches, medical work through hospitals and clinics. Today the Protestant churches are united in their relationship to the Ministry of Health through the secretary of the Protestant Churches' Medical Association. Close touch is maintained with Roman Catholic medical workers also.

Both these fields of public service in the name of Christ, education and medicine, were early mainstays of the Christian Council of Kenya; indeed, its first full-time secretariat only became financially possible through its educational work. The more recent service of the NCCK in the name of a very wide range of Protestant churches—possibly a wider range than in any other country in Africa—has been a response to many community needs: community centres and urban mission in Nairobi, famine relief in Turkana and among the Maasai, positive agricultural schemes aimed at obviating famine conditions in these areas, port mission in Mombasa, and the service of youth. These are but a few of its joint activities.

Yet it is in such united NCCK activity that tension, always a natural outcome of new growing-points, exists. These activities are undertaken with the full support of church representatives on the Christian Council, yet their local congregations, sometimes in the very town or village in which the serv-

150

ice is being rendered, may not be conscious that this is part of their own service and witness in common with the neighbouring congregations of other denominations. This is not to say that much-needed service must wait until all local Christians are consciously involved, but it points to the urgent need for those newly baptised into the Christian faith to be helped to understand that Christian discipleship reaches beyond their own denominational allegiance. It is here that young people are asking urgent questions, and will do so more pointedly when they become aware that the religious education syllabus throughout their school course speaks in the name of all the churches.

It is in planning and carrying out of the mission of the church in any town or local area, as something wider than, yet inclusive of, projects of community service, that there arise the biggest difficulties in working together. It is true that denominational boundaries are crossed by Christians of the same area on special occasions: the dedication of a new church, or the ordination of a local man to the ministry or priesthood. In some pioneer areas the same building is used by different churches for Sunday worship, and this includes the Roman Catholic Church. But full fellowship of shared worship and purpose in mission, to spread the Good News of Jesus Christ, does not find fulfilment in united action. There is one important exception to this. The East African Revival Fellowship surmounts the walls of partition. When its members in any one place meet together, then in a very real sense they feel themselves to be the church in that place. But when the spiritual needs of a new township in Nairobi, or of some distant area of northern Kenya, are crying out for understanding, there is little co-operation then even between member churches of the NCCK towards the best deployment of their limited resources. Genuinely spontaneous local councils of churches, whose denominational members would not be over-ridden by their national church authorities, would help towards the laymen's understanding of the felt needs of a neighbourhood for worshipping house groups; a Christian-inspired community centre and church building might then follow. What is required is an inner compulsion to witness; and such a compulsion led thirty pastors and laymen in Mombasa to meet for a full day's training course on Christian witness to Muslims on three occasions in 1971. On one Saturday in October, one group met from 8 a.m. until 5 p.m.; there were Anglicans, Roman Catholics, Pentecostals, Methodists, and African Brotherhood Church members among them; the lecturers were Roman Catholic and Methodist. This was local preparation for mission together.

Nationally, a growing-point exists potentially in St. Paul's United Theological College, Limuru. The college is supported by the Anglican, Presbyterian, Methodist and Reformed Churches, and has also in recent years trained ministers for the East Africa Yearly Meeting of Friends, the Church of God in East Africa, the African Brotherhood Church, the African Israel Church Nineveh, and the Holy Spirit Church of East Africa. As these men, trained together, become pastors in the future of neighbouring congregations, surely the unity of the church in mission will become more common.

A glance at what has been achieved in other countries of Africa, especially between Protestants and Roman Catholics, suggests that God uses the pressure of events to over-ride the innate conservatism of human nature. It is in the smallest African country, the Gambia, where the churches number in their membership a mere few thousand, that there exists a national Christian council in which Anglican, Methodist and Roman Catholic churches are joint foundation members, in a constitution whose basis of membership differs very little from that of the NCCK in Kenya. Again, it is in South Africa, where Christian students have felt the pressure of government policy, that the Christian University Movement, an associate member of the World Student Christian Federation, is jointly Catholic and Protestant. In Malawi, the Christian Service Committee, the arm of the churches in association with government schemes of development, is jointly Protestant and Catholic.

The challenge to the Christian churches of Kenya, of whatever tradition and theology, is surely to respond to the call of God in the urgent problems and deep needs of the country by taking positive action together in the spirit of Christ, rather than to wait for the pressure of events to compel us to do tomorrow what could be joyfully and freely undertaken today.

Grass-roots Christian unity: Christians from a dozen denominations in Bungoma meet for a united prayer service, 1972.

152

DOCUMENTATION

Full details of all inter-church co-operative bodies, councils and projects are given in Part V of this Handbook, the Directory of Christian Organisations in Kenya. Starting-points are the organisations whose initials are NCCK, KEC, KCS, ACC, CCEA, JEAREC, PCMA, UBS, WSCF, KSCF, CSC, YMCA, YWCA.

A second variety of co-operation, much more at the grass-roots or local level, is that in which all churches in an area get together for some specific purpose, usually evangelistic. In this category are four pioneering organisations, Eldoret Churches Unity, Mombasa Council of Christian Congregations, Nyeri Interdenominational Evangelism (see Inter-Christian Churches Denomination), and Chwele & District Ecumenical Group (all addresses given in Directory). The latter group recently sponsored two large open-air ecumenical prayer services at Chebukaka Catholic Mission (Bungoma) (see photograph), and at Chwele Market, attended by 2,000 Christians from every kind of local church (Anglicans, Friends, Roman Catholics, Salvation Army, Baptists, PEFA, PAG, Maria Legio, Assemblies of God, and others), and addressed by members of each church, preaching, praying, singing and testifying to the work of the Holy Spirit. These local united organisations express the impatience of grass-roots Christians regarding the slow progress of church union at the national leadership level.

All of these are primarily co-operative bodies between Western mission-related churches, Protestant and Catholic, with only a handful of African independent churches so far drawn in. It is important to note, therefore, that over the last 15 years in Kenya the independent denominations — now numbering over 150 — have made at least 14 attempts to form their own nation-wide council or federation, linked in some cases with churches outside Kenya — either Independent, or Eastern Orthodox (Greek), or Coptic Orthodox (Egypt), or Ethiopian Orthodox. Little success has so far been achieved, because of the absence of adequate funding, resources or trained personnel. These federations, several of which are now defunct or have emerged in new form under a different name, will now be listed. Addresses, officers and other details are given in the Directory.

COUNCILS OF AFRICAN INDEPENDENT CHURCHES IN KENYA

African Independent Communion Churches
Central Africa Christian Council (CACC)
Council of East African Evangelist Societies of God
East Africa Christian Alliance (EACA)
East African United Churches and Orthodox Coptic Communion
Ethiopian Orthodox Holy Spirit & United Churches of EA
Kenya African United Christian Churches
Kenya Independent Churches Fellowship
National United Churches Association of East Africa
United Churches of Africa
United Churches of East Africa
United Independent Churches of East Africa
United Orthodox Independent Churches of East Africa
United Orthodox Independent Zion Churches of Kenya

2

Part II

The Expansion of Christianity

The Expansion of Christianity in Kenya AD 1900 - 2000

In Kenya, 500,000 a year are joining the Christian faith, and there are 5 million practising Christians.

David B. Barrett

Christianity in Kenya: an overview

During the twentieth century, the Christian faith has been expanding in Kenya at a meteoric rate, and is still expanding faster than in almost all other countries of the world.

This is the conclusion we reach after an examination of the statistical findings of this survey, presented in summary form in Table 1 below, and in diagrammatic form in Figure 1. In these, we give statistics for the years 1900 and 1972, with projections ahead to the year 2000 where this can meaningfully be done based on existing trends. The reader wanting to discover immediately the present state of Christianity in Kenya can do so at a glance by reading from the table the most significant of the 1972 statistics, which we have printed in heavy type.

Since Christian missions did not arrive in strength in Kenya until well after the year 1900, this extremely rapid expansion is little short of phenomenal. How has this extraordinary state of affairs come about? Before we examine these summary findings in more detail, we must first consider the sources of this data, the methodology we have employed, and also certain basic questions as to the meaning of the term 'Christian'.

Sources of statistics

The sources of the statistics for this survey were sevenfold: (1) statistics reported by churches and missions in Kenya over the past eighty years, in

FIGURE 1: EXPANSION OF CHRISTIANITY IN KENYA, AD 1890-2000

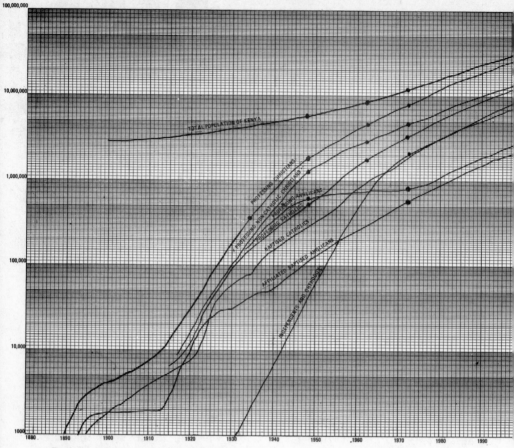

1. Semi-logarithmic graph paper (above) has a vertical scale whose steps, instead of increasing by equal amounts (1, 2, 3, 4, 5, 6, ... etc.), increase by multiples of 10, thus. 10, 100, 1,000, 10,000, 100,000, 1 million (see the left-hand scale). On such paper, a straight line represents a uniform annual rate of growth (such as that of the Independents and Orthodox above, who from 1930 to 1960 doubled roughly every three years, which means an annual exponential increase of around 20%).

2. For the sources and methodology behind this figure, see documentation at the end of this article.

3. The points marked with circles, derive from the two government censuses of 1948 and 1962, and also from certain quasi-censuses or surveys in 1913, 1920, 1934, and 1972.

4. The most detailed series of statistics shown here is the line 'baptised Catholics' for the period 1949-1969, for which Propaganda (Rome) published detailed statistics every two years. The dip in the line from 1961-1967 represents a loss of a minimum of 100,000 Catholics to independent churches as explained elsewhere in this Handbook.

5. Note the gradual falling off in the growth rates after 1940 as the churches become large compared with the number remaining non-Christian. By 1960, 50% of the country were Christians.

6. For a different kind of diagram illustrating the expansion of the two largest churches in Kenya (Catholic and Anglican) see Figure 3 in this article.

most cases published in items listed in our *Bibliography;* (2) answers to a standard questionnaire sent to all churches in 1971 by the *Kenya Churches Handbook*, and returned completed by 120 of Kenya's total then of 200 denominations, and tabulated here in Table 5; (3) field work by the editors, involving visits to the headquarters of 70 denominations, contacts with 30 more, and including our own head counts and statistical estimates of numbers of congregations, ministers, worshippers, and Christians; (4) the two government censuses of population in Kenya which have included a question on religion, namely 1948 (available, but never published) and 1962 (published), whose results are given in Table 2; (5) demographic projections for Kenya's future population made by government demographers, which were combined with the 1962 census figures for all Kenya's tribes and races to produce the figures of tribal religious profession in Table 4, as well as the projections to AD 2000 in Table 1; (6) records and annual returns held by the Kenya government concerning the 200 denominations registered under The Societies Act (also included in Table 5); and (7) a number of sample surveys and public opinion polls, in various parts of Kenya, which included questions on religious affiliation and practice.

In practice, it has been found possible to reconcile the statistics from all these sources, many of which appeared at first sight to be contradictory or incompatible. As a result, we can affirm that religious statistics in Kenya as kept by churches and government are of a remarkably high standard.

Of these sources, the government censuses, undertaken as they were by thousands of enumerators and field workers, probably yield the most accurate data; and the public opinion polls with their randomly-chosen samples are also reasonably accurate. But as the survey progressed, it became evident that the churches' statistics also were of high reliability, being based in most cases on grass-roots reality. Protestant figures, for example, were in many cases found to be based on head counts of participating persons physically present at services; this is evident in the high percentages given for Protestant Sunday attendances (see Table 5, column 11). Many African independent churches, it was discovered, only counted as members those who attended regularly; naturally, therefore, they reported that as high as 95 percent of all their members were in church every Sunday or Sabbath. Moreover, it was clear that many Protestant and independent churches kept 'clean' membership rolls, i.e. rolls from which non-participants (or members who have moved away or died) are regularly removed so that the rolls reflect actual current participation. Indeed, the requirements of the Kenya government -- the annual returns, the knowledge that every denomination may be called upon at any time to produce for the government a written list of all its members over 18 years of age, together with the Registrar-General's scale of annual fees (shs.5/- for up to 25 members, shs.10/- for under 100, shs.25/- for under 1,000, shs.50/- for 1,000 or over) -- all of these act as a powerful incentive to keep clean and current membership counts. The cleanest rolls

TABLE 1

CHRISTIANITY IN KENYA, AD 1900–2000

Year:

		Year:	• 1900	%	mid - 1972	%	2000	%
A.	**POPULATION OF KENYA**							
	1.	Total population	2,900,000	100.0	12,091,000	100.0	34,286,000	100.0
	2.	Africans	2,864,500	98.8	11,859,200	98.1	33,628,000	98.1
	3.	Arabs	8,000	0.3	30,800	0.2	87,000	0.2
	4.	Asians	27,000	0.9	155,000	1.3	442,000	1.3
	5.	Europeans	500	0.0	44,900	0.4	127,000	0.4
4	6.	Annual births	116,000	4.0	604,550	5.0	1,542,870	4.5
	7.	Annual deaths	104,000	3.6	205,500	1.7	342,860	1.0
	8.	Annual population increase	11,600	0.4	399,000	3.3	1,200,010	3.5
	9.	Annual persons reaching 15 years	40,000	1.4	260,000	2.2	809,200	2.3
	10.	Average age of nation	12		14.5		15.0	
	11.	Life expectancy	35		50		60	
	12.	Population in urban areas	9,000	0.3	1,260,000	10.4	5,740,000	16.7
	13.	Population of City of Nairobi	4,500	0.2	600,000	5.0	2,800,000	8.2
B.	**RELIGIOUS PROFESSION IN KENYA**							
	14.	Traditional (animists)	2,778,000	95.8	3,182,000	26.3	2,900,000	8.4
	15.	Muslims	100,000	3.4	770,000	6.4	2,400,000	7.0
	16.	Christians	5,000	0.2	8,000,000	66.2	28,600,000	83.4
	17.	Hindus	10,000	0.3	60,000	0.5	160,000	0.5
	18.	Jains	5,000	0.2	30,000	0.2	96,000	0.3
	19.	Sikhs	2,000	0.1	13,000	0.1	36,000	0.1
	20.	Baha'is	0	0.0	30,000	0.2	100,000	0.3
C.	**PROFESSING CHRISTIANS IN KENYA**							
	21.	Total all Christians	5,000	0.2	8,000,000	66.2	28,600,000	83.4
	22.	Catholics: total	2,700	0.1	3,400,000	28.1	14,000,000	40.8
	23.	Baptised Catholics	1,800	0.1	1,900,000	15.7	9,000,000	26.2
	24.	Unbaptised Catholics	900	0.0	1,500,000	12.4	5,000,000	14.6
	25.	Anglicans	2,000	0.1	800,000	6.6	3,000,000	8.7
	26.	Protestants	300	0.0	1,780,000	14.7	3,700,000	10.8
	27.	African Independents	0	0.0	1,760,000	14.6	7,000,000	20.4
	28.	Orthodox	0	0.0	260,000	2.2	900,000	2.6
	29.	First-generation Christians	4,500		2,400,000		4,300,000	
	30.	Christians in urban areas	800	0.0	945,000	7.8	5,170,000	15.1
	31.	Christians in City of Nairobi	400	0.0	450,000	3.7	2,520,000	7.3
D.	**AFFILIATED CHRISTIANS IN KENYA**							
	32.	Total affiliated (known to churches)	5,000	0.2	6,525,000	54.0	24,100,000	70.3
	33.	Catholics (and catechumens)	2,700	0.1	2,140,000	17.7	10,200,000	29.7
	34.	Anglicans	2,000	0.1	615,000	5.1	2,400,000	7.0
	35.	Protestants	300	0.0	1,750,000	14.5	3,600,000	10.5
	36.	Independents	0	0.0	1,760,000	14.6	7,000,000	20.4
	37.	Orthodox	0	0.0	260,000	2.2	900,000	2.6
	38.	NCCK-affiliated Christians	–		2,305,000	19.1		
E.	**PRACTISING CHRISTIANS IN KENYA**							
	39.	Practising Christians: churchgoing	2,000	0.1	4,578,000	37.9	15,000,000	43.7
	40.	Catholics	1,000	0.0	1,428,000	11.8	5,500,000	16.0
	41.	Anglicans	900	0.0	250,000	2.1	800,000	2.3
	42.	Protestants	100	0.0	1,300,000	10.7	2,600,000	7.6
	43.	Independents	–		1,500,000	12.4	6,000,000	17.5
	44.	Orthodox	–		100,000	0.8	500,000	1.5
	45.	Sunday church attenders (weekly)	2,000	0.1	2,400,000	19.8	8,000,000	23.3
	46.	Sunday radio service listeners	–		5,680,000	47.0		
	47.	Practising Christians: total all kinds	2,000	0.1	5,000,000	41.4	15,000,000	43.7
	48.	Annual weddings or liaisons among Christians	40		64,000		230,000	
	49.	Annual weddings in church	20		30,000			
F.	**CHURCHES AND CLERGY IN KENYA**							
	50.	Denominations	6		210			
	51.	Congregations	50		19,490		50,000	
	52.	Ordained clergy/ministers: total	53		6,218		20,000	
	53.	National clergy	3		5,354			
	54.	Expatriate clergy	50		864			
G.	**CHURCH GROWTH IN KENYA EACH YEAR**							
		Annual increase in						
	55.	Denominations	1		12			
	56.	Congregations	10		700		2,000	
	57.	Clergy/ministers	1		220		500	
	58.	Professing Christians	200		400,000		1,000,000	
	59.	Affiliated Christians	200		300,000		700,000	
	60.	Practising Christians	100		230,000		500,000	
	61.	Christians in urban areas	100		51,030		280,000	
	62.	Christians in City of Nairobi	50		25,650		140,000	
		Professing Christians:						
	63.	Annual new Christians	380		536,000		1,286,000	
	64.	Annual deaths	180		136,000		286,000	
	65.	Annual nett increase	200		400,000		1,000,000	
	66.	Annual baptisms: total	230		311,000		650,000	
	67.	Infant baptisms	150		132,000		450,000	
	68.	Adult baptisms	80		179,000		200,000	
	69.	Catholic (total)	120		114,000		350,000	
	70.	Anglican (total)	90		47,000		100,000	
	71.	Scriptures distributed annually			(1,100,000			

Note: Documentation on the sources and methodology employed in this table will be found at the end of this article, together with additional details and explanations concerning various lines in the above table.

Updating to mid-1973: It must be remembered that all the Christian numbers above, in the middle column, are increasing annually; professing Christians, and the churches, are growing at 4% per year. The national percentage of professing Christians increases by 2.1% each year, giving the following statistics for mid-1973: 8.4 million professing Christians (68.3% of the population of Kenya.

Boys (centre) and girls (top left) arriving in church for their weekly voluntary Christian instruction period. In addition, about 1.7 million of Kenya's 1.9 million primary school pupils receive regular religious education in state-run schools.

we examined were those of the Methodist Church in Kenya. Roman Catholics, on the other hand, kept by far the most comprehensive rolls of baptised persons at the congregational level; but, being exempt from registration along with several other of the larger churches, it was understandable that their rolls were usually less up-to-date and 'clean' than Protestant ones.

Methodology

Our approach to this material has been synthetic, i.e. attempting a synthesis or combination of all the different types of material that would make consistent sense of the total data. At many points, as mentioned above, it seemed at first glance as if we had irreconcilable data from different sources; further research into the exact meaning of the data showed that a synthesis was possible.

Secondly, after due consideration, we accepted the statistical returns of both government and churches as reliable, unless clear evidence of unreliability in any particular case was available. In some cases, it was necessary to check figures that we at first thought to be too large. In almost every case, however, detailed investigations showed that the claims were based on some sort of reality.

A third important principle behind the present analysis concerns the expansion of Christianity over the last seventy years. Large aggregate numbers such as church memberships do not normally expand by fits and starts, but grow gradually and smoothly over the years, as indeed whole populations themselves do. This means that graphs of church growth from one year to the next are usually smooth curves; any sudden rises or falls are probably due to church statisticians 'cleaning the rolls', or conducting a new survey, or some such methodological innovation. Moreover, church populations grow *organically*, in an exponential manner (1, 2, 4, 8, 16, 32, 64, 128, etc.), similarly to demographic growth (or compound interest on money in a bank). This means that the normal type of church growth, when plotted on semi-logarithmic paper as we have done in Figures 1 and 2, is a straight line. In practice, of course, historical and other factors are constantly changing, and so we get curves rather than straight lines. All of this means that our graphs can be interpreted in terms of actual historical events and forces. In several cases, the graphs illustrate well-known historical situations (e.g. the Kikuyu female circumcision controversy from 1929, which caused Presbyterian and Anglican membership to fall drastically: see Figure 2); but in other cases, the graphs reveal important changes that historians may not yet have noticed but must one day account for.

Who is a Christian?

The major problem that we encountered in handling these statistics was one of definition. What does the term 'Christian' mean? Who is entitled to be called a Christian? Who is a Protestant? Who is a Catholic? What sort of people can correctly be described as Christian? Can an infant be a Christian? Who has the right to decide which people are Christians, and which are not?

Our starting-point here is the fundamental right of the individual to the basic human freedoms, in their religious application. In Kenya, there has been a long tradition of religious tolerance. A century ago, by the Treaty of Berlin in 1885, Britain and Germany gave specific guarantees of freedom of conscience, religious toleration, and 'the free open exercise of all forms of worship', for their newly-acquired East African territories. A century later, the constitution of the Republic of Kenya had become even more explicit. In its chapter V, 'Protection of fundamental rights and freedoms of the individual', the constitution states in section 78: 'No person shall be hindered in the enjoyment of his freedom of conscience,... freedom of thought and of religion, freedom to change his religion or belief, and freedom... to manifest and propagate his religion or belief in worship, teaching, practice and observance'. This section is, of course, based on the United Nations' 1948 *Universal Declaration of Human Rights*, article 18: 'Everyone has the right to freedom of thought, conscience and religion; this right includes freedom to change his religion or belief, and freedom, either alone or in community with others and in public or private, to manifest his religion or belief in teaching, practice, worship and observance'. Clearly, this fundamental human right also includes the right to claim, and to state, the

TABLE 2

PROFESSING CHRISTIANS IN KENYA, 1948-1962

	1948				1962			
	Africans	Non-Africans	Total	%	Africans	Non-Africans	Total	%
TRADITIONAL (ANIMISTS)	3,550,800	0	3,550,800	61.2	3,179,721	0	3,179,721	36.8
MUSLIMS	242,740	52,957	295,697	5.1	606,560	74,456	681,016	7.9
CHRISTIANS:								
Roman Catholics	491,130	12,508	503,638	8.7	1,726,120	28,507	1,754,627	20.3
Protestants:	1,360,500	23,868	1,384,368	23.9	2,853,541	44,251	2,897,792	33.6
Anglicans	626,610	18,341	644,951	11.1				
Presbyterians	203,230	2,462	205,692	3.5				
Salvation Army	45,200	45	45,245	0.8				
Seventh-day Adventists	101,600	99	101,699	1.8				
Others (AIM, AICM, &c)	383,870	3,065	386,935	6.7				
OTHERS								
Hindus	0	45,304	45,304	0.8	0	97,841	97,841	1.1
Jains	0	6,149	6,149	0.1	0			
Sikhs	0	10,663	10,633	0.2	0	21,169	21,169	0.3
TOTAL POPULATION	5,645,000	154,846	5,800,000	100.0	8,365,942	270,321	8,636,263	100.0

This table gives the government census figures of religious profession for the two census years of 1948 (unpublished) and 1962 (published 1966) after which the question concerning religion was dropped. In 1948, non-Africans were counted in toto, whereas the African figures were obtained by sample census; in 1962, both groups were counted. Blank spaces indicate that a particular term (e.g. 'Anglicans') was not used during the census. 'Protestants' is used in the census to indicate all non-Catholics, although in this Handbook we follow the correct usage meaning only churches related to European or American Protestant missionary bodies. In 1962, there was no breakdown of 'Protestants' as there had been in 1948.

religion of one's choice, and the right to be called a follower of that religion.

A moment's reflection will show us how seriously we take the individual's choice in other important areas of life. We all know, for example, the power of the vote. Consider for a moment a political election in Kenya, such as a presidential election. Every adult has one vote. Every vote counts, irrespective of whether the individual voter is good or bad, clever or stupid, zealous or apathetic. The aggregate of such votes will elect or reject a presidential prospect, and he would be a foolish politician indeed who ignored large areas of the electorate on the grounds that they were illiterate, wrongly-motivated, merely nominal, or even non-practising party members. What ultimately decide the fate of the candidates are the freely expressed political choices of millions of individuals. In the same way, no Christian leader seeking to represent or mobilise Christian opinion can afford to dismiss the opinions of any section of the 8 million persons who claim to be Christians in Kenya today.

This elementary human right to decide one's own religion means, in addition, that every human being also has the right to have his decision respected and accepted by his family, by his neighbours, by his co-religionists, by the state, and by society at large. There is no difficulty here with most religions; if a man says he is a Muslim, or a Hindu, or an animist, nobody contests it. But the same should also be true if a man says he is a Christian, or a Protestant, or a Catholic; even if in your opinion, or in mine, he does not practise the Christian faith adequately, neither you nor I have the right to deny him the name Christian. We certainly do not have the right to dismiss him as merely nominal, still less to treat him as a non-Christian. A Christian, then, is any and every person who when asked what his religion is, for example by a government census enumerator, replies 'I am a Christian', or 'I am a follower of Jesus Christ', or (if he speaks Swahili) 'Ni Mkristo', or (if he is a Kamba) 'Ni mwitikili' ('I am a receiver of the Faith'), or any other such verbal profession or confession of faith. The fact that he may be a bad Christian, or an indifferent Christian, is not the point; he is a Christian. He may be a badly- or partially-instructed Christian, or even a completely uninstructed one; in that case, it is probably more the churches' fault than his own. More likely, in Kenya, he is one of millions of intending Christians, persons intending or attempting to start out on the life of church membership but who for one reason or another have not yet got there. Here, then, is the justification for our statement in Table 1 that there are 8.0 million Christians in Kenya by mid-1972; this is the estimated number of persons who, if a government census of religion were held today, would say 'Ni Mkristo' — 'I am a Christian'. To describe these persons, we use the term 'professing Christians'.

Of course, the churches also have the right, if they so wish, to define more exacting forms of Christian discipleship, and in practice almost all churches have categories of affiliated 'members', 'baptised members', 'communicant

Many of the 1,500 Anglican rural churches are too small to hold everybody, and so latecomers have to listen from outside. Children and even infants on their mother's backs (left centre) are regularly present, hence are counted in statistics of attendance.

members', 'active members', 'subscribing members', and so on, which are considerably smaller than the totals of all who call themselves followers of that church. We must now attempt to systematise such statistics, and to bring some order into what would otherwise be a very confusing field.

Three categories of Christians

If we consider, therefore, the various meanings of the term Christian, as understood by churches, governments, secular agencies, and individuals, we find that we can separate them into three main groups. We can distinguish three distinct categories of Christian, beginning with the category just described in the previous section. (1) *professing Christians*, those whose religious preference is Christian, and who profess 'I am a Christian', particularly in a government census or a public opinion poll; next, there are (2) *affiliated Christians*, i.e. Christians affiliated to churches, which means all those known to the churches, on the churches' rolls, books or records, and therefore claimed by the churches in their statistics; and lastly, there are (3) *practising Christians*, active Christians, or participating Christians, which means those who attend church activities regularly (weekly, monthly, or on the major Christian festivals), or who regularly join in broadcast worship services on the radio. Of these three categories, 'professing Christians' includes the other two categories, and 'affiliated Christians' includes 'practising Christians'. In Kenya in mid-1972, as Table 1 has illustrated, professing Christians number 8.0 million; affiliated Christians 6.5 million, and practising Christians 5.0 million.

Another important point concerns children and infants, especially the children of Christian parents. In some church statistics, they are always counted, as with Anglicans, Catholics, and Lutherans, in others, such as with Baptists, children are not counted. Either practice is perfectly correct and acceptable, but, since 49 per cent of the population of Kenya (and therefore of most churches) is under 15 years of age, it is vital to define clearly whether or not children are included in any figures we quote. In our three categories above, children and infants are included, as is also the case with the statistics in Tables 2 and 4, and Table 5, column 10.

A third essential point with statistics is that every figure must be accompanied by its related date or year. This is particularly important in a country like Kenya where Christianity is expanding at a rapid rate. Thus it is incorrect to say 'There are (or were) 4.6 million Christians in Kenya , we must specify the date, thus, 'There were 4.6 million Christians in Kenya *in 1962*, and there are 8.0 million Christians in mid-1972'.

* * *

We are now ready to draw attention to certain features in our data which illustrate the phenomenal expansion of Christianity in Kenya during the twentieth century, and which suggest that certain quite new interpretations are necessary. We will discuss four or five aspects in particular.

Instantaneous acceptance of the Gospel

It has often been asserted by Western historians, missionary writers and other observers, that the response of Africans to the Christian faith in Kenya was slow at first, only gathering momentum after several years or decades of missionary persuasion. Our data show that this is completely untrue. Two examples will suffice. The official PCEA historian (see Macpherson in *Bibliography)* gives the numbers of converts at Kikuyu and Tumutumu from 1907 on, and comments: "Growth was comparitively slow in the early years due to the "natural conservatism" of the Kikuyu people'. Similarly, of the early Catholic years in Meru, the Consolata history *Conquest for Christ in Kenya* comments: One often reads in mission magazines of "streams of conversions", but the registers in Meru show them to have been a mere trickle' Yet a glance at the actual statistics themselves of baptised converts in the PCEA and the Consolata dioceses of Meru and Nyeri, shown in Figure 2 plotted again on semi-logarithmic paper, illustrates the falsity of this widespread interpretation. Wherever the Word of God — the preaching of the Good News — went amongst the animistic tribal populations of Kenya, the response was instantaneous, immediate, and enormous. This is clearly brought out in Figure 2, where we show the initial growth rates in five missions in Kenya. In the very first days of the Gospel, the rate of growth of the Christian community — shown by the slopes of the curves in Figure 2 — was phenomenal. In some cases the Christian community doubled in size every three years. Then, as the graphs show, the initial enormously large growth rates began gradually to decrease as the churches got larger and as a majority of the people in the area became Christians. Yet so vast was the early response rate that even seventy years later it is still on average 5 per cent per year, or nearly double the demographic natural increase of the whole population.

On Palm Sunday about a million Catholics in 1,700 churches take part in processions of witness often, as in Eldoret in 1972, together with Protestants and Anglicans, carrying the traditional palms. Again, children participate (see infant with palm on his mother's back, lower right) and so are counted in statistics.

167

Although observers failed to notice the instantaneous growth of the churches in the earliest days, the huge numbers that resulted after twenty years soon changed their understanding. By 1913 in the Anglican church, and 1921 in the Catholic church (as Figure 1 illustrates), the enormous growth in western and central Kenya had overcome the slow growth of both churches at the strongly Muslim Coast; and by 1916 one can speak of a full-scale mass movement into the churches as having begun.

A short excursus is necessary at this point to avoid misunderstanding with regard to Roman Catholic baptismal statistics. In 1902 in the Consolata mission at Nyeri, the practice began of baptising as many dying persons as possible (in accordance with the doctrine that the unbaptised heathen went to hell at death). By 1917 these baptisms *in articulo mortis* had become a mass movement in itself, with 18,000 deathbed baptisms a year in Nyeri specially conducted by missionary sisters and lay persons, a rate 15 times larger than baptisms of live persons at that time. This practice — common in Catholic missions of that period throughout the world — continued until the doctrine disappeared in the 1950s. For our purposes, we should note that deathbed baptisms were never counted as living Catholics and so were not included in Catholic statistics of annual baptisms. These latter therefore reflect the actual growth of the Catholic community.

A genuinely African religion from the first

What this statistical analysis shows very clearly is that although the first seed was originally a foreign import, the resulting Christianity in Kenya cannot be thought of as a foreign transplant, but rather must be seen as an indigenous plant from the very first. Its expansion has not been due primarily to external forces (foreign missions, colonial pressures, Western education or civilisation); it has been due primarily to internal forces within the African churches themselves. In almost all areas and at almost all periods, growth has sprung directly, and measurably, out of the Christian community itself. Like shoots bursting up through fertile soil, the growing churches have expanded from the earliest days directly out of the first convert or groups of converts. This analogy of the seed is particularly appropriate, because Jesus himself used it. In his Parable of the Mustard Seed, he compared the future expansion of the Kingdom of God with the exceptionally rapid growth of the tiny mustard seed: 'It is the smallest of all seeds, but when it has grown it is the greatest of shrubs and becomes a tree' (Matthew 13.32). What this means is that the startling growth of the churches in Kenya -- and across the whole of Black Africa also -- is a sign of the arrival of the Kingdom of God in Africa in genuinely indigenous form. It is clear evidence that Christianity has been accepted by Africans from the earliest days as a genuinely African religion, with roots firmly in African soil. This is also striking refutation of the complaints still heard today that Christianity in Kenya is foreign, Western, the white man's religion — for, the statistical evidence clearly points to the fact that, from literally the very first days, the

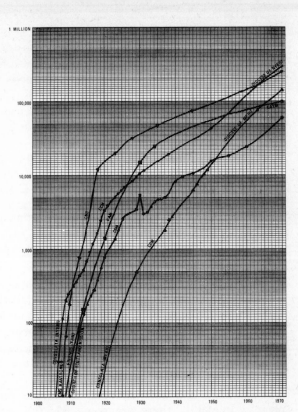

FIGURE 2:

**INSTANTANEOUS RESPONSE
TO CHRISTIANITY AMONG
FIVE KENYAN PEOPLES**

This diagram shows the growth of five denominational Christian communities (baptised members, including children, and catechumens) in five areas of Kenya, which began with the arrival of missions in the years shown below.

From the very first days, there were rapidly-growing groups of interested persons or enquirers around all mission stations. Statistics of all such interested persons were almost never kept, however, and membership statistics were measured more strictly and included only those who met certain criteria (completion of the catechumenate, or, as with the Friends (who do not baptise), admission to full membership). Such members were usually required to be instructed for from two to five years before they could be admitted (and therefore be counted in membership statistics). Further, at the start when there are less than 10 baptised members or converts, it is not possible to measure growth rates with any meaning. By the time growth rates have become measurable (in this case when the number of converts reaches 10), the rates are extremely large, doubling or even trebling every year (in figures, 69 or 110 per cent per year). Ten years after the first mission arrival, the rates in the graph have settled down to doubling every two years or so (35% per year). By 1970 these communities were on average doubling every 15 years (a growth rate of 4.6% per year).

The five missions shown in the graph began work in the following years.

1900 Church of Scotland Mission (CSM) among the Kikuyu, now the PCEA.
1902 Consolata Catholic Mission (CCM) among the Kikuyu, now the Diocese of Nyeri.
1902 Friends Africa Mission (FAM) among the Luhya, now the EAYM.
1906 Church Missionary Society (CMS) Kavirondo Mission among the Luo and Luhya, now the Dioceses of Maseno South and Maseno North respectively.
1911 Consolata Catholic Mission (CCM) among the Meru, now the Diocese of Meru.

The points marked on the lines in the diagram are totals of converts returned by the missions for the years shown. The bottom line represents 10 African converts or baptised members. The meaning of the graph is (for example) that the CMS Kavirondo Mission had 10 converts by 1908, which had increased to 64 by 1909, 175 by 1910, 750 by 1913, 12,000 by 1918, etc.

169

seed had successfully taken root in African soil; the converts attracted more converts, the Christian communities multiplied exponentially, and their churches grew organically precisely as seeds grow into shoots, then into plants and then into trees. In other words, Christianity in Kenya, in any of its major versions, can be regarded in no sense as a foreign transplant – from the very first days, it has been an indigenous growth springing directly out of African soil.

Acceptance of Christianity but not of denominationalism

Our next observation concerns the vast number of ecclesiastical schisms that have taken place in Kenya -- over 150 since the year 1914. For a certain number of missions and churches, the results have been numerically disastrous, as the data in this Handbook reveal. In 1930 the Presbyterian mission lost nearly half its members to the nascent AIPC and AOC independent churches, as Figure 2 shows. From 1914-1972, the Anglican church resulted in over 30 separatist bodies and lost over half its total membership. Serious disaffection within the Anglican church began around 1923, after which vast numbers of professing Anglicans disaffiliated themselves and began to form loose independent groupings although with no legal recognition. In the 1948 government census there were 640,000 professing Anglicans, though only 110,000 then were affiliated to the Anglican church. From 1960-1970 all these groupings of former Anglicans obtained legal recognition as independent churches, and by 1970 the enormous discrepancy between professing and affiliated had been reduced to normal proportions, as Figure 1 makes clear. In 1972, there are some 615,000 affiliated Anglicans (or about 800,000 professing), whereas members of churches that have seceded from Anglicanism number about 700,000 affiliated, as Table 5 illustrates. Another way of stating this same fact is to point out that whereas in the 1948 census Anglicans numbered 11 per cent of the whole country, by 1972 this

A packed congregation in Western Kenya engaging in 'simultaneous audible prayer', each praying separately, aloud (Pentecostal Assemblies of God, begun by Canadian mission). Protestant statistics of Sunday attendance are usually based on head counts and cover only adults, so when analysing statistics allowance must be made for the many children present.

Worshippers from several AICN congregations assemble beneath their local banners for a combined march through the Nyanza countryside. The only statistics collected by most independent churches are of the number of regular adult participants such as these.

had dropped to 6.6 per cent. Further, this mushrooming of independency from 1950-1972 has also been at the expense of the major Protestant missions of the early days — PCEA, AIM, MCK, SDA, EAYM, Salvation Army — all of whom would otherwise now be three or four times bigger and over the half million mark in membership. By contrast, the Catholic church has had a less turbulent history. Up to about 1951, professing Catholics numbered less than Anglicans; after 1951, they rapidly overtook Anglicans in numbers; but over the years 1959-1963 something like 100,000 Catholics were lost, mainly to Maria Legio of Africa (this drop can be clearly seen in Figure 1). Certain smaller Protestant missions have at times lost 80 per cent of their entire adherents. But independent churches also have suffered likewise, as the Musanda Holy Ghost Church did in 1939 when nearly half its members seceded. At present, it seems as though the Anglican church has learned from its past experience of schisms and has begun to expand again, whereas in several of the newer Protestant churches situations ripe for schism are rapidly developing.

The interesting thing is that, despite these convulsions, Christianity as a whole in Kenya has increased numerically over the years with a remarkable

Kenyan clergy of the African Orthodox Church assist their Archbishop a Greek (centre), at the **packed** dedication service of a large new Orthodox parish church. In Orthodox statistics, the faithful means the whole baptised community including infants.

smoothness. The schisms have not in the slightest affected adversely the rate of conversion of animists to Christianity. In other words, the schisms have been purely an internal affair, Christians of one denominational tradition shifting their allegiance to another. Equally startling is the fact that the initial responses to the Gospel, on the part of peoples of vastly differing cultures amongst whom had come foreign missions of widely varying ecclesiastical traditions, were almost uniformly enormous, as we have already seen (Figure 2). All of this indicates that what the populations of Kenya have accepted over the years has been not this or that version of Western denominationalism, but genuine Christianity — the basic essentials of the Biblical faith in the Risen Christ — and a Christianity only marginally interested in, or concerned with, or moulded by, the Western cultural and ecclesiastical trappings and accretions with which the Word of God had been brought.

If this is so, it casts a more favourable light on the excessive numbers of denominations at present in Kenya. To their practitioners and participants, this is not the scandal it would be in the Western world; it is not division nor denominationalism run riot — rather, it is diversity, the search for ever new and more valid indigenous expressions of Christian faith. It is in fact just the kind of diversity one would expect to find in a nation of fifty diverse ribes speaking fifty mutually unintelligible languages, and a nation into which at least 70 different foreign missionary societies from 30 nations have come.

The nominal fringe in Kenya

We move now to consider the discrepancy first noted in Table 1 between those who profess Christianity and those affiliated to churches. We have

Of the 700 new congregations begun in Kenya each year, about 300 construct mud or brick buildings in the African idiom, such as this one seating 100 persons (Church Army Training College, Nairobi).

Each year 180,000 adult Kenyans are baptised, many of them as here by immersion with its symbolism of dying with Christ and rising to new life with Him (PAG, Tsimbalo Assembly; on this occasion 250 were baptised in the presence of 3000 others.)

On two days in March 1971, Archbishop Makarios of Cyprus baptised into the Orthodox faith 5,000 persons of all ages (3 months to 90 years), using different methods — immersion, dipping, sprinkling, aspersion, pouring.

Many African independent churches in Kenya (such as the Vapostori here) baptise infants and children. In Table 5, in fact, 37 AIC denominations report infant baptism statistics.

shown that government statistics, projected to 1972, reveal a total of 8.0 million professing Christians; whereas the churches' statistics show a total of only 6.5 million affiliated. The contrast is particularly noticeable for the Roman Catholic Church: in mid-1972, that church knows of 2.14 million Catholics, including catechumens; but professing Catholics number 3.4 million. Who are these extra 1.26 million persons professing to be Catholics but unknown to the church? And, who, likewise, are the extra 185,000 who profess to be Anglicans and 30,000 who profess to be Protestants, but who are unknown to these churches also?

The explanation arises directly from the fact that both the Catholic Church and the other Western churches in Kenya are still expanding at the phenomenal rate of 5 per cent per year. Each year the Catholic Church baptises 110,000 new Catholics, and there are nearly twice that number of catechumens. But as with most Western churches in Africa, the Catholic Church requires of its converts a long period under instruction in the catechumenate, varying from one to four years; with similar figures for Anglicans and Protestants. And in practice, due to labour migration, difficulties of terrain, rainy seasons, sickness, family obligations, priority given to tilling the land, and so on, the average intending Christian, whether Catholic or Protestant, takes between five and ten years to reach the point of baptism. This means that for every newly baptised Catholic or Protestant, there are five or ten others waiting outside the churches. So, then, we reach the conclusion that the 'nominal fringe' in Kenya — the 1.26 million 'nominal' Catholics and 200,000 'nominal' Anglicans and Protestants — cannot properly be described as nominal at all; they are intending Christians who have already made some sort of break with pagan society, who have already decided 'Ni Mkristo', and who have already begun the long process of moving into the churches. The fact that it may take them up to ten years before baptism is probably less their fault than that of the churches, whose ponderous machinery of initiation cannot let in fast enough those who ask for instruction and baptism.

Not surprisingly, the independent churches in Kenya do not subject their converts to this kind of indignity, nor do they make it so difficult and lengthy a process to become a church member. Several of these bodies, in fact, have arisen precisely as a protest at this point against interminable delays before baptism. Consequently, there is no independent 'nominal fringe' — it is purely a Catholic, Anglican and Protestant phenomenon.

Christian practice in Kenya

Up to this point, we have maintained that the large numbers of professing Christians and affiliated Christians in the churches are not merely nominal lists, but represent a definite and active reality. What about actual statistics, then, of Christian practice? To what extent do Christians in Kenya practise their religion?

Statistics can only, of course, measure concrete realities such as the numbers who attend church every Sunday, or who listen to Sunday religious broadcasts on the radio. They can tell us little or nothing about the quality of Christian life, the depth of Christian conviction, or the extent of Christian involvement in nation-building or development. But the bare statistics are sufficiently striking, even though we must wait for theologians and sociologists in Kenya to tell us precisely how significant they are.

Our survey revealed that, in mid-1972, 20 per cent of the entire population of Kenya, 2.4 million people, attend Christian services regularly every Sunday; and something like 38 per cent (4.6 million) attend church at least once a year. In the towns and cities, these percentages are even higher, due to the greater ease with which Christians can find churches near them; a sample survey in 1971 in Nyeri township, for example, revealed that 50 per cent of the entire population attended church every Sunday (see *Bibliography* under C.A. Dutto). And a glance at the map *Churches and Temples in Nairobi* at the end of this Handbook will show the remarkable proliferation of 300 churches and congregations in the capital city, in a number of which well over 1,000 persons attend services each Sunday. With regard to that equally potent medium of Christian expression, Sunday religious broadcasts, 47 per cent of all adults in Kenya (2.3 million) listen regularly to Christian services broadcast over the Voice of Kenya and other stations, together with a roughly similar number of children under 18 years. Nor are they merely 'listeners' or 'radio Christians' — often they are full participants in the services, joining loudly in the hymns and prayers as the words come to them over the ether.

Other statistics of practice include 1,155,000 copies of Scriptures bought in 1971 from Bible House, Nairobi. But we should briefly note one apparently contradictory statistic of practice, namely the low number of church weddings every year. In any population, on average there are each year, for every 1,000 people, 8 couples who reach marriageable age and enter on some kind of marriage or liaison. As Table 1 (items 48-49) indicates, and as Table 3 elaborates for a number of Kenya churches and dioceses, the number of these liaisons or marriages in the Christian community which are celebrated as Christian weddings in church, is only a fraction of what it should be. It has often been assumed by Western Christians that this low figure reveals a rottenness at the core of African Christianity, a basic unwillingness to accept the implications of life commitment to Christ and to Christian marriage. This is far too glib an assessment. All one can say at present is that African Christianity has not accepted Western Christian marriage in church as either relevant to Africa or essential to the faith. When one considers the extent to which church weddings in the historical churches in Africa have become

176

ruinously expensive social displays, it is obvious that their small numbers cannot be regarded as a fair indicator of Christian commitment or practice.

Christianity in the year 2000

Lastly, we should ask what is likely to happen to these trends in Kenya over the next 28 years before the end of the twentieth century. Our starting point is the projected growth of the population, which is expected by Kenya government demographers to grow each year as shown in Figure 1 until it reaches 34 million in the year 2000. From this graph, we can easily make projections for the totals of Christians and our other variables, and the results are as we have shown in Figure 1 and in the last column of Table 1. Our assumption is that, with the present ecumenical climate of co-operation and understanding between Christians of all types, most churches are likely on average to treble in size by 2000; Protestantism may only double, but Catholics and Independents may well quadruple in size. Of course, future unions and mergers, or catastrophic schisms, may alter these proportions.

By the year 2000, then, it is likely that there will be 28 million Christians in Kenya, of whom perhaps 15 million will be practising Christians. What this implies must be left to others to find out, but at the very least it demands that the churches should embark immediately on realistic and sophisticated joint planning for development of their own resources as well as those of the nation at large.

What is happening in Kenya illustrates what is happening throughout Black Africa — 5 million baptisms a year (2.5 million adult), i.e. 100,000 every week, some 90,000 of which are in rural areas. The setting shown here is universal — the rolling countryside, the water, the praying church, the pastor (foreground), the arms raised in prayer, the earnest resolve on the candidate's face.

FIGURE 3: (OPPOSITE)
DEVELOPMENT OF ANGLICAN & CATHOLIC CHURCHES IN KENYA, 1844 - 1972.

1. This figure shows 'flow charts' or 'development diagrams' for the two largest churches in Kenya, indicating the creation of dioceses and other jurisdictions as the churches have expanded over the last one hundred and thirty years. Similar charts can be drawn for other large churches which have evolved complex structures over the decades. (Key to initials: PA = prefecture apostolic, VA = vicariate apostolic, D = diocese, AD = archdiocese).

2. The outer heavy lines symbolise the size of the whole church in Kenya at any particular year as shown on the scale at the top. Where the outer line is dotted, it indicates that part of the church in Kenya (defined on today's boundaries) was at that time in a jurisdiction based on another country; thus the top diagram shows that up to 1925 the Kavirondo or Nyanza area of Western Kenya was in the Vicariate Apostolic of the Upper Nile (Uganda). Similarly, the lower diagram shows that the same area, the Anglican Kavirondo Archdeaconry, was begun as part of the CMS Uganda Mission, which then became from 1898-1921 part of the Diocese of Uganda, before being transferred in 1921 to the Diocese of Mombasa.

3. Full vertical lines indicate the date of creation of new jurisdictions out of existing ones; dotted vertical lines indicate a change in the status, rank or name of a jurisdiction but with no change in its area or population.

4. Note also the creation of the following jurisdictions including the whole of Kenya:

Catholic Church: 1862, PA Zanzibar (1883, VA; 1906, changed to Zanzibar)
1953, Ecclesiastical Province of Kenya

Anglican Church: 1884, D Eastern Equatorial Africa
1960, Church of the Province of East Africa (Kenya, Tanganyika, Zanzibar).
1970, Church of the Province of Kenya.

5. Large arrows breaking the outer lines represent the major secessions or separatist movements that have left the churches to form independent bodies.

6. Similar flow charts (called 'fission diagrams') can also be drawn to illustrate the proliferation of African independent churches in Kenya since 1914; all the necessary data for drawing such charts will be found elsewhere in this Handbook.

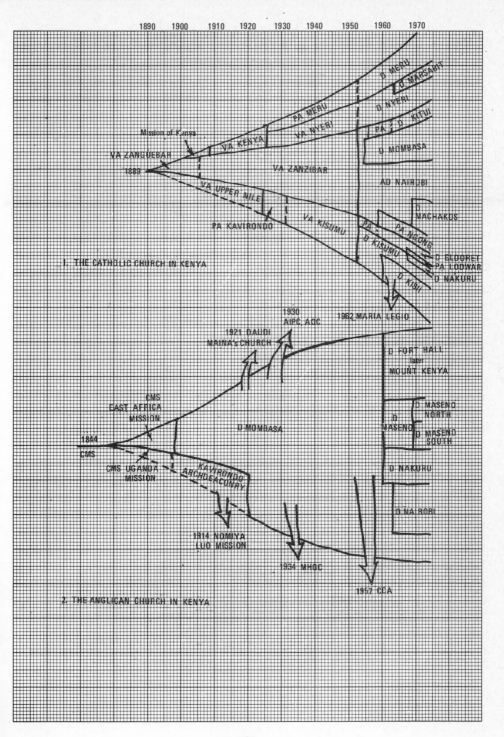

1890 1900 1910 1920 1930 1940 1950 1960 1970

D MERU
D MARSABIT
PA MERU
VA KENYA   VA NYERI   D NYERI
Mission of Kenya   PA   D KITUI
VA ZANGUEBAR   VA ZANZIBAR   D MOMBASA
1889   AD NAIROBI
VA UPPER NILE   D MACHAKOS
PA KAVIRONDO   VA KISUMU   PA   PA NGONG
D KISUMU   D ELDORET
PA LODWAR
D NAKURU
1. THE CATHOLIC CHURCH IN KENYA   D KISII

1930
AIPC, AOC
1962 MARIA LEGIO
1921 DAUDI
MAINA's CHURCH
D FORT HALL
later
MOUNT KENYA

CMS
EAST AFRICA   D MASENO
MISSION   NORTH
D
MASENO   D MASENO
1844   D MOMBASA   SOUTH
CMS
CMS UGANDA   KAVIRONDO   D NAKURU
MISSION   ARCHDEACONRY

D NAIROBI

1914 NOMIYA
LUO MISSION
1934 MHOC

1957 CCA
2. THE ANGLICAN CHURCH IN KENYA

179

TABLE 3
ANNUAL CHURCH WEDDINGS IN 19 ANGLICAN AND CATHOLIC DIOCESES IN KENYA

Church and diocese	Affiliated Christians (1970-71)	Annual church weddings. Expected	Actual	%
1	2	3	4	5
Church of the Province of Kenya:	582,000	4,660	1,382	30
D Maseno North	100,000	800	153	19
D Maseno South	150,000	1,200	102	9
D Mombasa	40,000	320	164	51
D Mount Kenya	199,900	1,599	571	36
D Nairobi	50,000	400	160	40
D Nakuru	42,700	342	232	68
Catholic Church in Kenya:	1,763,020	14,104	5,580	40
AD Nairobi	200,773	1,606	1,229	77
D Eldoret	64,210	514	187	36
D Kisii	236,218	1,890	345	18
D Kisumu	463,220	3,706	1,323	37
D Kitui	19,893	159	27	17
D Machakos	102,596	821	326	40
D Marsabit	4,033	32	13	41
D Meru	157,520	1,260	674	53
D Mombasa	70,066	561	159	28
D Nakuru	94,911	759	329	43
D Nyeri	340,000	2,720	946	35
PA Lodwar	1,090	9	1	11
PA Ngong	8,490	68	21	31

The rate at which marriages or other types of liaison take place each year in most parts of the world is .008 (8 marriages a year for every 1,000 population). This means that in a community of 1 million Christians (including children), about 8,000 marriages or liaisons between Christians are begun each year. We can therefore calculate the number of church weddings to be expected each year if all Christians got married in church (this is column 3, which is column 2 x .008). In practice, however, the actual number of church weddings is much smaller (column 4); examination of the resulting percentages shows that less than half of all Anglicans and Catholics marry in church (column 5, = column 4 ÷ column 3, x 100%).

NOTE

1. The actual number of weddings are for different years (Anglican, 1970; Catholic, 1968, except for Machakos, Marsabit and Meru, which are 1971), but the trends and results can properly be compared.
2. Note that the percentage marrying in church tends to be higher in cities (Nairobi, Mombasa, Nakuru), due to the status attached to weddings in large city churches.
3. A majority of all church weddings are marriages begun at the wedding in church; but a substantial minority are the blessing of marriages previously contracted according to traditional tribal custom. Thus in the Anglican diocese of Mount Kenya for the year 1970, 407 of the 571 weddings (71 per cent) were previously unmarried partners, whereas 164 were the blessing of former African tribal marriages.

4. Under the African Christian Marriage and Divorce Act, about 16,000 marriages each year are registered with government by 200 licensed ministers and priests (figure for 1970: 15,963 marriages by 195 licensed ministers). Catholic and Anglican marriages, which are probably nearly all registered, thus account for nearly half of the total registered each year.

TABLE 4

RACE, TRIBE AND RELIGIOUS PROFESSION IN KENYA, 1962-1972

The first two columns of figures show the size of the various races and tribes, expressed as a percentage of total population, for the two census years 1962 and 1969. The third column gives the 1969 census totals, which are then projected to mid-1972 and 1980 assuming uniform expansion among all tribes and races after 1969. The last eight columns give the percentages professing the various religions (Roman Catholic, Protestant (here including Anglican and independent), Muslim, Traditional). The figures for 1962 are from the census (previously unpublished); those for 1972 are then estimated based on current trends. To find the number of professing traditionalists (animists) in a tribe in 1972 (for example), multiply the mid-1972 population by the percentage in the last column (divided by 100).

| | Total Population | | | | | Religious Profession (%) | | | | | | | |
| | | | | | | 1962 | | | | 1972 | | | |
	1962 %	1969 %	1969	mid-1972	1980	RC	Pr	Mu	Tr	RC	Pr	Mu	Tr
Total population	100.00	100.00	10,942,705	12,091,000	16,053,000	20	34	8	37	28	38	6	27
Race:													
Kenya Africans	96.31	97.54	10,673,770	11,793,500	15,658,000	20	34	8	37	28	38	6	27
Asians	2.05	1.27	139,037	153,600	204,000	9	0	23	0	10	0	30	0
Other Africans	0.55	0.54	59,432	65,700	87,200								
Europeans	0.65	0.37	40,593	44,900	59,600	19	77	0	0	20	70	0	0
Arabs	0.39	0.25	27,886	30,800	40,900	0	0	99	0	0	0	99	0
Others	0.05	0.02	1,987	2,200	2,900	55	16	14	0	55	16	14	0
Tribe: *													
Kikuyu	19.01	20.12	2,201,632	2,432,600	3,229,800	20	40	0	40	26	47	0	27
Luo	13.30	13.91	1,521,595	1,681,200	2,232,200	33	46	1	20	39	50	1	10
Luhya	12.58	13.28	1,453,302	1,605,800	2,132,000	33	52	2	13	39	55	2	4
Kamba	10.81	10.95	1,197,712	1,323,400	1,757,000	10	42	0	48	14	47	0	39
Gusii	6.23	6.41	701,679	775,300	1,029,400	31	38	0	31	39	43	0	18
Meru	5.09	5.07	554,256	612,400	813,100	14	23	1	62	19	26	1	54
Mijikenda:	4.80	4.76	520,520	575,100	763,600	5	13	40	42	7	15	40	38
Digo	1.06	1.05	114,514	126,500	168,000	0	0	91	9	0	0	91	9
Duruma	0.94	0.93	102,022	112,700	149,700	8	22	25	45	4	24	25	42
Giriama	2.80	2.78	303,984	335,900	445,900	3	8	4	85	4	10	4	82
Kipsigis	3.96	4.31	471,459	520,900	691,600	27	30	0	43	34	34	0	32
Nandi	1.97	2.39	261,969	289,400	384,300	23	27	0	50	29	30	0	41
Somali	3.10	2.26	247,000	272,900	362,300	0	0	100	0	0	0	100	0
Turkana	2.10	1.86	203,177	224,500	298,100	2	0	0	98	3	1	0	96
Maasai	1.78	1.42	154,906	171,200	227,200	1	18	0	81	1	21	0	78
Tugen	1.27	1.19	130,249	143,900	191,100	6	29	0	65	8	33	0	59
Embu	1.11	1.08	117,969	130,300	173,100	30	30	0	40	38	34	0	28
Taita	1.03	1.05	114,818	126,900	168,400	13	46	5	36	17	50	5	28
Elgeyo	1.17	1.01	110,908	122,500	162,700	14	23	0	63	18	26	0	56
Pokot	0.89	0.85	93,437	103,200	137,100	2	6	0	92	3	7	0	90
Iteso	0.84	0.78	85,800	94,800	125,900	39	37	0	24	45	42	0	13
Marakwet	0.78	0.73	79,713	88,100	116,900	14	23	0	63	17	26	0	57
Kuria	0.48	0.55	59,875	66,200	87,800	20	30	0	50	25	34	0	41
Samburu	0.56	0.50	54,796	60,500	80,400	0	1	0	99	1	2	0	97
Tharaka	0.45	0.47	51,883	57,300	76,100	10	20	0	70	14	25	0	61
Mbere	0.44	0.45	49,247	54,400	72,200	10	15	0	75	14	20	0	66
Sabaot	0.32	0.39	42,468	46,900	62,300	39	37	0	24	45	42	0	13
Pokomo	0.35	0.32	35,181	38,900	51,600	0	13	85	2	0	14	85	1
Boran	0.68	0.31	34,086	37,700	50,000	1	2	90	7	2	3	90	5

* The list includes all tribes of over 34,000 in size in 1969, arranged in their 1969 order of size.

Following picture

'We receive this brother into the congregation of Christ's flock ... May he never be ashamed to confess the faith of Christ crucified ... May he continue, O Lord, Thy faithful soldier and servant unto his life's end' (Vapostori, Gospel of God).

TABLE 5

STATISTICS OF THE CHURCHES IN KENYA

This table lists all known Christian denominations in Kenya in mid-1972. A denomination is defined here as a church or sect with distinct members of its own belonging to no other church, with in almost all cases more than one congregation or church building, with in most cases legal status before government, and which usually is expanding, or intends to expand, by opening further out-stations or branch churches. If the reader expects to find a Kenya body here but fails to (e.g. Pentecostal Revival Church; or All Nations Gospel Tabernacle), this is probably because it is either (a) a defunct body, or (b) not a denomination but a single congregation affiliated to a denomination. A handful of the larger city congregations of this kind are given in Part V. Defunct denominations are given in Part IV. The actual situation can be quickly ascertained by using the Index at the end of the Handbook.

The statistics given here are those supplied or claimed by the churches themselves, mostly for the year 1971 for the smaller bodies, for the year 1970 for larger bodies whose statistics take one year to process, and for the beginning of 1970 in the case of the Roman Catholic Church. For the purposes of comparison, this table may thus be said to represent the statistical picture for the year 1970. At the end of the table, however, estimates are added for mid-1971 and mid-1972.

The accuracy claimed here by a statistic is easily assessed as follows. A round number, especially a string of zeros (e.g. 10,000), is clearly meant to be a rough estimate; but a number with other digits than 0 (e.g. 10,391) is based on some sort of aggregate count and therefore more accuracy is claimed. Likewise, small numbers (e.g. 83, or 471) are clearly based on head counts. In this table the editors have made a handful of estimates where no church figures are available. Blank spaces then indicate that no estimates of any kind were available although at the end of the table an estimate is made for the totals of all such missing data.

Key to columns on left-hand page

1. *Reference number* (the same as used in Part IV).
2. *Official name* of denomination as registered with government.
3. *Initials*, if used for the body by itself, or by others.
4. *Year denomination founded*, mission begun, or schism took place; for dioceses, year founded or formed under present name (c = circa, about).
5. *Type of denomination:* first letter = major Christian grouping (P = Protestant, i.e. linked to Western missions; R = Roman Catholic; O = Greek Orthodox; A = Anglican; I = Independent, or Indigenous). Next three letters = tradition followed, claimed, or adopted; namely, the first three letters of the following traditions: *Adventist, Anglican, Baptist, Disciples* (congregational), *Evangelical Anglican, Holiness, Interdenominational, Latin-rite Catholic, Lutheran, Mennonite, Methodist Mormon, Nationalist*, Pentecostal*, Ply*mouth Brethren, *Quaker, Reformed, Revivalist*, Roman Catholic, Russelite, Salvationist, Christian Science, Spirit*, Traditional - syncretistic, United.* (Those marked * belong to the typology of independent churches described in J. Murray's article, p. 128).
6. *Councils* on which membership held (. = no such membership):
First letter = world confessional families: *Anglican Consultative Council, Baptist World Alliance, Congregation for the Evangelization of Peoples (Propaganda), Friends World Committee for Consultation, Lutheran World Federation, Mennonite World Committee, Pentecostal World Conference, World Alliance of Reformed Churches, Salvation Army, World Methodist Council.*
Second letter = world Christian councils: W = World Council of Churches; I = International Council of Christian Churches.
Third letter = Kenya councils of churches: N = Member, National Christian Council of Kenya; P = NCCK Probationary Member; n = NCCK consultative associate; a = application for NCCK membership made; E = East Africa Christian Alliance; K = Kenya Episcopal Conference; F = Kenya Independent Churches Fellowship.
7. *Status in Kenya law as at 31 March 1972, with year when status was arrived at* (see explanation and analysis in Part V, in *Directory of Christian Organisations,* p. 280 under *Registrar of Societies.* For comments on the status of and reasons for unregistered churches, see p. 229).
   (a) under Societies Act (1953, 1968)
      r = registered
      e = exempted from registration
      a = application still being considered
      s = application refused
      c = former registration cancelled
      p = proscribed (prohibited)
        = unregistered
   (b) under Companies Ordinance
      i = incorporated (but not registered under Societies Act)
   (c) under Land (Perpetual Succession) Act
      u = incorporated (but not registered under Societies Act or Companies Ordinance)
   Note: A number of bodies are registered under all three of the Acts; in that case, reference is made below only to the Societies Act.
8. *Number of congregations* (churches, chapels, halls, open-air sites, regular preaching or worship points).
9. *Full adult members* or communicants (for the Catholic Church, baptised persons over 18 years old; such statistics are never collected by dioceses, so are here estimated to be total baptised x 43.5 per cent (the national % over 18); for most Protestant and Independent bodies, the figures are specifically for those over 18 years [as required by the Registrar-General]).
10. *Total Christian community* known to be affiliated to the denomination, including children, baptism candidates, fringe members, etc. (for the Catholic Church, baptised Catholics plus catechumens).
11. *Practising Christians* (regular attenders) as % all Christians or members (Anglicans, Protestants, = Sunday attendance; Catholics, = Easter communicants as % eligible communicants 7 years of age and over).
12. *Annual baptisms: Infants* (under about 7 years). Note: the sign — means infant baptism is not practised.
13. *Annual baptisms: Adults* (usually over 15 years, sometimes over 7 years).
14. *Ministers or priests* (full-time ordained): *Nationals* (Africans).
15. *Ministers or priests* (full-time ordained): *Expatriates* (non-Africans).

On right hand page
Descriptive and identifying notes (historical, geographical, tribal composition), including co-operating foreign missionary societies, if any. Note that when initials are mentioned, the full name can be immediately obtained from the Index of Abbreviations in this Handbook. For further information on each denomination see the *Directory of the Churches in Kenya,* in Part IV).

Ref	Official name of denomination	Initials	Year	Type	Coun	Status	Congs	Membership Adults	Total CC	P%	Annual Baptisms Infant	Adult	Ministers Nat	Exp
1	2	3	4	5	6	7	8	9	10	11	12	13	14	15
1	Africa Early Church		c1966	I	...	s1967	1	12	50					0
2	Africa Gospel Church	AGC	1935	P Hol	.. N	e1961	250	6,500	15,000	84	–	266	20	
3	Africa Gospel Unity Church	AGUC	1964	I Hol	.IE	r 1964	19	1,000	1,500	85	–	250	10	0
4	Africa Inland Church	AIC	1895	P Int	.. N	e1961	1,700	150,000	300,000	65	–	2,000	80	50
5	African Brotherhood Church	ABC	1945	I Nat	.. N	r 1954	342	30,869	64,030	68		1,010		0
6	African Christian Church & Schools	ACC&S	1947	I Bap	.. N	u1971	29	8,000	15,000			1,500	7	2
7	African Christian Church of East Africa		c1963	I Nat	...	r 1964		600	2,000					0
8	African Church	AC	1961	I Bap	.IE	r 1961	19	15,000	30,000	19			6	0
9	African Church Holy Spirit Independent			I Nat	...	s1971	1	100	300					0
10	African Church Mission	ACM	1941	I Ang	...	r 1960	12	2,000	3,000	35				0
11	African Church of Holy Spirit	ACHS	1927	I Spi	...	r 1957	54	3,352	5,455	75	80	90	3	0
12	African Church of Jesus Christ in Kenya		1970	I Ang	.. N	r 1970	4	300	1,000	50	271	460	29	0
13	African Coptic Orthodox Church			I	...				10		6	15	1	0
14	African Disciples Church	ADisC	1967	I Rev	.I.	c1971	6	150	500	80	–	16	6	0
15	African Divine Church	ADC	1949	I Pen	.. F	r 1955	82	2,000	3,850	95	106	186	21	0
16	African Eden Roho Society			I Spi	...	s1965		143	400					0
17	African Emmanuel Church New Salem			I	...	s1965		20	50					0
18	African Evangelical Presbyterian Church	AEPC	1962	P Ref	...	r 1962	30	338	800	67	20	30	8	0
19	African Holy Ghost Christian Church		1968	I Spi	...	r 1968	8	600	2,000		8	32		0
20	African Holy Zionist Church		1959	I Sal	.. F	c1972	3	1,200	3,000	90			20	0
21	African Independent Church of Kenya		1943	I Ang	.. a	c1969		500	1,000					0
22	African Independent Pentecostal Church of A	AIPC	1925	I Nat	...	r 1964	454	200,000	496,000			6,000	136	0
23	African Interior Church	AIC	1943	I Hol	.. N	r 1956	29	10,650	30,000	68	200	160	5	0
24	African Israel Church Nineveh	AICN	1942	I Spi	.. N	r 1956	274	36,904	70,000	80	83	160	91	0
25	African Mission of Holy Ghost Church	AMHGC	1961	I Spi	.. a	r 1961	14	2,500	7,000	99	50	120	14	0
26	African Nabi Roho Maler		c1965	I Spi	...	r 1965		100	300					0
27	African Orthodox Church of Kenya	AOC	1928	O Nat	GWn	r 1965	230	100,000	250,000	90	15,000	10,000	33	3
28	African Revelation Church St. Mission			I	...	r 1962		100	300					0
29	African Sinai Church		1965	I Pen	.. a	r 1965	4	350	1,000	95	20	10	1	0
30	All Ethiopian Church in East Africa			I	...				10					0
31	Apostles Christian Church of Africa		1968	I Pen	...	r1972	4	542	1,500					0
32	Apostolic Faith of Africa		1959	I Pen	...	r 1963	50	4,000	7,000	98	–		5	0
33	Apostolic Fellowship Church of God		c1966	I Pen	...	r 1967		93	300					0
34	Apostolic Hierarchy Church			I Rom	...	s1970		580	1,500					0
35	Assemblies of God, Kenya DC	KDCAG	1968	P Pen	...	r1968	212	3,000	12,000	50	–	876	4	4
36	Baptist Churches of Kenya	BCK	1956	P Bap	B.N	e1961	205	5,985	25,000	50	–	1,200	35	18
37	Believed Power of Jesus Christ in Kenya			I	...	s1972		100	300					0
38	Bible Fellowship Church		c1940	P Bap	.. N	r 1959		210	500					0
39	Catholic Church in Kenya:	RCC	1498	R Lat	C..		1,795	694,700	1,763,020	42	55,983	47,758	86	580
40	Archdiocese of Nairobi		1953	R Lat	C.K	u1930	71	76,040	200,773	56	9,338	6,161	8	86
41	Diocese of Eldoret		1959	R Lat	C.K	u 1971	115	23,340	64,210	41	2,522	2,086	1	24
42	Diocese of Kisii		1960	R Lat	C.K	u1962	228	100,050	236,218	35	6,386	4,408	12	33
43	Diocese of Kisumu		1925	R Lat	C.K	u 1968	251	197,910	463,220	32	11,602	5,264	13	91
44	Diocese of Kitui		1956	R Lat	C.K	u1965	135	7,150	19,893	52	623	2,226	1	37
45	Diocese of Machakos		1969	R Lat	C.K	u1970	153	34,580	102,596		2,204	4,060	6	35
46	Diocese of Marsabit		1964	R Lat	C.K		22	720	4,033	60	213	708	0	26
47	Diocese of Meru		1926	R Lat	C.K	u1962	312	61,900	157,520	47	7,400	7,500	14	49
48	Diocese of Mombasa		1955	R Lat	C.K	u1959	60	27,250	70,066	47	2,089	1,700	5	46
49	Diocese of Nakuru		1968	R Lat	C.K	e1968	165	31,540	94,911	48	4,173	2,818	1	52
50	Diocese of Nyeri		1905	R Lat	C.K	u1959	226	130,500	340,000	43	8,800	10,400	23	73
51	Prefecture Apostolic of Lodwar		1968	R Lat	C.K	e1968	6	240	1,090		28	87	0	13
52	Prefecture Apostolic of Ngong		1959	R Lat	C.K	u1961	51	3,480	8,490	45	605	340	2	15
53	Children of God Regeneration Church		1947	I	...	r 1965	90	1,000	3,542		52	124·	42	0
54	Chosen Church of the Holy Spirit in Kenya		1930	I Spi	...	r 1970	33	1,500	2,500	95	64	78	3	0
55	Christadelphian Bible Mission (Kenya)	CBMK	c1970	P	...	r 1971		50	150					0
56	Christ Evangelistic Association		c1959	I	...	r 1964		10,000	30,000					0
57	Christ Faith Evangelical Church			I	...	s1972		700	2,000					0
58	Christian Association			I	...	r 1970		1,100	3,000					0
59	Christian Brotherhood Church	CBC	1952	I Ang	.. a	r 1958	144	3,000	9,000	20	26	30	8	0
60	Christian Church in Africa			P	...	s1970		24	50					0
61	Christian Evangelical Church	CEC	1948	I Ang	...	r 1959	45	1,920	4,000	94	–	65	11	0
62	Christian Faith Mission of Kenya			P	...	s1970		85	200					0
63	Christian Holy Ghost Church of EA	CHGC	1934	I Spi	...	r 1960	18	660	1,500	95	–	60	9	0
64	Christian Science Church of East Africa		1925	P Sci	.. a	e1957	1	30	100	90			0	0
65	Christian Theocratic Holy Church of God		1958	I	...	r 1971	77	3,000	3,870	75			70	0
66	Church Group of Light			I	...	r1972	1	130	400					0
67	Church of All	CA	1971	I Nat	...	r1972		70	200					0
68	Church of Christ in Africa	CCA	1957	I Ang	.IE	r 1958	545	75,000	120,000	60	8,640	2,400	81	0
69	Church of Christ in the Word			I Pen	.. a		1	30	100		–			0
70	Church of Full Gospel in Africa			I Pen	...	s1970		250	700		–			0
71	Church of God in East Africa	CGEA	1905	P Hol	.. N	r 1964	385	40,000	260,000	75	–	1,800	375	5
72	Church of Holy Communion of God		1969	I Qua	...	s1969	30	550	1,700			60	30	0
73	Church of Jesus Christ of Latter-day Saints	LDS		P Mor	...		1	10	30					0
74	Church of Messiah		1948	I Bap	...		10	5,000	10,000					0
75	Church of Saviour. Diocese of Nvakeʑ		1968	I Ang	...	r1970	33	2,000	3,293	50	65	39	7	0
76	Church of Spirit in Grace & Truth in Africa		c1967	I Pen	...	c1972		600	2,000					0
77	Church of the Almighty (Kenya)			I Pen	...	s1971	1	35	100					0
78	Church of the Holy Apostles of the Lamb		1966	I Adv	...			200	500					0
79	Church of the Kenya Family		1948	I Nat	...	r 1968	13	1,049	4,000	75	96	54		0
80	Church of the Living God		c1964	I Bap	...	r 1965		429	1,200					0
81	Church of the Power of Jesus Christ		1966	I	...		22	40	200				8	0
82	Church of the Prophets (A-Nabii Church)		c1960	I Spi	...	r 1968	1	100	300					0
83	Church of the Province of Kenya:	CPK	1844	A Eva	AWN	r 1970	1,629	239,383	582,600	43	20,132	26,853	224	48
84	Diocese of Maseno North		1970	A Eva	.. N		400	20,000	100,000	50	1,000	1,000	37	3
85	Diocese of Maseno South		1970	A Eva	.. N		402	20,400	150,000	20	1,043	1,891	31	1
86	Diocese of Mombasa		1899	A Eva	.. N	u1925	75	15,000	40,000	70	1,000	800	33	4
87	Diocese of Mount Kenya		1961	A Eva	.. N		350	159,925	199,900	60	13,940	20,910	60	7
88	Diocese of Nairobi		1964	A Eva	.. N		105	15,000	50,000	20	1,700	700	23	22
89	Diocese of Nakuru		1961	A Eva	.. N		297	9,058	42,700		1,449	1,552	40	11
90	Church of the Truth			I Pen	...	s1967	1	20	50		–			0

184

1 A small Luhya independent group in South Maragoli.
2 Kipsigis church founded by WGM, autonomous in 1961. Five dioceses.
3 Kipsigis schism from AGC when moderator voted out of office.
4 Aided by AIM. Members: Kamba 33%, Kalenjin 27%, Kikuyu 20%, Coastal 12%, Maasai 5%, Luo 2%.
5 Large indigenous church, mainly Kamba but with congregations throughout Kenya.
6 Major Kikuyu schism from AIM. Has invited Canadian Baptist missionaries. Still 100% Kikuyu.
7 An independent church with Kikuyu and Meru members.
8 Kamba schism from AIM, first known as Kenya African Church.
9 Small independent group in Meru.
10 Schism from Nomiya Luo Church, permitting post-baptism polygamy.
11 Dini ya Msalaba (Religion of the Cross), expelled by FAM in 1927.
12 Kikuyu schism of Anglican background, linked with CCA.
13 Nominal group related to Ugandan Reuben Spartas, attempting to secure Coptic (Egyptian) aid.
14 Kamba revival movement with name Ikanisa ya Amanyiwa ma Yesu.
15 Maragoli schism in 1950 from PAOC over desire to wear uniforms.
16 Luo independent church formerly known as African Roho Mission.
17 Small Luo independent group in South Nyanza.
18 Founded by WPM, now five missionaries. 88% Kamba, rest Mbere and Embu.
19 One of the earliest Kikuyu churches from the Watu wa Mungu (People of God).
20 Luhya schism formerly called Africa Zion Church.
21 Kamba schism from Anglican Church, declining since 1960.
22 Original KISA-linked Kikuyu church; phenomenal growth since 1964 in rural areas. Four dioceses. .
23 Luhya schism in 1943 from Church of God mission.
24 Schism 1942 from PAOC. Membership: 51% Luhya, 49% Luo. Subdivisions: 23 Ministries, 68 Pastorates.
25 One of the earliest Kikuyu Spirit churches, formed from the Watu wa Mungu.
26 'African Prophet Holy Spirit'. Luo and Maragoli members.
27 Rapid expansion since 1965. Membership: Kikuyu 80%, Luhya 15%, Kalenjin 4%, Gusii 1%.
28 A small Luo independent group in South Nyanza.
29 Tiriki (Luhya) schism from African Divine Church over circumcision controversy.
30 Ephemeral grouping as focus for obtaining Coptic and Orthodox aid.
31 A recent Embu church with 4 parishes in a single Diocese of Riandu.
32 A Kikuyu schism from PCEA which has spread westwards through Pokot into Uganda.
33 A small Kikuyu independent church.
34 Kikuyu body formerly known as African God Worshippers Fellowship Church Society.
35 Schism from IPA led by two missionaries, first known as Kenya Pentecostal Fellowship.
36 Aided by BMEA, organised into eight Associations. Members: 1,500 Kikuyu, the rest Coast and Nyanza.
37 A small Luo independent movement in South Nyanza.
38 Independent congregation in Thika begun by former GMS woman missionary.
39 First mission in Kenya. Now 13 dioceses covering nation. 3.4 million professing Catholics (1972).
40 Catholics: Kikuyu 60%, Luhya 14%, Kamba 10%, Luo 10%, expatriates 6%.
41 Catholics: Bukusu 30%, Kikuyu 20%, Elgeyo 18%, Marakwet 15%, Pokot 5%, Luo 4%, Nandi 3%, 320 expatriates.
42 Catholics: Luo 52%, Gusii 47%, Kuria 1%. 3,000 Muslims also in this area.
43 Catholics: Luhya 47%, Luo 34%, Nandi 7%, Kipsigis 6%, Teso 6%, 430 expatriates.
44 Catholics: Kamba 99%, Tharaka 0.5%, 20 expatriates. 3,000 Muslims, 200 Hindus in area.
45 An entirely Kamba diocese experiencing very rapid growth.
46 Population (180,000) animists, except 4,000 Catholics, 1,300 Protestants, 6,000 Muslims.
47 Catholics: Meru 45%, Embu 45%, Turkana 4% (about 6,000).
48 Catholics: Taita 40%, Giriama 20%, Duruma 10%, Pokomo 5%, rest Luo and Kamba; 3,700 expatriates.
49 Catholics mostly Kikuyu, with 1,100 expatriates. About 400 Eastern Orthodox Christians in area.
50 Catholics almost all Kikuyu, with 300 expatriates.
51 Smallest diocese in Kenya, in extreme north-west of country.
52 Catholics: Kikuyu 40%, Maasai 14%, Kipsigis 12%, Kamba 10%, Luo 8%, Chagga (from Tanzania) 8%.
53 'Ayie Remb Yesu' ('I believe in the Blood of Jesus'). Members: Luo 95%, Bantu 5%.
54 Early Kikuyu movement, also known as Church of the Holy Spirit of God in Africa.
55 Small communities of believers called Ecclesias scattered across Kenya.
56 Luo movement originating in 1959, now experiencing rapid growth.
57 A Luo movement in South Nyanza with a considerable following.
58 A Luo independent group in South Nyanza.
59 Luhya schism from Anglican Church. Now 45% Luhya, 30% Luo, 18% Gusii, 6% Baganda.
60 A small group around Kitale with expatriate ministers.
61 First Balokole (Revival) schism among the Luo (1948), known until 1965 as CUEU or CUEF.
62 A mission from Louisville, Kentucky, USA.
63 Conservative wing of the Aroti (Seers, Dreamers) movement. Kikuyu members.
64 Single congregation, two-thirds African, linked with Mother Church, Boston, USA.
65 A Kikuyu independent church begun in 1958.
66 A small Luhya group with a single temporary church building.Name, Lurambi CG of L.
67 June 1972 changed to East Africa Divinity Church.
68 Large Luo Anglican schism, now 81% Luo, 10% Luhya. 8 Area Dioceses, 27 Areas, 90 Pastorates.
69 Indigenous Pentecostal body from Uganda with recent work in Mombasa.
70 A Kikuyu group also known as Full Gospel Church in Africa (Kenya).
71 A large national church. 31,000 Luhya, 8,000 Gusii, 500 Kalenjin, 300 Luo, 50 North Americans.
72 A recent Luhya schism from EAYM over tithing, polygamy, use of drums; called Friends of Light.
73 Handful of expatriate Latter-day Saints (Mormons) from USA.
74 Early Kamba schism from AIM, still led by founder. Congregations in Ukambani, Coast, Uganda, Tanzania, Rwanda.
75 Schism of majority of original Luo Anglican clergy from HTCA, itself schism from CCA.
76 Small Luo movement in extreme west of Kenya.
77 Independent church linked with Church of God (Universal), USA. Kikuyu members.
78 Luo schism from SDA Church. Members wear surplices with green epaulettes.
79 Embu movement characterised by healing ministryaand rejection of word 'Amen' after prayers.
80 Kamba schism from GFF, reporting decline from 560 members in 1964 to 429 in 1968.
81 Luo church 'Ayie kuom Yesu man gi teko' ('I believe in Jesus who has power').
82 Kikuyu schism from Kenya Foundation of the Prophets Church, in the Spirit tradition.
83 Autonomous province in Anglican Communion with six dioceses. All bishops, and 78% clergy, are Kenyans.
84 Membership: Luhya 90%, Kenya Teso 10%. Aided by CMS.
85 Members 94% Luo, 500 Kipsigis, 250 Gusii, 150 Luhya, 100 Europeans, etc. Mission: CMS.
86 Remnant of original Diocese. Members: 80% Taita, 20% Giriama, plus up-country labour migrants in Mombasa.
87 Formerly Diocese of Fort Hall. 99.5% Kikuyu, Meru and Embu; 500 Baluji and Boran, 330 Europeans.
88 City plus Kamba and Maasai rural areas. Many Anglican migrants to Nairobi are unknown to churches.
89 Rift Valley and North. Members: 55% Kikuyu, 20% Nandi, 10% British, 9% Luhya, 250 Pokot, 250 Samburu.
90 Formerly Gospel Proclaimers. Kikuyu group affiliated to Apostolic Faith, Portland, USA.

Ref.	Official name of enomination	Initials	Year	Type	Coun	Status	Congs	Membership Adults	Total CC	P%	Infant	Adult	Nat	Exp.
1	2	3	4	5	6	7	8	9	10	11	12	13	14	15
91	Communion Church of Africa		c1970	I Rom	...	r 1971		400	1,200					0
92	Cross Church of East Africa		c1940	I Ang	...	r 1970	70	5,000	15,000				10	0
93	Deliverance Church	YCAF	1969	I Pen	...	r 1971		1,000	3,000		–		2	0
94	Disciples of Christ in Africa		1970	I Pen	...	r 1970	15	700	2,000	90				0
95	Divine Christian Church of EA (Ludenyo)	DCCEA	1967	I Pen	..F	c1972	82	2,000	5,000	95	106	186	21	0
96	Divine Christian Church of EA (Masiza)	DCCEA	1962	I Pen	...	c1972	40	1,500	3,000	60		300	30	0
97	Dutch Reformed Church	DRC	c1948	P Ref	...		1	20	50				0	0
98	East Africa Pentecostal Churches	EAPC	1953	P Pen	...	u1964	74	10,000	20,000	80		7,000	117	2
99	East Africa Yearly Meeting of Friends	EAYM	1902	P Qua	F.N	r 1964	1,200	33,860	100,000	50	–	–	130	2
100	East African Church Roho Israel		1967	I Spi	...	r 1967	15	350	400	95	50	25	2	0
101	East African Israel Church		c1958	I Spi	...	r 1964		95	300					0
102	East African Mission	TEAM	c1970	P	...	r 1970		231	600					0
103	Ebenezer Gospel Hall		c1958	P Ply	...	r 1958	1	15	50		–		0	0
104	Eldoret Christian Fellowship Church		1948	P	...	e1961	1	15	30	70		0	0	2
105	Episcopal Church of Africa		1968	I Ang	...	r 1968	39	2,000	5,000				4	0
106	Evangelical Baptist Church in Africa		1966	I Bap	...	r 1967		232	600					0
107	Evangelical Free Mission in Kenya		1960	P Pen	P..	e1963	35	4,000	8,000	75		850	60	8
108	Evangelical Lutheran Church in Tanzania	ELCT	1967	P Lut	LWP	e1967		1,500	5,000					0
109	Evangelistic Church Universal of Africa	ECUA	c1963	I	...	c1965	1	35	100					0
110	Evangelistic Gospel Church of HM Star		c1969	I	...	r 1971		300	1,000					0
111	Evangelistic Association in Africa		c1962	I	...	r 1963		98	300					0
112	Faith Miracle Church			I Pen	...	s 1971		100	300					0
113	Fellowship of Believers			P Ply	...	a1971	1	13	40		–			0
114	Free Church of East Africa		1968	I	...	r 1968		304	946	75	12	40	0	0
115	Friends of the Holy Spirit	FHS	1946	I Rev	...	r 1960	3	336	1,000				6	0
116	Friends of the Holy Spirit (Kitui)		1948	I Rev	...			300	1,000					0
117	Full Gospel Churches of Kenya	FGCK	1949	P Pen	P.N	e1961	353	22,000	60,000	95		1,604	182	6
118	Full Gospel Fellowship Mission of Africa		c1964	I	;..	r 1965		829	2,500					0
119	God of Israel Zion Church			I	...	a 1971		85	200					0
120	God of the Universe Church	GUC	1962	I Pen	..a	r 1967	18	500	1,274	75	75	80	7	0
121	God's Last Appeal Church		1966	I Adv	...	r 1968	8	100	424	90	25	43	21	0
122	God's Word and Holy Ghost Church		c1940	I Spi	...	r 1958		100	300					0
123	Good News Church of Africa	GNCA	1958	I Bap	.IE	r 1968	120	11,050	30,000				60	0
124	Gospel Furthering Bible Church	GFF	1936	P Bap	...	e1968		3,000	10,000					0
125	Gospel Holy Spirit of East Africa		1927	I Spi	...r	r 1964	15	288	500	43		11	0	0
126	Gospel of God, The		1968	I Spi	...	e1968	30	800	1,800	95			20	0
127	Gospel Tabernacle Church		c1943	P Bap	...	r 1970	15	2,650	8,000				15	1
128	Holy Church of Africa (EA)		1968	I Rom	...	s 1969		1,000	3,000					0
129	Holy Church of Evangelistic Apostles Faith		1958	I Pen	...	r 1968	30	2,000	11,000	85	–	200	19	0
130	Holy Ghost Church of Kenya	HGCK	1934	I Spi	...	r 1958	30	6,000	10,000	90	100	100	31	0
131	Holy Ghost Coptic Church of Africa		1964	I Rom	...	r 1971	7	1,700	5,000	55			8	0
132	Holy Mission of Israel Church		1967	I Spi	...	r 1971	2	80	200					0
133	Holy Spirit Brotherhood Church		1960	I	...	s 1969		300	1,000					0
134	Holy Spirit Church of East Africa	HSCEA	1927	I Spi	...	r 1957	25	660	3,000	65	187	52	8	0
135	Holy Spirit Church of Zayun		c1962	I Spi	...	r 1963		470	1,500					0
136	Holy Trinity Church in Africa		1960	I Ang	..a	r 1965	174	20,000	50,000	55	1,000	600	15	0
137	Independent African Orthodox Church		c1955	I Nat	...	r 1965		968	3,000					0
138	Independent Assembly of God of Kenya			I Pen	...	c 1969		100	300		–			0
139	Independent Baptist Churches of EA	IBCEA	1964	P Bap	.IE	r 1970	28	400	2,400				7	2
140	Independent Churches of God of EA			I Pen	...	s 1967		100	300					0
141	Independent Lutheran Church	ILC	1961	I Lut	.IE	r 1966	20	500	1,000	80	25	31	1	0
142	Independent Pentecost Evangelistic Fellowship			I Pen	...	s 1969		1,860	5,000					0
143	Independent Presbyterian Church of EA	IPCEA	1946	P Ref	.IE	e1964	9	1,000	3,000					3
144	Independent United Churches of B of Christ			I	...	s 1971		105	300					0
145	International Church of God EF			I Pen	...	c 1969		945	3,000					0
146	International Fellowship for Christ	IFFC	1969	I Pen	...	r 1969	120	1,000	3,000				8	0
147	International Jerusalem Church	IJC	1968	I Pen	...			100	300					0
148	International Pentecost Church of CF	IPCCF		I Pen	...	a1971		750	2,000					0
149	Israel Assemblies of Kenya		1962	I Spi	..a	r 1969	15	1,000	3,000				80	0
150	Israel Holy Ghost Church of Kenya		1971	I Spi	...	a1972	16	936	2,000	90			12	0
151	Jehovah's Witnesses	IBSA		P Rus	...	r 1962	18	947	3,000			225	132	
152	Jerusalem Seventh-day Church of God		1959	I Pen	...	r 1971	20	1,020	3,000		–	30	15	0
153	Judah Israel Mission		1961	I Ang	...	r 1964	3	900	3,000	95	80	70	10	0
154	Kendu Roho Church Mission		1954	I Spi	...	r 1957	8	209	366				3	0
155	Kenya Church of Christ		1965	P Dis	...	e1968	26	600	2,000		–	340	0	12
156	Kenya Foundation of the Prophets Church	KFPC	1927	I Spi	...	r 1960	17	15,000	41,325	20	405	220		0
157	Kenya Revival Centre		c1960	P Pen	...	r 1961		400	1,200		–			0
158	Kenya Voice of Gospel Church		1965	I Pen	...	r 1967		150	500		–			0
159	Last Ministry Church			I Pen	...	s 1969		1,485	4,000					0
160	Lavington Church (United Parish)		1960	P Uni	...		1	500	1,500	50	30	20	0	1
161	Legion Catholic African Church		1962	I Rom	...	s 1964		3,500	5,000					0
162	Local Churches of Kenya, The		1960	I Pen	...	r 1970	102	2,000	6,000	60	50	500	52	1
163	Lost Israelites of Kenya		1960	I	...	r 1964		10,000	20,000	95		1,000	12	0
164	Luo Roho Church		1968	I Ang	...	r 1968	21	1,669	3,744	95	82	41	36	0
165	Lutheran Church in Kenya	LCK	1948	P Lut	L.N	e1966	69	4,204	9,000	50		250	8	2
166	Lyahuka Church of East Africa		1927	I Qua	...	r 1962		40	100					0
167	Magina Pentecostal Church in Africa		1969	I Pen	...	r 1970	8	150	300	90	13	8	5	0
168	Maranatha Church		1967	P Pen	...	r 1967	45	1,169	1,922		–	7	42	1
169	Mario Legio of Africa		1962	I Rom	...	r 1965	600	48,264	150,000				500	0
170	Methodist Church in Kenya	MCK	1862	P Met	WWN	e1967	624	18.729	100.000	75	1.989	2.258	30	10
171	Miracle Evangelistic Ministry		1970	I Pen	...	r 1970	5	80	250	75	–	80	9	0
172	Miracle Revival Fellowship PC		c1958	I Pen	...	r 1970		600	2,000					0
173	Muolo Roho Israel Church		1950	I Spi	...	r 1967	20	600	2,000				15	0
174	Musanda Holy Ghost Church of East Africa	MHGC	1934	I Spi	...	r 1960	65	1,673	5,073	64	111	80	13	0
175	Nairobi Baptist Church		1958	P Bap	...	e1959	1	140	1,500	83		6	0	2
176	Nairobi Undenominational Church		c1930	P Ply	...	e1961	1	45	150	55		8	0	7
177	National Independent Church of Africa	NICA	1929	I Nat	..a	r 1960	53	5,691	6,928	75	165	80	41	0
178	New African Canaan Church			I ·	...	s 1969	1	28	80					0
179	New East African Church		c1970	I	...	r 1971		3,500	10,000					0
180	New Roho Israel Church (Manyien)		1970	I Spi	...		1	30	90				1	0

186

91 Luo church with initially Catholic offices (cardinals, bishops), later changed to secular ones.
92 Roho Musalaba (Spirit Cross Church). Luo schism from MHGC.
93 An independent Pentecostal group stressing youth work, healing, shouting for victory.
94 Kikuyu schism from Apostolic Faith of East Africa, first known as Christian Evangelistic Church.
95 Separation from parent DCCEA in 1967, later winning property in court.
96 Luhya schism from ADisC. 1967, division. 1972, regrouped as Church of Jordan (see Part IV, Directory).
97 Former South African mission. Settler community, monthly service in Afrikaans.
98 Aided by Kenya Faith Mission. Members 80% Meru.
99 'Quakers'. Aided by Friends United Meeting. Largest Friends church outside USA. 98.7% Luhya.
100 Luo schism from Roho Church of God of Israel. 200 Luo members, 150 Luhya, Nandi and Kikuyu.
101 A Kikuyu body originally called Africam[
101 A Kikuyu body originally called African Israel Church Association (Dini ya Roho).
102 New American mission specialising in training pastors, ministers and evangelists.
103 'Mombasa Christians gathered to the Lord's Name'. Plymouth Brethren, related to Nairobi Chapel.
104 Single congregation, formerly expatriates but now with Africans. Decline over recent years.
105 Schism from CCA, 99% Luo. Diocese of Kenya, 3 parishes; work in Tanzania also.
106 Formerly called Baptist Evangelical Church in Africa. Members Kikuyu.
107 Aided by Swedish Free Mission, new name 1971. 2,300 Kikuyu, 1,350 Luhya, 200 Turkana, 150 Maasai.
108 Tanzania migrants from ELCT. Distinct from LCK, but merger talks are under way.
109 Small Luo group which has gradually declined in numbers since 1963.
110 'HM' = Holy Morning. Kikuyu body linked with Mantle Missions, San Diego, USA.
111 Luo organisation of itinerant lay evangelists, with loose congregational affiliations.
112 Independent movement first called Full Gospel Evangelistic Church (FEC). Luo members.
113 A small Plymouth Brethren fellowship group in Nairobi.
114 Multi-tribal movement: 132 Luhya members, 58 Kalenjin, 50 Luo, 39 Kikuyu, 18 Kamba, 10 Coast.
115 Arata a Roho Mutheru (=FHS). Kikuyu Anglican revival split, followers now throughout Kenya.
116 Kamba revival group, later split from Kikuyu FHS because latter registered. Unorganised local groups.
117 Widespread churches, membership 39% Luo, 33% Kikuyu, 14% Kalenjin, 9% Meru, 4% Luhya.
118 Luo independent church in South Nyakach.
119 Luhya movement calling themselves Zionists. Day of worship Friday; day for preaching Sunday.
120 Luo schism from PAG. Successful methods of evangelism through prophecy.
121 Luo title, Luong Mogik mar Nyasaye. Schism from SDA church stressing charismatic gifts.
122 One of the Kikuyu Spirit churches, split from HGCK due to polygamy.
123 Majority schism from GFF mission over polygamous wives. Kamba 50%, Kikuyu 25%, Coast, Kalenjin, Luhya.
124 1936, schism by missionaries from AIM. Strong among Kamba until massive GNCA schism.
125 Luhya Spirit revival group claiming origins in Kaimosi revival of 1927.
126 Vapostori (Apostles), a big Shona independent church from Rhodesia. Expected soon to merge with No. 129.
127 Kamba schism from GFF led by missionary. Now an indigenous church receiving GFF aid in Mombasa.
128 Attempted schism from Maria Legio of Africa by one of original prophetesses.
129 Offshoot from Apostolic Faith Mission of South Africa, affirming polygamy. Kikuyu 80%, Luo 7%, Maasai 5%.
130 Liberal wing of the Aroti (Dreamers, Seers), permitting modern attitudes. Name changed 1972 to HGCEA.
131 Luo movement employing Catholic terminology, with basilica and ecclesiastical HQ in South Nyanza.
132 A small Kikuyu group which broke in 1967 from AMHGC.
133 A Kikuyu group with 4 bishops, with a lengthy history of previous names.
134 Dini ya Roho. Luhya revival group, with some Kikuyu congregations. White robes and turbans.
135 Known as 'M' Aroti, due to red M and edges on robes, red or blue turbans; green 'forbidden'. Kikuyu.
136 First major schism from CCA over leadership. 15,000 Luo members, 2,000 Luhya, 1,000 Kikuyu.
137 Kikuyu body around Karatina and Nyeri. Schism from AOC over leadership.
138 A small Kikuyu group around Limuru, now in decline.
139 Mostly Kamba churches under national leadership, aided by Grace Independent Baptist Mission.
140 Kikuyu schism from Local Churches of Kenya over leadership difficulties.
141 Independent Luhya church, known until 1968 as African Lutheran Church (ALC), also Loyalist Religion.
142 A small Meru group around Rumuruti.
143 Kamba church north of Kitui, aided by IBPFM. 1957, WPM split in USA from IBPFM, then became AEPC.
144 A small group refused registration because of confusing name.
145 A small Kikuyu organisation in Central Province.
146 Indigenous Pentecostal organisation across Kenya. Links with USA and Canadian bodies.
147 Large faction in original IJC took over property in 1968, forcing leaders to adopt name PCCF. Mainly Meru.
148 Kikuyu body in Rift Valley.
149 Independent group in North Kinangop. Turbans worn. No water baptism.
150 Kikuyu Aroti group which split from AMHGC insisting on monogamy and water baptism.
151 Watchtower. In 1971, 335,643 hours spent witnessing, 118,463 magazines distributed in Kenya.
152 Kikuyu group linked with Church of God Seventh-day (Jerusalem, Israel), who ordained 17 Kenyans in 1970.
153 Bukusu schism by vice-bishop of DYM protesting violence. Main temple in Kimilili; prophecy, sacrifices.
154 Title in Luo, 'Chuny Kanisa Mochung' (Spirit Independent Church). Small Luo church in the Roho tradition.
155 American mission in Nairobi and Kakamega. Members 300 Kikuyu, 250 Luhya, 20 Kamba, 20 Luo.
156 One of original Kikuyu Spirit churches, still led by 92-year-old founder. Unusual prayer practices.
157 Mission from USA, formerly Muscoy Community Church Ministerial Fellowship.
158 Formerly known as Nakuru Full Gospel Church. Mainly Kikuyu members.
159 A Taita independent church stressing ministry in the last days before Second Coming of Christ.
160 Experimental union parish in Nairobi (Anglican, Methodist, Presbyterian). Wide variety of activities.
161 Part of original Maria Legio schism of 1962, which then broke off. Subsequent decline.
162 Pentecostal group of local congregations. Members: Luo 35%, Luhya 25%, Kikuyu 25%, Teso 15%.
163 'Israel with Ten Commandments'. Colourful flags, uniforms, marching. Followers across into Uganda.
164 Schism from NLC to assert glossolalia, healing and exorcism, plus Anglican features.
165 Aided by Swedish Lutheran Mission. Members: Gusii 85%, Luo 15%, some Kipsigis and Luhya.
166 Schism from FAM, until 1965 Church of Quakers in Africa, until 1971 African Church of Red Cross.
167 Luo schism from Norwegian Pentecostal Mission in Kenya, named after its location.
168 Aided by Swedish Maranatha ('Our Lord, come!') Mission. Near border with Tanzania.
169 Largest schism in Africa from RCC. Mainly Luo. 9 dioceses, 7 cardinals, 15,000 sisters.
170 Third church in Kenya (1862). Meru, Coast, and Nairobi Districts; new mission in northern Kenya.
171 A Luo Pentecostal movement begun in 1970 in South Nyanza.
172 Taita movement from Anglicanism after T. L. Osborn's 1957 crusades. 'Weni Mwanguvu' (People of Power).
173 Muolo = 'Peacefulness' (Luo). Split from AICN over food taboos. Luhya 60%, Luo 30%, Kalenjin 10%.
174 The first Luo Roho movement, stemming from martyr Alfayo Odongo. Major schism, RHGC, seceded in 1939.
175 Large Nairobi congregation, membership one-third Kenyans. 1971, Youth Church doubled attendances.
176 Known also as Nairobi Chapel; Christian (Plymouth) Brethren tradition, with associated chapel in Ofafa.
177 Embu and Meru ex-Anglican independents formerly in KISA and AIPC, revived in 1958.
178 Small Luhya independent group, first called Canaan Church in Kenya.
179 Recent Kamba schism at Mitaboni, claiming a large following.
180 Manyien = (New). Luo founder split 1962 from AICN, joined RCGI, split 1970.

Ref.	Official name of denomination	Initials	Year	Type	Coun	Status	Congs	Membership		P%	Annual Baptisms		Ministers	
								Adults	Total CC		Infant	Adult	Nat	Exp.
1	2	3	4	5	6	7	8	9	10	11	12	13	14	15
181	Nomiya Ligangala Mabith Sabato Church		c1970	I Ang	...	s 1972	1	50	150						0
182	Nomiya Luo Church	NLC	1914	I Ang	...	r 1956	420	65,000	120,000		3,504	2,076	31	0
183	Nomiya Luo Sabbath	NLS	c1957	I Ang	...	r 1958	184	6,800	10,680	68	860	340	23	0
184	Norwegian Pentecostal Mission in Kenya	NPMK	1955	P Pen	P.N	r 1966	74	5,200	15,000	65	–	924	60	
185	Peace & Mercy Church of East Africa		1962	I Adv	...	r 1963	1	200	600				1	0
186	Pentecost Africa Church		1967	I Pen	...	r 1970	10	500	1,500	90	40	100	4	0
187	Pentecostal Assemblies of God	PAG	1910	P Pen	P.N	e 1962	700	90,000	192,000	65	–	15,000	314	11
188	Pentecostal Christian Universal Church	PCUC	1968	I Pen	...	r 1968		970	3,000	70	–	40		0
189	Pentecostal Church of Christian Fellowship	PCCF	c1960	I Pen	...		5	100	300		–	30		0
190	Pentecostal Church, One Faith			I Pen	...	a 1969		150	500		–			0
191	Pentecostal Evangelistic Fellowship of A	PEFA	1938	P Pen	P.N	e 1962	791	48,200	150,000	65	–	5,000	526	9
192	Pentecostal Holiness Church of Kenya			I Pen	...	s 1968		150	400		–			0
193	Philadelphia Church of Africa			I Pen	...	s 1966	2	100	300					0
194	Power of Jesus Around the World Church		1955	I Pen	...	r 1965	200	10,000	30,000					0
195	Presbyterian Church of East Africa	PCEA	1898	P Ref	RWN	e 1964	350	60,000	100,000	80	5,000	2,450	33	6
196	Prophecy Evangelist Church of Africa			I Pen	...	s 1971	1	25	50					0
197	Reformed Church of East Africa	RCEA	1909	P Ref	R.N	e 1964	62	3,031	6,487	45	478	508	4	3
198	Religion of the Ancestral Spirits	DYM	1944	I Tra	...	p1968		10,000	50,000		–			0
199	Roho Church of God of Israel		1960	I Pen	..a	r 1963	25	13,000	40,000				36	0
200	Roho mar Nyasaye Mission		c1966	I Spi	...	r 1966	10	573	1,500					0
201	Roho Ngima Church of Kendu			I Spi	...	s 1971	1	50	150					0
202	Ruwe Holy Ghost Church of East Africa		1939	I Spi	...	r 1957	114	2,615	5,000	95	86	16	5	0
203	Sabato Maler mar Nyasaye Kanisa			I	...	s 1969		300	1,000					0
204	Sabina Church			I Spi	...	s 1968	1	700	2,000					0
205	Salvation Army	SA	1921	P Sal	SWN	i 1970	1,150	34,929	110,000	75	–	7,959	447	23
206	Salvation Merciful Church	WHC		I Sal	...	a1970		200	500					0
207	Scriptural Holiness Mission	SHM	1948	P Hol	...	r 1969	13	150	500				0	0
208	Seventh-day Adventist Church	SDA	1906	P Adv	..n	i 1970	861	82,569	171,023	64	–	9,846	105	16
209	SDA Church, Reform Movement	SDARM	c1968	I Adv	...	r 1969		400	1,000					0
210	Seventh-day Missionary Church	SDMC	1936	I Spi	...	r 1961	33	500	2,500	95	–			0
211	Sinai Church of East Africa	SCEA	1965	I Spi	..E	r 1965	6	350	1,200	50			3	0
212	Spiritual Church			I	...				10					0
213	Tanganyika Mennonite Church (Kenya)	TMC	c1962	P Men	M.N	r 1963	15	550	2,000	20		50	2	0
214	Three Holiness Israel Union Church		1965	I Pen	...	c 1970		98	300					0
215	Truth of the Apostles		c1966	I	...	a1967		300	1,000					0
216	United Pentecostal Church of Kenya	UPCK		P Pen	...	r 1972	1	20	50		–			0
217	Voice of Prophecy Church			I Adv	...	c1970		700	2,000					0
218	Voice of Salvation & Healing Church		1954	I Pen	...	r 1956	50	6,000	12,000	70			50	0
219	Water of Life Church	WLC	c1962	I	...	r 1964	8	201	500				7	0
220	Wokofu African Church	WAC	1966	I Sal	.IE	r 1966	120	3,900	15,000		–	160	35	0
221	World Christian Soldiers Church			I	...	a1971		300	1,000					0
222	World Revival Union Evangelistic Church		1965	I Pen	...	r 1970	8	52	120	60	27	13	5	0
223	World Salvation of Soul AHG Church		c1964	I Spi	...	r 1965	2	70	200					0
224	World-Wide Evangelistic Church			I	..a	a1968		120	600					0

Estimates for missing data (= blank spaces in table)							400	10	0		10,000	7,000	200	30
GRAND TOTAL (205 denominations: 1 RC, 46 Prot, 1 Ang, 1 Orth, 156 Indep)							**18,730**	**2,383,338**	**5,986,460**		**124,637**	**171,760**	**5,159**	**859**

SUB-TOTALS:

	Congs	Adults	Total CC		Infant	Adult	Nat	Exp.
Catholic Church (end-1969)	1,795	694,700	1,763,020		55,983	47,758	86	580
Catholic Church (mid-1971), estimated	1,900	787,000	1,998,000		60,000	50,000	90	580
Anglican Church (mid-1971)	1,629	239,383	582,600		20,132	26,853	224	48
Protestant churches (mid-1971)	9,600	636,270	1,698,300		9,000	62,000	2,800	225
African independent churches (mid-1971)	5,650	713,750	1,694,840		24,000	25,000	2,000	3
Orthodox Church (mid-1971)	230	100,000	250,000		15,000	10,000	33	3
NCCK-affiliated churches (mid-1971)	10,250	854,006	2,217,072		29,000	74,000	2,602	200
GRAND TOTAL MID-1971	**18,960**	**2,473,893**	**6,218,940**		**128,132**	**173,853**	**5,147**	**859**

Estimates for mid-1972:

	Congs	Adults	Total CC		Infant	Adult	Nat	Exp.
Catholic Church	1,950	842,000	2,140,000		62,000	52,000	95	580
Anglican Church	1,600	253,000	615,000		20,000	27,000	224	48
Protestant churches	9,900	660,000	1,750,000		10,000	64,000	2,900	230
African independent churches	5,800	755,000	1,760,000		25,000	26,000	2,100	3
Orthodox Church	240	105,000	260,000		15,000	10,000	35	3
NCCK-affiliated churches	10,500	890,000	2,305,000		30,000	75,000	2,700	200
GRAND TOTAL MID-1972	**19,490**	**2,615,000**	**6,525,000**		**132,000**	**179,000**	**5,354**	**864**

181   Luo schism from NLS; name means 'He gave me a sharp sword' and 'Sabbatarian'.
182   First independent church in Kenya (1914). Nomiya = 'The Word of God was given to us'. 3 Dioceses.
183   Reforming schism in 1957 from NLC in both Kenya and Tanganyika. Muslim features stressed.
184   Churches in western Kenya. Members: 2,500 Luo, 2,000 Kipsigis, 500 Gusii, 50 Luhya.
185   A 1962 schism among Gusii and Kipsigis from SDA Church; polygamous and sabbatarian. Declining.
186   Rapidly growing Luo movement emphasising faith healing and miraculous gifts.
187   Adherents: 140,000 Luhya, 20,000 Luo, 20,000 Gusii, 5,000 Kikuyu, 2,500 Kalenjin, 2,000 Coast, 500 Maasai.
188   Healing movement near Broderick Falls. 500 Bukusu, 200 Kalenjin, 100 Teso, 100 Luo, 70 Kikuyu.
189   Formerly known as IJC, name changed after 1968 controversies. Kikuyu, Meru members.
190   Coast group separated from Pentecostal Evangelistic Fellowship of Africa.
191   National church served by EMA and IPA missions; expanding at rate of 200 new churches each year.
192   A small Kikuyu group in Central Province.
193   Kikuyu movement emphasising praying for the sick.
194   Luo schism from Voice of Salvation and Healing Church after T. L. Osborn crusade in Uganda.
195   National church, widespread institutions. Kikuyu 60%, Meru 30%, Kalenjin 2%, Samburu 2.5%, expatriates 3%.
196   First called African Evangelist Fellowship Healing; Luhya group emphasising music.
197   Aided by Reformed Church of Netherlands. 1,600 Nandi, Elgeyo, Tugen; 900 Bukusu; 300 Kikuyu; 150 Turkana.
198   Dini ya Msambwa. Schism from FAM. Prohibited society in 1948 and again in 1968.
199   Schism from AICN, earlier known as World Spiritual Israel Church. Members: Luo 60%, Luhya 30%.
200   Small Luo group using Luo name meaning Spirit of God Mission. Members: Luo 90%, Luhya 10%.
201   Small group with Luo name, Living Spirit Church of Kendu Bay.
202   Major schism from MHGC over uniforms, setting up rival HQ at Ruwe.
203   Luo group with vernacular title, Holy Sabbath of God Church.
204   Kikuyu group led by three prophets. Name means Church of the Ark.
205   Members: Luhya (Maragoli, Tiriki) 70%, Kamba 20%, Kikuyu 5%. Organised as eleven Districts.
206   Luhya church with Swahili title Wokofu Huruma Church (WHC); schism from Salvation Army.
207   Mission from England dedicated to teaching doctrine of scriptural holiness.
208   Organised in four Fields. Members: Luo 45%, Gusii 45%, Kikuyu 5%.
209   Gusii schism from SDA Church, now linked to international schism SDARM (USA).
210   Early Kikuyu secession from HGCK changing worship from Sunday to Saturday.
211   Luhya schism in 1965 from AICN, growing slowly.
212   Nominal body serving as focus for uniting independent churches in Kenya.
213   Luo immigrants from Tanzania, now settled in South Nyanza since 1962.
214   Small secession in 1965 from African Israel Church Nineveh over leadership.
215   A Luo independent movement in South Nyanza begun circa 1966.
216   A recently-arrived mission of the United Pentecostal Church, USA.
217   Luo sabbatarian church led by blind charismatic prophetess.
218   An early Luo schism from the Africa Inland Mission over faith-healing.
219   A Luo organisation dedicated to a prayer ministry using English prayer cards.
220   Wokofu = 'Salvation'. Schism from SA; yellow uniforms. Luhya 60%, Kamba 30%.
221   A Luo movement requiring members to use musical instruments.
222   Mijikenda movement at the Coast to unite all Pentecostal denominations in the Harambee spirit.
223   Small Luo Roho group with three bishops. Membership declining since 1967.
224   Luo independent church first known as Salvation and Healing to All Nations.

DOCUMENTATION ON TABLE 1
('Christianity in Kenya, AD 1900-2000')

The following notes give (1) the sources of the statistics presented in Table 1, (2) notes on the methodology employed in constructing the table, and (3) some interpretative comments on the significance of the figures. Numbers on the left refer to the lines in the table. Note that the figures presented in this survey are intended to establish the general order of magnitude of the situation; accuracy to the last digit is not claimed. It should also be noted that percentages are rounded to the first decimal place, and so may not add up exactly to 100.0 per cent.

A. POPULATION OF KENYA   These figures are based on the published census reports of 1911, 1921, 1931 (all for non-Africans only), and (all races) 1948, 1962, and 1969; and the article 'The future growth of Kenya's population and its consequences', in *Kenya Statistical Digest*, IX, 2 (June, 1971), p. 1-8, and an updated article one year later (Statistics Division, Ministry of Finance and Economic Planning, Republic of Kenya). The 1971 article gives four alternative population projections for AD 2000. The first projection (34,286,000) is obtained by assuming no change from current fertility trends (age specific fertility); but if family planning programmes (which up to now have had no impact on the rate of population growth) are greatly multiplied and implemented, the population in 2000 could be reduced to around 30 million (a 13 per cent reduction). However, the higher figure is assumed here to be the more probable.

A.2.   The assumption made here (and for lines 3, 4, and 5) is that the proportions for all four races will remain approximately the same in the future as today.

A.6.   The percentage figures here (and for lines 7 and 8) show the annual rates; thus, the popultaion in 1972 is increasing at 3.3 per cent per year.

A.8.   Annual increase = births (line 6) minus deaths (line 7).

A.11.   Average life span of the individual, in years.

A.12.   *Kenya Population Census 1969*, Vol. II, 'Data on urban population'; and urban study group projections based on current expansion rates of 5.4 per cent per year (all urban areas) and 5.7 per cent per year (city of Nairobi). 'Urban population' is defined as the population living in towns of over 2,000 people in size (including Nairobi).

A.13.   Nairobi was founded in 1899 as a railhead camp. It is expected to reach 1 million in size in the year 1981. *Other data on Kenya*   Further 1972 description statistics for the whole population can be worked out using the following data. *Income* The per capita income is £50 (US$ 130) per year. The average family size (persons per household) is 4.92; hence the average family income is £240 per year. *Education* In the 1969 census, 27.1 % of the population had some school education, 72.9 % (including infants) had none. In 1968, 61 % of all children of primary school age were enrolled in schools, with a national target of 75 % by 1974 (see Kenya's *Development Plan, 1970-1974*). *Literacy* Of the adult population over 15 years old, 22.5 % were literate (in one language at least) in 1944, rising to 40 % by 1970; with a national target of 100 % by 1990. *Language comprehension* About 70 % of the population comprehend Swahili (to be the national language after 1975), and 25 % comprehend English (the official language at present). For further details on language and literacy, see Appendix 1 in this Handbook.

B. RELIGIOUS PROFESSION IN KENYA   Based on the religion figures in the census reports of 1948 (unpublished) and 1962 (published), as shown in Table 2, extrapolated to 1900, 1972, and 2000. The Baha'i statistics are not given in the censuses, but are those claimed by that community. In addition to the religions shown, there are tiny pockets of other religions: 700 Jews, 270 Parsees (Zoroastrians), etc.

B.14.   Note the survival and persistence of a sizeable core of 3 million persons professing (and often practising) African traditional religions.

B.15.   The vast majority of Muslims (including the Asian Ismailis (Khojas) are Kenya citizens.

B.17.   Many Hindus and other Asians emigrated out of Kenya during the period 1968-1971. About half the remainder are Kenya citizens.

B.20.   The Baha'i mission began in Kenya in 1951, and almost all its followers now are Africans.

C. PROFESSING CHRISTIANS IN KENYA   Derived graphically from the 1948 and 1962 censuses (as portrayed in Figure 1).

C.24.   'Unbaptised Catholics' are defined as those who profess to be Catholics in a census but are not yet baptised (catechumens, their children, fringe members, etc.).

C.26.   Note the probability of a gradually falling percentage of Protestants from 1972-2000.

C.27.   Note the probable increase in percentage of African independents, 1972-2000.

C.29.   First-generation Christians (converts whose parents at the time were non-Christians) numbered approximately 90 per cent of all Christians in 1900, and 30 per cent in 1972; and are likely to have dropped to 15 per cent by 2000.

C.30, 31. In Nairobi and other urban areas, Christians in 1962 numbered 59 per cent (*Kenya Population Census 1962*, Vols. III and IV), increasing to 75 per cent by mid-1972, and probably to 90 per cent by 2000. These figures are supported by various sample surveys and public-opinion polls.

D. AFFILIATED CHRISTIANS IN KENYA   The figures are taken from Table 5 in this article. Note that since 1971 (the date of most of the statistics in the Table), virtually all groups have grown perceptibly in size by mid-1972.

D.33.   Baptised Catholics on the church's rolls, and enrolled catechumens.

D.33-4. For a different kind of presentation of the expansion of the two largest churches in Kenya (Catholic and Anglican) during the 20th century, see Figure 3.

D.38.   The Christian Council of Kenya was begun in 1943, and now, as the NCCK, has 25 member denominations, as shown in Table 5

E. PRACTISING CHRISTIANS IN KENYA   'Practising Christians' are defined differently in the different churches. For Catholics (line 40) and Anglicans (line 41), the term here means Easter communicants plus unbaptised attenders (including infants) at the major festivals; for the other churches, regular worshippers (attending once a month or more). Weekly attenders (line 45), namely those actually in church every Sunday, are smaller in number, since many regular churchgoers are prevented from attending 52 Sundays a year (by sickness, family obligations, work, travel, rains, etc.)

E.39.   The sum of lines 40-44.

E.40.   Estimated by multiplying all Catholics by the Easter practice figure of 42 per cent.

E.46.   The 1972 figure is obtained by multiplying all regular radio listeners (77 per cent of the population - - see *VOK Audience Survey, Quick Reference Buyers Guide for 1970*, p. 3) by the proportion of these listeners who regularly tune in religious broadcasts (61 per cent, as found in the CCK Survey, *Radio listenership* (1965), Table 1. (77% x 61% - 47%). See also the article by Wesonga and Ward (p. 85) in this Handbook

E.47.   This is a minimum figure, based on line 39 plus a small fraction of line 46 to allow for a small number of regular radio listeners who, although not churchgoers, may yet be properly termed practising Christians.

E.48.   These figures = .008 multiplied by total Christians (since in every population of 1,000 persons, on average 8 couples each year reach marriageable age and enter on liaisons either temporary or permanent).

E.49.   Estimates, starting from Table 3 and including rough estimates for independent and other churches.

190

F.   CHURCHES AND CLERGY IN KENYA   The figures are obtained from Table 5, projected graphically.

G.   CHURCH GROWTH IN KENYA EACH YEAR'

G.55.   In addition to the proliferation of new denominations, new dioceses come into existance each year (see Figure 3 for illustration).

G.57.   Rough estimates of number of new clergy (ministers or priests) ordained each year, less number of deaths among existing ministers.

G.58.   The present increase rate is about 5.0 per cent per year.

G.61.   Urban Christians are assumed to share the general urban growth rate of 5.4 per cent per year.

G.62.   Assuming the Nairobi growth rate of 5.7 per cent per year.

G.63.   Note that new professing Christians are much larger than the actual increase (lines 58 or 65), due to deaths (in fact, line 65 = line 63 minus line 64).

G.65.   This line is the same as line 58.

G.66.   Taken from the end of Table 5 (similarly with lines 67-70).

G.71.   This is an average annual figure for 1971-72. For statistics on literacy and language, see the end of section A above.

Fields White Unto Harvest

Photographic Essay

Jesus said: "Do you not say, 'Four months more and then comes harvest'? But look, I tell you, look round on the fields; they are already white, ripe for harvest." — John 4.35.

Harvest and Harvesters

This page gives descriptions concerning each of the 38 photographs in the photographic essay following, using the numbers placed alongside the photos.

1. What the Bible calls the 'harvest field' — people in present-day Kenya. The average age of the nation is 14½ years, as with these youths; and the population increases each year by 399,000.

2.-4. Three more portraits of contemporary Kenyans.

5. In 1972 the churches of Kenya have around 5,350 Kenyan ministers, priests and pastors. (Right) The Rev. John Mpaayei, former secretary of the Bible Society in East Africa, and (Left) Pastor Esitsakha, Pentecostal Assemblies of God.

6. In April, 1968, the first Kenya Pastors Conference was held at Kenyatta College; 1,200 pastors attended, from the following churches: CPK (Anglican), 186,; PAG, 160; PEFA, 144; AIC, 129; CGEA, 100; PCEA, 88; Independents, 131.

   RURAL CHURCHES — 1: Kenya has 7,055,000 rural Christians and 19,000 rural churches.

7. This large rural denomination has 15,000 white-clad sisters or nuns (Maria Legio of Africa).

8. Bishop Raphael Ndingi (left) addresses some of the 103,000 rural Catholics in his former diocese, Machakos.

9. About 400 new rural church buildings are constructed each year through *harambee* (community self-help).

   RURAL CHURCHES — 2:

10. Most church headquarters are in the countryside, often at 'holy villages' such as Ninevah here with the AICN High Priest Kivuli (foreground) and some of his 60,000 followers.

11. On the door to the High Priest's residence at Ninevah is this representation of the AICN on the march.

12. Cardinal Maurice Otunga and Bishops R. Ndingi (centre) and J. Njenga process to Bishop Ndingi's enthronement over the rural diocese of Nakuru.

13. The President of Kenya, H. E. Mzee Jomo Kenyatta, gives the 'Umoja' (Unity) sign as he opens one of the countless new church buildings he has assisted in his time. Here, in May 1970, he opens a branch of the African Independent Pentecostal Church of Africa, which he helped to establish in the 1930s. On this occasion he donated £550 to the building fund.

   URBAN CHURCHES: Kenya has around 945,000 urban Christians in its towns and cities.

14. Salvation Army cadets train for urban witness at the Officer Training College, Nairobi.

15. The first Kenyan to become a Catholic bishop was Cardinal Otunga, now of the urban archdiocese of Nairobi.

16. With a population of 600,000 in 1972, Nairobi has over 300 churches and congregations, serving 450,000 Christians of whom about 100,000 adults and children are regular Sunday attenders.

    WE ARE PART OF THE WORLD CHURCH: international church leaders often visit Kenya.

17. Visiting Kisumu, international evangelist Dr. Billy Graham met three Luo *ajuoge* (medicine men).

18. In Kisumu, Dr. Graham's sermon was translated in Luo and Swahili by (left) Archbishop Festo Olang', at that time Bishop of Maseno: and (right) Ugandan evangelist the Rev. Festo Kivengere (now Bishop of Kigezi).

19. In 1971, Archbishop Makarios (President of Cyprus) visited Kenya, baptised 5,000 persons, and ordained a Kikuyu Kenyan citizen (centre) as a priest in the African Orthodox Church of Kenya.

20. The Archbishop of Canterbury meets students at the University of Nairobi in 1971.

21. The Archbishop of Nairobi, Cardinal Otunga, meditates on the Scriptures in his chapel.

22. A theological student blows a traditional Bajun *siwa* (trumpet).

23. Scott Theological College students accompany a Christian hymn with instruments both modern and traditional (centre, *abu*, centre back, *olwika).*

194

24. An open-air worship service in Western Kenya. The pastor (centre) claps to keep time.
25. Hand-clapping by leaders and drumming are the two normal means of producing lively and vigorous congregational singing in which all participate with a sense of the joy of the Lord (Assemblies of God).
26. A bishop preaching with an interpreter on a hot Sunday in Nyanza (Maria Legio of Africa).

MINISTRY TO YOUTH: 67 per cent of Kenya's 12 million people are under 25 years old.

27. Some of the 3,500 students at the University of Nairobi, outside the science block.
28. The Bishop of Mount Kenya greets students after a university service, Nairobi.
29. Every year, 100,000 young couples in Kenya reach marriageable age, and of these, 30,000 take Christian vows before God in a church ceremony.
30. Christian student leaders listen to Archbishop Michael Ramsey (University of Nairobi).
31. In the prime of life, countless young people each year accept a life's vocation to Christian work, witness, worship, and service to God and man.
32. Study of the Bible in groups by young people is assisted by many organisations, but not least by the Bible Society of Kenya which supplied these RSV Bibles at a greatly subsidised price.

BROADCASTING + COMMUNICATION + DEVELOPMENT = PROGRESS

33. Delegates to a joint Protestant/Catholic workshop in Nairobi on communication examine modern equipment.
34. A network of aircraft services to open up Kenya's vast northern deserts is operated by churches and missions.

SERVING THE COMMUNITY

35. Port Reitz school ministers to handicapped children, even enabling them to play regular football matches.
36. A Christian nurse serves in a local clinic.

GO YE THEREFORE ...   FEED MY SHEEP

37. A Young Christian hears the command of Christ to serve.
38. In service to the poor and needy, the hungry and the destitute, the orphan and the refugee, we serve the Lord Christ himself.

Okello-Olluoko, O., 237
Okelo, Bp. V., 246
Okite, O., 265
Okola, H., 276
Okullu, J.H., 240, 256, 276, 286
Okumu, J.M., 249
Okungu, P., 270
Okuyo, A., 274
Olang', Abp. F.H., 238, 240
Olang', Mrs. F.H., 276
Olloo, N., 236
Oloo, E.S., 251
Oloo, R., 232
Olsen, A.W., 241, 271
Olumide, Y., 255, 284
Olwande, Bp. E., 230
Omahe, C.M., 244
Omolo, J., 272
Omolo, J.D., 239
Omolo, S.K., 266
Omwansa, J., 250
Ondeng, R.O., 260
Ondeto, Bp. S., 246
Ondu, P.O., 232
Ongana, Abp. J., 250
Ong'idi, T., 230
Ongolo, Mrs. R., 276
Ongoma, A., 260
O'Otieno, Bp. B.T., 241
Onyango, J., 242
Opanga, S.O., 249
Opiyo, J., 236
Opolo, O., 241
Oriare, A., 246
Orina, Abp. K.,236
O'Rourke, N., 275
Orwa, J.P., 232
Orwa, Bp. M., 247
Osei-Mensah, G., 247
O'Sullivan, Sr. Aloysia, 270, 281
Otete, J., 274
Otieno, J., 231
Otieno, J.G., 242
Otieno, Abp. M., 238
O'Toole, P., 280
Otonglo, C., 240
Otunga, Cardinal M., 233, 271
Ouma, D.E., 251
Oundo, Abp. B., 247
Owago, Mrs. D., 276
Owalo, Abp. G.C., 247
Owalo, Abp. N.A., 243
Owino, Bp. J., 247
Owiti, J.A.S., 251
Owuor, H., 242
Oyango, P.A., 287
Oyieko, Bp. A., 251

Palliser, P.S., 245, 269
Patrick, Sr., 272
Paulo, Abp. J.A., 248
Pazia, N.E., 241
p'Bitek, O., 270
Peacock, H.F., 285
Pearce, B., 257
Pesa, J.W.S.J., 243
Petros, Mo. A., 259, 264

Philpot, D., 279
Pickstone, M., 276
Pollard, H., 259, 273
Pont, S.D., 259
Porcu, B., 262
Potvin, A.R., 262
Prendergast, Sr. M., 274

Rabari, S., 256
Reeper, Bp. J.de, 234, 278
Renata, Sr., 264
Rhines, C., 248
Rich, M., 283
Richards, W., 256
Richardson, D., 283
Ridout, J., 261, 287
Riess, J., 261
Riga, J., 263
Roberts, A.S., 236
Roberts, E.A., 256
Roberts, J.W., 242
Ross, S.L., 233
Roy, J., 280
Rutherford, B., 282

Sagide, E.O., 243
Sakwa, Bp. W.B., 236
Sanders, A.C.E., 256
Sartorelli, Abp. P., 257
Saunders, D.L., 269
Schoenecker, Sr. C., 274
Scholastica, Mo., 273
Scott, A.M., 273
Scott, J., 255
Scribbins, P.W., 277
Seii, J., 279
Sennot, S., 270
Sharp, M., 271
Shaw, E.M., 263
Shenk, J.C., 250
Shumaker, C.R., 255
Sickler, M.J., 248, 265
Silas, J.G., 238
Slade, R.P., 273
Smyth, M.I., 272
Snyder, F.J., 276, 283
Sperling, D.C., 284
Spurin, R.M., 260, 272
Stafford, R., 263
Stough, P. & Mrs., 274
Stovold, K.E., 240
Street, A.W.B., 284
Streng, Sr. L., 276
Strong, D.W., 286
Struble, R., 241, 284
Su, A., 256
Sulubu, S., 248
Sulumeti, Bp. P., 234
Sundh, B., 284
Swan, D.C., 255
Sykes, S., 236

Taiti, J., 248
Talitwala, S., 287
Tate, Van, 245
Taylor, A., 270
Tei, E., 248, 265

Teresa, Mo., 283
Thimes, E., 272
Thiong'o, E., 257
Thom, D.R., 237
Thomas, M., 277
Thompson, T., 285
Thuo, M., 245
Tidenberg, J., 257
Tonui, J., 260
Toror, M., 287
Tumbo, H., 243
Tuninetti, Mo. G., 262
Tveter, A., 248
Tyler, P., 287

Urungu, J., 284

Vail, D.W., 271
van Diepen, J., 281, 282
van Emmerick, J., 274
van Heerden, P.J.C., 236
van Rooij, T.C.M.J., 264
Varughese, T., 271
Verhoeven, A.H., 262, 286
Volz, P.M., 273

Wabande, Bp. S.M., 245
Wairegi, S.N., 230
Waithaka, Mrs. J., 256
Wakhu, S., 261, 262
Wakube, E.M., 266, 269
Waluoho, Abp. Y.B., 249
Wambogo, M.O., 247
Wambua, Mrs. J.J., 271
Wambugu, S., 258
Wanalo, W., 270
Wangai, F.K., 250
Wangendo, J., 242
Wangusi, B., 280
Wanjalo, E., 277
Wanjau, G.E., 282
Wanje, M., 233
Wanjohi, F., 286
Wanyonyi, J.M.W., 246
Ward, P.G., 260, 271
Wasike, M., 236
Waweru, D.N., 258
Weaver, E., 276
Weaver, L.M., 256
Welch, D.E., 264
Welch, F.G., 277
Welime, W., 249, 265
Wendell, K., 250
Were, Bp. I., 249
White, J.L., 278
Wilding, A.P., 260
Willy, E.N., 231
Wilson, B., 247
Wilson, F.E., 250
Wilson, R., 256
Woll, Mrs., 267

Yamo, C.O., 247
Young, A., 260

Zawadi, S.M., 245
Zenker, G., 259

343

Index of Kenya Towns and Cities

This Index lists all towns and cities in Kenya mentioned in the postal addresses of the Directories (Parts IV and V). It can therefore be used to locate all Christian bodies which have headquarters at or near a particular town.

Ahero, 230, 234, 239, 241, 242, 246, 248, 256
Athi River, 235

Bomet, 230, 235, 268
Bondo, 234, 239, 268, 283
Broderick Falls, 237, 248, 268
Bungoma, 234, 239, 260, 262, 272
Bura, 235, 259, 283
Busia, 234, 239
Butere, 239, 249, 263
Butula, 234, 239, 268

Chemelil, 240
Chogoria, 239, 258, 260, 268, 279

Doldol, 239

Elburgon, 235
Eldama Ravine, 230, 235, 240, 268, 283
Eldoret, 230, 233, 234, 240, 241, 249, 258, 260, 263, 265, 267, 268, 270, 274, 276, 277, 280
Emali, 235
Embu, 233, 235, 238, 240, 245, 247, 262, 270

Funyula, 234, 239, 268, 274
Fort Hall (see also Murang'a) 236, 267

Garissa, 235, 267
Gilgil, 235

Hoey's Bridge, 234
Homa Bay, 234, 239, 248, 251, 267, 272

Igoji, 268
Ishiara, 235
Isibania, 234
Isiolo, 235, 247, 262, 267, 268, 274
Iten, 234

Kabarnet, 230, 236
Kabondo, 240, 249
Kaimosi, 234, 264, 269
Kajiado, 230, 236, 240, 273
Kakamega, 231, 233, 234, 237, 238, 239, 258, 264, 266, 268, 278, 283
Kaloleni, 239, 258, 268, 282
Kangema, 239
Kangundo, 235, 237, 238, 268, 284
Kapcheno, 240, 276
Kapsabet, 230, 234, 240, 262, 268, 269, 269, 270, 283

Karaba, 240
Karatina, 236, 244, 268, 285
Karen, 278
Karungu, 236
Kendu Bay, 231, 242, 245, 247, 249, 250, 251, 255, 268, 270
Kericho, 230, 236, 239, 242, 255, 260, 271, 286
Kerugoya, 231, 236, 240, 267, 270, 276
Kevote, 235
Khayega, 277, 282
Khwisero, 236, 239
Kiambu, 233, 234, 240, 260, 267, 276, 280
Kianyaga, 236, 240
Kibwezi, 235
Kiganjo, 236, 249, 267
Kijabe, 230, 256, 268, 272, 275, 282
Kikambala, 269, 271
Kikima, 235, 243
Kikuyu, 233, 240, 241, 256, 268, 272, 277, 279
Kilgoris, 230
Kilifi, 235, 239, 248, 280
Kilome, 235, 240, 255, 268
Kimilili, 234, 239, 245, 268
Kinango, 235, 274
Kisii, 234, 237, 239, 246, 250, 262, 264, 266, 268, 272, 282, 284, 286
Kisumu, 230, 231, 232, 234, 236, 237, 239, 240, 241, 242, 243, 244, 246, 247, 248, 249, 251, 259, 260, 263, 266, 268, 270, 271, 272, 274, 276, 279, 280, 282, 287
Kitale, 234, 236, 240, 246, 258, 259, 268, 269, 270, 274, 285
Kithimani, 235
Kitui, 230, 234, 240, 268, 269, 272, 276, 280, 282, 286
Koru, 234, 242, 268
Kwale, 282

Limuru, 234, 240, 243, 244, 250, 257, 258, 261, 270, 273, 279, 282
Litein, 230, 268, 273
Lodwar, 236, 268, 269, 273, 274
Loitokitok, 236, 268
Lokitaung, 236, 273
Londiani, 248
Lorugumu, 268
Lumbwa, 248, 262

Machakos, 230, 231, 233, 235, 238, 240, 258, 260, 272, 273, 279, 283, 285

Makueni, 235, 273
Makuyu, 236
Malakisi, 234, 239
Malindi, 235, 239, 266, 268, 275
Maragoli, 230, 231, 232, 234, 238, 241, 243, 244, 246, 249, 250, 258, 268
Maragua, 236, 239, 267
Maralal, 235, 240, 259, 268
Mariakani, 235, 239, 247, 251
Marigat, 240
Marsabit, 235, 239, 240, 259, 268
Maseno, 234, 237, 239, 247, 258, 260, 261, 262, 268, 272, 274, 276, 282, 284, 285
Matathia, 237
Maua, 268, 275
Meru, 235, 241, 244, 247, 248, 258, 261, 262, 268, 269, 271, 275, 278, 279, 284, 286
Migori, 234
Migwani, 230
Mirogi, 233, 234
Mitaboni, 247
Miwani, 238
Molo, 236, 240, 250
Mombasa, 235, 239, 241, 243, 247, 248, 255, 259, 260, 261, 262, 263, 265, 267, 273, 275, 276, 280, 282, 286, 287
Moyale, 235, 239
Muhoroni, 242, 243, 248, 268
Mumias, 234, 239, 259, 268, 272, 276, 283
Murang'a (see also Fort Hall), 233, 239, 242, 257, 259, 263, 274, 276
Mwatate, 239, 245
Mweiga, 236, 267
Mwingi, 231, 235, 244, 268, 286

Nairobi, 230, 231, 232, 233, 234, 236, 237, 238, 240, 241, 242, 243, 244, 245, 246, 247, 248, 249, 250, 251, 255, 256, 257, 258, 259, 260, 261, 262, 263, 264, 265, 266, 267, 268, 269, 270, 271, 272, 273, 274, 275, 276, 277, 278, 279, 280, 281, 282, 283, 284, 285, 286, 287
Naivasha, 236, 240, 244
Nakuru, 235, 236, 240, 244, 245, 258, 260, 261, 262, 263, 264, 268, 271, 275, 276, 277, 278, 279, 280, 286
Nambale, 234, 239, 277
Nandi Hills, 234, 240
Nanyuki, 230, 235, 236, 239, 274

344

Narok, 230, 236, 268, 273
Ndori, 239
Ng'iya, 239
Njoro, 236, 242
Nkubu, 235, 278
North Kinangop, 236, 267
Nyeri, 231, 232, 236, 238, 248, 256, 258, 259, 262, 267, 268, 269, 279, 282, 284, 287
Nyilima, 238, 239, 246, 266, 268

Ol Kalou, 240
Othaya, 248
Oyugis, 234, 250, 251, 284

Pap Onditi, 236
Port Victoria, 234

Rabai, 239
Ramogi, 239
Ranen, 250

Ruiru, 231, 233, 237, 257, 267, 269, 283, 287
Rumuruti, 244
Runyenjes, 235, 237, 238, 240, 245, 268

Saba Saba, 239
Sagana, 236, 240
Sare, 234, 236, 238, 239, 251, 268
Shimba Hills, 235, 239
Siakago, 235
Siathani, 235
Siaya, 234, 237, 239, 268
Sondu, 230, 231, 232, 234, 265, 268, 274, 279
Songhor, 239, 268
Sotik, 235, 236, 239, 268, 273
South Kinangop, 230, 236, 278
Soy, 240
Subukia, 233
Suna, 238, 242, 246, 250

Taveta, 235, 239
Thika, 230, 231, 232, 233, 234, 236, 239, 240, 241, 244, 245, 258, 266, 267, 268, 269, 277, 280, 282, 283, 286, 287
Thompson's Falls, 236, 240, 245
Tiriki, 232, 234, 241, 266, 267, 268, 269
Turbo, 234, 257
Turi, 282

Ukwala, 234, 239, 248, 268, 284, 285
Uplands, 234, 286
Uranga, 239

Voi, 235, 239

Wanguru, 240
Wundanyi, 235, 239, 284

Yala, 230, 234, 237, 239, 268, 276, 282

Subject Index

This Index lists alphabetically all subjects and names mentioned in Parts I - III and VI or in photographs. It does not include items listed alphabetically elsewhere, for which the reader should consult Part IV (Directory of Churches), Part V (Directory of Christian Organisations), or Part VII (Bibliography).

Affiliated Christians, 160, 164, 165, 166, 170, 175, 190
Africa Acts, 94
Africa Christian Press, 94, 95
Africa Enterprise, 28
Africa Evangelical Literature Office, 98
Africa Gospel Church, 56, 88, 89, 90, 91
Africa Inland Church, 18, 37, 56, 70, 71, 72, 73, 74, 81, 82, 88, 89, 90, 91, 92, 94, 95, 96, 130, 133, 194
Africa Inland Mission, 22, 33, 35, 38, 75, 127, 130, 163, 171, 217
Africa Inland Press, 94
Africa Literature Centre, 94
African Brotherhood Church, 25, 56, 76, 90, 91, 92, 151, 218
African Christian Church of East Africa, 218
African Christian Church & Schools, 26, 56, 130, 131, 133, 134, 218
African Church, 218
African Church Mission, 218
African Church of Holy Spirit, 218
African Church of Jesus Christ in Kenya, 223
African Disciples Church, 223
African Divine Church, 26
African God Worshippers, 18
Africa Gospel Church, 77, 92, 96
African Holy Ghost Christian Church, 141, 223
African Independent Church of East Africa, 218
African Independent Church of Kenya, 25
African Independent Pentecostal Church of Africa, 24, 25, 36, 56, 127, 129, 130, 134, 138, 139, 170, 194, 218
African Israel Church Nineveh, 25, 73, 86, 90, 133, 135, 143, 151, 171, 194, 218
African Mission of Holy Ghost Church, 140, 218
African Orthodox Church of Kenya, 25, 28, 36, 56, 127, 129, 134, 170, 172, 174, 194, 218
Africa Sinai Church, 223
Aga Khan, 296, 297, 299, 308
Ahmadiyya, 225, 299, 300, 313
Akurinu, 124-127, 131
Alexander, Daniel, 25, 36
All Africa Conference of Churches, 27, 88, 90, 94, 102, 222
Allgeyer, Emile, 31

Alliance Girls High School, 60
Alliance High School, 24, 25, 35, 44, 111, 150
Alliance of Protestant Missions, 24, 35
AMECEA, 27, 28, 101, 105
Amoyo (Jerusalem), 137
Anabii (Prophets), 131
Andu a Iremba (Turban People), 131
Anglican Church, 18, 37, 38, 73, 75, 78, 79, 80, 88, 95, 96, 111, 116, 129, 131, 133, 136, 138, 151, 152, 153, 162, 163, 168, 170, 171, 175, 178, 180, 216, 221
Anglican Consultative Council, 28, 153
Apostolic Delegation of Africa, 24
Apostolic Delegation to British East and West Africa, 26
Apostolic Delegation to Eastern Africa, 27
Apostolic Faith Mission, 131
Apostolic Faith of Africa, 131, 218
Apostolic Nunciature, 27
Arabs, 21, 30, 31, 41, 181, 295
Arahuka Book Depot, 96
Archbishop of Canterbury, 23, 26, 194
Architecture, 59 - 64
Aroti (Dreamers), 24, 25, 124 - 127, 131, 134
Arya Samaj, 302, 303, 304, 305, 313
Asians, 24, 41, 87, 181, 295, 302, 303, 307, 309
Assemblies of God, 153, 194
Augustinians, 21, 29

Baha'i, 225, 313
Bakari, J.B. (Kabwere), 27
Balbo, A., 24
Balbo, G, 32
Balokole, 25, 26, 110 - 117
Baptist Churches of Kenya, 18, 56, 88, 89, 90, 92, 153
Barlow, A.R., 24
Bavaria Evangelical Lutheran Mission, 22
Baur, E., 31
Beecher, Abp. L.J., 27
Beecher Report, 26, 49
Berlin Conference, 22, 162
Bethany Bookshop, 96
Bible Churchmen's Missionary Society, 24, 35, 216
Bible Fellowship Church, 56
Bible House, 26, 27
Bible Society in East Africa, 27, 194

Bible Society of Kenya, 28, 97, 98, 176, 194
Bible translation, 21, 22, 23, 24, 25, 26, 27, 93, 97, 98, 99, 149
Biermans, J., 33
Bohoras (Bohras), 296, 299, 312
Brandsma, G., 25, 33
British East African Broadcasting Company, 24
Broadcasting, 27, 85 - 92, 149, 194
Butere Convention, 27, 113, 116
Buxton School, 27, 35
bwalo, 61

Camisassa, J., 24, 32
Campling, J.W., 33
Canadian Baptist Overseas Mission Board, 130
Catholic Bishops' Conference, 25
Catholic Church, 18, 38, 56, 57, 73, 74, 75, 81, 86, 90, 91, 92, 95, 97, 137, 151, 152, 153, 161, 163, 168, 169, 171, 175, 178, 180, 181, 215, 220
Catholic Mirror, 96
Censuses, 158, 159, 163, 170
Chilson, A., 24
Chogoria Convention, 113
Chosen Church of the Holy Spirit in Kenya, 124, 218
Christ Evangelistic Association, 218
Christian bookshops, 96
Christian Brotherhood Church, 218
Christian Churches' Educational Association, 26, 51, 56, 57, 150, 153
Christian Communications Congress, 28
Christian Council for Race Relations, 25
Christian Council of Kenya (CCK), (see also NCCK), 25, 37, 38, 70, 130
Christian Evangelical Church, 218
Christian Holy Ghost Church of East Africa, 133, 218
Christian literature, 93 - 99
Christian Literature Centre, 96
Christian publishing houses, 94, 95
Christian Universal Evangelistic Union, 26
Christian University Movement, 152
Christian Writers' Club, 94
Church Army (Anglican) 26, 90, 96, 173
Church Commissioners for Kenya, 26
Church growth, 160, 167, 191
Church Missionary Society, 22, 33, 34, 216
Church of Christ in Africa, 26, 56, 139, 143, 218

Church of God in East Africa, 23, 34, 56, 95, 151, 194, 217
Church of Messiah, 218
Church of Scotland Mission, 22, 33, 217 (see also PCEA)
Church of the Holy Apostles of the Lamb, 218
Church of the Kenya Family, 218
Church of the Province of East Africa, 38, 56, 90, 91, 92, 169, 178, 180, 194, 216
Church union, 25, 27, 28, 35
Church weddings, 176, 180
CMS Bookshops, 96
CMS Divinity School, 23, 25
Communications, 17, 100 - 105, 194
Conference on Christian Co-operation, 25
Conference on Church Union, 25
Consolata Fathers, 23, 25, 32, 215
Co-operation, 23, 25, 34, 44, 46, 51, 98, 104, 149 - 153, 177
Corcoran, E., 67
Cross Church of East Africa, 139, 141
Crossroads Mission, 28

Dasa Oshwals, 307
Daughters of St. Vincent, 32
Dawoodis, 300
Daystar Press, 95
de Courmont, J., 31
Deliverance Church, 223
Department of Philosophy and Religious Studies, University of Nairobi, 28, 52
Dervish orders, 297
Development, 17, 44, 46, 100 - 105, 194
Digambaras, 307, 308
Dini ya Jesu Kristo, 132
Dini ya Kaggia, 131, 134
Dini ya Mariam, 26
Dini ya Msambwa, 25, 26, 28, 218, 224
Disciples of Christ in Africa, 131
Diwali, 306

East African Consultation on Church Union, 28
East Africa Christian Alliance, 264
East Africa Scottish Mission, 22, 217
East Africa Venture Company, 97
East Africa Yearly Meeting of Friends, 56, 151, 153, 169, 171
Ecumenical organisations, 153
Ecumenical relations, 47, 70, 104, 108, 109, 123, 144 - 148, 152, 153, 177
Education, 17, 42, 44, 46, 49 - 58, 93, 102, 103, 130, 132, 150, 161, 299, 308, 309,
Education Act 1968, 50, 51, 53, 57
el-Farsy, Sheikh A.S., 45, 296
Elim Missionary Assemblies, 25, 27, 56, 217, 222
Emmaus Bible School, 89
Episcopal Church of Africa, 223
Ethnographic studies, 42
Evangelical Fellowship of Kenya, 146
Evangelical Literature Fellowship of East Africa, 98

Evangelical Lutheran Church, 222
Evangelism, 17, 21, 28, 33, 70, 96, 98, 101, 108, 222
Evangelistic ship, m/v Logos, 28, 222
Evangel Publishing House, 94, 95

Faith healing, 122, 133, 140 - 143
Female circumcision, 24, 36, 129, 162
Finnish Foreign Mission, 26
Fort Jesus, 21, 30
Francis, Carey, 25
Freedom of religion, 45, 48, 145, 162, 164
Freemasons, 314
Frere, Sir Bartle, 30, 31
Freretown, 22, 31
Friends Africa Industrial Mission, 33, 35
Friends Africa Mission, 217
Friends Bookshop, 96
Friends of the Holy Spirit, 26, 131, 141, 218

Gays, T., 32
Getonga, Joachim, 103
Gitari, David, 97
Gitau, Musa, 24
God of the Universe Church, 218
God's Word and Holy Ghost Church, 133
Gona, Johana, 22
Good News Church of Africa, 27, 218
Gospel Furthering Fellowship, 25, 217
Gospel Missionary Society, 217
Gospel of God, 174, 180, 223
Graham, Billy, 27, 194
Granth Sahib, 309, 311
Greek Patriarchate of Alexandria, 25, 129

Hanlon, Henry, 32, 33
Hannington, J., 22
harambee, 41, 57, 194
Hare Krishna, 225, 304, 305, 313
Heffernan, J., 31
Hindu Council of Kenya, 225, 303, 306, 313
Hinduism, 17, 150, 225, 302-306, 313
Hindus, 41, 163, 164, 302 - 306
Hinsley, Arthur, 24
Holy Church of Evangelistic Apostles Faith, 131, 218
Holy Ghost Church of Kenya, 133, 134, 218
Holy Ghost Coptic Church of Africa, 119, 223
Holy Ghost Fathers, 22, 31, 32, 33, 215
Holy Mother Maria, 137
Holy Spirit Church of East Africa, 151
Holy Spirit Church of Zayun, 133
Holy Trinity Church in Africa, 218
Horner, A., 31
Hotchkiss, W., 33
Houghton, J., 22, 30

IBEA Company, 22
Id-al-Fitr, 296
Id-al-Hajj, 296
Immaculate Heart of Mary Sisters, 32

Independent African Orthodox Church, 129
Independent church councils, 153
Independent Presbyterian Church, 56
International Council of Christian Churches, 27
International Fellowship for Christ, 223
International Pentecostal Assemblies, 25, 27, 217, 222
Isenberg, Samuel, 22
Islam, 17, 21, 49, 150, 224, 225, 295-301, 312 (see also Muslims)
Islam in Africa Project, 300
Ismailis, 296, 298, 299, 308, 312
Ithnasheris, 296, 298, 312

Jainism, 225, 307 - 309, 313
Jains, 163, 303, 305, 307 - 309
Jara, Joseph, 23
Jews, 225, 314
John XXIII, Pope, 46
Joint East African Religious Education Committee, 51, 153
Jones, William, 36
Judah Israel Mission, 218

Kabaa High School, 44
Kabare Convention, 113
Kabete Convention, 26, 113
Kabwere, Ali bin (Bakari), 27, 294
Kagaari Convention, 26, 113
Kaggia, Bildad, 131, 134
Kahihia, Benjamin, 130, 138
Kahuhia Convention, 25, 26, 27, 113
Kajiwe, 27, 224, 294
Kalume, Simeon, 35
Kalume, Thomas, 97
Kamau, J.C., 27, 38
Kamawe, Wanyoike, 23
Karanja, Phillip, 23
Kareri, Charles, 38
Kariuki, Bp. Obadiah, 26, 38, 47, 194
Kariuki, Petro, 141
Karuga, Daniel Nduti, 141
Karuri, Chief, 23
Kavirondo Taxpayers Welfare Association 24, 35
Kemango, T., 24, 32
Kendu Roho Church Mission, 138, 140, 218
Kenya African Keswick Convention, 25
Kenya Association for Liturgical Music, 67, 69
Kenya Catholic Secretariat, 27, 51, 88, 90, 102, 103, 153
Kenya Christian Teachers' Prayer Fellowship, 90, 91, 92
Kenya Education Commission Report, 54
Kenya Episcopal Conference, 25, 51, 153
Kenya Foundation of the Prophets Church, 133, 141, 218
Kenya Independent Churches Fellowship, 27, 146
Kenya Missionary Council, 24, 25
Kenya Pastors' Conference, 194, 222 •
Kenya Students Christian Fellowship, 153

Kanyatta, Mzee Jomo, 25, 27, 44, 47, 127, 128, 132, 134, 194, 296, 299
Kesho, 96
Kesho Book Centre, 96
Kesho Publications, 94, 95
Kestons, G., 32
Keswick Book Society, 96
Keswick Convention, 111
Kibicho, Samuel, 28
Kibukosya, Peter, 69, 84
Kikuyu Central Association, 127
Kikuyu Convention, 28, 113, 222
Kikuyu Independent Schools Association 129
Kitui Convention, 113
Kivuli, D.M.P.Z., 194
Kivengere, Bp. Festo, 194
Koi, David, 22, 31, 36
Krapf, J.L. 18, 21, 30, 33, 216
Kuamka (Awakening), 115, 116
Kufufuka (Awakening), 27, 115, 116, 222

Last Ministry Church, 223
Legio Maria, 27
Legion of Mary, 25
Leipzig Mission, 22
Lengo, 26, 97
Le Roi, A., 31
Local Churches of Kenya, 132
Lost Israelites of Kenya, 120, 121, 218
Luo Roho Church, 73, 136
Lutheran Church in Kenya, 56, 90, 91

Macdonald, Malcolm, 47
Macpherson, R., 166
Mahajanwadis, 225, 308, 309
Maina, Daudi, 24
Makadudi, E., 224
Makarios, Archbishop, 28, 174, 194.
Mangu High School, 44
Maria Legio of Africa, 27, 137, 143, 153, 171, 194, 218
Martyrs of Mombasa, 21, 215
Maseno Convention, 26, 113
Maseno School, 23, 35
Matogo, J., 67
Matthews, T., 32
Maupoint, A., 31
Mbila, Yohana, 23, 34
Mbotela, James, 23
McCarthy, Abp. J.J., 38
Medical work, 17, 33, 45, 102, 132
Medicine Men's Society, 224
Meru Convention, 113
Messianism, 136 - 138
Methodist Bookshop, 96
Methodist Church in Kenya, 38, 56, 90, 91, 92, 96, 116, 151, 152, 161, 171, 217
Mfuko ya Bwana, 115
Milad-al-Nabii, 296
Mill Hill Fathers, 23, 32, 215
Ministerial training, 22, 149
Ministry of Education, 44
M'Inoti, Phillip, 25
Miracle Revival Fellowship, 218

Missionary Aviation Fellowship, 27, 194, 222
Mission Volunteer Carrier Corps, 24
Mliwa, Shadrack, 34
Mng'ong'o, Ronald, 28, 38
Mombasa Convention, 27, 113, 222
Mosque College, 225
Mpaayei, John, 27, 97, 194
Mringe, 21, 30, 36
Mugwe, 224
Muinami, Samuel, 126
Mukurwe, 224
Mulwa, Wellington, 38
Mumbo cult, 23, 224
Mumias Convention, 113
Mung'ara, John, 126
Muolo Roho Israel Church, 140, 141
Musanda Holy Ghost Church of East Africa, 25, 138, 143, 171, 218
Muslim law schools, 297
Muslims, 17, 21, 86, 88, 163, 164, 168, 181, 295 - 301, 303, 307, 308 (see also Islam).
Muthirigu, 24,25
Mwangi wa Nyarari, 27, 36

Namdharis, 310
National Association of Religious Education Teachers, 52
National Christian Council of Kenya, 28, 45, 46, 89, 90, 91, 92, 98, 101, 102, 103, 105, 146, 151, 153, 190, 222, 300, 301.
National Holiness Association, 25, 217
National Independent Church of Africa, 129, 218
Nauvnathvanik Jains, 307
'Ndaragu Forest Affray', 25, 126, 132
Ndegwa, Boniface, 67
Ndiege, Zabulon, 136
Ndingi, Bp. Raphael, 28, 69, 194
Nduti, Ayub, 141
Neukirchener Mission, 22, 217
Neville, John, 31
New, Charles, 22
New East African Church, 223
New Roho Israel Church, 137
Ng'ang'a, Joseph, 126
Njenga, Bp. J., 47, 194
Njuri ya Mauku, 25
Njuri Nceke, 25
Nomiya Luo Church, 23, 136, 143, 218
Nomiya Luo Sabbath, 218
Nuru, 97
Nyerere, Julius, 102
Nzoka, Gideon, 37

O'Brollchain, C., 67, 69
O'Connell, J., 67, 69
Odongo, Alfayo (Mango), 24, 25, 36, 138, 143
Odundo, Matthew, 140
Ogol, Elijah, 138
Okite, Odhiambo, 97
Okullu, J. Henry, 97
Olang', Abp. Festo, 26, 28, 38, 45, 116, 194

Ominde Report, 49, 50
Ondeto, Simeo, 137, 143
Onduso, Mathayo, 23
Opoti, Shadrack, 100
Ordination, 22, 24, 32, 31
Osborn, T.L., 26
Otunga, Maurice Cardinal, 26, 28, 38, 45, 47, 194
Oundo, Benjamin, 136
Owalo, Johana, 23
Owen, W.E., 24, 35, 37
Owenga, Yohana, 23, 34, 36
Oxford Movement, 111

Pancha Oshwals, 307
Parseeism (Zoroastrianism), 314
Parsees, 225
Pentecostal Assemblies of Canada, 26, 217
Pentecostal Assemblies of God, 56, 131, 153, 170, 174, 194
Pentecostal Evangelistic Fellowship of Africa, 27, 56, 64, 153, 194, 222
Perlo, Filippo, 23, 32
Phelps/Stokes Commission, 24
Pesa, John Juma, 119
'Piga biti' movement, 27, 222
Plunkett, L. 32
Polygamy, 129, 132, 145
Portuguese, 21, 29, 30
Power of Jesus Around the World Church, 141, 218
Practising Christians, 160, 166, 167, 190
Prendergast, J., 32
Presbyterian Church of East Africa, 25, 28, 56, 90, 91, 92, 94, 116, 129, 131, 133, 151, 162, 163, 169, 170, 171, 194, 217, 222
Prince Philip, 47
Professing Christians, 160, 163, 164, 165, 166, 170, 175, 190
Protestant Churches' Medical Association, 102, 150, 152, 153

Quinn, Edel, 25

Ragot, Mariam, 26
Ramadhan, 296
Ramsey, Apb. Michael, 194
Rebmann, J., 21, 30, 33, 216
Reformed Church of East Africa, 56, 151
Religious education, 49 -58, 161
Religious Education Department, Kenyatta University College, 52
Revival, 24, 25, 26, 27, 28, 35, 37, 110 - 117, 131, 133, 216, 222
Ritchie, James, 300
Roberts, Oral, 28
Rock, 26, 97
Ruwe Holy Ghost Church of Africa, 25, 218

Saheb, Syedna M. B., 296, 300
Salvation Army, 24, 27, 56, 73, 90, 91, 92, 140, 153, 163, 171, 194, 217
Scott, Peter Cameron, 22

348

Scott Theological College, 27, 70, 71, 72
73, 74, 76, 77, 78, 80, 194
Scottish Mission, (See Church of Scotland
Mission)
Semler, Ishmael,. 36
Sempele, Molonket ole, 23
Seventh-day Adventist Church, 23, 56,
90, 91, 92, 163, 171, 217
Seventh-day Adventist Reform Movement
223
Seventh-day Missionary Church, 218
Sheikh Jundani, 225, 297
Shias, 298
Sikh Brotherhood (Khalsa), 309, 311
Sikhism, 225, 309 - 311, 313
Sikhs, 163, 303, 309 - 311
Slave trade, 22, 30, 31
Smith, Edwin W., 61
The Societies Ordinance, 26 .
Society of Saint Patrick for Foreign Mis-
sions, 26, 38
SODEPAX, 101, 102, 104, 105
South African Compounds and Interior
Mission, 22
Southern Baptist Convention (USA), 26
State of emergency, 26, 27, 37, 112, 133
Statistics, Part II, 155 - 191
Sthanakvasi Jains, 307
St. Paul's Minor Seminary, 25, 32
St. Paul's United Theological College, 26,
28, 130, 134, 151
St. Thomas Aquinas Seminary, 27

Sufis, 297
Sulaimanis, 300
Sunnis, 297, 312
Svetambaras, 307, 308
Swami Narayan, 303
Swami Prabhupada, 304, 305
Swedish Lutheran Mission, 26, 217

Tabatabai, Aqais, M., 298
Target, 26, 97
Tana River Independent Church, 27
The Societies Act, 28, 159
Thuku, Harry, 127
Today in Africa, 96
Torch, 97
Traditional music, 65 - 84, 107, 122
Traditional musical instruments, 28, 69 -
84, 194, 222
Traditional religions, 18, 27, 35, 36, 42,
66, 67, 74 - 83, 106, 107, 108, 109,
112, 122, 127, 132, 140, 141, 143,
163, 164, 181, 194, 224, 291 -294,
312
Trinitarian Bible Society, 28
Trinity College, 62, 88
Tumutumu Convention, 113
Tukutendereza, 113, 117

United Bible Societies, 28, 153, 222
United Churches of Africa, 146
United Missionary Conference, 23
United Nations, 104, 162

Uzima Press, 95

Waganga wa Miti Shamba, 224
Wamboi, Sister Giulia, 32
Watt, Stuart, 33
Watu wa Mungu, 24, 25, 132, 134
Willis, J.J., 33
Wokofu African Church, 28, 140, 223
World Alliance of Reformed Churches,28
World Council of Christian Education, 28
World Gospel Mission, 25, 217
World Methodist Congress, 28
World Revival Union Evangelistic Church,
27, 223
World Student Christian Federation, 152,
153
Wundanyi Convention, 113

Vapostori, 28, 174, 180
Vasco da Gama, 21, 29, 215
Vatican Council II, 46, 66, 67
Village Polytechnic Schools, 46, 100,
103, 222
Visa Oshwals, 307, 308
Voice of Kenya, 70, 73, 85 - 92, 105,
176

Xavier, St. Francis, 21, 29, 215

YMCA, 23, 63, 153, 217
YWCA, 153

Zanzibar, 22, 23, 31, 32, 297